THE ROUTLEDGE COMPANION TO SEVERE, PROFOUND AND MULTIPLE LEARNING DIFFICULTIES

The Routledge Companion to Severe, Profound and Multiple Learning Difficulties is a timely and rich resource with contributions from writing teams of acknowledged experts providing a balance of both academic and practitioner perspectives.

The book covers a myriad of topics and themes and has the core purpose of informing and supporting everyone who is interested in improving the quality of education and support for children and young adults with severe, profound and multiple learning difficulties and their families. Each chapter contains careful presentations and analyses of the findings from influential research and its practical applications and the book is a treasure chest of experiences, suggestions and ideas from practitioners that will be invaluable for many years to come. The chapters include many vignettes gathered from practitioners in the field and are written specifically to be rigorous yet accessible.

The contributors cover topics related to the rights and needs of children and young adults from 0–25 years, crucial features of high quality education, characteristics of integrated provision and effective and sensitive working with families to ensure the best possible outcomes for their children. Crucially, the voice of the learners themselves shines through. Historical provision that has had an impact on developing services and modern legislation aimed at improving provision and services are also discussed.

The contributed chapters are organised into six themed parts:

1   Provision for learners with SLD/PMLD.
2   Involving stakeholders.
3   Priorities for meeting the personal and social needs of learners.
4   Developing the curriculum.
5   Strategies for supporting teaching and learning.
6   Towards a new understanding of education for learners with SLD/PMLD.

This text is an essential read for students on courses and staff working in and with the whole range of educational settings catering for children and young adults with severe, profound and multiple learning difficulties, not just for teachers but also for support staff, speech and language therapists, physiotherapists, psychologists, nurses, social workers and other specialists.

Penny Lacey was a Senior Lecturer in the School of Education at the University of Birmingham, UK.

Rob Ashdown was Headteacher to three special schools for children and young people with severe, profound and multiple learning difficulties.

Phyllis Jones is an Associate Professor in the Department of Special Education at the University of South Florida, USA.

Hazel Lawson is a Senior Lecturer in Special and Inclusive Education at the University of Exeter, UK.

Michele Pipe is a Specialist Early Years Advisor for Dudley Local Authority, UK.

THE ROUTLEDGE COMPANION TO SEVERE, PROFOUND AND MULTIPLE LEARNING DIFFICULTIES

Edited by *Penny Lacey, Rob Ashdown, Phyllis Jones, Hazel Lawson and Michele Pipe*

Routledge
Taylor & Francis Group

LONDON AND NEW YORK

KH

First published 2015
by Routledge
2 Park Square, Milton Park, Abingdon, Oxon OX14 4RN

and by Routledge
711 Third Avenue, New York, NY 10017

Routledge is an imprint of the Taylor & Francis Group, an informa business

© 2015 P. Lacey, R. Ashdown, P. Jones, H. Lawson and M. Pipe

British Library Cataloguing in Publication Data
A catalogue record for this book is available from the British Library

Library of Congress Cataloging in Publication Data
The Routledge companion to severe, profound and multiple learning difficulties / edited by Penny Lacey, Rob Ashdown, Phyllis Jones, Hazel Lawson and Michele Pipe.

ISBN 978-0-415-70997-2 (hardback) -- ISBN 978-0-415-70998-9 (paperback) -- ISBN 978-1-315-71791-3 (e-book) 1. Learning disabled children--Education--Great Britain. 2. Learning disabled--Education--Great Britain. 3. Learning disabled--Services for--Great Britain. 4. Learning disabilities--Great Britain. 5. Special education--Great Britain. I. Lacey, Penny, editor of compilation. II. Ashdown, Rob, editor of compilation. III. Jones, Phyllis, editor of compilation. IV. Lawson, Hazel, editor of compilation. V. Pipe, Michele, editor fo compilaton. VI. Title: Companion to severe, profound and multiple learning difficulties.

LC4706.G7R68 2015

371.9--dc23

2014038939

ISBN: 978-0-415-70997-2 (hbk)
ISBN: 978-0-415-70998-9 (pbk)
ISBN: 978-1-315-71791-3 (ebk)

Typeset in Bembo
by Saxon Graphics Ltd, Derby

10/18/17

This book is dedicated to Penny Lacey, our friend and colleague, who died after a sudden and short illness in January of this year. The book is one of the fruits of Penny's dedication to improving the lives of children and adults with severe, profound and multiple learning difficulties and their families. She was the prime mover for this book, she perceived the need for it, invited contributions from among her many contacts, ensured that the voices of practitioners, families and learners were included, and did much of the editing as well as writing material for several chapters. Unfortunately, Penny never got to see the final proofs, but she was clearly proud of everybody's contributions. The irony is that she downplayed her own achievements. In practice, her outstanding contributions to the field of special and inclusive education will live on and people will be referencing her work in their teaching and research well into the future. We have lost a great thinker and a guiding light. She was a lovely person and a loyal, sincere and trustworthy friend to many. Penny was a remarkable woman, an inspiration to us all and will be greatly missed and we all hope that her family and friends and colleagues gain some comfort from the fact that this book will be part of her legacy.

CONTENTS

Contents

ABOUT THE CONTRIBUTORS

Chris Abbott taught in special and mainstream schools, was an Advisory Teacher for SEN and ICT and ran the Inner London Educational Computing Centre. Since 1994 he has been at King's College London, where he is Reader in e-Inclusion. He is also the Editor of the *Journal of Assistive Technologies*.

Richard Aird is a Consultant in special education and chairman of two charitable trusts. Prior to his retirement he served as Headteacher to four special schools over a 30-year period and continues to have a close involvement in all aspects of specialist provision.

Rachel Allan helped to develop an e-learning training resource, 'Making Sense of Mental Health' which was the outcome of a partnership between the University of Northampton and the National Association of Independent and Non-Maintained Special Schools. Rachel is now a Practice Lead for Mencap, developing the practice of staff working with adults with learning disabilities.

Caroline Allen has been Principal for 19 years of Orchard Hill College which is a specialist college for students over 16 with a range of learning difficulties/disabilities. She is also CEO of Orchard Hill College Academy Trust and has held other public roles. Her PhD research related to organisation culture and management in special education.

Carolyn Anderson is a Senior Lecturer at the University of Strathclyde. She has published in the fields of learning disabilities, children's eating/drinking difficulties, speech difficulties, and professional development.

Rob Ashdown was Headteacher of three special schools in England for learners with SLD and PMLD. He retired from teaching in 2013. He is an editor for the *PMLD LINK* journal. He is co-editor and author of books and papers in the area of education for learners with SLD/PMLD.

Julia Barnes (nee Rhodes) is the Sensory Needs Coordinator at Ravenscliffe High School and Sports College in Halifax. Julia first worked as a support assistant for teenagers with complex needs. After qualifying as a teacher, Julia has taught at Ravenscliffe for eight years. She has a Masters Degree in Severe, Profound, Multiple and Complex Learning Difficulties for which she did research on the contact experiences of learners with PMLD.

Rosemary Bird spent her entire professional life teaching in special education, particularly with learners with complex needs and physical disabilities. She enjoys the creativity of approaches to literature and storytelling. Over the last 10 years she has developed partnerships with schools in Africa, working on curriculum access.

Lana Bond is a Senior Teacher at The Bridge School in Islington, North London. Lana recently completed her Masters Degree in severe and complex learning difficulties and is currently studying for the UK mandatory qualification for teaching learners with visual impairment. Her special interests include all things PMLD, Intensive Interaction and well-being.

Hannah Brighton is currently in year two of the BA SEN and Inclusion Undergraduate degree at Northampton University. She is one of the student representatives for the School of Education sitting on the student experience committee.

Miranda Brookes is Senior Teacher in the Vision Support Team, Leicester City Council with responsibility for children and young people with visual or multi-sensory impairment and additional complex needs. She is regional Tutor for Birmingham University's Multi Sensory Impairment course for teachers, tutors and support staff working in schools and colleges. Contributor to the Visual Impairment and Multi Sensory Impairment courses at Birmingham University.

Erica Brown is Vice President of Acorns Children's Hospice and Research Fellow (Children and Family Applied Research) at Coventry University. She has been a senior manager and Headteacher in schools and Head of Special Education at Oxford Brookes University. Erica has lectured and published nationally and internationally. She was awarded Fellow of the Royal Society of Arts in 2013 in recognition of her national contribution to children's and young people's palliative care.

Julian Brown is a Physiotherapist at Wilson Stuart School, Birmingham. He has worked with babies, children and young people with cerebral palsy and other disabilities for well over 10 years. Spending half his clinical time at the special school, he also visits other schools and health centres.

Helen Burnford is a Speech and Language Therapist who is currently working as a Bobath trained Speech and Language Therapist at the Bobath Children's Therapy Centre, Wales, working with children with cerebral palsy and allied neurological conditions.

Richard Byers is a Lecturer in Special and Inclusive Education at the University of Cambridge Faculty of Education. He worked with learners with SLD/PMLD in various settings. His research interests include curriculum development, assessment, inclusion, social and emotional well–being, bullying, marginalisation and learners with special educational needs and/or disabilities.

Barry Carpenter is Honorary Professor at universities in the UK, Ireland, Germany and Australia. He has undertaken research with families of children with disabilities, motivated professionally and personally as the father of a young woman with Down's syndrome. He is currently writing on such topics as mental health and complex needs.

Margaret Corke is a Play and Creative Arts Therapist working in a primary special school. She is author of *Approaches to Communication Through Music* (2002) and *Using Playful Practice to Communicate with Special Children* (2012).

Anne Cradock has taught Physical Education to pupils with PMLD or complex needs since 1985. She helped develop the Elements programme and extension courses which focus on sensory learning. Anne taught in mainstream education and was a local authority Physical Education Adviser in Birmingham. She works as a Physical Education Consultant running training courses for national sports bodies and as a volunteer for the Disability Sport Organisations at national events.

Stephen Cullingford–Agnew was a PE teacher in special schools for 20 years and still provides training for school staff. He was Headteacher of two special schools and a local authority Senior School Improvement Officer for SEN. He is a Principal Lecturer at the University of Northampton and leads a SEN and Inclusion Team that supports teacher education programmes in developing students' knowledge and understanding of special school contexts.

Peter Danco is a Dance Teacher and Choreographer. He uses students' individual interests, strengths and talents to nurture their engagement in the learning process. Peter leads the post 16 unit of Sybil Elgar School, National Autistic Society, which provides a performing arts curriculum model for young people diagnosed with autism.

Barbara Dowson trained and practised as a mainstream PE teacher, has provided Home Tuition for Autistic Children and School Refusers but is now retired and works as a Voluntary RDA Side Walker. She is passionate about the importance of the benefits of animals in general and horses in particular in all our lives.

Trudy Duffield is Deputy Headteacher at Phoenix Community Special School, Peterborough. She has a keen interest in ensuring there are a range of meaningful extended school opportunities, including residential experiences, for all learners regardless of disability or family background. She views it as crucial the school's offer of a flexible and responsive curriculum that promotes the social and emotional development of every learner.

Jodie Dunn is a Special Educational Needs Teacher who holds a BA Hons degree focusing on 'Deaf Studies and Special Needs Inclusion in Society' from Wolverhampton University followed by a teaching qualification from Newman College and a Masters Degree in 'Special Educational Needs' from Northampton University. Jodie teaches at Castle Wood School, Coventry focusing on children with PMLD within the EYFS framework.

Kathrine Everett is Head of Learning Centre at Orchard Hill College where she manages a staff team and works with students to achieve work, independent living and community learning outcomes. Kathrine previously worked in an FE College where she was responsible for curriculum and delivery for students with special needs.

Ann Fergusson is a Senior Lecturer in SEN and Inclusion at the University of Northampton. Annie has a background in teaching and managing specialist and residential provision for learners with SLD/PMLD and challenging behaviours. She works and provides consultancy in school settings in the UK and internationally. Annie's research interests include PMLD, early learning and communication, inclusive research and the voice of the learner with SEN. Annie is an editor of *PMLD LINK*.

Graham Firth is the Intensive Interaction Project Leader, Leeds & York Partnership NHS Foundation Trust. Previously he worked as a care assistant in a large residential hospital for adults with learning disabilities and in further education. Along with Dave Hewett and Cath Irvine, he was a founding board member of the Intensive Interaction Institute.

Juliet Goldbart is Professor of Developmental Disabilities and an Associate Dean for Research at Manchester Metropolitan University where she teaches on the Speech Pathology and Therapy programmes. Her research interests include communication and interaction in children and adults with PMLD, augmentative and alternative communication, and service delivery models in the UK and in under-served countries.

Nicola Grove started life as an English teacher, changed into a speech and language therapist, set up the charity Openstorytellers and is now a Storyteller and Freelance Trainer specialising in communication, narrative, and signing with children and adults with learning disabilities.

Tom Hall is now in his third year as Sixth Form Teacher at Oak Field School and Sports College in Nottingham. Working with school leavers with SLD/PMLD, he has been keen to ensure appropriate Sex and Relationship Education as part of transition.

Jane Harwood works as a Project Leader for the charity Openstorytellers. Her specialism is supporting effective communication through personal narrative as a tool for interpersonal relationships and transition. Jane has been delivering Storysharing projects since 2006.

Elizabeth Henderson manages the Speech and Language Therapy team at Three Ways special school in Bath. She has worked with learners with PMLD in a variety of health and education settings and locations for over 20 years. Elizabeth is passionate about developing meaningful communication and interaction skills in those learners who face the most complex challenges, working alongside school staff and families.

Dave Hewett has been working nationwide for more than 20 years as an Independent Staff Trainer and Consultant to staff in all services who work with people who have severe learning difficulties and/or autism. Previously (1981–90) he was the Headteacher of Harperbury Hospital School, Hertfordshire. Dave is the Director of the Intensive Interaction Institute. His work on Intensive Interaction now takes him to many countries around the world.

Liz Hodges is the Senior Lecturer in Deafblindness at the University of Birmingham and also works as the advisory teacher for deafblind children in Hertfordshire. She is qualified as a teacher of pupils with severe and complex needs as well as of deafblind children. Her research, training, and teaching roles support each other in promoting best practice for the exceptional needs of deafblind people.

Fiona Holmes works in the West Midlands specialising in additional needs, inclusion and partnership with parents and young people. She has a wealth of experience supporting successful joint working practices and developing integrated working. For eight years Fiona ran projects focusing on disability and change management within Solihull Metropolitan Borough Council followed by two years facilitating the use of the Early Support approach.

Marie Howley is a Senior Lecturer in SEN and Inclusion in the School of Education at the University of Northampton. Marie has extensive experience teaching learners with autism and SLD of all ages. She has co-ordinated provision for children and young people on the autism spectrum in specialist settings. Marie has published widely in the field of autism and her research interests include eclectic classroom practice in special schools.

Peter Imray has worked in education for nearly 30 years, mainly as a teacher and school leader at The Bridge School in Islington for learners with SLD/PMLD. He is now an Independent Trainer and Advisor in the area of special educational needs. He is the author of articles relating to learners with SLD/PMLD and with Viv Hinchcliffe has written *Curricula for Teaching Children and Young People with Severe or Profound and Multiple Learning Difficulties* (2014).

Riana Jackson is a special needs teacher and Intensive Interaction Coordinator who supports students with severe and complex learning and communication difficulties aged from 3–19 years. She has over 12 years experience working with these students as well as implementing and embedding Intensive Interaction into a specialised school curriculum.

Kate Jones has been a practising Speech and Language Therapist since 1993. She has always worked in the South Wales area. She has worked with and learnt from learners with special needs and their parents and teachers throughout her career both in special schools and at the pre-school level.

Phyllis Jones is an Associate Professor in the Department of Special Education at the University of South Florida. Phyllis taught and was a Deputy Head in schools in the UK for 15 years before she entered teacher education. She is author of six books and journal articles related to inclusive practices, teacher education for teachers of learners with severe intellectual disabilities and/or ASD. She is co-editor of *International Journal of Whole Schooling*.

Rosie Jones switched careers following the birth of her third child, born with hearing and visual impairment and cleft palate. She spent 20 years as a Speech and Language Therapist working in specialist units and special schools across South Wales, specialising in Autistic Spectrum Condition. As a parent, teacher, therapist and former NHS manager, she tries to see special education from all sides.

Penny Lacey was a Senior Lecturer at the University of Birmingham, where she ran the 'Severe, Profound and Multiple Learning Difficulties' professional development programme. She also conducted research and wrote in the area of SLD/PMLD. Penny worked as a Coach and Adviser in a special school for one day a week and as a Consultant in many other schools around the country. She was an editor for *PMLD LINK*.

Hazel Lawson is Senior Lecturer in Special and Inclusive Education at the University of Exeter. She was formerly a primary and special school teacher and has research interests in curriculum development, pedagogy and pupil involvement for children and young people with SLD/PMLD.

Peter Limbrick established and directed the voluntary organisation, One Hundred Hours, in the UK to develop and validate joined-up support for families whose baby or young child had neurological impairment and consequent multifaceted disability. Peter developed and published the TAC model (Team Around the Child) and has since promoted this approach in the UK and abroad. He writes, publishes and continues his consultancy work to promote interagency collaboration in any country.

Daisy Loyd is a Drama Practitioner, Researcher and Teacher. She is passionate about the opportunities drama education can present and her PhD research focused on the participation of pupils with autism in drama education. She runs drama sessions in schools and has taught on MA courses in Special and Inclusive Education at the Institute of Education, University of London and the Higher Colleges of Technology, Abu Dhabi.

Dawn Male is a Senior Lecturer in Special and Inclusive Education at the Institute of Education, University of London. Previously, she was a teacher in mainstream and special schools and an educational psychologist.

Angela Mallett was former Deputy Head of Shepherd School, specialising in the education of pupils with PMLD. She is author of the sex education resource, 'Bodyworks'. She currently supports pupils with complex learning disabilities in mainstream schools in Nottingham.

Yvonne McCall is Headteacher of a primary special school. She has taught in mainstream and special schools, across age groups, and has taught adults with learning difficulties too. She aims to place the learner at the centre of everything that is done at school, and always to ensure that everyone reflects on their practice and explores new approaches, informed by evidence, so that learners are best prepared, not just for the here and now but for the future.

Mike McLinden is co-Director of the Visual Impairment Centre for Teaching and Research at the University of Birmingham and programme lead for the professional development courses in visual impairment. Mike's research interests have been primarily concerned with the identification and reduction of potential barriers to learning and participation for learners with sensory impairment including those with complex needs.

Ann Middleton became ICT coordinator in schools for learners with SLD after being the only person to read the instructions when the first computers arrived in the early 1980s. Since 2002 she has been an Advisory Teacher for ICT and SEN.

Sarah Moseley is Headteacher at Nancealverne School in Cornwall. She has more than 20 years' experience as a practitioner, including both mainstream and special needs classrooms, nationally and internationally. Her doctorate was focused on reading and pupils with SLD.

Lesley Mycroft has worked in schools and education services in England. She was Senior Lecturer in Initial Teacher Education at the University of Wolverhampton where she was instrumental in introducing a qualification (BEd Hons) for teachers in Early Years. She now works as a Freelance Consultant and School Assessor. Lesley is interested in the education of young children, in special education, and encouraging reflective practice for those in training and for qualified teachers.

Robert Orr is a Consultant in Groupwork at the Pen Green Centre for Children and Families in Corby and was Headteacher of RNIB Rushton Hall School. His book *My Right to Play* (Open University Press), came out in 2003 and he has both contributed to and edited a number of Pen Green publications.

Keith Park teaches young people with severe and profound learning difficulties, and is a specialist in visual impairment. He runs interactive multisensory storytelling workshops at the Globe Theatre in London and other cultural venues.

Laura Pease is Vice Principal of Whitefield Schools and Centre and Lead Tutor for the Whitefield/Kingston University courses in complex needs and multi-sensory impairment. She leads on curriculum development for Whitefield and has a particular interest in issues around making the curriculum meaningful for pupils with severe, profound and complex needs.

Melanie Peter is a Senior Lecturer in Education and Early Childhood at Anglia Ruskin University. She is a specialist in early learning and creativity, having trained originally as a teacher of children with learning difficulties. She has maintained involvement in special education for over 20 years and is a published authority in the field, known widely for her innovative approaches using the arts, especially drama.

Michele Pipe worked with learners with SLD/PMLD for 20 years and then as a Headteacher of a mainstream primary school and a local authority Specialist Early Years Advisor. Most recently she was a lecturer in SEN at the University of Birmingham. She is completing PhD research into children with SLD and early years' curriculum.

Jill Porter is Director of Research at the Department of Education, University of Bath. She taught in early years and special school settings prior to working in universities. She has undertaken a wide range of research in the field of disability and special educational needs and with particular interest and expertise in teaching number to pupils with severe complex and profound learning difficulties.

Kalvinder Rai is a Teacher in a school that caters for children with a broad range of learning and physical complex needs. Part of the job role is to support mainstream schools with developing their provision and support the Local Authority to develop its Inclusion practice.

Hollie Rawson is an Occupational Therapist currently working in mental health rehabilitation. She has a background in learning disability support, SEN research and family services, with a special interest in sibling experience.

Matthew Rayner is the Headteacher at Stephen Hawking School. He has worked with children with profound and multiple learning difficulties for 25 years in a number of special schools in both inner city and rural areas.

Michael W. Riley is a Doctoral Candidate in Special Education at the University of South Florida. He has taught in Florida public and charter schools since 2001, serving students with a range of needs from mild to intensive. His research interests include family–school partnerships, teacher education, and inclusive education.

Sana Rizvi is a Doctoral Student at the Graduate School of Education, University of Bristol. She has an MA in Education from the University of Birmingham and an MPhil in Educational Research from the University of Cambridge. Her background as a first generation Pakistani immigrant to the UK and a mother has influenced her PhD work, which focuses on South Asian maternal perspectives on their child's SEND. Her research interests include parent empowerment, disability and ethnicity.

Christopher Robertson is a Lecturer in Inclusive and Special Education at the University of Birmingham where he leads the postgraduate National Award for Special Educational Needs Coordination programme. His teaching and research interests include education policy, international perspectives on special and inclusive education, and all aspects of teacher education. He has written extensively on the role of the SENCO, has co-authored books on special educational needs and written articles pertaining to special and inclusive education.

Chris Rollings is Headteacher at the Hadrian School, Newcastle. He has co-authored a *Confident Parenting Handbook* and DVD on facilitating parenting groups. Hadrian Education and Development Services offers a range of training courses, including PE and rebound therapy. Chris is an executive member of the EQUALs charity.

Richard Rose is Professor of Inclusive Education at the University of Northampton. He is currently Director of Project IRIS, a longitudinal study of special and inclusive education in the Republic of Ireland. Richard has conducted research and consultancy in several countries including India, China, Malaysia and Georgia. He is author of several books and papers in the area of special and inclusive education.

Janet Sherborne has worked as a Senior Leader in further education for over 20 years developing a wide range of provision including vocational courses for students with learning disabilities, apprentices and higher education including teacher training. Janet uses her experience from working in the corporate private sector to ensure that courses are vocationally relevant and lead to the best opportunities for students to gain employment and progression into further and higher education.

Anthony Skipworth is currently working as a teacher in the early years at a school for pupils with severe and profound learning difficulties in Peterborough. His prime area of interest involves pupils with profound and multiple learning difficulties. He is an advocate for putting young people at the heart of their educational, social and emotional development; which includes an emphasis on working closely with families.

Fiona Smith is Assistant Headteacher at Mossbrook School in Sheffield, a primary community special school with learners who have a range of needs including autistic spectrum disorder (ASD), speech, language and communication difficulties, as well as learning difficulties. She graduated from Strathclyde University with a B.Ed and has postgraduate qualifications in Special Educational Needs and Early Years from Sheffield Hallam University. Fiona is particularly interested in the Early Years curriculum.

David S. Stewart is Headteacher of Oak Field School, Nottingham. He has worked with children with learning difficulties since 1970 and specialised in the field of sex education for 30 years. He is co-author of *Living Your Life*. He has research interests in the history of special education. David has an honorary doctorate from the University of Nottingham in recognition of his work in special education.

James Stonard has extensive experience arranging work experience placements for students with mild and severe learning disabilities, as part of their work based learning curriculum both at FE college and at Mencap Pathway. He is strongly committed to helping students with special educational needs to get a job.

Jean Ware started her career as a teacher of learners with PMLD shortly after they first became the responsibility of schools. She taught for 10 years before studying for a PhD at the Institute of Education in London. She has been following up her PhD work on 'Creating a Responsive Environment for People with PMLD' ever since! She is currently Reader in Education (Special Educational Needs) at Bangor University.

Debby Watson is currently carrying out research on playfulness and children with PMLD for a PhD at the Graduate School of Education, University of Bristol. She has a long-standing interest in children with profound and complex impairments and has several publications in this area. She was formerly a Research Fellow at the Norah Fry Research Centre, University of Bristol.

Lisa Wilson is qualified as a nursery nurse who has experience as a private day nursery manager, a midday supervisor and supply nursery nurse. She currently works as an Unqualified Teacher for primary aged children with SLD at Castle Wood School in Coventry.

Joanne Yarlett was previously a specialist Connexions adviser for young people with learning difficulties and disabilities, a Lecturer at Orchard Hill College and most recently Head of Learning Centre at the College's Southwark centre.

1

INTRODUCTION

Penny Lacey, Rob Ashdown, Phyllis Jones,
Hazel Lawson and Michele Pipe

Bringing together all these wonderful writers has been a very exciting project! However, an edited book is always difficult to join up seamlessly and with 39 chapters and more than 70 writers, this particular book has been especially challenging. We believe that we have achieved what we set out to do, which was to produce a textbook that would appeal to both students on advanced and postgraduate courses and to practitioners in schools, colleges and adult education provision. By practitioners, we do not refer just to teachers but also to support staff, speech and language therapists, physiotherapists, psychologists, nurses, social workers and other specialists interested in improving the quality of education and support for children and young people with severe, profound and multiple learning difficulties and their families.

We wanted to balance contributions from acknowledged experts in the field of severe, profound and multiple learning difficulties with encouraging newer writers and thus set up as many writing teams as possible. Most of the chapters have indeed been written by teams, especially on the topics where both academic and practitioner perspectives are important. For some chapters we have indicated the main writer/s and then added 'with…' for those who have provided examples from practice to illustrate the topic.

Each chapter has been reviewed three times by the editors, twice in chapter development where editors offered comments back to authors on clarity and coherence across the chapter. Chapter authors have engaged in this chapter development in a most gracious way, and we would like to thank them all for their willingness to engage in this process. We hope that in doing this, coherence and clarity across the book as a whole has been nurtured.

It was planned that there would be photographs of learners throughout the book and we have included as many for which we have permission. Where pictures are sparse, we hope you will substitute your own learners in your minds.

This book is about children and young people who have 'severe, profound and multiple learning difficulties'. We have shortened that phrase to SLD/PMLD in most places to save precious space. In this group, we include children and young people who have additional needs that often co-occur with SLD/PMLD, for example autism, sensory impairments, physical disabilities and a whole range of conditions and syndromes. Where an identified need is important to highlight, we have mentioned it, but throughout the book we have in mind a heterogeneous group of children and young people brought together by the severity of their learning difficulties.

As this book is about education, development and learning, the word 'learner' has been chosen to denote babies, children, pupils, teenagers, students and adults where actual age does not matter but have used specific terms where they are important or where it would be clumsy to make the substitution. The groups that are most often referred to are learners in schools, including early years settings, and colleges. However, much of what is discussed is relevant to adult learners in educational provision and to very young children not yet at school.

The chapter authors have used a range of terms to denote the practitioners involved in the education of learners with SLD/PMLD. Probably the term 'teacher' is used most often but we do stress that it does not necessarily denote a trained teacher but could mean anyone who is in a teaching role. Again, we affirm that the chapters are of relevance to a wide range of professionals from different disciplines, not just teachers.

The authors have written their chapters in such a way that they will not date rapidly. It is true that some chapters inevitably refer to newly introduced policies and legislation or innovative practices, but the content will stand the test of time. Indeed, the chapters convey long-established teaching approaches and methods that have not dated at all. Also, we do believe that the book will be entirely relevant to readers throughout the UK and abroad. We appreciate that most of the authors are based in the UK and the majority in England but we know that their writing is not limited to the UK context, except for some discussion on English legislation that will still be of interest to practitioners outside England. Moreover, a good many of the authors have strong connections with practitioners throughout the UK and abroad through consultancy and training activities and have international profiles through writing books and papers for journals.

When planning this book, we invited potential writers to tell us what topic they wanted to write on, rather than decide on the topics and find suitable writers. We were delighted by the response to the call and the richness of the proposed chapters. The result is a treasure chest of discussions, experiences, suggestions and ideas that we expect to provide support for students on courses and practitioners for many years to come. One of the difficulties with an open invitation is that we (the editors) struggled with finding a structure for the book that would be helpful for readers. Eventually we decided on six parts:

1   Provision for learners with SLD/PMLD.
2   Involving stakeholders.
3   Priorities for meeting the personal and social needs of learners.
4   Developing the curriculum.
5   Strategies for supporting teaching and learning.
6   Towards a new understanding of education for learners with SLD/PMLD.

We hope that you (the reader) find the part divisions helpful for finding your way around the topics.

Part I: Provision in the United Kingdom for learners with SLD/PMLD

The first part in this book introduces the nature of learners with SLD/PMLD and provides historical and current contextual information and perspectives on policy, provision and practice for these learners in the United Kingdom. Chapter 2 provides definitions and examples that describe learners designated as having SLD/PMLD. It also outlines related 'conditions' and terminology: Autism Spectrum Disorders, Complex Learning Difficulties and Disabilities and Challenging Behaviour. Provision over the past 70 years is discussed in relation to ideas around inclusion and 'quality of life' is suggested as a guiding principle regardless of placement. Chapter 3 brings us up to date with policy and legislation, particularly in the light of the Children and Families Act 2014 and subsequent Special Educational Needs and Disability Code of Practice 0–25 years. Chapter 4 takes us back in time to reflect upon the education of learners with SLD/PMLD from 1800–1970 exploring the prominence of medical views; the date of 1970 is an important milestone as legislation in this year meant that these learners were no longer considered 'ineducable'. Chapter 5 continues the journey from 1970 focusing on changes and developments in curriculum models to the present day – the introduction of a National Curriculum in 1989 was a particular challenge. The content of this book, however, goes beyond school-aged learners and Chapters 6 and 7 contextualise provision and practice for learners in Further Education (aged 16 years and over) and for those in Early Years provision (from birth to 5 years).

Part II: Involving stakeholders

Part II contains topics of differing perspectives related to learners with SLD and PMLD. Joint working across different disciplines can raise challenges and in Chapter 8, examples are given of successful strategies for joint working, as well as exploring issues, barriers and some underpinning theories. Chapter 9 raises the concern of involving parents and the wider family group. The authors consider how we can engage, strengthen and support our work with families and overcome difficulties that may occur. The theme of parents is extended in Chapter 10, where provision, needs and issues related specifically to learners and families from ethnic minorities are examined. The views of parents provide powerful insights into this topic. The importance of involving learners is considered in Chapter 11, where the voice of the children and young people are discussed, through the concepts of participation, citizenship and voice. Theoretical aspects are supported by real-life, successful examples of gaining learners' opinions. This part also includes two chapters related specifically to teachers of learners with SLD/PMLD. In Chapter 12, the training of teachers in special education is explored. Newly qualified teachers can face particular issues within the context of special education, and these are considered. In addition, the development needs of educators throughout their professional life are discussed. In Chapter 13 the voice of teachers is heard through research carried out. Teachers share their thoughts about working with learners with SLD/PMLD and the issues raised are discussed. Finally, in Chapter 14, the powerful voice of our learners is heard through interviews with students. The authors suggest more time and consideration of the learners' views need to be taken into account.

Part III: Priorities for meeting the personal and social needs of learners

In this third part, there are chapters that underpin learning in educational settings. They include topics that are important to understand before plunging into curriculum and classroom teaching. Chapter 15 contains advice on the effects of sensory impairments and suggests strategies that can be used when teaching learners with SLD/PMLD with sensory impairments. Chapter 16 focuses on the place of care in the curriculum; Chapter 17 considers sex and relationship education and Chapter 18 concentrates on physical contact and its nature in the lives of learners with SLD/PMLD. All three of these chapters have important messages to give on fundamental well-being topics. Chapters 19 and 20 continue this theme of well-being. The first is centred on behaviour that challenges and positive and proactive management of that behaviour and the second is designed to help practitioners to identify and address mental health concerns. The final two chapters in this part concern inner feelings. Chapter 21 deals with the roles played by faith, culture and ethnicity, alongside a more general view of spirituality, while Chapter 22 focuses directly on death, loss and bereavement: necessary but difficult subjects for learners with SLD/PMLD and their families.

Part IV: Developing the curriculum

This part, the largest part in the book, explores the broad concept of curriculum for learners with SLD/PMLD. Chapters 23 and 24 frame the part by presenting chapters on curriculum and progress. Chapter 23 offers a historical perspective of curriculum going on to discuss the tensions of developing a curriculum that responds to standards based curriculum and individual student need. Chapter 24 focuses upon recognising progress for this group of learners; it covers different types of assessment with emphasis upon formative assessment and principles/strategies for ensuring moderation and best use of assessment tools. The subsequent eight chapters each take a curriculum focus; three are focused on communication with Chapter 25 discussing the fundamentals of communication, followed by Chapter 26 giving a thorough overview of Intensive Interaction and Chapter 27 exploring the whole notion of inclusive talking and language learning. This is followed by five subject-focused chapters that illustrate the importance of planning enhanced curriculum opportunities for learners with SLD/PMLD. There are two focused on reading and literacy (Chapters 28 and 29), one on number (Chapter 30), one on Physical Education (Chapter 31) and the part ends with Chapter 32 taking a focus on drama. Across this part, educators of learners with SLD/PMLD are invited to engage with approaches to planning the curriculum that are both meaningful for individual learners and enriching in terms of access to planned learning experiences through a learner's education. The chapters offer examples of application to real-life classrooms to enable readers to envision the impact of the approaches in practice.

Part V: Strategies for supporting teaching and learning

This part provides support and advice for practitioners seeking to develop appropriate and stimulating environments for learners with SLD/PMLD. Over the last 30 years, technology, along with increased specialist knowledge about how to use it, has improved immensely. Chapter 33 explores how the use of technology enlivens teaching and provides access to learning in ways that cannot be provided by other means. Chapter 37 explores the opportunities provided by well-designed buildings and that of carefully planned use of resources, both indoors and outdoors. It is argued that learners with SLD/PMLD should be supported to learn through exploration in carefully designed environments that help them to begin to understand their world. Opportunities for learning through play are viewed as crucial and Chapters 34 and 35 explore the concepts of 'play' and 'playfulness' respectively. Chapter 34 explains why learners with SLD/PMLD struggle to play and play cooperatively with their peers. It suggests that it is not the case that they cannot learn to play but that they learn to do so differently and we must therefore teach them differently. Chapter 35 shows why playfulness is important and, with particular reference to learners with PMLD, how we can encourage learners' playfulness by naturally incorporating playfulness into our teaching practice and daily routines. The core subjects (mathematics, English and computing) are often prioritised at the expense of creativity and Chapter 36 reminds us why we must cherish creativity. Creativity, it is suggested, entails personalisation of learning which is essential both for teachers' planning to meet diverse needs and for learners' social inclusion and fulfilment.

Part VI: Towards a new understanding of education for learners with SLD/PMLD

This is the shortest part and contains just two chapters, one on research past, present and future and the other, a brief conclusion to the book and a glimpse into the crystal ball of the way ahead. A clear message from many chapters has been that there is a need for more research to throw more light on issues and to identify different or better solutions. Chapter 38 explores strengths and weaknesses in past studies and the new demand for research into evidence of what works in education to improve outcomes for learners. This chapter examines why teachers should get involved in research and how they might do their own studies. Finally, Chapter 39 records key themes that keep recurring throughout the book. It is suggested these themes must be fully explored and all issues addressed if there is to be a genuine impact on the quality of education for learners with SLD/PMLD and on their quality of life and that of their families.

Using this book

The book is not designed to be read from cover to cover in order, although that is, of course, possible. We expect readers to select chapters that are relevant to them at particular moments. There are references throughout the book to resources that can support and inform practice. Some are contained in the body of the chapter but others are listed at the end of each chapter. We hope that you will follow up the suggestions.

There are reference lists at the conclusion of each chapter in the hope that it will be easy for you to find a particular source that you would like to pursue. These sources are academically organised as we are attempting to appeal to students on professional courses as well as practitioners in educational settings. A glossary has been included to explain some key terminology and English governmental organisations and agencies.

We have included examples from practice where they are relevant, in the hope that, if applicable, you will be able to apply them to your own context and thus reflect on your own practice. The questions at the end of the chapters are also aimed at encouraging reflection.

The questions at the beginning of chapters are designed to give a brief overview of the chapter contents. Each writer or team of writers has addressed these introductory questions through the discussions and examples that follow. It is really useful to pay attention to the questions so you understand the line taken on each topic. All writers have had to select their themes very carefully and have, through word limitations, had to be succinct. Even with the 160,000 words in this book, it is impossible to cover every aspect related to the education and development of learners with SLD/PMLD.

A limitation of an edited book can be the lack of a single perspective on the education of learners. However, in the case of this volume we would like to argue that this is actually one of the book's greatest strengths. The writers clearly do generally agree on the basic principles of respecting and responding to the needs of individual learners with SLD/PMLD but they all have distinctive views and experience. We hope that you will learn from the combination of ideas found in this book. We especially hope that what we have all written here will be both inspiring and invaluable both to those who are just starting out on the road of educating learners with SLD/PMLD and to all of those who are at other points further along this road. As you can see, you are not alone on your journey!

PART I

Provision in the United Kingdom for learners with SLD/PMLD

2

LEARNERS WITH SLD AND PMLD

Provision, policy and practice

Dawn Male

In this chapter, the following questions will be addressed:

- Who are the learners described as having severe learning difficulties (SLD) and profound and multiple learning difficulties (PMLD)?
- What was past policy, practice and provision for learners with SLD and PMLD and what is present policy, practice and provision?

Who are these learners?

Danny is 13 years old. He is a sociable and popular young man who participates enthusiastically in all physical activities and who responds positively in social contexts. He enjoys being part of large activities and discussions: smiling, vocalising and responding to communications. Danny has some verbal language and uses a few recognisable words and a number of single word utterances which are understood by those who know him well. He gives some approximations of a few Makaton signs in context. He is able to write the first letter of his name independently and, with support, can be encouraged to trace other letters and shapes. He can count up to ten in rote fashion, using his own approximation of the words. Danny is very good at recognising pictures and photographs. He can point to pictures of people, objects and some animals and uses his own words to describe them. He uses a picture/photo album to demonstrate his wants and needs and uses a pictorial timetable to anticipate and signpost significant events in his day. He is able to eat independently using a spoon and is able to use the toilet, bath and shower with support and supervision. Danny has little sense of danger and so needs supervision to keep him safe.

Sarita is 10 years old. She shows positive responses to lively, bright and noisy TV programmes or activities and to music with a strong beat. She visibly relaxes and smiles when in the company of her parents, other family members, certain members of school staff and some pupils. She shows similar responses when in the soft play area and the hydrotherapy pool. When shown bright lights or brightly coloured shiny objects Sarita 'stills' and appears to concentrate and will visually track them as they are moved across her field of vision. She will also 'still' to sounds, smile in response to familiar voices and will participate in simple turn-taking games when an adult repeats her vocalisations. Sarita has a moulded matrix wheelchair in which she spends most of her day. She is unable to support her own weight and cannot move her legs independently but uses a standing frame for short periods each day. She has some movement in her arms and, with encouragement and allowing plenty of time, can bring her right arm to centre line and press a switch or hold an object in her hand. Sarita is able to grasp soft toys and small, hand–sized objects for up to a minute and can wiggle her fingers on a keyboard if her hand is placed there. She will also pull her hands away from some textures or tactile experiences which she appears to find unpleasant. Sarita does not use any recognisable words but makes some consistent vocalisations. She has seizures which are generally well controlled with medication and receives her nutrition via a gastrostomy. Sarita relies on others for all aspects of her personal care and safety.

Descriptions, definitions and characteristics

Children and young people such as Danny and Sarita have been described in a variety of ways, by different professional groups, in different countries and across time (MacKay 2009). In the United Kingdom (UK) practitioners working in educational settings are likely to describe Danny as having SLD and Sarita as having PMLD. In the context of health care Danny and Sarita would be likely to be described as having 'learning disabilities', a term which has had official status in the National Health Service (NHS) (MacKay 2009).

In the United States Danny and Sarita are likely to be described as having 'intellectual disabilities' of a severe or profound nature – a descriptor reflected in the revised fifth edition of the *Diagnostic and Statistical Manual of Mental Disorders* (DSM-5) (American Psychiatric Association 2013) in which the term 'intellectual disability' (intellectual developmental disorder) replaces the term 'mental retardation'; the parenthetical term 'intellectual developmental disorder' is intended to reflect deficits in cognitive capacity which first occur in the developmental period. Typically, deficits in cognitive capacity in individuals described as having SLD/PMLD are chronic, that is, persisting over the life span.

While it is acknowledged that learners described as having SLD/PMLD are an extremely heterogeneous group with a range of personal characteristics, abilities, strengths and challenges (Giangreco 2006), the terms SLD and PMLD generally imply significant weaknesses in learning abilities, communication, personal and social skills, and/or sensory and physical development (Westling, Fox and Carter 2014). Approximate intelligence quotient (IQ) scores according to international classification systems, such as DSM-5 and the tenth revision of the *International Statistical Classification of Diseases and Related Health Problems* (ICD-10: World Health Organization 1992), are 20/25–35/40 (severe), and below 20/25 (profound).

The Department for Children, Schools and Families (2009) (now the Department for Education) defined SLD and PMLD for England and Wales as follows:

> **Severe Learning Difficulty**: Pupils with SLD have significant intellectual or cognitive impairments. This has a major effect on their ability to participate in the school curriculum without support. They may also have difficulties in mobility and co–ordination, communication and perception and the acquisition of self–help skills. Pupils with SLD will need support in all areas of the curriculum. They may also require teaching of self–help, independence and social skills. Some pupils may use sign and symbols but most will be able to hold simple conversations.
>
> **Profound and Multiple Learning Difficulty**: Pupils with PMLD have complex learning needs. In addition to very severe learning difficulties, pupils have other significant difficulties, such as physical disabilities, sensory impairment or a severe

medical condition. Pupils require a high level of adult support, both for their learning needs and also for their personal care. They are likely to need sensory stimulation and a curriculum broken down into very small steps. Some pupils communicate by gesture, eye pointing or symbols, others by very simple language.

The American Association for Persons with Severe Handicaps (TASH), an organisation supporting 'equity, opportunity and inclusion for people with disabilities', defines individuals described as having SLD/PMLD with reference to their support needs:

> These people include individuals of all ages who require extensive ongoing support in more than one major life activity in order to participate in integrated community settings and to enjoy a quality of life that is available to citizens with fewer or no disabilities. Support may be required for life activities such as mobility, communication, self-care, and learning as necessary for independent living, employment and self-sufficiency. (Adopted by TASH, December, 1985, revised November, 1986)
>
> (reprinted in Meyer, Peck and Brown 1991: 19)

Similarly, the theoretical model of intellectual disability developed by the American Association on Intellectual and Developmental Disabilities (2010) has five dimensions: (1) intellectual abilities; (2) adaptive behaviour; (3) health; (4) participation; and (5) context, all of which are mediated by a support system that 'buffers' the individual's life. Furthermore, the functioning level of individuals may affect the support that they require for effective function. Thus, an individual's functioning is viewed as not being solely due to the characteristics of that individual, but also to the supportive context in which the individual operates (Westling *et al.* 2014).

Prevalence

The prevalence of individuals identified as having learning difficulties varies according to such factors as the population under study, geographical location, methods of assessment and criteria of assessment that are used. Emerson *et al.* (2011) reported estimates of 286,000 children and young people in England aged 0–17 years being described as having learning difficulties, with 180,000 of these being boys and 106,000 girls. Approximately 70,000 had a Statement of Special Educational Needs (SEN) (now called Education, Health and Care Plans; see Chapter 3), with one-third being described as having SLD and 1 in 10 being described as having PMLD. Learners from poorer families were more likely to be described as having a learning difficulty. Moderate learning difficulties (MLD) and SLD were more common among 'Traveller' and 'Gypsy/Romany' learners and PMLD was more common among 'Pakistani' and 'Bangladeshi' learners.

Both anecdotal and empirical evidence suggests rises in the number of learners identified with learning difficulties and disabilities, particularly PMLD. A national survey of SLD schools conducted by Male (1996) indicated that head teachers considered that the pupil population of their school was changing to include more learners with PMLD, challenging behaviour (CB), autism spectrum disorders (ASD), life-limiting conditions and learners with additional physical and sensory impairments. In a follow-up study (Male and Rayner 2009) head teachers again reported perceived increases in the number of learners with PMLD, CB, ASD and life-limiting conditions, with more than half of all head teachers considering that their PMLD and CB populations and learners with life-limiting conditions had increased 'significantly' or 'somewhat' in recent years. More than three-quarters of head teachers considered that their ASD pupil population had increased 'significantly' or 'somewhat' in recent years. Similarly, in a survey of 50 per cent of local authorities (LAs) in England conducted by the Audit Commission in 2002, a third of respondents perceived a significant increase in the number of learners with PMLD.

This perception of increases in the number of learners with SLD/PMLD appears to be supported by empirical data; for example, the Department for Children, Schools and Families (2009) reported that in England the number of pupils with SLD rose by an average of 5.1 per cent between 2004 and 2009 and the number of pupils with PMLD rose by an average of 29.7 per cent. Furthermore, factors such as increased survival rates have been identified which are likely to lead to further increases in the number of learners with SLD/PMLD in England over the next two decades, resulting in estimated sustained growth in the region of 14 per cent (Emerson and Hatton 2008).

Similar rises in the prevalence of learning difficulties in the childhood/young people population are recorded in Wales and Scotland. In Wales in 2009, 3,022 children aged under 16 were identified on LA registers as having learning difficulties, an increase in the region of 2 per cent from those registered in 2004 (Local Authority Register of People with Disabilities, 31 March 2009). Increases were also recorded in Scotland where, according to the 2007 Pupil Census, 13,913 pupils were identified as receiving additional support relating to learning difficulties, constituting a rate of 20.1 per 1,000 pupils, compared with 17 per 1,000 pupils in 2003.

Available data relating to the Northern Ireland pupil population indicate small but continuing rises in the proportion of pupils identified as having SEN (that is, 3.9 per cent in 2007/08; 4.0 per cent in 2008/09; 4.1 per cent in 2009/10; 4.2 per cent in 2010/11; 4.3 per cent in 2011/12; 4.4 per cent in 2012/13), with 2012/13 data indicating that 0.6 per cent of these (2,296) were described as having SLD/PMLD (source: Department of Education, Northern Ireland).

Autism spectrum disorders

Typically, autism spectrum disorders are characterised by impaired social reciprocity, atypical communication skills and repetitive behaviours; additional features include a high risk of epilepsy, vulnerability to self injury and hypersensitivity to sounds, textures, tastes, smell, temperature (Hyman and Levy 2013). The overall prevalence of learning difficulties among children and young people with ASD has been estimated to be in the region of just under a half to around two-thirds (Emerson and Baines 2010), with five times as many males as females being identified (Fombonne, Quirke and Hagen 2011). Individuals who have learning difficulties and ASD are included in the group of learners described as having SLD/PMLD, but individuals with conditions such as Asperger syndrome or high functioning autism (HFA) are not included as, by definition, they have average or above average intelligence (Wing 1998).

The prevalence rates of ASD have varied over time and place (Rutter 2005). Forty years ago ASD was considered to be a very rare, categorical condition (that is, an individual either had it or did not) and typical prevalence rates were reported to be in the region of four cases per 10,000 (Rutter 2005). However, Wing (1988) argued that autism lay on a continuum and that there was a spectrum of autism disorders. According to this view (as opposed to categorical view), the prevalence of autism was in the region of 10–20 per 10,000. Subsequently, Rutter (1994) reported prevalence rates of 30–60 cases per 10,000 and, more recently, Baron-Cohen *et al.* (2009) have reported estimated prevalence rates in the English school-based population in the region of 157 per 10,000. In the US the prevalence estimate is 1 in 88 (Centers for Disease Control and Prevention 2012). In addition to this adoption of a spectrum view of ASD, reported increases in prevalence and incidence have been attributed to changes in availability of services, age at assessment and increased awareness of the condition (Fombonne *et al.* 2011); Rutter (2005), however, argues that 'real' increases in prevalence and incidence rates of ASD cannot be ruled out.

Complex learning difficulties and disabilities

A second group of individuals who may or may not be included in the group described as having SLD/PMLD are those described as having complex learning difficulties and disabilities (CLDD). Carpenter *et al.* (2010) describe learners with CLDD as:

> those with co-existing conditions (e.g. autism and ADHD), or profound and multiple learning difficulties... those with difficulties arising from premature birth; those who have survived infancy due to medical advances; those with disabilities arising from parental substance and alcohol abuse; and those with rare chromosomal disorders. Many may also be affected by compounding factors such as multisensory impairment or mental ill-health, or require invasive procedures, such as supported nutrition, assisted ventilation and rescue medication.
>
> (Carpenter *et al.* 2010: 3)

While many learners described as having SLD/PMLD could also be described as having CLDD (Sarita being an example) there are individuals with complex learning difficulties and/or disabilities who do not have SLD/PMLD (Stephen Hawking – theoretical physicist, cosmologist and author being a frequently cited example). Rises in the number of learners being identified as having CLDD have been noted too (Blackburn, Spencer and Read 2010).

Challenging behaviour

Individuals such as Danny and Sarita are vulnerable to displaying challenging behaviours (CB), including self-injurious behaviours (SIB). The main forms of CB and SIB have been identified as aggressive/destructive behaviour, self-injurious behaviour, stereotypy, and other socially or sexually unacceptable behaviours (Hastings and Remington 1994; Qureshi and Alborz 1992). Causal hypotheses found in the research literature include: 'communicate needs' (e.g. 'if s/he wants something'); 'stimulation' (e.g. 's/he enjoys the feeling'); 'social' (e.g. 'lack of contact with other children – doesn't know how to behave with them'); 'biological' (e.g. 'pre-disposition because of syndrome'); 'environmental' (e.g. 'when s/he is in a crowded place') (Hastings, Reed and Watts 1997; Male 2003).

Studies into the number of individuals with learning difficulties who display challenging behaviours have indicated varying rates, but it is clear that a significant minority of individuals with SLD/PMLD display challenging behaviours (Jones and Eayrs 1993). Hogg *et al.* (1987) returned rates of CB ranging from 6 per cent ('engages in inappropriate sexual activity') to 43 per cent ('makes disruptive sounds or noises'); Kiernan and Kiernan (1994) returned rates of 2 per cent for 'extremely difficult or very difficult' behaviours and 14 per cent for 'moderately or least difficult' behaviours; Qureshi and Alborz (1992) returned rates of 10 per cent; Harris, Cook and Upton (1996) and Porter and Lacey (1999) returned rates of around 25 per cent. Male and Rayner (2009) reported that over 90 per cent of head teachers of SLD schools in England estimated that up to a quarter of their pupil population displayed challenging behaviours.

Specialist support services

An implication of the reported rise in the number of learners described as having SLD/PMLD, CLDD, ASD, those displaying challenging behaviours and those with degenerative/life-limiting conditions is an increased need for input from specialist support services. In a national survey of all maintained SLD schools in England conducted by Rayner and Male (2013) positive associations were found between the number of learners with PMLD and the number of hours of support provided by occupational therapy (OT), physiotherapy and speech and language therapy (SaLT); the number of learners with degenerative and/or life-limiting conditions and the number of hours of support provided by OT and physiotherapy; the number of learners with ASD and the number of hours of support provided by SaLT. Thus, learners identified as having more severe and/or complex needs received a higher level of support from specialist providers. Just over three-quarters of head teachers stated that they had a school nurse on site on a full-time, or near full-time, basis. Prior to this Male (1996) reported that just over half of all SLD schools surveyed (n = 57) employed a nurse on a full-time, or near full-time, basis and Evans and Ware (1987) reported that less than a third of SLD schools surveyed employed a nurse on a full-time, or near full-time, basis, indicating an increasing need for specialist support for learners' medical needs. Comments made by head teachers in the Rayner and Male (2013) study regarding input from specialist services indicated perceptions of inadequacy in terms of hours of support received, e.g. 'totally inadequate', 'never enough' and 'we need more'.

Past and present policy, practice and provision

Under the terms of the 1944 Education Act children and young people in England identified as having SEN were categorised by their disabilities (or 'defects of body or mind') according to medical terms. Those described as being 'severely educationally subnormal' (a continuation of the earlier descriptors of 'imbecile', 'idiot' and 'mental defectives') were considered 'ineducable'. At that time the responsibility was held by the Mental Deficiency Committees of the Local Authorities which also managed most of the long stay hospitals or asylums. The hospitals came under the Health in 1948 but the junior training centres remained the responsibility of the Local Authorities (LAs). In 1970, with the passing of the Education (Handicapped Children) Act, the responsibility for the education of some 32,750 'severely educationally subnormal' children in England and Wales was transferred to local education authorities (LEAs) (now LAs) which were then required to provide education suitable to their ages, abilities and aptitudes. These children were to be known as ESN-S (educationally subnormal – severe) and were educated almost exclusively in special schools, provided either by the LEA or a charitable institution. At this point there were thousands of children still in long stay hospitals but the majority were living at home either staying there all day or attending a junior training centre. The training of staff to meet these new responsibilities imposed immense challenges and the 1970s and 1980s were difficult times for many of the new schools and progress was difficult (see Chapter 5). Similar changes to legislation followed in Scotland with the passing of the Education (Mentally Handicapped Children) (Scotland) Act 1974 which was enacted in 1975. In Northern Ireland it would not be until 1987 that legislation changed with the passing of the Education (Northern Ireland) Order when responsibility transferred from Health to the Education and Library Boards.

In 1974 the Conservative Government set up the Warnock Committee to review special educational provision. The Committee recommended the abolition of all categories of 'handicap' and proposed, instead, a continuum of need ranging from learners whose difficulties could be met within mainstream classrooms, through to learners with more severe needs. Using evidence from various surveys (e.g. Rutter, Tizard and Whitmore 1970) the Committee recommended that planning for services for learners with SEN should be based on the assumption that about one in six at any time, and up to one in five (20 per cent) at some time during their school career, would require some form of special provision. Two per cent of learners (such as Danny and Sarita) were thought to have SEN of a more severe and probably long-term nature.

The 1981 Education Act (largely superseded by the Education Act 1993 and subsequently the Education Act 1996) was the legislative response to the Warnock Report. It brought about fundamental reforms to special educational provision, one of which was the presumption that learners with SEN should, wherever possible, be educated in mainstream schools alongside their same-age peers; consequently, the 1980s and 1990s saw enormous changes in the field of special education in England (Male 2011). In the case of special school placements, Norwich (1997) reported that by 1996 more than half (58.5 per cent) of all learners with Statements of SEN in England were placed in mainstream schools; this compares with 42.1 per cent in 1992, 47.7 per cent in 1993 and 51.7 per cent in 1994 (no data was analysed for 1995). Data from 1996 indicated that, when learners were placed in special schools, 47 per cent were in schools designated for pupils with SLD or PMLD.

Unsurprisingly, the 1980s and 1990s witnessed a concomitant decrease in the number of special schools; thus, according to Department for Education and Employment data (DfEE 1998), between 1986 and 1996 the number of maintained special schools fell by 15 per cent (from 1,405 to 1,191) while the number of non-maintained special schools fell by 18 per cent (from 88 to 72) for the same period.

In 1997 the New Labour Government published the Green Paper *Excellence for All Children: Meeting Special Educational Needs*, giving support to the UN statement on Special Needs Education 1994 which called on governments to adopt the principle of inclusive education (Department for Education and Employment 1997). In 2004 the government set out its vision on SEN in *Removing Barriers to Achievement* (Department for Education and Skills 2004: 37) in which it stated that, 'the proportion of children educated in special schools should fall over time'. Nevertheless, as noted in the House of Commons Education and Skills Committee Report (2006) on SEN, the proportion of learners placed in special schools plateaued. Recent figures indicate that, overall, 27 per cent of children with SLD and 18 per cent of children with PMLD are educated in mainstream schools. It is worth noting that actual numbers of pupils with PMLD who are included are small and rates of inclusion for these pupils are lower at older ages.

Giving evidence to the House of Commons Education and Skills Committee, the then Minister with responsibility for SEN (Lord Adonis) described the government as being 'content' if the 'roughly static position in respect to special schools continues' (House of Commons Education and Skills Committee Report 2006: 5) and that the government 'have no policy... of encouraging local authorities to close special schools' (para. 18, page 12). Currently, the most likely educational placement in England for learners with SLD/PMLD is a special school (Male and Rayner 2009; Emerson *et al.* 2011) and the indications for the future appear to be that this will continue to be the case. As we have noted elsewhere (Male and Rayner 2007, 2009), special schools for learners with SLD/PMLD appear to be here to stay. For example, the SEN Code of Practice (Department for Education and Department of Health 2014) states that special schools have an important role; and parents and young people with an Education, Health and Care Plan have the right to seek a place at a special school.

'Quality of life': a conceptual framework for informing future policy, practice and provision?

Most of all I want him to be happy and safe... I want him to be cared for by people who know him well... people who understand all his ways... teachers who will get the best out of him... I want him to have friends and things to do which he enjoys... I want his medical needs to be met... I want him to have the speech therapy and physiotherapy he needs.

(Maureen, mother of 10-year-old William)

Based on a model of quality of life proposed by Felce and Perry (1995), Petry, Maes and Vlaskamp (2005) considered the general validity of five basic domains in relation to individuals with PMLD and examined how parents and direct support staff operationalised these domains. They found that more than half of respondents spontaneously identified the five domains as being salient for the quality of life of individuals with PMLD and between 88 and 100 per cent considered them salient when asked explicitly. These five domains, and their operationalisation in respect to individuals with PMLD, are:

- Physical well-being: *mobility, health, hygiene, nourishment, rest.*
- Material well-being: *living environment, technical aids, transportation.*
- Social well-being: *communication, basic security, family bonds, social relationships, individual attention, social participation.*
- Development and activity: *involvement in activities, influence and choices, development.*
- Emotional well-being: *positive affect, individuality, respect, status and self-esteem.*

It will be noted that these domains – and their operationalisation in respect to individuals with PMLD – are consistent with Maureen's 'wish list' for provision for her son, William; Maureen does not concern herself with the '*where?*' of provision but focuses instead on the '*what?*', with the '*what?*' being William's quality of life.

Concluding comments

Learners with SLD/PMLD constitute one of the most vulnerable groups in society (Jones 2005) and much progress has been made in the last 40-plus years, perhaps particularly in terms of valuing these learners for who they are, rather than what they can do. In looking forward to possible policy, practice and provision for learners with SLD/PMLD maybe it is time to do as William's mother does, and focus our attention on providing quality of life for learners such as Danny, Sarita and William – whether it be in mainstream, 'special' or other settings.

Questions for readers

- What might be future policy, practice and provision for learners with SLD and PMLD?
- Does the concept of 'quality of life' offer a conceptual framework for informing future policy, practice and provision?

Acknowledgement

I thank Valerie Hobbs, teacher and researcher, for her observations of Danny and Sarita.

References

American Association on Intellectual and Developmental Disabilities (2010) *Intellectual Definition, Classification, and Systems of Support*, Washington DC: AAIDD.

American Psychiatric Association (2013) *Diagnostic and Statistical Manual of Mental Disorders*, 5th edn, Arlington, VA: American Psychiatric Publishing.

Audit Commission (2002) *Special Educational Needs: A mainstream issue*, London: Audit Commission.

Baron-Cohen, S., Scott, F.J., Williams, J., Bolton, P., Matthews, F.E. and Brayne, C. (2009) 'Prevalence of autism-spectrum conditions: UK school-based population study', *British Journal of Psychiatry*, 194: 500–509.

Blackburn, C.M., Spencer, N.J. and Read, J.M. (2010) 'Prevalence of childhood disability and the characteristics and circumstances of disabled children in the UK', *BMC Pediatrics*, 10–21.

Carpenter, B., Cockbill, B., Egerton, J. and English, J. (2010) 'Children with complex learning difficulties and disabilities: developing meaningful pathways to personalised learning', *The SLD Experience*, 58: 3–10.

Center for Disease Control and Prevention (2012) 'Prevalence of autism spectrum disorders – autism and developmental disabilities monitoring network, 14 Sites, United States, 2008', *Morbidity and Mortality Weekly Report*, 61, 3: 1–19.

Department for Children, Schools and Families (2009) *Schools, Pupils and their Characteristics*, Nottingham: DCSF Publications.

Department for Education and Department of Health (2014) *Special Educational Needs and Disability Code of Practice: 0 to 25 years*. Ref: DFE:-00205-2013. Online. Available: www.gov.uk/government/publications/send-code-of-practice-0-to-25 (accessed 12 July 2014).

Department for Education and Employment (1997) *Excellence for All Children: Meeting special educational needs*, London: The Stationery Office.

Department for Education and Employment (1998) *Special Educational Needs in England: January 1997*, Statistical Bulletin Issue No. 2/98, London: DfEE.

Department for Education and Skills (2004) *Removing Barriers to Achievement: The Government's strategy for SEN*, Nottingham: DfES.

Emerson, E. and Baines, S. (2010) 'The estimated prevalence of autism among adults with learning difficulties in England', Stockton on Tees: Improving Health and Lives. Online. Available: www.improvinghealthandlives.org.uk/projects/autism (accessed 29 June 2013).

Emerson, E. and Hatton, C. (2008) *Estimating the Current Need/Demand for Support for People with Learning Difficulties in England*, Lancaster: Centre for Disability Research (CeDR), Lancaster University.

Emerson, E., Hatton, C., Robertson, J., Roberts, H., Baines, S. and Glover, G. (2011) *People with Learning Disabilities in England 2010*, Learning Disabilities Observatory. Online. Available: www.improvinghealthandlives.org.uk (accessed 30 June 2013).

Evans, P. and Ware, J. (1987) *Special Care Provision: The education of children with profound and multiple learning difficulties*, Windsor: NFER–Wilson.

Felce, D. and Perry, J. (1995) 'Quality of life: its definition and measurement', *Research in Developmental Disabilities*, 16(1): 51–75.

Fombonne, E., Quirke, S. and Hagen, A. (2011) 'Epidemiology of pervasive developmental disorders', in D.G. Amaral, G. Dawson and D.H. Geschwind (eds) *Autism Spectrum Disorders*, Oxford: Oxford University Press.

Giangreco, M. (2006) 'Foundational concepts and practices for educating students with severe disabilities', in M.E. Snell and F. Brown (eds) *Instruction of Students with Severe Disabilities*, 6th edn, Columbus, OH: Pearson.

Harris, R.P., Cook, M. and Upton, G. (1996) *Pupils with Severe Learning Disabilities who Present Challenging Behaviour*, Kidderminster, Worcs: British Institute of Learning Disabilities.

Hastings, R.P., Reed, T.S. and Watts, M.J. (1997) 'Community staff causal attributions about challenging behaviours in people with intellectual disabilities', *Journal of Applied Research in Intellectual Disabilities*, 10(3): 238–249.

Hastings, R.P. and Remington, B. (1994) 'Rules of engagement: towards an analysis of staff responses to challenging behaviour', *Research in Developmental Disabilities*, 15: 279–298.

Hogg, J., Lambe, L., Cowie, J. and Coxon, J. (1987) *People with Profound Retardation and Multiple Handicaps Attending Schools or Social Education Centres*, London: Mencap PRMH Project, Report No 4.

House of Commons Education and Skills Committee (2006) *Special Educational Needs: Third report of sessions 2005–2006*, London: The Stationery Office.

Hyman, S.L. and Levy, S.E. (2013) 'Autism spectrum disorders', in M.L. Batshaw, N.J. Roizen and G.R. Lotrecchiano (eds) *Children with Disabilities*, 7th edn, Baltimore: Paul H. Brookes.

Jones, P. (2005) 'Teachers' views of their pupils with profound and multiple learning difficulties', *European Journal of Special Needs Education*, 20(4): 375–385.

Jones, R.S.P. and Eayrs, C.B. (eds) (1993) *Challenging Behaviour and Intellectual Disability: A psychological perspective*, Clevedon, Avon: British Institute of Learning Disabilities.

Kiernan, C. and Kiernan, D. (1994) 'Challenging behaviour in schools for pupils with severe learning difficulties', *Mental Handicap Research*, 7: 117–201.

MacKay, T. (2009) 'Severe and complex learning difficulties: issues of definition, classification and prevalence', *Educational & Child Psychology*, 26(4): 9–18.

Male, D.B. (1996) 'Who goes to SLD schools?', *Journal of Applied Research in Intellectual Disabilities*, 9(4): 307–323.

Male, D.B. (2003) 'Challenging behaviour: the perceptions of teachers of children and young people with severe learning disabilities', *Journal of Research in Special Educational Needs*, 3(3): 162–171.

Male, D.B. (2011) 'The impact of a professional development programme on teachers' attitudes towards inclusion', *Support for Learning*, 25(4): 182–186.

Male, D.B. and Rayner, M. (2007) 'Who goes to SLD schools? Aspects of policy and provision for pupils with profound and multiple learning difficulties who attend special schools in England', *Support for Learning*, 22(3): 145–152.

Male, D.B. and Rayner, M. (2009) 'Who goes to SLD schools in England? A follow-up study', *Educational and Child Psychology*, 26(4): 19–30.

Meyer, L.H., Peck, C.A. and Brown, L. (eds) (1991) *Critical Issues in the Lives of People with Severe Disabilities*, Baltimore: Brookes.

Norwich, B. (1997) *A Trend Towards Inclusion: Statistics on special school placements and pupils with statements in ordinary schools 1992–1996*, Bristol: Centre for Studies in Inclusive Education.

Petry, K., Maes, B. and Vlaskamp, C. (2005) 'Domains of quality of life of people with profound multiple learning difficulties: the perspectives of parents and direct support staff', *Journal of Applied Research in Intellectual Disabilities*, 18(1): 35–46.

Porter, J. and Lacey, P. (1999) 'What provision for pupils with challenging behaviour?', *British Journal of Special Education*, 26(1): 23–28.

Qureshi, A. and Alborz, A. (1992) 'The epidemiology of challenging behaviour', *Mental Handicap Research*, 5: 130–145.

Rayner, M. and Male, D.B. (2013) 'Specialist support services received by pupils in special (SLD) schools in England: level of support received and head teachers' perceptions of usefulness', *The SLD Experience*, 58: 14–20.

Rutter, M. (1994) 'Incidence of autism spectrum disorders: changes over time and their meaning', *Acta Paediatrica*, 1: 2–15.

Rutter, M. (2005) 'Aetiology of autism: findings and questions', *Journal of Intellectual Disability Research*, 49(1): 231–238.

Rutter, M., Tizard, J. and Whitmore, K. (1970) (eds) *Education, Health and Behaviour*, London: Longman.

Westling, D.L., Fox, L. and Carter, E. (2014) *Teaching Students with Severe Disabilities*, 5th edn, Columbus, OH: Pearson.

Wing, L. (1988) 'The continuum of autistic disorders', in E. Schopler and G.B. Mesibov (eds) *Diagnostics and Assessment in Autism*, New York: Plenum.

Wing, L. (1998) 'The history of Asperger syndrome', in E. Schopler, G.B. Mesibov and L.J. Kunce (eds) *Asperger Syndrome or High Functioning Autism?*, New York: Plenum.

World Health Organization (1992) *The ICD-10 Classification of Mental and Behavioural Disorders: Clinical Descriptions and Diagnostic Guidelines*, Geneva: WHO.

3

CHANGING SPECIAL EDUCATIONAL NEEDS AND DISABILITY LEGISLATION AND POLICY

Implications for learners with SLD/PMLD

Christopher Robertson

In this chapter, the following questions will be addressed:

- What was the rationale for introducing new special educational needs and disability legislation in England in September 2014?
- What is the definition of special educational needs?
- What are the implications for school placement and inclusion?
- What are the implications for policy of approaches to inclusive teaching (pedagogy)?
- What are the implications for the school curriculum?

Introduction

This chapter offers an overview of the special educational needs and disability (SEND) legislation in England introduced in September 2014. I reflect upon problematic issues related to the definition of special educational needs and learning difficulty, and implications both for school placements and for inclusive teaching and curricula. Different legislative frameworks are used in the other countries of the United Kingdom but it is hoped that the relevance of these reforms to a wider UK and international audience may be recognised.

Overview of special educational needs and disability legislation and policy – 2014

In Spring 2014 the *Children and Families Act 2014* (United Kingdom Parliament 2014) was given Royal Assent. Part of this new Act – that came into force on 1 September 2014 – is concerned solely with provision in England for learners with SEND. The Act is supported with detailed regulations, and perhaps more importantly, a new *Special Educational Needs and Disability Code of Practice: 0 to 25 years* (Department for Education and Department of Health 2014). The

Code also came into force on 1 September 2014. It sets out statutory guidance for schools, early years settings and post–16 education and training providers and other service providers in England. Advice in the Code will shape developments in SEND provision and practice for at least a decade, and perhaps through further iterations, for many more years.

Although signalled as a radical overhaul of a special education needs system no longer fit for purpose (Department for Education 2011) the new framework is not perhaps as radical as claimed. This was acknowledged, albeit inadvertently, by the Department for Education in a PowerPoint presentation (Department for Education 2014) sent to school leaders to help them to prepare to 'get ready' to work with new legislation: 'The SEND reforms build on the best practice over the past 13 years since the last Code of Practice was written.' This reminds us that new SEND legislation and guidance is evolutionary rather than revolutionary. It also suggests that some concepts and policies associated with previous legislation have been retained.

Arguably, the most important change in legislation, and one that should be most beneficial to learners with SEND and their families, is the requirement that 'joined up services' are in place from birth to 25 years of age. Other changes are designed to address concerns raised time and again over the past 15 years (Audit Commission 2002; House of Commons Education and Skills Committee 2006; Lamb 2009; Ofsted 2010). These concerns included:

- parents and professionals experiencing frustration about the complexity of the SEND support system with too much emphasis on inputs rather than outcomes for learners;
- a lack of real engagement with parents and learners in decision-making that affects their lives;
- longstanding concerns about the system of statutory assessment, including the length of time involved and the lack of a connection between assessment procedures and the focus of educational support;
- too many instances of young people, particularly those with the most complex needs, 'hurtling into a void' when they leave school and require support from adult services (Morris 1999; Department for Education 2011);
- systemic weaknesses in the quality of provision and support available to learners and their families;
- the over-identification of learning difficulties arising from the conflation of special educational needs with low attainment arising from teaching that did not set high expectations.

To improve matters radically, the government published a paper, *Support and Aspiration: a new approach to special educational needs and disability* (Department for Education 2011). This set out draft proposals for improving the SEND system. Following public consultation and significant redrafting, new legislation and new statutory guidance finally emerged in 2014, key features of which are:

- support across education, health and social care from birth to 25;
- requirements to ensure the participation of parents and learners in decision-making;
- early identification and intervention procedures and processes – to make sure support is in place as soon as it is required and can have optimal impact;
- the introduction of Education, Health and Care (EHC) plans – replacing Statements of special educational needs – with an emphasis on person-centred processes and outcomes;
- new duties to make sure that collaboration between education, health and social care is guaranteed and experienced as integrated support by parents and learners;

- offering more choice and control over the support that learners and their families may want through the introduction of personal budgets;
- high quality provision to meet the needs of learners;
- a focus on inclusive practice and removing barriers to learning;
- successful preparation for adulthood, including independent living, employment and community participation.

Taken at face value, the features of the revised special educational needs system are positive and seem to be particularly well targeted with regard to improving provision and longer time opportunities and outcomes for learners with SEND. However, I want now to discuss four issues that I think are inadequately addressed in SEND legislation, each of which will be considered in relation to learners with SLD/PMLD. In doing this, I will refer directly to guidance in the *Special Educational Needs and Disability Code of Practice: 0 to 25 years* (Department for Education and Department of Health 2014).

Defining special educational needs and disability

The 2014 Code of Practice (pp 15–16, paras xiii–xiv) uses a long-standing definition of special educational needs (SEN) – not a new one – but one that is confusing, and when considered alongside the Code's advice on assessment and intervention, inappropriately negative. The salient wording is:

A child or young person has SEN if they have a learning difficulty which calls for special educational provision to be made for him or her.

A child of compulsory school age or a young person has a learning difficulty or disability if he or she:
- has a significantly greater difficulty in learning than the majority of others of the same age, or
- has a disability which prevents or hinders him or her from making use of facilities of a kind generally provided for others of the same age in mainstream schools or mainstream-post 16 institutions.'

For parents, and some learners, confusion arises with regard to making a distinction between a greater difficulty in learning *or* a disability that prevents access to facilities. This confusion is exacerbated in the Code with its reference to the new duty placed on schools to support learners with medical conditions who also have special educational needs (p. 94, para. 6.11). A child or young person may therefore experience difficulties in learning that give rise to special educational needs. The same learner may also have a medical condition *and* be disabled.

To make matters worse, the Code of Practice notes (p. 16, para. xvi) that 'Post-16 institutions often use the term learning difficulties and disabilities (LDD). The term SEN is used in this Code across the 0–25 age range but includes LDD.'

Evidently, the authors of the Code have tried to integrate definitions and draw together different legislation (e.g. the Equality Act 2010 and the Children and Families Act Part 3, 2014). The result is a terminological compromise with a resultant experience of perplexity for parents, learners, and the many professionals providing support who may not be familiar with the nuances of definitions. The Code's compromise here is unlikely to address the concern referred to earlier in this chapter about the complexity of the 'support system' that families have to navigate.

The Code also provides less formal definitional guidance on 'broad areas of need', revising advice in the previous Code of Practice (Department for Education and Skills 2001b). Children and young people with learning difficulties are referred to under the 'cognition and learning' area of need:

> Learning difficulties cover a wide range of needs, including moderate learning difficulties (MLD), severe learning difficulties (SLD), where children are likely to need support in all areas of the curriculum and associated difficulties with mobility and communication, through to profound and multiple learning difficulties (PMLD), where children are likely to have severe and complex learning difficulties as well as a physical disability or sensory impairment.
>
> (pp. 97–98, para. 6.30)

This three-level description is familiar, but it is worth noting that children and young people with so-called moderate learning difficulties (MLD) were only included here after much debate. Earlier drafts of the 2014 Code of Practice preferred not to refer to MLD on the grounds that the needs of these learners were too easily conflated with low attainment arising from ineffective teaching. I welcome the acknowledgement that many children and young people do experience difficulties in learning that warrant the provision of additional support but am concerned that the Code (p. 97, para. 6.30) emphasises their slower place of learning when compared to that of their peers. Here, the Code slides into the discourse of deficit that is deeply problematic as we shall see in the discussion of teaching below. Before considering this, I want to examine the issue of inclusion as set out in the new Code.

Inclusive education provision

The Code of Practice clearly indicates that inclusive educational provision is back on the policy agenda (Robertson 2014a). It includes a section in the chapter on 'principles' titled *A focus on inclusive practice and removing barriers to learning* (pp. 25–28, paras 1.26–1.38). This reflects a decision to integrate previous statutory guidance on inclusive schooling (Department for Education and Skills 2001a) with other guidance on SEND. Positively, this section of the Code also refers to the UK government's commitments under articles 7 and 24 of the United Nations Convention on the Rights of Persons with Disabilities (United Nations 2006) actively to develop inclusive education for children and young people and progressively removing the barriers to learning and participation in mainstream education.

However, for learners with SLD/PMLD, the imperative of inclusion is trumped, in my opinion, by the government's view that parents of learners who have EHC plans have the right to express a preference for a mainstream or special school placement. This is in accord with its view – and that of the previous government (Department for Education and Skills 2004) – that special schools are an integral part of an inclusive education system and that learners can be 'educated effectively in a range of mainstream or special settings' (2014 Code of Practice, p. 28, para. 1.38). It is also consonant with the view of many special school based professionals (Department for Education and Skills 2003), the equivocal view of the national inspectorate (Ofsted 2006) and Warnock's well-publicised revisionist view of integration and inclusion (Warnock 2005; Warnock and Norwich with Terzi 2010).

My concern here is that despite using the rhetoric of removing barriers to learning and participation, the current government has no real commitment to challenging the status quo of provision and educational placement for the majority of children and young people with significant learning difficulties. This is reflected in the active encouragement being given to parents, professionals and organisations to open new special Academy and Free schools – premised on the idea of improvement through innovation and diversity – rather than through advice designed to enhance the quality of inclusive provision and practice in mainstream schools.

There is also newly emerging evidence that the number of learners attending special schools in England is beginning to increase (by 8,475 between 2007 and 2013) (Times Education Supplement 2014). This increase is small but could be significant because it reverses a slow long-term trend towards reduced special school placements, and is not simply explained by changing demographic patterns (e.g. increased survival rate of premature babies). More plausible explanations are likely to include one or more of the following:

- the perceived political ambivalence of the current government – in 2011 it clearly expressed the view that it intended to 'remove the bias towards' inclusion (Department for Education 2011);
- lobbying by some parents and organisations to increase the availability of specialist provision;
- increasing special school places in some local authorities due to demand from parents and mainstream schools;
- some mainstream schools seeking special school placements for learners because of perceived or real difficulties in being able to make appropriate curriculum provision (particularly in secondary schools);
- positive marketing of specialist provision by special school sector professionals.

Notwithstanding positive developments in special school-led inclusive practice initiatives (e.g. through collaborative activities with mainstream schools and a wide range of community-based activities) these are far from systemic in the way that Norwich (2008) argued for, and they are potentially fragile if, for example, a change of headteacher or a new Academy leadership team decides to downplay the value of inclusive provision.

I had hoped that new SEND legislation and guidance would be radical with regard to ensuring that more and more learners with a range of special educational needs, including learning difficulties, would be placed in mainstream schools as of right. The revised SEND framework does not, I think, open any new doors in this regard. The 2014 Code of Practice is at best cautious in its advice on educational placement and, although it refers to the concept of equality and the importance of countering discriminatory practice in education by adhering to provisions in the Equality Act 2010, it backs away from addressing arguments about the intrinsically discriminatory nature of specialist provision. In failing to do this, the Code only encourages mainstream schools and settings to develop inclusive provision without providing an imperative to do so. It also struggles to address the perennial problem of regular schooling that has at its core the need to marginalise and exclude some learners because of demands to focus on academic standards and the standardisation of provision to meet these (Cigman 2007; Slee 2011).

Inclusive teaching and learning

Having argued that the concept of inclusive education is poorly served by the 2014 Code of Practice, and that this has a particularly negative impact on children and young people with learning difficulties, I now want to consider the guidance the Code provides on teaching this group of learners.

The key vehicle for identifying, assessing and teaching learners with SEND is set out in Chapter six of the Code. It is referred to as the graduated approach and involves use of a four-part assess-plan-do-review cycle (pp. 100–102, paras. 6.44–6.56). The approach is a common sense one and can be applied through successive cycles to support different levels of teaching intervention according to the needs of learners. So far, so good, and the approach clearly lends itself to adaptation for learners with MLD, SLD and PMLD who may require teaching interventions of greater intensity by teaching staff with specialist knowledge (see chapters by Fletcher-Campbell, Porter, and Ware respectively in Lewis and Norwich, 2005 for detailed discussion of specialist teaching).

The difficulty in applying the graduated approach arises from the way that the new Code conceptualises the needs of learners who are making less than expected progress (Robertson 2014b). It refers to this as progress which:

- is significantly slower than that of the learner's peers starting from the same baseline;
- fails to match or better the learner's previous rate of progress;
- fails to close the gap between the learner and peers;
- widens the attainment gap. (p. 95, para. 6.17)

Without being stated explicitly, learners' difficulties are constructed in deficit terms and the 'real message' is that schools and teachers could do more to ensure progress is in line with age-related expectations of performance in core subject areas.

Reference is also made to 'progress in areas other than attainment – for instance where a pupil needs to make additional progress with wider development or social needs in order to make a successful transition into adult life' (p. 95, para. 6.18). This is welcome advice congruent with research recommendations (Douglas *et al.* 2012), but it does not have the same force as the persistent normative attainment narrative in the Code, government rhetoric more generally, and national inspectorate exhortations (Ofsted 2010, 2014).

Guidance in the Code on improving outcomes for learners with EHC plans is more neutral in tone, but is obviously linked to a narrowly conceived view of learning and progress. It refers, for example, to specific, measurable, achievable, realistic and time-bound (SMART) shorter-term outcomes or objectives (pp. 162–169, paras. 9.64–9.69), and in so doing, reflects a rather dated behavioural objectives approach to teaching and learning. What is missing here is a recognition that teaching approaches today can be richer, more responsive to the needs of learners, and be successful without being limited by SMART targets that can constrain learning. Examples of richer and more meaningful pedagogical approaches can be found in the social constructivist tradition (Watson 2000), the inclusive education tradition (Corbett 2001; Hart 1996; Hart *et al.* 2004; Loreman, Deppeler and Harvey 2010; Swann *et al.* 2012), and through the application of neurologically informed evidence (Claxton 1997).

Evidence from all these approaches highlights the limited value of prescribing outcomes and the benefits of co-constructing learning opportunities that can lead to the achievement of unintended but more powerful outcomes. Intriguingly, these approaches resonate with the following advice in the Code:

> When agreeing outcomes, it is important to consider what is important *to* the child or young person – what they themselves want to be able to achieve – and what is important *for* them as judged by others with the child's or young person's best interests at heart.
>
> (p. 163, para. 9.67)

The danger of course is that best interests are determined by those 'who know best' and in relation to demands of an assessment framework that may not be considered important to the learner, parents or possibly a teacher.

The Code's guidance on identification, assessment and intervention – or teaching – children and young people with learning difficulties is narrowly conceived and driven by particular assessment requirements. This is also a matter of concern with regard to teacher education, and the Code has little to say about this. We know, for example, that there is an outstanding need for teachers working with learners with SEND to enhance their own knowledge, skills and understanding (MacBeath *et al.* 2006; Hartley 2010; Ellis, Tod and Graham-Matheson 2011; Department for Education 2012).

Curriculum provision

The 2014 Code of Practice (p. 94, para. 6.12) briefly notes that 'all pupils should have access to a broad and balanced curriculum'. It then refers to the National Curriculum and the Inclusion Statement (Department for Education 2013), included in the National Curriculum framework introduced in England in September 2014. The statement has two dimensions. It places a strong emphasis on setting suitable challenges for learners and stresses the importance of responding to learners' needs and overcoming potential barriers to access and participation for individuals or groups of learners. With regard to suitable challenges for learners it says that teachers should:

- set high expectations for every learner;
- plan stretching work for learners whose attainment is significantly above the expected standard;
- recognise that they have an even greater obligation to plan lessons for learners who have low levels of prior attainment or come from disadvantaged backgrounds;
- use appropriate assessment to set targets that are deliberately ambitious.

This guidance is at best perfunctory, does little to acknowledge development work undertaken over many years to enhance access to the National Curriculum for children (aged 5 to 16) with learning difficulties (see Chapter 5 in this book), and yet again we see learners viewed from a deficit perspective.

With regard to overcoming barriers to access and participation, the Inclusion Statement reminds teachers of their responsibilities under the Equality Act 2010, and the importance of making reasonable adjustments in curriculum provision for learners with a wide range of needs (Robertson 2014c). The advice here is sound, but weakened because of the lack of more detailed guidance on National Curriculum access and participation, and the complete lack of guidance on what a broad and balanced curriculum might look like for children with significant learning difficulties.

Guidance in the Code on the curriculum for children in early years settings and young people in further education is minimal. This brevity might be regarded as positive if it affords teachers freedom to innovate, but there is a danger that, without more detailed advice, this might too easily be interpreted as 'just implement the graduated approach' in ways that I have cautioned against above. In the post-16 sector there is an additional concern that, following a national review of vocational education (Wolf 2011), a focus on core course provision in future will narrow opportunities for the learning opportunities for young people with learning difficulties that *they* want to help them fulfil their longer-term aspirations.

Summary

In this chapter I have provided a brief overview of SEND legislation implemented in England in 2014. I have argued that claims about its radical nature have been overstated and that, in many respects, it represents a cautious approach that focuses on making gradual improvements and refinements to the SEND system that is perhaps more fit for purpose than we might think (Lewis, Parsons and Robertson 2007).

It would be unfair to assess policy impact at the current time, given that it can take up to ten years to ascertain deeper level effects of key changes. However, I have presented a critical discussion of policy as set out in the 2014 Code of Practice. The weaknesses, as I view them, represent at best a missed opportunity in relation to the development of better provision for all children and young people with special educational needs. Furthermore, this missed opportunity will have a disproportionately negative impact on learners with SLD/PMLD. However, I do not want to conclude this chapter on a negative note. I take the view that teachers, parents and hopefully learners will find ways to navigate the new SEND system, making the most of its good features, and circumventing its weaknesses with imagination and resilience. Yet again though, they will do this in spite of rather than because of legislation or policy guidance.

Questions for readers

- Does the Code of Practice provide clear and accurate enough guidance for the people in your setting who have to implement it?
- What guidance and training has your local authority provided about the creation and delivery of EHC plans?
- Has your local authority published the 'local offer' about services available for learners with SEND?
- Does your local authority and/or your own setting have any statements about inclusive teaching and learning?
- If you do not live and work in England, what comparable frameworks and systems exist in your country?

References

Audit Commission (2002) *Statutory Assessment and Statements of Special Educational Needs: In need of review?* Wetherby: Audit Commission.

Cigman, R. (ed.) (2007) *Included or Excluded: The challenge of the mainstream for some SEN children*, London: Routledge.

Claxton, G. (1997) *Hare Brain, Tortoise Mind: Why intelligence increases when you think less*, London: Fourth Estate.

Corbett, J. (2001) *Supporting Inclusive Education: An inclusive pedagogy*, London: Routledge/Falmer.

Department for Education (2011) *Support and Aspiration: a new approach to special educational needs and disability. A consultation*. London and Norwich: TSO. Online. Available: www.education.gov.uk/schools/pupilsupport/sen/a0075339/sengreenpaper (accessed 20 August 2014).

Department for Education (2012) *Teachers' Standards*, London: Department for Education. Online. Available: www.gov.uk/government/publications/teachers-standards (accessed 20 August 2014)

Department for Education (2013) *National Curriculum in England – Framework document: for teaching. 1 September 2014–31 August 2015*, Online. Available: www.gov.uk/government/publications/national-curriculum-in-england-framework-for-key-stages-1-to-4 (accessed 20 August 2014)

Department for Education (2014) *A DfE Presentation Pack for School Leaders: The 0-25 special educational needs and disability reforms*, London: Department for Education. Online. Available: www.sendgateway.

org.uk/resources.a-dfe-presentation-pack-for-school-leaders-the-0-25-special-educational-needs-and-disability-reforms.html (accessed 20 August 2014).

Department for Education and Department of Health (2014) *Special Educational Needs and Disability Code of Practice: 0 to 25 years*. Ref: DFE:-00205-2013. Online. Available: www.gov.uk/government/publications/send-code-of-practice-0-to-25 (accessed 20 August 2014).

Department for Education and Skills (2001a) *Inclusive Schooling: Children with special educational needs*, Statutory Guidance, DfES /0774/2001. Online. Available: www.gov.uk/government/publications/inclusive-schooling-children-with-special-educational-needs (accessed 20 August 2014).

Department for Education and Skills (2001b) *Special Educational Needs Code of Practice*, Annesley, Nottingham: DfES Publications.

Department for Education and Skills (2003) *The Report of the Special Schools Working* Group, Annesley, Nottingham: DfES Publications.

Department for Education and Skills (2004) *Removing Barriers to Achievement: The Government's strategy for SEN*, Annesley, Nottingham: DfES Publications.

Douglas, G., Travers, J., McLinden. M., Robertson, C., Smith, E., Macnab, N., Powers, S., Guldberg, K., McGough, A., O'Donnell, M. and Lacey, P. (2012) *Measuring Educational Engagement, Progress and Outcomes for Children with Special Educational Needs: A review*, National Council for Special Education (Ireland) Research Report 11. Online. Available: www.ncse.ie/uploads/1/Outcomes26_11_12Acc.pdf (accessed 20 August 2014).

Ellis, S., Tod, J. and Graham-Matheson, L. (2011) *Reflection, Renewal and Reality: Teachers' experiences of needs and inclusion*, Birmingham: NASUWT.

Fletcher-Campbell, F. (2005) 'Moderate learning difficulties', in A. Lewis and B. Norwich (eds) *Special Teaching for Special Children? Pedagogies for inclusion*, Maidenhead: Open University Press.

Hart, S. (1996) *Beyond Special Needs: Enhancing children's learning through innovative thinking*, London: Paul Chapman.

Hart, S., Dixon, A., Drummond, M.J. and McIntyre, D. (2004) *Learning Without Limits*, Maidenhead: Open University Press.

Hartley, R. (2010) *Teacher Expertise for Special Educational Needs: Filling the gaps*, London: Policy Exchange. Online. Available: www.policyexchange.org.uk/publications/category/item/teacher-expertise-for-special-educational-needs-2?category_id=24 (accessed 20 August 2014).

House of Commons Education and Skills Committee (2006) *Special Educational Needs: third report of session 2005-06, Volume 1* [HC 478-1], London: The Stationery Office.

Lamb, B. (2009) *Lamb Inquiry: Special Educational Needs and Parental Confidence*, Annesley, Nottingham: DCSF Publications.

Lewis, A. and Norwich, B. (2005) *Special Teaching for Special Children? Pedagogies for inclusion*, Maidenhead: Open University Press.

Lewis, A., Parsons, S. and Robertson, C. (2007) *My School, My Family, My Life: Telling it like it is*, London: Disability Rights Commission.

Loreman, T., Deppeler, J. and Harvey, D. (2010) *Inclusive Education: Supporting diversity in the classroom*, London: Routledge.

MacBeath, J., Galton, M., Steward, S., MacBeath, A. and Page, C. (2006) *The Costs of Inclusion: A study of inclusion policy and practice in English primary, secondary and special schools*. Online. Available: www.teachers.org.uk/node/2269 (accessed 20 August 2014)

Morris, J. (1999) *Hurtling into a Void: Transition to adulthood for young disabled people with 'complex health and support needs'*, Brighton: Pavilion Publishing for the Joseph Rowntree Foundation.

Norwich, B. (2008) 'What future for special schools and inclusion? Conceptual and professional challenges', *British Journal of Special Education*, 35(3): 136–143.

Ofsted (2006) *Inclusion: Does it matter where pupils are taught? Provision and outcomes in different settings for pupils with learning difficulties and disabilities*, Ref: HMI 2535. Online. Available: www.ofsted.gov.uk/resources/inclusion-does-it-matter-where-pupils-are-taught (accessed 20 August 2014).

Ofsted (2010) *The Special Educational Needs and Disability Review: A statement is not enough*, Ref: 090221. Online. Available: www.ofsted.gov.uk/resources/special-educational-needs-and-disability-review (accessed 20 August 2014).

Ofsted (2014) *The Framework for School Inspection: The framework for inspecting schools in England under section 5 of the Education Act 2005 (as amended)*. September 2014 version. Online. Available: www.ofsted.gov.uk/resources/framework-for-school-inspection-january-2012 (accessed 20 August 2014).

Porter, J. (2005) 'Severe learning difficulties', in A. Lewis and B. Norwich (eds) *Special Teaching for Special Children? Pedagogies for inclusion*, Maidenhead: Open University Press.

Robertson, C. (2014a) 'Refocus on rights: inclusive provision and admissions for children and young people with SEND – updated Code of Practice guidance', *Special Educational Needs Hub*, Online. Available: www.optimus-education.com/refocus-rights-inclusive-provision-and-admissions-children-and-young-people-send-updated-code (accessed 20 August 2014).

Robertson, C. (2014b) 'Assess, plan, do review: a graduated approach to intervention', *Special Educational Needs Hub*, Online. Available: www.optimus-education.com/assess-plan-do-review-graduated-approach-intervention (accessed 20 August 2014).

Robertson, (2014c) 'Inclusion and the new National Curriculum', *Special Educational Needs Hub*, Online. Available: www.optimus-education.com/inclusion-and-new-national-curriculum (accessed 20 August 2014).

Slee, R. (2011) *The Irregular School: Exclusion, schooling and inclusive education*, London: Routledge.

Swann, M., Peacock, M., Drummond, M.J. and Hart, S. (2012) *Creating Learning Without Limits*, Maidenhead: Open University Press.

Times Education Supplement (2014) 'Increase in number of special school pupils reverses trend towards inclusion', Online. Available: http://news.tes.co.uk/b/news/2014/08/08/increase-in-special-school-numbers-reverses-trend-towards-inclusion.aspx (accessed 20 August 2014).

United Kingdom Parliament (2014) *Children and Families Act 2014 – Part 3: Children and Young People in England with Special Educational Needs and Disabilities*. Online. Available: www.legislation.gov.uk/ukpga/2014/6/contents/enacted (accessed 20 August 2014).

United Nations (2006) *United Nations Convention on the Rights of Persons with Disabilities*, New York/Geneva: United Nations. Online. Available: www.un.org/disabilities/convention/conventionfull.shtml (accessed 20 August 2014).

Ware, J. (2005) 'Profound and multiple learning difficulties', in A. Lewis and B. Norwich (eds) *Special Teaching for Special Children? Pedagogies for inclusion*, Maidenhead: Open University Press.

Warnock, M. (2005) *Special Educational Needs: A new look*, London: Philosophy of Education Society of Great Britain.

Warnock, M. and Norwich, B. with Terzi, L. (ed.) (2010) *Special Educational Needs: a new look*, 2nd edn, London: Continuum.

Watson, J. (2000) 'Constructive instruction and learning difficulties', *Support for Learning*, 15(3): 134–140.

Wolf, A. (2011) *Review of Vocational Education – The Wolf Report*. London: Department for Education. Online. Available: www.gov.uk/government/publications/review-of-vocational-education-the-wolf-report (accessed 20 August 2014).

4

AN HISTORICAL REFLECTION ON EDUCATION FOR LEARNERS WITH SLD/PMLD

1800–1970

David S. Stewart

In this chapter, the following questions will be addressed:

- Why was medical opinion allowed to hold sway for so long in determining the educability of learners with SLD/PMLD?
- Why have successive governments been so reluctant to provide appropriate training for teachers of learners with SLD/PMLD?

Introduction

The Individuality of the children is the first thing to be secured and respect for individuality is the first test of the fitness of the teacher.

(Benson 1934: 13)

It may be a surprise to the modern reader that when student teachers enrolled for a postgraduate teacher education course in Leeds and embarked on their training in the 'education of the mentally handicapped' in the mid-1970s, the set texts were Heaton-Ward's *Mental Subnormality* (1975) and Penrose's *The Biology of Mental Defect* (1972). Why such medical texts for an education course? It says much about the previous history of education for learners with SLD/PMLD. To assist me as a trainee teacher, a retired hospital chaplain gave me a copy of Jennie Benson's *Care and Training of Mentally Defective Children* (1934)! I had been a volunteer in a junior training centre (an establishment, run by the health department of the local authority, for children, at that time described as mentally handicapped) and had worked as a student at Darenth Park Hospital (variously described at that time as a hospital for the mentally handicapped or subnormality hospital), so I was well aware that provision for these children had been very different from that of other children. In this chapter I will explore that history, to give a better understanding of why this group of learners came so late to the state education system.

In the general history of special education, the education of learners with SLD/PMLD has sometimes been lost. There is no doubt that the early provision of education in the UK from the 1840s was for those children whose disability was more apparent. In an age when a large part of the population was unable to read or write, those with mild or moderate disabilities were less noticeable, from an educational point of view. Once universal education was provided from the 1870s, the issue of how to educate those with more moderate learning disabilities came to the fore, while those with SLD/PMLD were deemed to be ineducable, remaining so until 1970. Indeed in Pritchard's seminal text, they are no longer mentioned after his chapter on the 1944 Education Act (Pritchard 1963).

From the forests of Aveyron to the streets of Bath

Aug. 1, 1802. 'The Savage of Aveyron is a thousand times more interesting to me than Caliste. I have not read anything for years that interested me so much.'

(Hare 1894: 78)

Thus wrote the writer and educationalist, Maria Edgeworth to her cousin. Maria had been reading Dr Jean-Marc-Gaspard Itard's detailed account of his work with Victor, the Wild Boy (Itard 1806/1932). Itard's work should not be seen in isolation for, as in England, the Institute de France and the Society of Observers of Man were keen to pursue discoveries in sciences and the arts. This was also a time of radical rethinking in education philosophy and practice which had begun with Rousseau's *Emile* (1762). In the same year that Itard's book appeared, Pestalozzi published *How Gertrude Teaches Her Children* (Pestalozzi 1894). His starting point coincided with much of what Itard had found by experimentation with Victor, that all knowledge derived from sense impressions, which needed to be fostered and cultivated. Pestalozzi was truly ahead of his time when he wrote, 'We have no right to withhold from anyone the opportunities for developing all their faculties' (Pestalozzi 1827: 86).

In Paris, Itard felt that he had failed in his experiment for Victor, while making progress, had not been cured. This was not Rousseau's 'noble savage.' He would continue his work with the deaf until his death in 1838 (Lane 1977). During the late 1820s and1830s several people attempted to establish schools for so-called 'idiot' and 'imbecile' children in Paris, terms which we now find shocking. Felix Voisin, a keen phrenologist at the Bicetre asylum was one of these innovators. Another was Edouard Seguin, a favourite student of Itard, and he urged his mentor to share his practice and experience. These new experiments in education in Paris soon brought visitors from England and the United States and Voisin and Seguin wrote about their experiences (Voisin 1843; Seguin 1866).

In 1840 in Switzerland a young doctor, Johann Jacob Guggenbuhl had established a school for 'cretins' on the Abendberg. (The term cretin, derived from the word Christian, was given to those who presented with severely limited physical and mental growth. It was only later in the 19th century that the condition was found to be related to untreated congenital deficiency of thyroid hormones.) This attracted much interest from Britain, including Dr William Twining, of the tea firm, who presented his findings from a 1843 visit to the British Association for the Advancement of Science annual conference two years later. He reminded his audience 'that cretins can become healthy and intelligent has been proved by Dr. Guggenbuhl, in the success that his benevolent exertions… have met with' (British Association 1846: 79). The Vice President of the Association that year was the geologist, Roderick Impey Murchison, who had encouraged the attendance of women at the presentations. It was his nieces, Charlotte and Harriette White, who established the first school for idiot children in Bath in 1846.

I may mention that the first attempt made in England in behalf of this unfortunate class, was by Miss C. White – a young lady residing at Bath, who, partly at her own expense, and partly with the assistance of charitable friends, founded a school in that city, to which, for several years, she devoted all her time and energies. I have frequently had opportunities of visiting this institution, and of admiring the unwearied zeal which she brought to a task, then considered by many altogether hopeless.

(Cumming 1852: 38)

The Institution for Idiots, Bath

Established in 1846, in 1883 Harriette Newnham (nee White) reflected on the early days of the school:

> The Idiot Institution was originally an offshoot of the Deaf and Dumb School. Mute children were taken there whom it was found impossible to teach in the usual way. They were imbecile. My sister, then Miss Charlotte White, determined to try and train them separately. Nothing of the kind had ever been attempted in England, and it was amid great discouragements that the work was begun. In 1846 a house was taken in Walcot Parade, on her responsibility, but a public appeal was made for funds. Poor children only were admitted, at £12 a year.
>
> It was a rule strictly enforced that the children were taken for a walk every day. There was a perambulator for the use of the more infirm. A miniature gymnasium was erected at the foot of the so-called garden, consisting of a swing and hanging ropes, which by degrees the children got to enjoy. A swing which could be raised at will for the children to hang on was also placed in the door way of the schoolroom, and on wet days, the lady teachers, of whom I was one, remained to play with the children, who literally required to be taught the use of hands and feet. Learning to read was quite the exception, but intelligence was slowly developed. They learned to distinguish shapes and colours, and proved very susceptible of religious impressions.
>
> (*The Bath Chronicle*, Thursday, 18 October, 1883: 6)

The Darenth schools

Between 1847 and 1870 five larger regional charitable asylums for idiots and imbeciles were founded and there were some private establishments for a few children of the wealthy but in reality the majority of these children were at home, in the workhouse or in some cases in mental asylums. In 1865 the Commissioners in Lunacy stated 'that the association of idiot children with lunatics is very objectionable and injurious to them', advocating a distinct system of training and education (Commissioners in Lunacy 1865). This was to become very apparent in London when after the establishment of the Metropolitan Asylums Board (MAB) in 1867, workhouses discharged large numbers of disabled children to the new poor law asylums.

Urged by the Commissioners in Lunacy, the Managers of the MAB made arrangements first in Clapton in 1875 and then in purpose-built schools at Darenth in Kent, initially for 500 and later 1,000 children. Opened in 1878, the Darenth Schools became the first such establishments in the UK to be funded from the public purse. The first Chairman, Sir Edmund Hay Currie, was also Vice-Chairman of the School Board for London. Mary Jane Stephens, appointed as first head schoolmistress, established a regulated system of education. Unlike the voluntary aided institutions and similar schools in America, the Darenth Schools took children of all abilities, including those with the most significant need.

The Clapton and Darenth Schools

Miss Stephens recorded in 1875: 'Many attend school, and unfortunately can only be kept out of mischief and broken of bad habits; others attend to be amused; others to be educated, though to some their education will avail but little, they being too imbecile in mind or body; but were they not sent to school daily, they must either be allowed to run wildly in a most distressing way, or forced into an unnatural sitting-still – equally distressing. By attending school they are much brighter, more happy, and much more intelligent, and have so much more individuality.'

(MAB 1876, *Annual Report of Head School Mistress 1875*)

Dr Brewer, Chairman of the MAB spoke of the teachers in glowing terms. 'The teachers must possess and combine the indispensable qualifications of bravery, forbearance and moral courage, and be impressed with a sense of having consecrated their hearts on their admission to the object they have in view. All the teachers in the schools were women. It was women's work. Patience and gentleness were indispensable.'

(Brewer, *Dartford Chronicle*, 21 October 1876)

Almost as soon as the new schools were open, there was concern about the admission of the less able. In his annual report for 1883 Dr Beach of the Darenth Schools reported to the MAB that 'the building, I regret to say, is becoming more a receptacle for the care of the helpless and epileptic imbecile children, and is losing in the same degree the character of a training school.' He was also becoming increasingly exasperated with some managers who thought that palaces were being created for those who did not appreciate it: 'I suggest that those Managers who think the cost is high, should come and spend a day here' (cited in Stewart 1978: 15).

The report of the Department Committee on defective and epileptic children 1898 and its long-term consequences for learners with SLD/PMLD

Despite any direction from the Board of Education some school boards, such as Leicester, London, Nottingham, Birmingham, Bradford, Brighton and Bristol, had established schools for 'defective' children in the 1890s but there was no uniformity of procedure. Under pressure from the School Board for London, the Board of Education finally agreed to appoint a committee in 1896. There was only one teacher, Mrs Burgwin, on the committee. It heard evidence from teachers, doctors, inspectors, voluntary organizations and administrators. Its focus was on the education of 'feeble-minded and defective children' not under the charge of statutory guardians and not idiots and imbeciles. It was also to report on the means of discriminating between the educable and non–educable children.

The medical members of the committee quickly began to assert their influence and Drs Shuttleworth and Smith recommended that the term 'imbecile' be applied to all children who, by reason of mental defect, were incapable of being educated so as to become self-supporting.

This was more a social rather than an educational criterion. Evidence from witnesses showed that lack of proper assessment, coupled with lack of appropriate provision meant that certain children deemed to be ineducable were in fact being taught in special schools and classes and indeed in ordinary board schools. General Moberly of the London School Board noted that all the teachers could do was to keep them occupied, though they were sometimes 'taught to fetch and carry as a dog might be.' He noted, however, that they were 'exceedingly kindly treated by the other children' (Royal Commission 1889, Vol. 3: 868–9). The committee recommended that for school authorities the test must be 'incapacity to receive proper benefit from instruction in the special classes.' How was this to be determined? This was before the development of standardized intelligence tests. Miss Hoatson, by then Headmistress at Darenth, noted how difficult it was to classify children: 'A child may be able to read but cannot write, or be able to read a few numbers together but cannot either read or write, or may be intelligent in understanding simple things, and not be able to do anything but manual work' (Education Department 1898, Evidence of Hoatson 19 February 1897).

The doctors who gave evidence said they could assess imbecility by physical signs. The medical witnesses were in no doubt as to their superior knowledge in terms of assessment though Dr. Shuttleworth did concede that on occasion the teacher's view might be of the greatest importance. Mrs Burgwin fumed at their arrogance! The then Superintendent of Darenth, Dr. Walmsley, was particularly arrogant, saying that it was difficult to answer questions in terms that 'the lay mind' could comprehend. Other doctors concurred that they were the best people for assessment both medical and educational and, in the absence of other suggestions, the Committee concluded that selection of children for a special school or not should be undertaken by a doctor. The Elementary Education (Defective and Epileptic Children) Act 1899 re-affirmed their findings. Idiots or imbeciles would not receive education and decisions of selection would be by medical practitioners. The principles for the exclusion of children and young people with SLD and PMLD had been set for the next 70 years.

The Mental Deficiency Act 1913

Others have written about the rise of the Eugenics movement and the consequent demand for permanent exclusion of those with learning difficulties in the early years of the twentieth century (Jones 1972; Pritchard 1963; Kelves 1985). The Royal Commission on the Care and Control of the Feeble-minded, established in 1904, was in part a response to the fears for national efficiency highlighted by concerns about the physical and mental state of recruits for the Boer War in 1899. Similar concerns led to the provision of school meals and health inspections in schools. The Commission reported in 1908 but it was to be another five years before legislation was enacted. Vociferous voices such as Mary Dendy, Ellen Pinsent and Winston Churchill called for the permanent care of this section of society. Local Authorities urged the Government to Act. In February 1911, the Council of the City of Nottingham deplored 'the inadequacy of control of the adult feeble-minded, which… seriously reduces the mean average of the health, intelligence, the morality and physique of the race' (cited in Jones 1960: 62). It demanded 'permanent control of these unfortunates.' Josiah Wedgewood, MP, was appalled by these demands, feeling that the government had followed up the suggestions of the eugenic cranks and he painted a picture of children being taken away in spite of paternal protests and maternal tears to be 'locked up for life' (Wedgewood 1940).

The Mental Deficiency Act which followed in 1913, defined four categories of persons: feeble-minded; imbecile; idiot; and moral imbecile. The body appointed to oversee the implementation of this Act was the Board of Control. The Act did not apply to disabled children who were in workhouses. For the purposes of this chapter, it is the definition of the first two categories, which are of interest.

> Idiot – so deeply defective in mind as to be unable to guard against physical dangers (incidentally, there is still a question related to this on benefit forms to this day); and

> Imbeciles – incapable of managing themselves or their affairs, or, in the case of children, of being taught to do so.

There was no expectation of educability for these two groups and the sole provision was placement in a certified institution or under statutory guardianship. Clear responsibility was given to the local education authority (LEA) to notify the 'mental deficiency committee' of the local authority of all defective children over the age of 7 who had been ascertained to be incapable by reason of mental defect of receiving benefit or further benefit in special schools or classes, or who cannot be instructed in a special school or class without detriment to the interests of the other children. Recommendations could also be made for children leaving special school to be sent to an institution or placed under guardianship.

The 1914 Education (Defective and Epileptic Children) Act, which followed hard on, gave statutory responsibility to LEAs to provide special schools for the feeble-minded child. No sooner had the legislation been enacted, the First World War began and many of the proposals of the Act were hard to enact. Children who were recommended for admission to an institution were often still at home because places were hard to come by. Former homes for inebriates, such as Stoke Park in Bristol, were transformed for the new clientele but nationally there were insufficient places. Local mental deficiency committees were forced to contract for places in the workhouse for which parents were charged. So in the workhouse could be both pauper children with SLD, uncertified under the Act, and children whose parents were paying and who were certified as idiots or imbeciles. At Darenth, parents demanded different wards so the two groups did not mix!

Junior occupation centres

The one glimmer of light within the 1913 Act was section 48 which stated that voluntary societies could be funded to provide supervision of defectives. This gave the opportunity for voluntary organizations to come to the fore in providing services. Even before the Act, some attempts had been made to provide day centres, such as by Miss Arnould at Lillie Road, London and by Miss Woodhead in Brighton. The Central Association for Mental Welfare (CAMW), championed by the formidable Evelyn Fox, took on the task of establishing occupation centres toward the end of the war, although in 1914 Elfrida Rathbone had already established the Lilian Greg Centre in memory of her cousin. The CAMW took up the 50 percent grant offered by the Board of Control and by 1924 there were 55 centres nationally. Only one, in Norwich, had been set up by the local authority. The 1927 Mental Deficiency Act recognized that defectives needed not only supervision, protection and control but occupation and training too. Parents were given the power to make representations to the local authority that their child 'is in need of care and training which cannot be given at home.'

It is also very clear that it was not only children deemed ineducable who attended occupation centres. 'The provision of special schools is inadequate, and in some areas the occupation centre affords the only available means of training for numbers of children who are quite unable to benefit by the elementary school training' (Benson 1934: 12).

The Board of Control recognized the value of education and training. Ruth Darwin, one of their commissioners, noted in 1934 that 'to get down to the child's level and to discover some spark of interest which can be fostered and fanned into purposeful action requires, it is true, common sense and sympathy, but it also requires resources which can only be gained by practical experience of teaching methods' (Darwin cited in Benson 1934: x). County organizers from the CAMW, such as Jennie Benson in Staffordshire, would work with or badger local authorities to improve services for the least able children in the community, providing some of the first speech and language therapists and educational psychologists. The Wood Committee noted in 1929, 'the Supervisor is not generally a trained teacher, but is a woman with knowledge of dealing with children and ability to teach simple handwork, music and physical exercises. As a rule, she is given training by the Central Association for Mental Welfare in their special training centre or in an institution, or at one of the many Short Courses organized by the Association' (Board of Education and Board of Control 1929: 68).

The 1944 Education Act brought no inclusion for learners with SLD/PMLD. Section 57 excluded those 'whose disability of mind was of such a nature as to make him incapable of receiving education at school.' Decisions based on intellectual assessment became more prevalent. Hard on the heels of this Act came the National Health Service (NHS) in 1948. This had the disastrous effect of bringing residential institutions, in the main run by local authorities, under the NHS, reinforcing more strongly the medical model of learning disability. Ill funded and scandal ridden, it took another 50 years or more to return these institutions to local authority responsibility.

After the Second World War, parents began to take matters into their own hands and, dissatisfied with the CAMW's links with government, began to form their own support networks. Inspired by parents such as Judy Fryd and organizations such as the National Association of Backward Children (later Mencap) local groups were formed. Sheena Rolph's research in East Anglia on the early days of these groups is invaluable (Rolph 2002, 2005a, 2005b).

In 1959 the Mental Health Act appeared to give some compulsion to parents to send their child to a training or occupation centre. The term 'junior training centre' became the more usual term. This assumed of course that there was somewhere suitable to go. 'She attended an ordinary school for three years and was then classed as ineducable and promised a place at an occupation centre only to be told that there was no transport available and she must be content with a Home Teacher once in three weeks' (Rolph 2002: 55). The Act continued the separation of administrative responsibility for the education of school age children according to educability.

While a report on the 'Training of Staff of Training Centres for the Mentally Subnormal' (Central Health Services Council Standing Mental Health Advisory Committee 1962) recommended training for staff in junior training centres and hospitals, Enoch Powell, then Minister of Health, rejected the proposal saying that 'talk of training was premature and that in his experience ordinary people such as bus drivers were well disposed to these children' (Mittler 2012: 141). Fury at this led to the creation of a Department of Health 'Training Council for Teachers of the Mentally Handicapped.' However, by 1966, of 174 teachers attending a national training course, only 10 had been seconded from the hospitals and the rest were being financed by the local authorities. It was inferred in Parliament that the Ministry of Health had positively interfered in the secondment of staff from its hospitals to this training course. In Manchester, Mildred Stevens had begun a two-year training programme promoted by the National Association of Mental Health.

The groundswell of opinion for reform in the 1960s found a Labour government more prepared to listen. The Seebohm Committee recommended in 1968 that LEAs should assume 'responsibility for the education and training of all subnormal children' (Seebohm Report 1968: 116). This campaign for education was championed by Stanley Segal, the author of the seminal text, *No Child is Ineducable* (Segal 1967). The Education (Handicapped Children) Act was passed on 23 July 1970 by which all children in England and Wales, no matter the degree of disability, became the responsibility of LEAs. This was enacted on 1 April 1971. There was much to be done, not least being the training of teaching staff. A specialist three-year course was established with special one year courses for those holding the Diploma of the Training Council for Teachers of the Mentally Handicapped. Leeds Polytechnic and Redlands College, Bristol were permitted to provide a postgraduate certificate in education course. There would be many more battles to fight – sadly often the prejudice from other sectors of special education – but the principle of education for all had been set. The many successes and achievement of these learners over the last 40 years is an absolute vindication of those who championed their right to education.

Questions for readers

- Why is it important that we understand the history of this area of education in terms of planning for future? What are the ongoing issues and concerns?
- What does the history tell us about political and societal attitudes to the education of children and young people SLD/PMLD?

Further reading

Atkinson, D., Jackson, M. and Walmsley, J. (1997) *Forgotten Lives: Exploring the history of learning disability*, Kidderminster: BILD Publications.

Brigham, L., Atkinson, D., Jackson, M., Rolph, S. and Walmsley, J. (2000) (eds) *Crossing Boundaries: Change and continuity in the history of learning disability*, Kidderminster: BILD.

Carpenter, P.K. (2000) 'The Bath Idiot and Imbecile Institution', *History of Psychiatry*, 11(2): 163–188.

Carpenter, P.K. (2000) 'The Victorian Small Idiot Homes near Bath', *History of Psychiatry*, 11(4): 383–392.

Hurt, J.S. (1988) *Outside the Mainstream: A history of special education*, London: Batsford.

Rolph, S., Atkinson, D., Nind, M. and Welshman, J. (2005) *Witnesses to Change: Families, learning difficulties and history*, Kidderminster: BILD.

Stewart, D.S. (2000) 'Paved with good intentions: the Hampstead and Clapton Schools 1873-1878', *British Journal of Learning Disabilities*, 28(2): 54–59.

References

Benson, J. (1934) *Care and Training of Mentally Defective Children*, London: Law and Local Government Publications Ltd.

Board of Education and Board of Control (1929) *Report of the Joint Departmental Committee on Mental Deficiency (Wood Report)*, London: HMSO.

British Association (1846) *15th Report for the British Association for the Advancement of Science: 1845*, London: John Murray.

Central Health Services Council Standing Mental Health Advisory Committee (1962) *Training of Staff of Training Centres for the Mentally Subnormal*, London: Ministry of Health.

Commissioners in Lunacy (1865) *Annual Report of the Commissioners in Lunacy*, London: HMSO.

Cumming, W.F. (1852) *Notes on the Lunatic Asylums of Germany*, London: John Churchill.

Dartford Chronicle (1876) 'Speech of Dr. Brewer', *Dartford Chronicle*, 21 October 1876.

Education Department (1898) *Report of the Departmental Committee on Defective and Epileptic Children*, 2 vols, London: HMSO.

Hare, J.C. (1894) (ed.) *The Life and Letters of Maria Edgeworth, Vol 1*, London: Edward Arnold.

Heaton-Ward, W.A. (1975) *Mental Subnormality*, 4th edn, Bristol: John Wright and Sons.

Itard, J. (1806/1932) *The Wild Boy of Aveyron* (trans. G. Humphrey and M. Humphrey), New York: Appleton Century Crofts.

Jones, K. (1960) *Mental Health and Social Policy: 1845–1959*, London: Routledge and Kegan Paul.

Jones, K. (1972) *A History of the Mental Health Services*, London: Routledge and Kegan Paul.

Kelves, D.J. (1985) *In the Name of Eugenics*, London: Penguin.

Lane, H. (1977) *The Wild Boy of Aveyron*, London: George Allen and Unwin.

MAB (Metropolitan Asylums Board) (1876) *Annual Report of the Head Schoolmistress at Clapton Schools for 1875*, published in MAB minutes, 22 April 1876, London: Metropolitan Asylums Board.

Mittler, P. (2012) *Thinking Globally, Acting Locally*, Milton Keynes: Author House (purchasing information at http://mittlermemoir.com).

Penrose, L.S. (1972) *The Biology of Mental Defect*, London: Sidgwick and Jackson.

Pestalozzi, J.H. (1827) *Letters on Early Education: addressed to J P Greaves*, English Translation, London: Sherwood, Gilbert and Piper.

Pestalozzi, J.H. (1894) *How Gertrude Teaches Her Children: an attempt to help mothers to teach their own children and an account of the method, a report to the Society of the Friends of Education, Burgdorf* (trans. L.E. Holland and F. C. Turner), London: Swan Sonnenschein and Co.

Pritchard, D.G. (1963) *Education and the Handicapped 1760–1960*, London: Routledge and Kegan Paul.

Rolph, S. (2002) *Reclaiming the Past: The role of local Mencap societies in the development of community care in East Anglia, 1946–1980*, Milton Keynes: The Open University.

Rolph, S. (2005a) *Captured on Film: the history of Norwich and District Mencap Society, 1954–1980*, Milton Keynes: The Open University.

Rolph, S. (2005b) *A Little Glamour with Strict Tempo: The History of Cambridge Mencap, Vol. 1 1947–1990*, Milton Keynes: The Open University.

Royal Commission (1889) *Report on the Blind, Deaf and Dumb and Others of the United Kingdom*, London: HMSO.

Rousseau, J.J. (1762) *Emile, or On Education*, London: Penguin Classics.

Seebohm Report (1968) *Report of the Committee on Local Authority and Allied Personal Social Services* [chair Frederic Seebohm], London: HMSO.

Segal, S.S. (1967) *No Child is Ineducable*, London: Pergamon Press.

Seguin, E. (1866) *Idiocy and its Treatment by the Physiological Method*, New York: A.M. Kelley.

Stewart, D.S. (1978) 'A Short History of the Darenth Schools 1878–1978, Sidcup', Unpublished paper.

Voisin, F. (1843) *De l'Idiotie chez les Enfants et Autres Particularites d'Intelligence*, Paris: J-B Balliere.

Wedgewood, J.C. (1940) *Memories of a Fighting Life*, London: Hutchinson and Co.

5

PRIORITIES, PRODUCTS AND PROCESS

Developments in providing a curriculum for learners with SLD/PMLD

Richard Byers and Hazel Lawson

In this chapter, the following questions will be addressed:

- What is the historical development of curriculum for learners with SLD/PMLD?
- What different models for curriculum have been explored?
- Where does the National Curriculum fit in?

Introduction

This chapter describes the many changes and challenges over the last 50 years in curriculum development for learners with SLD/PMLD in the UK. Chapter 4 looked at the history of development in provision up to 1970. We take the account further and have inserted anonymised miniature vignettes of learners and practice drawn from the personal experiences of the lead author.

A 'care and therapy' model – before 1970

It is salutary to recall that, prior to 1971 in England and Wales, there was no education, in a formal sense, for those children and young people considered 'ineducable' in the terms of the 1944 Education Act. As a result, many learners with SLD/PMLD were placed in private institutions or simply stayed at home (DES 1971). Provision was also made for children, as well as adults, with SLD/PMLD in residential institutions.

In effect, there was no curriculum in the state's long-stay hospital provision because the young people were seen (officially and legally) as being 'too retarded' and therefore 'unsuitable' for schooling (Tilstone 1991). Practice in relation to them was conceptualised in terms of an institutional tradition in which 'subnormal' children were deemed to be primarily in need of 'care' rather than education. The therapy centres in the hospitals provided a form of occupational training for some of the residents considered to be 'more able' – training that usually consisted of carrying out mundane and repetitive tasks that attempted to mimic 'vocational' activity (such as packing plasticine in packets) with regularised 'tea' and 'lunch' breaks. Those who were deemed 'less able' were offered some relief from the tedium of life on the hospital wards in the form of part-time 'play' therapy. Life for residents was often characterised by many long and empty hours however (Oswin 1971).

I used to work at times, as a nursing assistant, on what were called the 'cot and chair' wards. These provided facilities for people with severe disabilities – what we would call 'PMLD' these days. I remember one girl called Beatty who used to spend most of her time confined to a play pen in the corner of the day room. She was dressed each day in a canvas boiler suit 'because she tore ordinary clothes'. She had no toys or play materials 'because she threw things'. When I took her out into the grounds on a sunny day, I was reprimanded because she would 'eat the grass', give herself an upset stomach and 'make a mess'. Somehow Beatty managed to maintain, in spite of this restricted environment, an optimistic view of life and a relentless craving for interaction.

Peter, another resident on the same ward, had spent so long lying on his side in bed that his joints had fused and his skeleton had flattened. Peter's only distractions resulted from being washed and dressed and from being lifted out, still flat because he was unable to adopt any other position, to lie across someone's lap to be fed. We did eventually discover that Peter had retained some movement in his hands and he was equipped with an early version of a pressure switch that enabled him to turn on lights and sounds in order to provide some stimulation that he could control.

Of course, enlightened people were challenging this status quo – both within the long-stay hospitals, as individuals and like-minded groups of colleagues, and outside, as commentators and policy makers. Although there were thousands of children in long stay hospitals, the majority were living at home either there all day or attending a junior training centre. Gunzburg (1963) championed the notion of 'training' for young people with learning difficulties in 'junior training centres' in the community; the establishment, in 1964, of the 'Training Council for Teachers of the Mentally Handicapped' acknowledged that 'teaching' was a possibility (Tilstone 1991); and Segal (1967) pioneered the movement towards education for all by arguing, from the position of a headteacher in a special school, that 'no child is ineducable'. From these interventions, it began to seem that education, and with it the notion of a curriculum, for learners with SLD/PMLD, was emerging as a possibility.

An 'all about assessment' model – during the 1970s

The Education (Handicapped Children) Act received Royal Assent in July 1970 and became effective from April 1971 (Furneaux 1973). Overnight, institutions in England and Wales that had previously been run in the community by the local health committees of local authorities as junior training centres became 'special schools'. These new schools catered for children who were deemed to be 'educationally subnormal (severe)'. Some of the staff in these settings converted from their roles as junior training centre supervisors and became teachers under the Department of Education and Science; other educationally qualified members of staff were recruited into these schools as teachers and senior managers. Schools were set up for children in the long-stay hospitals where schools had not existed before. Similar changes to legislation followed in Scotland in 1975 but in Northern Ireland it would not be until 1987 that legislation transferred responsibility to the Education and Library Boards. The new teachers in these special schools were rapidly confronted with the question of what to teach.

The answer came in the form of checklists of skills – checklists that were constructed by psychologists (Uzgiris and Hunt 1975; Bluma *et al.* 1976) and that purported to identify the 'milestones in learning' achieved by 'normally developing' infants and children. The rationale for using these materials was that these skills were seen as being essential prerequisites of learning. The more detail these checklists held, and the more minute the increments of progress between the skills they listed, the more valuable they were seen to be.

I worked in one of the early special schools set within a long-stay hospital and catering for the children living on the wards there. We had an educational psychologist who drove a long red sports car without any apparent sense of irony and who was determined to develop a checklist of skills for learners with SLD/PMLD that was absolutely exhaustive. The problem was, the checklist soon became too big to fit into the boot of the red sports car (and our educational psychologist was not about to start driving around in a van) and too big for us to use without getting utterly lost in minutiae.

We applied behaviourist principles to toilet training for Millie. We acquired a 'musical potty' that rewarded Millie with a jolly little tune every time a liquid completed an electrical circuit across the bottom of the potty. Millie was motivated by the music and we kept a chart that showed that Millie avoided wetting her pads for longer spells and had more successes on the musical potty. So far, so good. But the day came when the electrics of the musical potty expired – and no music greeted the flow of Millie's urine. My training in precision teaching soon rescued the situation, however, and I found myself spending parts of my day crouched outside the loo with my guitar, listening for the tinkling sound that would tell me it was time to burst into the opening chords of 'The wheels on the bus'. Mary was delighted. The chart continued to show progress. Unfortunately my relationship with the chord of G is still complex after all these years.

Despite the difficulties of finding exactly the right skills in the checklists to suit the needs of every learner, school staff used them in order to develop individual learning programmes for each individual. These programmes concerned themselves with areas of learning defined by the checklists, thus 'communication', 'cognitive development' and 'perceptual-motor skills' were deemed to be important. And just as the content of the programmes was therefore defined by the psychological research, so were the teaching methods. Behaviourism was the approved method and this led teachers onto courses that dealt with 'precision teaching' through the application of task analysis techniques and the use of rewards and sanctions.

Behaviourism, and techniques like backward chaining and shaping, certainly worked for teaching some skills. You could analyse the steps needed in putting on a coat and teach those in reverse order, with rewards for incremental successes. Children learned to stack blocks, thread beads and sort objects into colours using these techniques. Teaching learners the joys of interaction and communication through a skills-based, behaviourist route never seemed quite as satisfactory, however.

One of Nat's targets was 'to make eye contact' – something Nat was very reluctant to offer. But the item on the checklist was very clear. Nat needed this skill in order to move on. The skill was at the top of the list of targets on Nat's individual programme.

Acting on advice gleaned from one of my precision teaching courses, I took to sitting across the table from Nat, with a frequency recording chart and a tin of sweets, holding a dolly mixture up between my eyes and saying: 'Nat, look at me' enticingly. If Nat looked my way, he got the sweetie and a tick on the frequency chart.

The problem with this turned out to be that we were teaching Nat to look at sweets, not to make eye contact. If the sweets were not there, then nor was the looking – and the charts revealed regression back to a refusal to give eye contact.

This model of curriculum was characterised by individual programming. There were few shared learning activities (although there was shared play or singing). Learning activities were driven by the objectives in each learner's individual programme – and the objectives in the programmes were defined by the next item on the checklist. This was a way of working derived from the behaviourist psychological traditions with 'teaching' still appearing to be more like 'training' and the results of systematic testing defining success in the whole enterprise.

In this model, then, the curriculum was all about assessment, testing and re-testing. The resources used and the activities deployed were defined by the nature of the tasks and tests prescribed in the checklists. Training was focused on passing the next item in an ongoing hierarchy of tests and progress was measured by more testing. This was, in a sense, a curriculum defined as measurement with the aim of promoting acceleration of forms of development that were predicted to happen anyway – at least, for the 'normally' developing infants on whom the checklists had been standardised in the first instance.

An 'aims, objectives and outcomes' model – during the 1980s

The 1980s saw refinements and developments in this model. Criticisms of checklists designed for use with 'normally developing' infants were addressed by teams that produced packs of materials designed specifically for older children with difficulties in learning. Training courses, such as BATPACK and EDY, for teachers using such materials in their work with learners with SLD/PMLD were systematically evaluated for their effectiveness (Wheldall and Merrett 1985; Robson 1988). Special schools (running what was officially labelled as a 'developmental curriculum') started to develop their own curriculum materials. The Staff of Rectory Paddock School, for example, appropriately entitled their book *In Search of a Curriculum* (1981). The special schools were, indeed, in search of a curriculum – still using an objectives-driven model (Ainscow and Tweddle 1979) based on behaviourist principles, but focusing now on those outcomes that were deemed to be 'relevant' to learners with SLD/PMLD – often referred to as 'skills for life'.

This extension of behaviourist approaches offered great freedom to practitioners in the special schools to innovate and explore. Interestingly, this freedom tended to be limited by the capacity of staff in the special schools to imagine a life beyond school for their learners with SLD/PMLD. So the outcomes that defined the curriculum tended to focus on practicalities; preparation for an 'independent adult life' (or at least the kind of adult life that was assumed or predicted by members of school staff) was regarded as the ultimate goal. For these reasons, a great deal of teaching emphasised dressing and undressing, the cleaning of teeth, pouring drinks, making simple meals and going shopping. There was an emphasis on 'safety', on 'social sight vocabulary', on 'self care skills' and even 'household skills'. In some special schools, the freedom to innovate led to stagnation and a curriculum that was restricted to a narrow, functional set of goals set out in a further checklist.

If the checklist specified the aims and objectives that should be worked on next, teachers planned the content of their lessons, the 'subject matter' perhaps, and the experiences that would be offered to learners as vehicles for addressing those aims and objectives. The teacher's job was to organise activities and ways of working that would enable learners to gain (or consolidate) the relevant skills and then to measure success by evaluating progress in relation to those aims. This circular process, winding out from the checklist as a starting point and returning to it as a tool for assessment, amounted to a model for teaching founded on objectives, with the curriculum as a product of the work entailed in meeting those objectives and education as instrumental – a means to achieving a prescribed set of ends.

This approach led to some tensions and contradictions. Teachers working with older learners with SLD/PMLD found themselves teaching some of the skills of adult life while still treating their learners in other ways as 'developmentally young' or 'with the mental age of a toddler'. So, despite the pioneering work of people like Craft and Craft (1978), the vision of adulthood available to learners with SLD/PMLD was often a restricted one.

I remember one colleague who worked with teenage students in a school for learners with SLD/ PMLD. She was quite happy teaching her class to make a cup of tea, to count money or to cross the road safely (all good skills for 'adult life'). But if she caught any of her students holding hands at break time or kissing each other, she would 'send them to the moon' for the rest of the day by making them stand on the table. In her world, it was clear, adults with learning difficulties might make tea, but they should not be having relationships. And any sign that this might be happening would result in a swift return to firm control for the teacher and child status for the learners involved.

Some colleagues began to challenge the supremacy of the checklist of skills. A developmental curriculum, it was argued, should take account of developmental theories of learning and therefore the importance of experience and interaction with the environment. Sensory stimulation came to be seen as important by many professionals, especially for learners with PMLD (Longhorn 1988). Other teachers began to see other alternative futures, drawing perhaps on constructivist views about the importance of shared experiences in learning. If we are preparing young people for life 'in society' when they leave school, the reasoning went, why are we educating them in separate settings from their age peers? The 1980s therefore saw the initiation of some bold experiments in 'integration', with young people with SLD/PMLD being bussed onto mainstream school campuses in order to gain experience of a wider society from which they were otherwise largely shielded.

> There is no doubt that we were regarded as exotic, I think by staff and pupils alike, when we first started visiting mainstream schools for 'integration' experiences. It began with 'social times', like playtimes, and later the 'soft' subjects, like art and sport, where I presume it was reckoned that our pupils could have relatively little impact on learning for the mainstream pupils. Arriving in the inevitable white mini-bus, out of uniform, with mobility and sensory aids and manual sign language, they must have been like no other 'peers' the mainstream pupils had seen. It was also something of a shock for us special school teachers to realise that other schools had subject timetables, specialist teaching areas and syllabuses. Those ideas were all alien to us – but that situation was about to change.

A 'content for all' model – during the 1990s

When the first iteration of the National Curriculum was launched in 1989, it was presented theoretically as a 'curriculum for all' (NCC 1989). It quickly became apparent, as the National Curriculum folders began arriving in the special schools, that the teams responsible for actually writing the curriculum had not considered that 'all' would include learners with SLD/PMLD. Teachers in the special schools were startled to realise that they would be required to teach to programmes of study and attainment targets clearly designed for learners in mainstream schools. Indeed, they were shocked to realise that they would be expected to teach *subjects*, including science, history and design technology, for the first time.

Inevitably there was a backlash. Some teachers (indeed, the entire staff of some special schools) mounted fierce resistance and declared intentions to 'disapply' from the whole National Curriculum edifice, claiming that it had no relevance for their learners (Staff of Tye Green School 1991). An alternative response, from colleagues who saw problems with the checklist-driven approaches used in the special schools in the 1980s, was to attempt constructive engagement and to lobby for meaningful inclusion. The notion of 'entitlement' (expressed as a right to share in the same curriculum experiences as mainstream peers) became an important concept (Fagg *et al.* 1990).

Teachers and other commentators worked hard to demonstrate that the National Curriculum was accessible, appropriate and relevant for all learners (Ashdown, Carpenter and Bovair 1991). Official guidance on teaching the National Curriculum to learners with SLD/PMLD did emerge (NCC 1992). The first version of the special educational needs *Code of Practice* (DfE 1994) reminded stakeholders that the notion of teaching relevant skills, including skills in communication, mobility, behaviour management and daily functioning, for example, was still important and that individual education plans should be used to secure the teaching of key priorities for all pupils with learning difficulties. But the transition from objectives and functional checklists towards a liberal educational tradition founded on engagement with and learning about a wide range of topics was difficult.

I was curriculum co-ordinator in my special school when the National Curriculum first came out. I remember taking the big white folders around the school to my fellow teachers. One colleague had a particularly challenging class at the time, and I remember her looking uncomprehendingly at the folders while Nathan sat on the floor, flinging all the 'design and technology' equipment she was experimenting with back over his head item by item, and Nitin ecstatically ripped all her planning documents up into little pieces. We were deeply unsure about what was being expected of us.

One avenue that seemed to offer a way forward was the notion of the 'whole curriculum'. The opportunity for redefinition was welcomed by some (Sebba, Byers and Rose 1993) while others argued for the development of a wider curriculum that embraced the National Curriculum subjects in a harmonious combination with other elements (Carpenter and Ashdown 1996). In this approach, cross-curricular skills and themes were brought into relationship with the knowledge and understanding enshrined within subjects and arguably enabled staff in special schools to begin to secure balance and relevance in the curriculum along with the breadth that seemed to have been forced upon them.

There is no doubt, however, that, barely 20 years after their inception, the special schools for learners with SLD/PMLD were dealing, in the 1990s, with a revolution in their working practices. They were being expected to engage with a curriculum model primarily concerned with content – content that they were asked to accept, after a period of curricular autonomy, as a prescribed set of requirements. The key purpose of education in the special schools seemed to shift in these years from addressing what had been seen as 'needs' related to 'real life' towards a focus on acquisition of content. Teachers began to talk about their task as devising optimum methods, in the metaphor of the times, for the 'delivery' of that content to all learners. Education became, for some, a process of transmission – with success evaluated according to the levels achieved by learners in relation to attainment targets. Other, perhaps bolder, commentators began to see how a broad curriculum could offer opportunities for enlightenment, relief from the mundane drudgery of 'life skills', equality of access to knowledge and chances to be included in the process of developing a shared culture.

A 'learning process' model – the curriculum after 2000

The National Curriculum was revised for the new millennium in 2000, providing opportunities for greater flexibility in the curriculum and for an increased emphasis on aspects of personal and social development for all learners. Building on previous guidance (NCC 1992; SCAA 1996), a major new project resolved many of the issues relating to the education of pupils with learning difficulties within the National Curriculum. The resulting set of booklets (QCA/DfEE 2001; revised as QCA 2009) covered all subjects in the National Curriculum plus Religious Education, Personal Social and Health Education and Citizenship and Developing Skills. The materials provided coherent guidance on planning, teaching and assessing the curriculum for pupils with learning difficulties and encouraged staff, in special and mainstream schools, to seek to provide a balance in their approaches between teaching and therapy.

Also in 2001, the *Code of Practice* relating to special educational needs was revised (DfES 2001), re-emphasising that planning for learning for particular learners should focus on individual priorities set in terms of key skills such as communication, personal and social skills and learning to learn. The *Code* also highlighted requirements to involve both parents and learners in processes of planning, teaching, assessment and review. It began to seem that the revised structures would provide opportunities for staff to develop a genuinely 'integrated curriculum' for pupils with learning difficulties, offering access to shared experience while also addressing key priorities for individual learners.

In a sense, the new millennium brought with it, like the 1980s, real potential for innovation, this time with practitioners in mainstream and special schools working in constructive partnerships with learners and parents. There was potential for the curriculum, if not necessarily all schools, to become 'inclusive', with recognisably common elements balanced with opportunities to meet individual needs (Byers and Rose 2004). This was a vision of curriculum that was very different from the 1980s, however, because it moved away from 'individualised' programmes of learning in which each learner progressed, at their own pace, through their own set of objectives and instead provided shared experiences that were 'personalised' to enable each pupil, with and without learning difficulties, to address their own priorities for learning (Sebba 2009).

When I met Damien, he was using his wheelchair most of the time and he had a range of therapeutic and medical needs that were addressed as an integral part of his education. Staff used a hoist to move Damien out of his chair for toileting procedures and so he could have physiotherapy sessions several times a day. Damien was fed through a tube and his medication regime was monitored regularly. Damien gained a great deal from working on his sensory targets in a very well-equipped light and sound stimulation room; he also benefited from specialist approaches to communication using switches and computers. And the staff provided all this in addition to the shared sessions he enjoyed with 30 classmates working on the full range of National Curriculum subjects in the mainstream school where Damien was a full-time pupil.

Keisha was placed in a special school where staff assessed her attainments in relation to National Curriculum subjects using the P scales on a regular basis and where her progress relating to her individual targets (mainly, at this stage, for Keisha, to do with personal and social development, communication and interaction) was tracked and recorded on a cross-curricular system. Keisha worked on her targets in learning contexts that encompassed taught sessions in her special school, other parts of the school day (like break times and lunch times) and, with the support and involvement of her family, life at home and in the community. She also attended the local mainstream secondary school for part of her week. The work she did there on a horticulture project gave her the best opportunities, in many ways, of developing meaningful social interactions (and making progress towards her communication targets) with a group of friends who both motivated her and challenged her skills.

In the 2000s, then, we could argue that the dominant model of curriculum for learners with SLD/PMLD was a process-orientated model in which the focus was on promoting an improved capacity for learning itself (DCSF 2008). School staff in this decade enjoyed greater flexibility, liberated from the tyranny of both the checklist of skills (teaching to the next test item) and emancipated from the prescription of content (teaching to the programme of study). This flexibility enabled staff to select subject content, in their curriculum planning, that would allow them to support learning for each learner by providing appropriate contexts for the development of skills and knowledge. Similarly teachers working with learners with SLD/PMLD moved away from a single theory of learning and embraced a range of methods – ways of working from which they could select approaches that would facilitate the kinds of learning processes that they, together with parents and learners, deemed appropriate. Judgements about effectiveness, in confident schools, mainstream and special, implementing sophisticated approaches to curriculum like these, were made by evaluating the extent to which practice, entailing a combination of content, targets and methods, promoted learning processes, progress and development. The curriculum in these schools was not a static entity but encompassed a flexible range of possibilities that could be constantly re-aligned to meet the needs of all learners.

Questions for readers

- Can you envisage new relationships developing between 'special' and 'mainstream' schools, focused on shared interests in the further development of a common and inclusive curriculum?
- Can our interest in inclusion lead to a focus on participation in the learning process rather than on the location in which teaching takes place (Warnock 2005; Booth and Ainscow 2011)?
- Do you value the process of curriculum development itself, regardless of any products that might be generated, as a key form of co-operative professional development?
- Do you foresee a future in which schools, mainstream and special, are encouraged to dare to be different and to continue exploring flexibility in the curriculum (as envisaged by Norwich and Gray 2007)?
- And how might the voices of learners be given greater prominence, helping schools to make innovative, learner-led responses to 'whole person' issues?

References

Ashdown, R., Carpenter, B. and Bovair, K. (eds) (1991) *The Curriculum Challenge: Access to the national curriculum for pupils with learning difficulties*, London: Falmer Press.

Ainscow, M. and Tweddle, D. (1979) *Preventing Classroom Failure: An objectives approach*, Chichester: Wiley.

Bluma, S., Shearer, M., Frohman, A. and Hillard, J. (1976) *The Portage Guide to Early Education*, Wisconsin: Comparative Education Service.

Booth, T. and Ainscow, M. (2011) *Index for Inclusion – developing learning and participation in schools* (third edition), Bristol: CSIE.

Byers, R. and Rose, R. (2004) *Planning the Curriculum for Pupils with Special Educational Needs – a practical guide*, 2nd edn, London: David Fulton Publishers.

Carpenter, B. and Ashdown, R. (1996) 'Enabling access', in B. Carpenter, R. Ashdown and K. Bovair (eds) *Enabling Access: Effective teaching and learning for pupils with learning difficulties*, London: David Fulton Publishers.

Craft, A. and Craft, M. (1978) *Sex and the Mentally Handicapped*, London: Routledge and Kegan Paul.

DCSF (Department for Children, Schools and Families) (2008) *Personalised Learning – a practical guide*, Nottingham: DCSF.

DES (Department of Education and Science) (1971) *The Last to Come In* (Reports on Education No. 69), London: DES.

DfE (Department for Education) (1994) *Code of Practice on the Identification and Assessment of Special Educational Needs*, London: DfE.

DfES (Department for Education and Skills) (2001) *Special Educational Needs Code of Practice*, London: DfES.

Fagg, S., Aherne, P., Skelton, S. and Thornber, A. (1990) *Entitlement for All in Practice*, London: David Fulton Publishers.

Furneaux, B. (1973) *The Special Child*, 2nd edn, Harmondsworth: Penguin Books.

Gunzburg, H.C. (1963) *Junior Training Centres*, London: National Association for Mental Health.

Longhorn, F. (1988) *A Sensory Curriculum for Very Special People: A practical approach to curriculum planning*, London: Souvenir Press.

NCC (National Curriculum Council) (1989) *Curriculum Guidance 2 – a Curriculum for All: special educational needs in the National Curriculum*, York: NCC.

NCC (National Curriculum Council) (1992) *Curriculum Guidance 9 – the National Curriculum and Pupils with Severe Learning Difficulties*, York: NCC.

Norwich, B. and Gray, P. (2007) 'Special schools in the new era: conceptual and strategic perspectives', in B. Norwich (Ed.) *Special schools in the new era: how do we go beyond generalities? Policy Paper 2, SEN Policy Options Group 6th Series*, Tamworth: nasen.

Oswin, M. (1971) *The Empty Hours – a study of the week-end life of handicapped children in institutions*, London: Allen Lane.

QCA (Qualifications and Curriculum Authority)/DfEE (Department for Education and Employment) (2001) *Planning, Teaching and Assessing the Curriculum for Pupils with Learning Difficulties*, London: QCA.

QCA (2009) *Planning, Teaching and Assessing the Curriculum for Pupils with Learning Difficulties*, 2nd edn, London: QCA.

Robson, C. (1988) 'Evaluating the "Education of the Developmentally Young (EDY)" course for training teachers in behavioural methods', *European Journal of Special Needs Education*, 3(1): 13–32.

SCAA (School Curriculum and Assessment Agency) (1996) *Planning the Curriculum for Pupils with Profound and Multiple Learning Difficulties*, London: SCAA.

Sebba, J. (2009) 'Personalisation, individualisation and inclusion', in B. Norwich (Ed.) *Personalisation and special educational needs – Policy Paper 5, SEN Policy Options Group 6th Series*, Tamworth: nasen.

Sebba, J., Byers, R. and Rose, R. (1993) *Redefining the Whole Curriculum for Pupils with Learning Difficulties*, London: David Fulton Publishers.

Segal, S. S. (1967) *No Child is Ineducable – special education provision and trends*, Oxford: Pergamon Press.

Staff of Rectory Paddock School (1981) *In Search of a Curriculum – notes on the education of mentally handicapped children*, Sidcup: Robin Wren Publications.

Staff of Tye Green School (1991) 'Broad, balanced and relevant?', *Special Children*, 44: 11–13.

Tilstone, C. (1991) 'Historical review', in C. Tilstone (ed.) *Teaching Pupils with Severe Learning Difficulties – practical approaches*, London: David Fulton Publishers.

Uzgiris, I. C. and Hunt, J. McV. (1975) *Assessment in Infancy – ordinal scales of psychological development*, Urbana, Ill: University of Illinois Press.

Warnock, M. (2005) 'Special educational needs: a new look', *Impact No. 11*, London: The Philosophy of Education Society of Great Britain.

Wheldall, K. and Merrett, F. (1985) 'The "Behavioural Approach to Teaching Package (BATPACK)": an evaluation', *British Journal of Educational Psychology*, 55(1): 65–75.

6

FURTHER EDUCATION

Personalised destinations and outcomes for students with SLD/PMLD

*Caroline Allen, Kathrine Everett, Janet Sherborne,
James Stonard and Joanne Yarlett*

In this chapter, the following questions will be addressed:

- What are the purpose and benefit of FE for learners with SLD/PMLD?
- What are the key developments and challenges in the practice of the sector at this time?

The further education landscape

The contributors to this chapter are practitioners and managers from a further education (FE) sector college (Carshalton College) and from an independent specialist college (Orchard Hill College) both in England. We explored the above questions in discussions with other colleagues from the FE and specialist sectors.

The world of FE is a very exciting, dynamic and ever changing landscape with many colleges offering a diverse range of courses which are predominantly vocational. For many students this leads to higher education, employment and apprenticeships, which shows that FE provides for a wide range of students, ages and abilities. Every year colleges in England educate 3 million people with 853,000 16 to 18 year olds in learning from Entry Level to Level 3 (Association of Colleges 2013). Historically, most FE sector colleges have offered courses to learners with SLD and MLD, but now some sector colleges are providing programmes for learners with PMLD, or work collaboratively with specialist college providers in this area. Specialist colleges, known as independent specialist providers (ISPs), also provide learning programmes for learners with a range of learning difficulties, disabilities and additional support needs arising from autistic spectrum conditions and other social communication disorders, mental health issues, physical, sensory and medical issues, and communication difficulties including communication through challenging behaviours. Many ISPs are residential and include a strong focus on daily living skills. However, some of the contributors to this chapter are practitioners in a non-residential ISP (Orchard Hill College) which has a focus on providing learning programmes to improve local opportunities for learners in work (including supported, sheltered or voluntary), independent or supported living, community engagement and further learning. The focus for non-residential specialist FE providers is to provide learning close to where learners live and in very close partnership with local colleges, local authorities, local employers and others who can help to maximise opportunities for each individual.

Whether specialist or general FE, all colleges aim to provide an engaging and real life experience for the young person to become independent and follow successful progression pathways to FE and training, independent living and/or employment. This is underscored by the Department for Education's (DfE) 'Preparing for Adulthood' (PfA) programme (www. preparingforadulthood.org.uk) which notes five key messages (personalise your approach; develop a shared vision; improve post-16 options and support; raise aspirations; plan services together) which are crucial in improving the life chances of young disabled people. However, there have been challenges in FE in providing learning which is work related for this group of learners. The Ofsted evaluation of 'Progression post-16 for students with learning difficulties and/or disabilities' was critical of the sector. Its survey findings stated that 'work based learning provision was rarely considered an option' (Ofsted 2011: 6). Part of the difficulty may be a lack of consensus regarding employability.

> Relatively little is known about the career decision-making process of individuals with disabilities. Although attempts have been made in recent years to incorporate the disability element into existing theories of career choice and development, there have been relatively few efforts to develop models of career decision making that focus primarily on factors associated with disabilities.
>
> (Luzzo *et al.* 1999: 142)

Our view is that learners with PMLD are able to contribute to the workplace if a suitable match is made between a learner's skills and interests and the employers' needs. In addition, appropriate support is needed. In some cases this will mean that a learner carries out a specific element of a job in a 'job carving' approach (Griffin and Sherron 2006). Employment may take many forms including: paid or voluntary, part-time, social enterprise or supported.

'Since being at college I have been learning to be as independent as possible, as I am a wheelchair user. I have been using a switch to access the computer, I am now using a switch at home to use my Apple Mac computer. I can now support my eating by using a Neater Eater [manual self-feeding device], which the college have bought for me. I now use my Neater Eater at home also. I also go to work experience at a school every Tuesday, to listen to children read.'

Demi has been supported at college to visit a volunteering centre to find out what sort of volunteering placements are available for her in the area. This work, together with class tutorials, empowered Demi to make informed choices. She decided to have a volunteering work placement in her community listening to children read at a school.

The transition phase is key to the successful starting point for a learner entering a college, through links with their previous school or specialist institution, which may also include an ISP. Transition may include a menu of activities from taster days/observation at home or school, review of documentation or meetings with local authorities. Over the last few years there has been a shift in FE from providing education which is 'more of the same' classroom-based practice to a vocational education in which learners can develop through practical, simulation-based tasks in the first instance, and then through meaningful work/community/living experience. Life, employability and functional skills are embedded through this approach.

Learners often play a significant part in mainstream college life including through the student councils and the student union.

Destinations and outcomes

In FE, the purpose and benefit of learning has been much debated. The recent focus on 'destinations' and 'outcomes' has been reflected in the guidance and expectations for policy (DfE 2012a, 2012b) and from Ofsted (2012) and funding agencies (SFA 2013). It is acknowledged that the purpose of learning is to improve skills, knowledge and experience in order to improve the life of the learner in and beyond college both in terms of opportunities and also to improve confidence and enjoyment.

> In order for learning to have true meaning it must have a purpose and a relevance to the individual. The development of spontaneous, functional communication abilities and emotional regulatory capacities, which support all aspects of development and independence, are of the highest priority in educational and treatment efforts.
>
> (Prizant *et al.* 2006: 18)

Carshalton College's primary aim is to focus on progression and destination outcomes and all student targets are aligned to this. Progression might be defined as the learner's identification of and movement towards achieving their personal goals, supported by individualised education plans built around their needs and aspirations, while destination outcomes encompass measurable educational factors such as qualifications gained, a change of home living arrangements, a job. We are operating today in the context of a higher focus on rigour and outcomes, tighter budgets and a tough labour market, particularly for young people, including those with complex support needs. This has led to a review of the offer for students with learning difficulties by most colleges. While colleges had often been successful in ensuring that learners were able to travel independently and make choices, many learners were still coming to the end of their college life unable to make the successful transition from education into employment. The government strategy, 'Valuing Employment Now: real jobs for people with learning disabilities', raised concerns about this:

> The Learning and Skills Council (LSC) spends almost £330 million on education and training for 19–25-year-olds with moderate or severe learning disabilities. Yet too little of this education leads to jobs. Even where colleges do provide good work preparation, this is likely to be wasted if people do not transfer quickly into employment.
>
> (DoH 2009: 6)

While transition to mainstream education was in part successful, learners wishing to undertake an apprenticeship programme found that these were, for the most part, inaccessible due to the academic literacy and numeracy levels required. To overcome this barrier, some colleges have engaged extensively with learners and employers and introduced workplace programmes, following models of supported internships that provide a structured learning programme at a place of employment, enabling learners to develop relevant workplace skills and gain qualifications if they so choose, and thus increasing opportunities for them to move into paid work once their study is complete. These programmes enable learners to experience work placements, often initially within a safe college environment, with a view to establishing further opportunities externally. Figure 6.1 shows how Carshalton College has codified this approach:

Year 1:	Transition into College focusing on becoming independent, travel training, making choices, participating in vocational sessions integrated with skills building.
Year 2:	Developing independence and personal and social skills, together with a supportive internal work placement of vocational choice.
Year 3 and exit from the organisation:	Primary focus on external work experience placement with support from job coach, together with a college support programme to develop skills required to sustain voluntary or paid employment.

Figure 6.1   Transition template (Carshalton College Curriculum 2013)

Jane is a student with complex learning disabilities who joined the FE college on a three-year programme. In the first year she received intensive support in the skills of communication, integration and socialisation, and also undertook travel training. In the second year, she selected hospitality and catering as her vocational option and early in the year negotiated and began a substantial internal work experience in the college refectory focusing on developing her skills in customer service, communicating with others, building a work routine and understanding roles and responsibilities. In the third year she secured a voluntary placement at a local café. Support gradually reduced during the year. After leaving the programme she now works in the café independently of support on a voluntary basis as this suits her life choices; she has also moved into supported living.

The focus on qualifications and vocational outcomes for mainstream learners in FE has been mirrored in an emphasis on the identification of outcomes for learners with PMLD. In the specialist post-16 sector the journey to discover what a learner requires to achieve aspirational outcomes starts with holistic assessment which often involves all disciplines including, for example, therapy and nursing. However, the planned learning should not only take into account the individual's starting points but also identified outcomes/destination.

There are various ways of identifying what learning will be meaningful to learners who may find communication challenging. These can include, for example, sensory assessments, observation, Intensive Interaction (see Chapter 26 in this book) and the presentation of new and innovative learning opportunities. Pintrich and Schrauben (1992: 150–1) consider cognitive engagement ('extent to which students are attending to and expending mental effort in the learning tasks encountered'), behavioural engagement ('the extent to which students are making active responses to the learning tasks presented') and affective engagement (the level of students' investment in, and their emotional reactions to, the learning tasks, e.g. high levels of interest or positive attitudes towards the learning tasks).

Assessment of learning on entry to a provision is the key to any success in developing effective learning experiences for young people. The triangulation between learner preference, skills analysis, stretch and challenge and aspiration for the future, combine to create a bedrock on which effective adult experiences can be built.

'I am a people person. I like to interact with people. I like to be out and about. I like to use public transport, eat out, and visit different venues. I use my communication book and an I-pad to answer familiar questions, to make choices and to express likes and dislikes. I am a wheelchair user.'

Andrew accessed a part-time course to support him in moving from his family home into a supported living environment. The college staff have been working closely with Andrew and his family. In October last year his aim was achieved and Andrew moved into his new home! Andrew is now learning more about managing his new home environment and is working on a home living and community access course.

The learning underpinning this transition through levels of progress towards a destination/ outcome should be monitored and recorded in order to structure the learning stages to continue to stretch and challenge.

> In order to support young people's post-college learning and progression, more emphasis is needed on the exit strategy identified at the start of any learning programme and recorded in a young person's (individual plan). This will ensure that reviews concentrate on movement towards the next stage of transition into adulthood and allow for the development of potential pathways necessary to support the young person in future environments. For young people with complex learning difficulties, planning for the future should start as early as possible to improve outcomes and co-ordination.
>
> (Welsh Government Social Research 2013: 167)

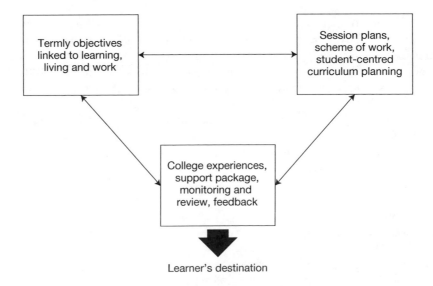

Figure 6.2 Learner destination

This model of destination-led planning is a personalised or 'person centred' approach which allows for teaching and learning to take place in context. There is a clear focus for both the individual and the practitioner working with him/her and an enthusiasm can be built around the student aspiration which can impact positively on engagement in the learning setting. Figure 6.3 details the different considerations that might go into formulating a person-centred plan.

Voluntary	Social Enterprise	Local authority PA Employability Programme	Supported paid/unpaid employment	Independent employment Paid/unpaid
Voluntary employment	Individual enterprise	1:1 employability support	Supported part time/full time	Part time/full time
Voluntary advocacy work	Group Enterprise	Group support programme	Supported advocacy employment	Group employment
Group voluntary advocacy		Quality checkers for LA	Group supported employment	Job coach/ Paid

Figure 6.3   Work destinations progress chart (Orchard Hill College Curriculum 2012)

Person centred

Work on person-centred planning (PCP) by the National Development Team (NDT 1998) led to it taking a central place in the White Paper 'Valuing People' (DoH 2001) and 'Valuing People Now' (DoH 2009), which was the 'refresh' of the white paper. The techniques of PCP are used to empower the individual with learning difficulties to make choices and express desires/dreams for their future and to ensure that the service is planned around the individual.

PCP is an approach to collaborative planning which assesses quality as 'set against desired outcomes that are specified by those using the service' (Parley 2001: 299). There are a number of approaches which follow the PCP principles, such as: 'Planning Alternative Tomorrows with Hope' (PATH) (Pearpoint, O'Brien and Forest 1992), 'Making Action Plans' (MAPs) (Forest and Pearpoint 1992; O'Brien and O'Brien 1998), 'Essential Lifestyle Planning' (ELP) (Sanderson *at al.* 1997) and 'Personal Futures Planning' (Mount 1984). PCP can offer a structure in which a learner may identify the tailoring of opportunities and lead the evaluation and, therefore, the development of those opportunities. However, the PCP approach will only be effective if organisations change the way in which they view and work with people with learning difficulties (Sanderson *at al.* 1997; Mansell and Beadle-Brown 2004; O'Brien 2004). Iles (2003: 76) advocates that organisations must adopt values which 'infuse all aspects of service design and delivery' and become 'learning organisations', which ask 'How do I/we improve my/our practice?' He warns that without this precondition, 'there is a danger that the new form of statutory services will be no better suited than previous incarnations to innovate in a person centred manner to provide services that are tailored to suit individual needs and desires' (Iles 2003: 75).

Research by Allen (2009: 82) concludes that the creation of organisations which enable collaboration and effective PCP requires 'the advanced social interaction abilities and maturity, described by some as "emotional intelligence".' A summarisation of the emotional intelligence framework can be found in Goleman, Boyatzis and McKee (2002). The inter-connectivity between FE's person-centred programmes and the broader PCP process has gained greater importance with the increased focus on destination/outcomes, since the need for partnership working around the learner becomes essential in order to achieve the transition from FE into destinations.

Partnership working using technology

If we are to secure best outcomes with learners, post–16 providers have to work very closely together with learners, their families, social workers and personal assistants in order to shape and develop a meaningful timetable of work, learning and leisure opportunities for each learner to move on to after college. One of the key challenges of partnership working is the time and communication required to create coherence (Allen 2001). In FE, providers are finding that learners and teachers can use technology to help communication and draw the learning and progression competencies together holistically. E-curricula vitae augmented with detailed e-portfolios are used in some colleges in order to clearly communicate a learner's achievements and skills and to support transition.

At Orchard Hill College, the design and build of our e-portfolio has been created specifically with partnership working in mind and relies heavily on other organisations contributing to its future planning sections. It is a software package that holds centrally all essential information about the student and has been designed to capture the range of information which learners with PMLD may need to communicate to show their aspirations, talents and support needs.

Coordination of planning is required to enable all parties to contribute to a productive and meaningful week designed with the learner, so that she/he may have an opportunity to contribute fully to community life. Planning and preparation are essential for transitions which involve multiple parties, as outlined in the Children and Families Act (2014). Pathfinders have engaged in a form of piloting and action research in order to prepare for implementation of the legislation. The report of the findings notes the limited evidence base and comments that in relation to 'close cooperation between all the services… through the joint planning and commissioning of services' pathfinders reported "mixed progress"' (DfE 2013: 113).

From a practical perspective, in the learner's final year at college it should be all partners' responsibilities to ensure that this timetable is in place and that the resources are in place for it to happen. This will need to occur well in advance, since many learners, especially those with PMLD, may require a 'slow transition' out of college. Providers should also work with and advise other placements of any resources that can be put in place to support learning opportunities in other contexts. Tools such as e-portfolios may be used to enable capture and ease of access to information including: 'My Future Plan', 'My Home Living Plan', 'My Work Plan', 'My Community Plan'. In this way e-tools may be used as a vehicle for focusing on destinations and achieving them through PCP, including personalised education programmes. This notion of coherent service is the rationale for the Children and Families Act (2014). The implementation of these intentions, however, remains complex, as noted by Allen and Burgess (2013).

Impact of policy, funding and regulation on person-centred collaboration

In the post–16 sector, providers continue to grapple with the complex and turbulent policy and funding landscape while seeking to improve provision and outcomes for students. Over the years funding has presented many issues for sector colleges delivering courses for learners with special needs. While it is acknowledged that there are emerging models of good practice, FE sector colleges have had to be creative in their planning and delivery. The funding for non-accredited programmes has varied and creates challenges for the provider. For example, the introduction of the 'Foundation Learning Tier' (LSC 2009), for those accessing education provision at Entry Level and Level 1, meant that in order to secure funding colleges focused on delivery of a plethora of qualifications, which Ofsted rightly challenged:

> The programmes reviewed by inspectors were too narrowly focused on accreditation and were not effective in enabling students to progress to open or supported employment, independent living or community engagement. This in many cases led to specialist staff focusing on the requirements of the awarding body away from the needs and aspirations of the students.
>
> (Ofsted 2011: 5)

In July 2012, guidance was issued to colleges advising of a significant change in additional support funding for students who have special needs, placing commissioning and funding decisions with local authorities (EFA 2012). The implementation of study programmes for young people aged 16–18 years (16–24 with learning difficulties), introduced in 2013, does provide more flexibility for learners which allows for preparation for work and/or independent living and encourages a work-based curriculum; however, this does not include learners over 25 years.

At this time of significant change and challenge within the policy, regulation and funding environment, much of the stated ideology of key developments and challenges in the sector achieves a synergy with our aims of effective collaborative work to achieve better outcomes for our students; 'giving frontline professionals the freedom to work together to develop better services for children, young people and families' (DfE 2012a: 66). And yet, the difficulties of enacting these aims in practice remain. It is perhaps ironic that the very policy, funding and regulation structures which state coherence with these aims often either form unintended barriers to the collaborative work required, or as Lacey (2001: 19) highlights, the legislation 'lacks compulsion'. In addition, the demands of person-centred partnership working continue to stretch us as we endeavour to put aside organisational self-protection in the pursuit of greater benefits for our students. The barriers to effective collaboration highlighted by Lacey and Lomas (1993) over 20 years ago remain challenges today: different cultures, funding, management, codes of practice, status tensions, communication failures. Delivery models and practice for destination-focused learning are also a work in progress. However, in spite of these constraints, the changes to our shared understanding of the purpose and benefits of FE for students with learning difficulties and disabilities have progressed, resulting in delivery of learning programmes becoming more focused on enabling the achievement of the destinations and outcomes to which our students aspire.

Questions for readers

- How can sector and specialist colleges build on their good work to improve the lives of young people and adults in terms of progression, including job outcomes?
- Will the introduction of the Children and Families Act help improve the lives and, in particular, the education and progression outcomes for young people?

Caroline Allen et al.

References

Allen, C. (ed.) (2001) *A Framework for Learning: for adults with profound and complex learning difficulties*, London: David Fulton.

Allen, C. (2009) 'Managing Creative Synergy in a Learning Organisation with People with Profound and Complex Learning Difficulties and/or Disabilities: A continuous quest for integrated development and holistic maturity', PhD Thesis, University of Birmingham.

Allen, C. and Burgess, Y. (2013) 'Funding of High Needs Support', *Academy Magazine*, 3(1): 22–3.

Association of Colleges (2013) *AoC College Key Facts 2013/14*. Online. Available: www.aoc.co.uk/about-colleges/research-and-stats/key-further-education-statistics (accessed 23 July 2014).

DfE (Department for Education) (2012a) *Support and aspiration: a new approach to special educational needs and disability. Progress and next steps*, London: Department for Education. Online. Available: www.gov.uk/government/uploads/system/uploads/attachment_data/file/180836/DFE-00046-2012.pdf (accessed 23 July 2014).

DfE (Department for Education) (2012b) *Building engagement, Building Futures*, London: Department for Education. Online. Available: www.education.gov.uk/childrenandyoungpeople/youngpeople/participation/a00200853/building-engagement-building-futures (accessed 23 July 2014).

DfE (Department for Education) (2013) *Impact Evaluation of the SEND Pathfinder Programme*, London: Department for Education. Online. Available: www.gov.uk/government/publications/impact-evaluation-of-the-send-pathfinder-programme (accessed 23 July 14).

DoH (Department of Health) (2001) *Valuing People – A New Strategy for Learning Disability for the 21st Century*, London: Department of Health. Online. Available: www.gov.uk/government/publications/valuing-people-a-new-strategy-for-learning-disability-for-the-21st-century (accessed 23 July 2014).

DoH (Department of Health) (2009) *Valuing People Now: A new three year strategy for people with learning disabilities*. London, Department of Health. Online. Available: http://webarchive.nationalarchives.gov.uk/ 20130107105354/http://www.dh.gov.uk/en/Publicationsandstatistics/Publications/Publications PolicyAndGuidance/DH_093377 (accessed 23 July 2014).

EFA (Education Funding Agency) (2012) *Funding guidance for young people: 2012/13 Funding regulations*. Education Funding Agency. Online. Available: http://webarchive.nationalarchives.gov.uk/20130903115227/http://www.education.gov.uk/aboutdfe/executiveagencies/efa/funding/fundings/a00209794/funding-guidance-2012-to-13 (accessed 23 July 2014).

Forest, M. and Pearpoint, J. (1992) 'Commonsense tools: MAPS and Circles', in J. Pearpoint, M. Forest and J. Snow (eds) (1993) *The Inclusion Papers: strategies to make inclusion work*, Toronto: Inclusion Press.

Goleman, D., Boyatzis, R.E. and McKee A. (2002) *Primal Leadership: Realizing the power of emotional intelligence*, Boston MA: Harvard Business School Press.

Griffin, C.C. and Sherron, P. (2006) 'Job carving and customized employment', in P. Wehman (ed.) *Life Beyond the Classroom*, 4th edn, Baltimore: Brookes Publishing.

Iles, I.K. (2003) 'Becoming a learning organization: a precondition for person centred services to people with learning difficulties', *Journal of Learning Disabilities*, 7(1): 65–77.

Lacey P. (2001) *Support Partnerships: collaboration in action*, London: David Fulton.

Lacey, P. and Lomas, J. (1993) *Support Services and the Curriculum: A practical guide to collaboration*, London: David Fulton.

LSC (Learning and Skills Council) (2009) *Foundation Learning Tier: 14-19 Delivery Guidance for 2009/10*. Online. Available: http://readingroom.lsc.gov.uk/lsc/national/provider_delivery_guidance_august_2009_final_version.pdf (accessed 23 July 2014).

Luzzo, D.A., Hitchings, W.E., Retish, P. and Shoemaker, A. (1999) 'Evaluating differences in college students' career decision making on the basis of disability status', *The Career Development Quarterly*, 48(2): 142–56.

Mansell, J. and Beadle-Brown, J. (2004) 'Person-Centred Planning or Person-Centred Action? A response to the commentaries', *Journal of Applied Research in Intellectual Disabilities*, 17: 31–5.

Mount, B. (1984) *Creating Futures Together: A workbook for people interested in creating desirable futures for people with handicaps*, Atlanta: Georgia Advocacy Office.

NDT (National Development Team) (1998) *Quality Is Our Business Too*, Manchester: NDT.

O'Brien, J. (2004) 'If Person-Centered Planning did not exist, valuing people would require its invention', *Journal of Applied Research in Intellectual Disabilities*, 17: 11–15.

O'Brien, J. and O'Brien, C.L. (1998) *A Little Book About Person Centered Planning*, Toronto: Inclusion Press.

Ofsted (2011) *Progression Post-16 for Learners with Learning Difficulties and/or Disabilities*. Online. Available: www.ofsted.gov.uk/resources/progression-post-16-for-learners-learning-difficulties-andor-disabilities (accessed 23 July 2014).

Ofsted (2012) *Going in the right direction? Careers guidance in schools from September 2012*. Online. Available: www.ofsted.gov.uk/resources/going-right-direction-careers-guidance-schools-september-2012 (accessed 23 July 2014).

Parley, F.F. (2001) 'Person-centred outcomes: Are outcomes improved where a person-centred care model is used?' *Journal of Learning Disabilities*, (5)4: 299–308.

Pearpoint, J., O'Brien, J. and Forest, M. (1992) *PATH*, Toronto: Inclusion Press.

Pintrich, P.R. and Schrauben, B. (1992) 'Students' motivational beliefs and their cognitive engagement in classroom academic tasks', in D.H. Schunk and J.Meece (eds) *Student Perceptions in the Classroom*, Hillsdale, NJ: Lawrence Erlbaum.

Prizant, B., Wetherby, A., Rubin, E., Laurent, A., and Rydell, P. (2006) *The SCERTS Model: a comprehensive educational approach for children with autism spectrum disorders, Vol. 1*, Baltimore, MD: Paul H. Brookes Publishing. Online. Available: www.scerts.com/index.php?option=com_content&view=article&id=2&Itemid=2 (accessed 23 July 2014).

Sanderson, H., Kennedy, J., Ritchie, P. and Goodwin, G. (1997) *People, Plans and Possibilities: Exploring person-centred planning*, Edinburgh: SHS.

SFA (Skills Funding Agency) (2013) *Business Plan 2013-14*, Crown copyright, Publication number, P – 130162.

Welsh Government Social Research (2013) *Post-19 Education Provision for Young People with Complex Learning Difficulties Living in Wales: levels of need and current provision*, Cardiff: Welsh Government. Online: Available: http://dera.ioe.ac.uk/18416/1/130510-post-19-education-provision-young-people-complex-learning-difficulties-levels-need-current-provision-en.pdf (accessed 23 July 2014).

7

BUILDING SECURE FOUNDATIONS WITHIN THE EARLY YEARS

Michele Pipe, Fiona Smith and Lesley Mycroft

In this chapter, the following questions will be addressed:

- How can early years theory be used to inform good practice for learners who have severe learning difficulties (SLD), particularly those in their early years?
- What is the relevance of early years principles to practitioners who support these learners?
- How can we create and maximise active learning opportunities for individual children in the early years phase?

Introduction

When working with children in their early years, the principles and practice of personalisation predominate and we argue that this includes learners with special educational needs (DfE 2014). Generally, it is acknowledged that the pace and pathways of development vary between learners, as reflected in the non-statutory guidance of Early Years Outcomes (DfE 2013). In England, the revised version of the Early Years Foundation Stage (EYFS) framework (DfE 2014) refers to *broad* and *overlapping* developmental bands of achievement (authors' emphasis), supporting the view that all children 'develop and learn in different ways and at different rates' (p. 6).

The principles apparent in the EYFS framework lend emphasis to our appreciation of the learner's individuality and uniqueness. These early years principles are particularly relevant to us as professionals working with children with SLD and PMLD. Practice built on such a basis will be evident in our later account of one teacher's experience. We very much agree that teachers should acknowledge differences between individual learners, but we would also strongly encourage the adults in these situations to see the many commonalities shared between children with SLD/PMLD and those who develop typically. We must remember that a child in their early years is a child first and foremost, regardless of any additional needs.

In this chapter, using a real-life example of good practice from the field, we aim to show the benefit of skilled practitioners, who interpret and apply theoretical knowledge and create active learning opportunities for an individual learner with SLD. In addition, we highlight the importance of excellent observation and interpretative skills in practitioners. We believe such skills are essential to support learning in the early years (Tilstone and Layton 2005; Nutbrown 2011).

An example from current practice in one setting

Our practice-based example concerns a boy named Brendan who has been identified as having SLD. When he starts at his primary special school at age 4 years, Brendan has some verbal communication skills; however his expressive socio-communication, intellectual and physical skills are under developed in comparison with typically developing children of his chronological age. These difficulties limit his interactions and involvement on a day-to-day basis, especially with other children. A consequence of this is that several members of staff observe that Brendan often plays on the edge of the group and generally seems 'afraid and sad'. His teacher wants to change this. She believes that the quality of his experience at school can be improved and begins to consider ways to support him further. She intends to motivate his learning and encourage him to enjoy his time at school.

Further observation of Brendan shows that he is able to walk but has a *very* unstable gait. The physiotherapist is keen for Brendan to strengthen his stability through crawling exercises, which she suggests will generally improve his motor skills. As well as acknowledging the importance of Brendan's need for mobility, his teacher knows she has a responsibility for his wider learning, and therefore she needs to extend his skills and knowledge on a holistic basis (Carpenter, Ashdown and Bovair 2001). However, at this point in time, she is unsure of a starting point to engage him in his learning.

Through further careful observations, Brendan's teacher notices that the only time Brendan smiles is when someone enters the room. When this happens, he becomes animated and flaps his hands in a very excited manner; he also demonstrates some socio-communication skills, such as vocalising and smiling. Several members of staff have noted that this response appears to be unrelated to any particular person entering the room, and they reach a conclusion that his change in behaviour seems to be associated with the door opening. His teacher decides to investigate this aspect of Brendan's interest more closely.

Having observed and discovered Brendan's responses to the classroom doors being opened, and knowing his physiotherapy target, staff decide to 'experiment' by combining these activities. They encourage Brendan to crawl a short distance towards the door … and it opens on his arrival.

This engages him and he participates with interest. This encourages the staff team to look for further ideas and they consider different contexts and areas of the curriculum where the theme of 'doors' can be explored and developed for Brendan. This process, taking the cue from the learner and responding to his interest, shows that the teacher has drawn on a truly child initiated learning opportunity, which promotes Brendan's willing participation. She works collaboratively with the staff team and they pool their observations and interpretations of Brendan's interactions. This information is used to explore and advance what Whalley calls 'possible lines of development' (Whalley 2007). This form of assessment and planning was developed at Pen Green Centre, where staff use this to establish a learner's interest and plan next steps of a child's learning.

Being aware of Brendan's competencies, current interest and information from their observations, the staff are creative in providing further opportunities to explore together the direction of his learning. Some of the participatory activities they identify, to extend Brendan's interest and learning around opening doors, are:

• using many resources, including the internet to research photos and pictures of doors;
• creating a book of doors with different pictures;
• making a model with opening and closing doors;

- introducing small world figures into the model to develop stories;
- introducing a symbol for Brendan to use to ask staff and children to shut the doors;
- collaborating in model-making of doors that open and that have numbers on them for Brendan to change;
- researching different doors around the school (sizes, colours and actions) and in the wider environment; teaching Brendan to take photos of the doors with a child friendly camera; and
- videoing a visit to a set of revolving doors in town and helping Brendan create a commentary on their return.

The highlight of this period of learning, for both Brendan and the staff, was the whole group visit to town to experience revolving doors. Before the visit, he 'talks' about it and seems excited, interacting with staff and children in a way not previously seen – Brendan came into school excited, his Mum told staff 'he hasn't stopped talking about it all evening and morning'.

He gave his teacher lots of hugs and when the head teacher passed him in the hall, he initiated conversation with her telling her where he was going, combining words in to short sentences such as 'Brendan go through revolving door'. Staff noted how responsive he is in the preparation stage, and also during the actual event. He was animated and excited in his demeanour, whereas normally he was quite a passive child.

On their return to school, Brendan continues to show interest in this topic and this enables staff to build on the experience. He spontaneously requests 'to make revolving doors'. Staff structure a session, providing stimuli (for example, photographs of the visit), materials, support and time to work with Brendan on the construction of a simple model.

With each event, staff observe Brendan being interested, lively and motivated. His enthusiasm begins to transfer to other aspects of his life in school, for example, he is happier around other children; he goes outdoors for the first time taking his door book to read; he volunteers to help say the end of day prayer in front of the whole school, along with the head teacher! In general, staff report he shows more assurance within his school environment and is much more willing to participate.

His increase in confidence and self-belief means Brendan also begins to explore situations and environments where he would have been fearful at the start of the school year. This enables both Brendan and the staff to extend further his learning opportunities. He is now motivated to crawl independently in PE sessions and participates in activities such as going on the mini trampoline with support and bending his knees to bounce; he asks for adult help to access higher surfaces in the ball pool, being motivated by a high door-like flap. This is a significant event, as the teacher knows that prior to the trip, Brendan was afraid of heights and would usually sit passively in the ball pool, seemingly afraid to explore this unusual environment. He volunteers to show his crawling at the end of the PE lesson one day and says, 'crawl like Shelley the tortoise' (the school tortoise!). As a result of his cooperation, the physiotherapist suggests that the staff teach him to get himself up from the floor and he happily cooperates and succeeds. These activities develop his mobility, physical skills and independence and he begins to achieve the targets set by the physiotherapist.

Brendan is also showing more confidence with his peers and he becomes friends with another child, Marc. This new friendship progresses and is particularly evident when Marc is absent. Brendan notices Marc's absence and cries. When Marc returns, Brendan hugs him in welcome. This demonstrates a considerable move forward in Brendan's peer–peer relationship building.

Brendan's parents are very supportive throughout and are delighted with his progress. There appears to be a shift or development of his interests at school and home. Brendan's curiosity of the world around him is beginning to broaden. As he leaves the Early Years department, he continues to develop interests and starts to investigate planets and space – something encouraged by both home and school.

Through the example given here, it illustrates that when something sparks a child's interest, however small and mundane this may seem to us as adults, it can be used to identify, explore and build the learning process. This is not achieved through any prescribed or fixed curriculum but through skilled adult observation. It involves continuous, ongoing assessment, where learning is fostered and extended, and is truly personalised for the individual. Hargreaves (2006) writes of 'deep learning' having three 'gateways', one of which is assessment for learning. He suggests that deep learning is 'at the heart of personalisation' and that such personalisation can 'transform the conditions of learning' (Hargreaves 2006: 7–8). It appears that engagement is a key part or precondition of this (SSAT 2012). The example of Brendan demonstrates all these influences in action.

From theory to practice

In the following section we consider the contributions of three researchers and the relevance of their work when supporting learners with SLD, particularly those in their early years. The writers are Urie Bronfenbrenner (considering his later works such as that published in 1995), Cathy Nutbrown (2011, writing on the theory under pinning schemas, based on Piaget 1962 and Athey 1990) and Margaret Carr (2001, who develops the idea of 'Learning Stories'). All three authors have a theoretical basis for their work, but also root their concepts in observations from their own practice, and illustrate the importance of a holistic view of the child. We think the principles being advanced apply as much to our context as they do when working with children without SLD. However, as these three authors do not specifically apply their work to learners with SLD, we draw on each and illustrate how their work is valid for this particular group. We do this through analysis of the actions of Brendan, his teacher and the other adults around him.

Bronfenbrenner – a later version of his ecological model

Bronfenbrenner's early works can be said to have a socio-cultural basis with the development of a specific ecological model (see Bronfenbrenner 1976). Bronfenbrenner gives emphasis to the impact of processes, persons and contexts in the environment of the developing child. In his later writings of the 1990s Bronfenbrenner's thinking has moved on to include the concept of time and he begins to refer to this as a bioecological model or paradigm. Bronfenbrenner (1995) puts forward two propositions, or basic elements, that define his model.

For his first proposition, he talks about enduring forms of interaction in the learner's immediate environment and he refers to these as proximal processes. Bronfenbrenner suggests that:

> Examples of enduring patterns of proximal processes are found in parent–child and child–child activities, group or solitary play, reading, learning new skills, studying, athletic activities, and performing complex tasks.
>
> (Bronfenbrenner 1995: 620)

In Proposition 2, Bronfenbrenner states that the proximal processes may vary depending on the form, power, content and direction involved and he 'identifies the three-fold source of these dynamic forces' as a) the developing person, b) the environment and c) the nature of the outcomes (1995: 621).

Applying Bronfenbrenner's ideas to the conceptualisation of our learners' needs, a particular process involves particular people in a particular context over a span of time. In our example, the teacher and other staff, having noticed Brendan's different reaction to the door opening, compare it with the way he fails to interact the rest of the time. The change in environment, brought about in response to his initiations is the catalyst to unlocking some of Brendan's potential. The staff carry this forward using the proximal processes of continual observation, feedback and adjustment. This learning experience could have been very different if, following their observation, everyone had just accepted that Brendan became excited when doors opened and this was simply 'what Brendan did'. Fortunately, investigation by staff meant they discerned more clearly Brendan's focus, and took the opportunity to build on this. Staff explored, shaped and led the possibilities for him, extending his experiences, knowledge and understanding. They were able to introduce meaningful learning experiences, from a seemingly simple interaction, and influence his development on a holistic basis.

In his later work, Bronfenbrenner adds the concept of learning over time to his original model. This is particularly important for those working with learners with SLD, as it is well documented that learning can take longer for this group (Porter 2006; Imray and Hinchcliffe 2014). In our example, Brendan's learning takes place continually and regularly over an extended period of the school year. We acknowledge the importance of routines in any child's life (DfE 2014; Daley, Byers and Taylor 2006; Gray and Macblain 2012), but we advise caution in using Bronfenbrenner to suggest that the time dimension means learners with SLD and PMLD need repetitive tasks, target-driven by adults in order to learn. While teachers need to have a clear understanding and give direction to the learning, the motivation and interest must come from the child in order for curiosity to play a part and learning to take place.

Nutbrown – theory and application of schemas

Nutbrown characterises schemas, initially using Piaget's (1962) definition of 'action, co-ordinated systems of movement and perceptions, which constitute any elementary behaviours capable of being repeated and applied to new situations, e.g. grasping, moving, shaking an object' (2011: 274). She continues, and explains how Athey takes this forward to explain schemas are 'patterns of behaviour and thinking in children that exist underneath the surface features of various contents, contexts and specific experiences' (Athey 2007: 5).

Athey (1990) also describes and identifies specific patterns of behaviour and development according to characteristics exhibited by the learner. Her list of suggestions (see Nutbrown 2011) includes two schemas that seem to apply to Brendan's thinking. These schemas are 'dynamic back and forth' (i.e objects or people moving backwards and forwards) and 'dynamic circular' (i.e. objects or people moving in a circular movement) (Nutbrown 2011: 14). At first, Brendan's schema might have been determined solely as a 'dynamic back and forth' as the door opened and closed, but this develops into the 'dynamic circular' schema with the introduction of revolving doors and into another related theme at a later stage.

In getting to know Brendan, the staff noticed his usual patterns of behaviour, such as being withdrawn etc., but most importantly they observed the change in his responses to the movement of the door. Having seen this, his teacher corroborates observations and interpretation with the team. When it is established that this is a repeated pattern of behaviour, they watch more closely and this raises questions for them. What exactly is stimulating this particular response in Brendan? Who comes through the door? Is it that Brendan wants to go through the door? Is it the opening of the door? Is it the motion of the door opening or closing? Is the noise of the action? The staff decide to test their hypothesis about the motion of doors and gather as much information relating to Brenden's reactions at this point. The staff then consider Brendan's forms of thought and how these can be encouraged through stimulating content (Nutbrown

2011) which is crucial to maintaining Brendan's engagement (Carpenter 2012). The staff decide to follow lines of enquiry around the movement of the door opening and look for ways to extend Brendan's interest and curiosity.

During the time the staff were working with Brendan on this schema, the content changed and they developed ways to understand his form of thought better. The staff had found a key to stimulating Brendan's curiosity and engagement in his environment. As we have recounted, Brendan did take his dynamic circular schema further by developing an interest in planets spinning and moving in space. The staff's hard work established a foundation for learning and given Brendan confidence to continue to explore and learn about his world.

Further evaluation of this learning process might have led the staff to explore other schema or lines of development related to dynamic back and forth or dynamic circular movements with Brendan. These could have included other moving, circular themes such as wheels, moving gears, globes, windmills, watermills, escalators lifts, whisks or mixers; or other back and forth themes such as swings, cranes, trains and train lines, robots, cars and roads, mechanical, and remotely operated toys for example. Brendan, now more self-motivating, developed his schema through a new topic of planets moving dynamically in space.

Carr – using learning stories

From our example it is clear that observation and assessment are crucial in the teaching and learning of children with SLD. When a staff team, such as those working with Brendan, come to write up, collate, share and communicate their observations, this leads to decisions about the next steps of action with the learner. This is where the Learning Stories of Carr (2001) have a significant role to play. She and her colleagues use this term to describe a particular approach to observations taken from everyday situations. These observations:

> provide a cumulative series of qualitative 'snapshots' which are recorded in five domains of learning disposition and then translated into actions: taking an interest, being involved, persisting with difficulty or uncertainty, expressing an idea or a feeling, and taking responsibility or taking another point of view.
>
> (Carr 2001: 96)

While this model was primarily established to use with typically developing children, analysis of our example shows how it can be applied equally well with learners who have SLD. Evaluation of the qualitative snapshots gathered over time illustrate:

- *Taking an interest:* Brendan showed a different reaction to a stimulus in his environment. His teacher interpreted this as an interest and began a more in-depth gathering of evidence.
- *Being involved:* Brendan was actively involved and engaged throughout because of his interest.
- *Persisting with difficulty or uncertainty:* The fact that this topic was sustained over such an extensive period of time could be said to be persistence on the part of both Brendan and the staff. He also overcame difficulties and faced new challenges, for example his motivation to explore the soft play room.
- *Expressing an ideas or a feeling:* Through the many activities Brendan was guided in expressing his ideas. His willing participation, changed responses and increase in self-confidence are all expressions of his enjoyment.

- *Taking responsibility or taking another point of view:* While this was evident as Brendan led his learning, this may be an area that staff consider further, providing learning opportunities and encouraging Brendan to explore in more depth (Edwards, Gandini and Forman 2011; Bruce 2011; Clarke 2013).

As our example of Brendan demonstrates, a range of lateral but related learning opportunities can motivate a child's interest over time, develop their curiosity and enhance their understanding of the world they live in. Assessment is a process that requires adults to develop skills of analysis, interpretation and decision making, thereby maximising possibilities for the child to progress (Nutbrown 2011; Nutbrown and Carter 2010)

Conclusion

Through the example of Brendan and his teacher, we have analysed early years pedagogic practices through the lens of three different early years theories. Brendan's progress demonstrates their efficacy. Learning for young children is a progressive journey, where each learner is unique and develops at their individual pace; however there are generalities that apply. As educators of learners with SLD and PMLD in their early years, we need to ensure our practice has sound pedagogical underpinnings and be willing to transpose the best ideas from early years practice in order maximise our learners' opportunities. To quote Loris Malaguzzi, founder of the Reggio Emilia approach:

> The wider the range of possibilities we offer children, the more intense will be their motivations and the richer their experiences. We must widen the range of topics and goals, the types of situations we offer and their degree of structure, the kinds and combinations of resources and materials, and the possible interactions with things, peers, and adults.
>
> (Malaguzzi 1998: 79)

As we see with Brendan, this can mean visiting the unexpected.

Questions for readers

- What is there within the Early Years Foundation Stage framework that you think relevant to educating children with SLD and PMLD in their early years?
- Some authors, such as Imray and Hinchcliffe (2014), have advanced alternative opinions on guiding the learning of children with SLD and PMLD suggesting a distinct and separate pedagogy? What are your thoughts on this?
- Consider children you know – how may knowledge of the theory of schemas help you further understand ways of teaching and learning?
- Can you see how 'Learning Stories' might add to the assessment processes you follow in your setting? What might be the advantages?

References

Athey, C. (1990) *Extending Thought in Young Children: A parent–teacher partnership*, London: Paul Chapman Publishing.

Athey, C. (2007) *Extending Thought in Young Children: A parent-teacher partnership*, 2nd edn, London: Sage.

Bronfenbrenner, U. (1976) 'The experimental ecology of education', *Educational Researcher*, 5(9): 5–15.

Bronfenbrenner, U. (1995) 'Developmental ecology through space and time: a future perspective', in P. Moen, G.H. Elder Jr and K. Luscher (eds) *Examining Lives in Context: Perspectives on the ecology of human development*, Washington DC: American Psychological Association.

Bruce, T. (2011) *Early Childhood Education,* 4th edn, Oxon: Hodder Education.

Carpenter, B. (2012) *Children with Complex Learning Disabilities: A 21st century challenge,* London: Specialist Schools and Academies Trust. Online: http//hwb.warwickshire.gov.uk/files/2012/04/Professor-Carpenter-Children-with-complex-learning-disabilities.pdf (accessed 28 July 2014).

Carpenter, B., Ashdown, R. and Bovair, K. (2001) *Enabling Access*, London: David Fulton.

Carr, M. (2001) *Assessment in Early Childhood Settings*, London: Paul Chapman Publishing.

Clarke, J. (2013) *Sustained Shared Thinking*, London: Bloomsbury Publishing.

Daley, M., Byers, E. and Taylor, W. (2006) *Understanding Early Years Theory in Practice*, Harlow: Heinemann.

Department for Education (DfE) (2013) *Early Years Outcomes – a non-statutory guide for practitioners and inspectors to help inform understanding of child development through the early years*. London: DfE. Online. Available: www.gov.uk/government/uploads/system/uploads/attachment_data/file/237249/Early_Years_Outcomes.pdf (accessed 28 July 2014).

Department for Education (DfE) (2014) *Statutory Framework for the Early Years Foundation Stage: Setting the standards for learning, development and care for children from birth to five*. Online. Available: www.gov.uk/government/uploads/system/uploads/attachment_data/file/299391/DFE-00337-2014.pdf (accessed 28 July 2014).

Edwards, C., Gandini, L. and Forman, G. (eds) (1998) *The Hundred Languages of Children: The Reggio Emilia experience – advanced reflections*, 2nd edn, Westport, CT: Ablex Publishing Corporation.

Gray, C. and Macblain, S. (2012) *Learning Theories in Childhood*, London: Sage Publications.

Hargreaves, D. (2006) *A New Shape for Schooling?* London: Specialist Schools and Academies Trust. Online: www.my-ecoach.com/online/resources/13729/a_new_shape_for_schooling_11.pdf (accessed 28 July 2014).

Imray, P. and Hinchcliffe, V. (2014) *Curricula for Teaching Children and Young People with Severe or Profound Learning Difficulties*, Oxon: Routledge.

Malaguzzi, L. (1998) 'History, Ideas and Basic Philosphy: An interview with Lella Gandini by Loris Malaguzzi', in C. Edwards, L. Gandini and G. Forman (eds) *The Hundred Languages of Children: the Reggio Emilia experience – advanced reflections*, 2nd edn, Westport, CT: Ablex Publishing Corporation.

Nutbrown, C. (2011) *Threads of Thinking,* 4th edn, London: Sage Publications.

Nutbrown, C. and Carter, C. (2010) 'The tools of assessment: watching and listening', in G. Pugh and B. Duffy (eds) *Contemporary Issues in the Early Years*, 5th edn, London: Paul Chapman Publishing.

Piaget, J. (1962) *Play Dreams and Imitation in Childhood*, London: Routledge and Kegan Paul.

Porter, J. (2005) 'Severe learning difficulties', in A. Lewis and B. Norwich (eds) *Special Teaching for Special Children?*, Maidenhead: OUP.

SSAT – Specialist Schools and Academies Trust (2012) *Redesigning Schooling*. Online. Available: http://social.ssatuk.co.uk/wp-content/uploads/2012/11/Redesigning-Schooling-October2012.pdf (accessed 28 July 2014).

Tilstone, C. and Layton, L. (2005) *Child Development and Teaching Pupils with Special Educational Needs*, 2nd edn, London: RoutledgeFalmer.

Whalley, M. (2007) *Involving Parents in their Children's Learning*, London: Paul Chapman Publishing.

PART II

Involving stakeholders

8

JOINT WORKING FOR LEARNERS WITH SLD/PMLD

Penny Lacey with Julian Brown, Fiona Holmes,
Helen Burnford, Kate Jones and Rosie Jones

In this chapter, the following questions will be addressed:

- What is joint working?
- What are the joint working strategies that seem to work?
- What are the chief barriers of joint working?
- What theoretical frameworks aid our understanding of joint working?
- What research evidence is there that joint working is effective?

Introduction

Working together in an organised manner is crucial, especially for children and young people who have complex disabilities and needs which require many people to be involved in their education and care. However, joint working is notoriously difficult to achieve and in this chapter we will be discussing why that is so. We will also be exploring what kind of strategies can be used by practitioners who attempt to develop joint working around the often complex needs of learners with SLD/PMLD.

Joint working

Policies

There have been many examples of supportive legislation and policy in England in the last 15 years. The New Labour Government (from 1997 to 2010) was clearly committed to facilitating joint working between health, social care and education, beginning with changing mechanisms to enable statuary agencies to pool budgets and jointly commission services and then creating structures to create integrated services (Cameron *et al.* 2014). The Coalition Government that followed in 2010 maintained the focus on joint working and the Children and Families Act 2014 has a strong emphasis on reforming children's services. The section on Special Educational Needs and Disability (SEND) specifically demands that services in a geographical area work together to produce a 'local offer' setting out the support for learners with SEND and their families. The Education, Health and Care Plans (EHC Plans) for learners with complex needs are a specific mechanism to support joint work as are the use of key workers to support parents and help them to have more control over what is happening to their children (Department for Education and Department of Health 2014). The views and aspirations of learners and their families are central to the policy. See Chapter 3 in this book for more detail on the SEND legislation and policy current in England in the summer of 2014.

Early support

Much of the effective practice on joint working has followed on from the Early Support policy developed under New Labour. There is a Multiagency Planning and Improvement Tool (MAPIT), which is designed to inform and underpin service improvement for disabled children, young people and their families (Early Support 2012). Other materials are designed to integrate Early Support as far as possible. For example, the *Developmental Journal for Children and Young People with Multiple Needs* (Early Support 2013) supports key working by providing a resource for everyone who is involved with a learner to share what they know and discuss how best to work together to support development and learning.

The following example shows how the Early Support experience has helped in the development of integrated services in one local authority.

Cornwall: Bringing about positive change in schools (www.ncb.org.uk/early-support/case-studies)

The use of Early Support in this Special Educational Needs and Disability (SEND) pathfinder area has been successfully established and embedded across services for young children for some years. The approach is now available for children and young people 0–19, with the aspiration to extend it 0–25, in line with the requirements of the Children and Families Act 2014. Development in schools and across services has been supported by investment in a small team, consisting of 1 x Early Support Development Coordinator, 3 x Early Support Coordinators and 6 x 0.5 Early Support Workers. The team sits in the Children's Social Work and Psychology Service. The families of 600 children and young people currently use the approach and service. Of these, 259 currently have a Statement of Special Educational Needs (due to become EHC Plans).

Despite the obvious policy support for agencies and practitioners to work together and the strategies introduced across England (and the rest of the UK), universal joint working has continued to be illusive in practice. The next section of the chapter is focused on defining exactly what joint working looks like in preparation for exploring the strategies that help its effectiveness and the barriers that can damage it.

Definitions

There are almost as many definitions of joint working as there are people who practise it and it has long been debated and discussed over the last 50 years. Lacey (2001) defines several different terms, divided into concept-based terms (such as multidisciplinary, interdisciplinary, transdisciplinary), process-based terms (such as liaison, cooperation, coordination, collaboration, keyworking) and agency-based terms (such as multidisciplinary, consortium, forum, centre, network, cluster and federation). All refer to different aspects of joint working that are suitable for use in different circumstances. There is no one way to working jointly that suits all situations and there is no research to suggest that one gives better results than others (Cameron *et al.* 2014).

Because terminology is used in so many different ways, there are some terms commonly in use in educational settings that would be helpful to define for this chapter. The information for the definitions comes from a range of sources (Lacey 2001; Law *et al.* 2002; Limbrick 2004; 2009; Limbrick-Spencer 2001).

Term	Definition
Multidisciplinary/ multiagency work	This is a generic term meaning a group of people who represent different disciplines and who work with the same learner. They may, or may not, work in collaboration (see below).
Networking	Agencies share information with each other and with learners and their families. Often the information is available on the web or on leaflets that are found in education and health settings.
Collaboration	Collaboration is the most advanced working together, implying sharing and joint purpose, mutual trust and support. Collaborative team members do not work hierarchically. They need a team leader, whose job it is to coordinate and motivate the team but it is not a hierarchical post.
Key working	One team member undertakes to coordinate the work of a team and be the point of contact for all who work with the same learner.
Team	A group of people work and meet together regularly. They work with the same learners in an educational setting in a collaborative manner.
Team-around-the-child (TAC)	A multidisciplinary team of practitioners established on a case-by-case basic to support a learner and his or her family. The TAC uses: joined-up assessment; a keyworker; a flexible team of people (that can alter with changing needs); coordination at the point of delivery; regular meetings and a team plan.
Consultative model	Specialists (such as speech and language therapists) work mainly as consultants with classroom staff to enable learners' therapy needs to be met on a daily basis. There is flexible use of direct, indirect work with learners, classroom focus and withdrawal accompanied by training for classroom staff.

The example below uses some of the terms above to illustrate how practitioners in educational settings can work together effectively.

In Apple Tree Nursery class there is a multidisciplinary team consisting of a teacher, a speech and language therapist, physiotherapist, occupational therapist and four teaching assistants. They work in a collaborative manner, meeting weekly to assess children, deciding on children's education, care and therapy goals, plotting progress and evaluating the programmes they write for individual children. They often work in the classroom together so they can observe and learn from each other and they share the class record keeping. Parents are an important part of the team and are consulted on all important aspects of their child's education, care and therapy in the manner of a TAC. Termly meetings are facilitated by managers, ensuring that time is set aside.

In the current climate of austerity, it is really hard to maintain the effective joint working seen in Apple Tree nursery class. Therapy services have been cut back and reorganised so many times that, in my (Penny Lacey) experience, educational settings are struggling to staff their multidisciplinary teams. The consultative model is being employed by many therapy services, but often is limited to passing on therapy skills to classroom staff, who then feel unskilled and unsupported (Miller and Lacey 2003). The collaborative aspects of the consultative model are being lost in response to dwindling funds and therapists.

Having defined some of the terms in the way they are used in this chapter, the discussions now move into the detail of joint working. How does it actually work? What strategies seem to support effective joint working and what seem to be the barriers that prevent it from being successful?

Joint working in practice

In reviewing the research on joint working between health and social care, Cameron *et al.* (2014) organised the factors that support or hinder joint working into three broad themes (see below). They point out that there is considerable overlap between the positive and negative factors and that often it is the absence of the positive factors that causes the problems. They also recommend much more research to test these factors in a more robust manner.

Effective joint work means:

Organisational issues
- Agreeing common aims between agencies and practitioners.
- Understanding and respecting each other's roles.
- Flexibility from partners in response to learners' needs.
- Minimising organisational differences.
- Mechanisms for communication and information sharing.
- Practitioners being co-located for ease of communication.
- The presence of strong management and appropriate professional support.
- A past history of joint working.
- Adequate resources to support joint working.

Cultural and professional issues
- Minimising different professional philosophies and ideologies.
- Breeding trust, respect and releasing some control over what happens to learners, to others in the team.
- Opportunities for teambuilding, team meeting and joint training.

Contextual issues
- Building relationships between agencies and practitioners.
- Minimising the problems of frequent reorganisation of services.
- Mitigating financial uncertainty and funding cuts.

The sheer length of the list indicates the complexity of joint working. Achieving partnerships and teams of people who can operate effectively demands deliberate effort at all levels (strategic, service and fieldwork). All services that work with learners with SLD/PMLD need to have a vision of sharing and joint purpose, mutual trust and support for each other. It is not sufficient for individual practitioners to desire to work with one another.

One of most common factors identified by researchers as important is the need for good communication between agencies and between practitioners (Vostanis *et al.* 2012; Davidson *et al.* 2012). Confidentiality is often cited as presenting difficulties as practitioners struggle with the tension between sharing relevant information and keeping the affairs of families with disabled children to themselves. However, sharing information is vitally important in joint working and ways can be found to do this sharing sensitively. The example below shows how one school manages communication between different agencies.

School A has an office to share between the therapists who come to the school. Although they are not always in the office at the same time, there is sufficient overlap each week for communication between them to be relatively easy. There is a communication book for queries and information that can be dealt with at other times. Teachers and therapists have timetabled slots for liaison, particularly when planning new education, health and care targets. There is one member of the leadership team who is responsible for facilitating the multi-agency work and there is a member of the support staff whose job it is to liaise between the school and home. She knows the families well and provides a consistent point of contact. In general the communication flow is excellent and learners' needs are identified and dealt with quickly. However, recently there has been a huge turnover of therapists who support the school, and their hours have been curtailed considerably which threatens to de-stabilise the arrangements. Relationships take time to build up and there needs to be constant investment of time as practitioners across the agencies get to know each other.

Establishing common goals among multi-agency partners is important, as is an understanding of the roles and responsibilities of everyone. There is a delicate balance between practitioners with different roles sharing their skills with each other and keeping a hold on professional integrity. In a context of shortages, it has become more and more necessary for agencies outside educational settings to adopt a consultative relationship with those inside. Visiting practitioners spend less time with individual learners and more time in training educational staff to meet learners' needs themselves (McCartney 2009; Vostanis *et al.* 2012). This can be seen as a positive step as the needs of individual learners can be met on a daily basis rather than waiting for the peripatetic member of staff to visit. But it can also be seen as a negative step if educational staff feel they are not sufficiently supported to perform a new role (Miller and Lacey 2003).

The example below shows how physiotherapists work jointly with classroom staff in a special school. It is a good example of the way in which skills are passed on to classroom staff in a supportive manner.

Group physiotherapy sessions

We are physiotherapists based within a special school and this gives us optimum contact with education staff. This means joint working can become not just a box-ticking exercise, but a purposeful and practical reality. Apart from their family, education staff are probably the only ones who see the learner every (school) day. They generally have them for the 'best' part of their day when they are most likely to be alert and energetic. So this makes any time we invest in working with school staff well worth it.

Setting and reviewing Individual Education Plan targets together with teachers and teaching assistants means the targets can be realistic, both in terms of what the learner is likely to be able to achieve and what is feasible to be worked on in the classroom setting within the confines of staffing and the curriculum.

Conducting group sessions, in which physiotherapy and class staff both handle the learners in a variety of positions, means that class staff can observe our handling and we can observe and modify theirs. Through working together over the years, staff gain insight and skills from each other, that inform the way they then work, even at the times when the other team members are absent. Often with learners with SEN, it is not clear who holds the key to the next door that needs to be unlocked, but joint working can really help with this, and often, once one door is unlocked, several become easier to open as development in one area has a knock-on effect.

Below is another example in which therapists have handed over some of their skills and expertise to classroom staff. This one is from speech and language therapy.

The BONES Language Curriculum

As speech and language therapists working in a special school in Wales in 2006/7, we were aware that the service was more likely to contract than to expand. With increasing numbers of learners with severe and complex needs coming into the school, much of the contracted therapy provision was taken up with the feeding and swallowing needs of the learners, leaving little time for hands-on individual and group communication therapy. We devised a simple individual communication profile, a box and arrow diagram, which was used for each learner. This covered six dimensions; feeding, alternative and augmentative communication (AAC), receptive language, expressive language, social skills and phonology.

To support the profile we produced a summary pupil profile for each level across each dimension, to give classroom staff the confidence to use the system. We then set about collecting simple therapy activities for each level, across each dimension. We also worked with IT specialists in the school to produce a number of interactive whiteboard games. The whole curriculum was put onto the school computer system and eventually made available in every classroom. It was well used.

The final example is a successful way of including families in the joint working that is the result of developing 'The Solihull Way'. The aim of this approach is for services to work jointly, from a user perspective, rather than a service perspective and has been in operation in Solihull since 2004.

George has SLD with autism and his family have been part of a Team-around–the-Family approach in which professionals and services have been working together to meet the family needs. The family has indicated that they have good support from their friends and would prefer for this assistance to be more formalised rather than receive a service provided by the local authority. It is important for George to be with people who know and understand his needs and for the family to be surrounded by friends rather than professionals. The result of this strategy is shared-care on a weekly basis with a family friend.

George was due to go into hospital and the team-around-the-family identified the need for George to have time to get to know the people who were going to be involved in his hospital stay as well as the environment in the hospital. George and his parents were able to visit the hospital. His parents took photos of the ward and the staff members that would be there during his stay. The school that George attends and the family were able to show the pictures to George in preparation for what was going to happen. The hospital also had access to the single page profile co-produced with the family. This information gave staff access to important information that supported him during his stay.

The team–around–the–child (TAC) model is now well-known but it is still hard to achieve, particularly as organisations need to create a 'horizontal' way of working in a world where the structures are largely 'vertical'. Limbrick (2012) argues that organisations, such as human services, have hierarchical structures based on positions of power, which mitigate against the flat structure needed for joint working. In a TAC, the practitioners and family members work as equals. There are no senior and junior members of the team and there is no withholding of information or struggles for power.

From the examples shared, it can be seen that practitioners have risen to the challenge of joint working in many special schools. It is relatively easy to facilitate ways of working together in an enclosed space, such as a special school or college but it becomes much more difficult where individual learners are educated in mainstream schools or colleges. There are so many more factors to be considered. For example, in many mainstream educational settings, learners are supported by teaching assistants (TAs) rather than by teachers. Sometimes TAs are insufficiently trained in meeting learners' education, health and care needs but yet are expected to manage all three (Morewood 2011). Targeted training and the facilitation of communication between classroom staff and visiting professionals can help to ameliorate some of the barriers to effective working (Hayes *et al.* 2011).

Theoretical frameworks

Following discussions around the practicalities of joint working, it might be helpful to consider some examples of theorising around the topic. Below are brief introductions to three different theories that can help in understanding how joint working operates and why it is so difficult to achieve. These include activity theory, discourse analysis and critical realism.

Activity theory

Activity theory offers a framework for understanding a system, such as a joint working (Engstrom 2007). Figure 8.1 shows how an analysis of the joint working system employs consideration of a range of different dimensions that influence the activity undertaken by individual or teams of people in their effort to produce an object (or objective) such as effective working together.

Human activity is mediated by several different factors. For example, joint working is influenced by artefacts (e.g. tools, documents used by team members), the organisation of the community (how the team works), rules that influence the community (which come from different working practices) and by the division of labour between team members (Daniels *et al.* 2007; Edwards *et al.* 2010).

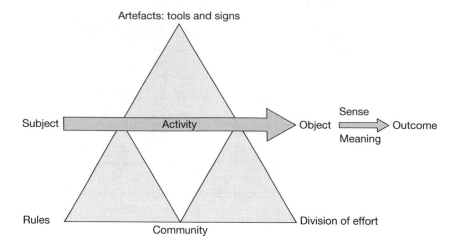

Figure 8.1 Activity System from Engstrom (2007)

Activity Theory is used by Davies, Howes and Farell (2008) to understand the difficulties and dilemmas of joint working in terms of cultural history and more practically, to help practitioners in finding solutions. Their project sought to enable teachers and educational psychologists to work together to improve inclusion through the use of Action Research. Tensions arose partly from the different expectations that the teachers and educational psychologists had of each other's roles in the project and this was partly solved through understanding the historical relationship between the two sets of practitioners and how it is gradually changing. From this theory, we can see that taking time to build understanding among team members is vital.

Discourse analysis

Another way of analysing joint working is through using the tools of discourse analysis developed by Foucault as is shown in the research by Forbes and McCartney (2010). Forbes and McCartney (2010) analyse the content of the discussions between teachers and speech and language therapists, demonstrating that although they use their professionally specific language, they do, in fact, develop language that is created between them to enable them to talk about joint working.

Critical realism

A third approach to theory in joint working is through critical realism as developed by Bhaskar and used by Hood (2012) in his analysis of complex situations. Hood explains that Bhaskar suggests that reality exists on three levels: the empirical, the actual and the real. 'Empirical reality' refers to the experience we have through our senses; the 'actual reality' refers to everything that happens, whether we can experience everything or not, and the 'real' refers to the underlying causes that generate events (Hood 2012). Critical realism accepts that reality is always subject to interpretation and using its theoretical perspective can help in understanding the complexity of joint working.

There are, of course, many other theoretical perspectives that can throw light on joint working, for example, theories around roles, team formation, group dynamics, team make up, leadership. Exploring any or all of these can increase our understanding of how and why joint working is effective or not (Lacey 2001).

Research evidence for effectiveness

Joint working has been discussed and researched since the 1960s but still it seems hard to achieve in practice and even harder to show evidence of efficacy. Hudson (2012) provides a very helpful historical review of the attempts of health and social care services to work together across the years, concluding that while both integration and competition exist side by side, there is little hope for joint working to develop effectively. Russell was a little more optimistic in 2008 when discussing the Children's Plan and commissioning services around the needs of the child (Russell 2008) but Cameron *et al.* (2012) and Morrison and Glenny (2011) suggest research about the effectiveness of joint working is not particularly encouraging. They point to the paucity of clear research evidence of better outcomes for the patients/clients from joint working. There are some studies where outcomes were measured and a few of these are briefly mentioned below.

A small study of family centred care in three services in Wales, conducted by Pickering and Busse (2010), found that regular TAC meetings contributed considerably to the satisfaction of the families involved. Other studies that concentrate on satisfaction of joint working include a Dutch study of Parent and Child Centres (Busch *et al.* 2013) where perceived advantages were found to be more continuity of care, shorter communication lines and good contact between professionals. A study from Northern Ireland by Davidson *et al.* (2012) found similar opinions in their evaluation of a particular project called 'The Champions Initiative'. The researchers report a positive effect on professional awareness and communication across the team.

Further examples of satisfaction include Bell *et al.* (2010)'s study of an early intervention transdisciplinary team that found waiting times for services had been reduced and more therapy had taken place through the more efficient utilisation of resources. Similar results came from a study by Nankervis *et al.* (2010) where joint working had reduced the length of time in hospital for very premature infants. Another positive example is an in-depth case study by Boroughs and Dougherty (2010) who demonstrate that providing a collaborative professional team for a child who was ventilator dependent meant that she was able to be cared for at home rather than in hospital.

Conclusions

Although the research evidence for the effectiveness of joint working is still small and mainly related to health and care services working together, there is no doubt that it is seen as the Holy Grail for agencies and practitioners who work in educational settings with learners with complex needs, such as those with SLD/PMLD. Recent governments have been committed to the production of legislation and policy that aid services in their quest to work together effectively and these have certainly given support to practitioners who desire to work together in a focused manner. There continue to be an enormous number of potential difficulties, especially those that relate to the current climate of financial austerity, large caseloads, unending paperwork and an often unrealistic view of the educational progress that can be made by learners whose needs are extremely complex.

The road to joint working may be hard and difficult to maintain across every organisation but it is definitely worth pursuing. Learners and their families need support from people who want to share their expertise among themselves. If their needs are to be met, they require help to navigate the service landscape that is both complicated and alien and assistance to obtain their rights.

Questions for readers

- What is the state of joint working in your organisation?
- What are your most successful strategies?
- What still requires development?
- Do you have a plan for evaluating the joint working on a regular basis?

References

Bell, A., Corfield, M., Davies, J. and Richardson, N. (2010) 'Collaborative transdisciplinary intervention in early years–putting theory into practice', *Child: Care, Health and Development*, 36(1): 142–148.

Boroughs, D.S. and Dougherty, J. (2010) 'A multidisciplinary approach to the care of the ventilator-dependent child at home: a case study', *Home Healthcare Nurse*, 28(1): 24–28.

Busch, V., Van Stel, H.F., De Leeuw, J.R.J., Melhuish, E. and Schrijvers, A.J.P. (2013) 'Multidisciplinary integrated Parent and Child Centres in Amsterdam: a qualitative study', *International Journal of Integrated Care*, 13(2). Online. Available: www.ncbi.nlm.nih.gov.ezproxye.bham.ac.uk/pmc/articles/PMC3718270/ (accessed 7 August 2014).

Cameron, A., Lart, R., Bostock, L. and Coomber, C. (2012) 'Factors that promote and hinder joint and integrated working between health and social care services', *Research Briefing 41*, London: Social Care Institute for Excellence.

Cameron, A., Lart, R., Bostock, L. and Coomber, C. (2014) 'Factors that promote and hinder joint and integrated working between health and social care services: a review of research literature', *Health and Social Care in the Community*, 22(3): 225–233.

Daniels, H., Leadbetter, J., Warmington, P., Edwards, A., Martin, D., Popova, A., Apostolov, A, Middleton, D. and Brown, S. (2007) 'Learning in and for multi-agency working', *Oxford Review of Education*, 33(4): 521–538.

Davidson, G., Duffy, J., Barry, L., Curry, P., Darragh, E. and Lees, J. (2012) 'Championing the interface between mental health and child protection: evaluation of a service initiative to improve joint working in Northern Ireland', *Child Abuse Review*, 21(3): 157–172.

Davies, S.M., Howes, A.J. and Farrell, P. (2008) 'Tensions and dilemmas as drivers for change in an analysis of joint working between teachers and educational psychologists', *School Psychology International*, 29(4): 400–417.

Department for Education and Department of Health (2014) *Special Educational Needs and Disability Code of Practice: 0 to 25 years*. Ref: DFE:-00205-2013. Online. Available: www.gov.uk/government/publications/send-code-of-practice-0-to-25 (accessed 20 August 2014).

Early Support (2012) *Multiagency Planning and Improvement Tool*. Online. Available: www.ncb.org.uk/media/925077/mapit_document_april_2013.pdf (accessed 25 July 2014).

Early Support (2013) *Developmental Journal for Children and Young People with Complex Needs*. Online. Available: www.ncb.org.uk/media/954319/mndj_part_i_overview_pages.pdf (accessed 25 July 2014).

Edwards, A., Daniels, H., Gallagher, T., Leadbetter, J. and Warmington, P. (2010) *Improving Inter-professional Collaborations: Multi-agency working for children's well-being*, London: Routledge.

Engstrom, Y. (2007) 'Putting activity theory to work: the change laboratory as an application of double stimulation', in H. Daniels, M. Cole and J. Wertsch (eds) *The Cambridge Companion to Vygotsky*, Cambridge: Cambridge University Press.

Forbes, J. and McCartney, E. (2010) 'Social capital theory: a cross-cutting analytic for teacher/therapist work in integrating children's services?' *Child Language Teaching and Therapy*, 26(3): 321–334.

Hayes, B., Richardson, S., Hindle, S. and Grayson, K. (2011) 'Developing teaching assistants' skills in positive behaviour management: an application of Video Interaction Guidance in a secondary school', *Educational Psychology in Practice*, 27(3): 255–269.

Hood, R. (2012) 'A critical realist model of complexity for interprofessional working', *Journal of Interprofessional Care*, 26(1): 6–12.

Hudson, B. (2012) 'Twenty years of health and social care joint working: a journey from Doctor Pangloss to Private Frazer?' *Journal of Integrated Care*, 20(2): 115–124.

Lacey, P. (2001) *Support Partnerships: collaboration in action*, London: David Fulton.

Law, J., Lindsay, G., Peacey, N., Gascoigne, M., Soloff, N., Radford, J. and Band, S. (2002) 'Consultation as a model for providing speech and language therapy in schools: a panacea or one step too far?' *Child Language Teaching and Therapy*, 18(2): 145–163.

Limbrick, P. (2004) 'Keyworkers are an essential part of a quality service for families. So why do most families not have one? Is the "Team around the Child" part of the solution?' *PMLD Link*, 16(2): 13–16.

Limbrick, P. (2009) *TAC for the 21st Century: Nine essays on Team Around the Child*, Clifford: Interconnections.

Limbrick, P. (2012) *Horizontal Teamwork in a Vertical World: Exploring interagency collaboration and people empowerment*, Clifford: Interconnections.

Limbrick-Spencer, G. (2001) *The Keyworker: A practical guide*, Birmingham: WordWorks in association with the Handsel Trust.

McCartney, E. (2009) 'Joined-up working: terms, types and tensions', in J. Forbes and C. Watson (eds) *Service Integration in Schools: Research and policy discourse, practices and future prospects*, Rotterdam: Sense Publishers.

Miller, C. and Lacey, P. (2003) *Wyre Forest Special Schools Working Together Agreement: Evaluation Report*, unpublished report, University of Birmingham.

Morrison, M. and Glenny, G. (2012) 'Collaborative inter-professional policy and practice: in search of evidence', *Journal of Education Policy*, 27(3): 367–386.

Morewood, G. D. (2011) 'Restructuring in light of budget restraints: optimise teaching assistants to maximise resources', *Assessment and Development Matters*, 3(1): 21.

Nankervis, C.A., Martin, E.M., Crane, M.L., Samson, K.S., Welty, S.E. and Nelin, L.D. (2010) 'Implementation of a multidisciplinary guideline-driven approach to the care of the extremely premature infant improved hospital outcomes', *Acta Paediatrica*, 99(2): 188–193.

Pickering, D. and Busse, M. (2010) 'Disabled children's services: how do we measure family-centred care?' *Journal of Child Health Care*, 14(2): 200–207.

Russell, P. (2008) '"Building brighter futures for all our children" – a new focus on families as partners and change agents in the care and development of children with disabilities or special educational needs', *Support for Learning*, 23(3): 104–112.

Vostanis, P., O'Reilly, M., Taylor, H., Day, C., Street, C., Wolpert, M. and Edwards, R. (2012) 'What can education teach child mental health services? Practitioners' perceptions of training and joint working', *Emotional and Behavioural Difficulties*, 17(2): 109–124.

9

WORKING WITH FAMILIES

Partnerships in practice

Barry Carpenter and Hollie Rawson

In this chapter, the following questions will be addressed:

- How is 'the family' perceived?
- What is the reality of family relationships?
- What are the needs of different family members?
- How can schools engage, involve and build relationships with families?
- How can schools strengthen and empower families?
- What are the ways families can support schools?
- What skills do professionals need in working with families?
- What are possible barriers to families' engagement with schools?

Changes in the perception of the family

The importance of the family in nurturing children came to the fore in the UK in the 1980s when educational practice perspectives began to move from being solely child-focused to more family-focused. This has since become increasingly emphasised through policy and in service approaches. The publication of *Supporting Families* (Home Office 1998) gave rise to the Family and Parenting Institute, founded upon the premise that, 'Families are at the heart of our society and the basis of our future as a country.' This thinking, combined with the writings of Dale (1996), Hornby (1995) and others, was hugely influential within educational practice, and generated a shift from professional control to family-centredness, and a higher level of parent participation (Carpenter, Rawson and Egerton 2012; Hutchinson 2005). However the 'family focus' tended to concentrate largely on the engagement and input of parents. Since the turn of the twenty-first century, this focus has moved to recognise the extended family, working with not only mothers and fathers, but also siblings and grandparents as well as a wider network of 'significant others' who are key supporters in the lives of the child and family. As Winton writes:

> Families are big, small, extended, nuclear, multi-generational, with one parent, two parents, same-sex parents, step-parents and grandparents. We live under one roof or

many... We become part of a family by birth, adoption, marriage, or from a desire for mutual support.

(Winton 1990: 4, cited in Carpenter 2001: 274)

Key as parents are to every child, the modern reality is that other family members undertake significant care-giving roles. In their work with families, therefore, professionals need to keep the pattern of real family relationships in mind. Role stereotyping by services can place limitations on families when they most need the self-support of their own internal structures. Consequently, it is important that schools shift the focus from talking only of 'partnership with parents' to 'partnership with families', that wider group of supporters who are involved in the cycle of upbringing. It is only by acknowledging the people who make up the family network and home environment that we can effectively work with families (Carpenter 2001).

To support and sustain the family as an interactive and holistic unit, it is important to appreciate the dynamics of the role and the potential contribution of each family member (Carpenter 1997). Schools may find themselves working with many 'self-defined' families, whose members may include grandparents, an older sibling, a stepfather or stepmother, or perhaps a family friend acting as a child-minder (Carpenter 2001). For example, Beresford (1994) reports instances where neighbours' informal support was very significant for parents. When unexpected difficulties or demands on the parent arose, neighbours would step in, providing child-minding or lifts to the hospital, for example. Close friends or work colleagues offered the informal emotional support parents needed, often more so than blood relatives who might not understand the child and the family's needs in the same way. Godparents may also play an important role in the support of the child and family, and may have been chosen for their particular expertise or backgrounds in disability, medicine and education with the hope of long-term involvement. This is particularly the case for families of children with life-limiting illness (Brown 2007). In empowering all family members through inclusive practices, professionals can strengthen and empower the whole family network.

Families – traditional, extended and self-defined

When we consider the family, we know mothers play a vital role in the development of their child with learning disabilities and are often the primary carers (Newman *et al.* 2010). However, because of this recognition, many schools make mothers their sole focus for communication, consequently increasing the ever present stress for mothers (Kingston 2007; Dossetor 2012). This excludes fathers from the dialogue preventing access to a major resource for the family (Carpenter and Towers 2008). In the past fathers have been referred to as the 'peripheral parent' (Carpenter 1997), the 'invisible parent' (Ballard 1994) or described as 'hard to reach' (McConkey 1994). However, it seems that fathers now have much more involvement in family life than previous research suggests (Towers and Swift 2006). Fathers emphasise the importance of being recognised and respected by practitioners for their contribution and being included in discussions and decision-making (Gore 2010).

Typically, every sibling relationship has its fair share of highs and lows. However when one sibling has a learning disability, the dynamic of the relationship can dramatically change (Contact a Family 2013a). Siblings who have a brother or sister with learning disabilities tend to feel a greater sense of responsibility, with many assuming additional roles of care (Conway and Meyer 2008; Rawson 2010).

I have to look after him if we're going out as a family and Dad's not there. I've become, sort of, not like a brother figure but more of a like a father figure – make sure he doesn't get in trouble, stays out of people's ways, and also make sure he's enjoying himself as well.

(Luke, age 21)

The accelerated level of maturity often found in siblings due to having to put their brother's or sister's needs first should not be underestimated by school practitioners; siblings may be very aware of and involved in the decisions around their brother or sister's life. As children often spend more time with their siblings than they do their parents (Contact a Family 2013a), siblings may be able to offer an alternative rich insights into their brother's or sister's education.

With that involvement come unique needs. For example, siblings with a brother or sister with learning disabilities may express feelings of guilt about their brother's or sister's disabilities and of isolation from not knowing others in the same situation as themselves. It should be acknowledged that not all siblings will want to be involved in their brother's or sister's life, and it is imperative that this is respected. While siblings need to be given the opportunities for involvement to help them decide, they may also need independent support to help them to express their needs rather than conforming to social pressures (Burke 2004). Schools are in a unique position to support and empower siblings in their developing relationship, should this be the route they choose (Conway and Meyer 2008).

Grandparents can play a vital role in any family. When a child has a learning disability, their valuable contribution often includes both emotional and practical support to family members from sharing feelings and allowing space to talk, through to child-minding and financial help (Contact a Family 2013b). However, they may have their own needs. Like parents, grandparents may struggle to come to terms with their grandchild's diagnosis and may grieve not only for the grandchild they have not had, but also for their own child whose world has changed for life (Limbrick, Meyer and Thomas 2009).

Often grandparents who are less involved tend to be the ones who have found the disability harder to deal with (Contact a Family 2013b), and may need some support to help them come to terms with the diagnosis. Encouraging grandparents' involvement with the school may provide them with opportunities to re-evaluate their existing views and ideas, but it is important that schools recognise and respect the dynamic of family relationships.

Support available to families, including local support, is 'crucial in determining their quality of life' (Mittler 1995: 51). For some families, support may come from their 'self-defined family' – comprising non-blood relatives, but carrying out traditional family functions (Carpenter 1998). In research carried out by Carpenter (1997), families of children with disabilities identified neighbours, friends, work colleagues, church members, teachers/assistants, link families and volunteers from charitable organisations among their significant others. Are schools flexible enough to welcome and interact meaningfully with a family's self-defined family members, allow parents to draw support from their presence in potentially stressful situations such as school meetings and reviews, and respect them as a significant source of information about the disabled member of that family?

What support do families need?

Effective family services promote family partnership, collaboration, affirmation and respect (Dempsey and Keen 2008). But how can this partnership be established? There are many routes to engaging family members and developing a functional, professional relationship, some of which are remarkably simple.

Davis (2007) suggests that families of children and young people with disabilities feel more positive about their relationship with school when:

- their views are listened to and taken seriously;
- they are given good clear information;
- they perceive that the school is doing something to help;
- they are involved in developing a shared approach to their child's progress;
- they have the support of others who understand or have been through similar experiences; and
- their own access needs are taken into account.

These are fundamental to a proactive and effective partnership.

Family members may find it hard to establish their side of the partnership if they do not know what is happening in school. Something as simple as a home-school diary can keep a regular dialogue between home and school, which is especially important if the learner has communication difficulties. It not only informs all parties about important developments in school and at home, but also promotes consistent approaches which can ultimately improve behaviour (Burton and Goodman 2011).

Modern technologies such as email, text messaging, websites and social networks can provide direct, convenient, even instant methods of sharing information, but these may not be for everyone. Finding out each families' preferred method of communication may aid partnership.

> The key with school is communication because Emma has no speech. She can't tell you what she's done at school, and she can't tell you her worries and concerns either. So, the home-school diary is really quite vital for us, so that we can discuss her day with her when she comes home, and if we've had problems with her at home or we think she's worried about something, we can write it in the diary and let teachers know. And if we have problems, you can come to school and try and hatch out a plan to manage behaviour or sort out something that she's not happy with.
>
> (Ruth, Emma's mother)

A Home-School Agreement given to families when their child starts at school could be a way of establishing the school's commitment to families and the expectation of families to contribute. This could be personalised to detail goals set and future aspirations. At Ellen Tinkham School in Exeter, this document is reviewed throughout the learner's school career. All parties are aware of the expectations and plans of action, and responsibility is mutual and understood.

As detailed above, different family members will have varying needs dependent on the family situation and the individual. Some schools may feel it is not their responsibility to provide support to family members for their personal and emotional issues. However, those that do are likely to witness higher levels of family engagement all round. Researchers in Wrexham started a Supporting Parents of Exceptional Children (SPEC) Group that facilitated a weekly discussion group for parents in school. The group provided a place where parents' social and emotional need to meet and talk informally could be met. It facilitated discussion among parents around: coping; issues with housing, benefits, annual reviews and other social and welfare issues; difficulties with their son or daughter. The group also supported their understanding of how to help their children, behaviour support strategies, child development, language and play, and how to work with their children at home. The project even offered a qualification in speaking and listening to those involved (McMinn and Britten 2005). This programme ran with great success and the authors reported parents particularly enjoying the social element of meeting those in similar situations. The authors felt that through opening and establishing these channels for communication, the foundations had been laid for a truly effective partnership.

It is wonderful that initiatives like this exist in attempts to engage and support parents, but what about other family members? As we have already seen, many families have invaluable support from siblings, grandparents, wider family and friends, but these may also need support. In recognition of this, some schools have set up groups that target specific family members. For example, many fathers have little contact with schools, perhaps because they are busy, shy, or feel marginalised and unwelcome. Having specific events for fathers may encourage those who are not yet involved to take a more active role in school life, and show fathers there are people there to listen and support them. Following a 'fun day' organized for fathers and their children, which they found enjoyable and supportive, two fathers commented on the benefits of fathers supporting other fathers:

> 'I've said loads and loads of times that there should be a sort of like a father support [group]... somewhere where dads can just drop in and have a chat...'
> 'That's what it's about: passing information on. I think men, once they break the ice and get to know it all, then yeah, the information starts flowing – it just takes a bit longer, really.'
>
> (Towers and Swift 2006: 48)

Similarly, facilitating opportunities for grandparents to meet enables them to share emotions and information with others without feelings of burdening their own family, and perhaps gain a broader perspective, leading to a more active role in their family (Seligman and Darling 2007). Grandparents may also want to become practically involved in school (e.g. through specialist craft, ICT, fundraising, political lobbying skills).

Supporting sibling needs may not be quite as straightforward, as their needs will vary widely with age (Burke 2004). Games and discussion activities such as 'Sibshops', developed by Don Meyer in the United States, may provide a unique way for siblings of different ages to meet, have fun and share their experiences in a non-judgemental environment (Sibling Support Project 2012), with reports of positive effects lasting into adulthood. The UK charity 'Sibs' (www.sibs.org.uk) provides workshops and training for practitioners working with siblings of all ages.

Research shows that step-families tend not to make use of family support services, often because they do not perceive themselves as core family members (Smith *et al.* 2001). However, their needs are just as valid – they may be experiencing the dual difficulty of adapting to life with a new member of their family having a disability, as well as coordinating involvement with that child alongside that with their own blood-family members.

As well as holding specific events for family members, there are other ways to involve them in the learner's school life. The school may have always had an open door policy for the whole family, but members other than parents may require invitations to feel welcome; for example to attend annual reviews or contribute a written report, to attend informal meetings and open days. Updates or photos of the learner's school activities could be sent to those living away from the primary family home, for example step-parents, siblings at university or grandparents. In one special school where iPads were used extensively to support learning, the learners were taught to make contact with their grandparents using Skype. Parents reported this had overcome so many communication barriers and reduced stress for the child and grandparent, firstly because the child could see their grandparent, and not just listen to a disembodied voice; secondly the grandparent could engage their grandchild by showing them things – a new toy ready for their next visit or the much-loved family cat.

To enable all family members to play a role, it may be important that the school not only makes clear who is welcome but also is flexible in accommodating all those who have expressed an interest in being involved. This may mean considering different days and times to allowing those who are interested to attend meetings, while being sensitive to any complex family situations (e.g. relationships between reconstituted family members).

Within the capacity of schools to resource and sustain initiatives, more creative means can be explored; for example, using modern technology to enhance involvement of family members who cannot always be there due to distance (e.g. Skyped comments at an Annual Review meeting).

Any form of meeting provides a valuable opportunity to involve family members, recognise their feelings and enable them to contribute to discussions and decisions. Whether the meeting is informal or formal, it is best to plan in advance to ensure information provided to the family is clear, ideas are conveyed effectively and adequate opportunities for the family to speak are made. Practitioners need to understand and be prepared for difficult interactions arising from family members' own negative school experiences, their concern about the meeting's contents, or anger about provision or decisions. One approach shown to be effective is structured conversations which can establish a more equal and productive partnership (Department for Children, Schools and Families 2009).

To facilitate an effective partnership, practitioners need skills of respect, empathy, genuineness, quiet enthusiasm, personal integrity and humility when working with families (Davis 2007). Other essential skills are around communication and interaction, including: concentration and active listening; prompting and exploration; empathic reasoning; summarising; enabling change; and the ability to negotiate and problem solve. These should ensure interactions are positive and focused, yet without an imbalance of power.

Twenty-first-century learners – challenges for schools and families

A new generation of learners is coming through the school system with complex combinations of disabilities and specific needs not previously seen (Carpenter *et al.* 2015). Due to medical advances, children with rare chromosomal syndromes and those born extremely premature are surviving into childhood, and presenting with unfamiliar configurations of development. Foetal alcohol spectrum disorder (FASD), unacknowledged in schools 10 years ago, is now considered to be the most common, non-genetic cause of learning disability (Carpenter, Blackburn and Egerton 2013).

The new wave of learners with complex learning difficulties and disabilities (CLDD) entering schools in the UK have brought with them new challenges to their families, far beyond those experienced by families of children with more traditional disabilities (Carpenter *et al.* 2015). These parents are truly pioneers, charting new pathways in raising their child with complex needs (Raca 2012). They will have created their own core pathways, therapeutic interventions and educational approaches, based on their deep and rich understanding of their child, long before any school-based professional ever comes into contact with them. By working with these families as equal partners, practitioners can make their role easier by learning from those who hold the most knowledge about what works best for their learners.

As the needs of school populations become more complex, educators are likely to work and liaise with more than just blood relatives. It is estimated that 80 per cent of children with FASD live with adoptive or foster families (Blackburn, Carpenter and Egerton 2012). Practitioners could therefore be liaising with several families for one learner, some of whom may only just be getting to know the child. Supporting these families and sharing information will be essential. Learners with life-limiting conditions may spend vast amounts of their time in the care of support workers at hospices or hospitals, meaning that educators may need to liaise with end of life staff and nurses as well as families (Brown 2007). Educators may also be working more closely with practitioners from different professional backgrounds such as social workers, therapists, and medical staff as learners' needs grow in complexity. It is not unusual nowadays for a teacher of learners with SLD/PMLD to find themselves liaising with a hospice on a weekly basis. The staff of the hospice become, as one parent said, 'just like family'.

Factors in family resilience

For learners with CLDD and their families, the impact of complexity may render them vulnerable, and their many issues and needs can create barriers to an effective partnership with schools. These can include: low income and poor living conditions; literacy or numeracy difficulties; health, illness or disability in the family; relationship or family breakdown; and drugs or alcohol misuse, or a complex compound of these (Cleaver, Unell and Aldgate 2011).

One in four adults will experience a mental health issue during their lifetime (Mind 2012). Alcohol or substance misuse may also be interlinked with poor mental health (Cleaver, Unell and Aldgate 2011). For some parents, caring for a child with a disability, concerns about their future and isolation from other parents raising children without disabilities can negatively affect their mental health. Many family members with mental health issues explain that the biggest factor in their reluctance to access services and engage with professionals is the stigma attached to their issues or situation (Pretis and Dimova 2008; Social Care Institute for Excellence 2011).

Learners with disabilities are three times more likely to have parents with disabilities (Blackburn, Spencer and Read 2010), perhaps due to genetic links (McGaw and Newman 2005). Parents with learning disabilities may feel vulnerable around people perceived as authoritative and, therefore, reluctant to engage with school staff (Cleaver *et al.* 2011). Unhelpful or negative attitudes and poor accessibility can also hamper these relationships (Maguire *et al.* 2009). Rather than making assumptions, talking with the parents themselves about what they require and making the necessary adaptations will reduce any perceived stigma and encourage more active involvement (Booth and Booth 2003).

Children in poverty are more likely to suffer poorer overall well-being and lower educational attainment than unaffected peers. Poverty puts a strain on relationships, and has a negative impact on physical and mental health (Centre for Social Justice 2011). The impact of poverty for learners with disabilities can be particularly severe (Blackburn, Spencer and Read 2010), especially in times of budget cuts and high unemployment. Their condition and needs may increase family costs in areas such as utility bills, clothing, travel costs and necessary equipment. As Carpenter *et al.* (2015) state, they can find themselves 'deprived, disadvantaged, and disabled'. Compounding issues for families may be their race, culture or religion (Centre for Social Justice 2011). Black and minority ethnic families and parents with learning disabilities who have disabled children, are more likely than the general population to experience poverty, worklessness and low-status employment (Tarleton, Ward and Howarth 2006; Blackburn, Spencer and Read 2010) as well as substantial inequality, discrimination and disadvantage (Hatton *et al.* 2004). Parents from ethnic minority groups may be put off engaging with schools due to language and cultural barriers, as well as physical and practical barriers such as time and transport (Harris and Goodall 2008). Professionals need to: acknowledge the cultural and situational experiences of these families; provide accessible written communications; involve staff who speak minority languages; and make efforts to reduce families' isolation by introducing them to supportive families of similar backgrounds.

More than most families, families with additional needs will require practical help, non-judgemental understanding and emotional support, alongside welcoming, confident and clear communication from school. Meetings may need more detailed planning and support, and general dealings require specific managerial input. Educators must be patient – for these families, trust may take longer to develop. For example, for parents of a child with complex and life-threatening health needs, beginning to trust that school staff have the training, resources and responsivity to keep their child medically safe throughout the day, and handing over responsibility for this, is a massive leap of faith.

Conclusion

For organisations and individual practitioners, families, in all their shapes, sizes and guises, should be at the heart of everything they do. It is important, that their interactions empower families rather than de-skill them. If they are empowered to believe in their abilities and not made to feel patronised or stigmatised, families are far more likely to take an active role in their child's education. How these partnerships within each school look may vary widely, but common to the most effective partnerships will be a foundation of enthusiasm and sincerity.

Questions for readers

The following questions may be interesting and useful to ponder in relation to a family you know:

* Who do you think the family relies on for support?
* What contact do you have with grandparents and other members of the family besides the parents in your daily practice? Consider the whole of the extended family. Is there more you could do to better embrace their needs?
* In what ways can all of the family be regularly informed about general goings-on around school and relating to their child?
* How well does your school support families? Carry out an audit of the school's current work with families.

References

Ballard, K. (ed.) (1994) *Disability, Family, Whānau and Society*, Palmerston North, NZ: Dunmore Press.

Beresford, B. (1994) *Positively Parents: Caring for a severely disabled child*, London: Social Policy Research Unit/HMSO.

Blackburn, C., Carpenter, B. and Egerton, J. (2012) *Educating Children and Young People with Fetal Alcohol Spectrum Disorders*, London: Routledge.

Blackburn, C.M., Spencer, N.J. and Read, J.M. (2010) 'Prevalence of childhood disability and the characteristics and circumstances of disabled children in the UK: secondary analysis of the Family Resources Survey', *BMC Pediatrics*, 10(21). Online. Available: www.biomedcentral.com/1471-2431/10/21 (accessed 26 August 2012).

Booth, T. and Booth, W. (2003) 'Self-advocacy and supported learning for mothers with learning difficulties', *Journal of Intellectual Disabilities*, 7(2): 165–193.

Brown, E. (2007) *Supporting the Child and the Family in Paediatric Palliative Care*, London: Jessica Kingsley.

Burke, P. (2004) *Brothers and Sisters of Disabled Children*, London: Jessica Kingsley.

Burton, D. and Goodman, R. (2011) 'Perspectives of SENCos and support staff in England on their roles, relationships and capacity to support inclusive practice for students with behavioural emotional and social difficulties', *Pastoral Care in Education: An International Journal of Personal, Social and Emotional Development*, 29(2): 133–149.

Carpenter, B. (1997) *Families in Context: Emerging trends in early intervention and family support*, London: David Fulton.

Carpenter, B. (1998) 'Defining the family: towards a critical framework for families of children with disabilities', *European Journal of Special Needs Education*, 13(2):180–188.

Carpenter, B. (2001) 'Enabling Partnerships; Families and Schools', in B. Carpenter, R. Ashdown, K. Bovair (eds) *Enabling Access: Effective education for pupils with severe, profound and multiple learning difficulties*, 2nd edn, London: David Fulton.

Carpenter, B. and Towers, C. (2008) 'Recognising fathers: the needs of fathers of children with disabilities', *Support for Learning*, 23(3): 118–125.

Carpenter, B., Blackburn, C. and Egerton, J. (eds) (2013) *Fetal Alcohol Spectrum Disorders: Interdisciplinary perspectives*, London: Routledge.

Carpenter, B., Rawson, H. and Egerton, J. (2012) 'Talking to families; listening to families (Module 1.3)', *Teaching Materials for Teachers of Pupils with Severe, Profound and Complex Learning Difficulties*, London: Teaching Agency. Online. Available: http://complexneeds.org.uk (accessed: 6 October 2013).

Carpenter, B., Egerton, J., Bloom, T., Cockbill, B., Fotheringham, J. and Rawson, H., Thistlethwaite, J. (2015) *Engaging Learners with Complex Learning Difficulties and Disabilities*, Abingdon: Routledge.

Centre for Social Justice (2011) *Mental Health: Poverty, Ethnicity and Family Breakdown*, London: Centre for Social Justice.

Cleaver, H., Unell, I. and Aldgate, J. (2011) *Children's Needs – Parenting Capacity. Child abuse: parental mental illness, learning disability, substance misuse and domestic violence*, 2nd edition, Norwich: The Stationery Office for Department for Education.

Contact a Family (2013a) *Siblings: information for families*, 2nd edn. London: Contact a Family. Online. Available: www.cafamily.org.uk/media/629582/siblingscurrentlastupdatedjan13_low_res_for_web.pdf (accessed 6 October 2013).

Contact a Family (2013b) Grandparents: information for families, London: Contact a Family.

Conway, S. and Meyer, D. (2008) 'Developing support for siblings of young people with disabilities', *Support for Learning*, 23(3), 113–117.

Dale, N. (1996) *Working with Families of Children with Special Needs: Partnership and practice*, London: Routledge.

Davis, H. (2007) 'The helping relationship: understanding partnerships', in P. Limbrick (ed.) *Family-Centred Support for Children with Disabilities and Special Needs*, Clifford: Interconnections.

Dempsey, I. and Keen, D. (2008) 'A review of processes and outcomes in family-centered services for children with a disability', *Topics in Early Childhood Special Education*, 28: 42–52.

Department for Children, Schools and Families (DCSF) (2009) *Achievement for all: the structured conversation, handbook to support training (National Strategies)*. Online. Available: http://dera.ioe.ac.uk/2418/ (accessed 6 August 2012).

Dossetor, D. (2012) 'How much do we value families and what impact does this have on children with intellectual disability?', *Mental Health and Intellectual Disability*, 2(3): 2–7.

Gore, N. (2010) 'Support for fathers of learning disabled children', *Community Care*. Online. Available: www.communitycare.co.uk/Articles/05/03/2010/113978/support-for-fathers-of-learning-disabled-children.htm (accessed 1 August 2012).

Harris, A. and Goodall, J. (2008) 'Do parents know they matter? engaging all parents in learning,' *Educational Research*, 50(3): 277–289.

Hatton, C., Akram, Y., Shah, R., Robertson, J. and Emerson, E. (2004) *Supporting South Asian Families with a Child with Severe Disabilities*, London: Jessica Kingsley.

Home Office (1998) *Supporting Families: A consultation document*, London: Home Office and Voluntary and Community Unit.

Hornby, G. (1995) *Working with Parents of Children with Special Needs*, London: Cassell.

Hutchinson, J. (2005) 'Early intervention for autism in Coventry', in B. Carpenter, and J. Egerton (eds) *Early Childhood Intervention: International perspectives, national initiative and regional practice*, Coventry: West Midlands SEN Regional Partnership.

Kingston, A. (2007) *Mothering Special Needs: A different maternal journey*, London: Jessica Kingsley.

Limbrick, P. with Meyer, D. and Thomas, J. (2009) 'An alphabet of helpful hints: G is for grandparents', *TAC Journal*, 2(7). Online. Available: www.teamaroundthechild.com/issue/issue-number-7.html (accessed 6 October 2013).

Maguire, R., Brunner, R., Stalker, K. and Mitchell, J. (2009) *Disabled Parents' Involvement in their Children's Education: an examination of good practice*, Reading: CfBT Education Trust.

McConkey, R. (1994) 'Early intervention: planning futures, shaping years', *Mental Handicap Research*, 7(1): 4–15.

McGaw, S. and Newman, T. (2005) *What Works for Parents with Learning Disabilities?*, Essex: Barnardo's.

McMinn, J. and Britten, G. (2005) *A different way of working with parents*. Online. Available: www.teachingexpertise.com/articles/different-way-working-with-parents-329 (accessed 17 August 2012).

Mind (2012) *About Mind*. Online. Available: www.mind.org.uk/about (accessed 23 August 2012).

Mittler, H. (1995) *Families Speak Out: International perspectives on families' experiences of disability*, Cambridge, MA: Brookline.

Newman, T., McEwen, J., Mackin, H. and Slowley, M. (Barnardo's Policy and Research Unit) (2010) *Improving the Wellbeing of Disabled Children (up to Age 8) and their Families through Increasing the Quality and Range of Early Years Interventions*, London: Centre for Excellence and Outcomes in Children and Young People's Services (C4EO). Online. Available: www.c4eo.org.uk/themes/disabledchildren/increasingquality/files/c4eo_improving_the_wellbeing_through_early_years_full_knowlege_review.pdf (accessed: 6 October 2013).

Pretis, M. and Dimova, A. (2008) 'Vulnerable children of mentally ill parents: towards evidence-based support for improving resilience', *Support for Learning*, 23(3): 152–159.

Raca, J. (2012) *Standing up for James*, London: Clarendon Publications.

Rawson, H. (2010) '"I'm going to be here long after you've gone": sibling perspectives of the future', *British Journal of Learning Disabilities*, 38: 225–231.

Seligman, M. and Darling, R.B. (2007) *Ordinary Families, Special Children: A systems approach to childhood disability*, 3rd edn, New York: Guilford Press.

Sibling Support Project (2012). Online. Available: www.siblingsupport.org (accessed 17 August 2012).

Smith, M., Robertson, J., Dixon, J., Quigley, M. and Whitehead, E. (2001) *A Study of Stepchildren and Step-parenting: Final report to the Department of Health, Unpublished*, London: Thomas Coram Research Unit, Institute of Education, University of London.

Social Care Institute for Excellence (2011) *Think Parent, Think Family: A guide to parental mental health and child welfare*. Online. Available: www.scie.org.uk/publications/guides/guide30/files/guide30.pdf (accessed 23 August 2012).

Tarleton, B., Ward, L. and Howarth, J. (2006). *Finding the Right Support? a review of issues and positive practice in supporting parents with learning disabilities and their children*, The Baring Foundation. Online. Available: www.baringfoundation.org.uk/Findingrightsupport.pdf (accessed 23 August 2012).

Towers, C. and Swift, P. (2006) *Recognising Fathers: understanding the issues faced by fathers of children with a learning disability*, London: Mental Health Foundation.

Winton, R. (1990) *Report of the New Mexico Home Memorial 5 Task Force on Young Children and Families: Report 1*, New Mexico: The New Mexico Home Memorial 5 Task Force on Young Children and Families.

10

PROVISION FOR CHILDREN WITH SLD/PMLD FROM ETHNIC MINORITY FAMILIES

Sana Rizvi with Peter Limbrick

In this chapter, the following questions will be addressed:

* What are South Asian families' experiences of special schools?
* What are the barriers preventing these families participating in school activity?
* What can schools and communities do about it?

Background

In recent decades, UK governments have promoted inclusion within health, education and welfare to expand ethnic minority access. For instance, the Education Health and Care Plan (EHCP), in effect, compels schools to view wider contexts before engaging with families (Department for Education and Department of Health 2014). The South Asian community, comprising ethnic-Indians, Pakistanis and Bangladeshis forms the largest ethnic minority group in the UK (Office for National Statistics 2011), with approximately 97 per cent living within major English conurbations like London and Birmingham (Cooper 2006).

Learning disabilities within ethnic-minorities vary across Special Educational Needs (SEN) categories (Strand and Lindsay 2009). For instance, Strand and Lindsay (2009) found Chinese learners were underrepresented in SEN categories, whereas Pakistani learners were overrepresented in the Profound Multiple Learning Difficulties (PMLD) category; incidentally, the prevalence of learners with PMLD within Pakistani and Bangladeshi communities is rising (Hatton *et al.* 2004).

Demographic changes in recent decades have necessitated acknowledgement of differences across and within ethnic-minorities when delivering culturally-appropriate services such as translation, same-sex carers and dietary needs (Shah 1995). Still, service uptake among ethnic minorities continues to be lower than White British families (Durà-Vilà and Hodes 2009), resulting in poor overall experiences and increased risk of exclusion. Croot (2012) notes the needs of ethnic minority families are similar to White British families: wanting their concerns addressed, trusting relationships with professionals, and better outcomes for their children. She adds culturally-appropriate services based on an essentialist assumption of ethnicity can lead to professionals pre-judging familial needs.

This chapter focuses on South Asian families because of the prevalence of learners with PMLD within this group (Emerson 2012); however, some PMLD literature from other ethnic minorities has been included. The first part of this chapter presents the findings of a small-scale case study Sana Rizvi (Rizvi 2011) undertook as an MA requirement at the University of Birmingham, examining the opinions of Bangladeshi parents and staff on improving home–school relations at an inner-city special school. The second jointly-written part of this chapter explores how schools can target services towards ethnic minority learners with PMLD.

Research and academic evidence

Many UK studies have examined South Asian families of learners with severe disabilities from a health and welfare perspective (Bywaters *et al.* 2003; Hatton *et al.* 2004; Croot *et al.* 2008). Sana undertook her case study because of the dearth of South Asian disability literature from an *educational* perspective (Strand and Lindsay 2009). Her findings are discussed below.

Background to the case study

I was initially interested in understanding the experiences of South Asian families of learners with disabilities within UK special schools. The research was conducted at Lincoln Special School in the West Midlands which had requested research into improving home–school relations with Bangladeshi parents, specifically exploring ways of increasing participation in the school's parent support groups and reasons for non-participation.

Method

Case study methodology was ideal because the research entailed considering multiple factors influencing home–school relations to facilitate an in-depth understanding of the experiences of staff and parents.

Access

After Lincoln School consented, I explained my background, research purpose and method of data collection via email, and then met the head teacher and pastoral manager to discuss the research focus; they wanted to improve home–school relations with Bangladeshi parents and increase their participation in parent support groups. With the focus agreed, the school identified 16 learners with SLD/PMLD from Bangladeshi families; I drafted a letter to them sent by the school, with my background and research aims, asking for their voluntary consent. Eight parents agreed to participate: two male and six female participants. Their children at Lincoln School ranged from nine to 18 years. Each household was single-income with mothers working as housewives and had on average four children. At an informal school meeting I reiterated my research objectives and my non-affiliation to the school.

Interviews were conducted at Lincoln School's primary and secondary sites and family homes. I obtained written consent from parents to participate and record interviews before commencing, and assigned pseudonyms to parents, although, since the school had identified my participants, total anonymity was impossible. I also interviewed five members of school staff, including the head teacher, to probe their understanding of parental involvement, if they thought ethnicity determined parental involvement, and to learn about their experiences with

Bangladeshi families. The school also allowed me access to learners' Individual Education Plans containing the school's correspondences with families.

Summary of findings

There were significant differences of perception about maintaining home–school relations between parents and staff. These differences centred on:

- divergent expectations of children's SEN;
- whether engagement in annual reviews, home–school diaries and parent groups constituted parental involvement;
- whether parental involvement had an ethnic context;
- whether barriers existed to participation.

Many parents disagreed with the description of their children's disability within Individual Educational Plans, while expressing concerns for their children's medical and educational needs. Many parents struggled to meet basic family needs, affecting their day-to-day experiences of supporting their children and their involvement with the school. Flawed cultural assumptions held by staff also affected home–school relations. Budgetary and personnel constraints restricted parental interaction. Parents displayed general satisfaction with the school's service delivery, although this may be equally attributable to parental passivity and a communication gap.

Discussion

Four main interlinked themes emerged after data analysis:

1 Parental and staff perceptions of SEN provisions.
2 Parental and staff views on parental involvement and parent groups.
3 Parental involvement in an ethnic context and comparison with other ethnic groups.
4 Perceived barriers to participation.

All parents held bio-medical views, considering impairment fundamental to their children's disability, and these influenced how they valued provisions. Initially, it seemed parental views were based on the 'child model', however, deeper probing revealed the learner's severity of impairment, and in some cases, complex medical needs also affected their lens. Parents described general difficulties which required the school's support such as toileting, independence skills, and communication. They also wanted guidance on medical support, safety, and post-19 provision.

All parents agreed that the school's expectations of parental involvement entailed attending annual reviews, utilising home–school diaries, and responding to enquiries. However, parents believed their existing involvement, based on supporting their children's primary medical needs, was satisfactory. Staff wanted greater proactive involvement from parents, rather than only when problems arose. The following comments are representative:

> Parents only contact us if there's a problem. We'd like them to use home-school diaries. Parents don't use them.
>
> (Class Teacher)

We're happy with what the teacher writes in the book, but if something happens we just tell the transport guide.

(Ms Hafiza)

I only write if there's some emergency, otherwise I don't think it's necessary.

(Mr Shakeel)

Such dichotomous views beg the question: what shapes parental involvement? All parents were concerned for their children's medical and safety needs, *so believed they were involved in their child's needs*. Parents, as first-generation immigrants struggling with basic family needs such as housing and food, and still decoding their children's learning difficulties, had not progressed to advocating for social needs like education which they outsourced to the school. Staff thought parent groups could teach parents proactive home-learning techniques and a skills transfer; most parents endorsed parent groups but pressing family needs restricted their participation. Their comments included:

It's a great idea but long working hours don't allow me to do anything else, so it wouldn't be convenient for me.

(Ms Hafiza)

I'm eager to be part of parent groups but they should arrange childcare.

(Mrs Ameera)

I don't have time for myself. I wouldn't mind attending [parent groups] but I have household demands.

(Mrs Zaib)

Ethnic and gender-mixed parent groups were cautiously welcomed by many parents. However, some, especially male, respondents felt uncomfortable opening-up to other Bangladeshi parents or publicly expressing their experiences. They would prefer one-to-one meetings.

I don't want to express my personal problems to other parents. My problem is my problem. I don't want to know other parents' problems.

(Mr Anis)

Most parents engaged primarily with the pastoral manager who was implicitly trusted. Parents and staff agreed the pastoral manager facilitated communication between them. However, the pastoral manager was concerned parents were being de-skilled and discouraged from approaching teachers directly.

Staff revealed inaccurate cultural assumptions about Bangladeshi parents which occasionally affected school policy. For instance, staff assumed school documents were not provided in Bengali because parents were probably not Bengali-literate, which all parents disputed (although this was not formally verifiable). Staff also revealed Asian (non-Bangladeshi) parent-governors informed them *someone* within Bangladeshi families was invariably English-literate. Their comments included:

You can't guarantee someone will read this [Bengali-translated correspondence] at home. They can speak Bengali but they can't read or write it.

(Pastoral Manager)

It [translation] was done before I worked here. Asian parent-governors tell us someone's fluent in English in Asian families, so we don't… [translate] school documents.

(Deputy Head Teacher)

Staff also assumed extended families prevented parents – especially mothers – from participating at school. However, with one notable exception, all parents said they lived away and had limited contact with extended family. Their comments included:

Extended family pressure might prevent… [parents'] participation in school-organised events.

(Teacher)

Mothers need to be liberated, they need to come out and see us. It's the fathers who come.

(Pastoral Manager)

Extended families give no support, mine does nothing for me.

(Mrs Rana)

The school also displayed disapproval of Bangladeshi parenting practices. Staff noted Bangladeshi parents removed their children from school during term time, assuming a disinterest in education compared to other ethnic minorities. Parents argued they were seeking alternative therapies or short-breaks where extended family in Bangladesh shared care responsibilities. However, it is possible lower travelling costs available during term time also determined their scheduling.

Staff and parents also identified barriers to developing ideal home–school relations, which are discussed below.

Implications for practice

We have identified three steps, which schools should consider when engaging with ethnic minority families unfamiliar with educational terminology and cultural norms using educational, health and social care literature touching on familial experiences of South Asian learners with PMLD (Shah 1995; Hatton *et al.* 2004; Katbamna *et al.* 2004). While not solely applicable to learners with PMLD, these engagement practices are a good starting point for educational practitioners. The following steps require professionals to anticipate familial contexts, and then change perceptions and actions accordingly:

1   Understanding the wider contexts
2   Communicating with families
3   Positive actions

Understanding the wider contexts

Such macro-environmental factors as immigration, education and welfare legislation, and micro-environmental factors like school policies, community networks, and parental well-being, continually shape familial support for their disabled children. Schools should consider the wider discourses affecting South Asian familial support including institutional racism, Islamophobia, immigration restrictions, and recession.

Institutional racism

Institutional racism occurs when systemic failures within an organisation obstruct equal access to services for the whole community based on race or ethnicity. For instance, in Sana's case study, Lincoln School did not translate documents into Bengali because it assumed Bangladeshi parents were illiterate. Moreover, Strand (2012), alarmingly, found lower expectations and differential treatment by educational practitioners contributed to Black Caribbean learners being least likely to achieve national academic benchmarks, while being most likely to face permanent school exclusion. Numerous studies (Shah 1995; Chamba *et al.* 1999) have revealed how institutional racism impedes ethnic minority access to services. Currently, Pakistani and Bangladeshi families have the lowest uptake of services despite being among the UK's poorest communities (Scope and ENC 2012).

Negative professional perceptions about culture, educational background and child-rearing practices create asymmetrical power relationships and promote the parent-deficit model in which professionals monopolise child-related expertise (Danseco 1997). Schools can subconsciously, rather than intentionally, discriminate between parents from different backgrounds (Page *et al.* 2007). For instance, consanguineous (first-cousin) marriages double the risk of children developing genetic disorders (Darr *et al.* 2013). However, Mir *et al.* (2001) contest whether consanguinity is *significant* for all South Asian families and suggest focusing solely on consanguinity can lead schools to blame parents for their child's disability while ignoring other macro-factors contributing to poor familial experiences. Discriminatory attitudes impede recognition of South Asian heterogeneity within language, culture, religion, and migration pathways.

Migration

Pakistanis and Bangladeshis migrated to the UK in the 1960s and 1980s respectively and are among the larger groups of new migrants annually (Blinder 2012). Despite large established communities, they still experience exclusion within employment, education and health (Kenway and Palmer, 2007). Pinson *et al.* (2010) suggest the extent of mainstream acculturation and respect accorded to immigrants determines their sense of belonging to society.

New migrants also face unequal access to education, health and social services (Stevens 2010). Ethnic minorities, subject to UK immigration control, experience two conflicting systems – immigration and social/welfare services – leading to confusion and distress. For instance, an asylum-seeking family with a disabled child cannot access statutory services until they have been granted permanent UK residency (Scope and ENC 2012). Arai (2005) suggests migrants downgrade the importance of education when facing food, housing or immigration uncertainty. Cultural unfamiliarity, poor English-proficiency and low socioeconomic status may all delay SEN identification and intervention. Thus, disability experience and migration experience are mutually-dependant (Scope and ENC 2012).

Research linking recently migrated status to awareness or uptake of services is limited. However, Katbamna *et al.* (2004) noted as a secondary finding that female Bangladeshi carers faced more acute problems if they were newly migrated. Accordingly, schools should reach out to newly migrated families because schools are among the first places new migrants experience their child's disability.

Religious and cultural factors affecting service uptake

Schools often suggest they cannot actively engage ethnic minority parents because of religio-cultural differences such as concerns about same-sex carers and dietary requirements (Hatton *et al.* 2004; Chamba *et al.* 1999). Dietary compliance issues may explain lower South Asian uptake of short breaks and residential care (Durà-Vilà and Hodes 2009), so acceding to such requests increases ethnic participation. However, parents want such services available within the mainstream, not as ethnically segregated provisions (Hatton *et al.* 2004). Professionals must, therefore, avoid stereotyping and appreciate South Asian diversity to deliver culturally competent services (Shah 1995).

Sometimes, religio-cultural differences are blamed erroneously. For instance, low service uptake among South Asians is commonly attributed to the presence of extended families, community networks, and different cultural preferences (Scope and ENC 2012). However, Hatton *et al.* (2004) and Katbamna *et al.* (2004) found parents of disabled learners reported isolation from their own communities (also noted in Sana's case study), suggesting flaws in delivering mainstream provisions were responsible for low uptake.

Housing costs

Kenway and Palmer (2007) found 55 per cent of Pakistani, 65 per cent of Bangladeshi, and 45 per cent of Black African households live in income poverty compared to 20 per cent of White British families. Such already-deprived families feel welfare cuts more acutely. Contact a Family (2012) found:

- caring for a disabled child costs almost three times more than a non-disabled child;
- almost one-third of families of disabled learners accruing debt to cover basic expenses;
- nearly one-fifth facing court action after debt defaults.

Poverty affects all facets of the lives of deprived families, especially housing and living conditions. South Asians, with larger families and higher likelihoods of single-wage households, are more likely to experience poor overcrowded housing. Homes may also have inadequate toilets, no downstairs bedroom for disabled children, threats to safety, limited therapy space, and poor access. Even houses in good condition require local authority permission for costly adaptations for disabled children which are often left incomplete (Chamba *et al.* 1999).

Recent migrants might use costly temporary accommodation for months before moving into appropriate housing. Schools are usually aware of the socioeconomic backgrounds of families they interact with and should appreciate that some families must fulfil basic needs before they can advocate for their child's education.

Communicating with families

Enhancing communication with ethnic minority parents extends beyond recruiting bilingual staff. Schools must attune to familial needs rather than assuming families will meet professional expectations. This requires practical and attitudinal shifts such as addressing language barriers, acknowledging differing aspirations and concerns for children, and developing relationships through home–school liaison officers.

Language barriers

Language barriers pose problems for South Asian parents from the disclosure process to securing SEN provisions. Disclosure is when parents are first informed within a medical–diagnostic setting their child has a disability (Hasnat and Graves 2000). Bywaters *et al.* (2003) link language barriers to poor understanding of disability during the disclosure process, specifically in South Asian mothers with poor English-proficiency. Hatton *et al.* (2004) found the disclosure process was conducted in English for two-thirds of South Asian families, despite preferences for ethnic languages. This meant disclosure took longer than for White British families. Also, only one-third of South Asian parents received written information, but again only in English. In Sana's case study most parents did not comprehend the extent of provisions offered in the SEN Statement. Clearer communication would have enabled parents to fully utilise the support.

When interpreting during consultations spouses often withhold vital information from mothers to protect them from 'unnecessary worry' (Mir *et al.* 2001). As primary carers, mothers must receive information firsthand. South Asian community members are also unsuitable interpreters since families of disabled learners are often stigmatised by their community. Shah (1995) suggests language barriers can antecede a complete parent–professional communication breakdown and recommends interpreters and translated documents during all consultations. However, high costs and long waiting times can limit access to professional interpreters (Alexander *et al.* 2004), so use of informal interpreters is condoned (Harry and Kalyanpur 1994).

In Sana's case study, teachers wanted formal interpreters whenever meeting culturally diverse families but interpreters were only available for external or medical meetings. The school argued that guaranteeing professional interpreters was wasteful since Bangladeshi parents frequently missed scheduled meetings. The school recognised the flaw in using non Bengali-fluent Asian teachers as informal interpreters and the need to recruit Bengali-proficient teachers. Parents felt uncomfortable having family members interpret. Some insisted the school had not arranged an interpreter despite their requests. Such viewpoints increased mistrust between parents and the school.

Different understandings of children's disability

When assessing parental involvement, schools need to appreciate that culturally diverse families might have different beliefs and goals about their child's disability. Hatton *et al.* (2004) found parental opinions, often formed during the disclosure process, evolve over time so poor disclosure can affect understanding of their child's disability. Only 20 per cent of South Asian parents could identify a specific diagnosis, while 45 per cent could only indicate an unspecified difficulty and 5.2 per cent could not name their child's disability (Hatton *et al.* 2004).

South Asian parents' understanding of their children's disability cannot be fully understood through the social model. The social model argues removing such extrinsic problems as structural barriers and disabling attitudes, enables the learner achieve a good quality of life. Academics debate whether bio-medical views, religio-cultural factors, and familial aspects shape ethnic minority understanding of disability (Singal 2010; Goodley 2013). Heer, Rose and Larkin (2012) suggest a fluid amalgam of medical, socio-cultural, and minority experiences influence parenting styles and attitudes to disability.

Croot *et al.* (2008) suggest Muslim parents, in their sample, held religious explanations for their child's disability contradicting their own bio-medical views. Moreover, their theological explanations often countered religious orthodoxy. American research on Christian parents indicates identical contradictions (Michie and Skinner 2010). Bywaters *et al.* (2003) suggest professionals should utilise religion as a positive factor to supplement the emotional support available.

Despite mothers (irrespective of ethnicity) being primary carers, there is scant research focusing on maternal perceptions of their children's disability. South Asian maternal perceptions are often developed through professional interaction frequently mediated through spouses. Schools could seek maternal participation in learning because maternal understanding of disability directly affects her and her child's wellbeing.

Home–school liaison

Studies on parent involvement have highlighted the benefits of home–school liaison officers and pastoral managers (Page *et al.* 2007). Home–school liaison officers, who may be formal or informal post-holders, have been found to improve home–school communication, overcome mistrust, and increase parental confidence and engagement in schools. Since they must develop effective personal relationships with parents it is critical schools choose approachable staff members. Pastoral managers organise services such as professional interpreters, communication with parents and providing material in preferred languages as per assessed needs (Page *et al.* 2007). Bilingual teachers can also mediate parental concerns, especially for recently migrated parents. Parents may also contact non-teaching staff members, such as teaching assistants and nurses.

Key workers can empower parents. They are named professionals, often from health educational or social care, offering practical help or advice and generally reducing barriers for parents (Greco *et al.* 2004; Chamba *et al.* 1999). Key workers are often social workers, aware of each learner's and each family's specific needs, ensuring parents' input is taken seriously. Parents functioning without a key worker have reported greater dissatisfaction with provisions and more unfulfilled needs (Sloper 1999).

Positive actions

Families on average engage with schools for 16 years, meaning schools strongly impact familial experiences of their children's disability. While limited resources can hinder schools introducing major projects, schools can nevertheless support parents and ultimately be agents of real change.

Support and advocacy

Since families of learners with PMLD require formal and informal support to improve their overall experiences (Hatton *et al.* 2004), service providers must adopt broad goals of support, advocacy and empowerment.

Parent support groups can offer practical and emotional support to help parents develop skills to support their children. They can raise awareness of available support by inviting to sessions such experts as occupational therapists, speech therapists and social workers (Ward and Tarleton 2007). Low turnout maybe problematic, but this may be due to poor awareness and accessibility rather than disinterest (Chamba *et al.* 1999). Schools could provide crèche and transport facilities to address these issues. Incidentally, Bangladeshi parents in Sana's research wanted to attend parent groups but were restricted by these childcare and transport issues.

Parents' groups can operate inexpensively if parent-governors or volunteers organise meetings. Parents can also organise meetings through community centres, especially as some parents are wary of visiting schools. This approach helps develop parental empowerment and autonomy in how the group operates.

Special Stars is a family support group set up by Calderdale Council for parents/carers of children with complex health needs from the Black and Minority Ethnic (BME) community. Originally set up using 'Aiming High' funding, group leaders Rizwana and Shahida encountered BME parents experiencing language and cultural barriers which prevented their accessing help. Some parents had children enrolled at the same school but had never met. Special Stars offers the opportunity for families to recharge their batteries, offering therapeutic massages or organising trips to theme parks with family members in specialised vehicles. Learners with complex needs can be part of a peer group whilst simultaneously building their independence and confidence. The group is a brilliant way to get families together to support each other, supporting 35 families with new mothers referred constantly. The mothers feel comfortable opening up to one another because everyone understands the barriers facing the BME community. The group gives out information about holiday activities, short-breaks, and other support group benefits (e-mail cyps.sis@calderdale.gov.uk).

Conclusion

This chapter has outlined various barriers to accessing services for South Asian families of learners with PMLD. However, we have not accounted for different barriers faced by other ethnic minorities. Schools facing growing ethnic diversity within the classroom, do so with reduced resources.

Schools must become acquainted with each family's uniqueness, anticipating their requirements without making assumptions. Schools should welcome and support new and existing learners and families effectively by making creative use of available human resources within school and the local neighbourhood. This collective endeavour will enrich everyone involved.

Questions for readers

- What resources are there in your community to support a school wanting to work better with South Asian families?
- How can a school best embark on learning more about South Asian families in its locality?
- What sort of innovative partnerships could a school develop in support of South Asian Families?

References

Alexander, C., Edwards, R. and Bogusia Temple with Kanani, U., Zhuang, L., Miah, M. and Sam, A. (2004) *Access to Services with Interpreters*, Joseph Rowntree Foundation, York: York Publishing Service.

Arai, L. (2005) *Migrants and Public Services in the UK: a review of the recent literature*, COMPAS Working Paper, Oxford, University of Oxford: COMPAS.

Blinder, S. (2012) *Settlement in the UK*, The Migration Observatory, Oxford: University of Oxford.

Bywaters, P., Ali, Z., Fazil, Q., Wallace, L.M. and Singh, G. (2003) 'Attitudes towards disability amongst Pakistani and Bangladeshi parents of disabled children in the UK: considerations for service providers and the disability movement', *Health and Social Care in the Community*, 11(6), 502–509.

Chamba, R., Ahmad, W., Hirst, M., Lawton, D. and Beresford, B. (1999) *On the Edge: Minority ethnic families caring for a severely disabled child*, University of Bristol: Policy Press.

Cooper, P. (2006) 'Supporting minority ethnic children and adolescents with social, emotional, and behavioural difficulties in the United Kingdom', *Preventing School Failure: Alternative Education for Children and Youth*, 50(2), 21–28.

Contact a Family (2012) *Counting the Costs 2012*. Online. Available: www.cafamily.org.uk/media/381221/counting_the_costs_2012_full_report.pdf (accessed 26 November 2013).

Croot, E.J. (2012) 'The care needs of Pakistani families caring for disabled children: how relevant is cultural competence?' *Physiotherapy*, 98(4), 351–356.

Croot, E.J., Grant, G., Cooper, C.L. and Mathers, N. (2008) 'Perceptions of the causes of childhood disability among Pakistani families living in the UK', *Health and Social Care in the Community*, 16(6), 606–613.

Danseco, E.R. (1997) 'Parental beliefs on childhood disability: insights on culture, child development and intervention', *International Journal of Disability, Development and Education*, 44(1), 41–52.

Darr, A., Small, N., Ahmad, W. I., Atkin, K., Corry, P., Benson, J. and Modell, B. (2013) 'Examining the family-centred approach to genetic testing and counselling among UK Pakistanis: a community perspective', *Journal of Community Genetics*, 4(1), 49–57.

Department for Education and Department of Health (2014) *Special Educational Needs and Disability Code of Practice: 0 to 25 years*. Ref: DFE:-00205-2013. Online. Available: www.gov.uk/government/publications/send-code-of-practice-0-to-25 (accessed 12 July 2014).

Durà-Vilà, G. and Hodes, M. (2009) 'Ethnic variation in service utilisation among children with intellectual disability', *Journal of Intellectual Disability Research*, 53(11), 939–948.

Emerson, E. (2012) 'Deprivation, ethnicity and the prevalence of intellectual and developmental disabilities', *Journal of Epidemiology and Community Health*, 66, 218–224.

Gillborn, D., Rollock, N., Vincent, C. and Ball, S.J. (2012) '"You got a pass, so what more do you want?": race, class and gender intersections in the educational experiences of the Black middle class', *Race Ethnicity and Education*, 15(1),121–139.

Goodley, D. (2013) 'Dis/entangling critical disability studies', *Disability & Society*, 28(5), 631–644.

Greco, V., Sloper, P. and Barton, K. (2004) *Care Co-ordination and Key Worker Services for Disabled Children*, Research Works no. 2004-01, York: SPRU, The University of York.

Harry, B. and Kalyanpur, M. (1994) 'Cultural underpinnings of special education: implications for professional interactions with culturally diverse families', *Disability & Society*, 9(2), 145–165.

Hasnat, M.J. and Graves, P. (2000) 'Disclosure of developmental disability: A study of paediatricians' practices', *Journal of Paediatrics and Child Health*, 36(1), 27–31.

Hatton, C., Akram, Y., Shah, R., Robertson, J. and Emerson, E. (2004) *Supporting South Asian Families with a Child with Severe Disabilities*, London: Jessica Kingsley Publishers.

Heer, K., Rose, J. and Larkin, M. (2012) 'Understanding the experiences and needs of South Asian families caring for a child with learning disabilities in the United Kingdom: an experiential–contextual framework', *Disability & Society*, 27(7), 949–963.

Katbamna, S., Ahmad, W., Bhakta, P., Baker, R. and Parker, G. (2004) 'Do they look after their own? Informal support for South Asian carers', *Health and Social Care in the Community*, 12(5), 398–406.

Kenway, P. and Palmer, G. (2007) *Poverty among ethnic groups – how and why does it differ?* Joseph Rowntree Foundation, York: New Policy Institute.

Michie, M. and Skinner, D. (2010) 'Narrating disability, narrating religious practice: reconciliation and fragile X syndrome', *Intellectual and Developmental Disabilities*, 48(2), 99–111.

Mir, G., Ahmad, W. and Jones, L. (2001) *Learning Difficulties and Ethnicity*, London: Department of Health.

Office for National Statistics, UK. (2011) *Ethnicity and National Identity in England and Wales 2011*. Online. Available: www.ons.gov.uk/ons/dcp171776_290558.pdf (accessed 26 November 2013).

Page, J., Whitting, G. and McLean, C. (2007) *Engaging Effectively with Black and Minority Ethnic Parents in Children's and Parental Services*, DCSF Research Report RR013. Online. Available: www.ethnos.co.uk/publications.html (accessed 26 November 2013)

Pinson, H., Arnot, M. and Candappa, M. (2010) *Education, Asylum and the 'Non-Citizen' Child: the politics of compassion and belonging*, Hampshire: Palgrave Macmillan.

Rizvi, S. (2011) *The opinions of ethnic parents and staff in how home-school relationships can be improved in a special school setting*, Unpublished Master's thesis, University of Birmingham.

Scope and ENC (Equalities National Council) (2012) *Over-Looked Communities, Over-Due Change: how services can better support BME disabled people*, London: Scope.

Shah, R. (1995) *The Silent Minority: Children with disabilities in Asian families*, London: National Children's Bureau.

Singal, N. (2010) 'Doing disability research in a Southern context: challenges and possibilities', *Disability & Society*, 25(4), 415–426.

Sloper, P. (1999) 'Models of service support for parents of disabled children: What do we know? What do we need to know?', *Child: Care, Health and Development*, 25, 85–99.

Stevens, C.S. (2010) 'Disability, caregiving and interpellation: migrant and non-migrant families of children with disabilities in urban Australia', *Disability & Society*, 25(7), 783–796.

Strand, S. (2012) 'The White British–Black Caribbean achievement gap: tests, tiers and teacher expectations', *British Educational Research Journal*, 38(1), 75–101.

Strand, S. and Lindsay, G. (2009) 'Evidence of ethnic disproportionality in special education in an English population', *Journal of Special Education*, 43(3), 174–190

Ward, L. and Tarleton, B. (2007) 'Sinking or swimming? Supporting parents with learning disabilities and their children', *Tizard Learning Disability Review*, 12(2), 22–32.

11

CITIZENSHIP, PARTICIPATION AND VOICE

Hazel Lawson and Ann Fergusson with Miranda Brookes, Trudy Duffield and Anthony Skipworth

In this chapter, the following questions will be addressed:

- What do we mean by 'citizenship', 'participation' and 'voice' in the context of learners with SLD/PMLD?
- What meaning can 'citizenship' have for this group of learners?
- What does 'meaningful participation' look like?
- How can learners' 'voices' be sought and listened to?
- How are these ideas being 'used' in practice? Are they realistic or token gestures?

Introduction

This chapter explores the three concepts of 'participation', 'citizenship' and 'voice' for learners with SLD/PMLD. Such concepts have not always been regarded as relevant for children, and, in particular, have been regarded as inappropriate or difficult to apply for this specific group of learners. As teachers working with learners with SLD/PMLD, and as academics and researchers, we have spent much of our respective careers exploring the theoretical and practical application and exemplification of these concepts (for example, Lawson and Fergusson 2001; Fergusson 2002; Fergusson and Lawson 2003; Byers *et al.* 2008; Lawson 2010; Fergusson 2013). We have noticed how these ideas now frequently form underlying principles in the way staff in educational settings engage in developing policy and practice, for instance, through person-centred approaches. Nevertheless, a number of issues and challenges remain and we explore some of these in this chapter.

Citizenship, participation and voice in the context of learners with SLD/PMLD

Emphasis on the participation and voice of children and young people now permeates many areas of public life. This builds upon the United Nations Convention on the Rights of the Child (UNCRC) (United Nations 1989), particularly articles 12 and 13, that children's opinions must be listened to seriously in all matters that affect their lives and that children have the right to express themselves freely and to access information. Article 7 of the United Nations Convention on the Rights of Persons with Disabilities (United Nations 2006) reiterates that right in relation to children with disabilities. Various aspects of educational legislation and guidance in England also convey the importance of pupil participation and involvement in decision making, for example, the Education Act (2002) and the special educational needs (SEN) Code of Practice (Department for Education and Department of Health 2014).

Citizenship

Citizenship is a contested concept (Lawson 2009) and this may be played out in schools in terms of the positioning of learners either as '*becoming* citizens' or as '*being* citizens already'. Are we preparing learners to be citizens upon reaching adulthood? This is in itself, perhaps, a problematic concept for some people with learning difficulties as adulthood holds connotations of productive activity, including economic self-sufficiency, non-dependent family roles, personal autonomy and having full responsibility for one's own life (Dee 2006). Or are we treating learners as citizens now and expecting them to enact citizenship as a member of the school community or other communities? We, the authors, have found the following distinctions (made by Kerr 2000) useful:

- education *about* citizenship – explicit curriculum knowledge and content;
- education *through* citizenship – active, participative experiences;
- education *for* citizenship – equipping learners through the first two for adult citizen status and life.

These different interpretations translate into different approaches within schools. As practitioners, we need to consider, with critical honesty, sensitivity and realism, that some aspects of curriculum knowledge and content (for example, understanding parts of legislation), that is, education *about* citizenship, may not be appropriate for some learners with SLD/PMLD (Lawson 2003). Instead we may place more emphasis on education *through* citizenship. This impacts on the way we construct and enact citizenship within the school and classroom, demanding a view of citizenship as 'an entitlement to recognition, respect and participation' (Neale 2004: 8), as 'encouraging and providing opportunities for young people to engage and participate' (Kerr and Cleaver 2004: 33). Thus the way we, as adults and staff members, behave and interact with learners and our expectations of learners are crucial.

Participation and voice

Thinking about learner participation leads to a number of questions – Which learners are participating? In what are they participating? How are they participating? Why? Do notions of participation refer to learners' *active engagement* in school activities and/or participation in *decision making processes* which lead to change, in particular decisions around their own lives? Response to these sorts of questions may indicate different levels of participation – from being aware, being informed, taking part and being consulted, to collaborating as reciprocal partners, and to leading (May 2004; Rudd *et al.* 2006). The degree and depth of this participation may depend upon a range of factors, for example, the learners' level of intentionality and the familiarity of the context.

Boundaries are often set which determine which learners can participate and what learners can participate in; this can lead to rather superficial or tokenistic participation. For example: the UNCRC (1989) refers to 'the child who is capable of forming his or her views'; in the Education Act 2002 children's views are also to be considered 'in the light of [their] age and understanding' (p. 105); and the SEN Code of Practice (Department for Education and Department of Health 2014: 9) reiterates the UNCRC in stating that children's views should be 'given due weight according to their age, maturity and capability'. Participation is thus conditional – if you are old enough, mature enough, and understand enough (May 2004). Here, then, the expectations of others determine what the learner can participate in and to what degree.

How, in this potentially limiting positioning, can we encourage and promote the participation of learners with SLD/PMLD? One response to this has been the increasing prominence of *person-centred* approaches. This transferred into the education context from health and social care services (see DoH 2001). A person-centred approach is described as discovering and acting upon what is important to a person from their own unique perspective, taking account of their wishes and aspirations (DoH 2009). Within education this approach is intended to ensure that everyone has a voice and to place the learner at the centre of planning and decision making processes. In our experience, many schools have embedded person-centred approaches into their annual review and individual education planning processes; others have positioned person-centredness as an underlying principle of their school's way of working. Learners are encouraged to develop skills of reflection and self-review, to negotiate or decide on their next steps and learning targets. Learners may work together; for example, to select work examples, photographs of their achievements or prepare presentations to share at annual review. On occasion, one learner may advocate for another peer. Such approaches promote and assume that the 'voice', the views, of the young person can be accessed and interpreted such that the learner is participating, and, at times, leading, in decision-making about their life.

The concept of 'voice', of course, needs a much broader interpretation than 'speaking' as many learners with SLD/PMLD use other modes of communication. Different approaches using a range of total communication methods have often been employed to try to access the learner's view; for example, photographs, video and Talking Mats (Murphy and Cameron 2008). Goodwin (2013) describes a process of observation, documentation (for example, using methods such as multi-media profiling or shared story-telling, in addition to photographs), reflection and interpretation of 'experiences and daily interactions' (p. 26) to support the continued understanding of a learner. Staff, family or independent advocates who know the child or young person well are frequently involved in eliciting/interpreting the learner's views. Of course, enabling learners to have a voice also requires that this voice is fully *heard* and responded to in some way.

Examples from practice

The examples presented below illustrate different aspects of participation and citizenship which try to capture an authentic voice of learners with SLD/PMLD.

Harrison – deciding on subject options for a personalised curriculum

Harrison is a Year 10 learner (aged 15) who attends an inclusive inner city mainstream secondary school. He is a young man with SLD on the autism spectrum and he communicates without words. In the main he uses signing, mostly at a single word level, with people who know him well and a word/picture bank to give answers or to share in conversations. He also relies heavily on a daily visual schedule and predictable routines. His frustrations around communication or unexpected changes sometimes manifest in anxiety levels and behaviour that are a challenge for staff to manage and for other learners to understand in a busy mainstream school.

Harrison, like many learners with SLD, has a 'spiky profile' – this means he demonstrates very wide variation in his knowledge, skills and understanding across different curriculum areas with specific strengths in some areas and considerable weaknesses in others. For this reason he spends his week following a personalised timetable with lessons split between the learning resource base and in subject lessons with his mainstream peers.

Staff worked hard to 'listen' to Harrison's preferences when selecting his subject options in Year 9. They wanted to ensure he had a timetable that reflected his personal interests and played to his strengths. Rather than make these decisions for him, school staff enabled him to take the lead in designing his own timetable. Using a similar approach to *Talking Mats* (Murphy and Cameron 2008), staff enabled Harrison to make his subject choices by offering him a visual structure of 'subjects he wanted to do' and 'subjects he didn't want to do'. They offered some tangible cues to support his decision-making from a combination of evidence of his own work (particularly his art work and artefacts), written subject labels (initially with pictures and photos of him in these lessons to support the text), along with spoken and signed dialogue. Through these approaches, Harrison was able to first express his likes and dislikes and then to prioritise his subject choices. To confirm the subjects he had selected, staff re-presented the subject choices a number of times and included his parents in the process too.

A year on, Harrison has followed and enjoyed his subject options. He has real strengths in Art, his favourite subject, where he is fully included and working on a par with his mainstream peers for his studies towards national exams at age 16 (GCSE). In some areas, especially around language and interaction, he continues to experience significant barriers to learning. He is attaining within the P scales for the majority of subjects, but can meaningfully access practical elements of subjects alongside mainstream colleagues (for example, science and PE).

Leah – listening to preferences to overcome barriers to learning and teaching

Leah was so sensitive to being touched it meant she regularly experienced great distress throughout her day as people prompted her to access learning or moved her between supported seating and activities. Her impaired vision and hearing, combined with her extreme tactile sensitivities, resulted in everyone really struggling to find ways to make the world more enjoyable and more meaningful for her. Her strong resistance to being touched challenged staff to make learning accessible – the usual ideas of prompting just did not work!

Aged seven years, Leah was working at the earliest stages of learning, her delayed development hampered partly by her multisensory impairment, but also because she was unable to interact with the physical world around her. Despite these huge obstacles, Leah was able to express some clear communications to others about what she liked or disliked. The visiting Sensory Support Teacher facilitated a very personalised intervention approach. She knew Leah well having supported her for many years and promoted an extremely consistent approach to intervening and responding to Leah in her world.

Through both staff and family really *listening* to Leah's communications (initially her strongest responses) some inroads slowly began to emerge. As a blind child who did not like being touched or to touch anything herself, she did respond to kinaesthetic sensations which did not involve direct human touch (for example, she consistently 'jiggled' to the 'Horsey horsey' nursery rhyme song). Leah adored Rebound Therapy (see Chapter 31) sessions, once over the distress of being hoisted and moved on to the trampoline. Solely in this context she would tolerate human touch because of her high motivation – she wanted the experience of bouncing. Staff followed a very consistent routine: using a cue at the start of her sessions consisting of drumming the trampoline bed so she could feel the vibrations and a countdown cue of '5, 4, 3, 2, 1, stop' in time with trampoline bounces at the end; and following a set sequence of activities linked to her 'favourite' songs. Throughout the sessions Leah was offered opportunities to have 'more' or 'stop' by vocalising or smiling and, after time, through co-active signing. Staff responded sensitively to her pace and her communications.

As Leah developed trust that people *listened* to her voice, her preferences and her pace, her extreme anxieties gradually reduced. This approach of scaffolding and responding to Leah's communications was transferred to other daily events. Staff would, for example, alert her and place objects on her tray or at her feet and let her decide if or when she was ready to explore them. A very structured and detailed plan of co-active signing/communication with Leah was planned to ensure this consistency and to be responsive to each context; this also offered Leah opportunities for progression. Being able to predict routines and receiving consistent staff responses meant Leah could respond in her own time and this enabled her to more fully participate in increasing opportunities to learn and enjoy the world.

Consulting learners and involving them in transition times

In the context of a *Moving On* project (Fergusson 2013; Davies 2013) Year 7 learners with SLD (aged 11–12 years) in three inclusive mainstream secondary schools were asked by researchers about their experiences of moving from primary to secondary school. The key message from these learners was that they wished they had been much more involved in the whole transition planning process from Year 5 onwards, for example, planning visits to the secondary school, choosing who to go with and being asked about their worries/concerns.

Discussions with researchers about issues learners felt to be important were facilitated using a visual structure provided by 'traffic lights' posters. Using drawings, written labels and/or photographs, according to learner need/preference, students placed these on the posters in the red (not OK), amber (neither good nor bad) or green (OK/good) areas. Photographs depicting elements of the school day were also used as a starting point when asking learners to review and compare their experiences in their old and their new schools – things such as dinner times, friendships and bullying or knowing who to talk to. The learners told the researchers about what should be improved and gave some ideas of what would have helped them. Their ideas directly informed some practical resources and suggestions for other learners preparing for this transition from primary to secondary schools. For example, Julia had difficulties finding her way around the new secondary school and could not use the diagrammatic map the school provided. The discussion group suggested that photographs could be taken of buildings and people at the new school and a map could be developed incorporating these photographs to show where different members of staff could be found (Fergusson 2013).

Participating in research as a member of an advisory reference group

What About Us? (Byers *et al.* 2008) was a two-year project which enabled young people with learning difficulties to act as researchers and become successful 'agents of change' in their own schools and colleges. By employing a person-centred approach, this research empowered young people in the project schools and colleges to identify and work to improve issues that were of real importance from their perspectives. Additional support was given to the overall project by an advisory reference group of eight young adults with learning difficulties – these young people were themselves 'experts by experience' and offered invaluable insight and expertise to the *What About Us?* research team.

For each meeting of this advisory reference group preparation time was provided with advocates facilitating the group, supporting them in developing their ideas and preparing an agenda. In the meetings, each person took a different role: three rotated the chair's role; others took an agenda item to lead. For example, Mark, a young man aged 19 with SLD and challenging behaviour, was responsible for the icebreaker game at the beginning of every meeting. This was a physically active game in which Mark was interested, enjoying the excitement of the game, the turn-taking element and being keen to lead – it involved different variations of passing a ball, balloon, inflatable globe or parcel around the group while saying participants' names. A number of methods were used to record the meetings in ways that were accessible to the reference group members – graphic facilitation, drawings along a flipchart timeline as the meeting progressed, and photographs (for example, of people, activities or resources) to enable reflection on the meeting and to help in planning future reference group meetings.

Being responsible citizens within the school community

Phoenix School, a community special school for learners with SLD/PMLD, provides a number of opportunities for them to participate as responsible citizens within the school community. When working towards the UNICEF Rights Respecting School Award (see Resources section), Phoenix School looked at the United Nations Convention's Rights of the Child (United Nations 1989). Learners across the whole school worked to decide what these rights might look like for them in their school. The School Council consists of learner representatives from each class across the school, some attending with support staff, with a teacher facilitator. Representatives took photographs of school activities involving learners, staff and family members and they selected photos that they felt demonstrated their ideas of learner rights. All learners in the school were involved in this selection through a voting system. Once agreed, these photographs were enlarged and displayed around the school to remind everyone about their rights and how to respect others.

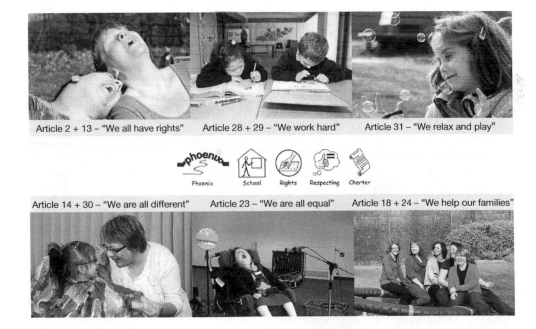

Figure 11.1   Phoenix School charter

Learners from the Upper School (aged 14–19 years) have opportunities to train as Play Buddies, with a role to facilitate good relationships and fun across the school. Each Play Buddy takes personal responsibility (with support if necessary) to promote friendly collaboration in the playground at break times and during the after-school clubs.

Learners are the 'face of the school'. So, at Phoenix School, learners routinely show visitors around the school and the have produced online virtual tours available on the school website (www.phoenix.peterborough.sch.uk), where they decided what and who were important to show on the school tours.

Discussion

The above examples illustrate a few ways in which practices around learner citizenship, participation and voice are developed and embedded within the learning opportunities offered in schools. In a study of the participation of learners designated as having moderate learning difficulties, Norwich and Kelly (2004) noted that adults tended to identify learner factors as barriers to participation (for example, cognitive competence). Learners, however, tended to identify school and teacher factors as barriers – for instance, not being able to control what is done with their views, teachers being unapproachable and token consultation. The examples in this chapter show how some of these school and teacher barriers may be challenged. The key points seem to be:

- getting to know and building a relationship with the learner;
- having open-ended expectations regarding the extent about learner participation;
- using multiple and creative methods;
- providing opportunities for, and facilitating, learners to develop and express their own opinions, views and aspirations and become confident communicators of these;
- having an institutional ethos and values which promote and enhance the status of every individual.

The example of Leah, in particular, illustrates the crucial importance of staff and advocates getting to really know learners. It is possible, however, that a facilitator can become so familiar that they stop looking and listening – the accuracy of their representation may then be questionable (Goodwin 2013). Thus, Goodwin (2013: 26) continues, we must 'constantly check and revise' our interpretations and continually listen and respond. Further, much communication with learners with PMLD may even be *constructed* rather than interpreted, so it is very difficult to ensure representation of a learner's wishes. It is often inferred from positive responses that learners therefore want to participate in that activity; similarly, negative reactions are assumed to indicate a wish not to participate. Ware (2004), however, cautions that while learners with PMLD may express like or dislike this does not amount to 'expressing a view'.

For this same learner group, where communicative repertoires are particularly limited, Forster (2011) suggests we may also be faced with ethical dilemmas by being *too* responsive to their 'voice'. She raises a challenging perspective for us to consider: are we listening and responding too much, to the potential detriment of the individual, particularly when the learner's voice is expressed through learnt behaviours? She offers an example of Belinda who at times enjoys the company of others but, in the main, routinely pushes people away. The accepted practice was to respect her communication and give her space alone. Forster suggested an alternative approach to Cameron, her support worker: to try to gently resist Belinda's push away and keep his hand in contact with hers, while being sensitive to her emotional responses. He was reluctant, but tried this.

> After just 20 seconds of persistent hand touching, Belinda's pushes became less forceful and there were moments of her allowing Cameron to rest his hands on hers. After a minute, she tentatively reached towards his hand.... [The] long established ethic of accepting when someone pushed away and respecting a person's wishes for personal space was in battle with a new possibility; persisting against Belinda's wishes opened up a new door for engagement with the world around her.
>
> (Forster 2011: 6)

It is important, therefore, that we maintain ethical awareness of this interpretative role (Connolly 1997), always thinking about whose agenda is being served, of the potential to be selective and uncritical in our use of learners' voices (Bluebond-Langner and Korbin 2007) and whether learner voice is framed in a form that serves professional decisions. We must not make assumptions or be too accepting of 'what is' just because it is, but continually engage in professional dialogue and review of our roles and our practice.

The use of multiple methods, activities, approaches and situations in which to ascertain learners' views (Lewis 2002) enables us to explore consistency in order to have greater confidence in these views. The example of Harrison showed how different media (art work, labels, photographs, spoken and signed dialogue) were employed in different situations (school and home) and on several occasions to confirm his subject choices. We need to be aware, however, that we all have a range of voices, multiple perspectives and changing points of view. This polyphony (Sidorkin 1999 cited in Fielding 2006) is important to recognise and encourage. We also need to consider that it is often more difficult for learners to express negative views and that 'some children may genuinely and freely prefer silence to voicing their views' (Lewis and Porter 2007: 224).

The *What About Us?* research and *Moving On* project both highlight the time needed to prepare for meaningful participation and that creative and responsive approaches are needed to ensure learners are included and able to use their voice in a way that is appropriate to them. The *What About Us?* research, for example, was carried out over two years and the young people involved from the schools and colleges and the members of the reference group demonstrated increased skills and confidence in asserting their views during that time.

The examples of responsible citizenship from Phoenix School show how the ethos and practices of the school need to embed and reflect clear values in order for the key principles of meaningful participation and learner voice to be integral to all aspects in the life of every learner within the school community. Neale (2004: 7) describes two ways of viewing children: as 'welfare dependants' or as 'young citizens'. As welfare dependants, children are viewed as dependants, as incompetent and vulnerable, as needing care, protection and guidance and their childhoods are determined by adults. Regarding children as young citizens, he argues, means children are viewed as people, with strengths and competencies, needing recognition, respect and participation and influencing their own childhoods. As educators, our own stance within this protection–participation tension determines our expectations of learners and in turn influences their potential. Newson (1978: 42) was clear that the very act of positively recognising a learner as a communicator, regardless of their (dis)ability, directly impacted on their likelihood of developing successful communication: 'it is only because [s]he is treated as a communicator that [s]he learns the essential art of communication.' Thinking and working from this position may actively impact on our understanding and ultimately improve our ability to promote and enhance greater participation and a stronger, more assertive learner voice.

Questions for readers

- How can participative opportunities be built into daily routines (so they become implicit, yet an explicit expectation of the way we work)?
- In what ways can learners work together, for example to support self-review, to advocate for each other?
- Are there limits to participation? How can we plan for progression within this area for every learner?

Resources

Mencap – Involve me: www.mencap.org.uk/involveMe
Moving on to secondary school – free to download suite of resources:
www.learningdisabilities.org.uk/our-work/employment-education/moving-on-to-secondary-school/
Participation works – www.participationworks.org.uk/
Person centred planning – www.helensandersonassociates.co.uk/what-we-do/how/person-centred-planning.aspx
www.fpld.org.uk/help-information/learning-disability-a-z/p/person-centred-planning/
Talking mats – www.talkingmats.com
UNICEF Rights Respecting School Award – www.unicef.org.uk/rrsa
What about us? www.whataboutus.org.uk

References

Bluebond-Langner, M. and Korbin, J. (2007) 'Challenges and opportunities in the anthropology of childhoods: an introduction to "children, childhoods and childhood studies"', *American Anthropologist*, 109(2), 241–246.

Byers, R., Davies, J., Fergusson, A. and Marvin, C. (2008) *What About Us? promoting emotional well-being and inclusion by working with young people with learning difficulties in schools and colleges*, London: Foundation for People with Learning Disabilities.

Connolly, P. (1997) 'In search of authenticity: researching young children's perspectives', in A. Pollard, D. Thiessen and A. Filer (eds) *Children and Their Curriculum*, London: Falmer Press.

Davies, J. (2013) 'Easing transition for those with SEN', *Behaviour and Pastoral Update*, 99, 11.

Dee, L. (2006) *Improving transition planning for young people with special educational needs*, Buckingham: Open University Press.

Department for Education and Department of Health (2014) *Special Educational Needs and Disability Code of Practice: 0 to 25 years*. Ref: DFE:-00205-2013. Online. Available: www.gov.uk/government/publications/send-code-of-practice-0-to-25 (accessed 12 July 2014).

Department of Health (DoH) (2001) *Valuing People: A new strategy for learning disability in the 21st century*, London: The Stationery Office.

Department of Health (DoH) (2009) *Valuing People Now: A new three-year strategy for learning disabilities*, London: DoH.

Fergusson, A. (2002) 'Developing citizen education', *SLD Experience*, 32, 2–5.

Fergusson, A. (2013) Moving on... to 'a giant big school', *Special Children*, 212, 8–10.

Fergusson, A. and Lawson, H. (2003) *Access to Citizenship*, London: Fulton.

Fielding, M. (2006) 'Leadership, radical student engagement and the necessity of person-centred education', *International Journal of Leadership in Education*, 9(4), 299–313.

Forster, S. (2011) 'An ethical dilemma of too much listening and responding', *PMLD Link*, 23(1), 5–6.

Goodwin, M. (2013) 'Listening and responding to children with PMLD – towards a framework and possibilities', *SLD Experience*, 65, 21–27.

Kerr, D. (2000) 'An international comparison', in D. Lawton, J. Cairns and R. Gardner (eds) *Education for Citizenship*, London: Continuum.

Kerr, D. and Cleaver, E. (2004) *Longitudinal Study: literature review – citizenship education one year on – what does it mean? Emerging definitions and approaches in the first year of national curriculum citizenship in England*, Annesley, Notts: DfES.

Lawson, H. (2003) 'Citizenship education for pupils with learning difficulties: towards participation?', *Support for Learning*, 18(3), 117–122.

Lawson, H. (2009) 'Promoting access to community and participation: What role can citizenship education play?', in J. Seale and M. Nind (eds) *Understanding and Promoting Access for People with Learning Difficulties: Seeing the opportunities and challenges of risks*, London: Routledge.

Lawson, H. (2010) 'Beyond tokenism: participation of/with pupils with significant learning difficulties', in R. Rose (ed.) *Confronting Obstacles to Inclusion: International responses to developing inclusive schools*, London: Routledge.

Lawson, H. and Fergusson, A. (2001) 'PSHE and citizenship', in B. Carpenter, R. Ashdown and K. Bovair (eds) *Enabling Access*, 2nd edn, London: David Fulton.

Lewis, A. (2002) 'Accessing, through research interviews, the views of children with difficulties in learning', *Support for Learning*, 17(3), 110–116.

Lewis, A. and Porter, J. (2007) 'Research and pupil voice', in L. Florian (ed.) *The Sage Handbook of Special Education*, London: Sage.

May, H. (2004) 'Interpreting pupil participation into practice: contributions of the SEN Code of Practice (2001)', *Journal of Research in Special Educational Needs*, 4(2), 67–73.

Murphy, J. and Cameron, L. (2008) 'The effectiveness of talking mats for people with intellectual disability', *British Journal of Learning Disability*, 36, 232–241.

Neale, B. (2004) 'Introduction: young children's citizenship', in B. Neale (ed.) *Young Children's Citizenship: Ideas into practice*, York: Joseph Rowntree.

Newson, J. (1978) 'Dialogue and development', in A. Lock (ed.) *Action, Gesture and Symbol: The emergence of language*, London: Academic Press.

Norwich, B. and Kelly, N. (2004) 'Pupils' views on inclusion: moderate learning difficulties and bullying in mainstream and special schools', *British Educational Research Journal*, 30(1), 43–65.

Rudd, T., Colligan, F. and Naik, R. (2006) *Learner Voice*, Bristol: Futurelab. Online. Available: http://archive.futurelab.org.uk/resources/publications-reports-articles/handbooks/Handbook132 (accessed 28 June 2014).

United Nations (1989) *Convention on the Rights of the Child*, New York: UN.

United Nations (2006) *Convention on the Rights of Persons with Disabilities*, New York: UN. Online. Available: www.un.org/disabilities/documents/convention/convoptprot-e.pdf (accessed 14 June 2014).

Ware, J. (2004) 'Ascertaining the views of people with profound and multiple learning disabilities', *British Journal of Learning Disabilities*, 32(4), 175–179.

12

TRAINING AND DEVELOPING THE INCLUSIVE TEACHER FOR LEARNERS WITH SLD AND PMLD

Melanie Peter

In this chapter, the following questions will be addressed:

- How are the rapidly changing policy and demographic contexts impacting on implications for training the next generation of special educators?
- What issues face newly qualified teachers (NQTs) wishing to enter special education?
- What are the implications for mentors supporting the emotional learning journey of those learning to teach in such challenging educational contexts?
- What characterises the pedagogical knowledge, skills and understanding of educators at different stages of their professional development, and their respective placement needs and mentoring implications?

Introduction

This chapter is aimed particularly at those involved in training special school teachers: course tutors, school mentors and senior managers. Government policy has resulted in a variety of routes into the profession and the increasing role of schools in training, so discussion is needed towards a shared vision of the special educator and a shared understanding of their development pathway. This chapter presents a model of professional development for the responsive, flexible, imaginative and nurturing educator of learners with SLD/PMLD. Creativity emerges as a key characteristic, endorsed by the views of trainees on evaluations following four-week developmental placements in special schools.

The developing background context

With no specialist initial teacher training (ITT) courses since the mid-1980s, the British government finally responded to the growing call ever since to strengthen support on SEN in ITT and introduced tomes of materials for undergraduate and postgraduate ITT courses for both Primary and Secondary (TDA 2008a, 2009). While certain areas of need were addressed (for example, autism and dyslexia), there was nothing specifically aimed at learners with SLD/

PMLD. It was an important initiative nonetheless and warmly welcomed within ITT. Principles were transferable and the accompanying financial support from the government enabled an additional limited number of extended four-week placements in special schools (TDA 2008b), including those for learners with SLD/PMLD.

Ofsted declared SEN a national priority from 2010, and the new inspection framework for schools identified SEN as a key area by which schools' effectiveness would be judged (Ofsted 2013). Further online training materials for experienced teachers were commissioned on five common areas of need: autism; MLD; speech and communication needs; social, emotional and behavioural difficulties; and dyslexia (DfE 2012a).

The Salt Review (DCSF 2010) meanwhile investigated provision for learners with SLD and PMLD, and significantly identified an aspiration that *'Teaching SLD/PMLD [should be] considered an area of specialist expertise, with high status and value, attracting some of the best applicants'* (p. 5). This led to further commissioning of an acclaimed ground-breaking, open-access online developmental training resource on severe and complex learning difficulties (DfE 2012b). Modules are not qualificatory although they can be used flexibly: within teacher training modules; to support school placements; by educators seeking self-help and self-directed study; and for staff development.

These developments are timely, as increasing numbers of children are being born with new conditions hitherto unknown and are now surviving premature birth and medical treatments. They will require an imaginative response, and their own personalised unique learning pathway. Carpenter (2012) reported the number of families affected as 700,000 in 2004, and 950,000 in 2010 – an exponential growth rate of 1.8 per cent a year. There are noticeable changes in the severity of needs of those young children entering the system, which is impacting through the education system: the Salt Review (DCSF 2010) highlighted that 25 per cent of children with SLD/PMLD are being educated in mainstream schools, such as those with Down Syndrome who previously would have been placed in special schools, and with a trend for children moving between two school rolls (Tutt 2007). Today's teachers need insights and experience to be able to engage with learners and colleagues across a flexible continuum of provision.

Issues for new special education professionals

The professional Teachers' Standards for England (DfE 2012c) identify generic attributes, knowledge and skills for working across contexts, which apply equally within specialist contexts. However, newcomers may undergo a steep emotional learning journey as they attune to the learners and complexity of the context. For many tutors of ITT courses, the challenges for supporting trainees will be considerable, not least because few will have prior teaching experience themselves in schools for learners with SLD/PMLD. Preparing trainees for educating learners with complex needs requires both tutors and trainees to be open-minded and inquiry-led, and to engage with research for 'new generation pedagogy' (Carpenter 2012). A characteristic of the special educator has to be flexibility to be able to respond 'in the moment' – an attribute that Craft (2001) and the DfEE (1999) regard as the hallmark of creative teaching and divergent thinking. While a tall order for the newcomer to special education, it is not the case that such teachers are necessarily 'born and not made'.

Unfortunately from first-hand experience of comments from trainees, there still seems to be confusing mixed views regarding newly-qualified teachers (NQTs) taking first appointments in special schools, and patchy support nationally during the first year in teaching remains a real concern. Some schools have openly stated to me that they prefer to appoint 'generalists', although many special schools also state the opposite too, preferring to mould the NQT and will appoint them for their aptitude and, encouragingly in some cases, for their training and prior placement experience. A placement in a special school with learners with SLD/PMLD can be valuable preparation for both mainstream and special education, for the pedagogical skills, emotional robustness and inclusive ethos. As one trainee commented, 'I now have the confidence to take risks and really push myself in all aspects'.

The following trainee indicated the personal and professional benefits from her placement in an outstanding school for learners with SLD/PMLD. She experienced explicit valuing of the creative teaching, while also revealing the importance of quality support.

> In principle the idea of completing this placement was a great challenge for me. I had no prior experience of working with children with special needs and certainly not within an SLD school. This concerned me greatly. The support of the University Placement Tutor was vital and her understanding of how I felt, plus the encouragement that I had to take the placement. My reaction to the children was also of great concern, as I was unsure if I would be distressed by the extent of the children's disabilities. The initial, accompanied visit certainly gave me more confidence to approach the first day. Once in the school, realising how much the staff were there to guide and advise me, my anxiety disappeared. It is, despite all the extra things staff have to be aware of, one of the most relaxed teaching environments I have worked in. This placement has provided a wealth of inclusive lesson ideas. I have seen innovative and creative lessons where the children were engaged and participating in despite the most severe difficulties. Visual and kinaesthetic activities were vital; also the breaking down of tasks into the smallest steps allowing all to achieve. Regarding inclusive provision in mainstream, I can certainly see now how it can be enhanced with the experience from this placement.

Another trainee likewise expanded on the transferable benefits from the special school for learners with SLD/PMLD to mainstream inclusion, from the creative injection to his teaching repertoire:

> I have learnt so much from this placement. There are so many strategies that I can now try to implement into mainstream teaching and I have also lost my 'fear' of working with children who have SEN-D. I believe that as a result of this placement I am now more prepared to teach well differentiated and inclusive lessons and now have a strong basis on which to build learning strategies to overcome barriers to learning. After this placement, I am now more excited than ever to get back into a classroom and teach again! I am really looking forward to implementing strategies into my future classes. I also really enjoyed how sensory the learning was and this is something I would really like to develop and transfer to towards mainstream teaching.

Supporting the emerging inclusive teacher

It is apparent from the comments above that appropriate support is crucial for overcoming a newcomer's initial starting point of 'fear' – whether a student on placement or a new but relatively inexperienced member of staff. Immersion experience in the complex environment of a special school for learners with SLD/PMLD will be risky without a graduated approach and regard for both emotional well-being as well as professional skill development. The emotional learning journey is integral: neuroscience informs us that experiences that are emotionally arousing will be more memorable (Iverson 1996). Korthagen (2010) explains how personal and professional development are inextricably linked, with insights from one's own struggle informing an embedded inclusive philosophy, as well as the emergence of the emotionally robust and sensitive professional able to attune to the individual learner.

Newcomers to the special school for learners with SLD/PMLD may be overwhelmed initially, not only by so many very disabled learners *en masse*, but also by the commitment and dedication of the staff to absolute child–centredness, which can be deeply moving. With smaller teaching groups and larger numbers of support staff in classes, relationships with staff and pupils are necessarily more intense. Trainees often comment on the keen interest and sensitivity shown to them as learners – directly experiencing first-hand the same 'teaching as caring' (Noddings 1992), as shown to the children. This collaborative, collegial approach can be inspirational, as another trainee stated: 'I hope to develop such a supportive ethos wherever I work in the future.'

This all begs a more humanistic model for training the special educator, rather than the traditional focus in ITT on pedagogical skills, and with more explicit holistic regard for the emotionality of the aspiring professional. In line with Maslow's (1954) principles, without priority attention to the emotional foundations for development, this will not result in the pinnacle outcome of a personally and professionally integrated and fulfilled inclusive educator (see Figure 12.1). Hargreaves (1998) underlines the need for training programmes to nurture trainees' inner drive and emotional growth, not just pedagogical skills and knowledge, and to create certain conditions to precipitate this. Special schools clearly can make a profound impact on trainees, and offer fertile learning contexts, albeit with quality mentoring support and centre-based preparation essential.

A clear overarching developmental training framework will provide a shared understanding of professional development for all involved, and avoid misunderstandings over the purpose of a placement and a trainee's role. It will give the aspiring professional reassurance and security regarding realistic, appropriate expectations for school placements. This fundamental feeling of *emotional safety* cannot be underestimated – each special school can be so different, that even with some prior experience, each new context may feel like one is starting again from scratch.

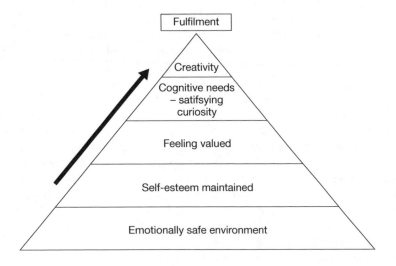

Figure 12.1 The emotional learning journey of the inclusive trainee

Experienced staff need to be available to talk through anxieties and issues without prejudice from the outset, both informally and in scheduled mentoring meetings. Timing of these ideally should avoid issues being taken home: a short daily debrief to talk through emerging themes from the busy day, and a more formal extended discussion towards the end of the week. Newcomers need planned and perhaps spontaneous time out of class, and systems to provide continuing support beyond school, such as access to online forums, and maintaining a reflective log.

New staff may feel very vulnerable, and their fragile *self-esteem* needs to be preserved, especially initially when anxious to do the right thing. Maintaining belief – focusing on positives and a 'can do' attitude – will be an important counterbalance to signposting constructively areas for development. Early briefing will enable newcomers immediately to implement personalised communication and behaviour strategies as part of the team, and to develop relationships. It will be important too for their professional face to be preserved: sensitively timing intervention to take over before a situation becomes critical, with a constructive debrief later in private. The 'shock factor' should not be underestimated, particularly when witnessing extremes of behaviour and positive handling of learners in non-negotiable incidents.

New staff to the teaching team, whatever their status, all need to *feel valued*, rather than a burden to their colleagues. Some may bring skills such as music, sport, gardening or cooking; others may have knowledge and insights from prior working or life experiences, such as a family member with a special need, and relish the opportunity to extend empathy to the learners' parents, for example greeting at the school gate or consultation evening. Early opportunity to take over an individual programme under supervision will instil feelings of being effective and making a difference. It may be too that they bring particular expertise that can be show-cased to colleagues, such as ICT skills – trainees' enthusiasm can be infectious and inject some life-blood into the special school!

With this emotional underpinning intact, the aspiring professional can engage conceptually with ideas and extend themselves *cognitively*. New staff should be challenged in their thinking, although timing of this needs to be paced. They will need plenty of time to get to know the learners, their needs, how provision is organised and the curriculum personalised, otherwise differentiated lesson planning will be ineffective. They will need opportunities to observe practice and quality teaching within the school, with staff prepared to discuss afterwards and answer questions. Curiosity may need nourishing too on sensitive topics, such as strategies for dealing with difficult parents and bereavement of learners with life-limiting conditions. Finding opportunity for talk can be difficult in the intensive, hectic special school day, so it may be useful to signpost to training materials for self-directed study, and where they may research their own answers to questions; for example, use of online training resources (DfE 2012a, 2012b), reflective tasks on aspects of the special school context and online discussions.

It will be apparent, that the confidence and ability to be *creative* will be a higher order need and skill, yet being innovative will be key to teaching inclusively: an aptitude to be imaginative, using a repertoire of teaching and learning styles and ways to overcome barriers to learning. Daring oneself to innovate in the special school context, often with unpredictable learners, can feel exposing at the best of times, although it is always possible to stop rather than battle on! Once settled, a new colleague should be given freedom to give vent to their latent potential, but with the important proviso that this happens without fear of negative judgement from colleagues if unsuccessful – or initial cynicism: just because something was tried previously, it does not mean that it won't work this time with new staff and a new context!

Countering the rigid ethos of highly structured approaches that may prevail in some special schools can be daunting, and indeed, regard is always needed for timing of the introduction of novelty with learners that expect and rely on routine. However, systems can be put in place such as an exclamation mark symbol to represent a surprise featuring on a visual timetable. The *Engagement Profile and Scale* (DfE 2012a) may be a useful structured tool for devising a personalised approach and tracking a child's progress that can then be implemented by colleagues and tried subsequently with other children with similar needs.

Developing the creative inclusive teacher – a training model

However desirable and essential creative teaching is for learners with SLD/PMLD, it is unrealistic to expect the newcomer to be able to spontaneously deliver a beautifully personalised and differentiated lesson to a class they barely know, weaving learners' responses skilfully to shape towards a learning goal, and presented in an imaginative way that engages and empowers the learners. Yet this perhaps is the aspiration ultimately of the expert special educator, who is able to respond intuitively in the moment with instant situational understanding, drawing on tacit knowledge and a wealth of prior experiences. They seem to deploy just the right teaching strategies, having swiftly appraised all those factors impinging on the teaching context, and with learners with highly diverse and idiosyncratic needs. It is important to remember that this teacher too was once a beginner, and needed to work systematically and analytically through all elements of their lesson plan, consciously trying out techniques and approaches gleaned through training, and with regard for policy and good practice principles.

A personalised professional development pathway will be needed for the emerging professional that nurtures their progression by building on prior experiences and learning. Developed from earlier models for training the empowering, interactive teacher working in the arts (Peter 1995; Peter and Walter 2010), Peter's (2013) five-stage model (see Table 12.1) distinguishes the characteristics to be acquired in four dimensions of the emerging creative and inclusive teacher:

- application of relevant theory, policy and pedagogical principles;
- recognising and responding to learning opportunities as they arise in the classroom;
- appraising all the factors that impact on the learning context (for example, resources, time, space, staff availability, group dynamics); and
- a repertoire of actual teaching strategies that could be deployed within any situation.

At each stage, in line with Dreyfus's model of occupational situational understanding (Dreyfus 1981, cited in Elliott 1991), one dimension in particular will be pivotal as the knowledge threshold for advancing to the next level. From this crude framework, it is possible to generate overarching outcomes in each of the four dimensions for stages within a developmental training programme. The framework can also provide pointers for descriptive vision statements to equate with the characteristics of the newcomer, advanced beginner, competent educator, proficient educator and developing expert respectively. The model is based on Vygotsky's (1978) principle of realising latent potential through being extended by a more experienced 'other' – here, a visiting tutor and/or school mentor.

The model can be used to inform not only clear generic, developmental placement outcomes, but also essential and desirable placement experiences, reflective tasks and mentoring implications. These all need to be differentiated to ensure a developmental scaffold for progression across training placements, broken down across the weeks. Initially, each new placement will involve starting afresh to familiarise with the structures; each time however, this will be informed from prior experience (Bruner 1986) and the learning curve from newcomer will be quicker.

Table 12.1 Professional development in inclusive teaching

	Theory and pedagogy	*Learning opportunities*	*Contextual factors*	*Teaching decisions*
Level 1 Trainee – newcomer	Understands theory and teaching principles for SEN-D	Aware of needs/ responses as lesson unfolds and engages child/ren in learning	Aware of factors affecting class organisation and management	Teaches a planned lesson, using suggested strategies
Level 2 Trainee – advanced beginner	Plans & teaches lesson(s) in literacy/ maths for a group with SEN-D	Responds to pupil initiative to shape towards learning and assesses progress	Organises the environment – groupings of children and staff, resources, timings	Draws spontaneously on familiar strategies to support social inclusion
Level 3 NQT – competent	Plans & teaches a series of linked sessions across the curriculum for inclusive groups	Adjusts challenge & approach in process to maintain engagement	Anticipates and prepares in partnership for possible known contingencies	Innovates approaches with support to personalise social inclusion
Experienced teacher – proficient	Fully inclusive differentiated planning, with personalised targets embedded	Varies approach in process for emerging needs/ contingencies with a familiar group	Adjusts flexibly and sensitively, in respect of the unexpected and holistic needs	Devises personalised interventions for individual needs in partnership
Senior teacher – expert	Secure inclusive theory and pedagogy – able to justify an intervention	Varies approach in process and shapes learning to maintain challenge with an unfamiliar group	Appraises factors impacting on a new/unfamiliar context	Responds intuitively using tacit prior knowledge

(based on Dreyfus 1981 in Elliott 1991, Peter 1995 and Peter and Walter 2010)

The newcomer special educator

Table 12.2 shows a summary framework (Peter 2013) for a two-week enrichment placement in a special school, in which a trainee may consolidate core knowledge and understanding of inclusive practices and awareness of some specialist approaches; it might also support induction of a new teacher or support staff. The priority needs are for plenty of observation of and reflection on good practice to understand key pedagogical concepts (University of Derby 2010–11; Teaching Agency 2012):

• management and organisation of classrooms;
• behaviour;
• communication;
• assessment; and
• the curriculum.

Table 12.2 Placement model for a two-week special school experience

Professional development needs – newcomer	Target pedagogical skills (placement outcomes)	Focus for mentoring & visiting tutor support (on line)
Theory into practice: Understand learning theory, relevant policy and inclusive teaching principles in the special school classroom	To know general approaches that inform planning, teaching and assessment for children with SEN-D within statutory frameworks	Feedback on understanding of the context: – engagement with policies, involvement in meetings – insights on general principles for promoting independence, fading out prompting, breaking down tasks – differentiation – how children show progress and implications for assessment – principles for personalising learning
Responsiveness: Recognise learning opportunities for child/ren with SEN-D and intervene towards a learning goal and to maintain their engagement	To recognise when child/ren with SEN-D are on and off task, and be able to engage them in their learning	Feedback on engagement strategies: – relationship-building with children, use of children's interests – questioning, positive praise, feedback to children on their learning – approach to monitoring child/ren's responses – Use of the *Engagement Profile and Scale*
Contextual factors: Awareness of factors affecting classroom organisation (time, space, resources available, staffing, group dynamics, individual needs)	To understand how contextual factors influence classroom management and organising for learning	Feedback on team working: – initiative, relationships with staff – regard for children's welfare and well-being
Teaching strategies: Engage with a range of techniques and multi-modal approaches for inclusive teaching and intervention	To use techniques under direction for inclusive teaching and for overcoming individual barriers to learning	Feedback on teaching decisions: – use of familiar techniques that have been demonstrated – use of personalised interventions for behaviour and communication

Table 12.2 (continued)

	Week 1: understanding the context			
Focus pedagogical concept	School and mentor input	Key activities in class	Desirable additional experiences	Reflective tasks
Pre-visit and Day 1 – The learning environment: Organisation of the environment	Induction from Senior Teacher (1–2 hours) • General introduction • Safeguarding and school approach to behaviour • Specialist staff & involvement with families Guided tour of the setting **Discussion with the class teacher (20 mins):** 1) Organisation of the environment for learning 2) Personalisation of resources Feedback to trainee on initiative and understanding of principles that guide practice	• Engage – join in – with general class routines and structure of the day • Carry out observations of the class/provision's layout/design, behaviour management • Support an individual child (case study)	Shadow an assistant member of staff Read the provision's prospectus and newsletters Read records and targets for a child Read policies on safeguarding and behaviour Engage with risk assessment procedures	**The learning environment** – *Carry out observations of:* – The physical environment of the whole setting – Organisation of the classroom/group room for learning and development – how personalised materials and resources are created and by whom On-line: share observations on organisation of the environment; discussion thread to compare & contrast
Behaviour	**Meeting with behaviour specialist (30 mins):** School policy and general strategies to promote positive behaviour; specific interventions for personalised behaviour needs **Debrief with the class teacher (30 mins):** Team approaches to behaviour; personalised interventions for individual children's behaviour Feedback to the trainee on use of strategies	• Keep a log of general staff interactions regarding behaviour – strategies used and impact • Time sampling of an individual child for their behaviour • Maintain 2 × ABC charts for when a child is on task and off task, and analyse for patterns	Read the setting's policy on Behaviour Read records for a child Make a relationship with a child with behavioural challenges – use positive language, note impact Use the Engagement Profile to assess a case study child when most and least engaged	**Children's behaviour** – Over the week, carry out observations: – General team approach, positive approaches, impact of staff responses on learning – Behavioural challenges, specific individual interventions and approaches – Behaviour of a case study child in formal and informal situations, with peers and with staff On-line: discussion thread on behaviour (how is policy reflected in practice?)
Communication	Talk/workshop: Communication / English co-ordinator(1 hr max) Communication approaches used in the setting Meeting with class staff (30 mins): general approach to communication; specific communication interventions for children Feedback to the trainee on use of language, questioning	Observe general communication approaches: visual supports / use of the environment spontaneous adjustments by staff Observe and participate in approaches used to promote communication Support a case study child with communication difficulties	Opportunity to familiarise with communication strategies and use of ICT Interaction with pupils in formal and informal situations Track case study child across the day, focusing on communication Observe/participate in a meeting between co-ordinator and school staff	Children's communication Observations of a case study child in formal and informal situations. Note: interactions with staff and children, use of communication strategies (planned and spontaneous), specific personalised communication interventions On-line: discussion thread on alternative and augmentative communication approaches and use of assistive technology, and their impact & transferability

Week 2: understanding practice

Focus pedagogical concept	Setting & mentor input	Key activities in class	Desirable additional experiences	Reflective tasks
Assessment	**Talk/workshop: Assessment co-ordinator (1 hour max):** identification and assessment of needs; setting's approach to assessment, progression & planning targets; assessment & tracking systems **Meeting with the class teacher (30 mins):** How holistic needs of children are understood (focus on case study child/ren), involvement of the family and professionals How learning goals are set for pupils and how they are decided; roles played by teacher and TA in assessing how far pupils have met objectives set for them	Support a group of children under direction – engage with their targets and Assessment for Learning Observe practical strategies to gather assessment data on children's achievements, noting roles of TAs Support case study child towards achieving a particular target	Shadow – observe - specialist staff working with children Discuss with specialist staff assessment tools used and how intervention is designed to address individual needs Read records, notes and assessment on an individual pupil, and how an understanding of the case study child has been reached Observe parent consultation / review & how targets are agreed	**Assessment** *Interview the class teacher and support staff:* Who decides what learning goals are set for pupils, and how they are arrived at On-line: – discussion thread on holistic assessment practices
The curriculum	**Guided walk: Senior teacher (1 hour)** *– could be combined with general intro in week 1* • approach to curriculum design across the setting – adjustments from NC & EYFS • specific curricula (eg Equals, forest schools, role of therapy) • enrichment activities and use of the community **Meeting with the class teacher (30 mins):** • How session content and strategies are decided • How learning goals are decided • How personalised targets are incorporated • Involvement of staff & children in planning	Support a group towards a curriculum learning outcome, engaging with how activities are differentiated and Assessment for Learning Engage with the teacher's planning, and lead part of a session planned by the teacher (eg literacy: tell and re-tell and story, using a range of interactive teaching and learning styles to overcome barriers to learning) Lead routine sessions (eg snack time, hello session)	Observe the differentiated curriculum experience in different classes across the school Look at examples of exemplary planning from across the school	**Planning and objectives –** *– interview the class teacher and teaching team:* How session content and strategies are decided; how learning goals for individuals are decided; involvement of staff and pupils in setting learning goals On-line: – discussions thread based on the NC 3 inclusion principles (learning objectives, teaching and learning styles, overcoming barriers)

Table 12.2 (continued)

Week 2: understanding practice

Focus pedagogical concept	Setting & mentor input	Key activities in class	Desirable additional experiences	Reflective tasks
The specialist professional	**Demonstration lesson and debrief by an outstanding teacher (1 hour)** (*could be by video conferencing*) – share planning with trainee, and Q & A on strategies **Debrief with the teacher on the trainee's teaching (20 mins)** – responsiveness to differentiated objectives, teaching and learning styles, strategies to overcome individual barriers to learning, organisation & management issues for the session	Plan collaboratively and co- teach a session with the teacher (to tell a story and re-engage children in re-telling) – *this could be a lesson previously observed, led by the teacher, which the trainee repeats* Receive feedback on teaching and learning styles & general strategies to sustain engagement and challenge Evaluate children's gains & the effectiveness of the planning, responsiveness, awareness of factors impacting, & strategies	Attend a team meeting, and note how professionals support one another and draw on respective strengths and expertise when planning Observe parent consultation / review – note how the setting learns from the family, and how sensitive issues are handled	**Excellence in practice –** Evaluate quality teaching – write a reflective commentary on learning points from the specialist context On-line: – discussion thread on dimensions of good practice – comment on: - Planning and assessment - Responsiveness to learning opportunities - Organisation for factors impacting on the environment - Teaching strategies

Newcomers benefit from access to key policies on behaviour, teaching and learning and communication, and receiving briefing from key staff responsible. This will enable them to apply strategies themselves with confidence and understanding under supervision. Working in a support role, and really getting to know a small group of learners (or an individual learner if a placement is restricted to one week or less) will enable them also to relate policies to practice to meet holistic needs (Lawson *et al.* 2013). Importantly, too, it will enable newcomers to recognise subtleties of when learners show signs of drifting off task. This will help develop their awareness of the importance of engagement in learning, their confidence in motivating and recognising when intervention is needed towards a learning goal.

From newcomer to advanced beginner

Over a four-week placement for a trainee or similar induction period for a new member of staff, a newcomer may progress to gain advanced skills for working with learners with SLD/PMLD. This goes beyond an initial two-week observation period, to dare themselves to 'have a go' independently. It may take up to four weeks to feel fully grounded and emotionally sufficiently well placed to confidently take the helm. The route there can be to take the lead in routine sessions such as the welcome 'hello' session. These tend to be ripe opportunities to focus on learners' behaviour, communication and social skills, which will enable the newcomer to consolidate their awareness of individual learner's priority targets and how to work on these inclusively in group contexts.

The priority target for the newcomer professional however, is to be able to plan and teach a lesson in a core curriculum subject area, albeit 'by the book' and rough at the edges, and with planning support from a mentor and the teaching team. Literacy or Mathematics tend to be more closely defined in terms of children's progression in small steps, which will be easier at first for the emerging advanced beginner to differentiate, as will focusing on addressing objectives and assessing outcomes for one or two children. Early forays into teaching the whole diverse group will need to prioritise using strategies to overcome barriers to learning for the focus children, taking confidence that using a range of multi-modal teaching and learning styles should enable others to access learning too.

From advanced beginner to competence

Over a longer induction period or final placement for a trainee (minimum 7 weeks), the aim should be acquisition of the specialist skill-set as befits a level of competence. By the end, they should be able to respond flexibly in process to extend or modify their approach, and to engage the learners and shape their responses towards a learning target. Importantly they should be able to do this for subject areas across the curriculum, including those where learners' progression is harder to pin down. The competent teacher will need to demonstrate contingency arrangements in their planning, with clear allocation of the roles of support staff, having taken account of known factors that could possibly impact on the teaching context. They should also deploy with confidence, specialist and personalised teaching approaches, particularly for communication and behaviour to support social inclusion, through collaboration with other agencies.

From competence to proficiency

Outstanding trainees and NQTs will show characteristics of an emerging proficient, experienced teacher, who is able to adjust practice swiftly and with versatility for the unexpected – as often happens within the special school context. The proficient teacher of learners with SLD/PMLD will be able to design personalised intervention in collaboration with specialist agencies, and innovate this with sensitivity to attune to and reach the individual learner. Teaching will be characterised by rigorous differentiation across the curriculum and with individual priority targets embedded throughout the school day. Support staff will be fully briefed, including on assessment strategies, and the experienced teacher will endeavour for the family to be involved too in continuing learning from home. The hallmark of the proficient inclusive teacher of learner with SLD/PMLD will necessarily be creativity: they will show imagination, ingenuity and flexibility in all aspects of their practice.

Conclusion

Learners with SLD/PMLD need educators who can support them to develop their potential and realise this through transferring and generalising learning from adult-led contexts into real-life situations. This requires a workforce that has the inner confidence and skills to work flexibly and responsively to encourage learners' autonomy and independence in spontaneous situations. Learners with SLD/PMLD also need educators that engender in them a feeling of empowerment and resourcefulness to become self-advocates as far as possible. They will need to develop this aptitude if they are to take their place within a fast-changing and increasingly diverse society; a society that requires adaptability and 'possibility thinking' (Craft 2001 in Craft *et al.* 2001), an ability to get on with others and enjoy fulfilment from their own latent creativity and potential.

This chapter has presented a rationale and framework for developing an inclusive teacher that recognises the integrated personal and professional emotional learning journey and pedagogical training pathway needed to be able to respond creatively to meet diverse needs. With this as the ultimate aspiration, implications for training educators of learners with SLD/PMLD have been considered within the rapidly changing legislative and also demographic context as the needs of learners become more complex, with ramifications permeating through the range of provision within the education system. Creativity is essential for professional survival and fulfilment, as well as for meeting learners' individual needs and maximising their potential.

Questions for readers

- What do you perceive to be your professional learning needs given the increasing numbers of learners with SLD/PMLD?
- What support would you wish for from a mentor that would help you with the emotional challenges of the work?
- What advice would you offer a new member of staff to your school for learners with SLD/PMLD?
- Using the model in Table 12.1 as 'best fit' indicators, where would you assess your current stage of professional development and priority target?

References

Bruner, J. (1986) *Actual Minds, Possible Worlds*, Cambridge, MA: Harvard University Press.
Carpenter, B. (2012) 'Training resources for Special Education in the 21st Century', keynote address – Dissemination conference. Stratford: University of East London, 2 May 2012. Unpublished paper.
Craft, A. (2001) 'Little c Creativity', in Craft, A., Jeffrey, B. and Leibling M. (eds) *Creativity in Education*, London: Continuum.

Department for Children, Schools and Families (DCSF) (2010) *The Salt Review: independent review of teacher supply for pupils with SLD and PMLD.* Nottingham: DCSF Publications.

Department for Education (DfE) (2012a) *Advanced training materials for autism; dyslexia; speech, language and communication; emotional, social and behavioural difficulties; moderate learning difficulties.* Online. Available: www.advanced-training.org.uk/ (accessed 12 August 2014).

Department for Education (DfE) (2012b) *Training materials for learners with severe, profound and complex learning difficulties.* Online: www.complexneeds.org.uk (accessed 12 August 2014).

Department for Education (DfE) (2012c) *The Teachers' Standards: Guidance*, London: DfE.

Department for Education and Employment (DfEE) (1999) *All Our Futures: The NACCCE Report*, London: The Stationery Office.

Department for Education and Skills (DfES) (2004) *Removing Barriers to Achievement*, Nottingham: DfES Publications.

Dreyfus, S.E. (1981) *Four Models v. Human Situational Understanding: inherent limitations on the modelling of business expertise*, US Air Force Office of Scientific Research, Contract No F49620-79-C-0063.

Elliott, J. (1991) *Action Research for Educational Change*, Milton Keynes: Open University.

Hargreaves, A. (1998) 'The emotional practice of teaching', *Teaching and Teacher Education*, 14(8), 835–854.

Hargreaves, A. (2001) *Changing Teachers, Changing Times*, London: Cassell.

Iverson, S. D. (1996) 'Communication in the mind'. Paper to the International Congress of Psychology XXVI Montreal, *International Journal of Psychology*, 31, 254.

Korthagen, F.A.J. (2010) 'Situated learning theory and the pedagogy of teacher education: towards an integrative view of teacher behaviour and teacher learning', *Teaching and Teacher Education*, 26, 98–106.

Lawson, H., Norwich, B. and Nash, T. (2013) 'What trainees in England learn about teaching pupils with special educational needs/disabilities in their school based work: the contribution of planned activities in one year initial training courses', *European Journal of Special Needs Education*, 28(2), 136–155.

Maslow, A. (1954) *Motivation and Personality*, New York, NY: Harper.

Noddings, N. (1992) *The Challenge to Care in Schools: An alternative approach to education*, Advances in Contemporary Educational Thought series, vol. 8. New York: Teachers College Press.

Ofsted (2013) *The Framework for School Inspection,* Manchester: OFSTED

Peter, M. (1995) *Making Drama Special*, London: David Fulton Publishers.

Peter, M. (2013) 'Training special educators', *Support for Learning*, 28(3), 122–132.

Peter, M. and Walter, O. (2010) 'Developing movement as inclusive pedagogy', *Support for Learning*, 25(1), 38–46.

Teaching Agency (2012) 'SEN School experience: framework outline and rationale', Handout (unpublished).

Training and Development Agency (TDA) (2008a) *Special Educational Needs and/or disabilities Training Toolkit: a training resource for initial teacher training providers – undergraduate courses.* London: TDA.

Training and Development Agency (TDA) (2008b) *A Guide to Extended Placements in Special Provision – primary undergraduate courses.* London: TDA

Training and Development Agency (TDA) (2009) *Special Educational Needs and/or Disabilities Training Toolkit: a training resource for one-year initial teacher training providers – post-graduate courses.* London: TDA.

Tutt, R. (2007) *Every Child Included*, London: Sage.

University of Derby (2010-11) *Placement in Special Schools – guidance booklet, B.Ed Stage 2.* Derby: University of Derby.

Vygotsky, L. (1978) *Mind in Society*, Cambridge MA: Harvard University Press.

13

TEACHERS TALKING ABOUT THEIR WORK WITH LEARNERS WITH SLD AND PMLD

Michael W. Riley and Phyllis Jones

In this chapter, the following questions will be addressed:

- What can be learned by listening to teachers' perspectives on their work with learners with SLD and PMLD?
- How can teachers be encouraged to reflect on and talk about their roles?

Introduction

Becoming and being a teacher is a complex developmental process involving a wide range of beliefs, experiences, knowledge, skills, and commitments (Bransford, Darling-Hammond and LePage 2005). Listening to the perspectives of teachers of learners with SLD and PMLD is vital to understanding how they make meaning of the work they do. Historically, this group of teachers has not had a strong voice in research (Jones 2004a) and it is important to appreciate teachers' perspectives when trying to understand what it is to be a teacher of learners with SLD/PMLD. There is a growing acceptance of the stories that teachers tell about their lives in the classroom and how this can inform professional learning (Kelchtermans 2009; Nias 1989; Tripp 1994). Over time, teachers' concepts of what teaching is may be shaped by their prior personal experiences with family and schooling, prior professional experiences including working with children and youths, their experiences teacher training and continuing professional development, their current teaching context and practices, and their vision of their future career path (Olsen 2008). Through these experiences teachers develop understandings of what teachers do, what teaching is, and these shape their professional beliefs, values and behaviours (Hammerness 2006). Soto *et al.* (2001) discuss how teacher attitudes toward disability impact on teaching in the classroom. They found that teachers highlighted feelings of discomfort and fear of working with learners with disability, personal insecurity, and fear of failure. While it is naturally vital to value all teachers' perspectives to support a greater understanding of the complex process of teaching all learners, this chapter is concerned with the perspectives of teachers who teach learners with SLD/PMLD.

The chapter authors, who currently reside in Florida, USA, acknowledge teachers' voices as the authority on their own professional lives and that their perspectives must influence the discussion about what it is to be a teacher (Goodson 1992; Kelchtermans 1993).

Listening to teachers of learners with SLD/PMLD

This section draws on to the voice of teachers of learners with SLD/PMLD. Our approach to this inquiry has not been on examining extant definitions of SLD/PMLD but, rather, to hear the perspectives of teachers related to their own practices in serving the needs of their pupils. Listening to teachers can inform us not only about what and how teachers work, but about how they conceptualize teaching, how they feel about the work they do, how they do it, and why they are doing it (Jones 2014). This may lead to better understandings of the teaching profession. There is a growing body of research reflecting the views of teachers of learners with SLD/ PMLD. This began in the nineties with the work of Corbett (1996). Her portrayals of life in a 'special care' classroom in the 1970s and 1980s, teaching learners with SLD/PMLD in the South of England, offered a vivid depiction of the teaching among this group of teachers. In her accounts, she recalls the language used by other teachers to describe her teaching and the learners she taught:

> The vocabulary being used in relation to this group was about 'care', 'nursing', 'comfort', 'respite for parents', 'occupy' and 'control'. This was the official language. The unofficial was expressed in terms such as 'dumping ground', 'sin bin', 'vegetables', 'shitty work' and 'baby minding'.
>
> (Corbett 1996: 9).

Although Corbett's recollections are from the 1970s and 1980s, they are affirmed in more recent research. The work of Jones (2004b) shared teachers' views about how they believed other teachers value the teaching they do with learners with the most complex disabilities. They voiced concerns similar to those of Corbett in feeling very undervalued as teachers.

Recently, the emphasis of teachers' views has become more curriculum, than care focused. De Bortoli *et al.* (2010) reviewed the research base on teachers' teaching practices with learners who have multiple and severe learning disabilities and who use augmentative communication. This analysis suggested that teachers' attitudes, perceptions and beliefs contribute to low frequencies of teachers facilitating communication and interaction with these learners. Narayan *et al.* (2010) explored teachers' views of assessments for learners with SLD/PMLD in America and India. Their study affirmed the importance of teachers understanding the way learners explore their environment and the learners' understanding of cause and effect, object permanence, memory, reasoning and choice making emerged as important. Teachers are sensitive to nuances in learners' behaviour and are able to recognise the significance of their actions and levels of engagement and progress. For example, they state that learners 'demonstrate this understanding through eye gaze, body posturing, vocalisations, gestures, movements, and increased oral motor activities' (Narayan *et al.* 2010: 273). For these teachers, the process of teaching involves a sophisticated interpretation of learner response and careful mediation of meaningful learning on an individual basis. The international similarity of teachers' perspectives is also borne out by the project by West *et al.* (2012) for teachers of learners with autism in regions of England, the US and Australia. Here teachers shared views about effective teacher learning, with much consensus across geographical boundaries. These include the importance of theory to practice application, mentoring, and learning about assistive technology at both the pre- and in-service levels. In listening to teachers' insights about their learning, we come to a better understanding of the lived experience of the teachers in the classroom.

Gathering the teachers' views

This project explores the views of seven teachers who teach learners with SLD/PMLD across five schools in England. The teachers met one of the chapter authors on a previous study tour to Florida. Ongoing communication was established, and 12 teachers were invited to participate in this study. Seven teachers participated and teacher demographics are detailed in Table 13.1, reflecting a spread of teaching experience across five special schools for pupils with SLD/PMLD. The teachers had a mixture of experiences that includes a range of teaching experience in general and in teaching pupils with SLD/PMLD in different contexts including mainstream and special schools.

Gathering their perspectives occurred in two ways: through either a virtual discussion venue or email communication. Teachers were encouraged to talk about/respond to the following prompts:

1   Tell us what it is to be a teacher.
2   Tell us what it is to be a teacher of students with complex disabilities.
3   Tell us about where and how you learn about teaching students with complex disabilities.
4   In your experience, where and how do teachers learn best to teach students with complex disabilities (list your top three)?
5   If you could provide policy makers with a top five list of what teachers need to know to teach students with complex disabilities, what would it be?

In conducting our analysis of the teachers' responses, we recognise that researchers act as interpreters and the lived experience of others is 'created in the social text written by the researcher' (Denzin and Lincoln 2008: 26). We attempt to present legitimate representations of the lived experience of others. We also acknowledge that this project shares the perspectives of a small group of teachers of learners with SLD/PMLD; these are not intended to represent all teachers, but highlight some issues that are particularly interesting for this group of teachers at this point in time.

Through collaborative analysis, four discrete themes emerged. Table 13.2 demonstrates the distribution of the themes across the teachers showing how they make meaning of the teaching they engage in with learners with SLD/PMLD.

Table 13.1 Teacher demographics

Teacher	School	Years of experience in teaching	Years experience teaching students with SLD/PMLD
T1	A	33	21
T2	B	29	20
T3	C	27	27
T4	C	3	3
T5	C	3	3
T6	D	7	7
T7	E	5	2

Table 13.2 Data distribution – being a teacher of learners with SLD/PMLD

Theme	Teacher response
Teaching as a vocation and making a difference	6 teachers T1, T2, T3, T4, T6, T7
Being different from mainstream teaching	6 teachers T1, T2, T3, T4, T5, T6
Identity as a teacher	7 teachers T1, T2, T3, T4, T5, T6, T7
Person-centred teaching	4 teachers T1, T2, T3, T6

Being a teacher of learners with SLD/PMLD

Being a teacher involves having and applying certain understandings and skills. The 'National Teachers' Standards' in England (DfE 2013) indicate that being a teacher involves having understandings of human development and learning as well as subject area content and curriculum, and that teachers demonstrate skills in planning, delivering and evaluating instruction, managing pupil behaviour and collaborating with other professionals and parents. Teachers have voiced the importance of these professional understandings and skills as part of their identity (Burn 2007; Sutherland, Howard and Markauskaite 2010) and these are the foundation of what we see teachers do each day with each of their learners.

While the teachers in this project did not refer to the teacher standards directly, they spoke of core elements common to teaching across contexts, including specialised skills to support learners with SLD/PMLD. As Teacher 1 said:

> I think all the qualities of what it is to be a teacher generally apply, but I think that to teach students with complex disabilities you need to be very flexible and keen to overcome different barriers, particularly barriers to learning.

Similarly, Teacher 6 commented:

> I think that being a teacher of students with complex needs requires an extra dimension of creativity, perseverance and patience to observe and learn from the student. Timing and responsiveness are key as is the designing and implementation of a meaningful, holistic curriculum.

Teacher 3 listed her priorities of what teachers of learners with SLD/PMLD need to know, including:

> How to build relationships with outside professionals and families to ensure consistency across all environments.

Teaching as a vocation

While all teachers in this project acknowledge the importance of the concrete teaching skills and commonality of motivations among all teachers, six shared a strong belief that being a teacher of learners with SLD/PMLD involved a vocation *to their specific profession*. They spoke of their own professional identities in terms of selecting to teach pupils with the most severe and complex needs as a vocation. For example:

> It is a vocation really, it's about making a difference and it's about changing lives. A vocation is about something that not everyone can do.
>
> (Teacher 2)

> I also think a vocation is probably something you've had for a very long time. For me, I always wanted to be a teacher.
>
> (Teacher 1)

In referring to all teachers, Beauchamp and Thomas (2009) found that one of the reasons any teacher chooses to enter the profession is an 'inherent passion and vocation for the job and interest and expertise in a subject area' (p. 3). Teachers in this project shared similar motivations, particularly with working with learners and families who have the greatest needs. Teacher 2 illustrates this:

> I think it's [teaching learners with PMLD] something that you have to have a passion for to make a difference. I do think it's not something that everybody can do.
>
> (Teacher 2)

Being different from mainstream teaching

Cimera (2003) points out that a particular difference between special and mainstream education is in the focus of each. She states, 'Special education is based upon the unique needs of individual students. Regular education, on the other hand, focuses upon the core content of the grade level or subject matter' (p. 6). As Cimera also points out, this does not mean that regular education teachers do not care about individual learners who are falling behind or require extra help. Imray and Hinchcliffe (2012) suggest that distinct kinds of teaching, distinct and separate pedagogies and curricula are required for teaching learners with SLD. Six teachers in the current project talked about teaching learners with SLD/PMLD as being different from mainstream teaching. While they acknowledged that special and general educators share some qualities, they voiced that teaching learners with SLD/PMLD is different in the steps involved in the teaching process. As one teacher said:

> In one sense, it is no different from working with mainstream learners as you still have all the same high expectations; and in another it is completely different as the methods and means you employ are so different and change is very much in small, very small steps.
>
> (Teacher 5)

Duffy and Forgan (2005) discussed unique knowledge and skills that special educators need to have. This unique knowledge includes specialised assessments, instructional practices, and understandings of medical characteristics of learners.

Another teacher says:

> [Being a teacher of learners with SLD/PMLD requires] a greater degree of conscious attempt at engaging the other.
>
> (Teacher 4)

While it may be common across the teaching profession for teachers to employ a variety of methods using small, graduated steps and making a conscious effort to engage others, these teachers perceive the necessity and demand for these as different from the experience of other teachers.

Another area where teachers saw differences between themselves and mainstream teachers is in the nature of the collaborative work they engage with on a daily basis. The complexity of learner need necessitates intensive collaborative partnering with other professionals and families. As Teacher 1 says about her role:

> I think to be a team player is different to being an individual teacher in a classroom where you don't really have to interact with that many adults.
>
> (Teacher 1)

This supports the idea of collaboration as an important part of teaching (Pugach and Johnson 2002). Indeed, it represents the reality of professional life of the teacher of learners with SLD/PMLD as managing a large network of professional and family partnerships. According to Aird (2000), there may be up to 25 different professionals involved in meeting the complex needs of a single learner with SLD/PMLD.

Identity as a teacher

There has been much research related to teacher identity and how teachers identify with the teaching profession. Some have reported the importance of emotion in the development of teacher identity (Nias 1996; Sutton and Wheatley 2003), others on the relationship of emotional knowledge about teaching and learning to pedagogical content knowledge (Zembylas 2007), and others on teacher motivation as a factor in teachers' self-definitions of professional competence (Kunter 2013). Teachers' evolving commitments to the profession and to social justice have also been highlighted as important to understanding teacher identity (Merseth, Sommer and Dickstein 2008; Olsen 2008), as well as an appreciation of contextual influences (Beijaard, Meijer and Verloop 2004; Gee 2001).

All teachers in this project spoke of their professional identity. For one teacher, her professional teacher identity began to take form at an early age:

> For me, it was always something that I always wanted to be a teacher. I remember when I was very young, you know, being at home and making my sister pretend we were in a classroom. And it was a real passion for me from a very young age.
>
> (Teacher 1)

Several teachers viewed teaching as a privilege with inherent rewards, seeing themselves as integral to the building of a better world by improving the lives of their pupils. For example:

It is a privilege to be moulding tomorrow's citizens. It gives me a sense of belonging to a community.

(Teacher 3)

To be a teacher is essentially a privilege; society has given us the opportunity to help mould, shape and influence the minds, souls and bodies of the next generation.

(Teacher 5)

[Teaching is] rewarding in the classroom, to see the joy learners get from their own achievement.

(Teacher 7)

These comments support Manvell's (2009) view that there is a privilege associated to spending time with other peoples' children for a large portion of the day with the responsibility to improve their lives. Our teachers indicated that it is important to be able to feel that they as teachers make a contribution to society.

For one teacher, understandings of professional identity are embedded in the emotional challenges she encountered as a teacher and the innovative and creative ways to respond in responding to those challenges:

[Teaching is] an emotional challenge in which you attempt to engage another human in a shared activity in which learning and experiencing something new is the focus.

(Teacher 4)

Another teacher commented on the challenges that extend beyond the classroom, reflecting on the demands on her as a teacher beyond actual teaching within the schoolhouse walls. In explaining the nature of teaching, she stated that teaching learners with PMLD is:

… exhausting outside the classroom in terms of the tomes of paperwork, which also makes it frustrating, because of the time it takes away from making resources for learners.

(Teacher 7)

In this teacher's view, the amount of time required to fulfil increased administrative requirements that are not essential to actual teaching of learners with PMLD reduces the amount of time, and thus inhibits her ability, to devote toward instructional design and lesson planning. This supports studies that indicate the additional paperwork required of SEN teachers contribute to reduced SEN teacher retention and job satisfaction (Antoniou, Polychroni, and Walters 2000; Billingsley 2004).

In speaking of their professional identities, four teachers in this project indicated that being a teacher of learners with SLD/PMLD requires patience, the ability to *think outside the box*, work with others, open-mindedness, and positive attitudes to a greater degree than their mainstream counterparts. For example:

Anybody who teaches, not just special needs kids, are the same person. But I do think you have to have a level of patience and an ability to think outside the box, and be prepared possibly to push the boundaries of what you're doing [more] than in a mainstream school, maybe.

(Teacher 1)

And, from another teacher:

> I think that people who work with children with complex needs do have very positive attitudes and are people who, the ones that are more effective, are people who can think outside the box and they're always striving to make things better and not really accepting of the status quo.
>
> (Teacher 2)

And from yet another teacher:

> Being a teacher of students with complex needs requires an extra dimension of creativity, perseverance and patience to observe and learn from the student.
>
> (Teacher 6)

Person-centred teaching

Teachers of learners with SLD/PMLD have responsibility for interpreting and assigning meaning to the behaviours of many of their pupils (Foreman *et al.* 2004). Four teachers commented on the importance of person-centred teaching in working with learners with SLD/PMLD. One teacher talked about the development of highly sophisticated personalised learning that emerged from the challenge of interpreting the National Curriculum for her school:

> That's when we came up with this idea of having personalised learning plans, and what they might look like. And it's developed from there really as we've moved on from just this idea of having a personalised curriculum to recognising that it's got to be about each child's engagement in the activities that you give them.
>
> (Teacher 2)

Although personalised learning plans are considered common in schools, this has not always been the case, as this teacher points out. It was this teacher's experience that personalised learning plans were a response to the National Curriculum and required a new way of thinking about educating learners with the most severe and complex learning needs.

Another teacher stated the importance of person-centred teaching simply as:

> I think firstly, that you need to listen to the young people themselves and their parents (and) teach individuals and not disabilities.
>
> (Teacher 1)

This teacher emphasised that, while understanding the common characteristics of a particular disability contributes to understandings that support teaching, it is understandings of the individual learner's needs and characteristics that are of greater importance in promoting optimum success for her students. This underlines the importance of teachers' knowledge and understanding of characteristics common to learners with SLD/PMLD, but also the need for teachers to provide a relevant, balanced, and broadly based curriculum through lesson planning and instruction that takes learners' individual needs into account.

And another teacher, speaking of what she believed policymakers should be aware of about teaching learners with SLD/PMLD, said:

> ... *it* is about identifying potential in everyone and engineering opportunities for that individual to try and reach that potential. It is about building the bridge between what is possible and what could be possible.
>
> (Teacher 6)

Person-centred teaching and learning is described as an educational process in which the teacher acts as a facilitator of learning through personalised and customised learning activities, social and emotional supports, learner self-regulation, and collaborative and authentic learning experiences (Hanover Research 2012). The teachers in this project are in agreement with this. Indeed, their views are akin to the Department of Health's (2010) advice for using person-centred teaching in schools. This highlights the importance of defining what content and skills are important for the learner in the present and in the future, as well as analysing which teaching practices are working and which are not and understanding why, particularly for the individual learner. Specifically, they cite the following as some of the practical implications of a person-centred approach:

a   identifying the most important ways in which to represent the subject matter.
b   creating an optimal classroom climate for learning
c   monitoring learning and providing feedback
d   acknowledging that all learners can reach criteria for success
e   influencing surface and deep learner outcomes.

Conclusion

We began this chapter by asking what we can learn by listening to teachers of learners with SLD/PMLD. This chapter shows that their perspectives can be a valuable contribution to professional understandings of teaching and learning for learners with SLD/PMLD. We have presented the perspectives of a small group of teachers who teach learners with SLD/PMLD. The teachers talked about what it is to be a teacher, and then, more specifically, a teacher of this group of learners. They also discussed what they considered teachers need to know to be successful in teaching learners with SLD/PMLD.

Through the teachers' voices we hear that teaching is viewed by them as a vocation inextricably linked to their identity as a teacher whose work makes a difference in the lives of others. As previously noted, this is similar to the researched views of mainstream teachers. However, for this group of teachers of learners with SLD/PMLD, it is the intensity of the collaborative and highly personalised teaching that, in their view, demarcates them from mainstream teachers.

Questions for readers

The study reported in this chapter raises additional questions about the perspectives of teachers of learners with SLD/PMLD which, when explored, will offer greater insights into how this group of teachers make meaning of teaching:

*   How do teacher perspectives of teaching learners with SLD/PMLD as a vocation contribute to their identity in collaborative contexts where there are a range of professionals working?
*   To what extent do teachers of learners with SLD/PMLD view mainstream teaching as different from what they do?
*   How can listening to teachers' voices make a difference in classroom practice?

Readers are invited to contact the chapter authors for further details on the methods of data collection used in this project.

References

Aird, R. (2000) 'The case for specialist training for learning support assistants employed in schools for children with severe, profound and multiple learning difficulties', *Support for Learning*, 15(3), 106–110.

Antoniou, A.S., Polychroni, F. and Walters, B. (2000) Sources of stress and professional burnout of special education needs teachers in Greece. Paper presented to the International Special Education Congress, 24–28 July 2000. Online. Available: www.isec2000.org.uk/abstracts/papers_p/polychroni_1.htm (accessed 23 March 2014).

Beauchamp, C. and Thomas, L. (2009) 'Understanding teacher identity: an overview of issues in the literature and implications for teacher education', *Cambridge Journal of Education*, 39(2), 175–189.

Beijaard, D., Meijer, P. and Verloop, N. (2004) 'Reconsidering research on teachers' professional identity', *Teaching and Teacher Education*, 20(2), 107–128.

Billingsley, B. S. (2004) 'Special education teacher retention and attrition: A critical analysis of the research literature', *Journal of Special Education*, 38(1), 39–55.

Bransford, J., Darling-Hammond, L. and LePage, P. (2005) 'Introduction', in L. Darling-Hammond and J. Bransford (eds) *Preparing Teachers for a Changing World: What teachers should learn and be able to do*, San Francisco, CA: Jossey-Bass.

Buchanan, E. (2009) 'Online survey tools: ethical and methodological concerns of human research ethics committees', *Journal of Empirical Research on Human Research Ethics: An International Journal*, 4(2), 37–48.

Burn, K. (2007) 'Professional knowledge and identity in a contested discipline: challenges for student teachers and teacher educators', *Oxford Review of Education*, 33(4), 445–467.

Cimera, R.E. (2003) *The Truth about Special Education: A guide for parents and teachers*, Lanham, MD: Scarecrow Press.

Corbett, J. (1996) *Bad-Mouthing: The language of special needs*, London: Falmer Press.

De Bortoli, T., Arthur-Kelly, M., Mathisen, B., Foremen, P. and Balandin, S. (2010) 'Where are teachers' voices? A research agenda to enhance the communicative interactions of students with multiple and severe disabilities at school', *Disability and Rehabilitation*, 32(13), 1059–1072.

Denzin, N.K. and Lincoln, and Y.S. (2008) 'Introduction: the discipline and practice of qualitative research', in Denzin N. and Lincoln Y. (eds), *Strategies of Qualitative Inquiry*, Thousand Oaks, CA: Sage Publications.

Department for Education (DfE) (2013) *Teachers' Standards*. Online. Available: www.gov.uk/government/uploads/system/uploads/attachment_data/file/208682/Teachers_Standards_2013.pdf (accessed 23 March 2014).

Department of Health (DoH) (2010) *Person-centred Planning: advice for using person-centred thinking, planning and reviews in schools and transition*, London: Department of Health Publications.

Duffy, M.L. and Forgan, J. (2005) *Mentoring New Special Education Teachers: a guide for mentors and program developers*, Thousand Oaks, CA: Corwin Press.

Farkas, S., Johnson, J. and Foleno, T. (2000) *A Sense of Calling: who teaches and why. A report from Public Agenda*, New York: Public Agenda Foundation.

Foreman, P., Arthur-Kelly, M., Pascoe, S. and Smyth-King, B. (2004) 'Evaluating the educational experiences of students with profound and multiple disabilities in inclusive and segregated classroom settings: an Australian perspective', *Research Practice for Persons with Severe Disabilities*, 29,183–193.

Gee, J. P. (2001) 'Identity as an analytic lens for research in education', *Review of Research in Education*, 25, 99–125.

Goodson, I. (ed.) (1992) *Studying Teachers' Lives*, London: Routledge.

Hammerness, K. (2006) *Seeing Through Teachers' Eyes: Professional ideals and classroom practices*, New York: Teachers College Press.

Hanover Research (2012) *Best practices in person-centered education*, Washington, DC: Hanover Research.

Imray, P. and Hinchcliffe, V. (2012) 'Not fit for purpose: A call for separate and distinct pedagogies as part of a national framework for those with severe and profound learning difficulties', *Support for Learning*, 27(4), 150–157.

Jones, P. (2004a) '"They are not like us and neither should they be": issues of teacher identity for teachers of pupils with complex learning disabilities', *Disability in Society*, 19(2), 159–169.

Jones, P. (2004b) 'Teachers' understandings of pupils with profound and multiple learning disabilities and the possible impact on assessment in the classroom', *PMLD Link*, 16(3), 19–23.

Jones, P. (2014) 'Whose insider perspectives count and why should we consider them?', in P. Jones (ed.) *Pushing the Boundaries: Developing inclusive practices through integration of insider perspectives,* London: Routledge College Press.

Kelchtermans, G. (1993) 'Getting the story, understanding the lives: from career stories to teachers' professional development', *Teaching and Teacher Education*, 9, 5–6, 443–456.

Kelchtermans, G. (2009) 'Who I am in how I teach is the message: self-understanding, vulnerability and reflection', *Teachers and Teaching*, 15(2), 257–272.

Kunter, M. (2013) 'Motivation as an aspect of professional competence: research findings on teacher enthusiasm', in M. Kunter, J. Baumert, W. Blum, U. Klusmann, S. Krauss, and M. Neubrand (eds), *Cognitive Activation in the Mathematics Classroom and Professional Competence of Teachers*, New York: Springer.

Manvell, E. (2009) *Teaching is a Privilege: Twelve essential understandings for beginning teachers*, Lanham, MD: Rowman and Littlefield Education.

Merseth, K.K., Sommer, J. and Dickstein, S. (2008) 'Bridging worlds: changes in personal and professional identities of pre-service urban teachers', *Teacher Education Quarterly*, 35(3), 89–108.

Narayan, J., Bruce, S., Bhandarià, R. and Kolli, P. (2010) 'Cognitive functioning of children with severe intellectual disabilities and children with deafblindness: a study of the perceptions of teachers and parents in the USA and India', *Journal of Applied Research in Intellectual Disabilities*, 23, 263–278.

Nias, J. (1989) *Primary Teachers Talking: A study of teaching as work*, London: Routledge.

Nias, J. (1996) 'Thinking about feeling: the emotions in teaching', *Cambridge Journal of Education*, 26(3), 293–306.

Olsen, B. (2008) 'How reasons for entry into the profession illuminate teacher identity development', *Teacher Education Quarterly*, 35(3), 23–40.

Pugach, M.C. and Johnson, L.J. (2002) *Collaborative Practitioners, Collaborative Schools*, Denver, CO: Love Publishing Company.

Soto, G., Muller, E., Hunt, P. and Goetz, L. (2001) 'Critical issues in the inclusion of students who use augmentative and alternative communication: an educational team perspective', *Augmentative and Alternative Communication*, 17, 62–72.

Sutherland, L., Howard, S., and Markauskaite, L. (2010) 'Professional identity creation: examining the development of beginning preservice teachers' understanding of their work as teachers', *Teaching and Teacher Education*, 26(3), 455–465.

Sutton, R. and Wheatley, K. (2003) 'Teachers' emotions and teaching: a review of the literature and directions for future research', *Educational Psychology Review*, 15, 327–358.

Tripp, D. (1994) 'Teachers' lives, critical incidents, and professional practice', *International Journal of Qualitative Studies in Education*, 7(1), 65–76.

West, E., Jones, P., Chambers, D., and Whitehurst, T. (2012) 'A multi-perspective collaborative on teacher learning for teachers of students with Autism Spectrum Disorder ', *Journal of International Special Needs Education,* 15(1), 24–40.

Zembylas, M. (2007) 'Emotional ecology: the intersection of emotional knowledge and pedagogical content knowledge in teaching', *Teaching and Teacher Education*, 23(4), 355–367.

14

UPS AND DOWNS

How learners with SLD/PMLD view their school experience

Elizabeth Henderson, Julia Barnes and Nicola Grove

In this chapter, the following questions will be addressed:

- Does the curriculum allow us to take the time for learners to tell us what they really feel about school?
- Do the learning challenges we set take account of the perspectives of the learners?
- How can we best find out about the real experiences of these young people?

Introduction

This book would not be complete without some representation of the views of the young people concerned; now regarded as good practice in a range of settings (Clark and Moss 2011; Lewis and Porter 2004; Franklin and Sloper 2009; Palikara *et al.* 2009; Roulstone and McLeod 2011; Ware 2004). Here, we present the views and experiences of four learners, gained through interviews with 'Talking Mats' (Murphy and Cameron 2008), and through participant observation.

Georgia, Lucy and Daniel – learners with SLD

Georgia, Lucy and Daniel, all aged 15, attend a special school, for learners with a wide range of Special Educational Needs. At the time of writing, they were preparing to move on from the main school into classes for young adults. Georgia is vivacious and giggly, and enjoys designing clothes, watching a popular TV soap opera, and eating chocolate. She is determined, and likes to be asked her opinion, rather than being told what to do. Lucy is bubbly, smiley, kind and sometimes cheeky. She enjoys dancing, especially to her favourite band, 'Steps'. Her understanding is helped by the use of simple language, and by being given time to plan her replies. Daniel is a confident, caring, hard-working charming young man. Even when challenged by his unpredictable behaviours and anxieties, he likes to have a sociable chat with those who are giving him the high levels of support he requires. He has a diagnosis of autism in addition to his learning difficulties. All three students are verbal communicators.

A Talking Mat is an interactive resource which provides a visual framework with photos and symbols to help people with communication difficulties think about topics and express their views. To illustrate, Daniel's Talking Mat measured 40cm × 60cm. Daniel assembled it during the interview described below, using 14 photos, each measuring 12cm × 9cm. The photos depicted particular places and activities. On the mat at the top were placed three symbols for 'like', 'not sure' and 'don't like'. The photos were placed in groups underneath these symbols as appropriate to Daniel's views.

Figure 14.1   Daniel's talking mat'

Georgia and Lucy were interviewed together, by their speech and language therapist (Liz Henderson), with a member of the class team present (Mr L). Daniel was interviewed separately with two staff members in support. All the sessions were filmed for later transcription. As preparation for use of the Talking Mat, we first played the 'sandwich making' game. Symbols of familiar food items were presented one at a time and the learners were asked to categorise them into the 'like', 'dislike' and 'not sure' areas of the mat. Well-known favourites and some highly unlikely items were included, in order to test reliability. All three learners responded reliably and consistently. What follows are their opinions of their school environment, curriculum and experiences, expressed in their own words.

Georgia and Lucy

	Liz:	Let's introduce ourselves first… I'm Liz and I work at TW school.
	Georgia:	I'm Georgia. At TW school.
	Lucy	My name is Lucy.
Sensory room	Liz:	Let's look at some photos of school. You decide where to put them. Tell me what you think.
	Georgia:	The sensory room. Yes, I like that one. I like the lights here. The lights show up nice.
Lift	Georgia:	That's a lift. I like it. Because of my knees, then yes.
	Liz:	How does the lift help your knees?
	Georgia:	Really good
	Liz:	What happens when you walk up the stairs?
	Georgia:	Pops out
	Liz:	You are worried that your knee will pop out?
	Georgia:	Yes. I like the lift best.
	Lucy:	I like it. Up… and down
	Liz:	Do you like the lift or stairs best?
	Lucy:	Lift
	Liz:	What is good about it?
	Lucy:	Pressing the buttons
Playground	Georgia:	In the playground, I don't like this bit (*points to main play area*). I like that bit…
	Liz:	The gazebo part?
	Georgia:	Yes, I can sit down and play with Briony
Art room	Georgia:	I don't like that.
	Liz:	You don't like the art room?
	Georgia:	No
	Liz:	Do you like doing art at all?
	Georgia:	No
	Liz:	We did painting last week. Do you like painting?
	Georgia:	No
	Lucy:	I like it – painting, in the art room
	Georgia:	(*Sighs and shakes her head, then puts her head on the table*)
	Liz:	Oh dear, Georgia, you really don't like art!
	Georgia:	No!

Science room	Liz:	That's the science room
	Georgia:	I like that one
	Liz:	Who is your teacher for science? Is it Miss K?
	Georgia:	Yes
	Liz:	What do you do in the science room?
	Georgia:	Don't know
PE hall	Georgia:	PE hall with Mr K. I like that one.
	Lucy:	(*Places photo on 'like' area of mat*)
	Liz:	Tell me about PE
	Lucy:	The cones, the bench. I walk and balance.
	Liz:	Who is your teacher for PE?
	Lucy:	Mr L
	Georgia:	No, it's not. It's Mr K.
	Lucy:	No, Mr L!
	Georgia:	No, Mr K!
	Liz:	Does Mr L help you during PE, Lucy?
	Lucy:	Oh, yes
	Liz	What do you like doing in PE, Georgia?
	Georgia:	Running and on the beams. Yes. I like that.
Food Tech room	Lucy:	Cooking – like it. Pizza and cheese.
	Liz:	Do you like to cook anything else?
	Lucy:	Kebab and chips
	Georgia:	I like it. It's good
Minibus	Liz:	Trips out in the minibus
	Lucy:	Aha – I like that!
	Liz:	Where do you go?
	Lucy:	Macdonalds
	Georgia:	And the park
	Lucy:	Yes and shops
	Liz:	Did we go somewhere with animals?
	Lucy:	Monkeys?
	Liz:	Yes, monkeys and lions
	Georgia:	Bristol
	Lucy:	Yes, Bristol
	Liz:	Bristol?
	Lucy:	Bristol Zoo!

Their own classroom	Lucy:	Miss M (class teacher) (*puts photo in 'like' area of mat*)
	Liz:	Yes, Miss M is in your class room. You like learning in your classroom?
	Lucy:	Yes, like Miss M
	Liz:	How does she help you?
	Lucy:	Have a drink and snack
	Liz:	Georgia, what do you like about your classroom?
	Georgia:	One thing is Miss M. But I don't like when she asks me hard questions. She doesn't do homework with me. She doesn't do French, Art, DT.
	Liz:	(*laughs*) You don't like art in the art room?
	Georgia:	No
	Liz:	What about DT? (*offers photo of Design and Technology room*)
	Georgia:	No, don't like (*places photo in 'don't like' area of mat*)
	Liz:	French?
	Georgia:	No
	Liz:	Do you have different teachers for these?
	Georgia:	Yes
	Liz:	Lucy, What do you think about DT? (*offers photo of DT room*)
	Lucy:	No, I don't like
Leisure centre (swimming) and school hydro pool	Georgia:	I like swimming but not here. This one I like (*leisure centre*) and this one not (*school pool*)
	Liz:	What do you learn to do?
	Georgia:	Miss H takes me there. Learn to float.
	Liz:	I wonder which Lucy likes best? School pool or the swimming baths?
	Georgia:	Lucy, you like school swimming or swimming baths?
	Lucy:	That one (*places swimming baths photo on 'like' area of mat*)
	Georgia:	That one? (*points*)
	Lucy:	Yes, I go on the coach
	Liz:	And then?
	Lucy:	My bag off. Get dry.
	Liz:	Get dry? You haven't been swimming yet!
	Lucy and Georgia:	(*Fits of giggles*)
	Liz:	Take your bag off and then…
	Lucy:	Go swimming
	Liz:	What do you learn?
	Lucy:	Going backwards

	Liz:	What do you do afterwards?
	Lucy:	Get dry. Back to school. Have lunch
Dining hall	Liz:	What about school lunch?
	Lucy:	I don't like it. I like packed lunch.
School toilet	Georgia:	The toilets. I don't like this
	Liz:	Tell me about it
	Georgia:	When you go to toilet, you can't even shut the door. People might see. Toilet at home is good. Shut the door and lock it!
	Lucy:	Toilet (*puts in 'like' area of mat*)
	Liz:	What do you think about the toilet?
	Lucy:	I wash my hands
Soft play room	Georgia:	Soft play room (*places in 'like' area of mat*)
	Liz:	Do you go there?
	Georgia:	No. Long time ago. Good. It has a trampoline.
	Lucy:	Soft play room. Balls. I like. And Georgia… throw ball at her (*laughing*)
	Georgia:	Yes. Throw balls! (*lots of laughing*)
Talking about people who help us	Liz:	Who helps you to learn at school
	Georgia:	Mr H (*a Teaching Assistant*)
	Lucy:	Mr L (*a Teaching Assistant*) and Miss M (*class teacher*)
	Liz:	Do your friends help you?
	Lucy:	Yes, when they give me cake and custard
	Liz:	When they give you cake?
	Lucy:	Yes!
Talking about school clubs	Liz:	Lucy, you go to some clubs at school? (*Georgia did not attend any school clubs at the time, but joined in discussing Lucy's*)
	Lucy:	Yes, football club
	Liz:	Any other clubs?
	Lucy:	Aha
	Georgia:	(*looking at Lucy and prompting her by counting off the clubs on her fingers*) Bike club
	Lucy:	Bike club
	Georgia:	And trampoline, don't you Lucy?
	Lucy:	Yes, trampoline, bounce bounce
	Georgia:	(*prompting Lucy*) And football with Mr H and trampolining with Mr H
	Lucy:	Yes with Mr H
	Georgia:	(*prompting Lucy again*) And running with Mr H?

	Liz:	Running too?
	Lucy:	Yes
	Liz:	Lots of clubs! Do you enjoy them?
	Lucy:	Yes and we have drink and snacks
	Liz:	Which is your favourite?
	Lucy:	Football with Mr H
Talking about moving to 'sixth form'	Liz:	Tell me about after the summer holidays. Is everything going to be the same... or different?
	Georgia:	Different
	Liz:	What will happen? Will you be in the same class?
	Georgia:	We'll be in sixth form
	Liz:	Are you going to sixth form too, Lucy?
	Lucy:	Yes
	Georgia:	Not Mr L though!
	Liz:	Is Mr L not going to sixth form with you? Oh dear.
	Mr L:	Yes I am
	Lucy:	Oh Mr L! (*lots of laughing*)
	Liz:	Will you still have clubs in sixth form?
	Lucy:	Yes. I like clubs.

Georgia and Lucy have some decided views, and individualised preferences. The focus is on specific areas of the school, but both are able to think beyond this and talk about what they do, and who with. Taking each in turn, Georgia is very conscious of her walking difficulties – going upstairs is a problem, and perhaps this is why she prefers to sit down with a friend in the playground; though we note that she enjoys structured exercise and trips. Some of our assumptions are challenged by Georgia's views: we can't be the only ones to think that art will be the favourite subject for learners with special needs! It is possible that Georgia's aversion to art is related to where it is usually taught (the specialist art room, upstairs), since she also doesn't like going to the first floor Design and Technology (DT) room. She prefers her classroom and the sensory room (on the same floor). Although she says that she likes the science room (upstairs), it seems that she is probably commenting on the subject, rather than the location, as she is actually taught science in her own classroom. Georgia also values places that used to be part of her curriculum and no longer are. Georgia is clear that school is a place for learning, and can involve hard questions. Finally, we see that in common with many other learners (IpsosMORI 2012) school toilets are to be avoided. Georgia's reflections on her need for privacy are very powerful.

Lucy's school experience feels more governed by sensory activities than Georgia's – specifically, food is a big preoccupation. Lucy does need to manage her diet, and this interview serves as a reminder of how all-consuming hunger is likely to be for some learners. Can you concentrate on learning when you are wondering where the next snack is coming from? However, to balance this, Lucy is also very keen on sport and physical activity. Both girls indicate the importance of the specific people who teach and support them. They mention the same staff repeatedly, in relation to activities and lessons that they enjoy. Lucy's favourite club is not just 'football' but 'football with Mr H'. Georgia and Lucy both speak about Miss M, their class teacher, when considering the photo of their (empty) classroom. We note also that their views on school are jointly constructed – as Small *et al.* (2013) point out, we form opinions through reciprocal interactions, not in isolation.

Daniel

The school exterior	Liz:	We're going to talk about school.
	Daniel:	I like school. I see my friends at school.
	Liz:	You like it?
	Daniel:	I do like it
	Liz:	And how do you get to school?
	Daniel:	I come to school on the bus every morning. With Steve (*school transport driver*). He picks me up every day. How nice!
School library	Daniel:	I like books.
	Liz:	You do?
	Daniel:	Because I want to learn to read the books properly.
Playground	Daniel:	I like to play outside with my friends, running around (*still holding photo*)
	Liz:	How do you feel about the playground?
	Daniel:	Hmmmm… not sure (*places photo in 'not sure' area of mat*)
Special 'safe' room	Daniel:	I don't like it. No, I don't like.
	Liz:	Can you tell me about it?
	Daniel:	Well, I go there on bad days.
	Liz:	When you have a bad day?
	Daniel:	Yes. Well, it's Mr L and Miss D that put me in there, when I am making bad choices. Well, what do I do? (*looks at Miss D*) What do I do? When I get mad, I go in there and I take my shoes off and Mr L does too – even him!
	Liz:	Does your special room help you?
	Daniel:	Yes. Because it helps me calm down a bit. Because it is hard talking about it and talking isn't any good at all. I'm not sure about the writing on the walls.
	Liz:	Do you write on the blackboards on the walls?
	Daniel:	No. It's someone else.
Soft play room	Daniel:	I came into this room years ago. I liked it. I came in with (*Miss*) K on every Wednesday. Mr L threw balls at me. And Miss D. We went crazy. I held up a cushion, like this. We threw the balls and threw the balls. Very funny. I want to go there again. (*Daniel is currently unable to safely access this room*)

PE hall	Daniel:	In the PE hall, I am anxious about the lights – the disco lights and the stage lights. Last year we did a story show in here. Mr L dressed up in a funny dress. It was Cinderella (*places photo in 'not sure' area of mat*)
	Liz:	You are not sure about the PE hall?
	Daniel:	I'm not sure, well it's on a Friday and I am anxious.
	Liz:	Do you enjoy PE?
	Daniel:	Yes I enjoy it. With Mr K in PE, I learn tricks. And he told me it is good to eat tomato salad to keep fit for PE. But I do like bacon and egg sandwich for breakfast.
Minibus	Daniel:	It's the minibus
	Liz:	Yes, going out in the minibus with your class
	Daniel:	It is great (*puts photo into 'don't like' area of mat*)
	Liz:	You don't like it?
Music Therapist	Liz:	Do you recognise this picture?
	Daniel:	It's A.. He comes every Wednesdays and he comes to my class.
	Liz:	What do you learn with A.?
	Daniel:	I learn music. I learn to play music with my friend, H. And I like Joseph and his dream coat music. You (*Liz*) talk about that with me in my class, don't you? We sing and I dance.
Classroom	Liz:	This is your classroom, Daniel
	Daniel:	Well, with Miss M, but she has gone.
	Liz:	Miss M isn't here today, is she?
	Daniel:	No. She's not well
	Liz:	What do you like in your classroom? What helps you to learn?
	Daniel:	I learn from my friends.
	Liz:	Your friends help you to learn?
	Daniel:	Yes, and my teachers help me. When I feel tired I sleep here, on my black beanbag. I did sleep today. Then I am happy. Before I was tired I had toast.
	Liz:	Daniel, where will you put the classroom?
	Daniel:	Here. I'm not sure about it.
	Liz:	Not sure?
	Daniel:	Yes. Not sure.
Swimming baths	Daniel:	Swimming. I don't go to swimming, it's in the big town. You know that place.
	Liz:	Bath?
	Daniel:	Yes. It's a special place. Too many people
	Liz:	Do you swim at school?

	Daniel:	No. I'll put it here. Not sure. (*Daniel was finding it challenging to participate safely in swimming at the time of the interview*)
IT room	Daniel:	I don't go to the computer room, because we have iPads in the classroom. I use an iPad like Ed (*points at 'camera man' and gives thumbs up sign*). So I've got three iPads. Respite have got one, school, and home. My Dad got one for his birthday.
	Liz:	So you don't need to go to the IT room, because you use the iPads?
	Daniel:	Yes I do. I like it. I want to go there.
Lift	Daniel:	The lifts are for my friends in the wheelchairs – R and H and C. And Miss T and Mrs McM and even Miss L. They go in there all together.
	Liz:	Do Miss T and Miss L need to go in the lift?
	Daniel:	Yes, because they push the wheelchairs (*places photo in 'like' area of mat*)
	Liz:	You like the lift, because it helps your friends?
	Daniel:	I really do, yes. And M (*another friend*). M loves lifts.
	Liz:	M does?
	Daniel:	Yes, because of the doors closing. M is in my class and he thinks it is funny.
	Liz:	Do you use the lift?
	Daniel:	No, the stairs.
Food technology room	Daniel:	The cookery room. I make cakes. I do them with eggs. And we do rice krispies
	Liz:	Rice Krispie cakes?
	Daniel:	Yes
	Liz:	Mmmm delicious
	Daniel:	With chocolate over the top
	Liz:	We've talked about all these things at school. Is there anything else that helps you at school?
	Daniel:	Well, being outside to play helps me to calm down.
	Liz:	Is there anything else you want to tell me about school?
	Daniel:	I am going to respite this afternoon. They have an iPad too. I will use it.
	Liz:	Does the iPad help you to learn?
	Daniel:	Yes, but only at school. At respite I use it to play.
	Liz:	Is there anything else you want to talk about?
	Daniel:	Yes, I would like to talk to my friends (*turns to face Mr L and Miss D, his support staff, grinning broadly and pointing at photo of soft play room*) I want to go to that room, please. Can I?

Daniel seems highly aware of both his strengths and his learning needs. He has strong views on what helps him to manage his outbursts – not talking, but physical activity. Like Georgia and Lucy, particular areas of the school have positive and negative associations for him; the 'special room' he sees as a punishment (despite the attempts of everyone to present the room as a safe place for time out); the sensory room and swimming that he loves but knows he cannot access are particularly poignant. Despite Daniel's difficulties, he expresses very positive attitudes to learning, to the efforts of staff to support him, and to his friends – it is noticeable that he makes more references to his peer group than Georgia and Lucy did. He is articulate about his complex emotions (anxious, happy, mad, calm, crazy, funny). And the conflicts in his life are very evident: the times he says one thing, but places an image in the opposite camp; the number of 'not sure' positions. So for Daniel, school seems to be somewhere where learning and play alternate, where there are great social possibilities, but where every experience is loaded with conflicting emotions, and places demands on his ability to manage them.

The insights gained from these three interviews lead us to question the extent to which we take on board the perspectives of young people as they go through school. Do we take enough account of their very concrete, sensory and immediate experiences of the school environment? Do we spend enough time learning from them about the strategies they find helpful in managing challenges (whether behavioural or to do with the 'hard questions' in learning?). Do our decisions about staffing arrangements and changes reflect the learning needs, styles and preferences of each pupil who will be affected? Do we acknowledge the loss of experiences as they move through their school lives – do we explain the differences clearly enough to them?

Sam: a learner with profound learning difficulties

Sam is a 14 year old with a strong mischievous personality who enjoys supporting Leeds Rhinos rugby club with his mum. He has cerebral palsy affecting all four limbs, shunt in situ, brittle bones, epilepsy, is registered blind but has some vision close up, and receives liquids and some nutrition through a gastrostomy. We explored Sam's school experience through participant observation: a volunteer who had experience of working with students with profound learning difficulties shadowed him throughout one school day, taking 200 photographs from his perspective, using an approach developed by Kaplan and colleagues (Kaplan and Howes 2004). The volunteer and his pastoral teacher Julia Barnes (who had taught him for two years and was aware of how he expresses himself) reviewed the photographs and identified those which showed Sam reacting, or not, to the different people and experiences in his day. This led to a lively discussion on what he was reacting to and how and what he was communicating. Twenty-seven photographs were selected to represent his day in chronological order, using captions which explained in the first person what was happening, e.g. 'I'm in the sensory room for ICT but the overhead lights are bothering me.' Sam was played a selection of tunes and his responses were interpreted to select a 'Glee' (a TV programme) song to accompany the slideshow of images and written captions. We do not think he can see the photographs clearly, but he responds to the music and looks towards a screen held close to his face as the images change. We were surprised how much information we elicited from the exercise.

He responded by clearly smiling and laughing at activities he enjoyed such as wheelchair dancing, live music, going over bumps in the road and using the trampoline. On two occasions he seemed to find the lighting in different rooms uncomfortable and communicated this by covering his eyes with his left 'useful' arm. He also communicated discomfort by placing his left hand behind his neck at his hairline and each time he did so someone responded to make him comfortable. This was interesting, as, although we are aware when Sam is uncomfortable, we did not have a key signal, and were responding intuitively. We were also surprised by the number of photos where he has his eyes shut until we realised that he does so to process a question or new/unexpected experience. This was something of which we had been previously unaware.

We noticed that Sam often appears with staff in the photographs rather than with his peers. Because of Sam's communication difficulties he has formed stronger bonds with the staff than his classmates. Other learners do interact with him, support him to use a communicator and chat to him. However none of this was captured on this particular day.

Sam was supported to use an iPad to show the slideshow at his transition annual review to show his mum and the professionals what a school day looks like, what he likes, what he didn't like (being uncomfortable and the lighting in some rooms), what he wasn't bothered about (having fluids given through his gastrostomy or being positioned by familiar people) and how he communicates this. They were all very positive about this insight into his school day. The slideshow will be used to support his transition into the next class, and to compose his communication passport (Millar and Aitken 2003).

It is a particularly challenging task to gain insights into the school experience of learners with profound disabilities. Here, tracking Sam and adopting his perspective on the world allows us to grasp the importance of environmental and physical aspects which we might not otherwise consider – the effects of light for example, which also affected Daniel. This reminds us of the critical significance of the role of building design in learning – several studies have been carried out on acoustic environments (Connolly *et al.* 2013) but lighting and visual environments appear to have received less attention and are ranked low in one relevant study (Barrett *et al.* 2013). We also learned from what was absent in the photos, the presence of peers, highlighting what may be a real ongoing issue for young people who are so dependent on staff to mediate their experiences.

Conclusion

Trying to adopt the perspective of learners with SLD/PMLD about their school experience leads us to abandon some preconceptions – for example, our focus on the academic curriculum – and to consider the sensory, physical and emotional aspects of education. The snapshots provided here are in no way presented as an overview or a generalisation. Rather they remind us of the unique individuality of each young person, and the need to ensure that our educational approach truly does put the learner at the centre of what we do.

The insights gained from our interviews and observations lead us to question the extent to which we take on board the perspectives of young people as they go through school. Looking at our original questions, our findings led us to conclude that we do need to make space within the curriculum and in target setting, for working with pupils: and that there are some useful tools now available to us for this purpose.

Questions for readers

- How do the learners you work with view your lessons and your interactions with them?
- What do they understand about changes in the learning environment as they move through school?
- How could you find out more about their perspectives?

Further reading

Roulstone, S. and McLeod, S. (eds) (2011*Listening to Children and Young People with Speech, Language and Communication Needs*, Guildford: J&R Press.

Acknowledgements

We are grateful to the young people concerned for the time they took to share their perspectives with us, and to Lucy Ratcliffe, who accompanied Sam during his school day.

Daniel, Georgia, Lucy and their parents wanted their own names to be used in this chapter as they are proud of their work together.

References

Barrett, P., Zhang, Y., Moffat, J. and Kobbacy, K. (2013) A holistic, multi-level analysis identifying the impact of classroom design on pupils' learning, *Building and Environment*, 59, 678–689.

Clark. A. and Moss, P. (2011) *Listening to Young Children: The mosaic approach*, London: National Children's Bureau.

Connolly, D., Dockrell, J., Shield, B., Conetta, R. and Cox, T. (2013) 'Adolescents' perceptions of their school's acoustic environment: the development of an evidence based questionnaire', *Noise and Health*, 15, 269–280.

Franklin, A. and Sloper, P. (2009) 'Supporting the participation of disabled children and young people in decision-making', *Children & Society*, 23(1), 3–15.

IpsosMori (2012) Young people in Scotland survey – Summary of findings for Scotland's Commissioner for Children and Young people. Online: www.slideshare.net/IpsosMORI/scotland-school-toiletsslides190313 (accessed 11 August 2014).

Kaplan, I. and Howes, A. (2004) 'Seeing through different eyes: exploring the value of participative research using images in schools', *Cambridge Journal of Education*, 34(2), 143–155.

Lewis, A., and Porter, J. (2004) 'Interviewing children and young people with learning disabilities: guidelines for researchers and multi-professional practice', *British Journal of Learning Disabilities*, 32, 191–197.

Millar, S. and Aitken, S. (2003) *Personal Communication Passports: Guidelines for good practice*, Edinburgh: CALL Scotland, University of Edinburgh.

Murphy, J. and Cameron, L. (2008) 'The effectiveness of Talking Mats® with people with intellectual disability', *British Journal of Learning Disabilities*, 36, 232–241.

Palikara, O., Lindsay, G. and Dockerell, J. (2009) 'Voices of young people with a history of specific language impairment (SLI) in the first year of post-16 education', *International Journal of Language & Communication Disorders*, 44, 56–78.

Roulstone, S. and McLeod, S. (2011) (eds) *Listening to Children and Young People with Speech, Language and Communication Needs*, Guildford: J&R Press.

Small, N., Raghavan, R. and Pawson, N. (2013) 'An ecological approach to seeking and utilising the views of young people with intellectual disabilities in transition planning', *Journal of Intellectual Disabilities*, 17(4), 283–300.

Ware, J. (2004) 'Ascertaining the views of people with profound and multiple learning disabilities', *British Journal of Learning Disabilities*, 32, 175–179.

PART III

Priorities for meeting the personal and social needs of learners

15

LEARNERS WITH SEVERE AND PROFOUND LEARNING DIFFICULTIES AND SENSORY IMPAIRMENTS

Liz Hodges and Mike McLinden

In this chapter, the following questions will be addressed:

- What is the effect of sensory impairments on learners with severe, profound and multiple learning difficulties?
- What strategies can be employed when teaching learners with SLD/PMLD and sensory impairments?

Introduction

In this chapter we examine the senses of vision and hearing and how these affect learning, development, communication, relationships and day-to-day life for learners with SLD/PMLD. Some key strategies and interventions are outlined, with key points illustrated through the examples of three people who have sensory impairment and learning disability: Victoria, Hikmat and Debbie.

Sensory impairment is sometimes described as being 'the least of their problems' when considering the needs of learners who have SLD/PMLD. Indeed, the dialogue of 'main presenting need' suggests that sensory impairment can be viewed as being a secondary or minor difficulty (Erin 2007). This chapter highlights, however, that sensory impairment can serve to compound, exacerbate, or even *cause* physical, cognitive or social and behavioural problems, and so should be considered at the heart of interacting needs and developmental difficulties. As an example, young children who do not see well may not be motivated to lift their heads to see what is going on around, thus not strengthening their necks, leading to difficulties in the development of trunk muscles, delay in balance and eventual physical delay. Similarly children who do not hear well may not be able to interpret the tone and mood of others, whether cross, or affectionate, or excited. Their emotional responses are therefore limited and they may appear to have social and relational difficulties.

The ability to use *remaining* (residual) vision or hearing may lead others to believe it is not a very significant problem or not to recognise it at all. Staff may not be prepared or trained in sensory losses. For someone with learning disability, hearing impairment, visual impairment or dual sensory impairment in fact affects all aspects of life. While glasses and hearing aids (including cochlear implants) can improve functional vision or hearing, and are essential where prescribed, hearing aids do not restore typical hearing and glasses frequently only solve some of the issues relating to vision.

Information and the distance senses

Vision and hearing are often described as being *distance senses* (for example, McLinden and McCall 2002). They provide information about the external world, such as who is talking (recognising the face, hearing the voice), or which train is coming (hearing the announcement, seeing the indicator). Perceptions of light travel through the retina (eyes) and sound vibration through the cochlea (ears) and are converted into electrical responses that go through the optic and auditory nerves to the brain. Notwithstanding the process in eyes and ears, without the brain, nothing is 'seen' or 'heard'. Of course, difficulties with the organs of eye and ear can affect the perceptions fed into the brain, but the brain receives and processes the information and allows the individual to act on it. Brain damage, whether congenital or caused by illness or trauma, may lead to related difficulty in sensory functioning. Adults with learning disability have been found to be 10 times more likely to have visual impairment than the rest of the population (Emerson and Robertson 2011) and somewhere between 40 and 89 per cent of people with learning disabilities may have hearing outside normal limits (Carvill 2001; Kerr *et al.* 2003).

A broad distinction is often made between *ocular* visual impairment and *cortical* (now usually called *cerebral*) visual impairment (McLinden and Douglas, 2013). Ocular conditions affect parts of the eye itself, and difficulties follow in functions such as the visual acuity and accommodation (how clearly things are seen, the ability to resolve detail and to focus) or field of vision (the area which can be seen), colour vision, and adaptability to light. Cerebral visual impairment (CVI) is where damage to the brain or the pathways to the brain results in difficulties in interpreting the visual environment (Corn and Erin 2010). CVI can also occur alongside ocular visual impairment and is a common cause of vision loss in people who have more complex needs.

Not everything that is the case for vision will necessarily have a counterpart in the field of hearing. Hearing is measured by intensity (volume) and frequency (pitch). The inability to hear sounds at certain volumes and certain pitches is diagnosed as hearing loss. The inability to interpret speech is not usually considered a hearing problem (for example, look up debates about Auditory Neuropathy Spectrum Disorder). There are three types of hearing loss: conductive (problems from the outer ear to the cochlea), sensori-neural (problems in the cochlea or the auditory nerve) and central (problems beyond the auditory nerve). It is possible to have combinations of these types referred to as mixed hearing loss (Watson 2003).

Deafblindness (dual sensory impairment, sometimes called MSI, or multi-sensory impairment) is a combination of impairments to vision and hearing, which causes problems with access to information, communication and mobility (Aitken 2000). Although most deafblind people have useful residual senses, either vision or hearing or both, the combination of combined mild impairments of vision and hearing has a multiplicative effect which causes far more difficulty than might be expected from the impact of each separately (McInnes and Treffry 1992). Most people use one sense to support the other, or those with a single sensory impairment use the other to compensate – people with deafblindness, however, usually cannot do this.

Victoria is three, she has cerebral visual impairment, profound and multiple learning difficulties and she does not walk. Her Education Health and Care Plan (EHCP) summarises her difficulties as follows:

> Victoria cannot see any fine detail in the world around her. She can see large bright or shiny objects when well contrasted with the background. At home she is attracted by bright moving images such as on TV. Given what she can reach for or notice in the environment, she is only distinguishing colour and movement from the TV.
>
> Victoria needs a structured environment in which to play with large, preferably yellow or orange toys, presented on a plain background. In supportive seating, which stabilises her trunk and enables her to use her arms, she can play briefly with an orange feather duster on her black tray, or a yellow ball (of about 25cm). She enjoys looking at toys which light up or shine and will lift her hands and arms (which is difficult for her) to interact with these.

Hikmat has Down syndrome. She has sensori-neural hearing loss, and sometimes glue ear (a conductive hearing loss). The following is part of her annual review:

> Following an intensive programme to support wearing of hearing aids, Hikmat has become somewhat more tolerant of them this year. Without them she frequently does not understand what is said and simply copies others. In context she can sometimes follow speech but in assembly or a class lesson, when asked, she has not understood much detail. In one to one sessions using her hearing aids her memory for sounds and instructions has improved a great deal. She can now complete 5 part sequences (matching a sound to a picture) and 4 part instructions in order. Her copying of speech has improved and this has made it easier to understand her.

Debbie has CHARGE syndrome. As with most people with CHARGE she has both impaired vision and hearing; her hearing loss is profound, and her vision poor. Her taste, smell, touch, balance and proprioception are also impaired. The following is part of her person centred plan:

> Debbie likes to sit with her feet on the speakers feeling the rhythmic vibration while very loud music plays. Very heavy rock is her favourite. She protests loudly about other music and bangs her head with her hands. She particularly likes looking at her family photographs while 'listening' in this way. She holds the pictures at odd angles and it helps if someone points out particular sections (marked on the back) of the pictures for her (which she apparently uses to identify them).

While Victoria, Hikmat and Debbie each have *some* residual vision/hearing, this must not be confused with having 'good' vision and hearing. Vision and hearing are key to development and to ongoing understanding of the world, with poor vision, poor hearing or both affecting the development and use of key skills (Miller and Hodges 2005).

Development and sensory impairment

As vision and hearing are so key to development and access to the environment, a loss of vision or hearing affects almost everything from getting up in the morning (not hearing a call to get up and being surprised when touched, difficulties in choosing clothes which match and are suitable to the weather), throughout the day, to going to bed (disturbed sleep patterns can result from lack of ability to perceive sunlight, taking off hearing aids when going to bed can make deaf people feel very vulnerable). A number of areas key to development and access to the environment are explored briefly below.

Movement mobility and orientation

Movement develops typically on the basis of visual stimuli, wanting to look at things, copying someone else running, hopping and jumping, and finally allows someone to see the places they want to go. Watching a young child crawl powerfully demonstrates the role of vision in motivating and co-ordinating movement (McLinden and McCall 2002). As the organs of balance are in the ear, deaf learners sometimes also have damaged balance systems. In addition, once mobile these learners are much more vulnerable when travelling as they cannot ask others where they should go if they get lost, for example.

> Victoria's mother uses a pop up tent with a variety of hanging materials, which are interesting to feel and hear (they are not all plastic) – such as a kitchen whisk, a bright feather boa, a dog lead. She puts Victoria in the tent to play (and does not interfere herself). As her mother leaves the objects in the same places, she helps Victoria to build up a picture of a predictable world. Victoria can find things herself and she develops her movement strategies to interact with them. In their home, her mother makes sure that she uses the same place for feeding Victoria, the same place for putting on her coat, and so on, to help Victoria develop an understanding of where things are in her world.

Communication

Communication through spoken language is learnt by most children through imitating what they hear around them. Eye contact and body language are perceived visually. Most people learn to speak without any specific teaching, having heard words thousands of times before they attempt to speak them (Watson 2003). People with hearing loss may hear only the tones of speech but not the distinct sounds of speech (so largely vowel sounds, which carry intonation such as happy, angry or puzzled) or they may hear the sounds of speech and enunciate better, but without much intonation. They may not hear enough to understand what is said. Their own speech may be very difficult for anyone to understand, or they may not hear at all. Alternative means of communication may be used, such as signs or symbols. However, if they are used only in structured 'teaching situations', opportunities for natural acquisition of these systems may be missed. As an example, staff working with learners with learning disabilities could have a policy of using Makaton when talking to one another so that the learners are able to see the system being used as a means of communication between other people.

Visually impaired individuals may not learn to look at the person they are talking to, or know whether someone is speaking to them or someone else, or how to take turns in a conversation (which is usually done by subtle visual cues) (Webster and Roe, 1998).

Given that Debbie has reduced information through both vision and hearing, staff gently get her attention first, before trying to communicate. Gestures have been agreed which are solidly linked to situations and they use these to tell Debbie what they want her to do, but only immediately beforehand as Debbie has not yet reached a level of communication where she could understand that an object represents an event especially in advance. For example, they stroke her arms before supporting her to stand up; her back before supporting her to sit down; her hand before raising it to her mouth when she is going to eat. Debbie can see things close to her, so staff use signs close to Debbie when they are talking to each other, encouraging her to touch their hands. She doesn't understand what they are saying but sometimes will put her hand in, as if to join the interaction.

Concepts

Young children learn concepts from different sources. For instance:

- experience – cars and cycles;
- observation – aeroplanes and rowing boats; and
- people talking about them – spacecraft and tanks.

Learners who have poor vision/hearing have much less access to learning from the environment than others (Hodges 2000). Concepts need to be deliberately presented to them, with specific teaching of the words or the items as well as being taught in different contexts.

For visually impaired people, things they cannot touch or see – such as roofs or rainbows – may be difficult to understand, and for hearing impaired people, abstract concepts which cannot be easily identified visually, such as 'later' or 'comfortable' can be hard to learn (Mason *et al.* 1997). Using touch to learn about objects is a very complex skill; as a person can only touch one part of something at a time, being able even to recognise a simple object requires the ability to remember, sequence and then to synthesise from this – something which is very difficult or impossible for some people with a learning disability (McLinden and McCall 2002).

Hikmat's teacher knows that due to hearing loss Hikmat cannot follow a description in class. When beginning a new topic of shopping, she asks an assistant to work one to one with Hikmat in a quiet environment to check her understanding of words and to teach her some new ones. Using pictures they rehearse some words Hikmat already knows, such as money, list, and supermarket, and using pictures, and real objects she helps develop an understanding of concepts such as till, bargain, stealing. In the class session Hikmat's teacher uses the radio system, remembering to turn it off when pupils are working in groups. She uses printed cards with phrases such as 'please help me' because she knows that Hikmat may not be understood when shopping more independently.

Social skills

Enjoying life, for many people, including those with learning disability, is about interaction and being with other people. These skills are harder to learn for people with sensory impairments. They are much less likely to be included in or understand the workings of a group (unless led by staff). They may not understand acceptable behaviour as they cannot necessarily see others to imitate, or understand which words are not appropriate (Palmer 1998).

Because of her visual impairment, Victoria only knows her mother is speaking to *her*, when her mother uses her name first and then gently touches her hands. In her pre-school group music session, Victoria's mother holds Victoria's hands gently when the other children are playing instruments, or helps Victoria to touch them, letting go when it is Victoria's turn. She shares short songs with silly noises (which Victoria loves) such as Old Macdonald, with lots of unusual animals. Sometimes Victoria will now make a sound indicating an animal she wants to hear about.

Exploration

Young children find out about things by interacting with them, *for example, a child poking a stone in a puddle with a stick* and an adult telling them about what they are doing, *'Look! You moved the stone with your stick, now the water is running'*. People with sensory impairments may not be able to see what is happening, or to hear the commentary, or to do these at the same time. As such, joint attention may be more challenging where people need to use their hands (touch), or their vision, or their hearing, both to understand someone else's comments (for example, by sign language, or lip reading) and to understand what is happening (for which they use eyes/touch). Sighted people rarely have a vocabulary which adequately describes what it is like to touch things, unrelated to visual stimuli. People with sensory impairments may therefore develop into more 'passive' than 'active' learners (Hodges 2000; McLinden and McCall 2002).

Debbie likes exploring the garden, sitting on the grass and pulling up plants. Staff are helping to develop a more constructive activity, but first she must familiarise herself again, as she cannot look at them while interacting with the environment. They show her what she can do, using her hands and theirs, signing some words though she doesn't understand these yet. When she turns away, they wait 2 minutes before trying to engage her again. They have learnt that she likes to take plants to bits so they have found harder plants to pick, thus developing her hand strength and flexibility.

Learning skills

Confidence, alertness, and interest are all essential to learning. People with sensory impairments have to concentrate much harder to obtain information and communicate within the environment and are far more likely to get fatigued, and need a break (Hodges 2000). It is often difficult to find resources which are as interesting to people with limited vision and/or hearing as to fully sighted hearing individuals. The confidence learners gain, by seeing and hearing positive recognition of their achievements, is also harder for those who do not see or hear well as they do not receive the immediate feedback that a typically developing child might.

Hikmat listens hard throughout a small group maths session. Despite the use of the radio system, she is tired at the end. Her teacher lets her do visual number matching on paper (a break from listening) rather than listening to the class plenary. Hikmat's work is given smiley face stamps to encourage her when she has done well. At the end of the morning, using a rhythmic counting song with flashing numbers on the whiteboard means Hikmat can join in through seeing the number sequence, though not hearing the words.

Using the environment

This final section presents some inclusive environmental adaptations and strategies, which can help people with hearing and/or vision impairment. In practice, a 'good' environment for people with hearing and vision impairment can help to include, interest and inform *everyone*. As examples, a quiet classroom helps everyone to hear the teacher's voice, and an uncluttered kitchen helps everyone to know where to find things and where to put them away. The following provides just a brief selection of strategies. For more detail, see the sources included in the websites referred to below.

Routes

Create clear routes, perhaps marked by coloured tape on the floor, so they are not impeded by furniture, or bags, to help everyone navigate and understand where they are.

Displays

Provide uncluttered displays, which include touchable and auditory elements, such as talking buttons and collage or sculpture. Information should be easy to find.

Lighting

Fit blinds/curtains and dimmable lights to give even lighting without glare, which makes features stand out better. Bright lights over some areas help to make some things clearer to see.

Reverberations

Reduce echo and reverberation by using carpets and soft furniture. On hard floors, rubber bungs on the feet of chairs can reduce sound dramatically.

Background 'noise'

Turn off noisy equipment such as fans, projectors and computers when not being used. Close windows and doors to decrease unhelpful noise from outside.

Increasing sound to noise ratio

Use or install systems, which produce an even level of sound through speakers (such as Soundfield). Loop systems for TVs can be linked to hearing aids for both home and school.

Quiet times

Ensure there are quiet times in a classroom to give an opportunity to hear (quiet spaces are not always possible).

Alternative and inclusive signage and communication systems

Provide alternative communication systems (for example, signs, photographs) at all times and in all conversations. Signage and display should include tactile information.

Specialist equipment

The correct use of specialist equipment is an essential feature of a good environment for people with sensory impairment. Have a system for checking, maintaining and dealing with damage for specialist individual equipment such as hearing aids and glasses, and ensure staff have clear responsibilities in relation to this. A support system should help individuals who can, to do this for themselves. Ensure all staff know about hearing aids and glasses being used in their group but also that training about the use of glasses and hearing aids is standard for all classroom staff.

Use devices such as magnifying lenses, or a magnification app on an iPad or similar to make small things bigger – such as a beetle in a science lesson or when it has just landed on the table!

Choose equipment carefully to increase independence. A scale using physical weights rather than a digital read off, or a microwave with a dial that can be tactually marked rather than visual display are easier than complex recorded language.

Use headphones for computers and CD players, and where possible link these directly to an individual's hearing aids. Some deaf people will use an FM ('radio') system, which should be working, charged and the right person should be wearing the microphone.

Some examples of these strategies from practice:

Victoria's mother always tells her when she is going from the sitting room to the kitchen. They always go the same way, through the dining room, as the kitchen smells are more distinctive. Going through the hall could confuse Victoria. Her mother has put a bead curtain across part of the space between the kitchen and dining room and always goes through it on the way into the kitchen, but not on the way back – so that Victoria has another clue as to where she is.

Hikmat's teacher checks her hearing aids with her every morning. They clean them every week. This has increased Hikmat's respect for her aids. In addition, for 15 minutes in every hour, they have 'quiet working' – not silent, but no background music, no computer sounds, and a space in which only one person speaks at a time.

The staff where Debbie lives have found a shady space in the garden with shiny items which spin in each corner. They don't think Debbie can hear the large wooden wind chimes but she likes banging them. They have included a carefully stacked 'sculpture' of plastic flower pots, which are painted in different colours and give Debbie something interesting to do.

Conclusion

At the end of this brief introduction to the needs of people with SLD/PMLD and sensory impairments we hope it is clear that sensory impairment affects all aspects of life and development. Some simple strategies and approaches which may help staff have been outlined. However, as each person is different and a wide variety of conditions cause sensory difficulty, knowledge of an individual is essential. Further investigations and reading, asking questions of staff with specialist knowledge (perhaps specialist medical staff, or in schools, specialist teachers for visually impaired, hearing impaired and deafblind pupils) will help to widen understanding of needs and match appropriate strategies to individual need.

Questions for readers

1   When considering the needs of the person to what extent would you agree with an often cited statement that sensory impairment is 'the least of their problems'?
2   In what ways would you say the sensory impairment interacts with his/her learning difficulties?
3   How do you think accessibility to the environment can be improved for him/her?

For further information and reading

The following websites can provide information about causes of sensory impairment, the working of the eye and ear, education in the UK and US, resources and provision, environmental audits, training information, video podcasts, and more.

Websites for major voluntary bodies in the field of sensory impairment (UK)

- RNIB, (Royal National Institute of the Blind).
- NDCS (National Deaf Children's Society).
- Sense (for deafblind people).

Websites for schools for learners with sensory impairment (USA)

Remember that 'learning disability' in the USA usually refers to dyslexia and similar conditions – try 'multiple disability' to search these sites.

- Texas School for the Blind (USA).
- Perkins School (USA).
- Gallaudet University (USA).

Other organisations

- National Sensory Impairment Partnership – NatSIP.
- Scottish Sensory centre (UK).
- Signature (UK).
- Seeability (UK).
- National Deafblind Consortium (USA).

References

Aitken, S. (2000) Understanding deafblindness, in Aitken, S., Buultjens, M., Clark, C., Eyre, J.T. and Pease, L. (eds) *Teaching Children who are Deafblind: contact, communication and learning*, London: David Fulton.

Carvill, S. (2001) Review: Sensory impairments, intellectual disability and psychiatry, *Journal of Intellectual Disability Research*, 45, 467–83.

Corn, A. and Erin, J. (eds) (2010) *Foundations of Low vision*, 2nd edn, New York: American Foundation for the Blind.

Emerson, E. and Robertson, J. (2011) *The Estimated Prevalence of Visual Impairment among People with Learning Disabilities in the UK*, Improving Health and Lives: Learning Disabilities Observatory report for RNIB and SeeAbility. Online: www.seeability.org/uploads/files/prevelence_vi_pld_full.pdf (accessed 15 June 2014).

Erin, J. (2007) Identifying the primary disability; are we all speaking the same language Speaker's corner, *Journal of visual impairment and blindness*, 101(10), 657–659.

Hodges, L.M. (2000) Effective teaching and learning in Aitken, S., Buultjens M., Clark, C., Eyre J.T. and Pease, L. (eds) *Teaching Children who are Deafblind: Contact, communication and learning*, London: David Fulton.

Kerr, A.M., McCulloch, D., Oliver, K., McLean, B., Coleman, E., Law, T., Beaton, S. Newell, T., Eccles, T.M. and Prescott, R.J. (2003) 'Medical needs of clients with intellectual disabilities require regular reassessment and the provision of client held reports', *Journal of Intellectual Disability Research*, 47, 134–145.

Mason, H., McCall, S., Arter, C., McLinden, M and Stone, J. (eds) (1997) *Visual Impairment: Access to Education for Children and Young People*, London: David Fulton.

McInnes, J.M and Treffry, T.A (1992) *Deafblind Infants and Children*, Toronto: University of Toronto Press.

McLinden, M. and Douglas, G. (2013) 'Education of children with sensory needs: reducing barriers to learning for children with visual impairment' in A. Holliman (ed.) *Educational Psychology: An International Perspective*, Routledge: London.

McLinden, M. and McCall, S. (2002) *Learning Through Touch*, London: David Fulton.

Miller, O. and Hodges, L.M. (2005) 'Deafblindness', in Lewis, A. and Norwich, B. (eds) *Special Teaching for Special Children? Pedagogies for Inclusion*, Milton Keynes: Open University Press.

Palmer, C. (1998) 'Social Skills' in Kelley, P. and Gale, G. (eds) *Towards Excellence: Effective Education for Students with Vision Impairments*, North Rocks Press: Sydney.

Watson, L.M. (2003) *Spotlight on Special Educational Needs: Hearing Impairment*, 2nd edn, Tamworth: National Association for Special Educational Needs.

Webster, A. and Roe, J. (1998) *Children with Visual Impairment: Social interaction language and learning*, London: Routledge.

16

CARE AS AN
EDUCATIONAL CONCEPT

Peter Imray and Lana Bond

In this chapter, the following questions will be addressed:

• What status does care have in an educational environment?
• Can care be an educational priority?
• Is care an area of the curriculum in which learners can succeed?

The need for care

All learners with PMLD and many with SLD will face a life in which care plays a considerable part. Given the complexity of their social and health needs, care features heavily among activities at school. This chapter seeks to discuss the nature of care in educational environments, the pedagogical opportunities provided by care activities and strategies for promoting all learners' independence in care situations. The need for this care is apparent 24 hours a day, seven days a week and can be an onerous burden for the caregiver. The implications of having to wake up every two hours throughout the night in order to turn their child with PMLD, who is physically unable to turn independently, will be known in detail by all parents in this position. And, while the demands are not so high for schools and school staff, they are still considerable. The tasks of changing clothes, dressing and undressing, toileting, padding, washing, regular positional changes, massage, stretching, and assistance with eating and drinking will probably apply for the vast majority of those with PMLD. In addition, school staff will need: some expertise in tube feeds (naso-gastric or via gastrostomy) and equipment such as pumps and giving sets; training regarding epilepsy and the administration of emergency medication such as rectal valium; tracheotomy training, especially around cleaning; setting up and administrating daily medication; and training in issues relating to degenerative conditions. While historically such clinical responsibilities have been carried out by a nurse or health care assistant, it is increasingly the case that educational staff will be trained to carry out these activities instead of, or in conjunction with, the medical staff. This enables education staff to have a holistic view of the learner and encourages a greater understanding of their world. It gives confidence to be able to work with the learner and know it is possible to keep them safe at all times. Such expertise also enables a class to go on trips, day or residential, and be prepared for all possible situations, for example a learner having a seizure or a feed pump breaking. Even in relation to general classroom activities, if a feed pump 'beeps' to indicate it has finished, being able to check, stop and turn the pump off is helpful. The alternative of waiting for the nurse to come and turn it off might be both time consuming and disruptive.

Care as an educational imperative

What are we therefore to make of this care and the need for care? Is this something that happens outside of the 'normal' curriculum? What status does it have compared to the 'normal' curriculum? The 'M' of PMLD, emphasising multiple difficulties and first suggested by Evans and Ware (1987), is missing in other descriptive 'labels' of this group of learners such as 'low incidence disabilities' in the US or MSID (Most Severe Intellectual Disabilities) in Australia (Lyons and Cassebohm 2012). Yet, there is a general assumption that the more intellectually impaired the learners, the more likely they are to have attendant and multiple physical disabilities (Ware 2003). Such additional physical disabilities may further deleteriously affect the learner's ability to learn. Goldbart and Caton (2010), for example, point out that a person's health, their sensory skills, and sensory difficulties, will critically affect their communication and their ability to communicate effectively. Imray and Hinchcliffe (2012, 2014) go further in suggesting that this combination of profound intellectual and physical difficulties has a direct effect on relevant pedagogy and curriculum and thus both should be fundamentally different from that normally on offer to learners who are developing typically.

Andrew Colley notes that:

> during our lives, we all, more or less, create our own narrative. The story of our lives. It's an unfinished story, but a story nevertheless, with many unpredictable twists and turns. Many joys and sorrows. Many successes and failures.
>
> Young people with PMLD don't often get the chance to do that. For practical reasons, they tend to be 'done to'. They are defined, analysed, restricted, contained, prescribed, followed and led.

> (Colley 2013, 30–31)

And it is this 'doing to' rather than 'doing with' which can lead to many lost learning opportunities. Also, it is suggested here that care should not be treated as a curriculum by-product but as a crucial element of the curriculum. Imray and Hinchcliffe (2014) argue that teachers should stop treating care as a necessary but time-wasting affair, something to be got over as quickly as possible, and recognise the pedagogical opportunities that care activities offer. Moreover, a sophisticated approach is necessary to address the social and health care needs of learners with PMLD. Carnaby and Pawlyn (2009) have suggested using a rigorous and continuous assessment cycle to ensure a holistic, person-centred approach and to decrease the likelihood of symptomatic changes in behaviour going unnoticed. To address the concern that poor care practices can also lead to the development of learned helplessness relatively easily, we have extended Carnaby and Pawlyn's model for complex care. Figure 16.1 attempts to show this more integrated approach to meeting learners' complex needs through a cycle.

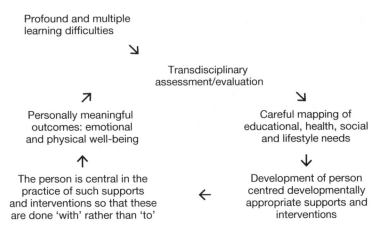

Figure 16.1 Complex educational care cycle
(based on Carnaby and Pawlyn 2009, p. 352)

The problem of 'learned helplessness'

Education for learners with PMLD is not simply an intellectual or cognitive process, since their multiple and often extremely complex physical disabilities *combined* with a profound intellectual impairment makes for a very different learning map. Part of this learning map is the notion that educators must *teach* learners to respond to the world as independently as possible, since (i) it is not a given that all learners will automatically strive for independence and (ii) it is extremely easy to dominate those with PMLD, even if that is not the educator's intention. The learner must be actively engaged in the process of care in the same way that they must be actively engaged in the process of art, or music, or literature or pressing a switch to communicate. Care must become something that the individual learns to take responsibility for so that that they become initiators and controllers rather than the merely receivers. We must be very careful that the current obsession with measuring progress does not force us into only teaching what can easily be measured and does not blind us to the fact that education for those with PMLD is a holistic process.

In 1975, the American psychologist Martin Seligman coined the phrase 'learned helplessness' to describe the condition where people actually learned to adopt helplessness when they were denied control over their lives, even when they did actually have the power and it was in their best interests to change things (Seligman 1975). This was especially evident in long stay mental institutions where staff, for a number of reasons, took control of even quite mundane things, such as making a cup of coffee, away from their patients. The same patients lost the will, and even the ability, to do these simple tasks for themselves, and thereby lost the ability to take control over their own lives. This in turn, Seligman noted, led to further, often quite deep, depression.

It is not difficult to imagine that such a state of affairs could be evident in very many 'care' situations where so much has to be done for learners with PMLD who tend to be passive and numerous writers (such as Barber 1994; Wilkinson 1994; Smith 1994; Collis and Lacey 1996; Hewett and Nind 1998; Ware 2003; Imray 2008) have argued strongly that addressing the issues of control inherent in caregiver/learner interactions are difficult for the teacher, but vital for the learner. Imray and Hinchliffe (2014) have suggested a number of pedagogical strategies which might be used to counteract such a potentially highly damaging state of affairs.

Strategies for counteracting learned helplessness in care situations

1 Build healthy attachments which allow for independent development

Every single person who works with someone with PMLD needs to look at each and every aspect their own day-to-day practice and ask themselves a very simple question: Can this person learn to do part, some, or all of this particular activity on their own, if I give them sufficient time, space and encouragement? A healthy attachment is indicated by answering 'yes' for the vast majority of cases.

2 Have high expectations

Having the expectation that a learner with PMLD can learn to do part, some or all of a particular activity is, by definition, having high expectations. This does not mean that the activity has to be unrealistic, since it recognises that succeeding for those with PMLD will probably take many hundreds and perhaps many thousands of opportunities to learn. Scaffolding will undoubtedly be an essential strategy.

3 Recognise the desirability of failure

Sometimes failure is feared because it is seen as a waste of time; one has set off on this target which has not produced any progress so all the time one has spent travelling there has been wasted. But hitting the target may be missing the point because the real point is – if one does not try one will *never* succeed. Learners with PMLD cannot, by definition, say what they can do and cannot do, what they might achieve and what they might not; teaching those with PMLD is so often guess work. It is educated guess work, but however skilled and knowledgeable one is, it may still be guess work. It is what makes working with those with PMLD so fascinating and so different. In this context, failure is inevitable, but this must not be an occasion for fear; the absence of failure is a sure indication that one has not been trying hard enough to maximise independence.

4 Provide predictable environments

Remembering Maslow's *Hierarchy of Need* (Maslow 1954), we need to be mindful that most who are profoundly disabled will find the process of learning extremely difficult if they are worried, anxious or fretful about what is happening, with whom and for how long. It is vital that one provides routine, order, structure and certainty *before* one can look to stretch learners into new ways of working and risk taking. The need to keep learners comfortable and safe is exemplified here by the case of Katie.

> Katie is 13 years old and has PMLD. Part of Katie's world is that she has very complex and ever changing health needs. Some days Katie is happy to engage in all activities and is able to participate fully with her postural management plan. On these days Katie will intentionally request an interaction by calling out and reaching towards the members of staff. Katie also has periods of very poor health, during which she sleeps for extended periods, and on these occasions she can also have extreme difficulties with breathing and tolerating her PEG (Percutaneous endoscopic gastrostomy) feeding tubes and feed. This requires a complete change in Katie's daily routine. The issues to be

considered are the positioning appropriate to Katie, duration of feed, medication and appropriateness of activities. During these times of fragile health, the primary aim of all staff is to keep Katie comfortable and safe.

All staff are aware that Katie has a fragile life expectancy. This can be a very difficult and challenging part of working with those with profound physical difficulties, and all organisations might want to look at the possibility of providing some form of staff counselling, should it be required. This does not have to be an overly expensive option, since there are numerous counselling training courses available, but it is a resource which might well have numerous benefits in the long term.

5 Elevate routines to become key learning opportunities

Routines are for the most part, things we do automatically and without thinking; unfortunately, they are often carried out automatically and without thinking *to* people with very high care needs rather than *with* them. Given the possibility that numerous opportunities to learn the same thing might be needed to enable the learner to master a particular skill, routines are clearly key learning opportunities as seen in the example of Lucy below. A learner who can roll on her hips after the count of three to enable carers to take off her trousers, or hold on to a spoon for five seconds to take food to her mouth, or remain calm and engaged in the organised chaos that is the normal school assembly, has learned valuable lessons. Such learning demands time, patience and a fairly strict adherence to a set pattern, so that there is consistency of approach, personnel, timings, language, and augmentative and alternative communication systems used. If we keep doing different things during the same learning opportunity, learning is unlikely to take place.

Lucy is 12 years old and there are many routines she must go through in a day:

- two positional changes in a morning;
- three bathroom changes throughout the day;
- medication – morning, lunchtime and afternoon;
- hand splints and ankle-foot orthoses for monitored periods of the day;
- a morning and lunchtime feed.

Lucy consistently followed the same process each day for each separate routine so as to ensure these routines could become learning opportunities. It was possible to observe over time Lucy's growing interest in these routines and the people supporting her through them. Lucy would look from the adult, making eye contact, to their hands and back to the adult to illustrate her growing understanding.

Each time Lucy's hand splints were put on she followed the same routine. Lucy was first shown the hand splints before receiving a hand massage and a light stretch with the hand splints left in view. Lucy was then shown her hand splints once more and told what they were before putting them on. As Lucy continued with this routine it was possible to see signs of anticipation and understanding of the routine as Lucy would move her fingers at the sight of the hand splint. Lucy was also able to anticipate within other routines. When the Nurse arrived with the medical trolley, Lucy would look from the Nurse to the trolley and back again, indicating she understood what was coming next.

Interestingly, the next leap in Lucy's understanding showed her rejecting the timings of particular routines, tightening and withdrawing her arms and hands when it was time for the hand splints, vocalising and shouting before a position change. This opportunity for Lucy to say 'not now' was listened to and appreciated. Lucy would then visibly relax, smile and laugh to indicate she was happy for the routines to continue. It is imperative to appreciate that this work (and these successes) were by no means instantaneous, but occurred over a five-year period.

6 Reward independent behaviours

Offer positive and entirely encouraging responses, and look out for them at every opportunity. It may be necessary to 'manufacture' independent behaviours in order to teach those who do not naturally recognise their significance. One might, for example, sing a favourite song to someone who looks at us accidentally; make a big fuss of a random vocalisation; encourage a learner to press the button on the hoist; give the learner time to eat his dinner as independently as he can, even if that takes much longer than everyone else. Structured routines, taking time, and using cues and prompts consistently may enable learners to take more of an active role in the process as in the case of Dan below.

A teaching assistant working closely with Dan, a 7 year old with PMLD, commented that she felt Dan seemed upset and cross each time a top was put on or taken off him. Dan would express this by a very slight and fleeting facial expression. To support Dan to understand the process of adding and removing clothing, and, as importantly, that he can take an active and controlling role in the process, specific touch cues and strategies were developed and used consistently. Dan has good mobility in his arms and is able to control the movement of them with an amount of processing time. As part of the new support strategies it was important, when adding or removing clothing, to position Dan's arms and elbows by the arm holes of his clothes to provide Dan with the opportunity to independently push and pull his arms through his top.

The routine for removing a jacket was:

- greet Dan in a happy tone;
- tell Dan what is about to happen and lightly touch the front of Dan's jacket;
- tell Dan 'this arm first' and lightly rub left arm;
- guide Dan's wrist and elbow so they are in line with the arm hole of the jacket giving Dan the opportunity to bring his arm through;
- stand in front of Dan and tell him you are going to bring him forward and lightly tap the back of Dan's shoulders, giving him the opportunity to help as the jacket is removed from Dan's back by another member of staff;
- the beginning stages are repeated for supporting the removing of the second sleeve of the jacket.

Over time, following the same structured routine of taking time, using touch cues consistently and using verbal prompts, Dan was able to take more of an active role in the process and expresses his happiness each time with a very big smile!

7 Communicate with learners at their level

Not just obviously, by working with learners on the floor or kneeling down if they are in their wheelchairs, but also by remembering that, if we use language too much and without thought, it can be a means of control by those who have it and against those who do not (Imray and Hinchcliffe 2014).

8 Recognise, respond to and reinforce learners' initiations

Those looking to extend their knowledge in this quite complex area would be strongly advised to spend some quality time with Jean Ware's book *Creating a Responsive Environment for People with Profound and Multiple Learning Difficulties* (Ware 2003) and Mark Collis and Penny Lacey's *Interactive Approaches to Teaching* (Collis and Lacey 1996). Both are designed to be interactive books and staff teams should be encouraged to go through them chapter by chapter during successive team meetings. Equally, class teams might also look at Barry Carpenter and his colleagues' *Engagement Scales* (Carpenter *et al.* 2010). They advocate detailed observation within the specific areas of *Awareness, Curiosity, Investigation, Discovery, Anticipation, Initiation* and *Persistence* in order to assess what a fully engaged learner might look like. As an essential base, learners need to be observed engaging in at least one activity which they personally find highly engaging and at least one activity which they personally find highly un-engaging. It may also be that those working with the learner will be able to utilise known motivators in all sorts of interesting ways to settle learners and increase their engagements in areas that they might previously have rejected.

9 Fade prompting

Providing essential support for learners to engage with an activity, such as hand–over–hand holding of a spoon at lunchtimes or holding an object of reference for the learner to touch before an activity takes place, is often second nature to all those working with persons with PMLD. But is one constantly thinking about reducing such prompts? Perhaps paradoxically, this can mean giving considerably more time and attention to the learner as well as more failures, but failure may be regarded as another chance to learn. Supporting adults need to think about the amount of assistance given to learners every day, and every part of every day, and look to pause before the assistance is given just to see if the learner makes an independent movement.

10 Provide real choices

Real choices – as opposed to superficial choices which have no real consequences for the learner – include teaching the learner how to negate. It is arguable that the power of saying 'no' and the power of being listened to when saying 'no' is a basic human right. Because those with PMLD are in such a vulnerable position, however, and because they are in need of so much care for so much of the time, their power to negate is crucially compromised (Barber 1994; Wilkinson 1994; Collis and Lacey 1996; Hewett and Nind 1998; Orr 2003; Imray 2008; Imray and Hinchcliffe 2014). This will naturally involve a great deal of sensitivity and reflection by teachers with the central question of 'Am I doing the right thing?' always to the fore. Teaching learners with PMLD is particularly challenging simply because it is so easy for the teacher to take control, to be didactic, and to limit learning rather than expand it.

11 Identify what the learner is interested in and use that as a basis for working with them

Motivation is the key here and we cannot expect learners with PMLD to find their own motivation (Carpenter *et al.* 2010). Activities, all activities, undertaken with a person with PMLD need to be intrinsically motivating to the individual learner if independent behaviours are to be encouraged (Bunning 1998; Ware 2003).

12 Take risks

Encourage learners not to be frightened of new experiences. This means that adults will need to build in much order, structure, routine and certainty within the existing way of working before introducing something new. Staff will need to build in considerable caution and take things very slowly if learners are to be encouraged to take risks. A long-term approach with many opportunities to experiment, built around having fun, may well be the best option. So, for example, a learner who is tactile defensive of cold, wet, slimy materials such as paint or wallpaper paste might need many opportunities to relax into an art session where the touching of such materials is not required. Once relaxed, you might bring in warmed–up wallpaper paste for her to touch, but only for the briefest moment, before carrying on with the relaxing, safe and familiar activity. Gradually, over what might become an extended period of time, perhaps several months, staff may encourage a more open and adventurous response.

13 Give the learner time to succeed

Of all the above strategies, this is the one that runs through everything one is likely to do. For this group of learners, it is a nonsense to assume that learning *will* take place in every lesson or session for *all* learners, since it may (is very likely to) take *much* longer than that. This is not only in terms of the lesson or session itself, but in recognising that learning timescales for those with PMLD may be vastly different to those of the rest of the school population, including those with SLD. Some things may take many months and maybe even many years of constant practice to even partially achieve. And of course, once one has given the learner time to succeed one then has to get used to the idea of giving him even more time!

Conclusions

Let us come back to the questions posed at the beginning of this chapter to see if there are any possible answers.

Firstly, what status does care have in an educational environment? It may be that care has a very low status, because it is perceived that this is not what education is for and it is not what teachers do; this, however, represents a very considerable danger for the learner with PMLD because it assumes that there are more educationally important things to do than take control of one's own life. Care must not be rushed so that the more important 'education' can be got on with!

Secondly, can care be an educational priority? We believe that ensuring the right approach to care and the increasing opportunities to work towards independence in care situations must be a priority if learners are to avoid becoming 'helpless'. Moreover, we argue that there is no greater educational priority; there may be equal educational priorities, but no greater one.

Is care an area that learners can succeed in? Most definitely yes, though this may not be measurable in any quantifiable sense. The tiny advance from touching the hoist switch, to holding the hoist switch, then to pressing the hoist switch may take a number of years to teach. Not teaching this process assumes that learners with PMLD cannot succeed. Not teaching this process, and innumerable others like it, condemns the learner to a life of being done to.

Questions for readers

- Am I thinking about how learners in my setting can maximise the control they exercise in relation to care?
- Am I turning those thoughts to action?

References

Barber, M. (1994) 'Contingency Awareness: putting research into the classroom', in J. Coupe O'Kane and B. Smith (eds) *Taking Control*, London: David Fulton.

Bunning, K. (1998) 'To engage or not to engage? affecting the interactions of learning disabled adults', *International Language and Communication Disorders*, 33, 386–391.

Carnaby, S. and Pawlyn, J. (2009) 'Profound intellectual and multiple disabilities: meeting complex needs through complex means', in Pawlyn, J. and. Carnaby S (eds) *Profound Intellectual and Multiple Disabilities: Nursing Complex Needs*), Oxford: Wiley-Blackwell

Carpenter, B., Cockbill, B., Egerton, J. and English, J. (2010) 'Children with complex learning difficulties and disabilities: developing meaningful pathways to personalised learning', *The SLD Experience*, 5, 3–10.

Colley, A. (2013) *Personalised Learning for Young People with Profound and Multiple Learning Difficulties*, London: Jessica Kingsley.

Collis, M. and Lacey, P. (1996) *Interactive Approaches to Teaching*, London: David Fulton.

Evans, P. and Ware, J. (1987) *Special Care Provision*, Windsor: NFER–Nelson.

Goldbart, J. and Caton, S. (2010) *Communication and people with the most complex needs: what works and why this is essential*, London: Mencap.

Hewett, D. and Nind, M. (eds) (1998) *Interaction in Action: Reflections on the use of Intensive Interaction*, London: David Fulton.

Imray, P. (2008) *Turning the Tables on Challenging Behaviour*, London: Routledge.

Imray, P. and Hinchcliffe, V. (2012) 'Not fit for purpose: a call for separate and distinct pedagogics as part of a national framework for those with severe and profound learning difficulties', *Support for Learning*, 27(4), 150–157.

Imray, P. and Hinchcliffe, V. (2014) *Curricula for Teaching Children and Young People with Severe or Profound and Multiple Learning Difficulties: Practical strategies for education professionals*, London: Routledge.

Lyons, G., and Cassebohm, M. (2012) 'The education of Australian school students with the most severe intellectual disabilities: where have we been and where could we go? a discussion primer', *Australasian Journal of Special Education*, 34(1), 79–96.

Maslow, A. H. (1954) *Motivation and Personality*, New York: Harper.

Orr, R. (2003) *My Right to Play: A child with complex needs*, Maidenhead: Open University Press.

Seligman, M. (1975) *Helplessness: On depression, development and death*, San Francisco CA: W H Freeman.

Smith, B. (1994) 'Handing over control to people with learning difficulties', in J. Coupe-O'Kane and B. Smith (eds) *Taking Control: Enabling people with learning difficulties*, London: David Fulton.

Vygotsky, L.S. (1978) *Mind in Society: The development of higher psychological processes*, Cambridge MA: Harvard University Press.

Ware, J. (2003) *Creating a Responsive Environment for People with Profound and Multiple Learning Difficulties*, London: David Fulton.

Wilkinson, C. (1994) 'Teaching pupils with profound and multiple learning difficulties to exert control', in J. Coupe O'Kane and B. Smith (eds) *Taking Control: Enabling people with learning difficulties*, London: David Fulton.

17

SEX AND RELATIONSHIP EDUCATION

David S. Stewart, Angela Mallett and Tom Hall

In this chapter, the following questions will be addressed:

- Do learners with SLD/PMLD have a right to sex and relationship education and why is it important?
- What are the benefits of working with parents, carers and families on issues to do with sex and relationships?

Introduction

Although we can shape (and mis-shape) sexual expression, sexuality is not an optional extra which we in our wisdom can choose to bestow or withhold according to whether or not some kind of intelligence test is passed.

(Craft 1987: 19)

In this chapter we wish to reflect on some of the issues in the teaching of sex and relationship education (SRE) for learners with SLD/PMLD. Much of the writing and research in this area has been with adults with learning disabilities and generally with articulate people with mild to moderate learning disabilities, e.g. McCarthy and Thompson (2007, 2010), McCarthy (1999), Abbott and Howarth (2005) and Thompson and Brown (2006). Yet this is such a vital part of young people's education for life. Our experience as staff in a special school is that mainstream schools rarely contact us about mathematics or history. What they do want to discuss are issues of inappropriate sexualised behaviours or student vulnerability.

While it may be over 25 years since Ann Craft wrote the words which preface this chapter, the teaching of SRE, as part of an entitlement curriculum for learners with SLD is as critical today. In England there is still insufficient national guidance to support schools, pupils and their families. Currently PHSE (Personal, Health, Social and Economic Education) is a non-statutory subject. In issuing the new guidance for the National Curriculum for 2014 the government felt it unnecessary to provide new standardised frameworks of study. With that in mind, we advise that schools follow the PHSE Association guidance on SRE (Brook, PSHE Association and Sex Education Forum 2014); otherwise children and young people risk being left untutored and vulnerable.

When even the *Daily Telegraph* (2013), hardly known for its liberal views in curriculum content, mounts a campaign to support the improvement of sex education in schools, albeit because of the issue of internet pornography, one realises the extent of the problem! The guidance for schools was last updated in 2000, with minimal reference to those with special educational needs (DfEE 2000). While new guidance was prepared for 2010, this was rejected by the incoming coalition government.

The Ofsted (2013) report, *Not Yet Good Enough*, highlighted the issue of sex education in schools.

> Sex and relationships education required improvement in over a third of schools, leaving some children and young people unprepared for the physical and emotional changes they will experience during puberty, and later when they grow up and form adult relationships. This is a particular concern because, as recent research conducted by The Lucy Faithfull Foundation indicates, failure to provide high quality, age-appropriate sex and relationships education may leave young people vulnerable to inappropriate sexual behaviours and exploitation, particularly if they are not taught the appropriate language, or have not developed the confidence to describe unwanted behaviours, do not know who to go to for help, or understand that sexual exploitation is wrong.
>
> (Ofsted 2013, p. 4)

Even more worrying is the lack of education in many schools to support learners in keeping themselves safe.

> In just under half of the schools, pupils learnt how to keep themselves safe in a variety of situations but not all had practised negotiating risky situations or applied security settings to social networking sites. Most understood the dangers of substance misuse but not always in relation to personal safety, particularly with regard to alcohol. These deficiencies in learning result in part from inadequacies in subject-specific training and support for PSHE education teachers, particularly in the teaching of sensitive and controversial issues.
>
> (Ofsted 2013, p. 4)

> Teachers have received little or no subject-specific training as a result they have, limited subject knowledge and are unskilled in teaching sensitive and controversial issues.
>
> (Ofsted 2013, p. 29)

If these are the findings for all learners, what then of those for learners with special educational needs (SEN)? The Ofsted researchers seemed heartened by the provision they observed for those with SEN.

> The great majority of schools provided good PSHE education for disabled pupils and those with special educational needs and for those whose circumstances made them vulnerable.
>
> (Ofsted 2013, p. 5)

They do not refer to SRE in particular and we would caution about being too complacent.

Our own research in Nottingham investigated the SRE provided for those with SEN in the city's mainstream and special schools (Bustard and Stewart 2002). Practice was inconsistent, while teachers identified a lack of training and resources. There was lack of clarity in terms of responsibility for ensuring the education was provided. Subsequent provision of resources and training did not necessarily lead to improved practice as follow-up research indicated five years later. Resources were lost, staff had moved on and teaching assistants reported that had not been given time to carry out support in mainstream schools.

There was, of course, good practice observed, but this was largely down to individual members of staff rather than a whole school approach. Special school practice was generally better than mainstream provision, but there was certainly no reason for complacency. From personal experience of providing training on a national basis, we would surmise that there is a very wide discrepancy in practice nationally and the lack of national guidance must be a major factor.

Rights and entitlements to sex education for learners with SLD

These are some of the principles, which should guide the education for these learners. It is important to recognise that knowledge of sex and sexuality is a basic human right and learners have a right:

- to be a sexual being;
- to grow up and achieve adult status;
- to form and break relationships;
- to acquire knowledge about sexuality and social behaviour such as they are able to assimilate;
- to privacy and dignity;
- to make informed sexual choices;
- to have opportunities to love and be loved and enjoy as full a range of satisfying human relationships as possible;
- to legal protection (including protection against exploitation).

Education staff must be creative in the ways learners are enabled to access their education entitlements, such as:

- to receive information about human development, with facts being presented in an objective, balanced manner, appropriate to the age, stage, level of maturity and learning needs of the individual;
- a structured framework of learning experiences designed to prevent unnecessary anxiety which includes learning to communicate about sexuality with appropriate language and vocabulary;
- to consider and receive specific training for relationships building and socio-sexual behaviour in order to promote greater social confidence; this would include realistic information on responsibilities and expectations of personal relationships;
- to be given information, advice and guidelines on inappropriate sexual behaviour (socially, legally and culturally unacceptable), and all aspects of exploitation.

Why it is important that learners receive education in schools

Our knowledge about sex, relationships and gender comes from a range of influences as we grow and develop. It will come from family, friends and peers at school. The media, television, books and magazines will all play their part and the internet is a major source of influence. Religion will have been a significant influence on some people's views. Formal education at school will have been very mixed for the reasons stated above. For some, in particular in the establishment of relationships, there will be experimentation and exposure to a wide range of emotions, all part of the learning process.

For learners with SLD, there can be many gaps in their opportunity to gain knowledge. A parent may feel embarrassed and unsure as to what to say. Siblings, too, may be less inclined to share information with their brother or sister. Many of the learners will have less access to friendships; indeed for many they will have little contact with peers outside of school. Loneliness may be a significant feature of their lives. Excluded from social opportunities, they may miss out on much of the natural incidental learning of young people as they grow up.

In terms of media, they may be exposed to a great deal of television but are they able to make the distinction between reality and fiction? 'Soaps' may purport to be educational but they are more likely to be sensational in their storylines, making it confusing for a young person. In terms of magazines and newspapers, for those who cannot read, they may have no context to the pictures they see. Pop music videos can be sexually explicit but are freely available. Learners with SLD are becoming more familiar with the use of the internet which has many benefits but clearly there are many pitfalls and, without sound education, they may be very vulnerable.

One can see from the many influences in a learner's life, it can be very difficult to make sense of all the different messages. If they do not receive sound and considered education at school, they can and do find themselves in all kinds of difficulties. This education must be supported by close working with families.

Working with parents and families

Adolescence is a period of change, and our adolescent teenagers can be very trying at times. It's natural if they want to shut themselves in their bedroom, lock the bathroom door and choose their own clothes and friends. They need to learn to be independent as they grow older. This can be a worrying time for parents and carers who have to tread the delicate line between allowing their children more freedom while trying to reduce the risks.

(Kerr–Edwards and Scott 2011a, p. v)

This quote is taken from the introduction to 'Talking Together about Sex and Relationships', an excellent resource from the Family Planning Association (FPA) for parents of children and young people with learning disabilities. Reporting on their research for the European Network for Health Promoting Schools, the National Foundation for Education Research (1997) reported that parents welcomed support from the schools. The report highlighted particular points for parents of learners with disabilities:

- A higher proportion of parents of learners in special schools than in mainstream schools said they found it quite or very difficult to talk to their children about these matters.
- Parents of learners in special schools appeared to place even more importance on school-based provision than other parents.

It is interesting to note that these researchers did not seem to consider the needs of those with disabilities in mainstream schools. It highlights the lack of overall research in this area.

Oak Field School – working with parents

To support its work in the area of SRE, Oak Field School set up a SRE Monitoring Group in 1985. The group, consisting of governors, staff, parents and community representation, liaises with staff on the delivery of the curriculum, creates new resources and runs regular courses for parents. In recent years the school has used the FPA 'Talking Together' books (for example, Kerr-Edwards and Scott 2011a, 2011b). These are an excellent starting point for parents and there are lots of useful ideas in them. On a practical note, most parents will not have heard of them, and certainly may not be able to purchase a copy. So the school makes an investment and, if parents attend the course, they are given the books free of charge. It is important that these are used at home. Parents of learners from other special and mainstream schools are invited as well as those from Oak Field School.

The course covers a range of topics. Appropriate language for body parts is a useful start, for parents in their embarrassment may give their child unhelpful words, e.g. calling a girl's vagina 'her fairy' could make story time very confusing. Discussion of friendships and social networks can prove upsetting when a parent acknowledges that all the people around her child are paid to be with him or her. Even a befriender can be a paid person. Subjects such as masturbation are often issues which parents seek advice on. It is important to establish with the parent that the message being given to the learner is that it is a private activity and that their child's bedroom is the private place. This will need to be reinforced by the family. If a physically disabled teenager masturbates and then has to rely on his mother to clean him up, this can be a real source of embarrassment for both mother and young person. Yet this is a real situation that people have to deal with. Staff working with families must be prepared to offer support on a wide range of issues. Sharing a problem can often be the first stage for a parent in tackling a situation with their child. Hearing another parent with the same problem makes the parent realise that their situation is not unique and the school is not shocked. It takes a brave parent to talk about their child smearing faeces for instance. They may feel shame and embarrassment but it is a critical area in which they need help.

The school provides a range of booklets for parents – 'Now They are Growing Up' (Oak Field School, 2009–2013) on a range of topics. There is also a booklet called 'Your Child's Right' (Stewart and Bustard 2012) produced by the school, which outlines the need for SRE. The school's SRE policy has an annex which addresses frequently asked questions to support parents' understanding.

Kerr-Edwards and Scott wish to empower parents, acknowledging their importance in education, suggesting that 'whatever their background, all young people will go through similar stages and will look for support from the most significant adults in their lives – their parents' (Kerr-Edwards and Scott 2011a, p. vi).

The curriculum

Valuing ourselves

Learners need to understand and value their bodies. They need to know about their gender and their physical development. There is a clear need for prophylactic education. For learners who find change difficult they need to understand the changes to their bodies. Preparing girls for their periods or boys for wet dreams is important so that they do not become anxious when it occurs.

Issues of disability

Learners have identified that there is often little discussion about their particular disability, physical or learning, and that needs to be part of their learning.

Life cycle

Their education needs to include the life cycle from birth to death. Learners need to be helped with dealing with bereavement and loss. They may wish to ask about abortion. More than one 'soap' has carried the storyline of a person being told that they are to have a disabled child and the dilemma then of whether to have an abortion. Education in school has to be responsive to all such occasions arising.

Emotions

Understanding one's own emotions and those of others forms a vital part of the education. It is alright to be angry; it is how one deals with the emotion that it is important. The mental wellbeing of learners is paramount and we know that people with learning disabilities are more likely to develop mental health difficulties (Carpenter and Morgan 2003) so their being able to express how they feel at any given time is important.

Relationships

In all their many forms relationships are the very stuff of our lives, but they are governed by a range of social norms and rules. Get them wrong and one can find life difficult. For many learners just trying to have a friend is a major challenge. If a couple wish to further their friendship into a more meaningful relationship, there can often be few opportunities unless given support.

Friendships

When learners leave school, friendships may be broken. This can be a very difficult time and can create a real sense of loss. Organisations for former students, which allow young people to keep in touch with one another, should be encouraged and supported.

Sexual expression

Issues of sexual expression need to be explored. Schools need to be clear on the support and advice they give to support learners. The law may say that a young person may have consensual sex at 16 but it is not compulsory and there needs to be discussion about what a learner feels comfortable with, not what they feel is expected of them.

Sexual orientation

Some learners may not identify themselves as gay for all the negative connotations the word brings but engage nonetheless in same sex activities. Some may experience same-sex relationships for reasons of opportunity as much as sexual orientation. They need to have an education, which keeps them safe. Schools have a duty to inform and support all learners.

Public toilets

Learners need to learn about keeping safe and also not putting themselves in the position of causing offence, such as a young man who stands at the urinal with his trousers around his ankles. Parents, anxious about going out for long periods of times because of issues with toilets, should be encouraged to use the National Key Scheme (RADAR Key) or Changing Places toilets (see 'Useful websites' below).

Personal safety

Teaching from a young age is vital. Children need to learn about modesty, dignity, choice making and the right to say no. Keeping their body healthy and hygienic is essential. Sexual health is equally important and pupils need to know where to go if they need help. We have already alluded to internet safety and pupils need to understand their vulnerability.

Oak Field School Men's Group

Oak Field School has a number of separate Men's and Women's Groups for key stage 4 and sixth form learners to learn about SRE. In the past the groups have been 'mixed ability' but currently they are organised according to learners' perceived needs and level of understanding. There is targeted small group work for learners identified as needing additional support, for example in relation to personal hygiene or inappropriate touching.

One of the Men's Groups consists of ten learners with SLD in Years 12 and 13 who will soon be leaving school. They work with a male teacher and three teaching assistants. The group meets once a week for about an hour.

It is important that staff are respectful of the fact that the learners are teenagers who have a right to their own opinions and sexual identities. This can be a challenge for both learners and staff, especially if they have known each other for a long time as it can represent a shift in their perception of one another. Deciding on an appropriate mix of staff is therefore essential.

The main assessment tool used with some adaptation is that developed by Rev Jane Fraser for the 'Not a Child Anymore' resource in the 1980s and now revised (Fraser and Dixon 2010). This enables a view of the knowledge and understanding of a young person.

As a framework for the course in recent years the school has used 'Living Your Life' (Bustard and Stewart 2011). For instance, a session may focus on issues of consent within friendships and relationships. This has led to discussion on the concept of consent, a topic some learners have trouble understanding. Other topics covered have included personal hygiene, sexual health and what it means to be a young man with a disability. We have found role play to be a very effective tool.

Staff have reported improved behaviour at break time as a result of the Men's Group sessions. Discussion about friendships take place in annual reviews with parents, where there is a focus on ways in which to encourage and nurture friendships beyond school. Within the classroom the teacher has created a 'confidentiality corner' where learners know they can talk confidentially in a one-to-one situation. Learners positively look forward to these sessions. They feel that they are taken seriously and treated as adults. It is important to keep parents informed about what topics are going to be covered so that they can reinforce positive learning.

Considerations for learners with PMLD

It is often difficult for parents, families and carers to gain knowledge about sexual matters related to learners with PMLD. Ideally, concerns will be shared with staff and together the best ways of managing issues of sexuality can be developed.

A crucial role can be played by parents, carers and other advocates in ensuring that the sexual and relationship needs of these learners are met. An advocate can include anyone who promotes the welfare of a person with profound learning disabilities. This could be a professional advocate or equally be a family friend, school friend or staff member who used to work with the person.

A Scheme for Learners with PMLD

'Sex in Context' (Downs and Craft 1997) is a very detailed resource which is still relevant. 'Bodyworks' (Mallett 2006) is a scheme developed at Oak Field School specifically for learners with PMLD. It covers a wide range of sexual and social issues in addition to health, protection, appearance, physical care and independence. There are four sections: Head and Face, Hands and Arms, Torso and Neck, Legs and Feet. Each section provides a comprehensive set of frequently asked questions.

Parents often appreciate discussing sexual issues with other parents of children with PMLD: a participant stated, 'I feel comfortable and at ease with other parents – I have learnt a lot from this group, especially from the parents of older children'.

Sometimes just one person makes decisions on behalf of a learner with PMLD and consequently can impose their own values. An 'advocate group' can help to ensure that a range of viewpoints are taken into account when addressing the most likely views of these learners. This can include choices and decisions in many areas including gender and sexual expression. Regular meetings, for example, once a month can take place, but when important decisions need to be made additional meetings may be necessary. Any decisions made by an advocate group will represent a range of different viewpoints.

Ongoing every day activities can provide awareness of sexual issues, therefore it is important that these are carefully planned beforehand to ensure the maximum benefit. Personal care time is an ideal time for people to learn about themselves. Appropriately positioned mirrors can help understanding of body parts, body changes, and periods. They can also help in the understanding of what the carers are doing during intimate care. This can be a rare time for learners with PMLD to explore their bodies if they wish. Carers can involve themselves in tasks such as folding clothing, sorting pads, etc. during this time.

Conclusions

There are still issues for the support of staff in delivering SRE. The PSHE Association (see 'Useful websites') is vociferous in its demands on government to ensure that this sensitive area of education is part of the National Curriculum and that staff receive appropriate training. The advice the PSHE Association gives is that schools should ensure the following:

- that staff teaching PSHE education receive subject-specific training and regular updates, including in the teaching of sensitive issues; and
- that the school delivers age-appropriate sex and relationships education that meets and contributes to safeguarding them from inappropriate sexual behaviours and sexual exploitation.

There may be many national challenges to counter in this work but those who work with learners with SLD/PMLD know that this is too important an area of their lives to be left to chance.

Questions for readers

- What constitutes a good programme of SRE?
- Does your own school's SRE programme include all learners?
- What are the challenges for schools in the context of an absence of statutory guidance for PHSE and a dearth of training for the delivery of SRE for learners with SLD?

Useful websites

Changing Places toilets is a national scheme established by the Changing Places Consortium – a group of organisations working to support the rights of people with profound and multiple learning disabilities to access their community. Information can be found on their website: http://changing-places.org.

National Key Scheme or RADAR Key was developed by the Royal Association of Disability and Rehabilitation aka Radar. Radar is now part of Disability Rights UK after merging with Disability Alliance and the National Centre for Independent Living in January 2012. Disability Rights UK now coordinates all things Radar key-related. https://crm.disabilityrightsuk.org

Oakfield School and Sports College has sex education information available on its website: www.oakfieldsportscollege.org.uk/index.php/about-oak-field

The Family Planning Association – a sexual health charity providing information, advice and support on sexual health, sex and relationships: www.fpa.org.uk/professionals/resources

The PSHE Association has much useful information on its website: www.pshe-association.org.uk/

Further reading

Allen, C. (2001) *A Framework for Learning for Adults with Profound and Complex Learning Difficulties*, London, David Fulton.

Fanstone, C. and Andrews, S. (2009*) Learning Disabilities Sex and the Law*, London: Family Planning Association.

Mencap (2008) *Fact Sheet – PMLD and Sexuality*, London: Mencap.

Scott, L. and Kerr-Edwards, L. (2010) T*alking Together… about Growing Up* London: Family Planning Association.

Stewart D.S. (2007) 'A penis is the man who plays the piano', *The SLD Experience*, 48, 15–18.

References

Abbott, D. and Howarth, J. (2005) *Secret Loves, Hidden Lives: exploring issues for people with learning difficulties who are gay, lesbian or bisexual*, Bristol: The Policy Press.

Brook, PSHE Association and Sex Education Forum (2014) *Sex and Relationships Education (SRE) for the 21st century: supplementary advice to the Sex and Relationship Education Guidance DfEE (0116/2000)*, Online. Available: www.pshe-association.org.uk/content.aspx?CategoryID=1172 (accessed 11 August 2014).

Bustard, S. and Stewart, D.S. (2002) 'Living your life: sex and relationships education for young people with special educational needs'. Paper presented at the 10th World Congress of the International Association for the Scientific Study of Intellectual Disabilities Disabilities (IASSID).

Bustard, S. and Stewart, D.S. (2011) *Living Your Life*, London: Brook.

Carpenter, B. and Morgan, H. (2003) 'Count Us In: the role of schools and colleges in meeting the mental health needs of young people with learning disabilities', *British Journal of Special Education*, 30(4), 202–206.

Craft, A. (1987) 'Mental handicap and sexuality: issues for individuals with a mental handicap, their parents and professionals', in A. Craft (ed.) *Sexuality and Mental Handicap: Issues and perspectives*, Tunbridge Wells: Costello.

Daily Telegraph (2013) 'Better Sex Education Campaign – More than 25k Sign Petition' *Article, Daily Telegraph*, 6 September 2013: 10.

Department for Education and Employment (2000) *Sex and Relationship Guidance*, London: DfEE.

Fraser, J. and Dixon, H. (2010) *Sexual Knowledge and Behaviour Assessment Tool*, Cumbria: Obtainable from Centre for HIV and Sexual Health, Sheffield. Online: www.sexualhealthsheffield.nhs.uk (accessed 11 August 2014).

Downs, C. and Craft, A. (1997) *Sex in Context*, Brighton: Pavilion.

Kerr-Edwards, L. and Scott, L. (2011a) *Talking Together … about sex and relationships*, London: Family Planning Association.

Kerr-Edwards, L. and Scott L. (2011b) *Talking Together … about contraception*, London: Family Planning Association.

Mallett, A. (2006) *Bodyworks*, Nottingham: Oak Field School/Nottingham City Council.

McCarthy, M. (1999) *Sexuality and Women with Learning Disabilities*, London: Jessica Kingsley Publishers.

McCarthy, M. and Thompson, D. (2007) *Sex and the 3Rs: rights, risks and responsibilities*, Brighton: Pavilion.

McCarthy, M. and Thompson, D. (2010) (eds) *Sexuality and Intellectual Disabilities – A Handbook*, Brighton: Pavilion.

National Key Scheme (RADAR Key) (https://crm.disabilityrightsuk.org)

National Foundation for Education Research (1997) *Parents Views of Health Education: survey of key findings for European Network for Health Promoting Schools survey of parents*, London: National Foundation for Education Research/Health Education Authority.

Oak Field School (2009–2013) *Feeling Grown Up*, Series of booklets for young people, Nottingham: Oak Field School.

Oak Field School (2009–2013) *Now They are Growing Up*, Series of booklets for parents, Nottingham: Oak Field School.

Ofsted (2013) *Not yet good enough: personal, social, health and economic education in schools*, London: Ofsted. Available: www.ofsted.gov.uk/resources/not-yet-good-enough-personal-social-health-and-economic-education-schools (accessed 11 August 2014).

Stewart, D.S. and Bustard, S. (2012) *Your Child's Right*, Nottingham: Oak Field School.

Thompson, D. and Brown, H. (2006) *Men with Learning Disabilities who Sexually Abuse: Working together to develop response-ability*, Brighton: Pavilion.

18

PHYSICAL CONTACT EXPERIENCES WITHIN THE CURRICULUM

Julia Barnes and Dave Hewett

In this chapter, the following questions will be addressed:

- What might be the nature of usual physical contact experiences for learners with SLD/PMLD?
- How crucial are positive touch experiences for the development of learners with SLD/PMLD?
- How may touch deprivation affect the development of learners with SLD/PMLD?
- How may the proper and appropriate use of physical contact be given due recognition in the curriculum in schools for learners with SLD/PMLD?

Introduction

The role of physical contact experiences has previously been little addressed as a curriculum issue (Hewett 2007; Rhodes and Hewett 2010), although the volume by Imray and Hinchliffe (2014) redresses the balance somewhat, with frequent mention of the significance and utility of physical contact experiences for learners with SLD/PMLD. This chapter firstly chronicles results and discussion arising from a small-scale study in one school and culminating in a Master's Thesis (Barnes 2012 [nee Rhodes]). It is suggested that the practical inquiry chronicled here, while small in scale and focused on learners with PMLD, nonetheless describes and illuminates something of the usual, general nature of physical contact experiences between members of staff in schools and learners with both PMLD and SLD.

In special schools, the use of touch with learners by staff is so frequent and extensive, it is submitted here that this aspect of practice must be regarded as teaching technique. The intended, assumed or likely effects of those touches upon learners may range, say, from a momentarily effective support or communication message to a profound developmental experience. Further, it will be argued that the receiving effect of those touches therefore is, or can be, contributing to learning for the learners. On various occasions, the effect of those touches might be considered to be, and intended to be, *the* learning. Secondly, then, this chapter asserts the perspective that nurturing touch, particularly, will likely be furnishing crucial developmental experience and learning to learners who are at early stages of development. Therefore, in a general and technical sense, physical contact experiences, the giving and the receiving, should be addressed as a major curriculum issue, both in practice and in documentation.

Learners' touch experience in the classroom and school

Julia Barnes is a teacher and Sensory Coordinator at a generic secondary special school. She and her class team long recognised the importance of their use of touch minute by minute in teaching learners with PMLD. Without touching learners they would be unable to physically support them to change positions, walk, eat, drink or have their personal care needs met. However, there is deep recognition that touch is necessary for more than meeting their needs; it is integral to the experience of being human:

> Touch sends unwritten messages which convey a wide variety of positive meanings; alternatively withholding of touch can transmit negative messages.
>
> (Dobson *et al.* 2004: 127)

Therefore, touch is used knowingly to support communication – either in formal ways such as using on-the-body-signing (Goold and Hummel 1993) or through naturalistic, enjoyable communication strategies such as Intensive Interaction (Nind and Hewett 2005). Touch offers learners at early developmental levels the opportunity to play through burst-pause interactions (Nind and Hewett 1994) such as 'Row-the- Boat'. If a learner is distressed, it is completely natural to hug, pat or stroke to support and calm them. For many learners, physical contact may be the most graphic, comprehensible communication experience, perhaps their main point of access to the crucial everyday experience of 'phatic' communication – chit-chat with others (Hewett 2012). See the example below.

Sam

Julia works with Sam who is a young man with very complex medical and learning difficulties including a severe visual impairment. He is very aware of who is around him and uses touch to initiate communication with the people he prefers. He will reach out to these staff members and hold onto them while laughingly enjoying the banter and physical bond his touch creates.

Studying the touch experience of learners with PMLD

Barnes' study (Barnes 2012) commenced in 2011 and researched the touch experiences of three representative learners with PMLD. All had profound learning difficulties plus physical and visual disabilities. An observation schedule was derived from the one used by Hodges and McLinden (2004), with their permission, but modified after trialling. During almost 13 hours of continuous observations Barnes recorded 315 different interactions involving 51 people; 176 of these interactions involved touch. The touch used in a large proportion of the interactions was analysed and classified in two main ways. Firstly, using Goold and Hummel's (1993) 12 categories of touch, but also with a simple categorisation of the touches as positive, neutral or negative in intent or effect (see Table 18.1).

Table 18.1 Touch categorisation

Qualities of Touch	Interactive Uses of Touch (From Goold and Hummel, 1993)	Number of Instances	%
Positive	Informative	56	67%
	Intimate	1	
	Nurturing	51	
	Recreational	5	
	Social	21	
Neutral	Habilitative	2	32%
	Extraneous	1	
	Protective	3	
	Requisite	59	
Negative	Malicious	1	1%
	Casual	1	
	Autocratic	0	

Note: There is a difference in total number of instances in Table 18.1 compared with the 176 interactions involving touch. Some interactions could be categorised in more than one way.

It was obviously reassuring to observe that positive touch occurred twice as frequently as neutral touch. It was anticipated that there would be a considerable quantity of neutral touch as this is the necessary, functional touch that people with high dependency require throughout their lives. Contrastingly, positive touch is not functionally necessary but is may be seen as critically concerned with communicating, reassuring, informing, playing and building relationships and is, arguably therefore, the touch that is most likely to create learning and development opportunities.

Alex

Alex is a teenager who uses a wheelchair, has limited movement of her head and limbs, vision in only one eye and receives her fluids and nutrition through a tube straight into her stomach. The school nurse met Alex in her classroom and greeted her by saying 'Morning Alex' then held her hand and had a chat with her during which Alex smiled in response. The nurse then stroked Alex's face before administering eye drops. Next Alex needed part of her wheelchair harness unfastening and her clothing rearranged so a giving set could be attached to her feed pipe. The nurse then syringed water through the pipe into Alex's stomach. Throughout this procedure the nurse chatted to Alex and gave reassuring, stroking touches. Alex remained relaxed and smiling. Once the water had been administered the nurse removed the pipe, gently rearranged Alex's polo shirt, fastened her harness and said goodbye.

In the above example the school nurse had to touch the learner to give her water and administer her eye drops, an example of 'requisite' touch fulfilling caregiving requirements and likely to be neutral (Goold and Hummel 1993). However, the nurse is experienced and has a strong relationship with Alex, so the touch, although requisite, was done in a 'nurturing' manner, with touch that also involved stroking and hand holding, thus making the experience positive rather than neutral. The time taken by the nurse is significant: without the positive, nurturing touch the procedures could have been completed in less than five minutes but Alex may not have responded positively.

The impact and implications of this study

For the school team, the effects of this simple study were various. Firstly, extensive discussion and further development of understandings within the team as to how staff deploy touch effectively to support learners' well-being and learning. This led to the team collaborating in writing a 'Touch' policy and guidelines document for the school. This document effectively 'institutionalises' staff touch practice as an aspect of curriculum. It clarifies the why, how, where of this crucial element of experience for all people who work in or attend the school. There was discussion of the tendency for special schools to employ 'touch professionals' (Appleton 2005) such as aromatherapists. However, the school team arrived at the orientation that all members of staff should understand the importance of using touch as technique in order to support and interact with learners in a considered yet ordinary and natural way throughout the day. For instance, the resolution to ensure that touches which might usually be requisite and neutral, became considered, nurturing and highly positive.

The desired state of affairs for staff practice is illustrated neatly in a simple Venn diagram (see Figure 18.1). The moments the school nurse spent with Alex were an example of her having technique in line with the spirit of the diagram. Could the whole team achieve this, during every requisite touch, all day?

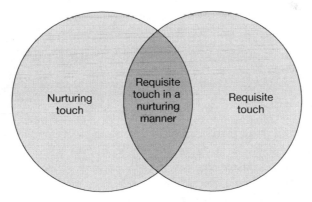

Figure 18.1   Requisite touch and nurturing touch

These issues are surely general to many learners with SLD/PMLDand to their schools. Clearly, everywhere, there is the operational issue of the sheer frequency with which staff touch learners. In this study the three learners were touched in 176 interactions in just less than 13 hours. Observing a high frequency of touching indicates its presence but it is the analysis of the types of touch which informs us about the role of touch in the lives of these learners. The three most frequently observed categories of touch were:

- Requisite – 29% of occurrences.
- Informative – 28% of occurrences.
- Nurturing – 25% of occurrences.

Requisite touch is necessary and its dominant frequency might be understandable due to the nature of the needs of the learners observed. However, informative touch occurred nearly as frequently as requisite and this is probably reflective of the team's existing strong practice of supporting learners with visual impairments through the use of tactile signs and hand-under-hand prompts to assist them to interact with their environment, e.g. by reaching out to press a switch. Correspondingly, there is a seemingly high incidence of nurturing touch used by the team, though further studies with other, similar teams are necessary to bear out this finding – this team had a known and pre-existing ethos of nurture and naturalistic interactions with learners. Nurturing touch combined with requisite touch may not be an obvious necessity. Its use is, therefore, a likely reflection of the relationships between the students and the staff members. Nurturing touch may be subconscious; its presence in an interaction demonstrating, perhaps, something of the respect and human connection between care-giver and student and the human, empathic qualities of the member of staff.

All touches, however, whether intentional or subconscious, communicate something by the qualities of the touch (Miles, 2003). So, conversely, touching in an uncaring way can communicate the opposite as Martin Pistorious is now able to describe for us:

> People revealed themselves in other ways too: in a touch that was gentle or caring or rough and unthinking… if they were angry, they would pull off my clothes just a little more roughly than usual.
>
> (Pistorious 2011: 101)

The importance of nurturing touch

Rhodes and Hewett (2010) write about members of staff seeming to have a sense of human 'knowingness' that giving physical contact to their learners of all ages who are at early stages of development, provides developmental goodness for them. The work by Hewett and Nind (e.g. Nind and Hewett 1994) and others on the continuing development and dissemination of Intensive Interaction partly flows from this posture of developmental pertinence. Intensive Interaction practitioners are comfortable with the giving and receiving of touch as an aspect of communication technique employing all available channels of communication. They are also comfortable with the outlook that learners of whatever chronological age are still at a stage of overall development where physical contact can have a sense almost of primacy for them and that its effects are likely to be, well, *developmental*. It seems obviously important that more studies should take place in the field of special needs in order to confirm this outlook of developmental pertinence and extend and develop practices accordingly. Those studies are awaited. However, the development of Intensive Interaction was influenced profoundly by a sense of developmental 'emulation' – scrutinising and borrowing from knowledge arising out of research on infancy, both for usually developing infants and for those identified as having learning difficulties from birth. This perspective focuses first and foremost on all of the potential for usual development which can occur in usual ways for a person who has SLD/PMLD.

From birth onwards, tactile stimulation plays an important role in health and development (Caplan 2005; Cigales *et al.* 1996). In the seminal study by Stack and Muir (1990) mothers were observed touching their infants over 80 per cent of the time they interacted with them and identified touch as a powerful component of social interplay. The stimulation provided by being held is known to affect infants' psychological and emotional wellbeing (Field 2010).

Touch is even more important for individuals who have deficiencies in one or more sensory channels (Hodges and McLinden 2004; Dobson *et al.* 2002). It has been proposed that individuals with congenital deafblindness may develop a language of touch and motion which is processed through the areas of the brain usually used to process visual and auditory stimuli (Hart 2012). Hart (2012) suggested that partnerships involving deafblind people require a common 'touchpoint' which lies within the perceptual experiences of both partners.

Alongside the psychological importance of touch for infants, touch has an important physiological role in growth and development (Montagu 1986). Touch deprivation therefore has an impact on an infant's physiological, psychological and cognitive development (Punyanunt-Carter and Wrench 2009). A range of psychological disorders in children and adults can be attributed to tactile deprivation (McCray 1978; Langton 2006; and Gupta and Schork 1995).

Modern medical advances are contributing to the 29.7 per cent increase in the population of learners with PMLD between 2004 and 2009 (DCSF 2010). 80 per cent of children born at less than 26 weeks gestation are now surviving with over 50 per cent of them having severe and complex learning difficulties often with neurological compromise and complex health needs (Marlow *et al.* 2005). Perhaps touch privation can arise from the very beginning therefore. Many of these learners began their lives in incubators where, although tactile interventions may be in place, they receive less comforting or soothing touch in comparison to new born 'healthy' infants (Law Harrison 2004). At this time parents are often dealing with the shock of the diagnosis (Myerson 2009). Parents frequently have to come to terms with the loss of the child they thought they would have and may experience feelings of failure from the difficulties in 'nursing' their infant (Hollander 2008). Therefore, from the very beginning, these infants can have very different touch experiences. The frequent need to use equipment to maintain good postural care (Mencap 2011) means that throughout their lifetimes many people with PMLD will spend a large proportion of their time in equipment which inhibits much of the nurturing touch such as hugging (Reid 2010). As Carpenter states:

> We must see beyond the tubes and medical equipment, beyond the physical apparatus to the child as a learner.
>
> (Carpenter 2010: 5)

The tactile sense is the first sense to develop followed by the auditory then visual senses, but as the child develops, the precedence of these senses is reversed (Montagu 1986). Learners with PMLD are recognised as functioning at overall early developmental levels (Welsh Assembly Government 2006). These early levels can compare to the normal developmental levels of a child of three days old to three years and four months old (Martin, Thomas and Price 2004). Therefore, a learner at these early developmental levels may still be using the tactile modality as their primary sense to engage with and comprehend the world around them. It may, therefore, be at least properly compensatory but, further, developmentally appropriate to offer some of the touch experiences that occur between infant and caregivers; 'up close, as close as possible' (Rhodes and Hewett 2010).

Within a developmentally appropriate approach learners are empowered and gain the confidence to reach out to others and trust being touched in return, such as Jude in the following example.

Jude

Jude is a strong young man with complex learning difficulties who because of his slight frame frequently gets mistaken as being of primary school age. He finds the whole school celebration assemblies overwhelming and indicates this by vocalising noisily, biting on his hands and vacating the hall. However if Jude is close to familiar people who he trusts he will frequently sit himself on their knees and initiate a repertoire of Intensive Interaction activities; clapping hands together, sharing quiet joyful vocalisations and the simultaneous swaying of bodies. In this manner Jude will frequently successfully sit amongst the rest of the school for 30 minutes to share the music and atmosphere of the assembly.

There are learners who may be described as 'tactile defensive' (Welsh Assembly Government 2006), who may avoid touch in some contexts or may respond in a negative way to some textures or touch. This may be due to hypersensitivity of the skin (Ayres 2005) which can affect the caregiver infant interactions as the touch causes pain and discomfort to the child who may then squirm or cry when held (Caldwell 2007). It may also be a learnt response which McLinden and McCall (2002) state can be due to inappropriate learning environments. Individuals with SLD/PMLD will nonetheless need requisite touch for the rest of their lives, so it is important to support them to tolerate and if possible enjoy a wider range of touch. It is important to therefore highlight a major aspect of touch technique that forms the basis of good Intensive Interaction practice – 'tuning-in'. The member of staff must tune into and read and assimilate the responses of the other person as sensitively and as humanly possible. Tuning-in can and should form the basis of good touch practices. Dobson *et al.* (2004) caution about the failure properly to read the participation and consent of the other person. Important, too, is at all times to be mindful of a usual sense of dignity for the other person (Calveley 2013).

Touch in the school curriculum

Natural, human, ordinary, physical contact experiences potentially provide opportunities for learners to develop knowledge and understanding about themselves, others, the world and how to communicate and socialise. In which areas of their curriculum would this learning be deemed irrelevant? Moreover, where in the curriculum does this understanding of 'self' fall? Probably within Personal, Social and Health Education, but given the already observed pervasive importance of touch experience in early learning experience, it seems inordinately limiting to allocate touch to a specific curriculum area.

Our field of work is probably still within a climate of uncertainty and 'moral panic' (Johnson 2000) on how to use touch with learners in education. The lack of clarity in policies and other documentation can only contribute to apprehension in staff members' approach to touch when meeting an individual's intimate and personal care needs (Carnaby and Cambridge 2006) and participating in Intensive Interaction (Culham 2004), while our colleagues in mainstream schools may agonise about touching appropriately when applying sun cream or a plaster to a child (Piper, Powell and Smith 2006). In their review of the research in adult services, Dobson *et al.* (2002) acknowledged that guidance and procedural policies relating to touch focus solely on the use of 'necessary' touch. They further state that staff are rarely trained in the use of touch in adult services other than to highlight risk and client privacy.

It is suggested here that there is a necessity for schools and other institutions to do what the team in Julia Barnes' study achieved and have a 'touch policy' which highlights the developmental appropriateness of touch and acknowledges what can be learnt and communicated through touch. Importantly, too, there should be guidelines around consent for touch and detail of safeguards. However, quality touch experiences rely partly on the natural and non-conscious communicative touch between consenting individuals so it is important that a touch policy does not hinder this by being too specific and applying arbitrary rules (Piper and Smith 2003). Safeguarding and physical intervention policies are frequently the sole documents in an institution which refer to touch at all. However, it is strongly suggested that the positive touch policy should stand independent of these others, emphasising developmental positives and the curriculum understandings; Hewett and Firth (2012) provide an example. A touch policy must also acknowledge the difficulties. Touch can be viewed as the most arousing of the senses (Schanberg 1995) and touch in everyday care and play can cause sexual arousal in individuals with learning difficulties whose avenues for sexual expression may be extremely limited (McCarthy 2006).

The positive utility of a touch policy will ideally be developed collaboratively by a team and shared with families in an environment of openness where differing views, opinions and concerns can be voiced and discussed. For instance, the outcomes of the study related here were shared with the school's parental support group. It was clear that parents' fears were more of physical or sexually abusive touches to their offspring, not of the natural and enriching touch experiences routinely offered. They discussed the nurturing touch that was commonplace within their homes and how that desired this to continue within the school day. One parent cited her son's experiences in a different school:

> (her son) is emotionally immature and when in mainstream wanted to hug teachers and they decided if he hugged them they wouldn't respond. I found that hard, he needed touch and without he felt lost, he didn't feel safe.

Summary and conclusion

Human touch is identified as crucial to the communicative, emotional and psychological developments of infancy. Our practices in special education should surely have a standpoint that embraces the importance of similar developmental experiences for those who have SLD/PMLD. Touch communication will be critically important for those who have sensory impairments where it may be their primary modality for experiencing and making contact with others. For individuals with profound and severe learning difficulties touch is at worst unavoidable and at best a way of communicating, expressing, nurturing, soothing, reassuring, informing and comforting. Schools need fully to acknowledge the array of touch experience these learners receive and provide documentation explaining the way in which touch experiences contribute to their quality of learning experiences throughout the school day.

A major aspect of this chapter is a review of the findings of one, small-scale research project and it is hoped that in the future there is further formal and informal inquiry into the physical contact experiences of learners with learning difficulties.

Questions for readers

- Do your school and team have an ethos of freely and warmly providing nurturing touch to people who are learners operating at very early levels of development? (While also recognising and applying all guidelines for safeguards).
- What can you do within your school, with your team, openly and realistically to commence discussion and knowledgeable evaluation of this area of practice and learning?
- What steps can be taken in all schools to document and make official these areas of practice and learning?

References

Appleton, J. (2005) 'Losing Touch', *The Guardian*, 9 February.

Ayres, J. (2005) *Sensory Integration and the Child: 25th Anniversary Edition*, USA: Western Psychological Services.

Barnes, K. (2012) *An Investigation of the Human-Touch Experiences of Students with Profound and Multiple Learning Difficulties and Visual Impairment at Crowshill School (a pseudonym): Site Study*, M.Ed. dissertation: The University of Birmingham.

Caldwell, P. (2007) *From Isolation to Intimacy: Making friends without words*, London: Jessica Kingsley.

Calveley, J. (2013) 'How are people with PMLD affected by dignity?' *PMLD LINK*, 25(2): 14–16.

Caplan, M. (2005) *To Touch is to Live: The need for genuine affection in an impersonal world*, USA: Third Eye Publishing.

Carnaby, S. and Cambridge, P. (2006) 'Staff Attitudes and Perspectives', in S. Carnaby and P. Cambridge (eds) *Intimate and Personal Care with People with Learning Difficulties*, London: Jessica Kingsley.

Carpenter, B. (2010) *Children with Complex Learning Difficulties and Disabilities: Who are they and how do we teach them?*, London: Specialist Schools and Academies Trust.

Cigales, M., Field, T., Hossain, Z., Pelaez-Nogureas, M. and Gewirtz, J. (1996) 'Touch Among Children at Nursery School', *Early Child Development and Care*, 126: 101–110.

Culham, A. (2004) 'Getting in touch with our feminine sides? Men's difficulties and concerns with doing Intensive Interaction', *British Journal of Special Education*, 31(2): 81–88.

DCSF (Department for Children, Schools and Families) (2010) *Salt Review: independent review of teacher supply for pupils with severe, profound and multiple learning difficulties*, Annesley: DCSF Publications.

Dobson, S., Carey, L., Conyers, I., Upadhyaya S. and Raghavan, R. (2004) 'Learning about touch: an exploratory study to identify the learning needs of staff supporting people with complex needs', *Journal of Learning Disabilities*, 8: 113–129.

Dobson, S., Upadhyaya, S., Conyers, I. and Raghavan, R. (2002) 'Touch in the care of people with profound and complex Needs: a review of the literature', *Journal of Intellectual Disabilities*, 6(4): 351–362.

Field, T. (2010) 'Touch for socioemotional and physical well-being: a review', *Developmental Review*, 30(4), 367–383.

Goold, L. and Hummel, J. (1993) *Supporting the Receptive Communication of Individuals with Significant Multiple Disabilities: Selective use of touch to enhance comprehension*, North Rocks, Australia: North Rocks Press.

Gupta, M. and Schork, N. (1995) 'Touch deprivation has an adverse effect on body image: some preliminary observations', *International Journal of Eating Disorders*, 17(2): 185–189.

Hart, P. (2012) *The Landscape of Touch*, Lecture, Multi-Sensory Impairment Network: Leeds, 13 October 2012.

Hewett, D. (2007) 'Do touch: physical contact and people who have severe, profound and multiple learning difficulties', *Support for Learning*, 22(3): 116–123.

Hewett, D. (2012) 'Blind Frogs, the nature of human communication and Intensive Interaction', in D. Hewett (ed.) *Intensive Interaction: Theoretical perspectives*, London: Sage.

Hewett, D. and Firth, G. (2012) *Intensive Interaction Curriculum Documents for Schools*, Puckeridge: Intensive Interaction Institute.

Hodges, L. and McLinden, M. (2004) 'Hands on – hands off! Exploring the role of touch in the learning experiences of a child with severe learning difficulties and visual impairment', *The SLD Experience*, Spring 2004: 20–24.

Hollander, J. (2008) 'A tale of two mothers', *The Guardian*, 8 March.

Imray, P. and Hinchcliffe, V. (2014) *Curricula for Teaching Children and Young People with Severe of Profound and Multiple Learning Difficulties*, Abingdon: Routledge.

Johnson, R. (2000) *Hands Off! The Disappearance of Touch in the Care of Children,* New York: Peter Lang.

Langton, E. (2006) 'Romania's children', *The Psychologist*, 19(7): 412–413.

Law Harrison, L. (2004) 'Tactile Stimulation of Neonatal Intensive Care Unit Preterm Infants', in T. Field (ed.) *Touch and Massage in Early Child Development*, San Francisco, CA: Johnson and Johnson Pediatric Institute.

Marlow, N., Wolke, D., Bracewell, M. and Samara, M. (2005) 'Neurological and developmental disability at 6 years of age following extremely preterm birth', *New England Journal of Medicine*, 352(1): 9–19.

Martin, K., Thomas P. and Price K. (2004) 'A comparison of P Levels and developmental assessment frameworks', *Communication Matters: UK Conference International Society for Augmentative and Alternative Communication*, University of Lancashire.

McCarthy, M. (2006) 'Sexuality and intimate and personal care', in S. Carnaby and P. Cambridge (eds) *Intimate and Personal Care with People with Learning Difficulties*, London: Jessica Kingsley.

McCray, G. (1978) 'Excessive masturbation of childhood: a symptom of tactile deprivation?' *Pediatrics*, 62(3): 277–279.

McLinden, M. and McCall, S. (2002) *Learning through Touch*, London: David Fulton.

Mencap (2011) *Postural care: protecting and restoring body shape.* London: Mencap Publications, Online. Available: www.mencap.org.uk/node/13296 (accessed 3 October 2013).

Miles, B. (2003) *Talking the Language of the Hands to the Hands.* Online. Available: http://nationaldb.org/library/page/1930 (accessed 9 September 2013).

Montagu, A. (1986) *Touching: The Human Significance of the Skin*, New York: Harper.

Myerson, T. (2009) 'Life and death decisions with a disabled child', *The Independent*, 10 November.

Nind, M. and Hewett, D. (1994) *Access to Communication: Developing the basics of communication with people with severe learning difficulties through Intensive Interaction*, London: David Fulton.

Nind, M. and Hewett, D. (2005) *Access to Communication: Developing the basics of communication with people with severe learning difficulties through Intensive Interaction*, 2nd edn, London: David Fulton.

Piper, H., Powell, J. and Smith, H. (2006) 'Parents, professionals, and paranoia: the touching of children in a culture of fear', *Journal of Social Work*, 151(6): 151–167.

Piper, H. and Smith, H. (2003) '"Touch" in education and child care settings: dilemmas and responses', *British Educational Research Journal*, 29(6): 879–894.

Pistorious, M. (2011) *Ghost Boy: my escape from a life locked inside my own body*, London: Simon and Schuster.

Punyanunt-Carter, N. and Wrench, J. (2009) 'Development of a validity testing of a measure of touch deprivation', *Human Communication*, 12(1): 67–76.

Reid, M. (2010) 'Spinal Column', *The Times Magazine*, 19 June, p. 13.

Rhodes, J. and Hewett, D. (2010) The human touch: physical contact and making a social world available for the most profoundly disabled, *PMLD Link*, 22 (2): 11–14.

Schanberg, S. (1995) 'The genetic basis for touch effects', in T. Field (ed.) *Touch in Early Development*, New Jersey: Lawrence Erlbaum.

Stack, D. and Muir, D. (1990) 'Tactile Stimulation as a component of social interchange: new interpretations for the still-face effect', *British Journal of Developmental Psychology*, 8: 131–145.

Welsh Assembly Government (2006) *Routes for Learning Additional Guidance: assessment materials for learners with profound learning difficulties and additional disabilities*, Cardiff: Crown Copyright.

19

CHALLENGING BEHAVIOUR AND THE CURRICULUM

Peter Imray and Dave Hewett

In this chapter, the following questions will be addressed:

- Why is addressing challenging behaviour not usually perceived as an integral part of the school curriculum?
- What should be the basis for a 'challenging behaviour curriculum'?
- How may teachers cope with challenging behaviour and help the learner?

Introduction

This chapter is about the positive and proactive management of challenging behaviour shown by learners with SLD/PMLD. There are certain assumptions made in this chapter, which would not be made were space to allow. Two of these are that, firstly, readers will have a broad understanding of what constitutes SLD and PMLD, and, secondly, they will understand what is meant by challenging behaviour in relation to these learners. Readers who do not would be well advised to first turn to either Harris, Hewett and Hogg (2001) or Imray (2008).

The pedagogy of behaviour

One of the major difficulties in addressing the behaviour of children, young people and adults with severe or profound learning difficulties[1] is working out where it lies in the education system. This means that we often try and teach it rather as we would teach maths: there are a number of rules which must be obeyed; there is only one answer to each question; as long as children learn the one answer all will be well. The failure of learners to follow these rules throws us into confusion, because Behaviour (with a capital B) is not a subject as such. There are Maths and English and Science; there are Geography and History and RE; there are Music and Art and ICT and PE; there is even PSHE (Personal, Social, and Health Education) and Citizenship; but there is not a subject called Behaviour.

Further, because behaviour does not exist with a capital B, there are questions as to whether it is part of the role of the education system to continue to teach learners how to behave appropriately if they aren't able to learn the basic rules. There will be some elements of preparing to learn, though this will largely be restricted to early years. By the time a child enters the education system proper, that is, at the age of 5 or 6 years, she/he should have learned the skills and strategies necessary for functioning within a classroom situation. But what if the pupil has not learnt these things?

There is virtually no guidance from the Department for Education (DfE), apart from recommendations from the Qualification and Curriculum Authority (QCA) that a curriculum for pupils with learning difficulties might include, for example, programmes to 'enable pupils to express preferences, communicate needs, make choices, make decisions and choose options that other people act on and respect' (QCA 2009: 6), and, of course, such objectives could equally apply to all pupils across all settings and certainly do not make the teaching of behaviour a specific priority. The introduction of 'personal priority needs' and 'therapeutic needs' which are 'central to their learning and quality of life' moves further into the behaviour field, but are classified under possible and additional therapeutic provision, which:

> enhances individual pupils' readiness to learn in many ways, for example by:
> - developing pupils' self-esteem
> - allowing pupils' behaviour and alternative ways of communicating to be acknowledged and understood.
>
> (QCA 2009: 7–8)

Here, the resolution of behaviour issues is seen as a concern of 'therapy', which will by its nature constitute an extracurricular activity. Even if it occurs within school time, it is likely to be conducted by specialist non-teachers who work through the medium of art or music or drama or dance movement and who are trained in a psycho-dynamic model. Movements to adopt therapeutic ideas into the education system are frequently met by a strong caucus which believes that such models have gained an increasing hold over education and have perverted its core from its traditional role of teaching knowledge (Ecclestone and Hayes 2009). The 'dangerous rise of therapeutic education' needs, they argue, to be kept in check.

Advice on behaviour programmes is often sought from educational psychologists, or psychiatrists and psychiatric nurses within a NHS funded team such as the Child and Adolescent Mental Health Services (CAMHS), or local authority funded behaviour advisory teams. The increasing use of physical restraint procedures through organisations such as Team Teach, SCIP or PRICE, potentially takes the responsibility away from the teacher and formalises a reactive policy. This is not to criticise organisations that provide training in restraint techniques, for such training is absolutely essential for when things inevitably go wrong. We are merely pointing out that such organisations were born out of a need for those working with learners, who habitually exhibit sometimes extreme challenging behaviours, to deal with crises. They are therefore, naturally reactive; their role is to give essential advice and training for when things go wrong, and we need to concentrate much more on creating the conditions for things going right and fully recognising the creation of these conditions as a curricular concern.

The actual management of the behaviour (and indeed the 'management' of the learner) can sometimes be a role passed on to senior teachers and school leaders or quite possibly teaching assistants so that the teacher has the time and freedom to do her job – teach. This further pushes the management of behaviour into a reactive setting, so that crucially, we as teachers, are effectively waiting for the behaviour to occur before we make any attempt at resolution.

Such reactive stances are, we argue, a direct result of not giving sufficient time and importance to Behaviour with a capital B, as a subject to be taught or addressed with learners as a curricular priority. This is especially so given our contention that 'challenging behaviour is normal' for those with SLD/PMLD (Hewett 1998a). This does not assume that every learner with SLD/

PMLD will display habitual challenges, though it does argue that given the depth of their difficulties, they ought to, and we must regard ourselves as being extremely lucky if they don't:

> Many challenging behaviours can be construed as (at least in the short term) coherently organized adaptive responses to challenging situations.
>
> (Emerson 2001: 3)

Estimates of the level and frequency of habitual challenging behaviour vary, but writers generally agree that there is a considerably higher than average chance of those with SLD or PMLD having attendant challenging behaviours (Allen *et al.* 2006). Harris (1995) estimated that between 10 and 15 per cent of the SLD school population will regularly exhibit challenging behaviour while Borthwick–Duffy (1994) suggests figures of 22 per cent of those with SLD and 33 per cent of those with PMLD. Male (1996) posits that the figure might be nearer 25 per cent overall. This same study also noted that some UK SLD schools reported 50 per cent of their population as exhibiting some form of challenging behaviour at various times in their school lives, a number supported by a similar study conducted by Porter and Lacey (1999). Einfeld and Emerson (2013) pooled studies conducted in the UK and Australia between 2005 and 2011 to posit that 29 per cent of those with an intellectual disability will also have significant emotional and/or social difficulties, and Emerson and Hatton (2007) noted that children with an intellectual disability were four and a half times more likely to have an additional ICD–10 diagnosis than those without.

Behaviour, learners' inner states and the curriculum

In the next two sections, we offer an outlook and value system on behaviour and curriculum which has been generated by decades–long experience of working with SLD schools and their teams, but also influenced by recent significant research. The views outlined here cannot belong solely to these two writers. These views have been fostered and nurtured by long thought and discussion with many wonderful practitioners who we agree, display 'incredible moral courage' (Rogers 2009). These practitioners often find that their aspirations for their pupils and their ambitions for their practices can seem to be at odds with the system of working they have been decreed. Our outlook has of course also been influenced by other writers, with a particular acknowledgement to the thinking of John Harris and his concept of 'everyday good practice' (Harris 1995; Harris, Hewett and Hogg 2001) and Geraint Ephraim's 'exotic communications' (Ephraim 1998).

We will, probably all too briefly, attempt to set out a practical orientation to a curriculum concept and the practices arising from this outlook, by itemising its basic principles. We suggest that this simple structure can form the basis for the operation and documentation of the 'challenging behaviour curriculum'. There are two basic and straightforward essentials, discussed below in order of priority.

First priority: cope

Please forgive the repetition of the word 'coping', but it *is* intentional. Coping means teamwork and attention to detail, doing all of the mundane, routine and down to earth things that are necessary, day by day, in order to cope with the reality of the way that the learner feels and behaves. Coping includes psychological preparation and orientation – 'challenging behaviour is normal', this is part of the job, this *is* curriculum etc.

Coping also infers a generalised orientation to the provision of an ordinary, everyday classroom social environment which exudes positive understanding, tolerance and nurture toward people who are still at very early levels of communicative, cognitive, psychological and emotional development.

Coping means being positive and having a positive culture. Effective teams put aside any thoughts of punishment and negative attitudes, developing ways of working *with* the learner who is exhibiting the behaviours rather than *against* her/him. This might even mean putting negative terms such as 'no' and 'don't do that' behind us (Imray 2012) because these do not tell the learner what he should be doing, they only upbraid him for being at fault... yet again.

Coping can be assisted by the 'one rule' rule. It is unusual for a learner who exhibits habitual challenging behaviour to just have a single behaviour which s/he only exhibits in one situation with one group of people and in one setting. If only life were that simple! Sometimes, there are various behaviours exhibited in a variety of situations and settings with lots of different people, but if we try to tackle them all at the same time, we are making life very difficult for ourselves, and almost impossible for the learner who we are asking to change. Effective teams prioritise, so they just deal with the most important, gradually moving on to tackle the others.

Coping implies being observant as to triggers for the learner's behaviour; the reasons behind the adoption of challenging behaviours may be complicated and complex but the triggers may be clearer.

- 'I don't want to do this.'
- 'I want more time from this person.'
- 'I don't understand this.'
- 'I've had enough of this, leave me alone.'
- 'There's too much noise/light/people.'
- 'I'm bored; give me something to do that interests me.'
- 'Can't you see I feel terrible today? Leave me be.'

Knowledge of what these triggers might be will only be found by looking at life from the perspective of the person with learning difficulties. You might think what you're asking the learner to do is reasonable; they obviously do not!

Coping will include helping the learner to resolve the behaviour before it re-occurs. Having established a prioritised list, we still need to accept that the reasons for the learner adopting the 'challenging' behaviour are perfectly normal; he wants us to listen to him. He has, probably over a period of time, adopted this behaviour(s) because we haven't listened to him. We need to remember that Behaviour has a capital B; it is a subject to be learned and we therefore have to approach this from a positive rather than a negative perspective; so this shouldn't just be 'Don't hit' or 'Don't bite' or 'Follow my instruction'. What do you think the learner could do instead of hitting or biting or refusing an instruction? How can we *help* the learner who is exhibiting the challenging behaviour? We must remember also that the learner has adopted the strategies of hitting or biting or refusing an instruction, because he has no other way of expressing himself so that the people in control (teachers, teaching assistants, bus escorts, meal-time supervisors, parents, siblings, Uncle Tom Cobley and all) will listen. In this context, helping the learner is not just about listening but actually doing something about it. Helping the learner might mean taking away the reason for the learner hitting or biting or refusing to follow an instruction. Logically, once the pressure on the learner has been taken away, the behaviour should cease, or at least drastically reduce (Imray and Hinchcliffe 2014).

Lastly, coping also critically includes sensible, practical, down to earth, incident management procedures – *all* members of staff understanding the techniques and sharing a common style when the worst happens and the team must attempt to manage a pupil's extreme feelings and behaviour. Hewett (1998b) recommends these principles of practice for staff style within challenging situations:

1 Attempt at all times to *avoid contributing* to the seriousness of the incident with the style of *your* behaviour.
2 *Stay calm.* You have the right to all sorts of feelings about the situation, but you do not have the right to allow those feelings to drive your practice. Your practice should be driven by reason and rationality.
3 Don't crowd around the learner. *One member of staff* at a time as the main communicator.
4 Work positively and look for *effective outcomes* rather than winners and losers. Avoid *unnecessary conflict* with the learner, remember and use techniques of *avoiding confrontation*, defusing (especially 'calming') and particularly, making options available where the *learner has power* to make decisions to end the incident.
5 Get your *priorities right.* The first priority is to manage the incident successfully and to have an effective outcome.
6 It may be expecting too much from the situation that it can be a *learning experience* for the learner who is being challenging, or that you may do something with *your* behaviour during the incident, which will cause it never to happen again.
7 Nonetheless, look *for opportunities* that the incident may provide for learning – particularly during the aftermath and any debrief with the learner.
8 You will probably handle the situation better if you attempt to see the world and the incident from the *point of view* of the learner who is being challenging.
9 Tune-in to the learner and *stay sensitive* to his/her varying levels of arousal.
10 Use *defusing techniques* for escalating arousal and stay aware of your own *body language*, movements and use of space.
11 Do *good evaluations* by reflecting, talking and preferably, recording in writing. Particularly, evaluate and record incidents with effective outcomes so that you can acknowledge what you did well and take the knowledge forward to the next incident.
12 *Don't expect* to manage all incidents successfully. It is all right to be fallible. Do think and reflect.

Second priority: help the learner

The team needs to be doing progressive, proactive things. Practical, routine, doable things, but things which may also be positive, insightful, human, humane, perceptive, therapeutic, psycho-dynamic, whatever: things that are aimed at helping the learner to progress, develop, move on, feel better, and adopt more positive and constructive ways of interacting with the world. This all needs to be documented – written up into a positive programme of action. The action plan should be founded on sensible and insightful appreciation of the state of mind and circumstances for the learner and it should be properly, regularly evaluated and recorded. The action plan *is* an aspect of curriculum.

It would be wonderful if you could find the cause of a learner's challenging behaviour. Then, you could do something about the cause and the behaviour would go away and it would probably be judged that highly effective work had taken place. Unfortunately, this operation is not possible because the cause does not exist. Or at least the single cause does not exist. People behave the way that they do, exhibiting both positive and negative behaviour, due to a wide variety of factors coming together to produce the behaviour. Hewett (1998c) sets out a detailed review of the factors as a practical concept which offers a model for understanding and action by staff. The factors are viewed as occurring in two dimensions, everything *inside* the learner ('personal factors') and everything occurring *around* the learner ('environmental factors'). A team of practitioners working effectively will pay thoughtful attention to the possibilities here. The core of a person-orientated approach will be observation of and sensitivity to the various factors for each individual learner and a preparedness to use this perception as the basis for helping that learner, particularly with personal factors, particularly their inner states.

In our field of work some personal factors have obvious significance. For instance, much of what we term 'challenging behaviour' can be viewed as the lifestyle of a person who is at a very early level of development in most respects, but often equipped with a fully developed body (Hewett 1998b). This perspective, i.e. people with SLD display those behaviours *because* they have severe learning difficulties or autism or both (Imray 2008), should surely flow through our orientations to meeting their needs.

Additionally, for any person, but crucially of course for learners who have SLD/PMLD and/or autism, the most significant personal factors in the production of difficult feelings and behaviour are likely to be communication difficulties. Communication difficulties that are then combined with the general nature of a learner's psychological and emotional development. These personal factors are then further combined with or confronted by, the environmental factor of the often extreme-feeling challenges of the situations they find themselves within.

Let us be reluctant here to view communication difficulties as a standalone issue of skill possession or the absence of these skills. There are recent exciting developments in the fields of neurobiology and cognitive neuroscience concerned with the general brain development consequences of communication learning experiences in infancy and the later outcomes in all cognitive, psychological and emotional development (Marshall and Fox 2006).

Studies in the field of developmental cognitive neuroscience have led since the late 1990s to a renewed interest in Bowlby's (1969) formulation of attachment theory and the parent–child interactions in which it is fostered and situated. Attachment is viewed increasingly from a perspective where psychological theories of attachment and biological theories of developmental ecology can be used together to understand behavioural outcomes (Bradshaw and Schore 2006). This perspective observes the relationship, or perhaps the feedback cycle, between the quality of early experiences, consequent generation of healthy brain chemistry, the development of attachment and affect – and the then further positive consequences in healthy neural development that produces further healthy brain chemistry, the positive behavioural consequences of all this, and so on (see Shore 1997; Schore 2001, 2002, 2008).

Sterkenberg *et al.*'s (2008) recent work in the Netherlands suggests that working to address attachment disorders and using positive behaviour interventions is more effective than just working on the difficult behaviour. Schuengel *et al.* (2009) describe an approach where the therapist 'makes verbal and tactile contact' and invites the child to 'engage in interaction' involving imitation and play. It is not difficult to visualise the sense in which the Intensive Interaction approach (e.g. Nind and Hewett 2005) can also be viewed as a multi-modal approach to the range of pupils' developing sensibilities, going beyond the development of communication routines per se and into realms of emotional well-being (Nind 2009, 2012; Hewett 2012). While Hewett and Nind contend that Intensive Interaction is teaching and learning and therefore part of the curriculum, rather than a therapeutic approach as described in the National Curriculum guidelines, they have no issues with the therapeutic nature of its applications and outcomes and the crossover between curriculum and therapy (Nind and Hewett 2005). Weare (2004 cited in Nind, 2009) says,

Thus staff need to foster environments where emotions are accepted as normal and unthreatening, discussed freely, expressed in safe ways, written about in policies and considered in decision-making.

(Nind 2009: 66)

Perhaps we special educators can now begin constructively to view a pupil's learning difficulty as more than just a diagnosed brain impairment. It can be a complex mix of the cognitive impairment, the resultant lack of experience of communication routines, and a reduced ability to connect with others. Therefore, there is a potential scenario of highly reduced access to usual early human interaction experiences where deep psychological and emotional (and neurological) underpinnings take place. This is followed by all of the well-being consequences of the challenge of going through childhood, life and our curriculum demands without some of these basic orientations in place.

Teams working well with from this standpoint have a form of communicative nurturance as the basis of their work. At the time of writing, we discern nothing new in this perspective, merely that it perhaps is not, as yet, general practice. Clegg and Lansdall-Welfare (1995: 302) suggested that 'facilitating secure attachment relationships for distressed clients may be difficult for professionals, but partial assuagement of their attachment needs is a realistic clinical goal.' It is perhaps disappointing that the developing culture of 'Nurture Groups' (Boxall and Lucas 2002) has not as yet seemed to have made major inroads into special education.

The way of working advocated here is not 'laissez-faire'. It will be expressed in written 'action plans' for each individual learner, outlining the perception of that learner's difficulties and factors and the detail of what the team does with her/him day by day. It will also be expressed in a general written rationale that outlines the nature of the social environment, the reasons for the nurturance emphasis, and the working and organisational practices thus occurring.

There is no doubt that this curriculum vision may imply changes for many classrooms and schools. There may be a change in practices in order to bring in more communication-based, nurturance and well-being experiences. For some learners, including those who display severe challenging behaviours, there may therefore be less emphasis on group work, less immediate emphasis on succeeding academically, and consequently more emphasis on building positive, nurturing relationships.

Summary and conclusion

For learners with SLD/PMLD, challenging behaviour should be perceived as normal. We should not be surprised, and it is nobody's fault, but challenging behaviour should be seen as an understandable consequence of the effects and experience of the learning difficulty. Learning about behaviour means that Behaviour and the emotional life that contributes to it must be regarded by schools as a subject, and for some this subject can be the most important in the whole curriculum. We cannot expect academic or scholastic progress to be made until we have helped the learner resolve the circumstances that give rise to what we call, challenging behaviours.

Because the reasons behind the behaviours are often multifarious and may well involve complex psychological and neurobiological factors, we can fall into the assumption that the resolutions must be therefore be complex and complicated too. Resist this temptation and adopt a 'less is more' policy, the two basic steps being coping and helping. We can't help if we can't cope and this is therefore an essential first step. We can't help if we insist that the learner has to do what we say; we can only help if we look at the world from the perspective of the learner with learning difficulties.

Questions for readers

- Is there a written policy, in your organisation, about the positive and proactive management of challenging behaviour that provides clear and unambiguous guidance as well as explicit aims?
- If so, was everyone involved in its development?
- What are the arrangements for helping everyone to prepare for dealing with challenging behaviour and mitigating the risks of it occurring?

Note

1   Whilst this is not a book or a chapter which is specifically dedicated to those with an autistic spectrum condition (ASC) we recognise that a large percentage of those who have an autism diagnosis will also have an additional learning difficulty, which is often severe. All that we aver here relating to those with learning difficulties and challenging behaviour, equally applies to those with autism, learning difficulties and challenging behaviour.

References

Allen, D., Lowe, K., Jones, E., James, W., Doyle, T., Andrew, J., Davies, D., Moore, K. and Brophy, S. (2006) 'Changing the face of challenging behaviour services: the Special Projects Team', *British Journal of Learning Disabilities*, 34(4): 237–242.

Borthwick-Duffy, S.A. (1994) 'Epidemiology and prevalence of psychopathology in people with mental retardation', *Journal of Consulting and Clinical Psychology*, 62: 17–27.

Bowlby, J. (1969) *Attachment and Loss, Vol. 1: Attachment*, New York: Basic Books.

Boxall, M. and Lucas, S. (2002) *Nurture Groups in Schools, Principles and Practice*, London: Sage.

Bradshaw, G.A. and Schore, A.N. (2007) 'How elephants are opening doors: developmental neuroethology, attachment and social context', *Ethology*, 113: 426–436.

Clegg, J.A. and Lansdall-Welfare, R. (1995) 'Attachment and learning disability: a theoretical review informing three clinical interventions', *Journal of Intellectual Disability Research*, 39(4): 295–305.

Ecclestone, K. and Hayes, D. (2009) *The Dangerous Rise of Therapeutic Education*, Abingdon: Routledge.

Einfeld, S. and Emerson, E. (2013) *Challenging Behaviour: Developing knowledge-based approaches to the prevention of challenging behaviours*, Sydney: University of Sydney.

Emerson, E. (2001) *Challenging Behaviour: Analysis and intervention in people with severe intellectual disabilities*, Cambridge: Cambridge University Press.

Emerson, E. and Hatton, C. (2007) 'The mental health of children and adolescents with intellectual disabilities in Britain', *British Journal of Psychiatry*, 191: 493–499.

Ephraim, G. (1998) 'Exotic communications, conversations and scripts – or tales of the pained, the unheard and the unloved', in D. Hewett (ed.), *Challenging Behaviour Principles and Practices*, London: David Fulton.

Harris, J. (1995) 'Responding to pupils with SLD, who present challenging behaviour', *British Journal of Special Education*, 22(3): 109–115.

Harris, J., Hewett, D. and Hogg, J. (2001) *Positive Approaches to Challenging Behaviour*, Kidderminster: BILD.

Hewett, D. (1998a) 'Challenging behaviour is normal', in P. Lacey and C. Ouvry (eds) *People with Profound and Multiple Learning Difficulties*, London: David Fulton.

Hewett, D. (1998b) 'Commentary: managing incidents of challenging behaviour – principles', in D. Hewett (ed.) *Challenging Behaviour: Principles and practices*, London: David Fulton.

Hewett, D. (1998c) 'Commentary: helping the person learn how to behave', in D. Hewett (ed.) *Challenging Behaviour: Principles and practices*, London: David Fulton.

Hewett, D. (2012) 'Blind frogs, the nature of human communication and Intensive Interaction', in D. Hewett (ed.) *Intensive Interaction: Theoretical perspectives*, London: Sage.

Imray, P. (2008) *Turning the Tables on Challenging Behaviour*, London: Routledge.

Imray, P. (2012) 'Saying "NO" to "no"', *The SLD Experience*, 64: 17–20.

Imray, P. and Hinchcliffe, V. (2014) *Curricula for Teaching Children and Young People with Severe or Profound and Multiple Learning Difficulties: practical strategies for educational professionals*, London: Routledge.

Male, D.B. (1996) 'Who goes to SLD schools?', *Journal of Applied Research in Intellectual Disabilities*, 9(4): 307–323.

Marshall, P.J. and Fox, N.A. (2006) 'Biological approaches to the study of social engagement', in P.J. Marshall and N.A. Fox (eds) *The Development of Social Engagement, Neurobiological Perspectives*, Oxford: Oxford University Press.

Nind, M. (2009) 'Promoting the well-being of people with PMLD', in J. Pawlyn and S. Carnaby (eds) *Profound Intellectual and Multiple Disabilities, Nursing Complex Needs*, Chichester: Wiley-Blackwell.

Nind, M. (2012) 'Intensive Interaction, emotional development and emotional well-being', in D. Hewett (ed), *Intensive Interaction: Theoretical perspectives*, London: Sage.

Nind, M. and Hewett, D. (2005) *Access to Communication: Developing the basics of communication with people with severe learning difficulties through Intensive Interaction*, 2nd edn, London: David Fulton.

Porter, J. and Lacey, P. (1999) 'What provision for pupils with challenging behaviour? A report of a survey of provision and curriculum provided for pupils with learning difficulties and challenging behaviour', *British Journal of Special Education*, 26(1): 23–28.

Qualifications and Curriculum Authority (QCA) (2009) *Planning, Teaching and Assessing the Curriculum for Pupils with Learning Difficulties: general guidance*, London. QCA.

Rogers, W. (ed.) (2009) *How to Manage Children's Challenging Behaviour*, London: Sage.

Schore, A.N. (2001) 'Effects of a secure attachment relationship on right brain development, affect regulation and infant mental health', *Infant Mental Health Journal*, 22(1–2): 7–66.

Schore, A.N. (2002) 'The neurobiology of attachment and early personality organisation', *Journal of Prenatal and Perinatal Psychology and Health*, 16(3): 249–264.

Schore, A.N. (2008) 'Integrating Attachment, Affect Regulation and Neurobiology.' Address to Lifespan Learning Institute, UCLA Campus, 9 March.

Schuengel, C., Oosterman, M. and Sterkenberg, P.S. (2009) 'Children with disrupted attachment histories: Interventions and psychophysiological indices of effects', *Child and Adolescent Psychiatry and Mental Health*, 3: 1186–1753. Online. Available: www.capmh.com/content/3/1/26) (accessed 23 June 2012).

Shore, R. (1997) *Rethinking the Brain: New insights into early development*, New York: Families at Work Institute.

Sterkenberg, P.S., Janssen, C.G.C. and Schuengel, C. (2008) 'The Effect of an attachment-based behaviour therapy for children with visual and severe intellectual disabilities', *Journal of Applied Research in Intellectual Disabilities*, 21(2): 126–135.

Weare, K. (2004) *Developing the Emotionally Literate School*, London: Paul Chapman.

20

HIDDEN BEHIND A LABEL

An uneasy relationship between mental health and special needs

Ann Fergusson, Marie Howley, Richard Rose and Rachel Allan

In this chapter, the following questions will be addressed:

- What is the relationship between special educational needs and mental health?
- How can we identify mental health concerns?
- Who is involved in identifying and addressing mental health concerns?

Introduction: SEN and mental health

A recognition of the mental health needs experienced by learners with special educational needs (SEN) has received much needed attention in recent years (Morgan 2007; Fergusson, Howley and Rose 2008; Reinke *et al.* 2011), and a number of complexities in relation to interpretation and understanding have been identified. Among the difficulties highlighted is the challenge of disaggregating those behaviours that may indicate a mental health issue from those often perceived as being symptomatic of a 'label' such as autism spectrum disorder or profound and multiple learning difficulty. The potential for 'overshadowing' (PAMIS 2011), i.e. attributing atypical behaviours to a diagnosed disability or learning difficulty rather than recognising them as symptomatic of a mental health problem, has been identified by a number of writers (Rose *et al.* 2009; Emerson, Einfeld and Stancliffe 2010). Sheehy and Nind (2005) suggest that the identification of mental health difficulties in learners with PMLD, and particularly learners who may have difficulty articulating their personal needs, often results in changes in behaviour being misinterpreted and a failure to attribute these to mental health issues.

Research suggests that the prevalence of mental health issues in learners diagnosed with some conditions associated with SEN may be particularly high, for example in relation to learners with autism spectrum disorders (ASD) (Simonoff *et al.* 2008). However, figures related specifically to learners with SLD/PMLD are much more difficult to obtain. This reflects the particular challenges of researching this particular population and also our continued limited understanding of their needs. As Ware (2004) and others (for example, PAMIS 2011; Carnaby 2009; Philip, Lambe and Hogg 2005; Davies and Hogg 2004) emphasise there are major challenges confronting those who wish to understand the feelings and experiences of this population associated with their limited ability to communicate and more especially our inability to interpret the messages that they may be attempting to convey.

The SEN Code of Practice (Department for Education and Department of Health 2014: 87) includes social, emotional and mental health difficulties as one of the broad areas of need and makes clear the responsibilities for identifying and addressing mental health needs as integral to the assessment of educational, health and social care needs for learners with SEN. Fergusson *et al.* (2008) argue that guidance for schools in identifying concerns is essential for a whole school approach. This chapter therefore presents a model for identifying and sharing mental health concerns

A model for identifying and sharing mental health concerns

Consideration of the individual learner and his or her family is fundamental to a holistic approach, together with careful observations and communication within the setting. As Weare points out:

> At the same time as mental health work is becoming more positive it is also becoming more holistic. This involves looking at environments rather than only at individuals, as a way both to understand and also to address problems. It promotes a concern with the relationships between problems rather than with single problems and encourages us to look at clusters of risk factors rather than single causes.
>
> (Weare 2005: 120)

Thus, a whole school systematic approach which includes consideration of multiple factors is necessary in order for teachers to develop skills in identifying risks to wellbeing and potential mental health concerns. An approach to identifying concerns should involve identifying what is 'usual' for the learner across all contexts in order to:

- identify 'changes' which have alerted concerns;
- use observation skills to clarify the nature of early concerns; and
- share and discuss early concerns with colleagues and family.

This approach is encapsulated in a model (Figure 20.1) which proposes a multidimensional approach firstly to identifying and recording concerns and then to sharing and signposting concerns in order to address potential risks to mental health. At the centre of this model is the need to share, communicate and record concerns at all stages of the process. By sharing concerns at the earliest stages, others can be made aware any changes in a learner and adults can undertake more focused explorations to help make decisions about best next steps in response to these early concerns. Establishing a common language that is accessible is essential to ensure cooperation between all parties. The notion of mental health difficulties continues to elicit anxiety and in some instances denial and it is therefore important that discussions are effectively managed in an empathetic manner and by a professional with experience of working with parents and learners who may be under considerable stress.

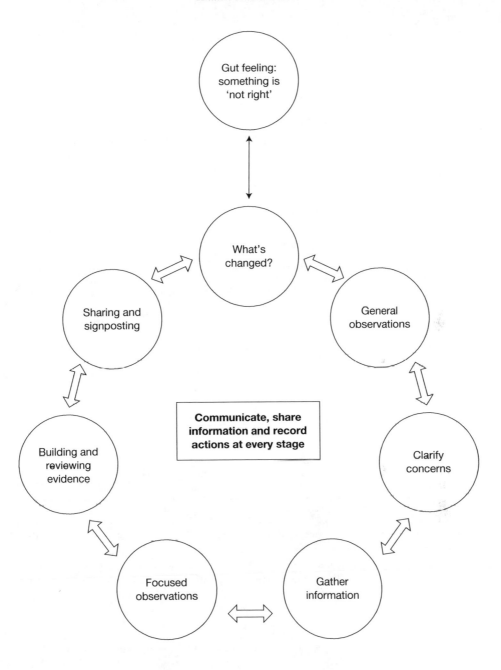

Figure 20.1   SEN and mental health: a model for identifying and sharing concerns

Identifying concerns

What is usual for the learner?

The starting point to identifying concerns is often an initial 'gut feeling' that something is 'not right' for an individual learner; this initial feeling may be determined by the teacher's knowledge of how the learner usually responds, learns and behaves. Observations should take into account the learner's skills, responses and behaviours in a variety of contexts in order to establish what is usual for them. Table 20.1 illustrates areas to consider when observing and recording what is usual for an individual.

Table 20.1 Recording what is usual

Individual factors	What's usual?
Physical signs and appearance	Posture, facial expression, body movements, appetite, sleep patterns
Daily activities	Levels of participation in everyday activities, interests, usual ways of responding
Communication	How does the learner communicate on a 'good' day?
Relationships	In what ways does the individual interact with adults and peers?
Emotions	How does the learner express his or her emotions?
Cognition	Attention span, making choices, problem solving
Behaviour	How does the learner usually behave?

Sally's usual skills, responses and behaviours
Sally is 10 years old. She lives at home and attends her local community special school. She has PMLD and is a wheelchair user. Consider what Sally's teacher has recorded as 'usual' for her:

Individual factors	What's usual for Sally?
Physical signs and appearance	Sally has cerebral palsy and is a wheelchair user. When she is in good health and physically comfortable, Sally can lift and keep her head up for long periods, turning to look at or follow people moving. When she is happy or excited, Sally becomes very active, waving her arms or rising out of her chair with giggles. She is alert most of the time – so she doesn't miss anything!!! Sally eats a soft, moist diet and plenty of drinks, with full support from someone who knows her well.
Daily activities	She enjoys spending time out of her chair – and especially loves physically active pursuits like swimming, rebound therapy, riding for disabled and, best of all, rough and tumble games. Sally is very sociable and likes to be in the heart of things, even if she might choose to be an observer of others. However, Sally also really enjoys opportunities for quality 1:1 time with her keyworker or with Alec [lunchtime assistant] when at school.

Communication	Sally has clear likes and dislikes and will convey these with obvious facial expressions, turning away or pushing things away if she doesn't like them or vocalising and reaching for things she likes. She can anticipate familiar routines and you will often see her lifting her head to vocalise long before the pause in songs or games she knows well. She can indicate 'more' by smiling, reaching or leaning towards you. When eating she can show you her pace, opening her mouth when she's ready for the next spoonful – and not before!
Relationships	It is important to Sally to be supported by people she trusts and knows well [and who know her well]. Her family is very important to Sally. She clearly enjoys being with them and talking about them. Generally, Sally is very sociable and loves spending time with people she knows well – you know this because she becomes very animated, with lots of smiles and vocalising [often shrieks of laughter!]. She tends to be quiet or sometimes anxious when with people she doesn't know.
Emotions	Sally conveys how she is feeling with clear facial expressions, often accompanied by vocalisations. Those who know her well can also 'read' her body signs, e.g. an increase or decrease in her movements, changes in her muscle tone and her general posture ['open' and bubbly; extended and tense or, more 'closed in' and subdued].
Cognition	Sally is beginning to use a switch intentionally to enjoy the class photo album on the interactive whiteboard or listening to her favourite music and stories. She responds to contextual and object cues for her favourite activities – particularly aromatherapy, rebound therapy and swimming. She loves to add the 'shouts' in familiar action games – like 'ready, steady…GO!'
Behaviour	Sally is nearly always happy! She is usually a bubbly and sociable youngster, keen to join in the fun. She can become quiet and still when she is feeling under the weather. If she goes somewhere new or is with someone new, she can quickly become tense and anxious. Reassurance from someone she knows staying nearby is often all it needs to allay her worries.

Information gathered about what is usual for a learner helps to establish their usual levels of wellbeing and how these present. This should be informed by teacher observations and also should involve communication with the individual themselves to seek their views (see Chapter 11 in this book), as well as with others who are in daily contact with the individual. A 'wellbeing section' as part of a 'personal passport' (see Chapter 25 in this book) is a useful way to record what is usual for an individual on a 'good day' and to summarise what an individual likes, does not like, how they communicate when happy, sad, anxious and so on.

What has changed? Interpreting intuitive feelings

The model presented in Figure 20.1 proposes an initial two-way process when you have an initial feeling about a learner that something is 'not right'. The two-way directional arrows indicate the imperatives both to observe the learner to identify any changes in what is usual for them and at the same time to share initial concerns with others. General observations in relation to each of the individual factors and in a variety of contexts should help to clarify initial concerns by identifying any changes and/or risk factors, including both individual and environmental factors. Communication with others is a vital part of the process in order to establish whether others have similar concerns. Asking others to observe the learner may help to identify any contextual factors which add to any risk to the learner's wellbeing. By observing and sharing information with others, clarification of the nature of early concerns may then inform any necessary actions. Information gathered at this early stage may highlight any catalyst to the noticed changes in behaviour or other factors – moving into a new bedroom at home, a bereavement or an undetected medical issue, for example.

Changes in Sally which led to concerns

Sally who was usually happy and bubbly with people she knew well, became much quieter and less responsive, even to her favourite activities. She seemed quite withdrawn and subdued. She had lost her appetite and had already shown some significant weight loss that was giving concern to school staff.

On speaking to her family, they had also noticed her reluctance to eat and the change in weight, but just thought she might still be under the weather from a chest infection. Mum also shared that Sally's sleep pattern had become erratic over the past three months – so she was probably also really tired and exhausted from this too.

Sally's teacher shared her observations about what seemed to be apparent changes over time in Sally's general mood and responsiveness, they all realised they had all seen similar changes – but because the changes had been gradual they hadn't been aware that these changes could put at risk Sally's wellbeing.

On seeing the bigger picture of what was different from usual for Sally, everyone agreed there was some cause for concern about her overall change in wellbeing and a need to explore things further. From the ongoing discussions between her family and the school, Mum raised the possibility that Sally was missing her older brother. Michael had left home a few months earlier to go to university – Sally was used to very regular cuddles and rough and tumble play with him.

As a first step, in Sally's case, her family took her to the GP for a general health check and review of her medication, to rule out any underlying medical issues. At school, her teacher introduced some activities that centred upon Sally and her brother Michael – they made up a photo album so that staff could regularly talk to Sally about him. They persuaded Michael to record some familiar songs and jokes that they often shared at home and Sally enjoyed using a switch to listen to these recordings. At home, Mum and Dad set up some regular Skype video 'chats' between Sally and Michael. All of these approaches seemed to alleviate Sally's subdued mood and gradually her other physical changes began to recover. At this stage observations continued to ensure that all action taken was having a positive impact on Sally's wellbeing.

Gathering information: observation skills and communication

While early identification and sharing of concerns may result in immediate action which restores or improves an individual's wellbeing, this is not always the case. In other situations clarification of concerns may identify further actions which require detailed information-gathering and more focused observations as in the case of Pravin below.

What's usual for Pravin

Pravin is 15 and he attends a residential, specialist school; Pravin has SLD and autism. Pravin's key worker, together with his family, has identified what is usual for Pravin in order to develop a wellbeing passport so that all who are in contact with Pravin are aware of his usual responses. What is usual for Pravin is summarised below:

Individual factors	What's usual for Pravin?
Physical signs and appearance	Pravin is usually physically active and alert. He is always moving, rocking, hand flapping and spinning, especially when he is happy.
Daily activities	Pravin loves to run outdoors and enjoys regular times to bounce on a trampoline. He is happy to join in most activities, and will join his peers for snacks and routine activities such as circle time. He loves helping to prepare snacks and simple meals at weekends.
Communication	Pravin uses a visual communication system; he seeks out his communication book and is increasingly using this to communicate his needs spontaneously. Family members are included in the book and Pravin will find an adult in class and point to family members in his book, enjoying hearing their names and simple conversations about his mum, dad and sister.
Relationships	Pravin has good relationships with familiar adults; he greets adults each morning with a 'high 5' and smiles. He has developed some social skills and is able to sit in close proximity to peers during familiar activities; he takes turns playing games and using the computer. Pravin has a particular attachment to his key care-worker.
Emotions	Pravin is able to indicate if he is happy or sad by selecting symbols; at times he expresses his emotions through his body movements and vocalisations. People who know him well are able to 'read' these signs and know when he is happy, excited, sad, upset.
Cognition	Pravin is able to recognise sight vocabulary and key words on his visual timetable. He has developed number concepts to 6 and is able to complete simple counting activities which he uses in his every day activities. Pravin is adept at matching and sorting and likes to complete independent tasks that use these skills.
Behaviour	Usually Pravin is alert, active and constantly moving. He shows no serious behaviour concerns and is described as willing to join in all activities. If he is upset, he sometimes will bang his forehead with the palm of his hand, but is easy to distract from this behaviour.

What has changed?

Pravin's teacher is concerned as she has noticed that Pravin has become less focused and he is seen at times to be staring into space. He is using his communication book less frequently and at the same time has been observed banging his forehead more frequently and has begun biting his hand. Pravin is less active and has been seeking out the quiet room where he sits for lengthy periods, refusing to join in activities.

By observing Pravin and sharing early concerns with school colleagues and care staff it became apparent that further observations were necessary as other staff had noticed similar changes in a variety of contexts. Early signs of some sort of distress indicated the need for more detailed information-gathering in order to gain insight into the difficulties he was experiencing. At this stage, observations focused upon his level of engagement in daily activities, his communication and his behaviours. Collated observations indicated that Pravin was withdrawing from activities, including those which were usually his favourites; for example, he would no longer participate in cooking at weekends. In addition, all were concerned about increased self-injury as Pravin was observed biting his hands throughout the day. Night care staff reported that he was agitated through the night and would often wake and begin biting his hand.

Pravin's mother felt uncomfortable in formal meetings so the key worker met with her at home to discuss concerns. It emerged from this conversation that Pravin was also withdrawing from preferred activities at home, he was refusing to leave the house at weekends and he had been biting his hand at home. The key worker recorded these impressions and having done so gave a copy to Pravin's mother for verification.

It was noted that one of the class teaching assistants had a good relationship with Pravin and so he was identified as a key person, together with Pravin's key care-worker, who would try to find out from Pravin how he was feeling. This included the use of symbol cards to depict daily activities and simple emotions (happy and sad) to try to identify if there were particular activities or contexts which were causing Pravin to withdraw.

As a result of this focused information-gathering it was agreed that an action plan needed to be established in order to address changes in Pravin. A short-term immediate action plan included: a medical check to find out if Pravin had any problems with his mouth (e.g. tooth ache, mouth ulcers) which may be causing pain; reversion to a 'first–then' visual timetable with photographs as staff knew that increased anxieties often lead to reduction in skills; independent activities were planned to be very brief and to make use of Pravin's strengths and interests (matching, sorting and super-heroes); increased access to the sensory environment where Pravin could sit quietly; increased deep massage activities which Pravin enjoyed. Whilst these immediate interventions reduced some hand biting and head hitting, all agreed that a longer term plan was needed. A collaborative approach was recognised as essential in order to take a holistic perspective and to plan effective longer term interventions.

Mental health is everyone's responsibility

The stories of Pravin and Sally highlight the importance of effective communication and information sharing when dealing with any concerns about the mental health and wellbeing of learners. The value of active collaboration within schools as a means of developing strong teams and promoting good communication and working relationships is key when considering the context of sharing and addressing concerns about the mental health of learners. Established practice of collaborative working is hugely beneficial in creating clear and open channels for information sharing and joint-working in order to successfully respond to such concerns.

Becoming aware or noticing something is 'not quite right' is the first step to supporting the positive emotional wellbeing of learners; the next steps are vital in addressing such concerns about potential mental health problems. In any school setting it is important for every member of staff to know with whom they should share such concerns and it is valuable for schools to devise and share clear communication channels. Weare (2005) offers the view of the school community as a jigsaw of interrelated factors that influence everyone's mental health and wellbeing. This jigsaw idea provides an overview of the many professionals [and others] involved in the lives of learners with SLD/PMLD and how they interface with each other directly or indirectly. Each learner will have a unique jigsaw of people contributing to their school life in some way, from the school cook at the counter in the dining hall to the bus escort who on a daily basis accompanies the individual on school transport to and from home. Having an awareness of your own personal 'jigsaw' (as a professional) can be helpful to indicate who may contribute to investigating the learner's situation further; this jigsaw will also enable you to be clear about the most appropriate avenues of help and guidance in sharing and responding to your concerns, as well as the support available to you as a professional.

Sharing information within and across the setting

Each member of staff needs to be aware of who to contact about any concerns, when they need to take this action and what information it is they need to share. Once the initial concern about a learner has been shared with a more senior colleague and the start of the systematic communication exchange has been instigated, decisions can then be made about how to develop a more accurate picture of the learner's situation. This communication is an ongoing and constantly two-way process, and at different points may include many others who are directly involved in the learner's life.

This multidimensional model suggests considering learners (and how they may have changed) from a number of interrelated perspectives. As indicated previously, evidence of changes in relation to a multiplicity of factors should be recorded; it is important to note that it is very rare that only one of these factors will be affected by a mental health problem. For example, in Pravin's case the difficulties he is experiencing are affecting: physical signs and appearance (staring into space); his daily activities (as he withdraws from what he is usually happy to participate in); his communication (as he ceases to use his communication book); relationships (as he engages less with adults and peers); emotions (as his usual happiness is replaced by withdrawal); cognition (which reduces his skills) and behaviour (as self-injury increases and he increasingly withdraws).

Should such explorations highlight concerns, then further focused and more detailed observations and explorations will be valuable to be clear about the frequency, intensity and duration of these different from usual responses and highlight other contextual factors that may be important parts of this holistic picture. At each point, school staff (and others possibly) convene to consider the information and evidence gathered and decide on the best, next steps. This may be seeking further clarification of the concern; or changing the learner's support plan or contextual factors that may be influencing the learner's situation; or by making decisions to refer the individual on to another professional. This may be an internal 'referral' (for example to a therapist who can help the learner to regulate anxiety) or, to seek more specialist help or services outside of the school setting (for example from a paediatrician or consultant or the local Child and Adolescent Mental Health Service (CAMHS) team). Such decision-making is not taken lightly and will involve senior school staff and the learner's family.

Identifying roles and responsibilities for responding to mental health concerns is very important. No single individual works alone and there are clear issues around safeguarding and confidentiality. Some responsibilities in the process will be shared (for example, observing and collecting information about the learner's behaviours), whereas others will have a distinct role for a senior member of the school team. Sharing concerns with families about possible mental health issues needs to be handled with utmost sensitivity and awareness of the impact of a potential dual diagnosis for the family. Schools may have clear roles for nominated people with the skills needed to lead in this sharing or to facilitate this with teachers and other school staff who have an established relationship with the family. Involvement of external services may be required to address ongoing concerns and decisions will be made as to what type of support or intervention is being signposted.

Conclusion

All teachers can take a constructive perspective by actively planning to promote emotional wellbeing and resilience for all their learners. Part of this strategy will include personalising records of what good mental health 'looks like' for each of their learners and being clear about the holistic needs of each individual to maintain and support positive wellbeing. When regularly reviewing and updating personalised records, steps can be taken to respond to any changed circumstances, however subtle, to ensure and maintain good mental health. The actual process of developing and reviewing these personalised documents will also highlight clear steps for learning and teaching opportunities for supporting individuals within their daily lives and routines at school, at home and in their community. Addressing such an important aspect of the 'whole learner' will underpin and enhance all learning, achievement and quality of life.

Questions for readers

- How do you record wellbeing for individuals in your setting?
- Is there a whole school policy on mental health and wellbeing?
- Is there a clear process for identifying and sharing concerns about mental health?

References

Carnaby, S. (2009) 'Mental health problems and people with profound intellectual and multiple disabilities', in J. Pawlyn and S. Carnaby (eds.) *Profound Intellectual and Multiple Disabilities: nursing complex needs*, Chichester: Wiley-Blackwell.

Davies, J. and Hogg, J. (2004) 'Count us in', *PMLD Link*, 16(1): 4–8.

Department for Education and Department of Health (2014) *Special Educational Needs and Disability Code of Practice: 0 to 25 years*. Ref: DFE:-00205-2013. Online. Available: www.gov.uk/government/publications/send-code-of-practice-0-to-25 (accessed 20 August 2014).

Emerson, E., Einfeld, S. and Stancliffe, R. (2010) 'The mental health of young children with intellectual disabilities or borderline intellectual functioning', *Social Psychiatry and Psychiatric Epidemiology*, 45(5): 579–587.

Fergusson, A., Howley, M. and Rose, R. (2008) 'Responding to the mental health needs of young people with profound and multiple learning difficulties and autistic spectrum disorders: Issues and challenges', *Mental Health and Learning Disabilities Research and Practice*, 5(2): 240–251.

Honey, A., Emerson, E. and Llewellyn, G. (2011) 'The mental health of young people with disabilities: impact of social conditions', *Social Psychiatry and Psychiatric Epidemiology*, 46(1): 1–10.

Morgan, H. (2007) *Mental Health and Children and Young People with Complex Needs – a policy briefing*, Online. Available: www.nasschools.org.uk/pages/welcome.htm (accessed 22 March 2014).

PAMIS (2011) *Responding to the Mental and Emotional Needs of People with Profound and Multiple Learning Disabilities*, Dundee: PAMIS.

Philip, M., Lambe, L. and Hogg, J. (2005) *The Well-being Workshop: Recognising the emotional and mental well-being of people with profound and multiple learning disabilities*, London: Foundation for People with Learning Disabilities.

Reinke, W; Stormont, M., Herman, K., Puri, R. and Goel, N. (2011) 'Supporting children's mental health in schools: teacher perceptions of needs, roles, and barriers', *School Psychology Quarterly*, 26(1): 1–13.

Rose, R., Howley, M., Fergusson, A, and Jament, J. (2009) 'Mental health and special educational needs: exploring a complex relationship', *British Journal of Special Education*, 36(1): 3–8.

Sheehy, K. and Nind, M. (2005) 'Emotional well-being for all: mental health and people with profound and multiple learning disabilities', *British Journal of Learning Disabilities*, 33: 34–38.

Simonoff, E., Pickles, A., Charman, T., Chandler, S., Loucas, T. and Baird, G. (2008) 'Psychiatric disorders in children with autism spectrum disorders: prevalence, comorbidity, and associated factors in a population-derived sample', *Journal of the American Academy of Child & Adolescent Psychiatry*, 47(8): 921–929.

Ware. J. (2004) 'Ascertaining the views of people with profound and multiple learning disabilities', *British Journal of Learning Disabilities*, 32 (4): 175–179.

Weare, K. (2005) 'Taking a positive, holistic approach to the mental health and well-being of children and young people', in: C. Newnes and N. Radcliffe (eds) *Making and Breaking Children's Lives*, Ross-on-Wye: PCCS.

21

SPIRITUALITY AND RELIGIOUS EDUCATION FOR LEARNERS WITH SLD/PMLD

Jean Ware and Erica Brown

In this chapter, the following questions will be addressed:

- Within the multicultural context of Britain, what are the roles played by faith, culture and ethnicity in approaches to disability, especially learning difficulties?
- What do we know about the development of spirituality in relation to people with intellectual disabilities?
- How can religious ideas be conveyed to learners with SLD?
- How can learners with SLD be helped to develop spiritual awareness?

We have tried to make clear links between responses to questions 3 and 4, without implying that religious education as a subject has sole responsibility for the development of children's spirituality. Death, bereavement and loss are dealt with separately in Chapter 22.

Some key terms and definitions

This section begins with a discussion of three key terms (religion, ethnicity and culture). We attempt to differentiate between these terms, and discuss what different groups of people mean when they use them; however, as will become clear, in practice, there is considerable overlap between these three areas. The word *religion* probably derives from the Latin 'religare', which means 'to bind' (Oxford Dictionary 2013). Most dictionaries agree that a *Religion* is an organised collection of beliefs, cultural systems, and worldviews that relate humanity to an order of existence; particularly where these beliefs include belief in a god or gods as creator of the universe. There is great diversity of religious belief in the UK, with the 2011 census showing that while 59 per cent of people describe themselves as Christian, the next largest group (25 per cent) say they have no religion. Other significant religious groupings include Muslims (5 per cent), Hindus (1.5 per cent), Sikhs (0.8 per cent) and Jews (0.5 per cent) (Office for National Statistics 2011). However, as commentators on the census have pointed out, a statement of one's religion carries a wide variety of meanings, from a statement of identification with a particular heritage to a statement of commitment to a particular belief system. Thus parents describing themselves to a school as members of a particular religion may not necessarily be active practitioners. Nonetheless, it is likely that the beliefs of that religion, including its attitudes to disability will have a profound influence on how they think and feel about their child's learning difficulties.

Like a number of words, *ethnicity* has both an everyday and a more technical meaning. In its more technical sense ethnicity is regarded as referring to a group of people that share distinctive features, such as origin of descent, language, culture, physical appearance, religious affiliation, customs and values (Portes and Rumbaut 2001). It is in this sense that it is used in this chapter.

There are numerous definitions of *culture*; in general, they tend to place emphasis on culture as a shared system of meaning, which derives from 'common rituals, values, rules and laws' (Ahmad *et al.* 2000). In this chapter, culture is defined as how people do and view things within the groups to which they belong. Culture also includes a set of shared values, expectations, perceptions and lifestyles based on common history and language, which enable members of the community to function together. Some aspects of culture are visible and obvious (Garrett 2006). These include dress, written and spoken language, rites of passage, architecture and art. The less obvious aspects of culture consist of the shared norms and values of a group, community or society. They are often invisible but, nevertheless, they define standards of behaviour, and the rituals around events such as birth and death. For many people, it is important for them that they are able to maintain their cultural values and practices, but cultures are not fixed and static. They change in response to new situations and pressures (Ahmad *et al.* 2000; Chand 2005).

Ethnicity and culture profoundly affect the way people view disability. For example, within some cultures, for a girl, marriage represents a transition from childhood to adulthood and failure to marry may be perceived as failure to fulfil this commitment and a financial burden on her birth family. In some communities, disability for a male may be viewed as a threat to masculinity and also to the prospect of marriage and family life (Bagum *et al.* 1994). There is also evidence that having a disabled family member in a BME[1] community may affect the marriage chances of siblings or the social standing of families (Ahmad *et al.* 2000). Chamba *et al.*'s (1999) study concluded that parents with a child with profound and complex disabilities were at multiple disadvantage compared with those who did not have a child with special needs. The study also revealed a consistent picture of families from BME communities with a disabled child as being poorer compared to the general population. Literature about disability and ethnicity is limited in both its volume and its scope. Furthermore, a fundamental weakness of the literature has been its insensitivity to the processes of change which occur as members of BME communities adapt to their new societies (Gatrad *et al.* 2008).

How individuals understand concepts such as 'learning disability/difficulty' or 'complex needs' arises from a complex interaction between a number of factors including personal experience, and faith, as well as the influence of ethnicity, religion and culture (Gatrad and Sheikh 2002; Kofman and Lukes 2009). The importance of each of these factors in a person's thinking may vary between cultures and between individuals; it is important to recognise that this is as true for school staff as for pupils' parents and carers. Furthermore, many people in Britain today have multiple ethnic and cultural identities, possessing mixed heritage, with parents, grandparents and great grandparents from different groups or communities. From a teacher's perspective, there are three critical issues:

- An individual, or family's perspective on learning disabilities will be influenced by their religious, cultural and ethnic heritage; however, these are not the only influences which have an important bearing on how learning disabilities are viewed, and on an individual or family's reaction to having a child with a learning disability.
- An individual or family's perspectives and beliefs cannot be assumed from their religious cultural or ethnic heritage, and many families have a mixed heritage.

- Schools need to be sensitive to all aspects of religious ethnic and cultural background, and not just those directly concerned with learning disabilities.

As a teacher, working either in a very diverse setting, or one which is much less diverse, but which receives a child from an unfamiliar background, it is easy to be overwhelmed by the difficulty of being conversant with a range of cultural and religious practices and beliefs. Leicester City Council has produced a resource (*Engaging with Faith Communities*) aimed at advising and supporting schools and teachers in this situation, which is freely available on the web, and which other schools may find useful (Leicester City Council 2012). This deals briefly and clearly with a range of aspects of Christianity, Islam, Hinduism and Sikhism, including helpful sections on 'do's and 'don'ts' for each grouping.

The development of spirituality

Despite the decline in religious belief reported in the 2011 census, the development of spirituality/spiritual awareness continues to be seen as an important aspect of education in the UK. In both England and Wales (DCSF 2010) the development of spirituality is explicitly stated to be one of the aims of the curriculum, and in Scotland religious and moral education is seen as making an important contribution to children's wellbeing (Scottish Government 2006) People who do not aspire to belonging to a faith may, nevertheless, have strong ethical and moral values and a sustaining spiritual dimension to their lives. Given the importance ascribed to this area in promoting children's well-being it is perhaps surprising that there is little literature which addresses the issue of how spiritual awareness develops and how its development can be facilitated. One problem is the lack of an agreed definition of what is meant by *spirituality* (Oman 2013); another is that, in general, definitions seem to demand an advanced level of intellectual understanding, for example that given by Shafranske and Gorsuch (1984, cited by Oman 2013):

> a transcendent dimension within human experience... discovered in moments in which the individual questions the meaning of personal existence and attempts to place the self within a broader ontological context.
>
> (Oman 2013: 28)

There are two distinct approaches in what has been written. On the one hand, the majority of past writing in this area takes a Piagetian perspective, and is more concerned with the development of religious concepts and children's religious thinking than with their spirituality. This work suggests that, as with cognitive development, and closely related to it, religious thinking goes through a series of stages. On the other hand, some more recent work illustrates attempts to look at children's spiritual experience from their own perspective; this work tends not to assume a link between cognitive development and spirituality (Ratclif and Nye 2006).

One notable exception to the lack of literature on facilitating children's spiritual development is the work of Rebecca Nye (for example, Nye 2009). Although Nye does not write explicitly about children with learning difficulties she does make it clear that, in her view, cognitive and spiritual development are not closely linked.

> Experiencing spirituality does not depend on how much we understand or can explain, but it is about our capacity for being – God's ways of being with us and our ways of being with God. So, in working with children and young people, engaging

with and nurturing their spirituality could be described as simply that: recognising and supporting God's ways of being with them, and their ways of being with God.

For Christians, this can help us to remember that spirituality starts with God – it is not something that adults (parents, teachers, church leaders) have to initiate. God and children (regardless of age and intellect) have ways of being together because this is how God created them. The difficulty comes in trying to appreciate, and support, the ambiguous forms these 'ways' can take – though, in fact, a lot of it may happen in very ordinary ways under our noses.

(Nye 2010: 2)

Writing from a specifically Christian perspective, Nye suggests that children's spiritual development can be facilitated by allowing them space, through a process approach, through the use of imagination, through their relationships with others, and through the development of intimacy and trust. Much of what Nye has to say is particularly relevant to teachers working with pupils with SLD/PMLD in the way in which it focuses on respect for the child's own experience and responses. In its emphasis on the need for space and time for reflection and on simply concentrating on the present moment, it has much in common with both 'Godly Play' and mindfulness. It is also reminiscent of the writing of Vanier and Nouwen about the spirituality of adults with learning difficulties (e.g. Nouwen 1997; Vanier 1988).

When *Routes for Learning* (Welsh Assembly Government 2006) was being developed there was much discussion about whether it should include ways in which the development of what was then referred to in the Curriculum for Wales as 'a sense of awe and wonder' could be assessed and facilitated. Those familiar with *Routes* will realise that this did not make it in to the final version! However, among the things suggested that might indicate the beginnings of that sense of awe and wonder were a child's surprised and delighted reaction to a rainbow-coloured shaft of sunlight falling across their body. Other such experiences might include the arrival of a brightly coloured goldfinch on the dead-looking thistles just outside the window, the scent of honey when lying in the flowering heather, the sky being lit up by fireworks. Of course, when a child cannot express their feelings at such an experience verbally, it is impossible to tell whether they are experiencing the beginnings of awe and wonder or simply responding to a novel and enjoyable stimulus. Such experiences, however, would fall within those mentioned by the School Curriculum and Assessment Authority (SCAA) in their 1996 discussion paper:

[t]he spirituality of young people can be developed in many ways: for example by religion, thinking, prayer, meditation or ritual. For some, spirituality is awakened through feelings of awe and wonder at nature and the universe. For others it comes through positive relationships with others.

(SCAA 1996: 6–7, cited in Best 2000: 10)

In the same paper SCAA asserted that 'the essential factor in cultivating spirituality is reflection and learning from one's experiences' (cited in Best 2000). Smith (2000) argues that if spirituality is to be developed through all aspects of the curriculum, then the teaching methods we adopt must take account of this. If this is the case there would appear to be strong links with both assessment for learning and the development of thinking skills. Work on thinking skills with learners with learning difficulties, particularly in Wales (Welsh Assembly Government n.d.), has demonstrated a variety of examples of good practice in helping them to evaluate the consequences of particular courses of action not only retrospectively but prospectively. There are also connections with the work of Jerome Berryman (1995) on Godly play, which aims to encourage children's spiritual growth through 'wondering questions' (see below).

It is important to mention one other recent development in the field of spirituality and its application to education, and that is *mindfulness*. Mindfulness is a technique based on an ancient Buddhist practice which means paying attention to the present moment in a non-judgemental manner, which aims to increase awareness, clarity and acceptance. It has gained in popularity in recent years, and has shown positive effects with a number of groups, for example those recovering from depression (Teasdale *et al.* 2000). There are few studies of the use of mindfulness with children and none with children with learning difficulties, However, a recent study conducted in 12 secondary schools found reduced stress levels, and fewer symptoms of depression post-intervention, and improvements were related to the extent to which mindfulness was practised by the participants (Kukyen *et al.* 2013). Additionally, a systematic review of 18 studies of the use of mindfulness with adults with learning difficulties and their carers found that positive effects were reported in all 18 included studies (Harper *et al.* 2013). Some studies in this review included participants with SLD/PMLD that suggests a potential for the use of this approach with this group of learners.

Religious education

Religious Education (RE) occupies a unique place within the curriculum in Britain as an essential part of the basic curriculum which all maintained schools must provide, but which (with the exception of reserved posts in some schools) teachers are free to decline to teach, and from which parents may withdraw their child. It is also the one subject area where different rules apply in special schools, in that special schools should provide RE so far as it is practicable. Perhaps this, in part, explains the comparative lack of resources for those working with learners with learning difficulties (DCSF 2010).

The most recent non-statutory guidance on RE in England (DCSF 2010) states that:

> RE is an important curriculum subject. It is important in its own right and also makes a unique contribution to the spiritual, moral, social and cultural development of pupils and supports wider community cohesion. The Government is keen to ensure all pupils receive high-quality RE.
>
> (DCSF 2010: 4)

In England, the most recent version of the Ofsted Framework for School Inspection (Office for Standards in Education 2014) continues to emphasise the importance of the spiritual, moral, social and cultural (SMSC) development of the pupils, and the role that various aspects of teacher and wider school practice have in promoting this. However, teaching RE to learners with SLD/PMLD may be regarded as a particular challenge by many teachers. For some that may be because of the nature of the subject; as the non-statutory guidance states:

> Religious education provokes challenging questions about the ultimate meaning and purpose of life, beliefs about God, the self and the nature of reality, issues of right and wrong, and what it means to be human. It can develop pupils' knowledge and understanding of Christianity, of other principal religions, other religious traditions and world views that offer answers to questions such as these.
>
> (DCSF 2010: 7)

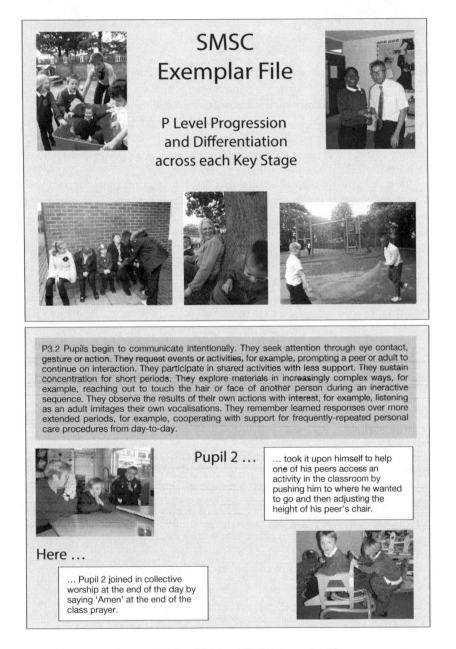

Figure 21.1 Abbey Court Community Special School SMSC Exemplar File

Although at one level these challenging questions involve very sophisticated patterns of thought and it is important that we help children and young people of all abilities to develop their thinking skills so that they can engage with such issues, these questions can also be *experienced* at least to some extent. Learners with SLD/PMLD who experience being treated with respect, dignity and love in the same way as all other learners are learning what it means to be human, as they are when we try and explain to them that it is someone else's turn to have their choice, or when we try and help them to occupy themselves quietly because another child is feeling unwell. At Abbey Court Community Special School in Medway this approach to SMSC is evident in the provision of an exemplar file that can be used for staff training, moderating pupil progress and sharing with other schools (Bosley 2013) (see Figure 21.1)

When Erica wrote her book *Religious Education for All* (Brown 1994), there was little available in this field to help teachers working with pupils with learning difficulties. Over the past 20 years, in addition to issuing of new non-statutory guidance in the different countries of the UK (for example, DCSF 2010; WAG 2008) and the updating of QCA's guidance on teaching pupils with learning difficulties (QCA 2009), a variety of approaches and materials have been developed and trialled specifically with pupils with learning difficulties. In the remainder of this section, we discuss these developments, and examine the evidence for their usefulness in the teaching of RE. It is also worth noting that there has been increase in academic research, for example at the Centre for Spirituality, Health and Disability at the University of Aberdeen (www.abdn.ac.uk/sdhp/centre-for-spirituality-health-and-disability-182.php) and an increase in discussions among faith groups about catering for diversity, including people with learning difficulties (for example, Fresh Expressions for Adults with Learning Disabilities, www.freshexpressions.org.uk/guide/examples/learning-disabilities) and we have included reference to these in the resources section as some readers may be interested to pursue them.

One important aspect of RE is knowledge about Christianity and about other religions. A number of approaches are concerned to increase learners' knowledge about Christianity, and in particular their familiarity with Bible stories. Park and Pilcher's Bible stories in cockney rhyming slang (Park 2008; Park 2009; Park and Pilcher 2010) both help pupils with SLD/PMLD become familiar with stories which are important in the Christian faith and give them the opportunity to become engaged in re-telling those stories in a religious context. This approach involves pupils in a way they find enjoyable in an activity which plays a central part in a number of religious traditions – the re-telling of stories which are central to that particular faith and its understanding of the part God has played in their history.

These versions of Bible stories would, perhaps, particularly appeal to older learners.

Park's approach could be adapted and extended by asking learners to write their own version of an episode from the Bible or other religious text, and through comparing different versions encourage reflection about the essential elements of the story.

Another approach which has been tried with learners with SLD is 'Godly Play' (Berryman 1995). Although this approach was originally designed for use with children by churches it has since been extended to a wider range of contexts (Davis 2010; Seaman 2005; Allen and Seaman 2010) including children with SEN. James (2012) has demonstrated in a small pilot study that it has potential to be adapted successfully for classroom use with children with SLD.

In Godly Play a familiar Bible story or religious rite is introduced, through a reflective retelling of the story, using a pre-prepared script and a box of resources which are provided specifically to go with that script. As James states:

> The purpose is that over time children will develop not just their knowledge of Christian stories and parables but also expand their inner lives by responding creatively to a series of 'wondering questions' which form part of the closing stages of each script.
>
> (James 2012: 20)

Bible stories in rhyming slang have been performed by pupils from a number of London Special Schools in several London churches, including both St Paul's Cathedral and Westminster Abbey. This account of the creation in the style of a town crier was performed at Westminster Abbey by pupils with SLD and PMLD from Charlton School, Greenwich in 2010.

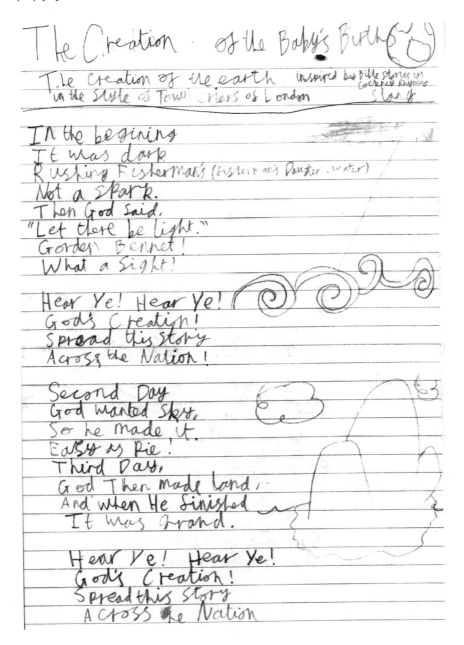

The Creation of the Baby's Birth

The Creation of the earth inspired by Bible stories in Cockney Rhyming Slang
in the style of Town Criers of London

IN the begining
It was dark
Rushing Fisherman's (Fisherman's Daughter. water)
Not a spark.
Then God said,
"Let there be light."
Gorden Bennet!
What a sight!

Hear Ye! Hear Ye!
God's Creation!
Spread this story
Across the Nation!

Second Day
God wanted Sky,
So he made it.
Easy as Pie!
Third Day,
God Then made land,
And when He finished
It was grand.

Hear Ye! Hear Ye!
God's Creation!
Spread this story
Across the Nation

Figure 21.2   Part of The Creation (from Genesis Chapter 1) in Rhyming Slang

Park and Pilcher (2010) Reproduced with permission from The SLD Experience Issue 57: 12–13

James found that both children and classroom staff responded positively to Godly play in her pilot study; she needed to adapt it to meet the needs of the group, however, she concluded that this could be achieved relatively easily.

Conclusion

This chapter has dealt with three rather different, but related areas: the role played by culture, ethnicity and religious belief in people's conceptualisations of, and attitudes to SLD/PMLD, the development of spirituality in people with SLD/PMLD and religious education for learners with SLD/PMLD.

Questions for readers

- How can you take account of the ways in which a learner's religious and cultural experiences at home, and in the wider community may influence their responses to events and activities in school?
- How can you provide opportunities to help all learners develop their spiritual awareness?
- How can ensure that your learners have the opportunity to learn about and develop respect for the cultural and religious views of others?

Resources

Godly Play

More information about Godly Play is available from a number of websites;

www.godlyplayfoundation.org/newsite/Main.php
(website address for the Godly Play Foundation in the United States)

Useful UK websites include:
www.godlyplay.org.uk/
www.shapworkingparty.org.uk

In the UK resources for Godly Play are available from:
www.spiritualchild.co.uk/resourcesgp.html
The Leicester City Council Materials are available from the engaging with faith communities
     website: http://ewfc.co.uk/
Jessica Kingsley publishers (www.jkp.com/catalogue/spirituality?next=46) publish a wide
     range of books about spirituality, religious education and disability including books by
     Rebecca Nye, John Swinton and Keith Park.

Centre for Spirituality, Health and Disability, Aberdeen University

'The centre has a dual focus on:

- The relationship between spirituality, health and healing and the significance of the spiritual dimension for contemporary healthcare practices.
- The theology of disability.

The centre aims to enable academics, researchers, practitioners and educators to work together to develop innovative and creative research projects and teaching initiatives.'
www.abdn.ac.uk/sdhp/centre-for-spirituality-health-and-disability-182.php

Note

Terminology used by authors and researchers referring to minority ethnic groups is inconsistent (Thoburn *et al.* 2005). Terms include: Black families, non-white families, ethnic minority families, minority ethnic families, non-indigenous families, ethnic families and in places permutations of the terms. There are also numerous references in the literature distinguishing people by place of birth or ancestry such as Indian, Pakistani, and Bangladeshi and to faith, for example, Muslim, Hindu, and Sikh. The Office for National Statistics (2011) uses the term Black and Minority Ethnic (BME) to describe persons from minority groups resident in the United Kingdom.

References

Ahmad, W., Atkin, K. and Chamba, R. (2000) '"Causing havoc among their children": parental and professional perspectives on consanguinity and childhood disability', in W. Ahmad (ed.) *Ethnicity, Disability and Chronic Illness*, Buckingham: Open University.

Allen, R. and Seaman, A. (2010) *Dementia and Godly Play*. Online. Available: www.godlyplay.org.uk/wp-content/uploads/2013/06/Dementia-and-Godly-Play.pdf (accessed 23 April 2014).

Bagum, N., Hill, M. and Stevens, A. (eds) (1994) *Reflections: The views of black disabled people on their lives and community care*, London: Central Council for Education and Training in Social Work.

Best, R. (2000) 'Introduction: where are we going with SMSC?', in R. Best (ed.) *Education for Spiritual, Moral, Social, and Cultural Development*, London: Continuum.

Berryman, J. (1995) *Godly Play*, Minneapolis: Augsburg Books.

Bosley, J. (2013) 'Spiritual, moral, social and cultural development (SMSC) at Abbey Court School', *SLD Experience*, 65, 28–29.

Brown, E. (1994) *Religious Education for All*, London: David Fulton.

Chamba, R., Ahmad, W., Hirst, M., Lawton, D. and Beresford, B. (1999) *On the Edge: Minority ethnic families caring for a severely disabled child*, Bristol: Policy Press.

Chand, A. (2005) 'Supporting South Asian families with a child with severe disabilities', *Child and Family Social Work*, 10(1), 88.

Davis, S. (2010) *Exploring the Connections between Godly Play and Special Education*. Online. Available: www.jbu.edu/assets/academics/journal/resource/file/2010/GodlyPlay.pdf (accessed 23 April 2014).

Department for Children, Schools and Families (DCSF) (2010) *Religious Education in English Schools: non-statutory guidance 2010*, Annesley: DCSF.

Garrett, A. (2006) 'Protecting children in a globalized world: "race" and "place" in the Laming Report on the death of Victoria Climbié', *Journal of Social Work*, 6(3), 315–336.

Gatrad, R. and Sheikh, A. (2002) 'Palliative care for Muslims and issues after death', *International Journal of Palliative Nursing*, 8(12), 594–597.

Gatrad, R., Brown, E. and Sheikh, A. (2008) *Palliative Care for South Asians: Muslims, Hindus and Sikhs*, London: Quay Books.

Harper, S., Webb, T. and Rayner, K. (2013) 'The effectiveness of mindfulness-based interventions for supporting people with intellectual disabilities: a narrative review', *Behavior Modification*, 37, 431–453.

James, L. (2012) '"Godly Play" as a tool for use in RE with pupils with SLD or PMLD', *SLD Experience*, 62, 18–26.

Kofman, E. and Lukes, S. (2009) *The Equality Implications of being a Migrant in Britain, Research Report 19*, London: Equality and Human Rights Commission.

Kuyken, W., Weare, K., Ukoumunne, O., Vicary, R., Motton, N., Burnett, R., Cullen, C., Hennelly, S. and Huppert, F. (2013) 'Effectiveness of the Mindfulness in Schools Programme: non-randomised controlled feasibility study', *The British Journal of Psychiatry* 1–6. doi: 10.1192/bjp.bp.113.126649

Leicester City Council (2012) *Engaging with Faith Communities*. Online. Available: http://ewfc.co.uk/ (accessed 4 February 2015).

Nouwen, H. (1997) *Adam: God's beloved*, London: Darton, Longman and Todd.

Nye, R. (2009) *Children's Spirituality: what it is and why it matters*, London: Church House Publishing.

Nye, R. (2010) Spirituality and space. *Roots: Children and Young People*, Issue 49 September/October 2010.

Office for National Statistics (2011) *Census 2011*, London: Office for National Statistics.

Office for Standards in Education (OFSTED) (2014) *The Framework for School Inspection* (Updated 2014) Online. Available: www.ofsted.gov.uk/resources/framework-for-school-inspection-january-2012 (accessed 23 April 2014).

Oman, D. (2013) 'Defining religion and spirituality', in R.F. Paloutzian and C.L. Park (eds) *Handbook of the Psychology of Religion and Spirituality*, 2nd edition, New York: Guilford Press.

Park, K. (2008) 'Bible stories in Cockney rhyming slang: from Adam and Eve to the resurrection in 40 minutes', *SLD* Experience, 50, 10–16.

Park, K. (2009) *Bible Stories in Cockney Rhyming Slang*, London: Jessica Kingsley.

Park, K. and Pilcher, P.J. (2010) 'Bible stories in Cockney rhyming slang', *SLD Experience*, 57, 12–15.

Portes, A. and Rumbaut, R. (2001) 'Not everyone is chosen: segmented assimilation and its determinants', in A. Portes and R. Rumbaut (eds) *Legacies: the story of the immigrant second generation*, Berkeley, CA: University of California Press, Russell Sage Foundation.

Qualifications and Curriculum Authority (QCA) (2009) *Planning, Teaching and Assessing the Curriculum for Pupils with Learning Difficulties: Religious education*. Online. Available: www.qcda.gov.uk/libraryAssets/media/P_scales_RE.pd (accessed 23 April 2014).

Ratclif, D. and Nye, R. (2006) 'Childhood spirituality: strengthening the research foundation', in E. Roehlkepartain, P. Ebstyne King, L. Wagener and P. Benson (eds) *The Handbook of Spiritual Development in Childhood and* Adolescence, Thousand Oaks, California: Sage.

Scottish Government (2006) *A curriculum for excellence 1. Building the curriculum: The contribution of subject areas* Edinburgh: The Scottish Government.

Seaman, A. (2005) *Godly Play: See things differently; do things differently*. Online. Available: www.shapworkingparty.org.uk/journals/index_0506.html (accessed 23 April 2014).

Smith, D. (2000) 'Spirituality and teaching methods: uneasy bedfellows?', in R. Best (ed.) *Education for Spiritual, Moral, Social, and Cultural Development*, London: Continuum.

Teasdale, J.D., Segal, Z.V., Williams, J.M.G., Ridgeway, V., Lau, M. and Soulsby, J. (2000) 'Reducing risk of recurrence of major depression using Mindfulness-based Cognitive Therapy', *Journal of Consulting and Clinical Psychology*, 68, 615–23.

Thoburn, J., Chand, A. and Proctor, J. (2005) *Review of Research on Child Welfare Services for Children and Minority Ethnic Origin and their Families*, London: Jessica Kingsley.

Vanier, J. (1988) *The Broken Body*. London: Darton, Longman and Todd.

Welsh Assembly Government Qualifications and Curriculum Group (Department for Education, Lifelong Learning and Skills) (2006) *Routes for Learning: assessment materials for learners with profound learning difficulties and additional disabilities*, Cardiff: WAG.

Welsh Assembly Government (2006) *Routes for Learning: Assessment materials for learners with profound learning difficulties and additional disabilities*, Cardiff: Welsh Assembly Government, Qualifications and Curriculum Group, DELLS (Dept of Education, Lifelong Learning and Skills).

Welsh Assembly Government (n.d.) *Developing Thinking for All Learners*. Online. Available: www.amdro.org.uk (accessed 23 April 2014).

22

DEATH, BEREAVEMENT AND LOSS

Erica Brown

In this chapter, the following questions will be addressed:

- How do the attitudes of professionals impact on the ways in which learners with SLD/ PMLD cope with bereavement and loss?
- How should professionals communicate with learners about death, bereavement and loss?
- How do learners with SLD/PMLD react to illness and loss?

Introduction

Children often do not live long before they encounter loss and change. Every year thousands of learners face bereavement. Adults are understandably so engrossed in their own grief that children's grief may be unnoticed. However, the way in which learners are supported when sad things happen may have a profound effect on how they are able to adapt to the death and is also likely to impact on the strategies they develop for coping with subsequent loss (Brown 2012).

Most of the literature in relation to how children and young people understand death is dominated by a Piagetian viewpoint. This involves conceptual understanding of death as a linear process linked to age, with an end point. Death is understood as a process that happens to all living things, caused by a breakdown in the healthy functioning of the body (Bluebond– Langner, Belasco and Goldman 2005; Klatt 1991). Kenyon (2001) defines a number of components for a mature understanding of death, namely:

- an understanding that all functions of life cease at death;
- the permanent and irreversible status of death;
- the universal nature of death;
- causal factors associated with death; and
- acceptance by an individual that they will die.

Oswin (1991), writing nearly a quarter of a century ago, said that it appeared that most learners with SLD/PMLD were not experiencing appropriate communication about death and dying. The same author argued this shortfall was largely due to an assumption that learners do not experience the same emotional responses as others do, and secondly the combination of a 'double taboo' of learning disabilities and 'death' has challenged society to the extent that they have been swept under the carpet. Furthermore, grief responses in learners with SLD/PMLD may be considered as part of abnormal behaviour associated with the learning disability rather than a universal human response (Brown 2007).

Authors have argued that there are three fundamental secrets kept from learners with SLD/PMLD, namely, sex, disability and death. 'The learning disability community is sadly underprepared for death and dying, which undermines a claim that concern for people stretch from the cradle to the grave' (Todd 2006: 15). Arguably, if the latter is disregarded, there is a risk that the life experience of some learners with SLD/PMLD is 'disenfranchised' (Brown 2007). Nevertheless, there is undeniably a challenge concerning how information might be given and by whom.

Research into how learners with SLD/PMLD react to life-limiting illness is limited; in the main research concentrates on adults in long-term residential care (Strachan 1981). McLoughlin (1989) believes that learners with SLD/PMLD are too often perceived as a homogeneous group with the result that their needs may be seen to be different than their mainstream peer group. Notwithstanding, one of the biggest dilemmas staff face is whether individual learners should be helped to understand the permanent nature of death (Todd 2004).

The England 'End of Life Strategy' (DoH 2008) made reference to the specific needs of learners with SLD/PMLD. Lascelles (2011) recommended that carers and professionals needed to be prepared to 'tune' into these needs and advocates that the attitudes and skills of practitioners determines how effectively learners are able to communicate. Munro (2011) supports this view, advocating that opportunities for the children's workforce to develop the skills and knowledge in communication is pivotal in achieving the best practice outlined in the Equality Act 2010. However, the value of listening to learners with SLD/PMLD is not just to ensure their needs are met through effective service delivery, but also 'to challenge professional assumptions and stereotypes about the lives of this unique group' (White and Choudhury 2010: 42).

Life-limited children and young people

Brown (2007) advocates that just as grief is considered to be a complex process with overlapping phases, so it is with understanding death. I also conclude that although learners with life-limiting conditions may not have a conceptual understanding of their illness, most are aware that something is physically wrong with their body. Furthermore, Bluebond-Langner (2000) and Judd (1995) write that children and young people who are life-limited may have a more mature understanding of death than their healthy peers. Herbert (1996) purports that a child or young person often understands they are seriously ill and then they gradually move towards a realization of acute, chronic and fatal sickness. Brown (2007) illustrates this idea in Table 22.1.

Table 22.1 Stages of children's understanding of life-limiting illnesses (Brown 2007)

1	2	3	4	5
My illness is serious	I am taking powerful drugs and they have side-effects	I know why I am having the treatment	I experience relapses and remissions	The pattern of relapses and remissions will end in death

Stage 1 is dependent on the learner observing how other people respond. After receiving treatment and visiting hospitals/clinics, the learner reaches **Stage 2** which may include a period of remission in the illness. After the first relapse, **Stage 3** is reached and, as a result of several more relapses and remissions, the learner accepts at **Stage 4** this is the pattern in their life. If the learner is aware someone else has died from the same illness, they may parallel their own experience and **Stage 5** is achieved.

Before discussing how the needs of learners with SLD/PMLD might be met, it is important to understand the impact of life-limiting or life-limited illness on the non-disabled child. The work of Black (1989) and Brown (2007) suggests that the way in which learners adjust is largely dependent on how well their primary carers cope, and how open family members are in communicating with one another. A study in special schools (Brown 2007) revealed a huge number of individual responses to death together with interrelated factors which have an impact on the way in which learners with special educational needs respond at the time of death and afterwards. One of these factors is that a life-limiting or a life-threatening condition can impact on a learner's identity.

Life-limited and life-threatened learners experience a number of events, which are unlikely to be experienced to the same extent by their 'healthy' peer group. These include:

- repeated GP, clinic and hospital visits and possible admission to hospital;
- repeated absences from school;
- long-term treatment/palliative care;
- distress and discomfort of medical procedures and possible side effects of treatment;
- chronic or continual episodes of pain;
- restricted social interaction or social isolation from their peer group. (Brown 2007)

Serious illness in the first year of a baby's life will almost always alter the development of the child's self-awareness. Parents usually find this particularly distressing because they are unable to offer the baby reassurance. During the toddler stage the most frightening aspects of life-limiting illness is likely to include separation anxiety and trauma if invasive procedures have to be carried out. Toddlers may regress in previously mastered skills and they may withdraw from primary carers and become easily agitated and angry.

Typically, young children react angrily (Brown 2012). This may include breaking toys, lashing out or biting people, and refusing to co-operate. Because the child's security is derived from routines, it is extremely important to maintain these as far as possible and to be consistent in approaches to behaviour management.

In the middle years, some children increase their autonomy and independence. If their illness interferes with their development, they may experience repeated frustration and failure. Some children in this age group will have an increased awareness of the significance of serious illness, and they may be developing an understanding of the permanence of death. Life-limited children may be aware of the fatal prognosis of their illness, even though they may not have been told. Most will be aware of the anxiety primary carers are experiencing.

Unlike young children, older learners may perceive death as irreversible. Therefore, acceptance of personal death is particularly difficult. However, knowing that death is approaching does not mean that children accept the inevitability. They may experience anxiety about dying and may withdraw emotionally as death approaches. Some may strive to achieve major accomplishments in an effort to maintain a sense of purpose in the face of impending death. Life-limited learners are often concerned about the well-being of their family and this may extend to aspects of the mental health of their parents and siblings.

Communication

Deciding how and when to communicate with a learner is one of the hardest decisions parents and professionals have to make (Dunlop 2008; Goldman 2007; Toce 2001). Arguably the extent to which a learner's experience is meaningful to them is dependent on the agenda for their care – more often than not this is an adult agenda that fails to empower learners with SLD/PMLD. Feiler and Watson (2011) believe children and young people may be vulnerable to others making assumptions about their needs.

Legislation endorses the importance of effective communication with children, young people and families. The ACT Charter (2004); ICPCN Charter (2008) and IMPaCCT (2007) purport that information should be appropriate to each person's need. Notwithstanding, Bluebond-Langner, Belasco and Goldman (2005) advocate that adult conversations with children with life-limiting conditions are often shrouded in *mutual pretence* where everyone concerned knows what is happening but nobody talks about the situation. It is important that adult fear and anxiety do not get in the way of open and honest communication (National Institute of Health 2006). The literature contains a plethora of guidance for those striving to engage learners in communication. However, there appears to be little published in relation to care for learners with SLD/PMLD. Sheir (2001: 35) proposes five components for involving learners:

- listening to what they communicate;
- supporting them in expressing their views;
- taking their views into account; and
- involving learners in their care.

Sinclair and Franklin (2000) cite several reasons for helping learners in decisions relating to their care, including upholding democracy and rights, improving service delivery, facilitating decision making, safeguarding, enhancing skills and enhancing emotional well-being. In many ways the communication skills of practitioners determines how effectively learners and their families are able to communicate (Brown 2000). However Matthews (2002) suggests there will be few professionals in primary care services with the knowledge and expertise that will enable them to best meet the holistic needs of learners with SLD/PMLD. Persaud (2006) stresses to service providers the importance of a workplace culture that reflects a commitment to enhancing the quality of life experience for children and families.

Active communication involves connecting with the whole 'experience' of the learner's world and appreciating the significance of the experience in the context of the learner's life (White and Choudhury 2010). Grieg, Taylor and McKay (2007) believe that being in touch with how learners communicate is one of the most neglected aspects of research. This view is supported by Christenson and James (2008) who make a plea for participatory methods that engage learners (see Chapter 11 in this book). Roulstone and McCleod (2011) remind readers there are two main aims for listening to children: to gain greater insight into the impact of complex needs on an individual, and to improve service design and provision so that they are relevant to the needs of children and their families. Some learners may have symbolic understanding and augmented or alternative communication systems can provide an effective means of communication (see Chapter 27 in this book). Systems include objects of reference, signs, together with grammatically spoken sentences, and symbol-based communication. Argyle (1998) asserted that non-verbal communication is five times more influential than verbal communication. Aspects of non-verbal communication include gesture, facial expressions, touch and posture. Regnard *et al*'s 2007 study found more than 20 changes in behaviour in learners when they encountered distress. Tuffrey-Wijne and McEnhill (2008) are of the opinion that although a person may have no verbal language, they are likely to be receptive to non-verbal communication. Gonzalez (2005) asserts that it is important for professionals working directly with learners to form meaningful relationships with them.

Difficulties with communication have been consistently reported as a barrier in supporting adults with learning disabilities around death and dying (Tuffrey-Wijne, Hogg and Curfs 2007). Cogher (2005) asserts that most learners with SLD/PMLD will encounter some difficulty with communication. Iacono and Johnson (2004) define these difficulties as speech that is either absent or difficult to understand, problems in listeners' understanding what has been said, and the learners' problems in expressing themselves because they have limited vocabulary or encounter difficulties forming sentences. Given that much of the language surrounding death and dying is shrouded in euphemisms and metaphors (Brown 2007), then it is hardly surprising that learners with SLD/PMLD are likely to encounter confusion.

Most definitions of quality of life agree that it 'can only be fully understood from an individual's perspective' (Markham 2011: 231). Parents and primary carers often have a rich and detailed knowledge of how their child communicates that allows them to make detailed observations of their child's responses from which they draw inferences about their child's needs (Goldbart and Marshall 2004). However, parents of learners with life-limiting or life-threatening conditions are likely to be experiencing anticipatory grief in relation to the death of their child and the atmosphere at home is therefore emotionally charged (Brown *et al.* 2013; Riches and Dawson 2000). Ware (2004: 103) cautions 'although those who are most familiar with an individual are most likely to interpret their reactions appropriately, they are also likely to be those with the highest degree of emotional involvement'.

Franklin and Sloper (2009) believe that learners cannot be assumed to be non-communicators or unable to indicate their needs and preferences. These authors stress a need to develop purposeful relationships with children and their families so that care is sensitive and responsive to their needs. This should extend to dimensions of care such as ethnicity and cultural needs and religious practices should be respected (Ali *et al.* 2011; Brown 2012; McLeod 2011).

Concluding remarks

This chapter has raised a number of questions and concerns about supporting learners with SLD/PMLD when they encounter loss and bereavement. Although reactions to loss are complex they are, in fact, normal human responses to unanticipated and frightening events. Professionals are not immune to grief and they should reflect on their own responses and recognise that another person's emotions may trigger unresolved losses.

Questions for readers

- Have you experienced death, bereavement or loss and how did you cope in these upsetting circumstances? Did people respond to you in ways that were helpful, or helpful at the time?
- What knowledge, skills and resources do you have that would help you to communicate with learners with SLD/PMLD and help support them in their grief?
- How would you recognise changes in learners' behaviour that may indicate bereavement or loss?
- If you were informed that a close family member of a learner in your class had died, how would you organise class team and wider school support for the individual?

References

ACT (Association for Children with Life-threatening or Terminal Conditions and their Families) (2004) *The ACT Charter for Children with Life-Threatening or Terminal Conditions and their Families*, Bristol: ACT.

Ali, Z., Fazil, Q., Bywaters, P., Wallace, L. and Singh, G. (2011) 'Disability, ethnicity and childhood: a critical review of research', *Disability and Society*, 16(7): 949–968.

Argyle, M. (1998) *Bodily Communication*, London: Methuen.

Black, D. (1989) 'Life-threatening illness, children and family therapy', *Journal of Family Therapy*, 22: 18–24.

Bluebond-Langner, M. (2000) *In the Shadows of Illness: Parents and siblings of the chronically ill child*, Princetown USA: Princetown University Press.

Bluebond-Langner, M., Belasco, J. and Goldman, A. (2005) 'Involving children with life-shortening illnesses in decisions about participating in clinical research: a proposal for shuttle diplomacy and negotiation', in E. Kodish (ed.) *Ethics and Research with Children: a child-based approach*, New York: OUP.

Brown, E. (ed.) (2000) *Baseline Assessment and Target Setting for Pupils with Profound and Multiple Learning Difficulties*, London: David Fulton.

Brown, E. (2007) *Supporting the Child and the Family in Paediatric Palliative Care*, London: Jessica Kingsley.

Brown, E. (2012) 'Around the time of death: culture, religion and ritual', in A. Goldman, R. Hain and S. Liben (eds) *Oxford Textbook of Palliative Care for Children*, 2nd edn, Oxford: Oxford University Press.

Brown, E., Kaur, J., Patel, R. and Coad, J. (2013) 'The interface between South Asian culture and palliative care for children, young people, and families – a discussion paper', *Issues in Comprehensive Paediatric Nursing*, 1: 1–24.

Christenson, P. and James, A. (eds) (2008) *Research with Children: Perspectives and practices*, London: Falmer.

Cogher, L. (2005) 'Communication and people with learning disabilities', in G. Grant, P. Goward, M. Richardson and P. Ramcharan (eds) *Learning Disability: A life-cycle approach to valuing people*, Maidenhead: Open University Press.

DoH (Department of Health) (2008) *The End of Life Care Strategy – promoting high quality care at the end of life*, London: Department of Health.

Dunlop, S. (2008) 'The dying child: should we tell the truth?' *Paediatric Nursing*, 20: 828–31.

Feiler, A. and Watson, D. (2011) 'Involving children with learning and communication difficulties: The perspectives of teachers, speech and language therapists and teaching assistants', *British Journal of Learning Disabilities*, 39(2): 113–20.

Franklin, A. and Sloper, P. (2009) 'Supporting the participation of disabled children and young people in decision making', *Children and Society*, 23: 3–15.

Goldbart, J. and Marshall, J. (2004) 'Pushes and pulls on the parents of children using AAC', *Augmentative and Alternative Communication*, 20(4): 194–208.

Goldman, A. (2007) 'An overview of paediatric palliative care', *Medical Principles and Practices*, 16(1): 46–7.

Gonzalez, N. (2005) *I am my Language: discourses of women and children in the borderlands*, Arizona: University of Arizona Press.

Grieg, A., Taylor, J. and MacKay, T. (2007) *Doing Research with Children*, 2nd edn, London: Sage.

Herbert, M. (1996) *Supporting Bereaved and Dying Children and their Parents*, Leicester: British Psychological Society.

HM Government Equalities Office (2001) *Equality Act 2010*. Online. Available: www.equalities.gov.uk/equality_act_2010.aspx (accessed 4 February 2015).

Iacono, T. and Johnson, H. (2004) Patients with disabilities and complex communication needs, *Family Physician*, 33(8): 585–9.

ICPCN (International Children's Palliative Care network) (2008) *The ICPCN Charter of Rights for Life Limited and Life Threatened Children*. Online. Available: www.icpcn.org/icpcn-charter (accessed 10 February 2015)

IMPaCCT (2007) 'IMPaCCT: Standards for paediatric palliative care in Europe', *European Journal of Palliative Care*, 14(3): 2–7.

Judd, D. (1995) *Give Sorrow Words: Working with a dying child*, London: Free Association Books.

Kenyon, B. (2001) 'Current research in children's conceptions of death: a critical review', *Omega Journal of Death and Dying*, 43(1): 63–91.

Klatt, K. (1991) 'In search of a mature understanding of death', *Death Studies*, 15(2): 177–87.

Lascelles, L. (2011) 'Tuning in to children with speech and language impairment', in S. Roulstone, and S. McLeod (eds) *Listening to Children and Young People with Speech, Language and Communication Needs*, Guildford: J and R Press.

Matthews, D. (2002) 'Learning disabilities: the need for better health care', *Nursing Standard*, 16(39): 40–1.

Markham, C. (2011) 'Designing a measure to explore the quality of life for children with speech, language and communication needs', in S. Roulstone and S. McLeod (eds) *Listening to Children and Young People with Speech, Language and Communication Needs*, Guildford: J and R Publishing.

McLeod, S. (2011) 'Listening to children and young people with speech, language and communication needs: who, why and how?' in S. Roulstone and S. McLeod (eds) *Listening to Children and Young People with Speech, Language and Communication Needs*, Guildford: J and R Publishing.

McLoughlin, J. (1989) 'Bereavement in the mentally handicapped', *British Journal of Hospital Medicine*, 36(4): 256–60.

Munro, E. (2011) *The Munro Review of Child Protection Interim Report: the child's journey*. Online. Available: www.gov.uk/government/publications/munro-review-of-child-protection-interim-report-the-childs-journey (accessed 4 February 2015).

National Institute of Health (2006) *Talking to Children about Death: Patient information*, Bethesda: CCNIH.

Oswin, M. (1991) *Bereavement and Mentally Handicapped People*, London: King's Fund Report KFC 81/234.

Persaud, M. (2006) 'Historical perspectives – care for people with learning disabilities over the past century', in S. Read (ed.) *Palliative Care for People with Learning Disabilities*, London: Quay Books.

Regnard, C., Reynolds, J., Watson, B., Matthews, D., Gibson, L. and Clarke, C. (2007) 'Understanding distress in people with severe communication difficulties: developing and assessing the Disability Distress Assessment Tool (DisDat)', *Journal of Intellectual Disability*, 51(4): 277–92.

Riches, G. and Dawson, P. (2000) *An Intimate Loneliness: Supporting bereaved parents and siblings*, Buckingham: Open University Press.

Roulstone, S. and McLeod, S. (2011) *Listening to Improve Services for Children and Young People with Speech, Language and Communication Needs*, Guildford: J and R Press.

Sheir, H. (2001) 'Pathways to participation: openings and obligations', *Children and Society*, 15: 107–17.

Sinclair, R. and Franklin, A. (2000) *How Quality Protects Research Briefing: Young people's participation*, London: Department of Health.

Strachan, J. (1981) 'Reactions to bereavement: a study of a group of hospital residents', *Apex*, 9(1): 20–1.

Toce, S. (2001) 'Ethical decision making for the child with a life-limiting condition', *Supportive Voice*, 7(4): 33–43.

Todd, S. (2004) 'Death counts: the challenge of death and dying in learning disability services', *Learning Disability Practice*, 7(10): 12–15.

Todd, S. (2006) 'A troubled past and present – a history of death and disability', in S. Read (ed.) *Palliative Care for People with Learning Disabilities*, London: Quay Books.

Tuffrey-Wijne, I., Hogg, J. and Curfs, L. (2007) 'End of life and palliative care for people with intellectual disabilities who have cancer or other life-limiting illness: a review of the literature and available resources', *Journal of Applied Research in Intellectual Disability*, 20(4): 331–44.

Tuffrey-Wijne, I. and McEnhill, L. (2008) 'Communication difficulties and intellectual disability in end of life care', *International Journal of Palliative Nursing*, 14(4): 189–94.

Ware, J. (2004) *Creating a Responsive Environment*, London: David Fulton.

White, S. and Choudhury, S. (2010) 'Children's participation in Bangladesh: issues of agency and structures of violence', in B. Percy-Smith and N. Thomas (eds) (2010) *A Handbook of Children's and Young People's Participation: perspectives from theory and practice*, London: Routledge.

PART IV

Developing the curriculum

23

CURRICULUM MODELS, ISSUES AND TENSIONS

Hazel Lawson and Richard Byers with Matthew Rayner, Richard Aird and Laura Pease

In this chapter, the following questions will be addressed:

- Are different curriculum models used by schools with learners with SLD/PMLD?
- What are some of the main issues and tensions to be considered in relation to curricula for learners with SLD/PMLD?

Introduction

'Curriculum' is generally taken to mean 'all the learning which is planned and guided by the school, whether it is carried on in groups or individually, inside or outside the school' (Kerr, quoted in Kelly 1983: 10); that is, the planned learning experiences through a learner's education. It is difficult to separate the *what* (what is taught – content), the *how* (how this is taught – process, pedagogy) and the *assessed outcomes* (product): curriculum, pedagogy and assessment are strongly interconnected. Here, although we focus on the *what*, this in itself encompasses different aspects, for example: curricular principles and aims; curricular divisions into areas of learning or subjects; ideas around the development of knowledge, skills and understanding; and methods of curricular organisation. The issues relate to what we should be teaching learners with SLD/PMLD and why. There are many factors which influence schools' decisions around these: external drivers, such as statutory requirements, local community interests and the specific composition of learners in the school. In addition, schools may involve staff, learners and families in discussing and agreeing curriculum values and priorities. In this chapter, we highlight an overarching tension between *commonality* and *individuality* and consider how some different curriculum models respond to and attempt to resolve these tensions.

Three curriculum models

We present three curriculum models as developed in three schools for learners with SLD/PMLD.

Curriculum model 1: Stephen Hawking School

Stephen Hawking School is a primary phase school for learners aged 2–11 years with SLD/ PMLD, many of whom have additional physical or sensory impairments. The headteacher, Matthew Rayner, describes here a recent process of curriculum development (see also Rayner 2011).

Designing a curriculum to meet the needs of all the learners proved to be a complex and difficult task. Not only did the needs of the learners have to be taken into consideration but also the statutory duties, for example the National Curriculum. The school also wanted to ensure that time within the school day could be allocated to other areas of learning such as movement therapy and sensory integration in order to support the learners' communication development and ability to concentrate and focus. The National Curriculum for England guidance (DfE 2013) states that there is time in the school day to go beyond its specifications; however, teachers stated that the National Curriculum expectations took almost all of the school day. A better balance had to be achieved.

Figure 23.1 shows the curriculum map that was created. This merged each of the National Curriculum subjects into five themes: communication, exploration, understanding my world, physical development (including therapy) and personal and social education (PSE). In particular, these themes were for learners working at P3(ii) or below. The school also considered when the themes should become more subject-focused and when they should broaden out into the full National Curriculum. It was agreed that from P4 to P6 the core subjects of the National Curriculum should be taught in full and the foundation subjects would be based around four themes: understanding the world; creative arts; physical education (including therapy); and PSE. From P7 all subjects of the National Curriculum would be taught in full. The P scales were used to define the limits of the themes as they are a nationally recognised system for the assessment of learners working below Level 1 of the National Curriculum. P 3(ii) was taken as a cut off for the five themes as, below this point, the P scales are not subject specific. Although the P scales are not seen by all as being totally appropriate (Imray and Hinchcliffe 2014), there is some acknowledgement that learners with PMLD tend to be working around the lowest P scales: P1(i) to P3(ii) (Aird and Aird 2006). Personal and social education (PSE) was included as a separate area with ICT being taught in a cross–curricular manner.

The size of the areas given to each curriculum subject in the curriculum map demonstrates the balance in the curriculum and the importance given to each subject. Therefore, the map shows that the majority of teacher time is given over to communication. Breadth is provided via the school's topic approach with areas such as the Victorians and Rivers being covered. Aspects of the National Curriculum are also protected by each topic having a focus on subsections of the programmes of study. An example of this is the topic on 'Ourselves' which focuses on life processes and living things in science and shape, space and measure in mathematics.

Subject Areas	P1(i) – P3(ii)	P4 – P8
PSE	PSE	
PE	Therapy	
PE	Physical Development	Physical Education
Art	Understanding my world	Creative arts
DT	Understanding my world	Creative arts
Music	Understanding my world	Creative arts
RE	Understanding my world	Understanding the wider world
Geo	Understanding my world	Understanding the wider world
His	Understanding my world	Understanding the wider world
Science	Exploration	Science
Maths	Exploration	Mathematics
English	Communication	English

Art, DT, Music, RE, Geo, His (P4–P8 far right column)

ICT

P1(i) | P1(ii) | P2(i) | P2(ii) | P3(i) | P3(ii) | P4 | P5 | P6 | P7 | P8

Figure 23.1 Curriculum map: Stephen Hawking School

Curriculum model 2: Barrs Court Specialist (SEN) School and College

Barrs Court is a secondary phase specialist academy for learners with moderate, severe and profound learning difficulties and other disabilities, aged 11 to 19 years. Richard Aird, the headteacher for many years, describes the curriculum in July 2013 as follows:

Aims of the curriculum

As a consequence of their participation in the curriculum, it is planned that learners will be better able to:

- Apply functional skills (including literacy, language, numeracy, independent living skills) in a range of practical contexts to help facilitate their social inclusion which may be evidenced by their ability to contribute to the completion of everyday and independent living tasks.
- Sustain relatively good standards of physical, mental and emotional well-being and be as fit as possible to participate in society, as may be evidenced by their active participation in health related regimes, therapeutic programmes, sustained, high attendance and low drop-out rates.
- Reflect on new experiences, make positive contributions to society, take responsibility for their personal actions and influence decisions relating directly to their future, as may be evidenced by their ability to engage in relationships, function effectively as part of a group and advocate their views to others.
- Be a successful learner who wants to continue to gain the knowledge, understanding and skills necessary to improve their life prospects, as may be evidenced by their rate of progress within accredited learning, a demonstrable sense of vocation and the ability to be purposefully employed.

Organisation of the curriculum

In order for learners to benefit from the aims described above, the curriculum offers a range of learning opportunities that can be readily personalised in terms of depth and breadth in response to the individual circumstances and learning styles of each individual. The curriculum range includes:

- developmental learning opportunities designed to minimise, or overcome, barriers to learning and so enable learners to achieve personal milestones in the acquisition of their functional and independent living skills;
- therapeutic learning for learners to bring about demonstrable improvements in their 'fitness' to participate;
- creative, social learning to ensure learners develop personality, respect for others, self-determination and a sense of self-esteem;
- differentiated, vocational learning that is linked to nationally benchmarked attainments, qualifications and awards.

Figure 23.2 shows the major components of curriculum content.

	Key Stage 3 (11–14 years)	Key Stage 4 (14–16 years)	Key Stage 5 (16–19 years)
Specialist Curricula	Early Thinking Skills – National Curriculum Mathematics & Science P1(i) – P4 Early Communication Skills – National Curriculum English P1(i) – P4 Early Motor Skills – National Curriculum Physical Education		
Creative and Inclusive Entitlement Curricula	Includes full coverage of the National Curriculum, but the breadth of coverage reduces from Key Stage 3 to 4.		Literacy and numeracy
	Schemes of Work are written to incorporate a set of basic principles to ensure teaching of entitlement curricula will: • provide enjoyable and hands on experiential learning; • include strong elements of sensory and cognitive learning; • be meaningful to learners who may be at different stages of development; • motivate learners to investigate, experiment and be curious; • have sufficient impact to provide lasting, memorable experiences; • stimulate learners to want to engage in other aspects of learning. Use of these 'inclusive and creative' principles helps facilitate the extent to which a learner enjoys an activity and the associated likelihood this will result in strong memory imprinting and retention of new information, together with an enhanced capacity for reflection, understanding and attainment.		
Personal, Social and Health Related Curricula	Includes a wide range of topics that learners opt into, or which are selected for them, as part of their transition to adulthood. Typical topics include: • Safeguarding and 'e' safety; • Sex and relationships; • Beauty and personal hygiene; • Independent travel training; • Leisure and hobbies; • Extra-curricular and extended school activities such as Duke of Edinburgh Club, Girl Guide Company, Friday Night Social Club.		
Vocational Curricula			Includes a range of work related learning, independent living skills, enterprise education and work experience that are all linked into a broad syllabus of accredited modules leading to relevant vocational qualifications.

Figure 23.2 Barrs Court School and College curriculum content

Curriculum model 3: Whitefield Schools and Centre

Whitefield Schools and Centre provides education for learners aged 3 to 19 years with complex needs including SLD/PMLD, multisensory impairment, autism and speech and language difficulties. The school has developed four related pathways within their overall curriculum model.

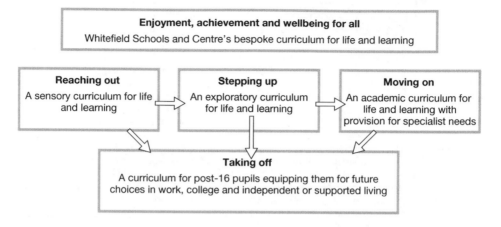

Figure 23.3 Whitefield Schools and Centre curriculum model

Laura Pease, Vice Principal, describes the development of the 'Reaching Out' sensory curriculum (see also Pease 2000, 2008). 'Reaching Out' was developed in order to provide small steps of learning for learners with complex needs including sensory and physical impairment. The school staff wanted a curriculum which would sit within the framework of the National Curriculum but, equally important, would build on learners' existing skills ('bottom up' rather than 'top down') and provide experiences which were meaningful to them and improved the quality of their lives. The school had already developed approaches based on the work of experts such as Lilli Nielsen (2001) and Jan van Dijk (1991; and Nelson *et al.* 2009) and the staff were determined to keep those approaches at the heart of their practice.

'Reaching Out' is essentially a developmental curriculum structured around six subjects – see Figure 23.4. Each subject underpins one or more National Curriculum areas and includes objectives linked to those subjects alongside the specialist curriculum and approaches for learners with PMLD and multisensory approaches. Each is summarised in a Programme of Study that structures teachers' planning and provides for personalized learning objectives. Lessons focus on one or two of the 'Reaching Out' subjects. Teachers select activities which motivate the learners to attend and lend themselves to the focus subject(s). Class groups may share an activity or learners may work in smaller groups. Individual learners may focus on a specific area of the curriculum within the group or may work separately to address an individual priority. All lessons include opportunities for learners to consolidate learning and generalise skills across the curriculum.

Some 15 years on from the introduction of this curriculum structure, Laura believes that it has stood the test of time. Its original aims can be summed up in the school's current Mission Statement, which sets out the aspiration for the school community – 'Enjoyment, Achievement and Wellbeing for All'.

Communication and Language	Helps learners establish a sense of agency and interact with others. The school aims to create the conditions through which learners are motivated to communicate and to progress through a hierarchy of communication modes from reflex responses to speech and sign. They develop behaviours which adults can interpret as communicative, make and communicate choices and, ultimately, develop intentional communication. Speech and Language Therapists collaborate with teachers to create personalised approaches.
Exploring and Ordering the World	Provides the opportunity for learners to develop their functioning senses and so respond to the world around them. Structured experiences are provided to help learners build skills in using sensory information and actively exploring the world within their reach.
Physical Development	Programmes aim to strengthen learners' awareness of their bodies and to help them exercise increasing control over their functional movement. The majority of learners accessing 'Reaching Out' benefit from postural management programmes to maintain flexibility and build physical strength. Physiotherapists and Occupational Therapists help to plan programmes and identify appropriate equipment.
Social and Emotional Development	Supports learners to develop self-confidence and self-awareness, to develop independence and to work alongside other members of the school community. Relationship and sex education is covered within this curriculum area.
Knowledge and Understanding of the World	Builds key concepts about the wider world. Learners develop an awareness of time through routine and change and an awareness of place through associating places with the activities which 'belong' to them. They begin to get a sense of the diverse community to which they belong through exploring features of different cultures and taking part in festivals and celebrations.
Creative Development	Enables learners to express themselves by exploring a range of media, making music and enjoying music and art created by others. Our music therapist, who leads the school's expressive arts team, ensures that expressive art across the school is fully inclusive.

Figure 23.4 Whitefield Schools and Centre: 'Reaching Out' curriculum subject areas

Issues and tensions

Common versus specialist curricula: should there be special/separate curricula for learners with SLD/PMLD?

Until the introduction of the National Curriculum in England, curriculum development for learners with SLD/PMLD was separate from that relating to other learners. The National Curriculum in England introduced notions of a common curriculum (for all) alongside age-related, standards-based attainment measures. Various modifications, adaptations and disapplications to the general curriculum have been permitted and developed over time in attempts to ensure relevance to all learners. At the same time, through the 1990s and 2000s, concepts and practices around rights, equality and inclusion also became more prominent. In this scenario 'commonality (inclusiveness, equality) and relevance (differentiation)' are both important aspects and 'the aim is to have it both ways as far as possible' (Norwich 2010: 132). But this creates a tension. The tension can be illustrated by the following two quotations. On the one hand:

> To achieve inclusive learning pupils must be included in the curriculum.
>
> (O'Brien 2001: 182–183)

On the other hand:

> The priority for children with SEN ... must be that they have access to curricula which are appropriate for them, not that they are fitted in to a curriculum designed for the mainstream population which may not meet their particular needs.
>
> (Hornby 2001: 6)

How much should we strive for, develop and respond to a common curriculum for all (a national curriculum) and how much are there/should there be special curricula for learners with SLD/PMLD incorporating areas which are considered to be specifically relevant (for example, life skills, hydrotherapy, sensory stimulation)? Should any such areas be additional to or instead of 'mainstream' curriculum areas? How far can a general curriculum be modified to include *all* learners?

The curriculum models for the three schools described above each respond to this tension in different ways. They all relate to and draw upon the National Curriculum. The Stephen Hawking School curriculum uses the National Curriculum as a *starting point*, then merges some subject areas into 'themes' for learners working at 'earlier' levels. In the Barrs Court curriculum, the core National Curriculum subjects are explicitly included through being *incorporated into* development areas – mathematics and science into Early Thinking Skills and English into Early Communication Skills. Whitefield's Reaching Out curriculum is described as 'sitting within the framework of the National Curriculum' and six areas ('subjects') are delineated which 'underpin one or more National Curriculum areas' – the Reaching Out 'subjects' seem to be regarded, then, as a *foundation for* the National Curriculum.

Each of the curriculum models, however, also includes curriculum areas in addition to the National Curriculum (for example, therapies, functional skills) and each suggests prioritisation of some areas over others. For Stephen Hawking School this is evident in the time allocation to particular areas; for Barrs Court School National Curriculum physical education, as part of Early Motor Skills, is one specialist curricular area. In this way, a common curriculum is made relevant through specialist focus and through intensification of some areas over others. This leads on to a consideration of breath and balance at an individual level.

Curriculum entitlement, breadth and balance, and individual need: how can these be reconciled?

The issue here is an extension of the common–specialist curriculum tension outlined above but relates more to an individual pupil level:

1   ensuring curriculum entitlement/s while also emphasising individuality;
2   meeting needs that are common to all pupils and, at the same time, responding to individual needs (O'Brien 1998); and
3   maintaining a broad and balanced curriculum, while also prioritising individual relevance.

As O'Brien (1998: 147) states: 'to understand individuality we have to be able to place it within a holistic concept of commonality'; the tension here is reconciling and balancing the two.

The notion of entitlement itself needs examination as it is interpreted differently. The first iteration of the National Curriculum in 1989 was developed as an entitlement curriculum in the sense that all learners had the right to, and were expected to, participate in this curriculum. In this way the National Curriculum was regarded as prescriptive and entitlement was interpreted as a right. In the 2014 National Curriculum there are four 'entitlement areas' at Key Stage 4 (arts, design and technology, humanities and modern foreign language) and learners have 'a statutory entitlement to be able to study a subject' in each of those four areas (DfE 2013: 7). They are not *required* to study these areas but they *must have the opportunity* to be able to do so. The Barrs Court School curriculum includes 'Creative and Inclusive *Entitlement* Curricula' with underlying principles, noting that breadth of coverage reduces over Key Stages. Here, entitlement seems to suggest that learners must be able to study these areas with the proviso that breadth and balance may vary according to a pupil's age, enjoyment, perceived meaningfulness to the pupil and impact upon the pupil.

The concepts of *breadth* and *balance* have been integral features of all iterations of the National Curriculum, including the 2014 version: each school must offer a broad and balanced curriculum. The Stephen Hawking School curriculum development process describes a balance between individual learners' needs and 'statutory duties' (to provide the National Curriculum). Breadth is provided through a topic approach and balance in overall curriculum emphasis is suggested by the size of the areas on the curriculum map. What constitutes breadth and balance, and how this might be determined as common or as different for all learners, however, may be problematic. Should the type of breadth or the particular balance be different for different learners? Barrs Court School curriculum emphasises personalisation of learning opportunities and personalisation of learning objectives is a feature of the Whitefields' model.

Imray and Hinchcliffe (2012: 154) suggest that 'desire to ensure breadth and balance are the very things that are preventing deep and meaningful learning within a needs-led curriculum from taking place', perhaps arguing for more in-depth focus on specific areas at the expense of breadth. These authors have subsequently taken these arguments further (Imray and Hinchcliffe 2014), suggesting that learners with SLD/PMLD 'deserve and need separate and distinct pedagogies' and that a 'mainstream type curriculum is not appropriate'. Imray and Hinchcliffe (2014) argue for a focus in the curriculum on 'fundamental learning skills' such as cognition, communication, thinking and problem solving. A danger in such an approach, however, may be a narrowing of the curriculum, for example, deciding that particular functional curricular aspects (say, 'life skills' and 'independence skills') should be prioritised for some/all learners, which may ignore opportunities in creative arts or humanities. This approach also appears to ignore the fact that more inclusive curriculum models also provide opportunities to gain key cross-curricular skills.

Developmentalism: should curricula be based on models of development?

Many curricula in England in the 1980s were based on 'normal' developmental milestones. The National Curriculum is also criticised for following a particular 'linear, development or academic model' (Imray and Hinchcliffe 2012: 154) and for therefore being unsuited to learners with PMLD. In a 2011 survey of 49 special schools for learners with SLD/PMLD, Lacey (2011) asked respondents to indicate whether their curriculum fitted the categories of 'alternative', 'developmental' and/or 'adapted mainstream'. The curriculum for learners with SLD was most frequently described as 'adapted mainstream' (presumably, adapted National Curriculum), although several schools did select 'developmental'. For learners with PMLD the most chosen category was 'developmental'. This designation is interesting – the National Curriculum model is critiqued for being *developmental* in one way, yet schools are also choosing a *developmental* model for working with learners with PMLD. Is the issue, then, about being a developmental model *per se* or about the stage or level of development incorporated in the curriculum model?

The curriculum model examples in this chapter relate to notions of development: Whitefield's 'Reaching Out' curriculum is described as 'a developmental curriculum'; Barrs Court School curriculum refers to 'developmental learning opportunities' and includes development areas which are defined as 'early'. The understanding here seems to be that learners with SLD/PMLD are at earlier levels of development. Does this mean earlier than other learners? A notion of 'normal' development seems to be apparent. Perhaps we should be contemplating 'different' rather than 'earlier' development? Universal development theory is critiqued (for example, by Burman 2008) as seeking to identify broad and general patterns of development, as applying these to all learners regardless of context and as failing to provide enough subtlety for every learner.

A linear curriculum is rarely appropriate for learners with SLD/PMLD as they tend to have spiky learning profiles. However, if 'developmental' is interpreted not as a linear pathway but instead as being in opposition to a step-by-step skills-based curriculum with pre-designed outcomes, a different position is possible. In this way a developmental curriculum may alternatively be regarded as creating the best conditions for a learner's development through appropriate relationships, activities, scaffolding and stimuli so that learning take place in a way that reflects the individual.

Subjectness: how relevant and useful are subject divisions?

Debates around the possibility and usefulness of dividing curricula according to subjects (for example, mathematics, science or history) go well beyond the field of teaching learners with SLD/PMLD, asking broader questions about the distinctiveness of forms of knowledge (for example, Young 2008). In schools for learners with SLD/PMLD, prior to the National Curriculum, it was rare to conceive of the curriculum according to subject-specific organisation. In many such schools, a functional skills-based curriculum was divided into areas such as cognitive skills, language and communication skills, motor skills and life skills. Following the introduction of the National Curriculum that took a subject orientation, and Ofsted school inspections that tended to align to this, the curricula (and timetables) developed and delivered in these schools also frequently employed a subject-orientated organisation. There continues to be considerable debate regarding subject-based learning for learners with SLD/PMLD (Grove and Peacey 1999; Byers 1999; Goss 2006).

The materials developed in the 2000s around the education of children and young people with learning difficulties within the National Curriculum (QCA/DfEE 2001; revised as QCA 2009) also took a subject-focused orientation, including a booklet for each National Curriculum subject. In the development of these materials, Lawson, Marvin and Pratt (2001) note that each subject was approached from two angles: 1) through the extension and exemplification of the National Curriculum subject programmes of study and 2) by considering the needs of learners, for example, questioning what each subject meant at the earliest stages of learning. This was thus another attempt to focus on entitlement to a commonality of learning experiences (the National Curriculum) and, at the same time, to ensure relevance to learners' individual needs via a focus on priorities for learning addressed in the context of subject-orientated lessons (see also Byers and Rose 2004).

In the three curriculum examples in this chapter there seems to be a view that, for learners with more profound learning difficulties, division by subject as defined in the National Curriculum is not appropriate but amalgamations or new titles for clusters of subjects are established.

Concluding comments

There is a pendulum-like main theme threaded through this chapter swinging between the extremes of common curricula for all and specialist separate curricula. This vacillation, and all stages in between, has occurred over periods of time, influenced by national and global policy drives, for example around accountability, and broader societal impulses, for example around inclusion. It is perhaps best viewed as a continuum. Individuals also have their own views and as Lacey (2011) found in her survey, 'People who express their views at either end do so strongly, feeling that children's needs can only be met at one extreme or the other'.

The 2014 National Curriculum seems to denote a knowledge-based curriculum (perhaps less accessible to learners with SLD/PMLD), but reiterates that 'The National Curriculum is just one element in the education of every learner. There is time and space in the school day and in each week, term and year to range beyond the National Curriculum specifications' (DfE 2013: 5). Indeed, the National Curriculum has never been stated as the whole curriculum (Sebba, Byers and Rose 1993; Rose *et al*. 1994) although it has often been interpreted as such.

There is no one agreed curriculum for learners with SLD/PMLD across the country and, as in the 1980s, many schools seem to be developing their own curricula. Is this a retrograde step? At the time of the introduction of the National Curriculum in 1990, teachers were concerned that existing 'good practice', for example the emphasis on life skills and personal and social education, would be lost (Ashdown, Carpenter and Bovair 1991). However, most commentators and teachers would now acknowledge the wider opportunities and different perceptions of achievement that participation in the National Curriculum has enabled. Laura Pease comments: 'I absolutely see our curriculum in the context of the National Curriculum – I wouldn't have said that 20 years ago!'

In England, there are now a number of different designations of schools, including academies and free schools. Academies and free schools are still required to offer a broad and balanced curriculum, but are not obliged to follow the National Curriculum. These flexibilities may offer exciting opportunities for new and different types of curricula but also afford the possible danger of narrowing the curriculum for learners with SLD/PMLD. Freedom to innovate can also lead to stagnation. As O'Brien (1998: 147) argues, 'The curriculum must be a challenging agitator as well as a supportive and affectionate mediator if it is to respond to need, provide access and extend learning.' Understandings and views of curricula are underpinned by values and assumptions – about the importance and nature of knowledge, about theories of learning, about cultural values (for example, in relation to special educational needs and disability), about the needs of learners, and about learning outcomes (Norwich 2013).

Questions for readers

- Should there be special/separate curricula for learners with SLD/PMLD?
- How can the different values of curriculum entitlement, curricular breadth and balance and of meeting individual needs be reconciled?
- Should curricula be based on models of development?
- How relevant and useful are subject divisions?

And in addition:

- How much do, or should, accreditation schemes and assessment criteria define the curriculum for learners with SLD/PMLD?

References

Aird, R. and Aird, K. (2006) 'Distinctive pedagogy and the development of specialist curriculum matter in the education of pupils who have profound and multiple learning difficulties', *SLD Experience*, 46: 15–19.

Ashdown, R., Carpenter, B. and Bovair, K. (1991) *The Curriculum Challenge: Access to the national curriculum for pupils with learning difficulties,* London: Falmer.

Burman, E. (2008) *Deconstructing Developmental Psychology*, London: Routledge.

Byers, R. (1999) 'Experience and achievement: initiatives in curriculum development for pupils with severe and profound and multiple learning difficulties', *British Journal of Special Education*, 26(4): 184–188.

Byers, R. and Rose, R. (2004) *Planning the Curriculum for Pupils with Special Educational Needs: A practical guide*, 2nd edn, London: David Fulton Publishers.

Department for Education (DfE) (2013) *The National Curriculum in England: framework document*, London: DfE. Online. Available: www.gov.uk/government/publications/national-curriculum-in-england-framework-for-key-stages-1-to-4 (accessed 4 February 2015).

Goss, P. (2006) 'Meaning-led learning for pupils with severe and profound and multiple learning difficulties', *British Journal of Special Education*, 33(4): 210–219.

Grove, N. and Peacey, N. (1999) 'Teaching subjects to pupils with profound and multiple learning difficulties', *British Journal of Special Education*, 26: 83–86.

Hornby, G. (2001) 'Promoting responsible inclusion', in T. O'Brien (ed.) *Enabling Inclusion: blue skies… dark clouds?,* London: The Stationery Office.

Imray, P. and Hinchcliffe, V. (2012) 'Not fit for purpose: A call for separate and distinct pedagogies as part of a national framework for those with severe and profound learning difficulties', *Support for Learning*, 27(4): 150–157.

Imray, P. and Hinchcliffe, V. (2014) *Curricula for Teaching Children and Young People with Severe or Profound and Multiple Learning Difficulties – practical strategies for educational professionals*, London: Routledge.

Kelly, A. V. (1983) *The Curriculum: Theory and practice*, London: Paul Chapman.

Lacey, P. (2011) 'Educational Provision for Pupils with Severe and Profound Learning Difficulties', Unpublished Report, Birmingham: MENCAP/University of Birmingham.

Lawson, H., Marvin, C. and Pratt, A. (2001) 'Planning, teaching and assessing the curriculum for pupils with learning difficulties: an introduction and overview', *Support for Learning*, 16(4): 162–167.

Nelson, C., van Dijk, J., Oster, T. and McDonnell, A. (2009) *Child Guided Strategies: The van Dijk approach to assessment*, Louisville, Kentucky: American Printing House for the Blind.

Nielsen, L. (2001) *Early Learning Step by Step: Children with visual impairment and multiple disabilities*, 3rd edn, Copenhagen, Denmark: Sikon.

Norwich, B. (2010) 'Dilemmas of difference, curriculum and disability: international perspectives', *Comparative Education*, 46(2): 113–135.

Norwich, B. (2013) *Addressing Tensions and Dilemmas in Inclusive Education: Living with uncertainty*, London: Routledge.

O'Brien, T. (1998) 'The millennium curriculum: confronting the issues and proposing solutions', *Support for Learning*, 13(4): 147–152.

O'Brien, T. (2001) *Enabling Inclusion: blue skies… dark clouds?* London: The Stationery Office.

Pease, L. (2000), 'Creating a communicating environment', in S. Aitken, M. Buultjens, C. Clark, J.T. Eyre and L. Pease, L. (eds) *Teaching Children who are Deafblind*, London: David Fulton.

Pease, L.D. (2008) 'Curriculum success for learners with complex needs', *Insight*, 13: 10–13.

QCA (Qualifications and Curriculum Authority)/DfEE (Department for Education and Employment) (2001) *Planning, Teaching and Assessing the Curriculum for Pupils with Learning Difficulties*, London: QCA.

QCA (Qualifications and Curriculum Authority) (2009) *Planning, Teaching and Assessing the Curriculum for Pupils with Learning Difficulties*, 2nd edn, London: QCA.

Rayner, M. (2011) 'The curriculum for children with severe and profound learning difficulties at Stephen Hawking School', *Support for Learning*, 26(1): 25–32.

Rose, R., Fergusson, A., Coles, C., Byers, R. and Banes, D. (eds) (1994) *Implementing the Whole Curriculum for Pupils with Learning Difficulties*, London: David Fulton.

Sebba, J., Byers, R. and Rose, R. (1993) *Redefining the Whole Curriculum for Pupils with Learning Difficulties*, London: David Fulton.

Van Dijk, J. (1991) *Persons Handicapped by Rubella: Victors and victims*, Amsterdam: Swets and Zeitlinger.

Young, M. (2008) *Bringing Knowledge Back In: From social constructivism to social realism in the sociology of education*, Abingdon, Oxon: Routledge.

24

RECOGNISING PROGRESS

Assessing outcomes for learners with SLD/PMLD

Ann Fergusson and Richard Byers

In this chapter, the following questions will be addressed:

- What are the different purposes of assessment?
- Why is formative assessment so crucial?
- What frameworks for assessment are available to show learners' attainments and their progress no matter how slight?
- What guidance is available to develop best practice in assessment for learners with SLD/PMLD?

A brief history of guidance on assessment for learners with SLD/PMLD

Assessment regimes prior to 1970, and indeed in the newly created special schools for learners with SLD/PMLD in the years after 1970, were based on checklists of skills originally designed for measuring progress towards developmental milestones in typically-developing infants (see Chapter 5 in this book). The materials in use in those times included Uzgiris and Hunt's (1975) work on assessment in infancy and the Portage early education programme (Bluma *et al.* 1976). The Progress Assessment Charts (PAC) developed by Gunzburg (1974) represented a pioneering and influential effort to create assessment materials of direct relevance to people with learning difficulties. Whelan and Speake (1979), among others, built on this emerging trend for focusing on 'skills for life' with their scales for assessing 'coping' and 'work' skills. Kiernan and Reid (1987) contributed innovative schedules for assessing pre-verbal communication for learners with PMLD. But these valuable materials all took individualisation as a starting point.

The launch of the National Curriculum (NCC 1989) was informed by a commitment to shared experience (infamously called a 'curriculum for all') and understandings on various forms of assessment developed by a Task Group on Assessment and Testing (DES 1987). These forms of assessment included:

- initial assessment – that might be conceived of as providing a baseline against which to measure future progress;
- diagnostic assessment – that can be understood as enabling professionals to identify any problems, difficulties or barriers that might confront a learner;

- formative assessment – that essentially represents the kinds of assessment that inform planning for future learning;
- summative assessment – that provides a retrospective account of attainments at the end of a given period of learning.

Despite recommendations about the key significance of formative assessment (see Black and Wiliam 1998), the National Curriculum, with its attainment targets and level descriptions, was founded on an essentially summative system of assessment. Learners with SLD/PMLD were, from 1990, theoretically included in the new curriculum but there were no National Curriculum assessment materials for any levels below Level 1 (broadly representing the subject-related attainments of typically developing six-to-seven-year olds). Therefore, teachers and parents became accustomed to living with the phenomenon of young people who were clearly learning but who were, of necessity, recorded officially as constantly 'working towards Level 1'.

The first signs of a change came with the publication of guidance on whole-school target setting (DfEE 1998). This booklet offered scales for measuring attainments in English, mathematics and personal and social development which were 'designed for use by teachers when making summative assessments' but not to support 'day to day assessments' (DfEE 1998: 19). The guidance introduced the notion of teachers making 'best fit' judgements about their pupils' learning and the concept of measurable progress leading to Level 1. Taking account of criticisms and representations from practitioners, the P scales (as these materials came to be known) were soon revised and extended to all subject areas. The new versions of the P scales provided performance descriptions for eight levels leading to Level 1 for all subjects of the National Curriculum plus religious education and personal, social and health education and citizenship). They were published together with comprehensive guidance to support planning, teaching and assessment for pupils with learning difficulties (QCA/DfEE 2001). The target setting materials, with guidance on recording and reporting, were re-launched in same year (DfEE 2001).

These publications coincided with revisions to the National Curriculum itself. Ongoing problems with the P scales and contradictions in the official policy positions on assessment and target setting for learners with SLD/PMLD were set out in a report based on the views of practitioners, inspectors and school leaders (Byers 2004). Again, these perspectives were acknowledged and led to further revision of the P scales and the publication of formal guidance on using the P Scales (QCA 2005). In 2007, the P scales became part of the National Curriculum and schools were required to provide data gathered using the P scales for all learners attaining below Level 1 (including those with SLD/PMLD). The suite of guidance booklets on planning, teaching and assessing pupils with learning difficulties was updated in accordance with the requirements of an updated National Curriculum (QCA 2009a). The guidance on using the P scales was also revised and updated with the provision of video exemplars showing learning at each of the levels from P1 to P8 (QCA 2009b; QCDA 2011).

The structure of the P-scales

In response to calls from teachers for greater differentiation at the earliest levels, the descriptions for P1 to P3 were further divided into two steps – P1(i), P1(ii), P2(i), P2(ii), P3(i) and P3(ii). These performance descriptions are common across all the subjects in the National Curriculum. They outline general performance that pupils with learning difficulties might demonstrate and are based on research into communication, interaction and cognitive development by contributors including Coupe O'Kane and Goldbart (1998), McInness and Treffry (1982), Aitken and Buultjens (1992) and Ware (1996).

Although the descriptions at P1 to P3 are generic, subject-focused examples of responses are included in the descriptions, in italics, to illustrate 'some of the ways in which staff might identify attainment in different subject contexts' (QCA 2009a). The descriptor for P1(ii) in English, for example, says: 'Pupils show emerging awareness of activities and experiences. They have periods when they appear alert and ready to focus their attention on certain people, events, objects or parts of objects, *for example, attending briefly to interactions with a familiar person*. They may give intermittent reactions, *for example, sometimes becoming excited in the midst of social activity*.' In science, the core elements of the description at P1(ii) remain the same ('show emerging awareness', 'give intermittent reactions', etc.) but the subject related examples are *'looking towards flashes of light or turning towards loud sounds'*, and *'sometimes withdrawing their hands from changes in temperature'*.

The implication here is that, even at this level, teachers need to be aware of (and ready to record) the subject context in which responses occur since they may indicate early forms of subject knowledge.

The descriptions at levels P4 to P8 explicitly focus on responses that suggest 'the emergence of skills, knowledge and understanding in each subject' (QCA 2009a). The descriptions at P4 to P8 enable staff to recognise new gains, consolidated or generalised learning and are different in each subject, with separate elements for 'speaking and listening', 'reading' and 'writing' in English and for 'using and applying mathematics', 'number' and 'shape, space and measures' in mathematics. Arguably at P4 to P8, it is possible to describe performance in a way that indicates the emergence of subject-focused skills, knowledge and understanding and to reveal progress that is clearly related to a subject area. The descriptions provide examples of how this can be done, although the descriptions do not cover all the areas of learning that should be covered by the curriculum in any given subject. The description for P6 in mathematics, for example, says: 'Pupils sort objects and materials according to given criteria. They begin to identify when an object is different and does not belong to given categories. They sort simple patterns or sequences, *for example, a pattern of large and small cups, or a drumbeat*.'

Key issues in using the P-scales

The P-level descriptions were designed to be applied using a 'best fit' approach (QCA 2009a). This represented a shift in approach for colleagues who had experience of the precision teaching and checklist-driven assessment. Indeed, there have been tendencies to return to the atomisation and quantification of learning by breaking the performance descriptions of the P scales down into hierarchies of sub-levels and mini-attainments. Thus, the use of materials such as CASPA, PIVATS, and B-Squared has found favour in some settings (see Ndaji and Tymms 2009) but in many senses seems to run counter to the spirit of the central guidance.

Learning at levels P4 to P8 recognisably represents the kind of learning, based on the acquisition of new skills, noted by White and Haring (1980), for example, in their work on precision teaching. By contrast, the range of responses at P1 to P3 is understood as occurring prior to the acquisition of skills and is orientated towards the kinds of experiential learning explored by Brown (1996), Ouvry and Saunders (1996) and Byers (1999). This continuum covers the following possibilities:

- **Encounter:** Learners are present during an experience or activity without any obvious learning outcome, although for some learners, their willingness to tolerate a shared activity may, in itself, be significant.
- **Awareness:** Learners appear to show awareness that something has happened and notice, fleetingly focus on or attend to an object, event or person.
- **Attention and response:** Learners attend and begin to respond, often not consistently, to what is happening, demonstrating the beginning of an ability to distinguish between different people, objects, events and places.
- **Engagement:** Learners show more consistent attention to, and can tell the difference between, specific events in their surroundings.
- **Participation:** Learners engage in sharing, taking turns and the anticipation of familiar sequences of events, although these responses may be supported by staff or other pupils.
- **Involvement:** Learners actively strive to reach out, join in or comment in some way on the activity itself or on the actions or responses of the other pupils.
- **Gaining skills and understanding:** Learners gain, strengthen or make general use of skills, knowledge, concepts or understanding that relate to their experience of the curriculum.

In the guidance from QCA (2009a), this continuum is illustrated with examples that are designed to support staff in recognising the kinds of responses that learners with SLD/PMLD may make (e.g. the withholding of attention, self-absorbed vocalisation, the eye-tracking of movement, making exploratory hand movements). The use of responses like these as a foundation for the P scales ensures that the progress of all learners, including those with the most profound difficulties, can be recognised within an inclusive assessment framework. However, the P-scales are not without their critics and their value in comparison to other assessment tools has been downplayed (e.g. by Imray and Hinchcliffe 2014).

Significantly, the P scales were designed to allow staff to recognise forms of learning that are not necessarily dependent upon the progressive acquisition of new skills, knowledge and understanding. The P scales facilitate, for example, the recognition of both linear and lateral progress (QCA 2009a) where:

- linear progress is represented by increasing levels of subject specific attainment leading towards attainment at National Curriculum Level 1;
- lateral progress is recognised when learners demonstrate the application of related skills at similar levels in subject contexts across the curriculum.

This core possibility that learners may make progress without necessarily gaining new subject-specific skills, knowledge or understanding is important for learners with SLD/PMLD. The QCA guidance (2009a) provides examples of the kinds of progress that may be made when learners:

- demonstrate the same achievement on more than one occasion and under changing circumstances;
- demonstrate an ability to maintain, refine, generalise or combine skills over time and in a range of circumstances, situations and settings;
- demonstrate a reduced need for support in carrying out particular tasks;
- show a reduction in the frequency or severity of behaviour that inhibits learning.

The guidance emphasises that some learners at some times may decide not to participate or respond – and that this may represent progress of a kind for some. The guidance also makes clear that developing 'a range of responses to actions, events or experiences' constitutes a form of progress for learners with SLD/PMLD, even where 'there is no clear progress in acquiring knowledge and skills' that relate to the subjects of the curriculum.

This is a crucial consideration for staff who are also trying to implement the requirements of the new Special Educational Needs and Disability Code of Practice: 0–25 Years (DfE/DoH 2014; and see Chapter 3 in this book) which reminds us that we must ensure that the priorities for learning that are identified for learners are matched to their individual needs. Taken in association with the guidance on assessment in relation to the shared curriculum (see Byers and Rose 2004), this means that teaching and learning for learners with SLD/PMLD can provide:

- breadth of experience – an entitlement for all to a shared curriculum that includes those learners who may not make rapid or sustained progress towards subject–related attainments;
- relevance to individual needs – enabling staff, parents and pupils to identify and pursue priorities for learning for each learner, whether these relate to subject content or not;
- an integrated approach – in which personalised priorities for learning are addressed in the context of experiences founded in the shared curriculum.

Assessment in practice

There are some valuable principles and frameworks to support any form of assessment within the school setting, described in the guidance developed to support the use of P Scales. Such tools for professional reflection can be useful with many assessment approaches. They offer a structure to support the development of more systematic assessment practices resulting in teacher assessment being more accurate and more useful to plan for progression. QCDA (2011: 2) offers a set of important guiding principles when describing a national approach to assessing pupils' progress (APP): the learner is at the heart of assessment; assessment needs to provide a view of the whole learner; assessment is integral to teaching and learning; and assessment includes reliable judgements about how learners are doing in relation to national standards and expectations where appropriate. The APP approach depends on ongoing professional reflection and teacher judgement of the insights gained from day-to-day practice and how these are used to improve learning and teaching over time.

Viewing 'assessment for learning' (AfL), or formative assessment, as an integral part of the planning, teaching and assessment cycle, recognises that it is central to classroom practice. In order to develop as full a picture as possible about each of our unique and individual learners, it is essential to have an accurate view not only about what has been learnt but, as importantly, how. Practitioners will want information about all factors that positively promote or enhance learning: how individuals prefer to learn; what motivates them to respond and learn; and what are the most successful conditions or types of support to enable them to learn. AfL approaches enable us to focus on a more comprehensive view of the whole learner, how they learn, their progress and potential next steps. This type of assessment promotes learning goals and encourages the involvement of learners in the process of learning.

Building on baseline assessment information

A sound baseline will include insight of prior learning, of individual barriers to learning and the unique contributing factors such as learning styles, motivators and other preferences that influence or promote learning. Baselines enable us to consider developmental needs of a learner as well as the impact of their barriers to learning and altered experience of life. This view enables us not only to plan next steps of learning and longer-term progression, but also to develop a more focused view of what indicators to look for in day-to-day activities when considering personalised learning outcomes from each learner. However, undertaking baseline assessment will often highlight the need for further, more detailed observations or specialist assessment.

Schools, and indeed teachers, need a wide-ranging battery of assessment tools to collect evidence and information to build accurate pictures of their learners (Imray and Hinchcliffe 2014). Such resources can vary in form and generate different views: for example, informal and structured teacher observations, school-based tools and profiles, specialist or published materials. Practitioners need to be eclectic and select accordingly to gather appropriate information to add the next level of detail of their focus in question. Chapter 25 by Goldbart and Ware in this book offers valuable examples of assessment resources to construct a profile of a learner with PMLD. For example, they describe the use of Routes for Learning (Welsh Assembly Government 2006) and Quest for Learning (CCEA 2011) to clarify the unique spread of responses and learning within a developmental framework. This framework offers insight into the very distinctive nature of opportunities or activities that facilitate responses from learners as well as their very context-specific responses. The Affective Communication Assessment (ACA) (Coupe *et al.* 1985) offers potential to dig deeper, to the next level of detail about those very specific responses. The very structured focus of the ACA enables us to identify the range of clustered responses made by a learner to various stimuli, with a view to interpreting or attaching meaning (intentional or otherwise). However, teachers can develop even further this unique baseline picture of a learner by continued observations and discussions with families and others who know them well, about valuable supplementary 'puzzle pieces' which over time continue to build the bigger picture. From the initial baseline, evidence of different or repeated responses may indicate signs of new/emerging skills or consolidation and potentially, progress. 'Strengths and Needs' analyses aid review based on careful observation and evidence involving those who know the learner well (e.g. Lacey 2010; QCDA 2011).

Evidence of learning and progress

Teacher assessment based on evidence from everyday practice offers a wealth of information. It supports us to make more secure and reliable judgements of learning and progress and valuably informs future planning and target setting. However, the appropriateness of the evidence determines its usefulness in meeting these needs. QCDA (2011) helpfully suggests that to be of greatest benefit evidence should ideally:

- be gathered over time and from a wide range of differing contexts (ideally beyond the classroom or school);
- include a variety of formats (e.g. artefacts, photos, digital records, observations and informal notes);
- be supported by annotation, offering significant contextual information;
- involve contributions, views and interpretations of others, e.g. families, therapists, residential or other social care staff;
- involve learners themselves wherever possible.

By developing the assessment cycle and accurate profiles of learners, practitioners do become increasingly skilled at selecting the most significant evidence of learning and progress. With the support of focused annotation, such evidence provides valuable insights into factors (often context-specific) that may influence or promote learning for individuals.

Maddie

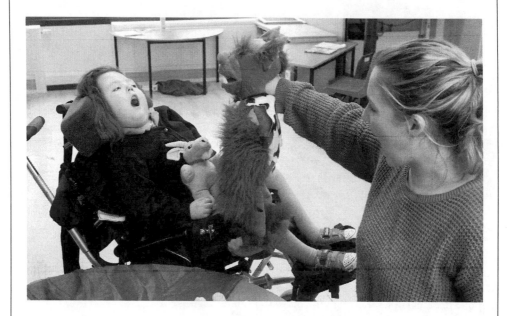

Maddie opened her mouth really wide and for the first time, sighed loudly when the puppet came close to her face during her daily interactive games with Hannah (very familiar teaching assistant). This particular game with the puppet is really motivating to Maddie.

Frameworks for assessment and progression

Working within a structure or framework can potentially offer a more systematic approach to assessment and the review of our teaching practices. The value of frameworks is considered in Chapter 20 in this book by Fergusson and Howley and their colleagues where they create a model to support the systematic examination of observations and explorations in response to concerns about the mental health needs of learners.

Content-free models allow practitioners to draw on the structure to examine chosen areas and can be particularly useful in acknowledging small steps of change, less predictable outcomes or the idiosyncratic behaviours of learners with SLD/PMLD. Similarly they may offer multidimensional perspectives on learning and development to acknowledge and support achievements that do not follow conventional, hierarchical or linear progress. An example is the framework for recognising attainment of learners with PMLD (QCA 2009a) described earlier in this chapter. This continuum lends itself particularly well to evidencing interaction and engagement offering a qualitative view of interacting or perhaps working with others (for an example, see Firth's (2004) adaptation for Intensive Interaction).

Joel

During the class' daily story (Big Bug), Joel seemed to relax and 'look' towards the book in front of him as Anthony opened the page with the big pop-up flower. He was aware of the page being turned and despite his visual impairment, Joel appeared to be attending to the book/story.

A continuum perspective can provide a multi-layered view of learning and progress (e.g. Fergusson 1998; Sissons 2010). It acknowledges learners may be functioning at multiple points simultaneously, while demonstrating lateral progress within each point: for instance, as learners broaden their 'repertoires' of skills (e.g. new ways of responding, increased vocabulary of signs/symbols) or use existing skills in additional contexts. Sissons (2010) (described by Imray 2013) develops this further in MAPP – a two-part assessment resource (learning intentions, skills development continuum) addressing learning and progress for learners with SLD (at approximately P-levels P4–P8).

As also noted above, we should look for evidence of broader learning and lateral progress (QCA 2009a), when a learner remains at the same level of attainment, for example the same P level or Routes/Quest milestone. We have noted that evidence of progress might be that a learner demonstrates the same skill but with less support or in a new situation or with greater independence/confidence. Similarly we may consciously enable progression to be demonstrated by planning small steps that scaffold the transfer of skills from a familiar context to one that is similar but not identical; for instance, we may change one factor, such as a different adult supporting the learner, the same activity but in a new venue, or a new action song with a similar sequence or pattern.

Alia

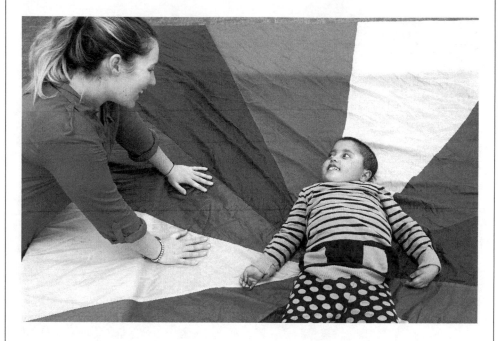

Alia is used to interacting with Hannah (teaching assistant) only in the classroom. She really enjoys rebound therapy and was supported by Hannah for the first time in this rebound session. Ready to make the 'drumming' cue to start the session, Hannah put her hands on the trampoline and said 'ready…' (pause). Alia looked at Hannah, tensed her body and smiled in anticipation at the cue to start.

PARTY

When considering factors that may impact on successful learning, Fergusson and Brookes (2015) offer their simple aide memoire, PARTY (see below), to prompt focus and reflection on key information about progress. This encourages practitioners to consider key needs or tailored conditions that ensure learners are 'ready to learn', such as physical/postural management to facilitate 'comfort for learning' or access to the activity, sensory regulation, arousal state and emotional well-being as prerequisites to effective learning (see also Longhorn (n.d.). Practitioners are asked to consider contextual factors including:

P   People, place, position, particular situation or conditions.
A   Aims, activity or event observed, approach used, arousal state – attention/engagement level, anticipation, active involvement.
R   Resources, response – anything about what learner did; new response, repetitions, or your interpretations of response – intentional, learner-led, turn-taking.
T   Time-related information – processing time, duration, time of day, pace, pause time, how long learner was engaged.
Y   YOU! Anything about your role or approach, type of support/prompts used, your positioning, learner or adult-led.

This focused review of learning enables practitioners to identify what promotes successful learning outcomes – what works well/not so well? What makes the difference to the learner? What factors can we use again to maximise chances of success? Sometimes it can be unplanned, unexpected or novel elements that lead to achievements.

Amos

During a visit to London Zoo, Amos noticed a penguin swimming. He stopped running around, moved to the side of the tank and watched it intently for almost five minutes (not usual!).

Using assessment information

Progress files, personal portfolios and learning journals are a valuable method to present annotated evidence of learning (both linear and lateral progress) over time and a range of contexts. Selecting evidence can involve the learner themselves in reviewing items to be included. These collections can provide a valuable point of reference particularly when making judgements against shared milestones (such as P scales or Quest/Routes for Learning or MAPP).

Frameworks, such as those discussed, offer a valuable structure for conversations with families and other professionals; they are especially useful when a learner may not have made linear progress up to the next level, but their achievements can be shared facilitated by the focus of a framework for reflection. By engaging in collaborative dialogue as part of this review process, our judgements become more consistent and reliable and these professional discussions impact directly on our practice, leading to improved opportunities for learning and progress.

Questions for readers

1   To what extent is it possible to identify subject–related attainment at levels P1 to P3?
2   How useful, for learners with SLD/PMLD, is the notion of the 'subject context' within which other forms of learning can be promoted, assessed and recorded?
3   How important, for learners with SLD/PMLD, is the identification and assessment of learning that is not related to the shared curriculum?
4   To what extent and in what ways can learners with SLD/PMLD be involved in assessing their own progress as learners?

References

Aitken, S. and Buultjens, M. (1992) *Vision for Doing*, Edinburgh: Moray House Publications.

Black, P. and Wiliam, D. (1998) *Inside the Black Box: Raising standards through classroom assessment*, London: King's College.

Bluma, S., Shearer, M., Frohman, A. and Hillard, J. (1976) *The Portage Guide to Early Education*, Wisconsin: Comparative Education Service.

Brown, E. (1996) *Religious Education for All*, London: David Fulton Publishers.

Byers, R. (1999) 'Experience and achievement: initiatives in curriculum development for pupils with severe and profound and multiple learning difficulties', *British Journal of Special Education*, 26(4): 184–188.

Byers, R. (2004) 'Developing the P–Scales – performance descriptions in eight levels from P1 to P8 outlining attainment leading to level 1: executive summary, report and recommendations.' London: DfES.

Byers, R. and Rose, R. (2004) *Planning the Curriculum for Pupils with Special Educational Needs – a practical guide*, 2nd edn, London: David Fulton Publishers.

CCEA (Council for the Curriculum, Examinations and Assessment) (2011) *Quest for Learning: guidance and assessment materials – profound and multiple learning difficulties*, Northern Ireland Curriculum, Belfast: CCEA.

Coupe, J., Barton, L., Collins, L., Levy, D. and Murphy, D. (1985) *The Affective Communication Assessment*, Manchester: M.E.C. Available from Melland High School, Holmcroft Rd., Manchester M18 7NG.

Coupe O'Kane, J. and Goldbart, J. (1998) *Communication before Speech: development and assessment* (second edition), London: David Fulton Publishers.

DES (Department of Education and Science) (1987) *National Curriculum Task Group on Assessment and Testing: a report*, London: DES.

DfE (Department for Education) (1994) *Code of Practice on the Identification and Assessment of Special Educational Needs*, London: DfE.

DfEE (Department for Education and Employment) (1998) *Supporting the Target Setting Process: guidance for effective target setting for pupils with special educational needs*, London: DfEE.

DfEE (Department for Education and Employment) (2001) *Supporting the Target Setting Process: guidance for effective target setting for pupils with special educational needs*, 2nd edn, London: DfEE.

DfE/DoH (Department for Education and Department of Health) (2014) *Special Educational Needs and Disability Code of Practice: 0 to 25 years*. Ref: DFE:-00205-2013. Online. Available: www.gov.uk/government/publications/send-code-of-practice-0-to-25 (accessed 20 August 2014).

Fergusson, A. (1998) 'Planning for Communication', in R. Rose, A. Fergusson, C. Coles, R. Byers and D. Banes (eds) *Implementing the Whole Curriculum for Pupils with Learning Difficulties*, 2nd edn, London: David Fulton.

Fergusson, A. and Brookes, M. (2015) 'A reason to PARTY: recognising the importance of context to maximise learning and engagement', *PMLD Link*, forthcoming.

Firth, G. (2004) *A Framework for Recognising Attainment in Intensive Interaction*, Leeds: Leeds Mental Health NHS Trust.

Gunzburg, H.C. (1974) *Progress Assessment Chart of Social and Personal Development*, Bristol, Indiana: Aux Chandelles.

Imray, P. (2013) 'Alternatives assessment and pupil progress indicators to the P scales for pupils and students with SLD or PMLD', *The SLD Experience*, 66: 7–16.

Kiernan, C. and Reid, B, (1987) *Pre-Verbal Communication Schedule*, Windsor: NFER-Nelson.

Lacey, P. (2010) 'Smart and Scruffy targets', *The SLD Experience*, 57: 16–21.

Longhorn, F. (n.d.) 'Sensory Happiness Check Sheet', cited in RNIB (nd) *Working with Complex Needs in the Classroom*. Factsheet. Online. Available: www.rnib.org.uk/services-we-offer-advice-professionals-education-professionals/guidance-teaching-and-learning (accessed 10 August 2014).

McInness, J. M. and Treffry, J. A. (1982) *Deaf-blind Infants and Children*, Toronto: University of Toronto Press.

NCC (National Curriculum Council) (1989) *An Introduction to the National Curriculum*, York: NCC.

Ndaji, F. and Tymms, P. (eds) (2009) *The P Scales: assessing the progress of children with special educational needs*, Chichester: Wiley-Blackwell.

Ouvry, C. and Saunders, S. (1996) 'Pupils with profound and multiple learning difficulties', in B. Carpenter, R. Ashdown and K. Bovair (eds) *Enabling Access: Effective teaching and learning for pupils with learning difficulties*, London: David Fulton Publishers.

QCA (Qualifications and Curriculum Authority) (2005) *Using the P Scales: Assessing, moderating and reporting pupil attainment in English, mathematics and science at levels P4 to P8*, London: QCA.

QCA (Qualifications and Curriculum Authority) (2009a) *Planning, Teaching and Assessing the Curriculum for Pupils with Learning*, 2nd edn, London: QCA.

QCA (Qualifications and Curriculum Authority) (2009b) *Using the P Scales: Assessing, moderating and reporting pupil attainment at levels P1 to P8*, 2nd edn, London: QCA.

QCA (Qualifications and Curriculum Authority)/DfEE (Department for Education and Employment) (2001) *Planning, Teaching and Assessing the Curriculum for Pupils with Learning Difficulties*, London: QCA.

QCDA (Qualifications and Curriculum Development Agency) (2011) *Using the P Scales to Assess Pupils' Progress*, Coventry: QCDA.

Sissons, M. (2010) *MAPP: Mapping and Assessing Pupil Progress*, North Allerton: The Dales School.

Uzgiris, I. and Hunt, J. (1975) *Assessment in Infancy – ordinal scales of psychological development*, Urbana, Ill: University of Illinois Press.

Ware, J. (1996) *Creating a Responsive Environment*, London: David Fulton Publishers.

Welsh Assembly Government (2006) *Routes for Learning: Assessment materials for learners with profound learning difficulties and additional disabilities*, Cardiff: Welsh Assembly Government, Qualifications and Curriculum Group, DELLS (Dept of Education, Lifelong Learning and Skills)

Whelan, E. and Speake, B. (1979) *Scale for Assessing Coping Skills,* Rochdale: Copewell Publications.

White, O.R. and Haring, N.G. (1980) *Exceptional Teaching,* Columbus, Ohio: Charles E. Merrill Publishing Co.

25

COMMUNICATION

Juliet Goldbart and Jean Ware

In this chapter, the following questions will be addressed:

*   What is communication?
*   How does communication develop?
*   How might this differ in learners with PMLD?
*   What assessment approaches are most useful?
*   What approaches to teaching are useful for these learners?

Introduction

In this chapter we want, as far as possible, to present both a practical and an evidence-based approach to communication and interaction in relation to children and young people with PMLD. We say 'as far as possible' because there is not always sufficient research for us to draw on; in the absence of robust research, we will draw on theoretical work based on an understanding of the development of communication in typical infants and very young children. We will finish our account at the point where children are starting to use some formal means of communication, whether that is through single words, signs or symbols. A list of useful resources are given at the end of the chapter.

What is communication?

Communication, and the interaction between staff and learners and among learners themselves, is fundamental to education and is acknowledged to lie at the centre of the curriculum for this group (e.g. Bradley 1998; Imray and Hinchcliffe 2014). A simple definition of communication is the exchange of information between two or more participants. This definition is often extended to suggest that the two participants can be defined in terms of whether they are the sender or the receiver of a particular piece of information. Underlying this definition is a view of communication as a process in which a piece of information is encoded by the sender (for example as words or signs) and decoded by the recipient (Grove *et al.* 1999). A more useful definition, however, is given by Bunning: 'communication is about two or more people working together and coordinating their actions in an ongoing response to each other and the context' (Bunning 2009: 48).

The idea of communication as a joint effort, in which both participants take a share of the responsibility for reaching understanding, is a critical one in theories of the development of early communication (e.g. Bremner 2008), since it suggests that from very early on communication is embedded in social interaction and is a joint rather than a solo effort. Thus for communication to be successful, both partners need to adjust to each other, rather than the more competent (adult) partner taking sole responsibility. Given this view of communication it is unsurprising that difficulties with communication are often part of the defining features of learners with PMLD (e.g. Bellamy *et al.* 2010; Iacono *et al.* 2009), as teachers and other classroom staff are all too aware.

We take a rights-based perspective; effective communication is a human right. The responsibility of teachers, speech and language therapists (SaLTs) and other practitioners is to provide the optimal input and environment for communication to flourish. As Bunning says:

> Communication is the conduit between the individual and the world. It is the very cornerstone of identity formation, social engagement and human relationships... In this respect, people with profound intellectual and multiple disabilities (PIMDs) are no different to the typically developing population. The real differences lie in the scope and level of sophistication of available skills and the role performed by significant others (the people who engage with them on a daily basis).
>
> (Bunning 2009: 46)

The development of early communication

It is important to remember that communication involves both output and input. In becoming communicators, children learn to listen and understand and also to express themselves. Of course, in everyday interaction, the roles of listener and 'speaker' (whether that is through gesture, sounds, words, etc.) are exchanged during the course of the interaction. This turn-taking is fundamental to communication. From the early weeks of a baby's life, caregivers model this for the baby by using a burst-pause pattern, not just in speaking, but for all sorts of activities. Typically, the caregiver waits for a pause in the infant's activity before they begin an action (a turn) of their own. They then leave a space for the baby to fill (the baby's turn) before they take another turn themselves. In this way, infants participate in turn-taking before they are able to initiate or direct it themselves.

Communication can be seen as having its roots in both social and cognitive development. Socially, in addition to turn-taking, an interest in, or at least an awareness of, other human beings is important. In terms of cognitive development:

- in the first few months babies become aware of objects around them, their characteristics and properties (this is a necessary step towards forming a concept of the object and so being able to learn its name);
- by about five months of age they are beginning to act purposefully and to be aware of cause and effect;
- by nine months they begin to search for objects which have vanished and to try again when an action which has been successful before (e.g. pressing a switch to work a toy) is unsuccessful;
- by about 18 months, typically developing children can reproduce actions they have seen someone else do in the past and are attempting to solve problems, for example by trying an alternative strategy when an old one fails.

As can be seen from Figure 25.1, for typically developing children clear parallels can be seen between the development of cognition and that of communication. For example, babies begin to make different sounds themselves at about the same time as they notice and respond differently to different stimuli.

Hearing and Understanding	Talking
Birth–3 Months Startles to loud sounds Quiets or smiles when spoken to Seems to recognise your voice and quiets if crying Increases or decreases sucking behaviour in response to sound	**Birth–3 Months** Makes pleasure sounds (cooing, gooing) Cries differently for different needs Smiles when sees you
4–6 Months Moves eyes in direction of sounds Responds to changes in tone of your voice Notices toys that make sounds Pays attention to music	**4–6 Months** Babbling sounds more speech-like with many different sounds, including p, b and m Chuckles and laughs Vocalises excitement and displeasure Makes gurgling sounds when left alone and when playing with you
7 Months–1 Year Enjoys games like peek-a-boo and pat-a-cake Turns and looks in direction of sounds Listens when spoken to Recognises words for common items like 'cup', 'shoe', 'book', or 'juice' Begins to respond to requests (e.g. 'Come here' or 'Want more?')	**7 Months–1 Year** Babbling has both long and short groups of sounds such as "tata upup bibibibi" Uses speech or non-crying sounds to get and keep attention Uses gestures to communication (waving, holding arms to be picked up) Imitates different speech sounds Has one or two words (hi, dog, dada, mama) around first birthday, although sounds may not be clear

Figure 25.1 Birth to one year old. What should a child be able to do? (American Speech and Hearing Association n.d.)

Implications of profound and multiple learning difficulties

Little is known about the extent to which learners with PMLD follow this typical developmental trajectory, though in a study by Vandereet *et al.* (2010), children with *severe* learning difficulties produced significantly more protoimperatives (requesting behaviours) than protodeclaratives (behaviours drawing the other person's attention to something interesting), and used more sophisticated forms to do this. This may relate to difficulties in developing shared understanding and is likely to have negative implications for later language learning.

Why might learners with PMLD develop communication and language differently from typically developing children? In addition to profound cognitive impairments, learners with PMLD are likely to experience a range of additional difficulties:

- Visual impairment, experienced by 85 per cent (van Splunder *et al.* 2003) – learners with PMLD, especially those who were born prematurely, may have damage of various types to the brain's visual system (Hoyt n.d.) so that their eyes may appear to function normally, but they experience severe challenges in making use of the incoming visual information.

- Hearing impairment, affecting 25–35 per cent (Evenhuis *et al.* 2001) – this is likely to adversely affect the development of speech and language, yet many parents of children with SLD and PMLD report delays and inadequacies in obtaining appropriate audiological services for their children (McCracken and Turner 2012).
- Motor delays and impairments (Lancioni et al. 2010), including cerebral palsy, which limit learners' opportunity to access and interact with the world around them.
- Atypical patterns of attention (Munde and Vlaskamp 2010) which mean that learners may not be sufficiently alert to respond to stimulation and events around them.
- Epileptic conditions which are diagnosed in around 50 per cent of learners with PMLD (Lhatoo and Sander 2001).

All of these can have an effect on both the social and the cognitive aspects of communication development we described earlier. For example, a learner's visual difficulties may be sufficiently severe that they cannot distinguish between the teacher facing towards or away from them. So their attempts to interact might go unnoticed much of the time and they are at risk of giving up. A learner with significant motor impairments will need additional support from parents and school staff to ensure they have the rich and varied experiences of objects and of making things happen that they need to develop an awareness of cause and effect.

Although quite a lot is known about these additional difficulties experienced by learners with PMLD, we do not have detailed descriptions of their developmental stages and trajectories. So, we will use information from typical development, along with a sceptical view, bearing in mind possible differences.

Helpfully, the American National Joint Committee for the Communication Needs of Persons with Severe Disabilities (1991) stated that 'Communication may be intentional or unintentional, may involve conventional or unconventional signals, may take linguistic or non-linguistic forms, and may occur through spoken or other modes' (www.asha.org/policy/GL1992-00201.htm). This allows us to consider all learners, no matter how great their difficulties, to be communicators.

Assessment of early communication

Parents and staff who work regularly with a particular learner will have considerable knowledge about that learner's communication skills; what they understand, what and how they can express themselves, and how their communication is used in interaction with others. It is helpful, however, to draw this knowledge into a more structured form, test it out, and make it available to others. A range of assessment approaches is available to support this process. If you have access to a SaLT, assessing learners together and agreeing teaching approaches based on your joint findings is likely to be a good strategy.

Routes for Learning (Welsh Assembly Government, 2006)

Routes for Learning (see web address on page 267) is an assessment specifically designed for classroom use. Since its publication in 2006 it has been used by teachers not simply to assess a learner's initial level of communication, but to assess ongoing progress, and some schools have developed additional tools to help them use it in this way (see below for examples). 'Routes' is designed to assess communication and cognition. It is based on observation of the learner's responses to a range of activities and situations, the great majority of which would be familiar to teachers of learners with PMLD. The structure of Routes attempts to take account of the fact that learners with PMLD may well not follow typical developmental trajectories, although it also identifies behaviours which the development team believed all learners would pass through.

The Routes materials include a DVD which provides examples of all the behaviours which make up the assessment, with particular attention to helping teachers differentiate between behaviours which appear similar but which indicate different stages of development. Suggestions for how a learner can be moved towards a particular step are also included; for example, even staff who know the learner well may be doubtful about whether or not a learner is recognising a particular voice as *familiar* (Routes: Box 8), or simply responding to the sound of *an adult* talking, so the Routes DVD uses two video clips to show how a learner responds differently to a person she knows from one who she does not. Teaching strategies for helping the learner achieve this step include ensuring that every member of staff has a personal identifier, and consistently using the learner's name to encourage voice recognition.

Routes is designed to assess learners up to about 18 months of developmental age, although the 'steps' are rather sparse in the later stages. More recently, the Welsh government has brought out a literacy (and numeracy) framework which is designed to be an assessment of communication linking Routes into the Foundation Phase (Welsh Government 2013).

A school in Swansea (Ysgol Crug Glas) has been using Routes for Learning as their main assessment tool for some years. A portfolio of evidence is built up for each learner; demonstrating not only the learner's level, but the evidence on which staff have reached their conclusions.

Joanna Ciuksza from Brooklands School in Surrey started using Routes for Learning, following an Ofsted inspection, as the system they were using did not show the achievement for the learners with PMLD she was working with. She quickly realised that she needed more from the Routes approach and through focus group meetings with teachers of learners with PMLD in other SLD schools in Surrey she learned about an Excel spreadsheet which was developed by Clifton Hill School. The spreadsheet allowed Brooklands staff to create a baseline of achievement and then track each child's progress by breaking down each Routes Step into five progress steps and then giving each a percentage score. Through the SLD Forum (http://lists.education.gov.uk/mailman/listinfo/sld-forum) and with permission from Clifton Hill this work has been disseminated to a very wide audience. See also Turner and Ciuksza (2014).

Quest for Learning

Quest for Learning (Council for the Curriculum Examinations and Assessment, 2011) is very largely based on Routes for Learning but includes more on certain aspects of communication (such as Intensive Interaction) and additional materials (accessible on the web) which schools can conveniently use to record learners' progress.

Affective Communication Assessment (Coupe et al. 1985; Coupe-O'Kane and Goldbart 1998)

The Affective Communication Assessment (ACA) is an observation or video-based assessment developed by teaching and therapy staff working with learners with PMLD. People who know the learner well make detailed observations of the way a learner responds to a range of stimuli (e.g. smells, tastes, sounds, tactile), events and experiences using a form which prompts the observers to look at the learner's face, hands and body, and listen for vocalisations. The observers also report what they think the learner's affective (emotional) response is to the stimulus. This allows evidence to be built up for identifying typical ways of responding which familiar people can interpret as, in the earliest stages, *like*, *dislike*, *want* and *rejection*. These are regarded as hypotheses which are then tested out in a second set of observations by observing the learner's responses to other, both similar and different, stimuli, events etc. Research by Hogg *et al.* (2001) shows that, despite some inconsistencies, ratings of affective communication by familiar observers suggest some level of agreement. Thus the staff team and parents/carers working together are likely to be able to interpret a learner's behaviours more accurately than an individual working in isolation.

The ACA allows us to identify behaviours or clusters of behaviours which may start as responses, but which can be responded to systematically by parents and teachers with the aim that the learner begins to use them as signals. For example, we observe that when Jenny likes the drink she is offered, she smiles and turns towards the person giving her the drink, giving them eye contact. We respond to that by giving Jenny another taste of the drink. After many exchanges like this, we might wait a little while to see if Jenny will use turning to the teacher, smiling and making eye contact to show that she wants more of the drink.

Communication Matrix (online version; Rowland 2013)

The Communication Matrix, like Routes for Learning, is available as a free internet download. It is designed to assess communication in children and adults at early developmental stages; typical of children from 0 to 24 months. It uses many familiar concepts such as pre-intentional and intentional communication. The Matrix works by asking how the learner expresses each of four communicative functions or 'reasons to communicate': to *refuse* things; to *obtain* things; to engage in *social* interaction; and to give or seek *information*. This information is coded at one of seven levels, each clearly defined:

Level I   Pre-Intentional Behaviour.
Level II   Intentional Behaviour.
Level III   Unconventional Communication (pre-symbolic).
Level IV   Conventional Communication (pre-symbolic).
Level V   Concrete Symbols.
Level VI   Abstract Symbols.
Level VII   Language.

These levels can be mapped quite easily against those from the book *Communication Before Speech* (Coupe-O'Kane and Goldbart 1998) and the progression in Routes for Learning, but one useful variation is Level 5. Rowland (2013) argues that typically developing children bypass this stage, moving directly from Level IV to Level VI, perhaps occasionally using a concrete symbol together with a word or gesture. For example, saying 'Mummy brrm' to mean Mummy is in the car, or patting their nappy and saying 'poo' to mean they have a dirty nappy. For some learners, however, concrete symbols (which include any concrete representation such as a real object, a toy object, a photo), can be a stage on the way to understanding more abstract symbols (such as words, signs or abstract symbols on a communication aid). For others, concrete symbols will continue to offer a means for communicating in the long term.

The Matrix is completed by answering 24 questions about how the learner communicates the four 'reasons' given above. One limitation to the Communication Matrix, however, is that it provides little guidance on comprehension, to what learners understand, but we can draw on typical development to provide parallel stages to the levels in the Matrix, described above.

1   Responds to emotional tone in voice. For example, Sam smiles when his teacher welcomes him in a friendly voice, but gets distressed when another learner shouts angrily.

2   Extracts meaning from others' intonation and facial expression. For example, Asif waves his arms in excitement when his teaching assistant looks at him with an expectant face and says 'Mummy's coming!' He does not understand the words, but he realises that something good is about to happen.

3   Understands nonverbal communication and contextually cued language. For example, Karen understands what is meant when the teacher says 'home time' and holds up her coat.

4   Understands some single words and abstract symbols without any contextual support, but a wider range if there is some clue from the context.

5   Because this stage is not part of typical development, we do not really know what learners at this stage understand, but it is likely to be a range of single words, signs and/or symbols.

6   Understands short phrases without a supporting context, such as 'your turn,' or 'find the big one.'

7   Understands quite complex language but may still struggle with particular structures, such as double negatives (if you don't finish tea, you can't go out), if-then, why-because etc.

Learners with PMLD are more likely to experience pain and disruptions to their health, to show fluctuating levels of arousal, and to be inconsistent in their responses to stimuli. As a result, we (along with Chen *et al.* 2009) would argue that learners with PMLD need to be assessed over time, by familiar people and in supportive environments that allow them to demonstrate both the best they can achieve and more typical levels of performance. The majority of the assessments we have described are designed to be used in this way. A one-off assessment by someone who does not know the learner well is unlikely to generate useful information, but the involvement of several people who know the learner well, including parents, not only provides a detailed picture of the learner's abilities, but also helps that group of people to come to a shared understanding.

Van Walwyk (2011), in a helpful worked example, suggests that it is useful to supplement the school's main approach to assessment with aspects taken from other assessments. Using the strengths of different approaches gives a more complete picture of the communication of learners with PMLD.

Options for teaching communication

Once a profile of a learner's communication skills and competences has been carried out, using any one or more of the assessments we have described, you are ready to plan your teaching approach. We can conceptualise this intervention as a set of general strategies for promoting communication and social interaction in the classroom and/or a specific plan for an individual learner or group of learners.

General strategies

From looking at the way in which typical babies become communicators, it is clear that they need sensitive contingent responding from the people around them. We would argue that this is the same for learners with PMLD. The parents and family carers in Goldbart and Caton's (2010) interviews and focus groups agree. Their consensus was that people with the most complex needs needed familiar, responsive partners who cared about the person with whom they were communicating. So, how do we go about providing this kind of sensitive communication environment in a busy classroom? We would suggest that a key component is attitude; this has been demonstrated through a Finnish project, OIVA (Koski *et al.* 2010). Some resources for OIVA are available on the internet (see resources section). We need to think of the young people we work with as communicators and provide opportunities to interact with them. This will include using information from assessments like the ACA or Routes to sensitise ourselves to ways in which particular individuals respond. Some suggestions of ways in which this can be done within a classroom context can be found in Ware (2003).

Specific interventions/teaching approaches

In a review conducted for Mencap, Goldbart and Caton (2010) identified a range of approaches used with children and adults with complex communication impairments, including those with PMLD. They present the evidence base for each of these approaches. Three of the formal teaching approaches identified by Goldbart and Caton are singled out here: switch-based approaches (e.g. Jones and Maltby n.d.), Intensive Interaction (e.g. Nind and Hewett 2006 and Chapter 26), and Objects of Reference (McLarty 1997; Park 1997). Other approaches identified in Goldbart and Caton (2010) include the use of music, narrative or story-based approaches, symbols and the modification of children's environments through, for example, sensory rooms.

Switch-based approaches and cause and effect

Switches and other cause–and–effect activities are ways of helping people with PMLD understand that their actions have consequences; that they can make things happen. Learning to make things happen can be seen as a step on the way to making things happen by communicating with other people. Researchers (e.g. Lancioni *et al.* 2006a and b) have also shown that children and adults with PMLD can learn to use switches to make and convey choices and attract the attention of other people. One snag with this work is that most of it has been carried out in research settings rather than everyday contexts, though Barber (e.g. Barber 1994; Barber and Goldbart 1998) has discussed their use in classroom settings and one paper by Lancioni's team (Singh *et al.* 2003) does evaluate switching for mealtime choices for one child at home. As well as matching the type of switch to the abilities of the learner, it is important that what the switch operates is motivating. At very early stages, this is likely to be a sensory experience such as vibration, lights, sounds or a fan. Learners with PMLD are likely to need quite a lot of experience of their action on a switch having a consequence before they understand the association, but this needs to be established before expecting them to learn that they can affect the behaviour of other people by operating a switch.

One application of this work on switches with which teachers will be very familiar has been the development of the BIGmack, a single message communication device. Many teachers will use these to enable a learner to respond in the right place, for example in a class greeting song or a story. More importantly, however, they can be used to gain the attention of other people for social contact (e.g. Lancioni *et al.* 2009). Researchers suggest that the use of switches is an approach which needs to be developed further (Mansell 2010).

The use of switches can be seen as a precursor to the use of more complex alternative and augmentative communication systems (AAC), including voice output communication aids. Ideas for moving on from cause and effect and single messages are available from a number of authors and organisations (see resources section).

Intensive Interaction

Many teachers will also already be familiar with Intensive Interaction (e.g. Hewett, Firth, Barber and Harrison 2011; Nind and Hewett 2006; see also Chapter 26 of this volume). Intensive Interaction is seen primarily as a way of building up enjoyable interactions between people with complex communication needs and significant others in their lives. From our account of typical development, Intensive Interaction can been seen as promoting the social aspects of communication development, and interest in other people and a desire for social interaction are very important for communication to develop. Intensive Interaction can result in rapid increases in social engagement (Zeedyk *et al.* 2009), but it may be hard to embed in daily routines (e.g. Samuel *et al.* 2008) and it should be combined with trying to ensure that learners experience a generally responsive communicative environment (Ware 2003) through the whole of the day, rather than just during Intensive Interaction sessions.

Objects of Reference (e.g. Jones et al. 2002; Park 1995, 1997)

The idea behind Objects of Reference is that the object (or even a smell or taste) has significance for the learner at an earlier developmental stage than would be required for formal symbols. Objects of reference have a number of uses. They can be used to signal to the learner what is about to happen, for example giving the learner a cup would show that is snack time. They are also used to offer choices; giving the learner a choice between a cup and a spoon to show their choice between a drink and a snack. A development on from this would be the use of a visual timetable with objects of reference for the activities that were available or due to happen during the morning. As well as this use of objects to help the learner make sense of what happens around them, the learner may learn to use the objects to request things or events.

Park (1997) details a useful way of classifying objects of reference, going from those that are easiest for the learner to understand to those which are most abstract:

- *Index*: objects are used which are a direct part of the event they refer to, e.g. the actual spoon with which Mary eats her dinner for 'dinner'. When we are sure that Mary has learned the significance of her spoon, we could try using a range of spoons to develop her understanding, before moving on to the next stage.
- *Icon*: objects are used which have a concrete relationship or a visual or tactile resemblance to the target object, but are not part of the event. For example, a miniature cup for 'drink', a plate mounted on a piece of card for 'dinner' or a piece of seatbelt webbing for going out in the car. It is especially important to be aware of how the object appears to the individual. A miniature horse may be an icon for horse-riding for a learner with good vision, but for one who is blind it may be a 'symbol' (see below), because there is no tactile connection between the plastic miniature and the real horse. A piece of leather rein attached to a card might be much more appropriate as an icon for this second learner. When the learner shows understanding of a number of icons, we can consider moving on to the use of symbols.

- *Symbol*: here, the object has an arbitrary link to the target object or event, and the learner has to learn the association. While you might start with a symbol that is special to your class, you could consider moving on to a formal symbol system as described in Chapter 27.

There is very little research evidence in relation to the effectiveness of objects of reference, although a recent article by Harding *et al.* (2011) describes a case study with one young learner with PMLD, in which his communication skills were shown to have been developed through an intensive intervention which focused on objects of reference, but also included other components. Interestingly, this skill development included expressive communication, but was very costly in terms of staff time.

Conclusion

In concluding we would want to stress the need for communication between teachers, parents, SaLTs and all other members of the staff team in developing the communication of these learners, and of the need for training to be available for teachers, parents and everyone in regular contact with them in the use of these approaches, in order to ensure the best possible outcomes for the learners.

Questions for readers

How can you, as a teacher, ensure all learners have the opportunity to develop and use their communication skills?

This will involve several aspects, for example: how can you ensure:

- your classroom provides a positive environment for communication and interaction?
- everyone who interacts with your learners can recognise their attempts to interact and communicate?
- all learners have opportunities both to initiate and to respond to the communication of others?
- your communication assessments provide an holistic picture of learners?
- you are able to select appropriate evidence-based teaching approaches for your learners?

Resources

Assessment materials

Routes for Learning

The resources are available in both English and Welsh. The English language versions of the routemap poster, routemap planner, example sheet, assessment booklet, and additional guidance booklet are available free of charge as downloadable pdfs:

English language version: http://wales.gov.uk/topics/educationandskills/schoolshome/ curriculuminwales/additionaleducationalneeds/routeslearning/?lang=en

Welsh language version: http://wales.gov.uk/topics/educationandskills/schoolshome/ curriculuminwales/additionaleducationalneeds/routeslearning/?skip=1&lang=cy

Enquiries regarding the routes for Learning DVD should be addressed to: assessment@wales. gsi.gov.uk

Quest for Learning

Free downloadable materials and additional materials from: www.nicurriculum.org.uk/
inclusion_and_sen/assessment/pmld.asp

The Communication Matrix

The Communication Matrix is available as a free download from: www.communicationmatrix.
org/

Intervention approaches

Intensive Interaction

Information about training and publications is available from: www.intensiveinteraction.co.uk/

OIVA Interaction Model

Information in English about OIVA can be found on the following websites:

www.kehitysvammaliitto.fi/in-english/training-and-development/oiva-interaction-model/
http://papunet.net/tikoteekki/in-english/oiva-interaction-model.html

Using switches to develop communication

The following organisations provide resources for developing communication through the use
of switches and on augmentative and alternative communication in general.

Call centre (Scotland) http://callcentre.education.ed.ac.uk/Home/
Communication Matters www.communicationmatters.org.uk/
Priory Woods School and Arts College www.priorywoods.middlesbrough.sch.uk/page_
viewer.asp?page=resources&pid=4

References

American Speech and Hearing Association (n.d.) *Birth to One Year*. Online: www.asha.org/public/speech/
development/01/ (accessed 23 May 2014).
Barber, M. (1994) 'Contingency awareness: putting research into the classroom', in J.Coupe-O'Kane and
B. Smith (eds) *Taking Control: Enabling people with learning difficulties*, London: David Fulton.
Barber, M. and Goldbart, J. (1998) 'Accounting for failure to learn in people with profound and multiple
learning disabilities', in P. Lacey and C. Ouvry (eds) *People with Profound and Multiple Learning Disabilities*,
London: David Fulton.
Bellamy, G., Croot, L., Bush, A., Berry, H. and Smith, A. (2010) 'A study to define: profound and
multiple learning disabilities (PMLD)', *Journal of Intellectual Disabilities*, 14(3): 221–235.
Bradley, H (1998) 'Assessing and developing successful communication in P. Lacey and C. Ouvry (eds)
People with Profound and Multiple Learning Disabilities, London: David Fulton.
Bremner, G. (2008) *Theories of Infant Development*, Oxford: Wiley.
Bunning, K. (2009) 'Making sense of communication', in J. Pawlyn and S. Carnaby (eds) *Profound
Intellectual and Multiple Disabilities: Nursing complex needs*, London: Wiley-Blackwell.

Chen, D., Rowland, C., Stillman, R. and Mar, H. (2009) 'Authentic practices for assessing communication skills of young children with sensory impairments and multiple disabilities', *Early Childhood Services*, 3(4): 328–339.

Council for the Curriculum, Examinations and Assessment (2011) *Quest for Learning: Guidance and assessment materials – profound and multiple learning difficulties*, Northern Ireland Curriculum, Belfast: CCEA.

Coupe, J., Barton, L., Collins, L., Levy, D. and Murphy, D. (1985) *The Affective Communication Assessment*, Manchester: M.E.C. Available from Melland High School, Gorton Education Village, 50 Wembley Road, Manchester M18 7DT.

Coupe-O'Kane, J. and Goldbart, J. (1998) *Communication Before Speech*, London: David Fulton.

Evenhuis, H.M., Theunissen, M., Denkers, I., Verschuure, H., and Kemme, H. (2001) 'Prevalence of visual and hearing impairment in a Dutch institutionalized population with intellectual disability', *Journal of Intellectual Disability Research*, 45(5): 457–464.

Goldbart, J. and Caton, S. (2010) *Communication and People with the Most Complex Needs: What works and why this is essential*, London: Mencap. Online: www.mencap.org.uk/all-about-learning-disability/information-professionals/communication (accessed 23 May 2014).

Grove, N., Bunning, K., Porter, J. and Olsson, C. (1999) 'See what I mean: interpreting the meaning of communication by people with severe and profound intellectual disabilities', *Journal of Applied Research in Intellectual Disability*, 12: 190–203.

Harding, C., Lindsay, G., O'Brien, A., Dipper, L. and Wright, J. (2011) 'Implementing AAC with children with profound and multiple learning disabilities: a study in rationale underpinning intervention', *Journal of Research in Special Educational Needs*, 11(2): 120–129.

Hewett, D., Barber, M., Firth, G. and Harrison, T. (2011) *The Intensive Interaction Handbook*, London: Sage.

Hogg, J., Reeves, D., Roberts, J. and Mudford, O.C. (2001) 'Consistency, context and confidence in judgments of affective communication in adults with profound intellectual and multiple disabilities', *Journal of Intellectual Disability Research*, 45(1): 18–29.

Hoyt. C. (n.d.) 'Delayed Visual Maturation and Cortical Visual Impairment'. Online: http://content.lib.utah.edu:81/cgi-bin/showfile.exe?CISOROOT=/ehsl-nam&CISOPTR=854&filename=855.pdf (accessed 14 May 2014).

Iacono, T., West, D., Bloomberg, K., and Johnson, H. (2009) 'Reliability and validity of the revised Triple C: Checklist of Communicative Competencies', *Journal of Intellectual Disability Research*, 53: 44–52.

Imray, P. and Hinchcliffe, V. (2014) *Curricula for Teaching Children and Young People with Severe or Profound and Multiple Learning Difficulties: Practical strategies for educational professionals*, London: Routledge/Nasen.

Jones, A. and Maltby, M. (no date) Online: http://talksense.weebly.com/uploads/3/0/7/0/3070350/switching_to_communication.doc (accessed 23 May 2014).

Jones, F., Pring, T. and Grove, N. (2002) 'Developing communication in adults with profound and multiple learning difficulties using objects of reference', *International Journal of Language and Communication Disorders*, 37: 173–184.

Koski, K., Martikainen, K., Burakoff, K. and Launonen, K. (2010) 'Staff members' understandings about communication with individuals who have multiple learning disabilities: a case of Finnish OIVA communication training', *Journal of Intellectual & Developmental Disability*, 35(4): 279–289.

Lancioni, G., O'Reilly, M., Singh, N., Oliva, D., Baccani, S., Severini, L. and Groeneweg, J. (2006a) 'Micro-switch programmes for students with multiple disabilities and minimal motor behaviour: assessing response acquisition and choice', *Developmental Neurorehabilitation*, 9(2): 137–143.

Lancioni, G., O'Reilly, M., Singh, N., Sigafoos, J., Didden, R., Doretta, O. and Severini, L. (2006b) 'A microswitch-based program to enable students with multiple disabilities to choose among environmental stimuli', *Journal of Visual Impairment and Blindness*, 100(8), 488–493.

Lancioni, G., O'Reilly, M., Singh, N., Sigafoos, J., Didden, R., Doretta, O., Campodonico, F., de Pace, C., Chiapparino, C. and Groeneweg, J. (2009) 'Persons with multiple disabilities accessing stimulation and requesting social contact via microswitch and VOCA devices: new research evaluation and social validation', *Research in Developmental Disabilities*, 30(5): 1084–1094.

Lancioni, G., Singh, N., O'Reilly, M., Sigafoos, J., Oliva, D., Smaldone, A., La Martiree, M., Stasolla, F., Castagnaro, F. and Groeneweg, J., (2010) 'Promoting ambulation responses among children with multiple disabilities through walkers and microswitches with contingent stimuli', *Research in Developmental Disabilities*, 31(3): 811–816.

Leaning, B. and Watson, T. (2006) 'From the outside looking in – an intensive interaction group for people with profound and multiple learning difficulties', *British Journal of Learning Disabilities*, 34(2): 103–109.

Lhatoo, S.D. and Sander, J.W. (2001) 'The epidemiology of epilepsy and learning disability', *Epilepsia*, 42 (Suppl 1), 6-9; discussion 19–20.

Mansell, J. (2010) *Raising our Sights: Services for adults with profound intellectual and multiple disabilities*, London: Department of Health. Available online at http://kar.kent.ac.uk/24356/1/DH_2010_Raising_our_ sights.pdf (accessed 24 May 2014).

McCracken, W. and Turner, O. (2012) 'Deaf children with complex needs: parental experience of access to cochlear implants and ongoing support', *Deafness & Education International*, 14(1): 22–35.

McLarty, M. (1997) 'Putting objects of reference in context', *European Journal of Special Needs Education*, 12(1): 12–20.

Munde, V.S. and Vlaskamp, C. (2010) 'Alertness observations in children with profound intellectual and multiple disabilities', *International Journal of Child Health and Human Development*, 3(1): 115–124.

National Joint Committee for the Communication Needs of Persons With Severe Disabilities. (1991) 'Guidelines for Meeting the Communication Needs of Persons With Severe Disabilities'. www.asha. org/policy/GL1992-00201.htm#sthash.VstvRz3q.dpuf (accessed 24 May 2014).

Nind, M. and Hewett, D. (2006) *Access to Communication*, 2nd edn, London: David Fulton.

Park, K. (1995) 'Using objects of reference: a review of the literature', *European Journal of Special Needs Education*, 10(1): 40–46.

Park, K. (1997) 'How do objects become objects of reference? A review of the literature on objects of reference and a proposed model for the use of objects in communication', *British Journal of Special Education*, 24(3): 109–114.

Rowland, C. (2013) 'Communication Matrix'. www.communicationmatrix.org/ (accessed 23 May 2014).

Samuel, J., Nind, M., Volans A. and Scriven, I. (2008) 'An evaluation of Intensive Interaction in community living settings for adults with profound intellectual disabilities', *Journal of Intellectual Disabilities*, 12(2): 111–126.

Singh, N.N., Lancioni, G.E., O'Reilly, M.F., Molina, E.J., Adkins, A.D. and Oliva, D. (2003) 'Self-determination during mealtimes through microswitch choice-making by an individual with complex multiple disabilities and profound mental retardation', *Journal of Positive Behavior Interventions*, 5: 209–215.

van Splunder, J., Stilma, J.S., Bernsen, R.M.D. and Evenhuis, H.M. (2006) 'Prevalence of visual impairment in adults with intellectual disabilities in the Netherlands: cross-sectional study', *Eye*, 20: 1004–1010.

Turner, S. and Ciuksza, J. (2014) 'Ten heads are better than one: improving collaborative practice for teachers of pupils with profound and multiple learning difficulties', *SLD Experience*, Issue 69: 14–18.

Vandereet, J., Maes, B., Lembrechts, D. and Zink, I. (2010) 'Eliciting proto-imperatives and proto-declaratives in children with intellectual disabilities', *Journal of Applied Research in Intellectual Disabilities*, 23: 154–166.

Van Walwyk, L. (2011) 'Measuring progress in children with profound and multiple learning difficulties', *SLD Experience*, 60: 9–16.

Ware, J. (2003). *Creating Responsive Environments for People with Profound and Multiple Learning Difficulties*, 2nd edn, London: David Fulton.

Welsh Assembly Government (2006) *Routes for Learning: Assessment Materials for Learners with Profound Learning Difficulties and Additional Disabilities*, Cardiff: Welsh Assembly Government, Qualifications and Curriculum Group, DELLS (Dept of Education, Lifelong Learning and Skills).

Welsh Government (2013) *National Literacy and Numeracy Framework*. Online: http://learning.wales.gov. uk/resources/nlnf/?skip=1&lang=en (accessed 26 May 2014).

Zeedyk, M.S., Caldwell, P. and Davies, C. (2009) 'How rapidly does Intensive Interaction promote social engagement for adults with profound learning disabilities?', *European Journal of Special Needs Education*, 24(2), 119–137.

26

INTENSIVE INTERACTION

Developing fundamental and early communication abilities

Dave Hewett, Graham Firth, Lana Bond and Riana Jackson

In this chapter, the following questions will be addressed:

- What is Intensive Interaction – aims, outcomes, processes?
- How is Intensive Interaction different from other approaches?
- How can schools address these differences, both practically and theoretically?

'At its simplest level Intensive Interaction is a process that aims to enable communication and sociable interactivity' (Firth 2012: 14). However, the simple nature of Intensive Interaction practice within classrooms can seem to confront the orthodoxy of the way all other established activities are carried out.

Intensive interaction: history and development

The story of the development of Intensive Interaction is fully chronicled elsewhere (see Nind and Hewett 1994, 2005; Irvine 2010; Firth 2012). This will therefore be a brief resume. The starting point in the early 1980s was a practical curriculum quest by teachers in a hospital school for learners with SLD. There was a recognition that for the majority of the learners, the absolute basics of being a communicator was the priority. Yet these needs were unaddressed in existing practices. There was also a desire to move away from the rigidity and severity of the then ubiquitous reliance on behavioural approaches. At first, the development resided simply in classroom practice becoming more relaxed and more playful. The brief, significant input from psychologist Geraint Ephraim in 1983 had the effect of bringing research on infant communication learning into the processes of the project (see Schaffer 1977 for one seminal point of access to this literature).

The development work continued throughout the 1980s with project leaders commencing the production of publications (Nind and Hewett 1988) and promulgation of the approach at conferences (Hewett and Nind 1988). School-based research projects on the approach were carried out over a period of approximately two years from 1988–90 (Nind 1993; Hewett 1994). Since the early 1990s, the project has become something of a nationwide movement, also increasingly rippling to other countries around the world via numerous publications, the website (www.IntensiveInteraction.co.uk) and the gradual founding of the Intensive Interaction Institute.

Who is intensive interaction for? What does it do? How does it do it?

The learning intentions and outcomes of Intensive Interaction are usually summarised as the 'Fundamentals of Communication' (FoCs) (see Figure 26.1). While the FoCs make a usable description of learning outcomes for most practical teaching considerations, it is worthwhile to note Hewett's (2012a) caution that these are simply descriptions of the visible, outer behaviours of a communicator and that the learning rather resides in the overall development of the cognitions that support the production of the FoCs. This essentially neurological/cognitivist standpoint is central to Intensive Interaction curricular issues.

The learners are clearly therefore those who have the most severe learning difficulties and/ or are at early stages of development as social communicators. Again, caution. This group has been described as pre-verbal, even by Nind and Hewett (1994), but this is certainly not always the case. Increasingly it is realised that there are large numbers of learners who perhaps have a diagnosis of autism, are verbal, even seemingly accomplished with spoken words, yet not necessarily using speech in a meaningful and connected way for interpersonal communication.

Another central curriculum issue is surely this. A perusal of the FoCs list promotes a realisation that this is a brief description of major aspects of the first learning for all human beings. Further, this is surely part of the most critical learning for a person. This learning comes first and in usual development it seems to be foundational and underpinning to most other subsequent learning. Learners who have SLD/PMLD characteristically have not completed these attainments, yet, until the advent of the use of Intensive Interaction, standard curricula and working practices in schools for pupils with SLD mostly did not address this learning need.

From the earliest stages of the development of Intensive Interaction, it was clear that the teaching/learning activities would be extremely social, often fun-filled, dynamic exchanges of behaviour, though serene at times too. It was quickly realised that the best, perhaps only way to learn how to interact, is by and through repeated positive experiences of genuinely interacting. This practical development was reinforced and theoretically underpinned by immersion in the research literature on the 'natural model' of parent–infant interaction and its detailed descriptions of the micro social-ecology of infant communication learning (Schaffer 1977). In particular, these studies gave detailed analysis and description of what it is that the teacher (parent/ caregiver) literally *does* with their social behaviour, in order to elicit, promote and support the learner's development of communication knowledge and performance.

Enjoying being with another person
Developing the ability to attend to that person
Concentration and attention span
Learning to do sequences of activity with another person
Taking turns in exchanges of behaviour
Sharing personal space
Using and understanding eye contacts
Using and understanding facial expressions
Using and understanding physical contacts
Using and understanding other non-verbal communications
Vocalising and using vocalisations meaningfully (including speech)
Learning to regulate and control arousal levels
Fundamental emotional learning
(Probably) the development of neural links

Figure 26.1   The fundamentals of communication

In Intensive Interaction, the teacher's face, voice, body, presence, personality and way of being is the major teaching resource. The activities are experiential, practical, enjoyable rehearsals of interaction and communication. As detailed by Hewett (2012a) this 'natural model' brings with it a departure from the traditional desire evident in special needs education to control and programme learning in a linear fashion. The emphasis of the learning is on process – the process of each activity and the repetitive, cumulative process of the activities. The learning outcomes do not drive the activities; the activities do not work *toward* them as objectives. Rather, the learning outcomes are emergent over time as a result *of* the activities.

Intensive Interaction and the Bridge School experience

The Bridge School in London caters for learners with SLD/PMLD, including many with a diagnosis of autism. This is a description of the structure and organisation of a class of six secondary age learners with PMLD. Intensive Interaction is timetabled to happen throughout the week but its principles are entrenched into the everyday practice of the staff as a 'way of being' with the learners throughout the day. This 'way of being' facilitates the exploration of differing communications that naturally occur during the process of being involved in activities. For example, the learner may express thoughts and feelings, pre-intentional or intentional, about the music session, feeding, changing, transitioning, etc. The staff support this communicative expression by ongoing communicative availability – treating all initiations and expressions as potentially meaningful and intentional, and by allowing the learner to express and explore the FoCs throughout the school day.

In order to support the natural flow of sessions where one-to-one engagements take place, team members take turns to be 'Main Facilitator'. This person keeps overview of the session, stepping in to be the number two for hoisting, advising on technique, guiding groups into finishing, facilitating the swapping of interaction partners and ensuring all important timings are kept. There is a board in the classroom that has a daily list of the times and routines for each learner; medication, feeds, splints, standing frames and ankle-foot orthoses.

At the end of the activities the staff team are involved in the write-up and evaluations of sessions and learning outcomes arising. When evaluating, the following questions are reflected upon:

- What happened last time?
- What happened this time?
- What (if anything) was different?

The school has been looking closely at the way the curriculum for learners with PMLD and SLD is organised and how learning and progress is monitored and assessed. Lacey (2010) asserts that people with PMLD are poor consumers of SMART targets (Specific, Measurable, Achievable, Realistic and Timed). She instead proposes SCRUFFY (Student-led, Creative, Relevant, Unspecified, Fun, For Youngsters) targets. This system was adopted by the school and the SCRUFFY targets were re-named Potential Learning Outcomes (PLOs) to highlight the areas of potential learning. In order to devise successful PLOs for a learner, firstly detailed information must be collected through observation in both class activities and solo play. All the information on the social and communication skills of the learner and the physical and sensory information is then consolidated and put into the learner's Pupil Educational Profile (PEP). The second stage in identifying PLOs is looking at the PEP and previous observations and asking:

- Is the learner doing more of something?
- Is the learner attending to anything for longer?

As well as the PLOs for each learner being defined by staff observations of what the learner is generally doing, they also look to include the kinds of activities for which they have previously shown some inherent inclination or interest. In practice this means that the learners, through showing the staff their own activity when socially engaged and self-directed, are enabled to lead the process of setting or defining their own emergent PLOs.

Kirsty (a 15-year-old girl who uses a wheelchair) has cerebral palsy and a cortical visual impairment. Kirsty started to vocalise more throughout the day and started to laugh during the Intensive Interaction sessions when she heard her own sounds being echoed back. Kirsty would vocalise, then pause and smile; when she heard her sounds she would laugh. Staff reported on the evaluation sheets a feeling that when Kirsty was laughing she was thinking 'I knew you were going to do that...' evidencing anticipation of a meaningful social response.

The PLO became: 'Kirsty could call out to initiate an interaction.' Once the PLO is identified the teaching strategies to support the learning are devised and incorporated consistently throughout the school day. The supporting teaching strategies were: (a) take part in Intensive Interaction sessions; and (b) join in with all vocalisations throughout the day.

The concept of the PLO has helped this school, the class team and individual members of staff, gradually to become comfortable with the operational practicalities of activities, which are not driven by or structured around short-term objectives or medium-term targets. Instead, through observation and repetition of activities, emergent learning can be identified. The adult joins in with the learner in the cycles of activities and uses delicate scaffolding techniques that support the learner in practicing and extending their skills across a range of areas. Informing these activities are cycles of observation and review through individual sessions and tracking sheets, group discussion and video analysis. This diligent assessment ensures emergent targets and PLO can be identified and easily shared within the class team.

The overarching structure of the classroom is a 'Process–Central' model (Hewett 2012a: 139). This requires all staff to be actively involved in and knowledgeable about the students and their developing and emergent learning. An emergent outcomes model requires constant observation and critical analysis, and encourages staff to take the time to think and reflect on student learning. Fine-tuned observation during sessions, or subsequent video analysis, makes it possible to identify more detailed aspects of an interaction, such as fleeting eye contact or slight changes in facial expression. This crucial aspect of identifying learning is highly rewarding and motivating for the staff.

Another consequence of the Intensive Interaction sessions is what has been identified as 'spill-over' (Nind and Hewett 1994). This is when staff and learner build up a rolling repertoire of activities within the Intensive Interaction sessions which gradually 'spill over' into other aspects of the school day, even those activities which are more goal-directed. Additionally, the many, incidental, naturally occurring interactive moments throughout the day are recognised as being a crucial aspect of learning and are therefore deliberately acknowledged within the planning and organisation of the classroom.

Utilising the principles of Intensive Interaction within the day-to-day practice of the classroom as a 'way of being' creates a respectful environment where all communications and initiations are celebrated and responded to. This has had a positive effect on all the learners in the class and has led to increased smiling and laughing (for staff too!) within the discrete Intensive Interaction sessions and also throughout the school day.

Intensive Interaction and the Perseid School experience

Perseid School is a school for pupils with SLD and PMLD where many of the learners have additional physical and sensory impairments and/or an additional diagnosis of autism. Effective communication development for each learner is embedded within every classroom through a 'total communication approach' – drawing on most of the known communication methods and strategies allowing teachers to individualise the communication programme to the individual learner's specific communication needs.

The organisation of the learning environment is focused more on organising for effective one-to-one interactions rather than operating in larger groups. All team members are able to carry out Intensive Interaction with all pupils, ensuring that each pupil has four or five knowledgeable interaction partners available. Learning activities are set up in the specific zones around the classroom to provide a variegated experience as learners move from one activity to the next. These zones include areas such as an exploration area in which sensory toys are available for learners to explore and interact with, as well as a sensory massage area wherein learners are able to experience body awareness by linking Intensive Interaction with approaches such as Sherborne Developmental Movement (Sherborne 2001).

Effective room management throughout lessons ensures that quality one-to-one interactions take place as well as creating a learning environment wherein learners feel safe and are nurtured to develop their full potential. The room manager uses sensitive overview to, for instance, direct colleagues to opportunities for one-to-one interaction, identifying when to move on to another activity as well as making sure that all other daily routines such as toileting and postural management take place within the rhythm. This results in a smoother running of lessons with fewer moments of crisis or unrest as both staff and learners are content within the safe environment in which learning can take place.

One-to-one work does not always imply leaving the room although a quiet area may be beneficial during the early stages of establishing a connection with learners who are easily distracted, anxious or difficult to reach. However, if the aim is to establish Intensive Interaction as occurring regularly and frequently enough to achieve progress, then it is essential that the majority of Intensive Interaction activities takes place within the normal, regular daily routine and situation. Supporting such learning ensures that learners become more fluent in their interactions with a range of adults (staff) as well as being able to generalise their communicative skills within a variety of settings. It is also important to remember that, if Intensive Interaction is seen as part of a learner's communication routine, it cannot be something that only takes place on special occasions in a special place.

Class practice is underpinned by an atmosphere of trust, respect and confidentiality among staff. Colleagues (teachers and support staff) work closely alongside each other, slipping in and out of differing roles throughout the day. Members of staff strive to be positive, playful, engaging and animated when working with the learners, and every interaction is seen as a potential teaching opportunity.

Members of each class team are continuously supported by each other to self-evaluate by expressing their opinions and reflecting on their Intensive Interaction practice. By doing this, the team continues to be sensitive observers, picking up on the smallest signals of pleasure and negativity while being encouraged to think analytically. Each class team holds regular meetings focusing on Intensive Interaction within the classroom. This is the forum where effective planning, discussion and evaluation take place.

Intensive Interaction activities are video recorded regularly (at least fortnightly) and analysed within the staff teams in order to identify differences in staff practice as well as identifying progress in learners' communicative performance. Solo videos are also filmed to track progress of learners' self-directed behaviour when on their own within the learning environment. Various tools and methods of data collection and analysis are used, depending on the purpose of the video analysis and discussions between staff. These tools not only aim to make analysis and data collection as simple and objective as possible, they are also a useful tool for monitoring staff development as well.

To monitor observable changes in behaviour that the learner may present when not interacting with staff, an 'Observation Form' is completed during analysis of the solo videos of the learner. Staff complete a 'Session Evaluation Form' that captures qualitative data by highlighting significant occurrences (progress) that takes place during the Intensive Interaction sessions when the learner interacts with an adult. The form aims to answer questions such as 'What did the session look like?', 'Did anything new happen (significant occurrences)?', 'What was successful/unsuccessful' and 'Any ideas or thought for the future?'

Significant occurrences are then collated from completed Session Evaluation Forms and mapped onto a Monthly Progress Tracker that tracks the progress over a period of time. The Tracker informs staff at a glance of the progress the learner has made. This supports staff to continuously reflect on their own practice to ensure that they always maintain the momentum and repertoire of interactions that take place.

In order to monitor and support staff development as reflective practitioners and fluent communicators, a 'Style Checklist' is completed during the Intensive Interaction video analysis. This form assists staff by making them aware of areas/skills that need to be drawn upon when working with learners, especially during Intensive Interaction sessions. These areas/skills include timing and allowing for pauses, constant scanning of the learner, exaggerated facial expressions, creating a 'social bubble' by using appropriate body positioning, having a positive relaxed approach and most importantly having fun. It is essential for video analysis to take place as subtle changes such as pausing during Intensive Interaction sessions, bending down to the learner's level and staff allowing learners to initiate or respond to an interaction is now increasingly taking place.

Members of staff are continuously becoming more proactive, needing less encouragement to communicate and interact with learners. A significant aspect of the use of Intensive Interaction has been increased staff confidence and improved communication with each other. Thus it contributes further to a more consistent approach in meeting the needs of the pupils more effectively.

General communication issues and the curriculum

The primary developmentalist ideal of progress with the FoCs (Nind and Hewett 1994, 2005) can be seen as in keeping with the broad traditions of special needs work. From a learning or skill acquisition perspective, the communication development supported by Intensive Interaction is assumed more or less to follow the developmental trajectory of usual human communication learning. Moreover, the knowledge and skills acquired in learning the FoCs are also identified as the foundation for subsequent communication and indeed other learning (for a visual representation see Figure 26.2).

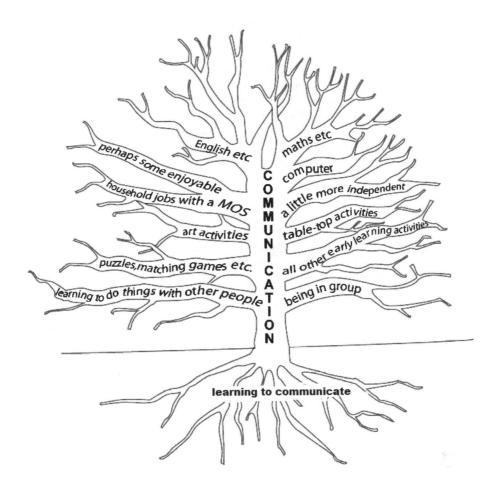

Figure 26.2 Learning the Fundamentals of Communication is underpinning to subsequent learning
Note: MOS means Members of Staff.

There is an identifiably broader curriculum imperative however. Making progress by taking part in Intensive Interaction activities implies wider lifestyle outcomes than our 'developmentalist ideal'. The practitioners who carry out Intensive Interaction also purposefully look to extend a person's inclusion in social processes that are simply integral to the quality of daily life for all of us, and to help them appreciate the roles that they can fulfil as active members of a wider social network.

The issue of active social participation of learners with severe or profound intellectual disabilities highlights a wider issue for those of us concerned with their present and future well-being. Access to regular Intensive Interaction allows a learner to repeatedly take on the role of an active participant within a supportive social nexus, a process that is vital in terms of relationship building, but also central to the construction of an individual's esteem and sense of social agency. The issues of learning and the development of an individual's identity and esteem are closely related, this relationship being acknowledged by educationalists Lave and Wenger, who stated that '… learning and a sense of identity are inseparable: they are aspects of the same phenomenon' (Lave and Wenger 1991: 115).

The pedagogical issue already highlighted within this chapter is that Intensive Interaction was a departure from previous orthodox practices. Intensive Interaction cannot be viewed as an objectives-based approach that requires the setting of predetermined and precisely defined outcomes. Instead, Intensive Interaction is best described as a 'process-central' approach (Hewett 2012a: 139) where the learning outcomes are seen as the SCRUFFY (Lacey 2010) and emergent products of the naturalistic spiralling, cumulative, transactional process, within which the teaching and the learning are continuously negotiated and concurrently developed.

The cumulative learning outcomes of Intensive Interaction could be viewed as the sequential development of an individual's understanding of the techniques and procedures of human social communication and interactivity. Within this process the learner incrementally constructs their understanding of the different aspects of social communication through repeated engagement in social interactivity in partnership with more experienced social communicators (their teachers or carers). Firth (2008) visualised this as the 'dual aspect process model' of Intensive Interaction (see Figure 26.3). Social communication development (i.e. learning) is dependent on the initial social inclusion of the learner in authentic social experiences, which will obviously include regular access to Intensive Interaction.

Once successfully engaged in mutually affirming social transactions, the learner is then enabled to use their current social understanding at the most developmentally advanced level possible. At such a developmental level activities should be concurrently both reassuringly familiar and acceptably challenging, so that the learner can repeatedly successfully practice their social skills and also then develop their understanding still further. As a process of regular Intensive Interaction proceeds for an individual learner, the resulting cumulative development gradually becomes apparent as 'these [Intensive Interaction] activities, perhaps simple and brief at first, transform into longer, more sophisticated, more complex periods of shared, mutual attention and exchanges of behaviour' (Hewett 2012b: 32).

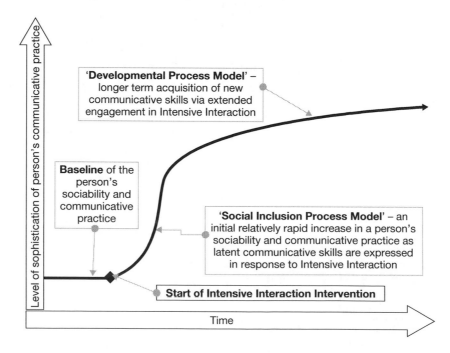

Figure 26.3   A visual representation of the 'Dual Aspect Process Model' of Intensive Interaction (Firth, 2008)

Despite widespread uptake, the use of Intensive Interaction is still not general enough to serve all the learners who need it. Online training materials for teachers in England posted by the Department for Education in England (Department for Education 2013) note that: 'Intensive Interaction is one of the most important advances of the past 20 years. It has made a significant contribution to the development of effective communication curricula for those with complex learning and communication difficulties.' In a number of countries Intensive Interaction has achieved the status of general, but not ubiquitously seen, practice in special education (e.g. the UK, New Zealand and Australia).

The further implementation of the approach requires the acceptance or development of a flexible 'process-based' curriculum structure seen in action in the work of the two schools described above. This structure first enables and then continues to support and further develop meaningful social engagement for the learner. To sustain this process the teaching staff need to continuously and collectively reflect on their own social practices, supporting the development of a range of flexible and dynamic social situations centred on and personalised to each learner. As Barber (2002: 8) notes: 'It is not the flexibility of the learner's skills that enables interaction to occur, but the flexibility of the situation that allows the inclusion of the learner.'

Questions for readers:

- How many of the learners in my school have completed learning the FoCs?
- Does my school curriculum specifically describe work on the FoCs? If not, why not and could we adopt Intensive Interaction?
- Can my school curriculum easily accommodate objectives-driven teaching and a Process-Central approach simultaneously?

References

Barber, M. (2002) *The teacher who mistook his pupil for a nuclear incident: environment influences on the learning of people with profound and multiple learning disabilities.* Online. Available: http://drmarkbarber.co.uk/theteacherwhomistook.pdf (accessed 16 January 2014).

Department for Education (2013) *Training materials for teachers of learners with severe, profound and complex learning difficulties: Module 2.3. The Curriculum Challenge, Resource on Intensive Interaction.* Online: www.complexneeds.org.uk/modules/Module-2.3-The-curriculum-challenge/All/m07p040b.html (accessed 11 July 2013).

Firth, G. (2008) 'A Dual Aspect Process Model of Intensive Interaction', *British Journal of Learning Disabilities*, 37: 43–49.

Firth, G. (2012) 'Background to Intensive Interaction', in D. Hewett, G. Firth, M. Barber and T. Harrison (eds) *The Intensive Interaction Handbook*, London: Sage Publications.

Hewett, D. (1994) *Understanding and writing a methodology of Intensive Interaction – teaching pre-speech communication abilities to learners with severe learning difficulties: a naturalistic inquiry using qualitative evaluation methods.* Unpublished PhD Thesis. Cambridge Institute of Education/UEA.

Hewett, D. (2012a) 'What is Intensive Interaction? Curriculum, process and approach', in D. Hewett (ed.) *Intensive Interaction: Theoretical perspectives*, London: Sage Publications.

Hewett, D. (ed.) (2012b) 'Preparing for Intensive Interaction', in Hewett, D., Firth, G, Barber, M. and Harrison, T. *The Intensive Interaction Handbook*, London: Sage Publications.

Hewett, D. and Nind, M. (1988) 'Developing an interactive curriculum for pupils with severe and complex learning difficulties', in B. Smith (ed.), *Interactive Approaches to the Education of Children with Severe Learning Difficulties*, Birmingham: Westhill College.

Irvine, C. (2010) 'What is the history of Intensive Interaction?' in G. Firth, R. Berry and C. Irvine (2010) *Understanding Intensive Interaction: Context and concepts for professionals and families*, London: Jessica Kingsley.

Lacey, P. (2010) 'Smart and scruffy targets', *The SLD Experience*, 57: 16–21.

Lave, J. and Wenger, E. (1991) *Situated Learning: Legitimate peripheral participation*, Cambridge University Press: Cambridge.

Nind, M. (1993) *Access to Communication: Efficacy of Intensive Interaction teaching for people with severe developmental disabilities who demonstrate ritualistic behaviours.* Unpublished PhD Thesis. Cambridge Institute of Education/UEA.

Nind, M. and Hewett, D. (1988) 'Interaction as curriculum', *British Journal of Special Education*, 15(2): 55–57.

Nind, M. and Hewett, D. (1994) *Access to Communication: Developing the basics of communication with people with severe learning difficulties through Intensive Interaction*, London: David Fulton.

Nind, M. and Hewett, D. (2005) *Access to Communication: Developing the basics of communication with people with severe learning difficulties through Intensive Interaction*, 2nd edn, London: David Fulton.

Schaffer, H.R. (ed.) (1977) *Studies in Mother-Infant Interaction*, London: Academic Press.

Sherborne, V. (2001) *Developmental Movement for Children*, London: Worth Publishing Ltd.

27

INCLUSIVE TALKING

Language learning

Carolyn Anderson and Penny Lacey with Kalvinder Rai,
Helen Burnford, Kate Jones and Rosie Jones

In this chapter, the following questions will be addressed:

- What are the pre-requisites for talking, based on typical development?
- What assessments arc useful for learners at the pre-linguistic stage?
- What are some of the difficulties specific to language learners with SLD?
- What are the most effective ways of teaching the stages of language development from the first word to combining words for learners with SLD?
- When and how should Augmentative and Alternative Communication (AAC), including Picture Exchange Communication System (PECS), be used?

We have chosen to entitle this chapter 'Inclusive Talking', although there are many learners with SLD who do not use speech. They might use signs, pictures or symbols to 'talk' to and understand what other people are saying. They might use low or high tech to 'talk' for them. Whatever the actual medium employed we want to include all learners in our interpretation of 'talk'.

Prerequisites for 'talking'

Typical language development is a useful guide for assessment and intervention as learners with SLD tend to follow similar but delayed patterns. Typically developing children begin to say their first words about 12 to 18 months of age. There are certain prerequisites that must be in place before they begin to talk, including intentionality, joint attention and contingency awareness as discussed in Chapter 25. Children usually understand about 50 words before they produce their first word. They will have been babbling and vocalising for some months before they say the first word, and using turn-taking, both verbally with vocalizations and non-verbally, in play and routine exchanges. They will have been expressing some communication functions by gestures, gaze, facial expression and vocalizations. These functions include requesting objects or actions, gaining attention, refusing, greeting, and commenting by showing an adult something they are interested in such as pointing to a toy. They will recognize familiar objects and understand their use and demonstrate their understanding mainly through play. For example, they may cuddle a doll, hold a real or toy phone to their ear, put their teddy to bed or pretend to drink out of an empty cup. Sheridan, Sharma and Cockerill (2008) and Bee (2010) outline the developmental sequence for areas including communication, interaction, play and motor milestones. A number of websites outline typical language development stages and some examples are listed at the end of this chapter.

Assessments for the prelinguistic stage

Assessments and checklists based on typical development may help identify whether a learner is ready to start talking; these include the *WellComm Toolkit* (Sandwell PCT 2010), *Schedule of Growing Skills II* (Bellman, Lingam, and Aukett 2008), *Receptive-Expressive Emergent Language Scales* (Bzoch, League and Brown 2003), *Rossetti Infant-Toddler Language Scale* (Rossetti 2006), *Bayley Scales of Infant and Toddler Development* (Bayley 2005), and the *Preschool Language Scale* (Zimmerman, Steiner and Pond 2002). Formal assessments such as the ones listed should give an indication of the stage learners have reached in their understanding of language. As noted above, the developmental age for talking is about 12 months with an understanding of about 50 words. If a learner scores below this age level, some of the tests listed also give an indication of what should come next in development. This information can be useful in planning intervention to support the learner to the next stage.

Difficulties specific to learners with SLD

Although learners with SLD are often very effective communicators, it can be very helpful to understand the specific difficulties they face. Learners with SLD are likely to have language processing difficulties due to reduced or variable attention and listening, a slower rate for processing auditory information, problems with short-term memory, specifically phonological working memory, and difficulties in generalising their learning to other situations (Harding 2012). Hearing and vision difficulties may affect language learning. Learners with syndromes may have specific difficulties including those with Down syndrome, Fragile X, Williams syndrome, and Autism Spectrum Disorders (Paul and Norbury 2012). For example, learners with Down syndrome or Fragile X may have specific difficulties with vocabulary development and recall as well as learning to use grammatical markers. Learners with Williams syndrome may begin to use single words but may not have used pointing in early development. In some syndromes, expressive language may exceed the learner's verbal understanding.

Many learners with SLD and autism do not understand the need to communicate and can only react to situations they like or don't like (Jordan 2013). They can develop challenging ways of reacting to what they are feeling, for example Carl head bangs because he is hungry or Amir bites people because he wants to be squeezed or Maria screams because the environment is too loud for her.

Some learners with SLD and autism can learn to use spoken language but it is usually slow to develop. Some learners repeat what they have just heard and are said to be 'echolalic' (Preece and Jordan 2010). Echolalia or imitation of something just said is a stage all children go through before they learn to use spontaneous words with meaning. However, some learners with autism can get stuck at this stage for some time and it is often an indication that they do not understand what is being said. One reaction to a learner echoing a phrase is to treat it as if it had meaning, as in the example below (Jordan 2013):

> The adult asks 'Do you want a biscuit?' and the child repeats it. The adult behaves as
> if it is a request for a biscuit. Once there is a good connection between 'Do you want

a biscuit?' and getting a biscuit, the adult can start shaping the phrase into a more conventional request 'I want biscuit' or maybe 'Can I have a biscuit?'

Learners with Down syndrome have a different language profile. Buckley (2012: 17) shows how children with Down syndrome vary in their milestones from typical children. They have significantly delayed language skills, despite their keenness to communicate from a very early age. They usually have strengths in learning non-verbal skills such as signing, gesture, body language but they have particular difficulties with speech. Often their understanding of language is greater than their ability to produce it and their speaking difficulties indicate a deficit rather than a delay. Vocabulary is learned slowly as is early grammar and hypotonia in the muscles in the mouth and tongue contributes to poor articulation (Buckley 2012). Buckley (2012) goes on to argue that it is essential for interventions that all the specific difficulties faced by individuals with Down syndrome are understood and deliberately targeted. The following example is taken from a primary special school.

Emma has Down syndrome with SLD. She is 8 years old and has not yet started to speak. She has a moderate hearing loss and finds all learning that involves listening particularly hard. She has a small vocabulary of individual signs but uses natural gesture to help get her meaning across. She loves books and will sit with any adult willing to 'read' to her. She points to pictures readily but only really understands the names for 8 objects when they are both spoken and signed. She can match pictures that are exactly the same and select pictures of the 8 objects when requested. She loves the homemade books that include her 8 objects and wants to 'read' them frequently.

Effective ways of teaching talking to learners with SLD

A number of effective intervention strategies are supported by research evidence. The Better Communication Research Programme (Law *et al.* 2012) found strongest research evidence for Milieu teaching strategies, with moderate support for Hanen parent programmes (e.g. *It Takes Two to Talk*), Makaton signing, PECS (Bondy and Frost 2009), and *Talk Boost Early Talk 0-5* (ICan; www.ican.org.uk/en/What-we-do/Early%20Years.aspx), among others. There is limited but indicative evidence for *TEACCH* (Mesibov, Shea and Schopler 2004), *Derbyshire Language Scheme* (www.derbyshire-language-scheme.co.uk/), Intensive Interaction (Nind and Hewitt 2005) and *Living Language* (Locke 1985). The *See and Learn* programme developed for children with Down syndrome has a small amount of research evidence for success specifically related to that group (Burgoyne *et al.* 2012a). Prelock, Paul and Allen (2011) reviewed the effectiveness of interventions for children with autism and found evidence for parent and joint attention training including Hanen *More Than Words*, Milieu teaching strategies, *PECS* and discrete trial interventions.

Milieu teaching strategies are illustrated in Table 27.1 and include organising the environment so learners have plenty of opportunities to communicate, ensuring that language targets are at the right level and responding contingently with motivating rewards when they communicate (Kaiser and Roberts 2013). Readiness for interaction focuses initially on comprehension skills to ensure that learners understand at least 50 words consistently before there are any expectations of verbal expressions. As Milieu language teaching strategies are supported by extensive research (Kaiser and Roberts 2013; Kaiser and Trent 2007), the key strategies for teaching first words are listed below.

Early intervention by parents and teachers is recommended with the aim of promoting language development and interaction (Goswami 2008). The aim of training is to increase parental responsiveness to their children's communication attempts when they are ready to interact as responsiveness has been shown to be predictive of language development (Warren *et al.* 2010). Adults need to persist in responding as children and young people with SLD can learn that their behaviour causes a response but may take longer to make the connection (Odom 2007).

Table 27.1 Milieu teaching strategies that are most effective for teaching 1st words

---

Direct modelling; Name it! Name the object or action and ask the learner to imitate the word
Learner is playing with a car.
Adult says "That's a car. Say "car".

Follow-in directive; Do it! Ask the learner to do something with an object
Learner is playing with a ball.
Adult says "Give/show me the ball" or "Throw/roll the ball".

Imitating; Copy me! Imitate learners immediately after they have vocalised so they get a response to their verbal attempt. This is a good strategy to use when adults don't know what they are talking about
Learner says "aba."
Adult says "aba".

Linguistic mapping; Hear it! Say what learners might say if they could talk. Use language just above their level
Learner says "a" while holding up hat.
Adult says "Hat".

The environment should be adapted with the aim of increasing the amount and accuracy of intentional non-verbal communication such as putting toys/objects out of reach but in view so learners have to request them (Paul and Norbury 2012). If you have played a game or activated a toy the learner enjoys, wait before repeating the action to see if they will make eye contact or take your hand to the toy, or request repetition by another signal. Add a verbal label such as 'Again?' or 'More?' when they have signalled nonverbally. The most successful activities for learning opportunities are likely to be those that have meaning in context and are functional for individual learners.

Additional visual aids, including gestures, pictures, signing and the written word, can help vocabulary and grammar learning, especially for learners with Down syndrome (Zampini and D'Odorico 2009; Burgoyne *et al.* 2012b; Paul and Norbury 2012). For learners with Foetal Alcohol syndrome, Kalberg and Buckley (2007) recommend using daily schedules, colour coding for task completion, and reducing distractions in classes with identified work areas.

Teachers and parents help children develop language by talking to them, especially about things that interest the learners in their environment. Once learners have started to use some words, adults can add language to any activity by following the learner's lead and talking about what they are playing with or doing. To aid early language development, adult language should be simplified so it is just above the learner's level of expression and about their level of understanding. It is also important to slow the rate of language, as learners with developmental delays often need longer to process information. Responsive strategies to help learners move from single words to two words are shown in Table 27.2.

Table 27.2 Responsive strategies that are most effective for teaching two and more words together

Descriptive talk; Describe the Action. Say what you or the learner is doing so the learner is hearing language related to what they are playing with or doing.
Learner and adult are playing with farm animals. Adult puts a cow into a barn.
Adult says "The cow is going in the barn"
Learner is washing her hands. Adult says "You're washing your hands. They are wet."

Expansions; Add a word. Repeat what the learner has said, adding one or 2 relevant words so learners are hearing the level of language that they might use next.
Learner says "car" while holding a blue car.
Adult says "A blue car."

Recasts; Good grammar. Repeat what the learner has said, using adult grammar so the learner can hear a correct model.
Learner says "Brush dolly hair"
Adult says "Brushing dolly's hair."

Targeted teaching of language

Although teaching 'talking' in natural contexts is successful, many learners with SLD also require very specific language interventions in addition. They may require many repetitions of target words to take into account limitations with short-term memory. The following example is taken from a primary special school.

Class 4 had the story of Mrs Wishy Washy. It is very short and repetitive. Some of the children were learning the names of the animals 'cow', 'pig' and 'duck' and others were learning to put two words together 'wash cow', 'wash pig', 'wash duck'. 'Dirty' and 'clean' were selected as two important concepts and some of the activities focused on getting things dirty and washing them clean.

To ensure sufficient repetition for the children to learn the words, there were pictures and small world animals to match and name and games to play where the same words were used over and over again, for example, hiding games, Kim's Game, role play and songs.

Some of the children struggle with verbs so there was an activity to reinforce 'the pig is rolling', 'the cow is running'. The Language Master (audio recording and playback unit) was available to hear words over and over again. There was a game on the interactive whiteboard and another on the iPad that involved matching animal sounds to animal pictures and in one activity, some children were asked to provide a caption for the pictures from the book.

This vocabulary was targeted over several weeks and all the children made progress in their receptive language and some in their expressive language.

Some schools and services have written their own language programmes, for example the *Basics Of New and Emerging Skills in communication (BONES) language programme*, which was developed by a team of speech and language therapists in a large regional special school in South Wales.

BONES consists of an individual pupil profile across receptive and expressive verbal language; receptive and expressive augmentative and alternative communication; two way social communication and auditory and oro-motor skills. There is an emphasis on input and output as separate pathways within each dimension. The pathway has three broad levels, pre linguistic, early language and higher language levels; a correspondence map of the key developmental texts, to identify levels for intervention and reduce teacher administration; a collection of staged communication activity programmes for each dimension, for both input and output across all levels and checklists and advice sheets to support delivery of the programme.

If you have not developed your own language programme, you might find it helpful to use *WellComm* (Sandwell PCT 2010) or *See and Learn* (Down Syndrome Education International, www.seeandlearn.org/en-us/language-and-reading/).

Augmentative and alternative communication

Children and young people with SLD are likely to spend much longer than typically developing learners at each language stage. As a result, AAC may need to be considered to support language understanding, as well as a means of expression, when a learner is non-verbal or has unintelligible speech. There is consistent evidence in the literature that AAC use by nonverbal learners does not inhibit spoken language development (Miller, Light and Schlosser 2006). AAC use may also reduce behaviour that is considered challenging (Walker and Snell 2013) by giving a learner a means of expression that is more easily understood. Dealing with parental and teacher concerns and training are essential if AAC use is to be successful (Harding 2012). Paul and Norbury (2012) outline measures that have been shown in research to predict speech development; use of these measures will help predict which learners would benefit from learning an AAC system and which should concentrate on speech sound production.

There are a number of types of AAC from sensory cues and objects of reference to visual symbols and signing, with advantages and disadvantages for each type; see Romski *et al.* (2010) for choice of modality and Downing (2005) for introducing AAC. Using gesture can support vocabulary learning (Zampini and D'Odorico 2009), while signing at the early pre-linguistic stage helps develop language in children with Down syndrome (Rondal and Buckley 2003). PECS has been shown to increase initiations and requests but not other language functions and there is limited evidence of speech development (Gordon *et al.* 2011; Howlin *et al.* 2007). Use of speech-generating devices show increases in vocalising and expression (Mirenda 2003), and VOCAs (Voice-Onset Communication Aids) help increase learners' understanding of words introduced in joint attention routines (Brady 2000). iPhones and iPads apps have picture displays for pointing to, to develop a core vocabulary of frequently recurring functional nouns and verbs that the learner is motivated to use. There is information on additional AAC websites at the end of this chapter.

True Object-Based Icons

TOBIs (True Object-Based Icons) may be the first AAC to be introduced in educational settings for children and young people with SLD who are beginning to learn to understand and use language. A TOBI is a photograph of an object that is cut out to the same shape as that object and can offer a bridge between a 3-D object and a 2-D picture. The example below illustrates how successful TOBIs can be with some learners.

Parminder has shown some interest in photographs of the other learners in her class but when staff tried to teach her to use photographs of snack items so she could choose what she wanted to eat and drink, she did not seem to associate the photos with the real objects. They tried TOBIs and she looked at them very carefully. It took several weeks but she was able to associate her own cup with the exact matching TOBI. She has yet to learn to request a drink or a snack but she gets excited when the TOBIs appear and know that the drink and snack are coming next.

There is very limited research involving TOBIs and none that specifically provides evidence for their use. However, Taylor and Preece (2010) successfully introduced a TEACCH structure using TOBIs for three students with multiple disabilities and visual impairment, helping these students to understand what was happening around them.

Picture Exchange Communication System

PECS (Picture Exchange Communication System) can provide functional communication to people with a range of communication difficulties (Ganz *et al.* 2012). The programme can offer a good structure for learners to learn to 'ask' for what they want. Two people are required to use PECS as intended: one to prompt the learner to give the card (with the photo/symbol on) to the other person who will give the learner the item. It is important to use items that are really desirable or the learners will not be motivated to complete the exchange. The following example has been adapted from a home to a classroom situation from Jordan (2013).

1   David loves grapes and is used to being given grapes at snack time.
2   One day there are no grapes in his bowl but an adult is holding out her hand beside a Tobi of a grape.
3   A second adult takes David quickly to the TOBI and prompts him to take it and hand it to the first adult.
4   The first adult immediately puts grapes into David's bowl, maybe saying the phrase 'want grapes' at the same time.
5   If this is repeated day after day, it becomes a routine.
6   Once it is established the prompts become less and less until David is automatically going to the first adult, picking up the card and handing it over.
7   After that, the first adult can make David work harder for his grapes by dropping her hand or moving away so he has to actively make her take the card.
8   Once active handing over is established it is clear that David understands the process. At this point, he can move onto using another TOBI at a different time.

Eventually he can make a choice from a menu of cards on a board or in a book.

Communication books, related to PECS, can range from containing a single card to a whole set of cards, divided into topics. Sometimes learners can attain a huge visual vocabulary and they may need to divide up all the words into different books. Jordan (2013) reminds practitioners not to include things the learners cannot have all day long (like sweets) in a choice board/book because they must have a genuine choice of things they can have. If you have to say 'no' to something they request (or say 'later'), they will give up and may revert to screaming or biting to get what they want.

PECS is not necessarily useful for every learner and every situation, particularly if the learners already understand the function of communication. They may require the use of photos, pictures or symbols to get their message across but they do not need to go through the early stages of PECS. The following example shows possible limitations of PECS and indicates how we must continually consider ways of teaching more effectively.

A school for children with PMLD and SLD was successfully using PECS with non-verbal communicators. A teacher had taught PECS to Phase 4 with a boy and girl who had SLD and autism; the children were able to request, for example, using 'I want X' structures consistently. The girl's favourite game was being chased by the teacher and she often used 'I want chases' to request this activity which the boy also enjoyed. One day, the girl gave the PECS request strip to the boy instead of the teacher. The teacher was distressed to see the boy look at the symbols, all of which he understood, and then hand the strip to her instead of chasing the girl. She realized that he had only learned to request but responding to requests was not included in PECS training. The girl never gave the boy another request strip. The teacher discussed ways of encouraging other language functions with the speech and language therapist.

Inclusive talking

In the last 25 years, schools have had less focus on teaching speech and language than on literacy (Lacey *et al.* 2007). There have been very few resources for focused language teaching and some of the useful language programmes have gone out of print and not been replaced. Recently, schools and colleges have renewed their interest in teaching 'talking' and want to develop their skills. New programmes are available and staff are exploring activities to promote language acquisition such a drama (see Chapter 32), story telling (see Chapter 29), film making (see Chapter 29) adventurous activities and learning outside the classroom (see Chapter 37).

To learn to be an 'inclusive talker', learners need three things: something to communicate with, someone to communicate with and something to communicate about.

Questions for readers

- Are you using teaching strategies based on research evidence of techniques that are effective for developing talking?
- Are parents involved in their child's language programme and do they know how to support their child's language learning?
- Do you know how to decide whether a learner should use AAC to communicate or whether they need specific help for speech sound production?

Useful websites

Communication and Learning Enterprises Ltd: www.candleaac.com/page1.htm
Call Scotland: www.candleaac.com/page1.htm
ECAT Every Child a Talker: http://earlylearningconsultancy.co.uk/resources/

National Institute on Deafness and Other Communication Disorders: www.nidcd.nih.gov/
health/voice/pages/speechandlanguage.aspx
Speech and Language Therapy dot com: www.speech-language-therapy.com/index.
php?option=com_content&view=article&id=34:ages&catid=11:admin&Itemid=117
See and Learn: www.seeandlearn.org/en-gb/
The Communication Trust: www.thecommunicationtrust.org.uk/early-years/resources/
resources-from-our-consortium.aspx

References

Bayley, N. (2005) *Bayley Scales of Infant and Toddler Development®*, 3rd edn, San Antonio, Tx: PsychCorp.
Bee, H. (2010) *The Developing Child*, 12th edn, Boston, Mass: Allyn & Bacon.
Bellman, M., Lingam, S. and Aukett, A. (2008) *Schedule of growing skills II: User's guide*, 2nd edn, London: NFER Nelson Publishing Company Ltd.
Bondy and Frost (2009) The Picture Exchange Communication System. In Mirenda, P. and Iacono, T. (Eds) (2009) *Autism Spectrum Disorders and AAC*, Baltimore, MD: Paul H. Brookes.
Brady, N. (2000) Improved comprehension of object names following voice output communication aid use: Two case studies, *Augmentative and Alternative Communication*, 16: 197–204.
Buckley, S (2012) *Speech and Language Development for Individuals with Down Syndrome: An Overview*, online e-book: http://store.dseenterprises.org/collections/ebooks/products/speech-and-language-development-for-individuals-with-down-syndrome-an-overview-pdf-ebook
Burgoyne, K., Duff, F.J., Clarke, P.J., Buckley, S., Snowling, M.J. and Hulme, C. (2012a) Efficacy of a reading and language intervention for children with Down syndrome: a randomized controlled trial, *Journal of Child Psychology and Psychiatry*, 53(10): 1044–1053.
Burgoyne, K., Duff, F., Clarke, P., Smith, G., Buckley, S., Snowling, M. and Hulme, C. (2012b) *A Reading and Language Intervention for Children with Down Syndrome: A Teacher's Handbook*, Portsmouth: Down Syndrome Education International.
Bzoch, K., League, R. and Brown, V. (2003) *REEL 3 Receptive Expressive Emergent Language Scales*, 3rd edn, San Antonio, Tx: PsychCorp.
Downing, J. (2005) *Teaching Communication Skills to Students with Severe Disabilities*, 2nd edn, Baltimore, MD: Paul H Brookes.
Ganz, J.B., Davis, J.L., Lund, E.M., Goodwyn, F.D. and Simpson, R.L. (2012) Meta-analysis of PECS with individuals with ASD: Investigation of targeted versus non-targeted outcomes, participant characteristics, and implementation phase, *Research in Developmental Disabilities*, 33(2), 406–418.
Gordon, K., Pasco, G., McElduff, F., Wade, A., Howlin, P., and Charman, T. (2011) A communication-based intervention for nonverbal children with autism: What changes? Who benefits? *Journal of Consulting and Clinical Psychology*, 79: 447–457.
Goswami, U. (2008) *Learning difficulties: Future challenges*. A paper prepared as part of the Foresight Review on Mental Capital and Wellbeing. Online: www.bis.gov.uk/assets/biscore/corporate/migratedD/ec_group/101-08-FO_on (accessed 8 February 2015).
Harding, C. (2012) Children with severe learning disabilities, in J. Wright and M. Kersner (eds.) *Speech and Language Therapy: The decision-making process when working with children*, Abingdon, Oxon: Routledge.
Howlin, P., Gordon, R., Pasco, G., Wade, A. and Charman, T. (2007) The effectiveness of Picture Exchange Communication System (PECS) training for teachers of children with autism: a pragmatic, group randomized control trial, *Journal of Child Psychology and Psychiatry*, 48: 473–481.
Jordan, R (2013) *Autism with Severe Learning Difficulties*, 2nd Edn, London: Souvenir Press.
Kaiser, A. and Roberts, M. (2013) Parent-implemented Enhanced Milieu Teaching with preschool children who have intellectual disabilities, *Journal of Speech, Language, and Hearing Research*, 56: 295–309.
Kaiser, A. and Trent, J. (2007) Communication intervention for young children with disabilities, in S. Odom (ed.) *Handbook of Developmental Disabilities*, New York: Guildford Press.
Kalberg, W. and Buckley, D. (2007) AUTISM: What types of intervention and rehabilitation are useful? *Neuroscience and Biobehavioural Reviews*, 31: 278–285.

Lacey, P., Layton, L., Miller, C., Goldbart, J. and Lawson, H. (2007) What is literacy for students with severe learning difficulties? Exploring conventional and inclusive literacy, *Journal of Research in Special Educational Needs*, 7(3), 149–160.

Law, J., Lee, W., Roulstone. S., Wren, Y., Zeng, B. and Lindsay, G. (2012) *'What works': Interventions for children and young people with speech, language and communication needs*, London: DfE. www.education. gov.uk/publications/standard/publicationDetail/Page1/DFE-RR247-BCRP10 (accessed 4 February 2015).

Locke, A. (1985) *Living Language*, London: NFER-Nelson.

Mesibov, G., Shea, V., and Schopler, E. (2004) *The TEACCH Approach to Autism Spectrum Disorders*, New York: Springer.

Miller, D., Light, J. and Schlosser, R. (2006) The impact of augmentative and alternative communication intervention on the speech production of individuals with developmental disabilities: A research review, *Journal of Speech, Language and Hearing Research*, 49: 248–264.

Mirenda, P. (2003) Towards functional augmentative and alternative communication with students with autism: Manual signs, graphic symbols and voice output communication aids, *Language, Speech and Hearing Services in Schools*, 34: 203–217.

Nind, M. and Hewitt, D. (2005) *Access to Communication: Developing the basics of communication with people with SLD*, 2nd edition. London: David Fulton.

Odom, S. (2007) *Handbook of Developmental Disabilities*, New York: Guildford Press.

Paul, R. and Norbury, C. (2012) *Language Disorders from Infancy through Adolescence*, 4th edn, St Louis, Missouri: Mosby Elsevier.

Preece, D and Jordan, R. (2010) 'Obtaining the views of children and young people with autism spectrum disorders about their experience of daily life and social care support', *British Journal of Learning Disabilities*, 38(1), pp. 10–20.

Prelock, P., Paul, R. and Allen, E. (2011) Evidence-Based treatments in communication for children with autism spectrum disorders, in B. Reichow, P. Doehring, D. Cicchetti, and F. Volkmar (eds) *Evidence-Based Practices and Treatments for Children with Autism*, New York: Springer.

Romski, M., Sevcik, R., Adamson, L., Cheslock, M., Smith, A,, Barker, R. and Bakeman, R. (2010) Randomized comparison of augmented and non-augmented language interventions for toddlers with developmental delays and their parents, *Journal of Speech, Language and Hearing Research*, 53: 350–364.

Rondal, J. and Buckley, S. (2003) *Speech and Language Intervention in Down Syndrome*, London: Whurr.

Rossetti, L. (2006) *Rossetti Infant-Toddler Language Scale*, East Moline, Il: Linguisystems.

Sandwell PCT (2010) *WellComm: A Speech and Language Toolkit for the Early Years*, London: GL Assessment.

Sheridan, M., Sharma, A. and Cockerill, H. (2008) *From Birth to Five Years: Children's developmental progress*, London: Routledge.

Taylor, K. and Preece, D. (2010) Using aspects of the TEACCH structured teaching approach with students with multiple disabilities and visual impairment Reflections on practice, *British Journal of Visual Impairment*, 28(3): 244–259.

Walker, V. and Snell, M. (2013) Effects of augmentative and alternative communication on challenging behavior: A meta-analysis, *Augmentative and Alternative Communication*, 29(2): 117–131.

Warren, S., Brady, N., Sterling, A., Fleming, K. and Marquis, J. (2010) Maternal responsivity predicts language development in young children with Fragile X Syndrome, *American Journal on Intellectual and Developmental Disabilities*, 115(1): 54–75.

Zampini, L. and D'Odorico, L. (2009) Communicative gestures and vocabulary in 36-month old children with Down's syndrome, *International Journal of Language and Communication Disorders*, 44: 1063–1074.

Zimmerman, L., Steiner, V. and Pond, R. (2002) *Preschool Language Scale*, 4th edn, San Antonio, Tx: PsychCorp.

28

THE TEACHING OF READING TO LEARNERS WITH SLD

Sarah Moseley

In this chapter, the following questions will be addressed:

- What do we know about teaching reading to typically developing learners?
- What are the particular difficulties faced by learners with SLD?
- How have learners with SLD benefited from the use of traditional multisensory approaches to reading?

Introduction

The more that you read, the more things you will know. The more you learn, the more places you'll go.

(Dr. Seuss, *I Can Read With My Eyes Shut!*)

Unlike learning to speak, which appears to require no direct teaching, the complex task of learning to read has been described as the 'single most important educational challenge learners face during the first two to three years of formal education' (Muter 2003: 2). This chapter presents a brief overview of current educational debate surrounding the teaching of reading to learners with SLD. The important role that learning to read plays within education and society is highlighted, alongside a brief discussion of how typically developing learners learn to read. The purpose of this chapter is to provide practitioners with the knowledge and strategies to translate theoretical debate into classroom practice.

Research and academic evidence

The teaching of reading for typically developing children

Reading has been defined as a 'message getting, problem solving activity which increases in power and flexibility the more it is practised' (Clay, 1991, p. 6). Throughout our lives we are surrounded by print; it is embedded into everything we do regardless of our ability to access it. Reading is emphasised to be the key to education, and education the key to success in our society through the creation of self-generated learning opportunities (Wigfield and Guthrie 1997).

Figure 28.1   Reading to or with an adult

Simple view of reading

Reading is a highly complex cognitive task, involving higher level (language comprehension) and lower level (decoding of letters and words) processing skills (McCutchen *et al.* 2000). By understanding how children learn, it is hoped that educators can develop clearer ideas about how learners may be best taught (Stuart 2006). The outcomes of the Rose Review (Rose 2006) have had an influential impact on current approaches to the teaching of reading within mainstream education. The review advocates the model proposed by the *Simple view of reading* (Gough *et al.* 1996) and this is embedded into current UK practice.

Current research focusing on learners with Down syndrome emphasises that, 'effective (reading) instruction is imperative to enable all children to reach their full potential' (Burgoyne *et al.* 2012: 1). Reading has a positive influence on many aspects of development of these learners, such as spoken language (especially expressive spoken language), short-term memory, self-esteem and general cognitive development (Bird and Buckley 1994). Government-led strategies and initiatives have highlighted the importance of reading to raising attainment within education. According to this framework, reading comprises two dimensions of printed word recognition and language comprehension (Rose 2006). The model distinguishes between the processes required for each of these two dimensions. For example, the importance of teaching phonics as well as knowledge and repetition of tricky words to develop the word recognition dimension alongside specific activities to teach comprehension to develop the language dimension.

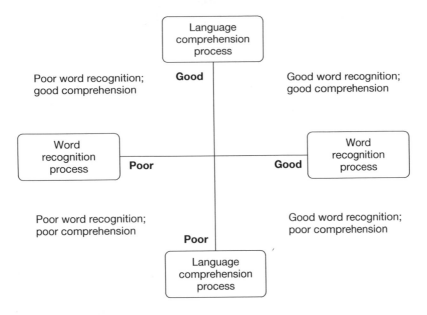

Figure 28.2   The simple view of reading

Neurological damage and implications for learners with SLD

Children and young people with learning difficulties are not a homogenous group. They may approach the task of reading with uneven patterns of language skills, due to a variety of reasons, in comparison to typically developing children (Laing and Hulme 2001). Problems or damage prior to or during birth can lead to cognitive processing difficulties in specific or general skills (Goswami 2004). Learners with SLD may have a mixture of structural and processing deficiencies, which may make learning to read a difficult, if not impossible, skill to acquire.

Reading requires familiarity with the language system and awareness of the relationship between letters and sounds, therefore learners with hearing impairments will have problems at the input level. The output stage requires muscular ability to produce the information through speech. Learners with SLD may have deficits in both of these areas. This will result in complex learning patterns and needs (Lewis 1999). This awareness should inform rather than deter practitioners from using specific approaches.

Reading and learners with SLD

Historically, it was thought that learners with SLD were incapable of learning to read. Where reading was taught, a narrow definition of the construct was often found (Kliewer and Landis 1999; Lacey *et al.* 2007). The focus was upon teaching learners with SLD to recognise a limited vocabulary of functional words (Kliewer and Landis 1999). This was often not combined with the teaching of word-attack or language comprehension skills, meaning reading can never be truly functional (Elkins 1992).

Research into effective reading instruction for children with learning difficulties has been lacking in the past (Byrne, MacDonald and Buckley 2002), although this is beginning to increase specifically relating to research with learners with Down syndrome (Burgoyne *et al.* 2012), with some interesting and exciting findings. Research has shown that individuals with Down syndrome and other intellectual disabilities actually continue to develop cognitively into adolescence, making this an important time for literacy learning.

Stanovich (1986) used the term 'Matthew effect' when discussing reading opportunities and environments provided for pupils with learning difficulties. The term is a reference to the Gospel according to Matthew. The story tells of the rich getting richer and the poor being left to become even poorer (Stanovich 1993/4). He applied this idea to the relatively deficient educational opportunities offered to struggling readers (Stanovich 1986).

Characteristics of learners with poor reading skills

Learners become confident readers through reading. Unfortunately, poor readers may never achieve this confidence (Clay 2000). The initial underlying cause of their reading problem can result in reading becoming a slow, laborious and unrewarding task, which leads to a lack of motivation or even fear of future reading activities. The result is that the less the learners learn, the less they are able to learn due to an impoverished knowledge base and opportunities (Mastropieri, Scruggs and Fulk 1990).

Learners who have had limited language experience may end up with limited vocabulary and poorly developed speaking and listening skills. This will make engaging in questioning, discussions and reasoning difficult, causing frustration and lack of motivation towards reading activities (Buckley and Bird 1993; EQUALS 2011). In many instances the majority of poor readers appear to have lowered self-concept and self-esteem.

Mainstream approaches to reading and learners with SLD

Research into the teaching reading to particular groups of children with learning difficulties, specifically those learners with Down syndrome, has been extensive; it no longer focuses on whether this population can learn to read but on the most effective approaches for all (Bochner et al. 2001).

This work has provided a valuable insight into effective ways of teaching and learning for this group of learners that may have value for other learners with SLD (Buckley and Bird 1993; Moni and Jobling 2001). Current research has shown that targeted reading interventions based on structured mainstream good practice can raise attainment in reading for learners with Down syndrome (Burgoyne et al. 2012). Research focusing on a wider range of learners with SLD, using targeted mainstream approaches based on established good practice (e.g. phonics and whole word learning), has also been shown to have a positive impact on learners' ability to learn to read as well as on their self-concept and self-esteem (Moseley 2009). Also, the mainstream classroom has been emphasised as providing learners with SLD the chance to be exposed to a structured reading curriculum where such intense approaches are used (Byrne et al. 2002).

Research focusing on literacy within the specialist school classroom

There is concern that the conclusions of documents such as the Rose Review (2006) and research that highlights the importance of a more structured systematic approach to the teaching of reading for all learners may not be suitable for all learners with SLD (Lacey et al. 2007). A review by Miller, Lacey and Layton (2003) into literacy practices within special schools for learners with SLD concluded that the use of multiple approaches is essential. A review of practice by Lacey (2006) divided strategies observed within schools into six key approaches. These ranged from the more conventional approaches using traditional orthography, such as letter identification, through to more specialist activities using symbols and augmentative and

Figure 28.3   Symbols as a support for reading a visual timetable

alternative speech systems. Due to increases in technology there has been an expansion in what can be used and how learners can be supported within the classroom (Lacey 2006).

Penny Lacey and colleagues conducted research into literacy for learners with SLD/ PMLD and articulated the concept of 'inclusive literacy', which refers to a range of activities and artefacts, which transcend the conventional view of literacy as related only to reading and writing text (Lacey 2006; Lacey *et al.* 2007). From their reports, it was clear that teachers lacked training in literacy in relation to learners with SLD/ PMLD.

Reading Pictures

Learning to read pictures is important in its own right, as well as being seen as a stage on the way towards reading words. It may be tempting to think that, if learners cannot read the words in a book, they can look at the pictures. They can indeed look at the pictures but it is by no means certain that they understand what they see, especially when the pictures are very stylized. There seem to be several aspects to be taken into account when planning to teach learners to read pictures: the developmental stage of the learner; visual perception; attention skills and working memory available.

In developmental terms, for instance, black and white patterns are apparently attractive to very young babies. Eventually children learn to associate familiar objects with photographs of a single familiar object on a plain background and then realistic drawings of the same (see also Chapter 27). Gradually there can be more distractions in the pictures as children become more adept at picking out the relevant part of the illustrations.

Visual perception is a complex process and learners with SLD/PMLD may have difficulties in this area. The process involves, for example, the ability to distinguish different colours, recognise shapes, interpret the position of one object in relation to others, differentiate between parts and whole objects and complete and incomplete object. Visual perception is more than seeing, it is 'understanding' what you see.

Paying attention to the relevant parts of a picture is also very important. Many learners with SLD/PMLD find focusing on relevant aspects of objects and pictures very hard. Some learners with autism may be attending to the shine on the page rather than the picture on it. Other learners may simply not understand what they are meant to be focusing on.

Even if learners are paying attention to the picture on the page, they may need to spend some time learning to recognise one object at a time before they can put those together to understand the illustrations in a story book. A good working memory is required to be able to make sense of several parts of a picture. You scan the picture for main clues and then put these together to 'make' the story illustrated. Almost by definition, learners with SLD/PMLD have difficulties with working memory and need to learn to make the best use of what they have.

It is necessary to put together all of these aspects to develop a systematic programme for teaching learners with SLD/PMLD to read pictures. For some learners this kind of programme is important in its own right as they will go on to use picture interpretation as their main literacy skill. Books Beyond Words (www.booksbeyondwords.co.uk) use pictures to tell stories that engage and empower people with learning difficulties on topics that are of social or health importance, such as death and dying or crime. The illustrations are developed through consultation with adults with learning difficulties and although there are suggestions for words to use, the books are essentially pictures only.

Objects and Multisensory Literacy

Learners with SLD/ PMLD require a concrete approach to their education. Activities based purely on language or abstract ideas are rarely successful but add sensory experiences, pictures and active manipulation of objects and the meaning behind the activities become accessible. Bag Books (Fuller 1999) were developed specifically for learners with SLD/PMLD and the multisensory approach has been adopted across the age range from babies to adults. Pamis (http://www.pamis.org.uk) have developed their own brand of multisensory stories on sensitive topics, such as sexuality, transition and growing up.

The use of symbols

Symbols are a more abstract form of pictures and are used widely in special schools to support the teaching of traditional orthography (Carpenter 1991; Detheridge and Detheridge 2002). Lacey (2006) found that 96 per cent of the schools visited used symbols in some form; but most frequently they were used within picture communication systems. Symbols can be used to support and enhance the meaning of text as they provide the reader with increased visual information (Carpenter and Detheridge 1994). Symbols can help to increase learners' ability to access literacy activities in a meaningful way, increasing autonomy, which in turn may have a positive impact on their social, emotional and personal development (Abbott and Lucey 2005).

In terms of using symbols as an aid to the teaching of reading, rather than purely as a way into communication, some research has found that they may not be overly useful (Sheehy 2001). It has been argued that the additional cues provided by the image may cause a blocking effect to the learning of single words and more complex text. For many learners the learning of symbols does not transfer to later word recognition, with systematic teaching required for them to be used effectively (Abbott and Lucey 2005).

Implications for practice

It is clear that the definition of reading needs to be widened to include a range of literacy experiences and learning opportunities. Then in order to find out if an approach to reading will work, we need to try it. The idea of a 'continuum' of pedagogies proposed by Lewis and Norwich (2000, 2005), where a broad framework is adjusted according to the needs of the learner, is useful for today's inclusive classrooms. The following strategies form part of this continuum, creating a framework where inclusive and more intense approaches to the teaching of reading are adapted and used where appropriate.

The classroom environment

Immersing learners in a broad and rich literacy environment, where they are provided with a wealth of opportunities to encounter traditional and non-traditional orthography, is a starting point. Readers learn best within a community of readers, where an awareness of literacy is given priority and celebrated (Miskin 2012). This environment requires a multi-sensory approach using visual, tactile and auditory experiences to promote the engagement of all learners (Department for Education 2012; Grove 2005).

A text-rich environment with opportunities for wide and exciting literacy experiences will help to ensure that the Matthew effect is avoided. Daily exciting, inspiring and interesting literacy experiences that encourage, support and challenge learners will help them move them on to becoming emergent readers and, in some cases, on to being fluent readers of basic texts (Miskin 2012). Within this environment learners should be provided with opportunities to tune into sounds through the use of music and rhymes. Grove (2005) emphasised that encouraging learners with SLD to become storytellers, using personal experiences, provides a way into literacy for all. Park (2004) places importance on interactive approaches to storytelling, making use of drama to bring literacy to life, and emphasises that learners should be supported and encouraged to develop communication and awareness of stories both within and around them. The example offered by Elizabeth Searle illustrates this.

Creating personal stories

Within my class of secondary aged learners with SLD, I use ICT to immerse all my learners within a literary world. I enable learners to become story tellers within their own right. The Clicker 6 programme (symbol support package) is widely used within my class to allow learners to recognise and annotate pictures they have selected. The stories created range from known, familiar tales to news events, to stories created through the use of story boxes. The learners love to record their own voices reading what they have written. The learners can then present these story books to the whole class and, when printed, they can be kept in the library adding to the individuals' kudos by becoming an author.

(Elizabeth Searle, Year 9 teacher, Mont a L'Abbe School, Jersey)

Learning should be encouraged through making and sharing experiences. Learners should be provided with opportunities to not only tell but also create personalised representations based on their experiences, using a flexible approach to the awareness of print (Lacey 2006). The use of personalised story boxes, boards, talkers, books and sacks that are based on the learner interests and experiences supports reading to teach talking from the outset. For many learners the encouragement of home–school involvement will have a positive impact, with learners taking home some form of literacy experience to share and bring back to school (news activities with symbols to support, big books, story boxes, sacks, reading books, etc.) (Miskin 2012). The 'See and Learn' intervention programme provides a useful framework which emphasises the importance of learners knowing what they are reading about, ensuring they build up an understanding of language and its relationship to print from the start (Burgoyne *et al*. 2012).

Using ICT to enhance learning

The expansion and increased use of ICT within today's classrooms allows learners with SLD to participate in all aspects of literacy. This can extend from writing their own stories, rewriting familiar stories, recording responses, celebrating what has been learnt, creating new and exciting environments, to listening to and interacting with stories and poems among the expanding uses (Hannah 2001; Lacey *et al*. 2007). There is a wealth of support and ideas concerning the use of ICT, giving learners with SLD a voice to enhance literacy for all. These would include: apps for iPads, all forms of tablets, interactive whiteboard/table/floor resources, podcasts and websites. This is illustrated in the example provided by Mathew Dingle.

Creative use of ICT in the classroom

I use ICT in every session to engage, motivate and provide cutting edge experiences for all my learners. The learners in my class all have SLD. When I introduce a new story, initially I introduce new vocabulary related to the new book. I show the learners the hard copy of the book, and see whether the learners can hold the book the correct way, and whether they can share a book with an adult and gain the experience of the book. The story is brought to life on the interactive whiteboard, as I turn the pages of the digital copy of the book; I check whether the learners can follow my lead. Learners are given laminated vocabulary mats made using Communicate in Print 2 and Clicker 6 communication packages/props and other sensory cues to the book. Learners then engage in matching activities, with the teacher modelling vocabulary, pointing at the picture/word/symbol and encouraging learners to say word or initial letter sound. There is repetition of initial letter sounds and key vocabulary pictures/words for reading focus for the week. This activity can be differentiated according to level. (Using individual pictures and objects or matching symbol to symbol, word to picture, word to word, etc.). Assessment methods include use recording books, linked to photographic evidence, voice recordings (Clicker 6 grids 'Listen and say') and questioning. Learners take home a copy of the vocabulary sheets to share with parents and carers (differentiated according to pupil need). Since using a structured approach brought to life through ICT, one learner has said her first whole word and others have continued to make progress in their recognition of sight words and correct pronunciation of key topic related vocabulary. I have found increased levels of concentration and the ability to focus and attend to a group activity.

(Matthew Dingle, Year 4 teacher, Mont a L' Abbe School, Jersey)

Figure 28.4 Comparing the pictures from a book with a digital copy on the interactive whiteboard

Multi-media

The use of multi-media resources in literacy learning is still under development for learners with SLD/PMLD (see Chapter 33). For example, Frank Wise School involves learners themselves in filmmaking and the films made by them have won well-deserved prizes (see the school's website: www.frankwise.oxon.sch.uk/news-media/video-gallery).Video can provide the means by which learners may both enjoy fiction and non-fiction and 'write' for themselves. However, it is important to bear in mind still the issues about learning to read still pictures. What is the developmental level of the learners, how well can they attend to the moving pictures, how good is their perception and their working memories? Videos are no more universally accessible than pictures.

Approaches to sight word learning

If learners begin to develop a meaningful awareness of text, more formalised ways into sight word learning should be introduced, again using multisensory approaches to ensure understanding and motivation are maximised. A systematic programme of assessment, teaching, further assessment and celebration of achievements should be applied (Burgoyne *et al.* 2012). At this point learners will be building up a number of sight words recognised, understood and used. These should be recorded and celebrated in many ways (e.g. using word boards, displays, word mats and word books/boxes).

Word recognition and decoding should be taught alongside comprehension, using support material (e.g. see the EQUALS (2011) guide to Literacy), 'See and Learn' materials (www. seeandlearn.org), and 'Letters and Sounds' (Department for Education and Science 2007). This knowledge requires initial errorless learning to build up skills and establishing an awareness of reasons for learning the words (Burgoyne *et al.* 2012).

Reading books and published schemes, to support word recognition and language comprehension, can then be used alongside homemade books and materials. There are number of schemes which are designed to support learners with SEN, using clear structures and progression alongside opportunities to revisit and over learn specific aspects. Many of these schemes have exciting visual images, stories and characters designed to motivate older readers (e.g. Project X CODE (Oxford University Press), Rapid Reading Scheme (Pearson) or Literacy and Life Skills (SEN Press)). Regular opportunities to participate in guided reading activities will provide a bridge for learners between independent and shared reading. Sharing the same book (story sack, box or sequence) in small groups or alone with an adult enables shared learning to take place; where experiences of language can be scaffolded and reinforced. If tracking learners' progress shows that no sight words have been retained, teaching should revert back to using more inclusive approaches but with continued access to sight words. At all opportunities bring literacy learning to life, don't forget the importance of rich, exciting and imaginative literacy experiences! The example offered by Frances Moseley demonstrates the benefits of a structured approach.

Figure 28.5 Using symbol/word cards to teach word recognition

The benefits of a structured approach

The year 7 group of learners with SLD in my class have a mixture of abilities and have many challenging behaviours. Over the years I have found that there is a lack of support to help me teach reading to this group of youngsters. Participating in a research project a few years ago looking at how useful a more structured approach to reading was for learners with SLD, gave me the confidence to teach sight words alone. I had always thought that giving learners symbols alongside words would help them to read the words and develop reading skills. The confidence to try words alone meant that I saw how some learners were able to read words, and others could just recognise symbols whatever word was with them. The outcome was a number of my pupils quickly learnt to read a number of sight words, which we later made into a book. This was taken home and read to siblings to the joy of both learner and parents.

(Frances Moseley, Year 5 teacher, Mountjoy Special School, Dorset)

The teaching of phonics

As awareness of print develops learners need to experience multisensory activities to consolidate and extend their awareness of sounds. Opportunities to tune into sounds, through rhyme and song, should be an established part of the daily routine. If learners can recognise a number of sight words alone, then more systematic phonics learning is appropriate. Burgoyne *et al.* (2012) recommended 30–40 words recognised as an indicator. Learners can develop phonic skills using traditional multisensory approaches that are based on established good practice for all, based on a synthetic approach (Department for Education and Science 2006, 2007; Drifte 2004; Lloyd 1998). Learners require the opportunity to listen and remember sounds, becoming more aware of differences between them (through alliteration, segmentation and blending). It is essential to develop prerequisite skills including auditory discrimination between sounds as well as memory skills. Through experiencing and talking about sounds, they are able to develop vocabulary and language comprehension skills (Johnston and Watson 2004).

The teaching of phonics must be part of a broad, rich and exciting reading curriculum, which begins with speech and moves onto the sounds contained in words. A review on effective practice in phonics teaching emphasises that any approach needs to be applied systematically, be well planned, evaluated and reviewed at regular intervals (Ofsted 2010).

Figure 28.6 Teaching blending with letters for eading simple words

Conclusion

In summary, what has been emphasised is that a multisensory approach alongside a diverse and rich range of experiences, creates the ideal word learning environment for all learners struggling with reading. The emphasis is not on the rejection of SEN knowledge or specialist approaches but on the inclusion of these pedagogies as one aspect of learning for all (Davis and Florian 2004). The term 'inclusive literacy', suggested by Lacey (2006), refers to literacy in its widest sense, incorporating all aspects of reading experiences from storytelling to theatre visits to reading pictures. A wider, more inclusive approach is also advocated here to enhance teaching and learning. The importance of further systematic, rigorous research that focuses on the applicability and effectiveness of a range of pedagogies for learners with SLD is advocated. Further research is necessary to further our knowledge and understand concerning how teaching and learning can be enhanced through combinations of approaches in different contexts and for different purposes.

Questions for readers

• What do you consider to be appropriate reading experiences for learners who may never learn to read printed words?
• What visual or tactile representations do you use as alternatives to written words or to augment them?
• What do you do to provide a text rich environment with a range of engaging literacy experiences for all?

Useful resources

www.equals.co.uk – provides useful examples of how to map and assess progress.

www.leics.gov.uk or www.kenttrustweb.org.uk – these provide examples of activities to support learners in reading within P levels.

www.gov.uk/government/publications/letters-and-sounds – the 'Letters and Sounds' structures provide a good early learning framework for phonics.

www.bugclub.co.uk or www.oxfordowl.co.uk – these provide examples of eBooks and interactive stories.

References

Bird, G. and Buckley, S. (1994) *Meeting the Educational Needs of Children with Down's Syndrome: A resource for teachers*, Portsmouth: University of Portsmouth.

Buckley, S. and Bird, G. (1993) 'Teaching children with Down Syndrome to read', *Down Syndrome Research and Practice*, 1(1): 34–39.

Burgoyne, K., Duff, F., Clarke, P., Smith, G., Buckley, S., Snowling, M. and Hulme, C. (2012) *A Reading and Language Intervention for Children with Down Syndrome – teacher's handbook*, Down Syndrome Education International. Available from www.dseinternational.org

Carpenter, B. (1991) 'Unlocking the door: access to the English national curriculum for children with severe learning difficulties', in B. Smith (ed.) *Interactive Approaches to Teaching the National Curriculum Subjects*, Bristol: Lame Duck Publishing.

Carpenter, B. and Detheridge, T. (1994) 'Writing with symbols', *Support for Learning*, 9(1): 27–32.

Clay, M. (1991) *Becoming Literate: The construction of inner control*, London: Heinemann Educational Books.

Clay, M. (2000) *The Concepts about Print Test*, Portsmouth, NH: Heinemann.

Davis, P., and Florian, L. (2004) *Teaching Strategies and Approaches for Children with Special Educational Needs: a scoping study. Research Report 516*, London: Department for Education and Skills.

Detheridge, T. and Detheridge, M. (2002) *Literacy Through Symbols: improving access for children and adults*, 2nd edn, London: David Fulton. Reprinted 2013 by London: Routledge.

Department for Education and Science (2006) *Primary Framework for Literacy and Mathematics*, London: Department for Education and Skills.

Department for Education and Science (2007) *Letters and Sounds: Principles and practice of high quality phonics*, London: Department for Education and Skills.

Department for Education (2012) *Statutory Framework for the Early Years Foundation Stage Setting the standards for learning, development and care for children from birth to five: DfE*. London: Department for Education.

Drifte, C. (2004) 'Top of the phonics', *Special Children*, March issue: 10–11.

EQUALS (2011) *The EQUALS Guide to Literacy: supporting access for pupils working towards Level 1 of the National Curriculum*, Tyne and Wear: EQUALS.

Goswami, U. (2004) 'Neuroscience, education and special education', *British Journal of Special Education*, 31(4): 175–183.

Gough, P., Hoover, W.A. and Peterson, C. (1996) (eds) *Some Observations on a Simple View of Reading*, Mahwah, NJ: Lawrence Erlbaum.

Grove, N. (2005) *Ways into Literature: Stories, plays and poems for pupils with SEN*, London: David Fulton.

Hannah, L. (2001) *Teaching Young Children with Autistic Spectrum Disorders to Learn: A practical guide for parents and staff in mainstream schools and nurseries*, Crowes, UK: National Autistic Society.

Johnston, R., and Watson, J. (2004) 'Accelerating the development of reading, spelling and phonemic awareness skills in initial readers', *Reading and Writing: An Interdisciplinary Journal*, 17: 327–357.

Kliewer, C. and Landis, D. (1999) 'Individualizing literacy instruction for young children with moderate to severe disabilities', *Exceptional Children*, 66(1): 85–100.

Lacey, P. (2006) 'What is inclusive literacy?' *The SLD Experience*, 46 (Autumn): 3–7.

Lacey, P., Layton, L., Miller, C., Goldbart, J. and Lawson, H. (2007) 'What is literacy for students with severe learning difficulties? exploring conventional and inclusive literacy', *Journal of Research in Special Educational Needs*, 7(3): 149–160.

Laing, E. and Hulme, C. (2001) 'Learning to read in Williams Syndrome: looking beneath the surface of atypical reading development', *Journal of Child Psychology and Psychiatry*, 42(6): 729–739.

Lewis, A., and Norwich, B. (2000) *Mapping a Pedagogy for Special Educational Needs*, Exeter: University of Exeter.

Lewis, A., and Norwich, B. (2005) *Special Teaching for Special Children? pedagogies for inclusion*, Maidenhead: Open University Press.

Lloyd, S. (1998) *The Phonics Handbook: A handbook for teaching, writing and spelling*, Chigwell: Jolly Learning.

Mastropieri, M.A., Scruggs, T.E. and Fulk, B.J.M. (1990) 'Teaching abstract vocabulary with the keyword method: effects on recall and comprehension', *Journal of Learning Disabilities*, 23(2): 92–96.

McCutchen, D., Abbott, R.D and Green, L.B. (2000) 'Beginning literacy: links among teacher knowledge, teacher practice, and student learning', *Journal of Learning Disabilities*, 35(1): 69–86.

Miskin, R. (2012) 'Early birds catch the words', Online: Available: www.senmagazine.co.uk/articles/1019-ruth-miskin-on-what-schools-need-to-do-to-ensure-children-both-learn-to-read-and-keep-reading.html (accessed 4 February 2015).

Moni, K., and Jobling, A. (2001) 'Reading-related literacy learning of young adults with Down Syndrome: findings from a three year teaching and research programme', *International Journal of Disability, Development and Education*, 48(4): 377–394.

Moseley, S. (2009) The Effect of Reading Instruction on the Self-concept and Self-esteem of Pupils with Severe Learning Disabilities, Unpublished PhD thesis, London: University of London Institute of Education.

Muter, V. (2003) *Early Reading Development and Dyslexia*, London: Whurr Publishers.

OFSTED (2010) *Reading by Six; how the best schools do it*, London: Office for Standards in Education.

Park, K. (2004) 'Interactive storytelling: from the Book of Genesis', *British Journal of Special Education*, 31(1): 16–23.

Rose, J. (2006) *Independent Review of the Teaching of Early Reading*, London: Department for Education and Skills.

Sheehy, K. (2001) 'Teaching non-readers with severe learning difficulties to recognise words: the effective use of symbols in a new technique', *Westminster Studies in Education*, 24(1): 61–71.

Stanovich, K. (1986) 'Matthew effects in reading: some consequences of individual differences in the acquisition of literacy', *Reading Research Quarterly*, (Fall): 360–397.

Stanovich, K. (1993/4) 'Romance and reality', *The Reading Teacher*, 47(4): 280–291.

Stuart, M. (2006) 'Learning to read: developing processes for recognizing, understanding and pronouncing written words', *London Review of Education*, 4(1): 19–29.

Wigfield, A. and Guthrie, J. (1997) 'Relations of children's motivation for reading to the amount and breadth of their reading', *Journal of Educational Psychology*, 89: 420–432.

29

LITERATURE AND STORIES IN THE LIVES OF LEARNERS WITH SLD/PMLD

Nicola Grove, Jane Harwood, Elizabeth Henderson, Keith Park and Rosemary Bird

In this chapter, the following questions will be addressed:

- Are literature and stories important for all young people? Why might this be so?
- How can we tell stories with those who find spoken and written language hard to understand?

Introduction

The telling of stories appears to be a universal human phenomenon. One leading developmental psychologist has argued that narrative drives the acquisition and elaboration of the language system (Tomasello 2008). Yet narrative has not been a significant priority in the teaching of language and communication to learners with SLD/PMLD. Therapy and teaching have emphasised: basic vocabulary in either speech, sign, graphics or pictures (Locke 1985; Picture Exchange Communication System: www.pecs.com; Makaton Vocabulary: www.makaton. org); putting words together (Derbyshire Language Scheme: Knowles and Masidlover 1982); interaction (Nind and Hewett 2005); social skills (e.g. Kelly 1997); and basic wants and needs (see Bunning *et al.* 2011). Even today, one widely used curriculum-based assessment (www. bsquared.org.uk) regards narration as a skill which only comes into play once children have verbal language (Grove 2014a), although research into child development shows that infants are engaged in scaffolded narration from very early on (Ellis 2007; Miller and Sperry 1988). In this chapter we will consider the role of both literature and personal recounts in the lives of children and young people with SLD/PMLD.

Barriers to learning

It may appear self-evident that learners whose communication is preverbal, or who have severe expressive and receptive language difficulties, will be incapable of either narrating themselves, or of understanding stories told to them. However, experience suggests that the main barriers are often our expectations, our confidence, and what is prioritised in the curriculum. In the English National Curriculum, there is an emphasis on functional literacy skills and the structural aspects of narrating, whether oral or written, which can disadvantage young people functioning at very early levels of communication. Teachers in the SEN sector have developed creative inclusive approaches to literacy and storytelling which successfully challenge this narrow perspective (Grove 2005; Lawson *et al.* 2012) using research on early communication. Comprehension is particularly important.

Comprehension models

Information processing models see understanding as a process of decoding – that is, the brain waits for a signal to come in (via the senses) and then checks it against the store of meanings filtered through a grammatical processor (e.g. Knowles and Masidlover 1982; Pinker 1994). The system must be intact to operate effectively. For learners with complex communication difficulties, this model is less useful than those that include the role of inference (Sperber and Wilson 1986), social interaction, and context (Bloom 1993; Bruner 1990). Bloom, for example, identifies the earliest understanding as 'episodic', where the baby learns what sounds and intonated phrases are associated with key events; Bruner characterises early language as first 'enactive' (that is, based in active movement), then 'iconic' (imagistic) then 'linguistic'. This is helpful when considering how the oral telling of a story calls on participation through movement and sound, and calls up images through the use of sound, gesture and highly concrete use of language. Language can of course be simplified so that learners who can only decode basic information can grasp something of the storyline, but we can also use language in a musical and poetic way, to which they respond through the senses and emotions. For example, Park (2010) and Grove (2005) provide examples of young people quoting bits of Shakespeare with evident enjoyment, ('Fair is foul and foul is fair…') without necessarily being able to analyse it. Poetry can be appreciated for its rhythmic, musical qualities without the listener always being able to analyse or explain its effects. The very structure of an orally told story contains within it the affordances for early communication that provide the foundations of later language and social development (Coupe O'Kane and Goldbart 1998) – as long as stories are presented in ways that invite active response. Figure 29.1 provides examples of these key behaviours.

- Consistency and repetition – because of the typical structure of stories (beginning, high point, conclusion, often with three part repetitions) these are a strong vehicle for providing consistent input of events:
- Attention (call/beginning)
- Response from the audience
- Turn taking
- Imitation: echoing of rhymes, key phrases, gestures, sounds and movements
- Contingency awareness (if this happens, then that happens)
- Anticipation
- Expression of feelings
- Body movements, vocalisations, gestures and facial expressions
- Recall of events
- Sequencing of events
- Symbolic understanding – recognition of objects and pictures (used simply and selectively to illustrate the story)
- Basic cognitive skills such as object permanence – appearance and disappearance of props in the story.

Figure 29.1 Features of oral storytelling that support early communicative and cognitive development

In particular, for busy teachers and speech and language therapists, part of the value of story is in the opportunity it provides for work on the foundations of communication and cognition (Grove and Park 1996, 2001). Through story, work on communication can be generalised in a way that feels purposeful and natural, enabling staff to respond consistently and with interest themselves (storytelling is a lot of fun!). This enthusiasm and relevance transmits itself to the learners. Storytelling enables us to resolve the tension between teaching a subject and teaching skills, and provides us moreover with meaningful cultural experiences to share. Learning about the lives of others can be done through storytelling, providing opportunities for links with home (for example, finding stories that are told by grandmothers across different ethnic backgrounds). Oral storytelling can and does lead into literacy – see for example, how Beth McCaffrey (2013) used a range of stories over the course of a year to develop both telling and writing in her learners – but it is vital to recognise the importance of oracy in its own right.

Using literature and fictional stories

Here we will outline two approaches which have proved useful to teachers in adapting works of fiction across the range of ability: call and response interactive storytelling, and multisensory storytelling.

Call and response storytelling

Interactive Storytelling (Park 2010) is an approach based upon a call and response method, where the storyteller will call out a line which is then repeated by the group. Non-speaking learners participate in many ways – signing, clapping, vocalising, rocking and so on. The story is divided into short sections, each ending with a climactic word, phrase or sound effect, thus making each episode into an anticipation game. It began as a way of including children and young people with very complex needs in community storytelling, as a performing art rather than an exercise in literacy. For example, it has been used in the deafblind community, with children and adults with SLD/PMLD, and their staff and family members. The story content is made as varied as possible: Shakespeare; pantomime in a local theatre and Bible Stories in Cockney rhyming slang. Where possible, the stories are also performed in context: Shakespeare at The Globe Theatre, Bible Stories at Westminster Abbey, Dickens at Rochester Cathedral, Chaucer at Canterbury Cathedral, and Ovid's story of 'Marsyas' in Tate Modern, directly underneath the Anish Kapoor 'Marsyas' installation. A recent development has been to encourage stories from people with learning disabilities and autism (Park and Pilcher 2013). These workshops are scripted and led by people with disabilities.

Multisensory storytelling

This has become a term in general use for the ways in which teachers adapt fictional works to include music, textures, smells, tastes and visual images. Such approaches, used with discrimination to avoid sensory overload, have proved successful across the range of ability (Mitchell and van der Gaag 2002; Grove and Park 1996). Story sacks (www.storysacks.org.uk), for example, can provide a key set of props for specific stories that allow children to handle and recognise key characters. It must be said that these are not generally available for secondary level texts such as, say, *Romeo and Juliet*, *Gulliver's Travels*, or Michael Morpurgo's *War Horse*, but teachers are adept at finding and using props to tell these stories in similar ways (Grove 2005). To fill the gap in resources for fictional storytelling for learners with profound learning difficulties and sensory impairments, Fuller (2013) developed Bag Books (www.bagbooks.org); these stories are original, specifically designed and carefully structured to meet the needs and interests of this population, though they are more akin to reading aloud than oral storytelling. This is because, however dynamically they are told, the focus is on the book and the teller simultaneously; in oral telling there is no divided attention. Barbara Fornefeld (2013) also uses custom-made props and sensory inputs, this time to tell traditional stories (Grimms' tales or the Arabian nights) and Bible legends. An example of multisensory storytelling is provided below.

Multisensory storytelling in action: Oliver Twist

The book was chosen as a text for a variety of reasons: the strong storyline and range of characters; the richness of the language, and the opportunities for sensory input (atmospheric sounds and smells and tastes – think gruel); the historic relevance (workhouses, after all, became the institutions which housed people with learning disabilities), and cultural immediacy: popularised by the musical and recent films there are many opportunities for learners to access the story outside school. The story was developed over two terms to allow learners enough time to familiarise themselves with it and to explore themes. For example, a teenager who finds it hard to think about herself as a young woman was encouraged to take on the role of Nancy. The approach combined narration and drama, with learners taking active roles as characters, memorising lines from the original text and singing songs from the musical.

Evaluating progress

Learners' responses to such rich events are complex and multilayered, and it can be frustrating when the assessment framework only includes transactional targets. Grove (2005) developed a multidimensional framework that attempts to present a rounded picture of the learner's learning, comprising 'engagement', 'affective', 'cognitive' and 'aesthetic' elements. Examples are provided in Figure 29.2 of how two learners functioning at different levels of development responded in the lesson.

Anna is nineteen, and has Down syndrome and a severe hearing loss. She functions educationally at approximately the level of a typically developing 5 year old though language is more delayed, with her best performance being usually two to three word/sign sentences. Simon is seventeen, and has spastic cerebral palsy. He communicates nonverbally, using smiles, vocalisation and eye gaze, and functions at approximately a 12-month level of cognitive development. The learners were observed during an hour-long lesson dramatising the penultimate chapter: Oliver's kidnapping from his new home by Bill Sykes, and Nancy's decision to help him escape.

Figure 29.2 allows us to see some of the strengths of these learners that might be missed when the targets are overly structural, cognitive or linguistic: for example, Anna's rhythmic and creative abilities; the impact of Simon's communication on his peers. It also highlights some areas for development: for Anna, working on more spontaneous use of language, and communication of a wider range of emotions (in both cases, it would be important to see if she can do this in other settings, since she was functioning largely in active listener role and was rapt with enjoyment, both factors which certainly contribute to this profile). For Simon, it was exciting to see him actively recalling an event and intentionally activating his communication aid; we might also want to see if there is any way of helping him to differentiate his vocalisations, maybe even to achieve jaw closure.

	Anna	Simon
Engagement	**Achievement**	**Engagement**
Using the original framework devised by Brown (1996)	Gaining, consolidating, practising skills, showing knowledge and concepts.	Directed attention, focused looking, listening, showing interest, recognition, recall
Affect	Communicates strong feelings; uses emphasis in signing to convey importance; laughs with enjoyment, stills to show seriousness, Range somewhat limited; she does convey anger and expectation but minimally. This is probably just because she is enjoying the whole thing so much, she can't suppress the sense of fun	Contrastive use of smiling and laughing and stilling. Alternated gaze appropriately between his TA support, the action and the film show.
Imitation	A lot of repeated signs and speech for important aspects of the story show she is tuned in and attending; the basis of empathy	
Empathy	Demonstrated through her attention, riveted on the film and the action, her joining in with looking for Oliver 'where' singing in a contrastive way Oompapa, and Where is love	Seemed to remember that 'where's Oliver' was on his communication aid, and tried to activate this at the appropriate time.
Feelings shown	Happiness Enjoyment Serious/sad Uncertainty 'DON'T KNOW' in role Anger (imitating the right expression for Bill) Strength (muscles) Wistful (singing) Fear (shakes body on demand, though facial expression does not change).	Fun and enjoyment
Thinking and language		
Recall	Correctly answers several questions relating to the events of the story eg answers 'London' to question where are we? ; volunteers that Oliver is 'at HOME' (ie with Mr Brownlow, who has adopted him)	Seemed to remember that 'where's Oliver' was on his communication aid, and tried to activate this at the appropriate time.
Problem solving, hypothesising and imagining	Can refer to events that are removed in space and time.	
Instructing and explaining	Tells Bill to stand up. Guides a friend in showing the missing poster round the class	

Reasoning, debating	NA	NA
Vocabulary used spontaneously	Names of individuals and places (Oliver, Fagin, London); specific terms eg pickpocket Question WHERE Mostly single word and sign answers and imitations	
Forming words and sounds	NA	May have been trying to articulate 'oompapa' – his bottom jaw moved up to contact upper lip consistently on the final word of the song.
Aesthetics		
Creativity	'Bill, Bill, Stand up!' is Anna's own input	Attempted to activate communication aid spontaneously to contribute.
Congruence (responses that are appropriate and which reinforce the atmosphere)	Beautiful rhythmic singing and signing to the music, a real feel for the right expression. Repeats WHERE, WHERE, with emphasis GONE/disappeared imitated with feeling	Stilled at serious moments, laughed at moments that were energetic or funny. Allowed his arms to be moved rhythmically and seemed to be anticipating this.
Impact (how the learner's creativity affects others)	She takes a lead in the 'search' for Oliver, acting as a model for her peers.	When he did activate the communication aid to call 'where's Oliver' in the final scene, this was echoed by a fellow learner, creating a lovely moment of community.

Figure 29.2 Response to literature by two learners
NA = not applicable, blank = no example observed

Although only two learners were profiled in depth, there was much evidence of active participation and enjoyment by their classmates, who performed extracts at the final assembly of the year, attended by parents.

Personal stories

The telling and sharing of personal stories, sometimes termed 'recount narratives', helps us process small – and larger – events that happen in our lives, and to build relationships and empathy with others. Research shows that such narratives predominate in the communication of children as they grow up (Preece 1987; Wilson 1997). McCabe *et al.* (2008) maintain that if we want to enable children to apply skills in everyday life, then we should prioritise personal over fictional narratives. Multisensory storybooks and multisensory storytelling techniques can be used to develop real as well as fictional stories, as demonstrated by Lambe and her colleagues (Lambe and Hogg 2013).

Over the last ten years, we have been developing a systematic approach – Storysharing® (Grove 2014b) – to the recounting of both personal and fictional narratives. Learner and story partner work together to share the telling: through the encouragement of active listening, others are included in the story. Narratives are 'scaffolded' (Vygotsky 1978) and co-narrated using a range of techniques that can include objects of reference, sensory props, communication aids, iPads, signing, repetition and sentence prompts. Storysharing requires staff to avoid direct questioning, and use a more supportive and conversational approach to elicit communication (see Antaki 2013 for a similar approach). There are no prerequisite skills required in speaking and listening or narrative, and the approach can be used with preverbal learners functioning at the earliest levels of communication. However, the emphasis changes as learners develop skills and abilities: at first the learner contributes minimally, and impact of the stories is seen mainly on the audience, as they develop more awareness of who this young person is. Verbal learners functioning nearer their chronological age will only require occasional prompts and supports and will be using the techniques spontaneously themselves to interact with peers and sometimes to support their friends or younger learners.

Storysharing strategies can be used within planned sessions, but also across the curriculum and in informal settings: such as playground interactions, advocating for oneself or others in school council meetings, to demonstrate achievement in review meetings and in reporting events and experiences (for example, field trips, science, geography). Families are involved as they contribute anecdotes from home, and listen to the stories that learners bring back from school.

Storysharing in action

The following examples are taken from a three-year intervention programme in a special school of 170 learners, around half of whom would be described as having SLD/PMLD.

Choosing Stories: Where communication needs are high, personal stories will not be spontaneously reported. Stories will need to be gathered. For this to happen effectively everyone involved in the process needs to agree on a common definition of a 'story' – something worth sharing. A simple 'story sheet' records a snapshot. We look for 'the sparkle' – a reportable event (Labov and Waletzky 1976), which sits in the heart of the story. Often stories are funny: sometimes sad, or difficult. Achievements can be celebrated and changes acknowledged. We acknowledge every story that learners bring in, however small. We cannot judge the importance of a story to the individual. The links between our stories help us to build friendships, learning that we have similar experiences, emotions and responses. Figure 29.3 shows an outline lesson plan.

Structuring the session: Storysharing sessions can be short, even impromptu (you can reinforce awareness by using storysharing as events happen); individual or group. Group sessions enable turn taking and active listening, a skill that is developed alongside storysharing. The session may last up to 45 minutes, but will include varied activities such as breakout work or resource making.

Resources: Objects of reference have a specific link to the story being told and may have been part of the actual story. They trigger sensory memories and have a clear connection to the event. For example, a trowel and some compost help tell a gardening story. Props are used more casually, in a reactive manner – they introduce a sensory, tactile element that can be shared around the listeners (for example, seashells and an ocean drum for a seaside story). A props bag for recurrent story themes can be created. Communication aids (such as Big Macks) and iPads enable participation with both verbal and non verbal groups, though it is important to take care that the learner does not become fixated on the digital technology, but is paying attention to others in the group.

Connecting through story: Stories often naturally follow a theme or echo each other. Through facilitation and response, the leader can identify patterns and build a web of stories – recognising an interconnection of experience and shared responses. Remembered events strengthen a feeling of community. An archive of stories told is a useful tool for an individual, community or class, for memories and sharing with visitors.

---

1 Introductory song, acknowledging who is present and inviting people to tell their stories.
2 Recap of previous stories, if relevant.
3 New stories are shared in turn, around the circle. Everyone is encouraged to join in with active listening techniques. The audience are not just 'waiting for their turn', they are leaning forward, echoing what's said, joining in with gestures and actions, and reacting with exclamations, often recorded on the Big Mack.
4 Break out work – in groups or one to one. This is a time to develop stories, create resources, and use iPads.
5 The group reconvenes to share and show.
6 Closing – a song, and goodbyes.
7 Debriefs with staff and forward planning.

Figure 29.3 Storysharing outline plan

Evaluating progress

Currently there are no truly inclusive, developmentally based narrative assessments available. In the school we look at learners' individual education plans and profiles on the National Curriculum framework, identifying skills to be targeted within the sessions. This forms the basis of tick sheets that are used by staff after each session. We are looking for levels of engagement, both with telling and joining in (evidencing listening). We have used film at regular intervals (before, during and after interventions) to demonstrate change in learners' communication styles and unexpected outcomes. Bunning and her colleagues (2014) found positive changes in pupils' narrative skills post intervention. It is helpful to gain more than one viewpoint. We ask different people for their feedback, including families. It can take a long time for change to happen: in our current project we are seeing dramatic differences in the ability of the first group of learners we taught, 18 months after the focused intervention – thanks to the ongoing support of the teaching staff. The progress rate and unexpected outcomes vary with every group. It's helpful to keep a running document of reflective practice, to keep notes of new ideas; what went well and not so well; things to change and introduce. Two learners who have benefited from the intervention are Callum and Helen.

Callum is 19, a young man who communicates using single words, can understand short phrases in conversation, and who functions at approximately the level of 36 months in cognitive development. At the beginning of the intervention, he preferred to interact with adults rather than his peers. He is on the point of leaving school. His teacher says that, 'since he began storysharing, Callum has added to the repertoire of stories he tells about himself, evidencing memory. His questions and responses used to be very limited and repetitive – he's moved on. He's had more opportunity to reflect on interesting things that have happened in his own life. He joins in with other people telling their stories – building empathetic skills, engaging with other peoples' experiences, make links with his own. He's developed his skills as an active listener and supportive friend. It's extended his repertoire of topics to engage with other people about'.

Helen is a 13 year old who can understand short phrases in conversational language, but often presents at a more reactive and concrete level of development. She is a non-verbal communicator, choosing to express herself through body language and gesture. She is functionally blind and can appear withdrawn, isolated from her peers. She relies heavily on interactions with adults. Helen's story developed over several weeks, as she gained new skills in the hydro pool. Photos of her were used to create a comic strip book of her story. This was sent home to her parents, who reciprocated by sending in more stories. Using objects of reference and tactile props, a 'mini hydro pool' full of warm water enabled Helen to tell her stories to others, lifting a look-alike doll in and out of the water, splashing, and drying with a towel. Adults filled in the gaps of this story as she demonstrated the sequence of events. A simple one message communication aid enabled her to add to the narrative. A film of her telling this story was shown in assembly. She also shared it in her annual review, as it represented new skills gained – a significant opportunity for her to contribute to her own decision making processes.

Recording stories

Because we cherish and retell the stories we share, it's helpful to make creative, tactile records of these stories together. Most simply, a story can be represented by key words, photos, pictures and symbols, which can be laminated, cut up, and used in collages or books. Other ideas that have proved effective in classrooms and residential settings include:

- Story trees, with each branch representing a person: hung with colourful leaves, a story written on each.
- Story boxes, made from shoe boxes: decorated inside and out, containing tactile objects, switches and so on.
- Story clouds, with names, key words and pictures, suspended from the ceiling, which move gently as people walk around the room.
- Story houses, with a window for each person in the group, opening to reveal stories.
- Films of stories being shared, to watch and show others.
- iPad apps – a range of story based apps are available, and more are coming on the market all the time.
- Comic books made with Comic Life software (www.comiclife.org). This is popular with teenagers.
- Life sized me: draw around a person, cut them out, decorate with colours and paste on their stories.

Conclusion

The telling of stories, both fictional and personal, has proved transformative for many young people who have been enabled to develop their skills as listeners, as tellers, actors and writers. After telling a personal story in his review, and demonstrating his skills as an actor in *Oliver Twist*, Callum was seen as someone capable of going to college to study drama, rather than to a day centre. Now that Anna has become a confident storyteller in sign and speech, she is keen to write stories down. She is also using her storytelling skills to support a classmate who is deaf and often finds it difficult to process what is going on. Elsewhere, in a multisensory book group run by the Openstorytellers charity, a young woman started to say 'no' and to assert her choices independently. Staff saw this as a direct outcome of hearing many legendary and fictional stories in which women asserted themselves. Stories help us to make sense of our own lives and to empathise with others, skills that are at the heart of educational achievement for all learners.

Questions for readers

* How does a multisensory approach help learners to understand and enjoy a story?
* How much should we simplify the language of stories, poetry and plays to suit the understanding of learners?
* How many of the learners you teach can narrate a personal experience?
* What are the implications for learners growing up, if they are unable to recall and tell their own stories with others?

Acknowledgements

Thanks are due to the learners and teachers whose insights have contributed so much to this chapter, in particular Nigel Pooley who with Rosemary Bird devised the scenarios for Oliver Twist.

The Storysharing project at Threeways School was managed by Openstorytellers, and funded by the Paul Hamlyn Foundation and the Rayne Foundation, with in house support provided by the school.

Openstorytellers (www.openstorytellers.org.uk) run courses and provide certificated and in-service training in Storysharing®.

References

Antaki, C. (2013) 'Two conversational practices for encouraging adults with intellectual disabilities to reflect on their activities', *Journal of Intellectual Disability Research*, 57: 580–588.

Bloom, L. (1993) *The Transition from Infancy to Language: acquiring the power of expression*, New York: Cambridge University Press.

Bruner, J. (1990) *Acts of Meaning*, Cambridge, MA: Harvard University Press.

Bunning, K. (2014) Taking part through telling stories: a pilot study of Storysharing. *Paper presented at the 4th IASSIDD Europe Congress Pathways to Inclusion*, 14–17 July 2014.

Bunning, K., Smith, C., Greenham, P. and Kennedy, C. (2011) 'Examination of the communication interface between learners with severe to profound and multiple intellectual disability and educational staff during structured teaching sessions', *Journal of Intellectual Disability Research*, 57: 39–52.

Coupe O'Kane, J. and Goldbart, J. (1998) *Communication Before Speech*, 2nd edn, London: David Fulton.

Ellis, L. (2007) 'The narrative matrix and wordless narrations: a research note', *Augmentative and Alternative Communication*, 23: 113–125.

Fornefeld, B. (2013) 'Storytelling with all our senses: mehr-Sinn® Geschichten', in N. Grove (ed.) *Using Storytelling to Support Children and Adults with Special Needs: Transforming lives through telling tales*, London: Taylor and Francis.

Fuller, C. (2013) 'Multi-sensory stories in story packs', in N. Grove (ed.) *Using Storytelling to Support Children and Adults with Special Needs: transforming lives through telling tales*, London: Taylor and Francis.

Grove, N. (2005) *Ways into Literature*, 2nd edn, London: David Fulton.

Grove, N. (2014a) 'Personal oral narratives in a special school curriculum: an analysis of key documents', *British Journal of Special Education*, 41: 6–24.

Grove, N. (2014b) *The Big Book of Storysharing*, London: Speechmark.

Grove, N. and Park, K. (1996) *Odyssey Now*, London: Jessica Kingsley Publishers.

Grove, N. and Park, K. (2001) *Social Cognition Through Drama and Literature: Macbeth in mind*, London: Jessica Kingsley Publishers.

Kelly, A. (1997) *Talkabout: A social communication skills package*, Milton Keynes: Speechmark Publications.

Knowles, W. and Masidlover, M. (1982) *The Derbyshire Language Scheme*, Derby: Derbyshire County Council.

Labov, W. and Waletzky, J. (1976) 'Narrative analysis: oral versions of personal experience', in J. Helm (ed.) *Essays on the Verbal and Visual Arts*, Seattle: University of Washington Press.

Lambe, L. and Hogg, J. (2013) 'Sensitive stories: tackling challenges for adults with profound intellectual disabilities through multisensory storytelling', in N. Grove (ed.) *Using Storytelling to Support Children and Adults with Special Needs: Transforming lives through telling tales*, London: Taylor and Francis.

Lawson, H.A., Layton, L., Goldbart, J., Lacey, P., and Miller, C. (2012) 'Conceptualisations of literacy and literacy practices for children with severe learning difficulties', *Literacy*, 46(2): 101–108.

Locke, A. (1985) *Living language*, Windsor, Berks: NFER Nelson.

McCabe, A., Bliss, L., Barra, G., and Bennett, M. (2008) 'Comparison of personal versus fictional narratives of children with language impairment', *American Journal of Speech-Language Pathology*, 17: 194–206.

McCaffrey, B. (2013) 'What can teachers learn from the stories children tell? The nurturing, interpretation and evaluation of stories told by children with language and learning difficulties', in N. Grove (ed.) *Using Storytelling to Support Children and Adults with Special Needs: transforming lives through telling tales*, London: Taylor and Francis.

Miller, P. and Sperry, L. (1988) 'Early talk about the past: the origins of conversational stories of personal experience', *Journal of Child Language*, 15, 293–315

Mitchell, J. and van der Gaag, A. (2002) 'Through the eye of the Cyclops: evaluating a multisensory intervention programme for people with complex disabilities', *British Journal of Learning Disabilities*, 30: 159–165.

Nind, M. and Hewett, D. (2005) *Access to Communication: Developing the basics of communication with people with severe learning difficulties through Intensive Interaction*, 2nd edn, London: David Fulton.

Park, K. (2010) *Interactive Storytelling*, 2nd edn, Milton Keynes: Speechmark Publications.

Park, K. and Pilcher, P. (2013) *Special Stories*, Wootton, Beds: Flo Longhorn Publications.

Pinker, S. (1994) *The Language Instinct: How the mind creates language*, New York: William Morrow and Company.

Preece, A. (1987) 'The range of narrative forms conversationally produced by young children', *Journal of Child Language*, 14: 353–373.

Sperber, D. and Wilson, D. (1986) *Relevance: Communication and cognition*, Blackwell: Oxford.

Tomasello, M. (2008) *Origins of human communication*, Cambridge, MA: MIT Press.

Vygotsky, L. S. (1978). *Mind in Society: The development of higher psychological processes*, Cambridge, MA: Harvard University Press.

Wilson, M. (1997) *Performance and Practice: Oral narrative traditions amongst teenagers in Britain and Ireland*, London: Ashgate Publishing.

30

USING NUMBER IN EVERYDAY LIFE

Jill Porter

In this chapter, the following questions will be addressed:

* What do we know about the very earliest stages and the activities that sensitise learners to an awareness of number?
* How do learners acquire the skill of counting and an understanding of what it means to count?
* How can learners use these skills, understanding, and awareness in everyday life?

Introduction

In everyday life we are surrounded by numerical information, much of which provides important cues that enable us to make sense of events, yet these are largely taken for granted. The church clock chimes and without conscious counting the quarter or half hour is noted. Equally I automatically perceive that a book is missing, that two rest on the table where once there were three. Such knowledge enables me to anticipate that one may thankfully have been returned to the library. As importantly, I see that I have only two teabags left – I must buy some more. These examples demonstrate how numerical skills and understanding of a very basic nature are woven into everyday tasks that are meaningful and goal directed for me as an individual. Number, or numerousness, provides important cues in the environment enabling us to predict and anticipate and take appropriate action. Equally, research has highlighted the importance of number skills in the lives and wellbeing of adults with learning difficulties (Farragher and Brown 2005).

There is, however, little research that explicitly addresses the development of numeracy in learners with SLD (Porter 2005b). That which does exist is often specific to particular groups such as children with Down syndrome (not all of whom will have SLD). It is therefore important to understand typical development and to consider how this might be influenced by particular difficulties that learners with SLD experience. These can include difficulties with language, with processing verbal and auditory material and with working memory; learners with different conditions have different profiles of strengths (Paterson *et al.* 2006). We need also to consider the environment we provide for learners, how we use number words and how we draw attention to quantity, as opposed to colour or size. Children in nursery settings are provided with a rich environment in which number words are used in a whole variety of practical and concrete contexts and children are usually gradually inducted into these special and precise meanings through interactions with adults, siblings and peers that centre around activities including play, games and routines. We may want to be more targeted in our approach but this emphasises the need for number to be experienced across activities.

Learning about number draws particularly on working memory – the short-term store that allows us to hold information in mind while we perform some mental operation on it. If, for example, a learner is asked to give eight items, they have to hold the number 8 in mind while simultaneously counting out, 1, 2, 3, 4 etc., until they reach a match for the target number. If this parallel task is well practised and easily executed then the demands on memory are lessened. There is evidence, however, that, even at the earliest stages of learning the count words, the child may have problems in remembering the sequence (Porter 1996; 1999). This may be particularly true for learners who have difficulty distinguishing between the sounds or who have auditory sequential memory difficulties. It is likely that visual or tactile cues may support learners better than oral cues and reduce the load on memory.

Earliest stages

In order to understand the development of number in children with SLD it is important to start with the earliest stages that start well before children reason through language. Competing debates and explanations abound for the way that typically developing children acquire the foundations of mathematical skills and understanding. At the heart of these lies the place of visuo-spatial skills, with one view being that an awareness of differences in *magnitude* supports later developments in the manipulations of number including arithmetic skills. The other explanations build on *tracking* individual items which are held in mind separately – which could be linked to the ability to understand 1:1 correspondence and to ordinal aspects of number. This has important implications for how we shape the earliest contexts for learning, whether for example the learner is presented with items all together or as a sequence.

Research by developmental psychologists demonstrates how infants as young as six months are able to distinguish differences in arrays where the ratio is 1:2 even where this involves large numbers such as 8:16. As they get older this process becomes increasingly precise so that by 8–9 months they can make distinctions between ratios of 2:3 (Cordes and Brannon 2009).

If we turn to studies where items are presented sequentially, Wynn (Wynn 1992; McCrink and Wynn 2004) reveals that infants discriminate between the auditory sequence of two and three drumbeats and between the physical actions of a puppet jumping two or three times. In a series of ingenious studies using a puppet and a screen she also found that young infants were able to predict the outcome of adding and subtracting one, to one and two puppets. The infant, as judged by an independent observer, shows surprise when he sees one puppet join another puppet but the screen goes back to indicate that instead of two puppets, inexplicably (courtesy of a trap door) there is only one. These studies have been confirmed by neuroscientists looking at changes in the brain activity of infants. Number can be highly salient.

Other research by Feigenson and colleagues shows infants can apply this in meaningful contexts choosing between containers when they see one or two crackers inserted or between two and three crackers at the age of 10–12 months. They also reveal the limitations as infants of this age are unable to process information that relates to 4. Older infants of 14 and 15 months have been found to retrieve objects that they can no longer see by making an appropriate number of reaches and by spending longer searching when one disappears thus further demonstrating the ability to represent and reason about number (Feigenson and Carey 2003; 2005).

Early Number Activities

Zack is learning about 3. One of his favourite games involves two rice bowls. We take it in turns to hide 1 or 3 items in each, move them round on the table, and then guess which one had 3 items in it. Sometimes we put a symbol on the top of the rice bowl lid (one or three dots or sometimes we make up our own signs) so that we can track the movement of the bowls.

Zack also has a number 3 book, with each page having different items, some are identical, some vary by colour and size and some share the same category (e.g. three cats). Zack adds to the pictures in his book by choosing from cards showing one or three. In looking through the book he has to find where one of the items has 'dropped off'.

Heidi is learning about 2. In the splash pool we submerge two ducks under the bubbles then release them one at a time to pop up, we leave a pause before the second duck to encourage her to anticipate that a second will arrive.

Early development and SLD

As we can see from the above activities research with young infants has started to inform work with learners with SLD and draws attention to differences between individuals in the way they respond to visual number tasks (Porter 2005a). Research has been carried out to investigate contexts to draw children's attention to small quantities and to use this awareness to promote problem solving in learners with complex needs (Porter 2005a, 2010). Following a series of case studies it has become clear that contexts for learners at the earliest stages need to be individually tailored to their needs and interests. A vital element is to find situations which will arouse learners' interest and hold their attention in order to encode numerical information – for example, learners need to sustain their looking if they are to register that more than one item is available. The context also needs to invite a response that is within the learners' repertoire. This individualisation requires a curriculum that draws attention to the ways in which learners' awareness and understanding develop but does not prescribe the activities through which this can be achieved. The excerpt below illustrates the development of a game with a non-verbal child, which encourages her to register numerical information (two puppets) with actions.

Sheila's interest in puppets and her readiness to reach out to touch them (albeit to grab them and throw them over her shoulder) are incorporated into a new game. The puppets appear one at a time at opposite sides of the table saying 'hallo Sheila' as they arrive, to ensure that she has registered the appearance of each one. She turns from the first puppet to the second indicating that she has registered that there are two, *as it is impossible to see both puppets at once.* As she then pushes them off the table, they respond 'goodbye Sheila'.

The game is developed further with the puppets each holding a maraca which they shake on arrival and departure. On two of four presentations, she pushes one then turns to push the second puppet.

Taken from Porter (2005a)

Learning to count

The developments and activities that have been discussed so far do not require counting, but here I turn to look at what we know about this skill – again from work with typically developing young children. If we start with considering the task of learning the number string, then acquisition is dependent on hearing the sequence again and again. There is no predictive pattern of sounds until the child has learnt the number string from 1–13. The words are learnt as a serial list, like learning the alphabet, so that they are acquired as a linked series of sounds, with one number word becoming the cue for the next word in the sequence. Fuson, Richards and Briars (1982) provide us with an outline of the process of acquisition, one that we might identify with if we have recently attempted to learn the words in another language. Table 30.1 sets out the sequence together with the implications for teaching.

Research carried out with pupils with SLD has highlighted how this is often a difficult task, especially for the group of pupils with Down syndrome. They may know the number words, but not be able to reliably produce them in the correct order. While children with SLD often have a similar number vocabulary to typically developing nursery-aged pupils their count strings are significantly shorter (Porter 1996). If we listen to the counting of some children with SLD, we can hear that certain words are produced clearly and distinctly, and others are poorly articulated. 'Eight', for example, is a nice clear sound to produce, while 'five' may be indistinguishable from 'four'. Again, if we draw a parallel with learning a foreign language, we can understand how difficult it is to remember a word that we have problems pronouncing. If we have some kind of hearing loss, then that sound may be only slightly distinguishable from others.

If learners are experiencing particular difficulties with the counting task, there are strong arguments to be made for supporting their learning with visual material: for example, the use of numerical symbols or the use of pictorial representations of the numbers. A parallel to this process is the use of written words to support language development in pupils with Down syndrome. With number, as with words, it is possible to provide cues within the number symbols with dot patterns contained within the symbol and these are available commercially.

Learners have also to learn the rules of counting in order that the skill becomes a useful tool. Not only do they have to produce the count words in sequence but they also have to use them to tag each item once and once only. In addition, they have to learn that the last number used

Table 30.1 Stages in acquiring the count string (drawn from Fuson, Richards and Briars, 1982)

1 Number words learnt first as a chant or song
   Children don't fully perceive the gaps between number words and, therefore, are not able to co-ordinate words with pointing. Teachers need to consider how intonation and melody help the production of these sounds.

2 Produce a sequence of individual number words but cannot break into the sequence
   Children have to begin the count from one (or their first word in the number sequence); they are better able to co-ordinate pointing with saying the number words.

3 Children are able to break into their sequence, producing parts of the sequence starting at different points
   Children can be prompted to produce what comes 'next' and can count on with concrete objects.

4 Children are fluent in their counting and can simultaneously keep track of the number words said
   Children can count up three from four etc., keeping track of the number of number words said.

5 Children can move easily both up and down the number chain
   Children can count both forwards and backwards through the number word sequence.

in the sequence indicates the number of items in the group. It is conventional to make this task as easy as possible for the learner by placing the items in a line and encouraging them to move sequentially down the line. This helps to reduce the load on memory of recalling which items have been counted and which have not. Experience also indicates that items need to be placed at a suitable distance apart. Too close together and the learner is unsure which item he or she has tagged. Too far apart and he or she has to hold onto the next number word in the sequence too long. Some teachers encourage pupils to count while putting items away, but as we have seen, pace is important and if learners are not fluent the extra dimension to the activity may distract them.

Research with typically developing children suggests that there may be an order of difficulty whereby learners at the earliest stages find objects laid in a row the easiest situation in which to co-ordinate the count process. It is not until children are a bit older and more fluent in their production of the number words, that putting objects away elicits more accurate counting. We know from research by McEvoy and McConkey (1991) that children with learning difficulties do find it hard to co-ordinate counting and pointing. Learners may, therefore, be best introduced to counting by sharing the task which will enable them to become more fluent in each aspect of it although this should not be at the expense of all solo experience.

It is vital, if learners are going to acquire the rules, that the support we give them initially is withdrawn as they become increasingly proficient. While we might start learners by using small groups of items in rows and sharing the count process so the learner does the tagging and we say the number words (or vice versa) it is important that these arrangements are altered. Learners need to experience counting in a whole variety of contexts if they are to realise that the rules of counting don't include putting items out in a row — that this is merely a strategy that they may not always need.

Understanding cardinality

Cardinality can be understood at many different levels and in many different contexts. At an early level children need to understand that it indicates the number of items in the set, or the number of activities, sounds or events in total. Children may learn that they have two shoes, two gloves, and one scarf and thereby be able to use number words as a descriptor. However, they also have to learn the link between counting and cardinality — that counting is used to find out: how many items there are in the group; activities in a day; rings of the bell for the start of school etc. Typically developing children are described as passing through stages whereby they say a single number after counting but it is not usually the last one uttered (indeed it could be a 'favourite' number). This is followed by a phase of recounting the items when asked how many items, even though they have just counted them. It seems at this stage as if children think that the question 'how many?' is an instruction to count the items. They then return to producing a single digit in answer. Research with pupils with SLD suggested that they too followed a similar pattern albeit that there were additional responses made (Porter 1999), including reciting the number words rather than recounting the items. Making a variety of responses seems quite a useful indication that the child is actively trying to work out what the correct answer might be — and, therefore, what the rule is.

So how do learners learn that counting is done to find out how many there are? There seems to be no single answer to this. One way is for adults to explain it and model it for them. Another is to make the connection using small sets which the learner is able to visually recognise. Thus, they can see that there are two items and when they count the last number reached is also two. Again, this suggests that learners might best learn about counting using small groups of items. Teachers need to measure progress by what they can do and in which contexts rather than focusing on how many numbers the learner knows.

Having learnt that counting is a tool for finding out 'how many', learners then have to learn to use the skill to solve problems. The challenge of this is reflected in the relative difficulty of learning to use counting to make sets. Developmentally this is a considerably more advanced task than being able to count a given set and tell you how many there are. To make a set, one has to hold the target number in mind while counting out items, mentally comparing each number said with the target number. One also has to keep in mind what the requirements of the 'task' are. Learners with SLD can take a while to learn to use counting in this way – the task is suddenly more difficult. Again, it is likely that keeping set sizes small best helps learners. This difficulty also reflects the partial understanding that learners may have of counting. Research with typically developing five and six year olds has shown that many are confused if asked how many items there would be if we counted starting at the opposite end of the set or if we counted alternate ones and then came back and counted all the rest. Gelman (1982) has termed this understanding the order-irrelevance principle, the understanding that it does not matter what order items are counted in, the number remains the same. This demonstrates how important it is that we do not always expose learners to the same conditions for counting as, inadvertently, we may be limiting their developing understanding.

Simple arithmetic

Counting is also an important tool for adding and subtracting. It is important that these arithmetic skills are underpinned by an understanding of the process. One method of introducing these skills is to encourage the child to mentally represent the process. A seminal study by Martin Hughes (1986) involving bricks in a closed tin has been developed and adapted by others to form an informal addition and subtraction activity. The tin, bag or box is shown to the child with a small number of items in, say, one or two bricks. The child then sees the addition, or indeed subtraction, of items by an adult and, without being able to see the result, has to say how many items there are now in the container. Research with children whose counting skills are poor provides surprisingly accurate results as they are required by this procedure to visualise 'the sum'. Notably the task draws on earlier visual spatial skills of magnitude representation rather than being a language-based task of counting. The task prompts an understanding of the inverse relationship between subtraction and addition, which will underpin their acquisition of more formal procedures.

Again we have seen the importance of introducing concepts through the use of small numbers of items that learners can mentally represent visually. Hughes' studies have revealed how children succeed on this task and make the development to adding when the items have a concrete referent but are not actually there. For example, 'how many are two cups and one cup more' is solved well before learners can respond to 'how many is two and one,' a sum which makes little sense or meaning. Studies of children with learning difficulties suggest that they follow similar stages to typcially developing pupils in the development of their strategies for adding and subtracting, and that these are dependent on acquiring the underlying concepts. For example, in learning to count two sets of items, children initially count out each of the amounts to be added, the addendums, and then count all the items, starting from one. This is often referred to as '*counting all*'. It appears in part to reflect the child's ease with producing the count string for, as we shall see, the next strategy is to '*count on*' from the first addendum. Thus, if the learner was asked to add two beans and six beans, having counted out each set, he would then count on two… three, four five etc. Finally the learner comes to realise that it doesn't matter which order the addendums are summed, because the answer is the same, and with time will count on from the largest. In the above sum, therefore, the learner would add, six... seven, eight. Studies have suggested that this strategy is often elicited first where the sum includes adding one, for example adding one car and five cars (Baroody 1996).

Hanrahan and Newman (1996) suggest that the dot notation numerals can also support the transition to adding without the need for concrete items. Thus learners would be encouraged to place their pencil or finger on the dots in the symbol while adding two numbers. This, however, raises questions about whether pupils are able to generalise this method and in particular it may be counterproductive when encouraging learners to acquire strategies for subtraction. Indeed there is an argument to be made for carefully considering the introduction of symbols in adding and subtracting activities. It is likely that, for many learners, the relevance of these skills lie with their concrete application.

Research by Nye, Buckley and Bird (2005) has cautiously pointed to the efficacy of 'Numicon' a visual approach to teaching to support the development of early number concepts in children with Down syndrome and in particular the way that it enabled children to develop skills of calculation for the first time. Rather like Cuisenaire rods, Numicon, devised by Tony Wing, enables learners to understand number bonds – as they can physically put together shapes of different sizes together.

Conclusion

This chapter has emphasised the importance of devising activities that encourage learners to form a mental representation of number as a tool through which to anticipate, predict and problem solve. Instead of focusing purely on right answers we can shift attention to 'what happens if'. Rather than conceiving of number as something that is simply taught in a maths lesson, examples have been given that encourage the reader to think about developing activities that are underpinned by an understanding of how typically developing children progress while also being aware of the challenges for some learners. For many learners we need to consider building on other pathways. We can be guided by drawing on their strengths and interests, capitalising on both their engagement and the meaning. There have been a number of points in this chapter where 'sharing the task' has been suggested, or role reversal. In understanding how best to support the pupil we must also become the learner ourselves.

Questions for readers

- How far does your numeracy curriculum reflect the many stages to developing an awareness and understanding of number?
- What additional activities could you introduce to encourage learners to recognise number as a tool to anticipate, predict and problem solve in situations that are meaningful to them?
- What strategies can you introduce to support learners overcome some of the challenges they encounter and how would you then phase out their use?

References

Baroody, A.J. (1996) 'Self-Invented addition strategies by children with mental retardation', *American Journal on Mental Retardation*, 101(1): 72–89.

Cordes, S. and Brannon E.M. (2009) 'The relative salience of discrete and continuous quantity in young infants', *Developmental Science*, 12(3): 453–463.

Farragher, R. and Brown, R.I. (2005) 'Numeracy for adults with Down syndrome: it's a matter of quality of life', *Journal of Intellectual Disability Research*, 49(10): 761–765.

Feigenson, L. and Carey, S. (2003) 'Tracking individuals via object-files: evidence from infants' manual search', *Developmental Science*, 6(5): 568–584.

Feigenson, L. and Carey, S. (2005) 'On the limits of infants' quantification of small object arrays', *Cognition*, 97: 295–313.

Fuson, K., Richards, J. and Briars, D.C. (1982) 'The acquisition and elaboration of the number-word sequence', in C.J. Brainerd (ed.) *Children's Logical and Mathematical Cognition*, Springer-Verlag: New York.

Gelman, R. (1982) 'Basic numerical abilities', in R.J. Sternberg (ed.) *Advances in the Psychology of Intelligence*, 1: 182–205.

Hanrahan, J. and Newman, T. (1996) 'Teaching addition to children', in B. Stratford and P. Gunn (eds) *New Approaches to Down Syndrome*, London: Cassell.

Hughes, M. (1986) *Children and Number*, Oxford: Blackwell.

McCrink, K. and Wynn, K. (2004) 'Large-number addition and subtraction by 9 month old infants', *Psychological Science*, 15(11): 776–781.

McEvoy, J. and McConkey, R. (1991) 'The performance of children with a moderate mental handicap on simple counting tasks', *Journal of Mental Deficiency Research*, 35: 446–458.

Nye, J., Buckley, S. and Bird, G. (2005) 'Evaluating the Numicon system as a tool for teaching number skills to children with Down syndrome', *Down Syndrome News and Update*, 5(1): 2–13.

Paterson, S.J., Girelli, L., Butterworth, B. and Karmiloff-Smith, A. (2006) 'Are numerical impairments syndrome specific? Evidence from Williams syndrome and Down's syndrome', *Journal of Child Psychology and Psychiatry*, 47(2): 190–204.

Porter, J. (1996) *A Study of Procedural and Conceptual Understanding of Counting by Pupils with Severe Learning Difficulties.* Unpublished PhD, University of London.

Porter J. (1999) 'The Attainments of Pupils with Severe Learning Difficulties on a Simple Counting and Error Detection Task', *Journal of Applied Research in Intellectual Disabilities*, 12(2): 87–99.

Porter, J. (2005a) 'Assessing awareness and coding of numerosity in children with severe and profound learning difficulties: three exploratory case studies', *British Journal of Learning Disabilities*, 33(1): 1–5.

Porter, J. (2005b) 'Severe learning difficulties', in A. Lewis and B. Norwich (eds) *Special Teaching for Special Children?* Maidenhead: Open University.

Porter, J. (2010) 'Developing number awareness and children with severe and profound learning difficulties', *SLD Experience*, 57: 3–7.

Wynn, K. (1992) 'Addition and subtraction by human infants', *Nature*, 358: 749–750.

31

PHYSICAL EDUCATION FOR ALL LEARNERS

Stephen Cullingford-Agnew with Anne Cradock, Chris Rollings,
Barbara Dowson and Hannah Brighton

In this chapter, the following questions will be addressed:

- Are all learners are able to effectively access a full range of physical education (PE) activities?
- What approaches can be used to engage learners?
- What opportunities for inclusive education are available?

The value of PE

When constructing a physical education (PE) curriculum, fundamentally you need to believe in the value of PE for all learners. The document 'Planning, Teaching and Assessing the Curriculum for Pupils with Learning Difficulties: PE' (QCA 2009) clearly explains the value of PE within the curriculum. PE can offer real opportunities for inclusion too, such as working with learners from other schools or colleges or with learners from another class. It just needs some careful thought, enthusiasm and preparation including a timely induction. In addition, PE offers opportunities to further develop a range of cross-curricular skills such as expressive and receptive language, mathematics and literacy, etc. Of course, there may be special considerations: for instance, ensuring all learners are provided with access to a range of opportunities involves finding sufficient time within the school curriculum; and for some learners this means allowing additional time for lifting and handling or other physical management activities.

In terms of encouraging general fitness, there is some research evidence for specific approaches used with learners with SLD/PMLD. For example, a study by Hinckson *et al.* (2013), using a specialist fitness programme for young people with learning difficulties, found that the participants ate less chocolate; had fewer hospital visits and fewer missed days in schools. Similarly, Tomporowski, Lambourne and Okumura (2011) found that physical activity interventions can optimise physical fitness, promote health-related behaviour that offset obesity and facilitate mental development. The FeelGood programme for children with autism, which was evaluated by Stockley (2010), was found to be effective for letting off steam, weight management and it was a fun way to practise social skills and learn life-long leisure pursuits.

Specialist approaches

There are a number of specialist approaches that can be used to enhance opportunities for all learners to engage in PE, some of which are described in this chapter. A particular influence was the work of Veronica Sherborne (2001). Much of Veronica's teaching was based around the work of Rudolph Laban, especially the motion factors into which all movements and expressions can be analysed. Laban himself recognised that four different aspects of how we move do not only distinguish movement. He states that: 'Movement is a feature of all man's activities... Through the movements of our bodies we can learn to relate the inner-self to the outer world' Laban (1963: 14–24). These additional elements involve communication, constructing relationships with others, developing self-confidence, self-knowledge and meeting social and emotional needs. Laban further developed theories of natural movement within young children, and he notes that living within an environment in which these are suppressed may adversely affect self-confidence, and diminish the ability to relate to the environment and to other people.

> The flow of movement fills all our functions and actions; it discharges us of detrimental inner tensions; it is a means of communication between people.
>
> (Laban 1963: 97)

Sherborne Developmental Movement (SDM)

SDM is applicable and accessible for all learners, including those at the earliest levels of development or those with sensory disabilities (Sherborne 2001). It enables learners to be active and helps them to build relationships and develop communication. It uses the movement of the bodies of caregivers (adult helpers and other learners) to develop support, using free-flow activities such as rocking from a caregiver or from one caregiver to another, building a rapport between partners and other elements such as communication, constructing relationships with others, self-confidence, self-knowledge and meeting social and emotional needs.

Veronica Sherborne used Laban's movement analysis to construct her theories on developmental movement (Sherborne 2001). Her developmental approach was built upon basic objectives:

- Awareness of self
    - Body awareness
    - Spatial awareness
    - Confidence in self and a positive self-image
- Awareness of others
    - Relationships with a partner
    - The three elements of relationships
    - Trust and confidence in self and others

Fundamentally, Veronica Sherborne developed a notion of relationships within movement:

- With – Relationships: the ability to contain, support and use free-flow and building a rapport between partners.
- Shared – Relationships: where partners alternately support each other and demonstrate confidence.
- Against – Relationships: to help the learner to focus, channel energy and develop determination.

Movement work, done with a partner or within small groups, focuses upon some of the following:

- Awareness of the ground – this includes lying, rolling, creeping, spinning, and falling and pushing.
- Awareness of the centre of the body – this includes rocking, being contained by a partner.
- Whole body experiences – this includes swinging (in blankets), rocking on backs, tunnels, sliding, maintaining a stable position against others, jumping and falling.
- Awareness of hips – includes sitting and spinning, spinning and falling, making bridges, rocking on hips, and pushing and pulling.

Initial sessions with learners might be short in duration, perhaps 10–15 minutes, or might not take place in a large hall but perhaps a smaller, more familiar environment. Sustaining an activity is not insisted upon; sometimes a reaction clearly demonstrates that the learner does not like the activity or will only tolerate it for short periods of time. Allowing time for the learner to realise that other learners are enjoying this activity might alleviate their anxiety or fear. Most of all the movement sessions are fun for all concerned and always look for ways of introducing creative and innovative ideas from the learners or adults. The teacher assesses the qualities of movement, however small, and skills are developed over a period of time. The teaching emphasis is on 'sensitivity' and 'observation'. Miles and Riggio (1999) note that having respect for the subtleties of learners' behaviour is a skill that we all should seek to develop.

Movement can be seen as a 'conversation' that goes back to the fundamental interactions between people or between a parent/carer and child. Many learners may need additional support to facilitate this conversation, e.g. physical guidance, augmentative communication systems, careful positioning, etc. It is the realisation that movement can be used to develop relationships and communication, in order to feel a sense of wholeness and not to be concerned only about the movement of separate parts of the body, that sets SDM apart from other approaches to PE.

SDM has been the subject of several small-scale evaluations. Konaka (2007) designed a structured approach to SDM specifically for 100 young people with autism and SLD. After his six-week programme, he found that there were definite improvements in eye contact, joint attention, shared experiences, attention span and turn taking. Marsden, Hare and Weston (2007) compared young children using SDM with a control group using typical PE found in the early years. The researchers found that although both programmes led to improvement in gross motor skills, social development improved more in the SDM programme. They attributed those gains to the partner work that is so important in SDM.

Halliwick Swimming

Halliwick Swimming is a based on known scientific principles of hydrostatics, hydrodynamics and body mechanics. It provides a fun and safe way of offering access to swimming that encourages water confidence and structures the teaching of swimming for all, especially those with physical and/or learning difficulties. Children and young people learn to swim and control their balance in water without the use of floatation aids. This development is promoted by a one to one assistant who supports the swimmer and provides minimal adjustable support during the swimming lesson. The water activities provided involve a series of group and individual games and activities that are based around a ten-point programme. An essential element is that the swimmer is always able to return to a safe, breathable position. Using the Halliwick 'concept' over many years, learners develop water confidence leading to independent swimming. Halliwick has similarities to SDM as it contains elements of group working, develops confidence in self and others and can be delivered at a pace that is consistent with the needs of the learner. The approach appears effective and it clearly motivates learners. The games and activities, while fun, also serve a purpose and are built around ten points that can be found on the Halliwick Association website. It is important that those using the Halliwick concept are fully trained and information about training can be found on the website.

Mortimer, Privopoulos and Kumar (2014) summarise research into Halliwick swimming and suggest that improvements in social interaction and behaviours for children with autism can be claimed, despite the small-scale nature of most of the research. One such study undertaken by Pan (2010) showed that a ten-week exercise swimming programme using Halliwick principles had not only effected physical fitness but also social competence.

Rebound Therapy

Rebound Therapy is the term used for the therapeutic use of a trampoline in order to develop and promote motor skills, body awareness, perceptual skills, movement co-ordination and communication. It can be a powerful and effective tool in education and therapy and a favourite activity for those who have the opportunity to access it. It is designed to accommodate learners' individual abilities and disabilities as well as previous experience, personal likes and dislikes. It makes a huge contribution to improving personal health and fitness and to forming trusting relationships and communication skills with difficult to reach pupils. Developed initially in the UK by Eddy Anderson over four decades ago, it has been widely applied to children and adults with SLD/PMLD in the education and healthcare domains.

Rebound Therapy has to be seen in action to truly appreciate the impact it makes on youngsters' movement development, their ability to accept direction, motivation and potential to communicate using symbols, sign language, social cause and effect and speech. Those interested in sensory integration activities or Intensive Interaction (see Chapter 26) will find so many parallels with the therapeutic work in Rebound Therapy. It goes beyond a physical intervention tool; used wisely it can also promote concept development and physical learning. At its best it needs to be used regularly, at least weekly, to build up and sustain the muscle memory and movement vocabulary for individuals.

Based upon the therapeutic effects of vibration, Rebound Therapy stimulates the body producing remarkable effects. It can reduce high muscle tone and can stimulate the tone of those learners with low tone. It can fatigue learners with high levels of energy and bring down their high arousal levels, thus allowing them to move from the trampoline to compatible activities with much more success. It can help support learners with complex healthcare needs and ensure that their airway management and lungs are kept in good condition. It can help relax learners and reduce anxiety and provide a safety valve for learners with a range of emotional and behavioural needs. It is not unusual to come across non-communicating learners who have been actually motivated to use speech on the trampoline in order to gain physical vestibular rewards such as high bouncing or fun activities over physio balls on the trampoline.

Rebound Therapy is quite complex and must only be undertaken by coaches who have completed an accredited Rebound Therapy training course. The training allows the coaches to assess and write individual programmes for a range of learners moving from basic positional and passive stretching work through to the early stages of trampolining skills. Once experienced, never forgotten!

Elements

The Elements course was developed, and delivered, by those working with young disabled people with profound and multiple impairments. The course was initially based around facilitated workshops designed to provide practical ideas and strategies around physical activity for staff working with young people who have profound and multiple impairments. It was developed by the Youth Sport Trust and a working group of practitioners. This programme has been devised to meet the needs of learners with PMLD. Training is provided through the Hardian School, Newcastle (www.headstraining.co.uk/trainingcourses). It is the intention that these activities provide a link between other existing and excellent programmes devised by Flo Longhorn (www.flolonghorn.com/index.php/flo-publications) and Veronica Sherborne (2001).

EARTH – games-based activities

- Sensory environment encouraging individual reaction and movement.
- Supported interaction developing basic skills.
- Group settings to promote participation, anticipation and interaction.

Examples of these would be:

- Sensory Gazebo – create an environment in the classroom, school hall or outside where a theme is followed through, for example taking ideas from travel brochures of a country.
- Marbles – place a row or line of circle of plastic space markers with balls of different colour, size and texture on top of each. One at a time alternating players around the circle, or teams at opposite ends of the centre line, throw balls, or aim using a ramp and Boccia Balls, to knock a ball off the marker. Keep any balls knocked off to keep personal or group score.

WATER – water-based activities

- Promoting confidence and relaxation.
- Achieving stillness and balance.
- Stimulating movement and independence.

Examples of these would be:

- Turbulent Gliding – the swimmer, floating on their back, is assisted to move by the helper providing turbulence under their shoulder blades. (c.f. Halliwick swimming)
- Whirlpool – this is created by the group moving in a circle. Swimmers take it in turns, one at a time, floating on their back in the centre of the Whirlpool to be swirled around.
- Treasure Hunt or Relay Challenges – objects are placed on the poolside for swimmers to collect. A variety of objects with different colours, textures, scents, etc. Swimmers may move independently or be assisted.

AIR – Outdoor adventure

- Preparation of learners and staff.
- Specific equipment considerations.
- Supporting and encouraging.

Examples of theses would be:

- Sensory Trail – making use of the journey from classroom to dining hall or the hydrotherapy pool. Objects of reference are found en route to prompt the learners about the activity coming next, following a colour trail, made from arrows or coloured ribbons or ropes, to objects such as arm bands, swimming costume, pool toys, shampoo, etc.
- Come Outside – explore the school grounds which vary with the season (trees, leaves, flowers, fruit, etc.), the time of day, the weather; explore shadows; use the wind; listen to the rain on gazebo roof, under an umbrella etc. There are links with the Forest Schools programmes (www.forestschools.com) which encourage learners to become comfortable with an outdoor approach to education and play both in familiar surroundings but also in woodland settings.

FIRE – Dance and movement

- Using movement, sound and vibration to direct big movements
- Assisted and directed movement
- Self-expression and independent movement

Examples would be:

- Folk Dance, Meet and Greet, Turn and Travel – learners explore ways of meeting and greeting (high fives, shake hands, fist to fist), turning with a partner (two hands, linked arms, over and over, under one arm, etc.), travelling with a partner (side by side linking arms, following, facing holding two hands, back to back, etc.). Then they create a reel, e.g. facing partner, meet and greet of choice twice, forwards, backwards and repeat, top couple travel down the set while everyone else claps and move up, then everyone turns their partner twice on the spot; repeat until original top couple are back at the top.
- I Am Me – body part awareness songs (e.g. Heads and Shoulders, Tony Chestnut (Touch Toe, Knee, Chest, Head, etc.). Any action songs that are age appropriate and can be signed along with the singing; DJ version for older students.

Riding for the disabled – therapeutic horse riding

Another specialist approach where there is some evidence of efficacy is therapeutic horse riding, which not only focuses on the therapeutic nature of riding but also the development of a relationship between horse and rider. Although Davies *et al.* (2009) found no clinically significant impact on the physical skills of children with cerebral palsy, some of the families in the study did feel that horse riding was beneficial to their children.

The Riding for the Disabled Association (RDA) has a motto: 'It's what you can do that counts.' The motto speaks for itself and is at the core of what RDA does. RDA, founded in 1969, has 489 member groups across the UK who help disabled people, throughout the spectrum, to take part in riding, carriage driving and vaulting activities. The aim is to give each rider the chance to gain therapeutic benefits and provide enjoyment and opportunity to achieve. It is fun, it is character building, it is sociable and it is therapeutic. Self-esteem is enhanced and the equestrian disciplines and games of which there are many provide the opportunity.

'Hippotherapy' use the movements of a horse to provide kinaesthetic experiences for learners, allowing for hands-on learning. Within therapeutic riding activities, elements of hippotherapy can be included in the form of games and exercises in order to improve learners' fitness and posture. Even when the concepts of horseback riding for people with disabilities were being introduced in the 1960s, the exercises being used were designed to 'give the rider confidence, a sense of balance and co-ordination, and teach him how to use his body and muscles naturally, with the minimum amount of force or tension' (Davies 1967: 68). Many of these exercises, or elements from them, are used in hippotherapy, therapeutic and 'riding for the disabled' classes today.

'Exergames'

There is some evidence to suggest that using computers to motivate learners to exercise can be helpful. For example, combining exercise with digital game play, known as 'exergames', has contributed to overall fitness (Staiano and Calvert 2011; Lin *et al.* 2010). The use of the Wii has been studied and results have shown that two learners with SLD and physical disabilities improved the duration of maintaining the correct standing position during balance games (Shih, Shi and Chu 2010). A larger study was carried out using the Wii with 105 children with Down syndrome and results show that the learners improved their sensorimotor function through the games using, for example, jumping, striking and catching (Wuang *et al.* 2011).

PE and Assessment for Learning (AFL)

> Assessment for Learning is the process of seeking and interpreting evidence for use by learners and their teachers, to identify where the learners are in their learning, where they need to go and how best to get there.
>
> (QCA Assessment Reform Group 2002: 2)

Developing the skills of observation and the collection of annotated evidence are crucial if we are to understand how learners are developing their skills and confidence in PE. A video clip, photograph or observation can all indicate progress but the key is annotation. This might include notes that demonstrate if a learner is responding with prompting or other forms of support or is using secure or established skills more confidently or independently and applying these skills in new contexts or settings or with different people.

The document 'Planning, Teaching and Assessing the Curriculum for Pupils with Learning Difficulties: PE' (QCA 2009) contains PE-specific P scales to support periodic and formative assessment. It provides a framework that may be used to map the progress of learners as part of the cycle of planning, teaching, learning and assessment; to acknowledge linear progress through the P levels but also opportunities for lateral progress within a P level. Consider how to capture comments or commentaries from learners themselves or from their peers. When making best-fit judgements using the P levels, teachers need to rely on annotation to take account of prior attainment, the levels of support, modelling or prompting learners receive and other contextual issues that might influence learning and responses. Factor in the effects of the barriers to learning experienced by learners and which learning contexts or type of environment offers most success. In this respect think about what motivates the learners and how to offer success at the same time as challenge in a sensitive manner.

In terms of observing learners, remember that it may not only be a direct observation of the activity that elicits or demonstrates progress but what a learner might do around the periphery of a group. An example of this comes from observation of a learner in a movement session at the end of her activity. She finished her turn and, while the adult was working with the next learner, she was observed to get up and make a very conscious effort to indicate that she wanted another go. This could have been missed or interpreted as challenging behaviour; instead it indicated a clear preference/choice in a way that was unusual for her and therefore represented some very important evidence about her ability to make a choice. Think about what it is about an adult or the way they work that guarantees a successful experience; think how these factors change the nature (and perhaps the level) of the learners' responses rather than merely enable the learners to participate.

Securing reliable judgements through moderation

There is no single way of securing reliable judgements, but assessment-focused discussions are key to making consistent and secure judgements. As a teacher of PE, you will need to give some thought to the prior knowledge of learners (which P level is secure? which is emerging?) and what overall level are you considering. Consider developing over time individual learner portfolios of evidence or developing a PE subject portfolio which provides exemplars for others who teach PE.

Using assessment information

Remember that the key purpose of assessment is to inform teaching and promote further learning. Having assessed learner progress through the moderation process, consider how to use assessment information to inform learning and teaching and embed this into everyday practice. Identify the strengths, needs and interests of the learners and the conditions that enable successful learning to take place. Remember that PE will also be a vehicle that provides progress information about other subject areas; try not to miss these rich opportunities.

Continuing professional development training and PE

An important aspirational target, supported by the National College for Teaching and Learning (NCTL), an agency for the English Department for Education, would be to offer all Initial Teacher Education (ITE) trainees an opportunity to undertake a placement within a special school. This is becoming particularly important as special schools struggle to appoint teachers with some experience within a special school context and the need to recognise and value training on SEND (special educational needs and disabilities). As an example, PE specialists studying at the University of Northampton undertook a half-day placement over four weeks in a special school which was designated to meet the educational needs of primary aged pupils with severe and profound multiple learning difficulties, autism, multi-sensory impairment and physical difficulties. Other students on the one-year post-graduate certificate in education course were provided with a one-week placement in a special school and students on a BA degree course leading to qualified teacher status had a four-week placement. Importantly, students were provided with an induction programme prior to the placement, which is a vital element if it is to be successful. It also included a DVD made by a special school and the university, introducing the school and showing the learners working in different activities, including PE and swimming.

One student commented: 'It is just amazing how little you know until you get to experience it yourself' and 'I have more confidence working with children who have SEN/D which will help in my other placements'. The student comments demonstrate their positive attitudes towards the placement and, even though it was time limited, it impacted upon their confidence and understanding of working with learners with SEN/D which was an inspiration.

Resources

There are now many websites that contain resources specifically designed so that learners can access PE. Websites for Sport England, Speed Agility Quickness (SAQ), and other organisations contain information and resources to provide access to PE. A resource for all phases is the document 'Success for All: an inclusive approach to PE and school sport' produced by the Department for Education and Science (2003) in conjunction with the English Federation of Disability Sports, the QCA, and the Youth Sport Trust and Inclusion. The resource and CD-ROM contains a wide range of resources for PE teachers in primary, secondary and special schools. The CD contains nine case studies, filmed in mainstream and special schools around the country, and other audio and text resources including information related to many different PE activities, such as swimming, dance, gymnastics, etc., and lesson plans. EQUALs, a national charity that has now been offering its services to schools for 20 years, has developed a scheme of work for PE written by teachers who have expertise in special education and PE (EQUALs 2007). Details about the scheme of work, as well as 'best practice workshops' in PE, including SDM, Rebound Therapy, etc., are available on the EQUALs website.

Questions for readers

- Is PE truly for all?
- How can you differentiate or modify activities so that all learners are able to make progress and access PE?
- Do you provide sufficient time to enable movement conversations to take place within the context of PE?

Useful websites

EQUALs: http://equals.co.uk/
Flo Longhorn Publications: www.flolonghorn.com
Forest Schools programmes: www.forestschools.com
Halliwick Association of Swimming Therapy: www.halliwick.org.uk
Rebound Therapy: http://reboundtherapy.org.uk
Riding for the Disabled Association: www.rda.org.uk
Sherborne Association UK: www.sherbornemovementuk.org/
Speed agility quickness: www.saqinternational.com/ (please note that there are many website links to a variety of organisations)
Sport England: www.sportengland.org

References

Davies, J. (1967) *The Reins of Life: An instructional and informative manual on riding for the disabled*, 1st edn, London: J.A. Allen & Co.

Davis, E., Davies, B., Wolfe, R., Raadsveld, R., Heine, B., Thomason, P. and Graham, H.K. (2009) 'A randomized controlled trial of the impact of therapeutic horse riding on the quality of life, health, and function of children with cerebral palsy', *Developmental Medicine & Child Neurology*, 51(2): 111–119.

Department for Education Science (2003) *Success for All – an inclusive approach to PE and school sport*, Nottingham: DfES.

EQUALS (2007) *Schemes of Work for the National Curriculum for pupils with learning difficulties: Preview Physical Education*, Tyne and Wear: EQUALS.

Hinckson, E. A., Dickinson, A., Water, T., Sands, M. and Penman, L. (2013) 'Physical activity, dietary habits and overall health in overweight and obese children and youth with intellectual disability or autism', *Research in Developmental Disabilities*, 34(4): 1170–1178.

Konaka, J. (2007) 'Developing social engagement through movement', in E. Marsden and J. Egerton (eds) *Moving with Research: Evidence-based practice in Sherborne Development Movement*, Clent: Sunfield Publications.

Laban, R. (1963) *Modern Educational Dance*, 2nd edn, revised by L. Ullmann. London: MacDonald and Evans. (First published 1948).

Lin, J.D., Lin, P.Y., Lin, L.P., Chang, Y.Y., Wu, S.R. and Wu, J.L. (2010) 'Physical activity and its determinants among adolescents with intellectual disabilities', *Research in Developmental Disabilities*, 31(1): 263–269.

Longhorn, F. (2014) 'I.E. Info Exchange Magazine', retrieved August 2014 from www.flolonghorn.com/index.php/flo-publications.

Marsden, E., Hare, M. and Weston, C. (2007) 'Improving the movement vocabulary and social development of children in the early years', in E. Marsden and J. Egerton (eds) *Moving with Research: evidence-based practice in Sherborne Development Movement*, Clent: Sunfield Publications.

Miles, B. and Riggio, M. (1999) *Remarkable Conversations*, Massachusetts: Perkins School for the Blind.

Mortimer, R., Privopoulos, M. and Kumar, S. (2014) 'The effectiveness of hydrotherapy in the treatment of social and behavioral aspects of children with autism spectrum disorders: a systematic review', *Journal of Multidisciplinary Healthcare*, 7, 93.

Pan, C.Y. (2010) 'Effects of water exercise swimming program on aquatic skills and social behaviors in children with autism spectrum disorders', *Autism*, 14(1): 9–28.

QCA (Qualifications and Curriculum Authority) (2002) *School Based Assessment: Assessment for learning: research into practice*, London: QCA.

QCA (Qualifications and Curriculum Authority) (2009) *Planning, Teaching and Assessing the Curriculum for Pupils with Learning Difficulties – PE*, London: QCA.

Sherborne, V. (2001) *Developmental Movement for Children*, Duffield: Worth Publishing.

Shih, C.H., Shih, C.T. and Chu, C. L. (2010) 'Assisting people with multiple disabilities actively correct abnormal standing posture with a Nintendo Wii balance board through controlling environmental stimulation', *Research in Developmental Disabilities*, 31(4): 936–942.

Staiano, A.E. and Calvert, S.L. (2011) 'Exergames for PE courses: physical, social, and cognitive benefits', *Child Development Perspectives*, 5(2): 93–98.

Sterba, J., Rogers, B., France, A. and Vokes, D. (2002) 'Horseback riding in children with cerebral palsy: effect on gross motor function', *Developmental Medicine & Child Neurology*, 44: 301–308.

Stockley, C. (2010) 'The FeelGood PE programme: designing an autism-friendly PE curriculum in a residential school setting', *Good Autism Practice (GAP)*, 11(2), 18–26.

Tomporowski, P. D., Lambourne, K. and Okumura, M. S. (2011) 'Physical activity interventions and children's mental function: an introduction and overview', *Preventive Medicine*, 52: S3–S9.

Wuang, Y. P., Chiang, C. S., Su, C. Y. and Wang, C. C. (2011) 'Effectiveness of virtual reality using Wii gaming technology in children with Down syndrome', *Research in Developmental Disabilities*, 32(1), 312–321.

32

DRAMA EDUCATION FOR LEARNERS WITH SLD/PMLD

Daisy Loyd and Peter Danco

In this chapter, the following questions will be addressed:

- What is drama education?
- Why is drama education important for learners with SLD/PMLD?
- How can drama be used to develop performance work with learners?
- How can the teaching style from drama education be applied in other areas of the curriculum?

Introduction

Drama is an art form in which the defining feature is 'enactment' (acting out) with the purpose of making and sharing meanings. It is about making sense of the world and encapsulating the interpretation of experience by drawing on performance practices derived from theatre. Drama is focused towards an audience – comprising peers, the class teacher or visitors to a production – and the response of the audience forms an important part of the process. Making and sharing meanings through drama involve interaction, flexible thinking and engagement in make-believe which can be particularly challenging for learners with severe, profound and multiple learning difficulties (SLD/PMLD), many of whom have additional communication and interaction problems including autism. This chapter considers approaches to enable this group of learners to participate meaningfully in drama education.

What is drama education?

In both mainstream and special schools, drama plays an important cultural role. Drama productions, whether they are annual or more frequent, provide an opportunity to bring the school community together and showcase talent. However, drama's status in schools as a subject and learning medium varies considerably. It depends very much on school ethos and individual teaching styles, as well as the extent to which the government in power values drama as a subject and learning medium that can promote creativity and learning. 'Drama education' refers to drama as an educational subject area where the focus is on learning about performance practices in preparation for a shared performance (Hornbrook 1998; Neelands 1984; Winston

334

and Tandy 2001). Since the introduction of the National Curriculum in 1988, drama as an educational subject area sits within English where it is considered to have an important role in the development of communication, particularly spoken language (Department for Education 2013a, 2013b). The drama element is compulsory for maintained schools, which means learners educated in England in maintained mainstream and special schools are supposed to engage with drama at some level and guidance has been developed for teachers to facilitate drama with learners with special educational needs (Department for Education & Science 2005). 'Drama-in-education' refers to drama as an enlivening teaching tool and learning medium that can be used across the curriculum, and does not need a formal performance element (Bolton 1984; Heathcote 1984; Peter 2003). It uses improvisation and conventions derived from theatre to bring a 'living through' quality to enable exploration within a fictitious context of aspects relating to human experience, for example to bring to life themes in history, geography and religious education (see Park 2004 and Peter 1995 for examples). Drama education and drama-in-education (also known as 'process drama') are approaches to working with drama within an educational framework. This contrasts with 'drama therapy' which is the intentional use of drama to meet specific psychological and therapeutic needs (Leigh *et al.* 2012). Although there are overlaps between drama approaches, this chapter is about drama education to develop performance work with learners with SLD/PMLD, including those with autism.

Why is drama education important for learners with SLD/PMLD?

Making and sharing meaning through drama is a uniquely human experience and an important part of cultural life. With this in mind, the importance and relevance of drama education for learners with SLD/PMLD is broader than its current place in the National Curriculum implies. Drama education enables learners with SLD/PMLD to participate in a uniquely human experience, which Ware (1994: 72) suggests should be a core aim in choosing activities for this group of learners. It also provides a context in which this group of learners can participate in cultural life and be given the opportunity to develop and use 'creative, artistic and intellectual potential, not only for their own benefit, but also for the enrichment of society' (United Nations 2006).

In addition to a cultural argument for the importance of drama education with learners with SLD/PMLD, there is a developmental argument. Typically, developing children learn about the social world through interaction and engagement in make-believe with others (Rieber and Carton 1993; Trevarthen 1995; Vygotsky 1976) whereas those with SLD/PMLD may not do so spontaneously (Jarrold 2003; Jordan and Powell 1995). Vygotsky highlights the importance of interaction with more capable others to stimulate development. He explains the process of learning through interaction with a concept he refers to as 'the zone of proximal development' (ZPD) which operates on the principle that what an individual can do with help today, they can do independently tomorrow (Vygotsky 1978: 86). Vygotsky observed particular opportunities from interaction in a social play context where there is engagement in make-believe. Firstly, it can help an individual learn to act independently from immediate perception and detach word meanings from their objects and actions. This supports an understanding of how representation and symbolism works. Secondly, it can raise self-awareness and self-control because an individual becomes consciously aware of their own actions and aware that every object and action has a meaning. Thirdly, it can encourage an individual to create their own ZPD where their behaviours are seen to be more advanced than they are typically. This is because in make-believe an individual can imitate cultural conventions, explore them and push boundaries (Vygotsky 1976). Drama education supports learners with SLD/PMLD to participate in interactive and make-believe contexts and potentially enjoy the same benefits as typically developing learners.

Empirical evidence relating to outcomes from drama, both with typically developing learners and learners with SEN, is limited (Anderson and Donelan 2009; Jindal–Snape and Vettriaino 2007; Kempe 2011). It is also very challenging to capture the complexity of interactions in drama and attribute accurately change to activities in a drama context (Jindal–Snape and Vettriaino 2007; Mitchell and van der Gaag 2001). However, case studies and small-scale studies show that in drama activities learners with SLD/PMLD can be supported to interact, think flexibly and engage in make-believe spontaneously (Clethero 2001; Loyd 2011; Mitchell and van der Gaag 2001; Park 1998; Peter 2009; Sherratt 2002). Sherratt and Peter (2002) draw on findings from neuroscience to explain positive responses by this group of learners in drama. They contend that the emotional engagement in drama activities has the potential to stimulate the amygdala which is the part of the brain responsible for processing and evaluating meaning. This part of the brain has been found to be under-functioning in learners with autism (Damasio 2003; Ramachandran 2003).

How can drama be used to develop performance work with learners?

Depending on the context, dedicated drama sessions may form part of the literacy/English curriculum or be part of a vocational curriculum such as *OCR Life and Living Skills* where units include engaging in creative activities and taking part in a performance (OCR 2013). Learners are also able to work towards personalised goals that may relate to social interaction, communication or flexible thinking.

When drama is a subject in its own right, it involves learning about performance practices and working towards a performance or culminating activity. Learning about performance practices includes building group awareness; sharing and showing to others; responding to the work of others; learning about facial expressions and body language; playing drama and movement games and practising different drama and movement techniques. Working towards a performance or culminating activity includes deciding what to perform; building movement sequences and scenes; rehearsing movement sequences and scenes and performing in front of an audience whether this is the teacher, the school or a wider audience. The idea of a performance with a group of learners with SLD/PMLD can raise challenging questions. What is the purpose of the performance? Is it to showcase the learning and the talents of the learners involved? Can this learning and these talents be appreciated if, as Kuppers argues, 'when disabled people perform, they are often not primarily seen as performers, but as disabled people' (Kuppers 2001: 26). These questions can make some practitioners feel uneasy and their hesitance often depends on the nature of the audience. However, working towards a performance or culminating activity is a valuable motivator for both teachers and learners, and can be a celebration of the community. Importantly, it should be a way of drawing together and reflecting the skills of learners and the art that they are able to create using their skills and interests. If a performance is being worked towards, it can be more meaningful if it is developed with the learners rather than imposed upon them. This can be done in three ways. Firstly, the theme of the performance can draw on learner interests. Secondly, the framework for the script or sequences can be tailored to the learners by drawing on their interests and the ways in which they communicate. Thirdly, when the performance is being put together, teachers can draw on learner feedback to incorporate suggestions and use how learners respond to shape the script and sequences.

Whatever the content of drama sessions, consistency in structure is important so that learners can identify the session as drama and become familiar with it. This then allows for flexibility within each component of the structure. The structure can be introduced to the group at the beginning of each session and it can be supported by the use of visuals. The following five-step structure can be used as a guide.

- **Step 1 – sit as a group:** The teacher welcomes the learners and asks them to sit in a circle on the floor.
- **Step 2 – greeting:** The teacher shakes hands with each learner and greets them to the class. This is important for acknowledging and reinforcing who is in the group.
- **Step 3 – warm-up/drama and movement games:** Led by the teacher, at least one warm-up and game before moving onto the main drama activity helps to relax learners, get their attention, build group awareness and establish a safe and secure environment. Examples include walking around the room and incorporating 'as if' ways of moving or passing a bean bag around the group adding in modifications such as changing pace (see Peter 1994 and McCurrach and Darnley 1999 for further examples).
- **Step 4 – drama activity:** The teacher engages learners in a drama activity that focuses on learning about performance practices or working towards a performance. The activity may be a whole-group activity, small group or one-to-one activity with learners taking it in turns to perform and be in the audience. Drama activities need to be structured carefully with teachers working sensitively to enable meaningful participation.
- **Step 5 – reflection and relaxation:** The teacher closes the session by bringing the learners back together as a group and reflecting on the session either by recapping on activities or by asking learners individually how they feel about the session. The teacher then turns the lights down, puts music on quietly and asks the learners to relax for a few minutes.

Two examples from practice with learners with SLD and a diagnosis of autism show how drama can be used to develop performance work.

Learning about performance practices where the goal is for learners to improvise a performance using parameters

The teacher brings together a group of learners and they sit on the floor in a circle. She explains that each learner is going to show a performance with some music and a piece of fabric that they can choose. The teacher demonstrates by choosing some music and a piece of fabric and then in the centre of the circle she performs an improvised sequence to the group in which she uses the fabric in different ways. She spins around and wafts the fabric over the learners, she wraps the fabric around her as if it is a dress and she puts it over her head as if she is a ghost. All the time she talks through the movements and actions she is doing to explain them. The teacher finishes the performance when the music finishes. She asks who in the group would like to go first. On gaining a response, she explains the task again and asks each learner to perform in turn. She supports the learners where necessary starting with open questions such as, 'What can you do with the fabric?' and moving on to choices where an open question may be more difficult, 'You could put it on your head or drop it on the floor'. She gives encouragement to the learners throughout their performance reinforcing what they are doing or saying and encourages the group to clap at the end of each performance in recognition of each learner's contribution. The teacher extends the task in future sessions by grouping learners together in twos or threes to create a performance with the same parameters.

In this example, the teacher challenges the learners to think flexibly and create their own performance but she gives clear parameters and guidance to help them meet this challenge. This is an important part of the teaching style in drama education and for learners with SLD/PMLD it can present opportunities for them to develop their thinking and ways of expressing themselves.

Preparing one learner for a performance

Richard is an active young man who could be described as having severe autism as well as profound learning difficulties. He appears unresponsive and unable to follow verbal guidance. In order to engage Richard with something that is meaningful for him, the teacher reminds himself of Richard's interests listed as 'likes' in his behavioural support plan. One of the likes is Richard's deep interest in the boy band 'N Sync and the teacher suggests he uses this as the basis of his performance. To develop Richard's performance, the teacher projects a video clip of an 'N Sync song on the wall using an iPad and a mini projector. Richard is then asked to stand in front of the projection and copy the movements of the band singing the song. Richard's performance is built incrementally and enhanced through repetition as well as the teacher giving positive encouragement and modelling steps for him, 'I like the way you do this'. Richard's peers are encouraged to clap at the end of each performance. As sessions progress, Richard becomes more aware of the audience responding to their applause with excitement and the audience becomes an additional motivator for him to perform. As Richard's movements become more precise, the projection is gradually withdrawn. Richard is subsequently introduced to a variety of performing environments in which to perform the movements independently and experience being a 'live' performer showcasing his talents and interests.

In this example, the teacher uses the learner's interest as the basis for engaging the learner in a performance activity. Through this interest the learner is able to be supported to develop a dance performance and perform it in front of others. In the process of creating and performing the dance, the learner develops his awareness of his own actions and of the fact that he is performing to others.

Both of these examples have highlighted aspects of the teaching style in drama education, which deserve closer attention. This teaching style has parallels with interactive educational approaches and interventions such as Intensive Interaction (Nind and Hewett 1994), music therapy (Berger 2002) and Integrated Play Groups (Wolfberg and Schuler 1993) and fits within the SPELL framework for learners with autism – structure, positive, empathy, low arousal, links with parents (Mills 1999; Siddles, Mills and Collins 1997). However, research focusing on aspects of the teaching style that elicit and/or enable interaction and flexible thinking with learners with autism has revealed that it has distinctive components which emerge from drama being a group activity that engages and develops the contributions of different learners for performance purposes (Loyd 2011). The teaching style includes:

1   **Flexibility within structure which is enhanced by the presence of an audience:** Sessions are structured but there is flexibility in the structure which results from both teachers adapting how they develop work according to learner contributions and the impact that an audience – in the form of teachers, peers and/or visitors – has on learner performance and response.

2 **Teaching through the action of the whole body:** Teaching is active in drama with learning taking place through 'doing' in a safe and secure environment. This means learners can experience abstract concepts and make-believe scenarios in a physical way, use their bodies to represent ideas and as Grove and Park (2001) contend, understanding can emerge through that experience.

3 **Employing a wide variety of modes of communication:** Drama is a multimodal, multi-sensory activity (Baldwin and Fleming 2003; Longhorn 2000) in which teachers can use a variety of modes of communication including gaze, gesture, movement/stance and speech as well as physical props and music which in turn provide learners with different pathways through which to access and engage with activities.

4 **Balancing interests and competencies of individual learners and the group:** Teachers in drama engage with learner interests and competencies balancing those of individual learners and the group to shape warm-up activities, drama and movement games and performances. Engaging with learner interests is an important motivator for learners with SLD/PMLD and provides an opportunity for teachers to build on an individual's prior experience, broaden their interests into useful activities and preserve the real of their experience (Jordan and Jones 1999).

5 **Using performance to enhance learning:** The process of learning in drama education is interactive with the notion of performance adding dimensions of interaction between the learner as a performer ('I am performing'), between performers in a performance ('I am performing with others') and with the audience during a performance ('I am performing to others'). This interaction can raise self-awareness and self-control in the way Vygotsky (1976) suggests occurs in social play and can help learners remember themselves as part of an activity and consider themselves in relation to others as part of that activity.

6 **Challenging learners and supporting them in their learning:** Teachers challenge learners in drama and then 'scaffold' them to meet challenges using approaches that encourage flexible thinking and using their own ideas. Scaffolding approaches include instructions with multiple steps, open questions and modelling. These approaches exemplify Vygotsky's notion of working within a ZPD and supports learners in moving from concrete thinking to abstract thinking, raising self-awareness and self-control and creating their own ZPD which are key features of social play (Vygotsky 1976, 1978).

7 **Harnessing group trust:** Trust plays an important role in drama, both between teachers and learners and within the group. Trust needs to be based on mutual respect and involves teachers having high expectations of learners, presuming competence and allowing them to learn in their own way (Kasa-Hendrickson 2005). Group trust is harnessed by the teacher coordinating group and collaborative activities and allowing more experienced learners to set an example and support less experienced learners in paired and group activities.

How can the teaching style in drama education be applied in other areas of the curriculum?

There are valuable examples of drama as a learning medium across the curriculum for those with SLD/PMLD (Grove 2005; Park 2004; Peter 1994, 1995). These focus on enabling learners to access different areas of the curriculum and promote early communication and social understanding. The examples given below consider how the teaching style in drama education described in the previous section can be applied in other areas of the curriculum. The examples focus on literacy and numeracy and developing concepts of letter and shape through drama, again with learners with SLD and a diagnosis of autism.

Signing one's own name

Marcus is a learner with developing fine motor skills and limited understanding of conventional verbal communication who likes dance and music. Marcus is able to vocalise some sounds such as letters M, P, B and most of the vowels. The main objective for the lesson is to explore the letter shapes of his name using local and general body movements and perform it to the group. Local movements are movements related to a body part rather than a whole body.

Marcus is given instructions to recognise his own name from three options so the teacher is challenging Marcus and then supporting him to achieve the task. Marcus is then asked to spell his name while he is encouraged to make sounds with the help of a variety of modes of communication including a feather, a voice recorder and verbal and gestural prompts.

Marcus is subsequently encouraged to shape the letters of his name by taping it onto a mirror in the dance room. The teacher gives visual demonstrations of the next step and traces the letters taped on the mirror using his index finger. To encourage understanding of the task the teacher sticks a piece of the same tape on the index finger nail. Once Marcus is able to trace the letters with less support he is asked to do the same from different locations in the room. The further step is to transfer the tape to different body parts such as knee, elbow and forehead, and use these to trace the taped letters through local movement. The taped name is then transferred onto the floor and Marcus is encouraged to walk on it and trace it. The level of visual and verbal support is then withdrawn gradually until Marcus can trace his own name independently and perform it to the group.

Identifying geometrical shapes

A group of young learners are learning about geometrical shapes. They have limited abilities to associate names with corresponding shapes when learning through conventional table-based tasks. They also do not seem to be motivated to sit at a table and work on worksheets. The teacher is knowledgeable about what motivates the group. Tractors and cars seem to be motivators that the group has in common. The teacher introduces large cardboard cut-outs of cars and tractors and places them around the room. He then shows the learners cardboard shapes of triangles, squares, rectangles and circles and asks the learners to put these on the cars and tractors. Modelling the task, the teacher instructs the learners to trace the shape of the wheels with fingers, elbows and different body parts so they have to think flexibly about how to trace the shapes. Once practised, the teacher adds verbalisations and shouts out 'circle' every time the learners trace the wheels. This is repeated several times. The learners are encouraged to verbalise 'circle' while on task so they associate the name with the shape. Once the learners seem to have understood the task, the same exercise is repeated while relating to triangles, rectangles and squares. The task culminates in 'the shape game' where a shape or name of a shape is shown or shouted out by the teacher and learners are asked to trace the corresponding shape with various body parts depending on the individual skills and understanding of each participating learner.

In these examples, the teacher engages learners through a variety of modes of communication. He encourages them to experience the concepts of letter and shape in a physical way and think flexibly about how to trace them with different parts of their body. This physical approach helps the learners to access areas of learning that are otherwise more difficult. Incorporating a performance element provides a route through which learners can rehearse their learning and demonstrate it to others.

Conclusion

Drama education and the teaching style within it offer opportunities for learners with SLD/PMLD to engage meaningfully with the curriculum. This supports in the challenging task of personalising learning approaches, making education more innovative and responsive to their needs and raising achievement for all learners (Humphrey and Lewis 2008). However, research about drama education with learners with SLD/PMLD continues to be behind other aspects of educational practice, and there is a need to understand more about how different groups of learners may access and engage in drama and the longer-term outcomes from doing so.

Questions for readers

- How is drama regarded in your setting?
- What strategies do teachers use in drama to enable learners with different needs to participate?
- How do learners with different needs respond in drama sessions? Where are there similarities and differences between learners?
- What do you observe as outcomes for learners with SLD/PMLD from participation in drama?

References

Anderson, M. and Donelan, K. (2009) 'Drama in schools: meeting the research challenges of the twenty-first century', *Research in Drama Education: The Journal of Applied Theatre and Performance*, 14: 165–171.

Baldwin, P., and Fleming, K. (2003) *Teaching Literacy through Drama: Creative approaches*, London: Routledge Falmer.

Berger, D. (2002) *Music Therapy, Sensory Integration and the Autistic Child*, London: Jessica Kingsley Publishers.

Bolton, G. (1984) *Drama as Education*, London: Longman.

Clethero, S. (2001) 'An exploration into creativity', *Good Autism Practice*, 2: 45–51.

Damasio, A.R. (2003) *Looking for Spinoza: Joy, sorrow and the feeling brain*, New York: Harcourt.

Department for Education (2013a) *National Curriculum in England: English programmes of study – key stages 1 and 2*, Available: www.gov.uk/government/uploads/system/uploads/attachment_data/file/260491/PRIMARY_national_curriculum_-_English_RS2.pdf (accessed 19 January 2014).

Department for Education (2013b) *National Curriculum in England: English programme of study – key stage 3*, Available: www.gov.uk/government/uploads/system/uploads/attachment_data/file/244215/SECONDARY_national_curriculum_-_English2.pdf (accessed 20 January 2014).

Department for Education & Science (2005) *Speaking, Listening, Learning: working with children who have special educational needs*, Norwich: HMSO.

Grove, N. (2005) *Ways into Literature: Stories, plays and poems for pupils with SEN*, London: David Fulton Publishers.

Grove, N. and Park, K. (2001) *Social Cognition through Drama and Literature for People with Learning Disabilities*, London: Jessica Kingsley Publishers.

Heathcote, D. (1984) *Collected Writings on Education and Drama*, London: Hutchinson.

Hornbrook, D. (1998) *Education and Dramatic Art*, London and New York: Routledge.

Humphrey, N. and Lewis, S. (2008) 'What does 'inclusion' mean for pupils on the autistic spectrum in mainstream secondary schools?', *Journal of Research in Special Educational Needs*, 8: 132–140.

Jarrold, C. (2003) 'A review of research into pretend play in autism', *Autism*, 7: 379–390.

Jindal-Snape, D. and Vettriaino, E. (2007) 'Drama techniques for the enhancement of social–emotional development in people with special needs: review of research', *International Journal of Special Education*, 22: 107–117.

Jordan, R. and Jones, G. (1999) *Meeting the Needs of Children with Autistic Spectrum Disorders*, London: David Fulton Publishers.

Jordan, R. and Powell, S. (1995) *Understanding and Teaching Children with Autism*, Chichester: Wiley.

Kasa-Hendrickson, C. (2005) 'There's no way this kid's retarded': teachers' optimistic constructions of students' ability', *International Journal of Inclusive Education*, 9: 55–69.

Kempe, A. (2011) 'Drama and the education of young people with special needs', in Schonmann, S. (ed.) *Key concepts in theatre/drama education*. Rotterdam: Sense Publishers.

Kuppers, P. (2001) 'Deconstructing images: Performing disability', *Contemporary Theatre Review*, 11: 25–40.

Leigh, L. Gersch, I. Dix, A. and Haythorne, D. (2012) *Dramatherapy with Children, Young People and Schools: Enabling creativity, sociability, communication and learning*, London: Routledge.

Longhorn, F. (2000) *Sensory Drama for Very Special People*, Bedfordshire: Catalyst Education Resources Limited.

Loyd, D. (2011) 'Perspective taking in individuals with autism in the interactive context of drama education', unpublished thesis, Institute of Education, University of London.

McCurrach, I. and Darnley, B. (1999) *Special Talents, Special Needs: Drama for people with learning difficulties*, London: Jessica Kingsley Publishers.

Mills, R. (1999) 'Q&A Spell', *Communication*, Winter: 27–28.

Mitchell, J.R. and van der Gaag, A. (2001) 'Through the eye of the Cyclops: evaluating a multi-sensory intervention programme for people with complex disabilities', *British Journal of Learning Disabilities*, 30: 159–165.

Neelands, J. (1984) *Making Sense of Drama: A guide to classroom practice*, London: Heinemann Education.

Nind, M. and Hewett, D. (1994) *Access to Communication: Developing basic communication with people who have severe learning difficulties*, London: David Fulton Publishers.

OCR (Oxford, Cambridge and RSA Examinations) (2013) *OCR Entry Level Life and Living Skills*, Available: www.ocr.org.uk/Images/76954-centre-handbook.pdf (accessed 4 February 2015).

Park, K. (1998) 'Dickens for all: inclusive approaches to literature and communication with people with severe and profound learning disabilities', *British Journal of Special Education*, 25: 114–118.

Park, K. (2004) 'Interactive storytelling: from the book of Genesis', *British Journal of Special Education*, 31: 16–23.

Peter, M. (1994) *Drama for All: Developing drama in the curriculum with pupils with special educational needs*, London: David Fulton Publishers.

Peter, M. (1995) *Making Drama Special*, London: David Fulton Publishers.

Peter, M. (2003) Drama, narrative and early learning, *British Journal of Special Education*, 30: 21–27.

Peter, M. (2009) 'Drama: narrative pedagogy and socially challenged children', *British Journal of Special Education*, 36: 9–17.

Ramachandran, V. (2003) 'The Emerging Mind: Lecture 5 – Neuroscience, the new Philosophy', *Reith Lectures 2003*: BBC Radio 4.

Rieber, R.W. and Carton, A.S. (eds) (1993) *The Collected Works of L.S. Vygotsky: The fundamentals of defectology (abnormal psychology and learning disabilities)*, New York: Plenum Press.

Sherratt, D. (2002) 'Developing pretend play in children with autism: A case study', *Autism*, 6: 169–179.

Sherratt, D. and Peter, M. (2002) *Developing Play and Drama in Children with Autistic Spectrum Disorders*, London: David Fulton Publishers.

Siddles, R., Mills, R. and Collins, M. (1997) 'SPELL – The National Autistic Society approach to education', *Communication*, Spring: 8–9.

Trevarthen, C. (1995) 'The child's need to learn a culture', *Children & Society*, 9: 5–19.

United Nations (2006) Convention on the Rights of Persons with Disabilities: UN General Assembly.

Vygotsky, L.S. (1976) 'Play and its role in the mental development of the child', in J. Bruner, A. Jolly and K. Sylva (eds) *Play: its role in development and evolution*, New York: Penguin.

Vygotsky, L.S. (1978) 'Interaction between learning and development', in Cole, M., John-Steiner, V., Scribner, S., and Souberman, E (eds), *Mind in Society: the development of higher psychological processes*, Cambridge, MA: Harvard University Press.

Ware, J. (1994) *The Education of Children with Profound and Multiple Learning Difficulties*, London: David Fulton.

Winston, J. and Tandy, M. (2001) *Beginning Drama 4-11*, London: David Fulton Publishers.

Wolfberg, P.J. and Schuler, A.L. (1993) 'Integrated Play Groups: A model for promoting the social and cognitive dimensions of play in children with autism', *Journal of Autism and Developmental Disorders*, 23: 467–489.

Further reading

Kempe, A. (1996) *Drama Education and Special Needs: a handbook for teachers in mainstream and special schools*, Cheltenham: Stanley Thornes Publishers Ltd.

Smidt, S. (2009) *Introducing Vygotsky: a guide for practitioners and students in early years education*, London and New York, Routledge.

PART V

Strategies for supporting teaching and learning

33

TECHNOLOGY SUPPORTING LEARNING

Chris Abbott and Ann Middleton

In this chapter, the following questions will be addressed:

- What technology is currently used with learners who have severe or profound learning difficulties?
- How is this technology integrated into the curriculum?
- How does the use of this technology provide access to learning in ways that cannot be provided by other means?

Technology and learning difficulties

During the last 30 years, there has been an expanding range of technology available in schools. As well as the growing proliferation of computers for recording and data entry, there has been increasing provision of resources designed specifically for disabled people, as well as a wide range of materials available via the internet. Government funding since 1988, when Information and Communication Technology (ICT) was included in the National Curriculum for England and Wales, has ensured that almost all schools have a wide range of computers, interactive whiteboards and other hardware. This has aimed to mirror the provision available in the wider world to enable learners to take their place in society. The assumption has been that good specialist provision will make the best use of the equipment available to all, as well as maximising the achievements of learners through the use of adaptive technology designed specifically for people with disabilities (as opposed to other assistive technologies that may have other aims, as is discussed below).

It is striking to note the ubiquity of technology in all our lives today, but perhaps especially when considering the needs of those with SLD/PMLD. Computers, sensory rooms and interactive toys have been available in special schools since the early 1980s and have led to progress by learners which could not have been envisaged otherwise. Despite many examples of good practice and innovative uses of technology across the country, there has been no sustained centralised effort to look at 'what works' and is worth recommending to others. The tendency of schools for learners with SLD/PMLD to be isolated from one another and to develop their own curricula means that teachers may have fewer chances to share good practice than those in other types of school. However, there have been efforts by experienced practitioners who specialise in this area to share their skills with others. Millar (2009), as well as giving advice on the types of technology that are useful for teachers to have within the classroom when working with learners with PMLD, lays out the theoretical foundations of using that technology. She stresses the use of switches to develop contingency awareness, not as an end in themselves, but as part of the pupil's acquisition of intentionality and development of interaction with others. Ware and Thorpe (2007) also examine the development of early cognition and communication in learners with PMLD by the development of contingency awareness through the use of technology. They describe their research project, set up not only to specifically teach contingency awareness to pupils at the earliest stages of development, but also to allow teachers to record progress in the minutest detail.

While some special schools may have a large range of equipment, it is not always apparent that staff training has kept pace with innovation. Mumtaz (2000) found that teachers' beliefs about teaching and learning were as important as their technical knowledge when integrating technology into the classroom. Sometimes, an expensive piece of equipment is not being used because the person who was originally trained in its use has left, or because repairs are too expensive. The online training materials (DfE 2012) developed by the government following the Salt Review (DfES 2010) cover access to technology and alternative and augmentative communication (AAC) systems but there has been no research to show how many people are using these.

A taxonomy of technology use

Attempts to classify and describe assistive or learning technologies by technology or by their use with learners with particular impairments have met with varying degrees of success. A taxonomy of use has been put forward by Abbott (2007a, 2007b) and this has been used by others, for example Galloway (2009), when discussing the ways in which technology can be used. A further development of the taxonomy (Abbott *et al.* 2014) breaks down technology uses by people with learning difficulties and disabilities into three broad areas:

- Technology uses to train or practise.
- Technology uses to assist learning.
- Technology uses to enable learning.

In a sense, these could be seen as chronological stages in the development of assistive (learning) technologies. The term 'assistive technologies' is now widely used and covers technologies for learning and for daily life and independence. The growing use of the term 'assistive learning technologies' is a result of the need to consider these separately from the quite different 'assistive living technologies' such as medication monitors, fall detectors and smart home devices for independent living. The taxonomy above is not designed to describe development over time but to highlight alternative styles of use. However, it is certainly the case that '*technology uses to train or practise*' were among the earliest developments in technology-mediated learning, perhaps because much of that stage of development was led by programmers and designers rather than educators. Unlike educators, with their in-depth knowledge of how children learn, it is more likely that developers and designers will adopt a simplistic behaviourist framework emphasising drill and practice to underpin software. Although drill and practice software is not generally popular today, it is still true to say that there is a role for it at a variety of levels where the aim is the practising of a skill rather than the acquisition of it. For example, speech and language therapists have found that screen displays representing vocalisation can alert learners to their progress in generating sound and improving articulation. Researchers working with learners with autism have shown that using specific computer-based learning environments has led to increases in communication and social interactions (Keay-Bright 2008; Herring 2009). This is currently a very active field of research, previously characterised by exploration of the potential of virtual reality but now often linked to teams working on robotics for social communication.

Much of the research in this area of technology use tends to be devoted to the evaluation of a particular device or software title, rather than to understanding the way in which each can be used in an educational context. However, this is beginning to change; for example, a conference paper by Brown and Standen (2011) considered the role of games software in the practising of mathematical skills. Working with learners across a wide age range, using a matched pairs design, the team found increases in understanding of a particular topic (fractions) among the group who played relevant games, but not among members of the control group who did not. Bober (2004) points out that outcomes from using technology effectively in the classroom may not be adequately measured by the existing testing regime, although we suggest that this could be said to apply to aspects of progress made by this group of learners in all subject areas.

Perhaps the most significant potential to be found in this area awaits us in the future – although perhaps the near future – because of the rapid development of alternative interfaces, such as those utilising 'eye gaze' or 'brain control', that will enable non-reading, non-textual learners to interact with technologies at a deeper level than is currently possible. The prospective use of 'virtual environments' (Standen, Brown and Cromby 2001; Standen and Brown 2005) will allow learners to rehearse appropriate behaviours in such places as restaurants or holiday resorts without having to visit them regularly. Lee, McGee and Ungar (2001) reported on the effectiveness of a teaching programme for personal safety for learners with severe and complex needs. The programme considered the language necessary for discussions of personal safety to take place, and the difficulties of following a role model approach with these learners. The authors go on to describe how they used technology to more effectively address these areas and there has been much development in this area since that date.

There is a growing literature on design principles for inclusion (Abbott *et al.* 2011), looking at the whole context of the use of technology rather than at specific products. Assistive technology, as it is often known, has tended to be impairment-related, with much development having taken place around the technologies that can assist those with particular sensory or physical difficulties. Where the emphasis is more on the use of technologies than on the progress made by the learner, much that is important has been discovered. An example of this was the work by McGuinness and Farrand (2010) which showed that the use of VOCAs (Voice Output Communication Aids) was much less effective when users had learning difficulties in addition to communication needs. Text and keyboard interfaces have always proven to be a barrier to some learners and the rapid development of touchscreens on mainstream devices has been welcomed within the learning difficulties community, where more basic versions of such interfaces have been used for many years.

The advent of tablet and mobile computing devices such as the iPad and smartphones has led to a revolution in how users access information. This m-learning (the 'm' stands for 'mobile') has the potential to revolutionise the way schools work (Melhuish and Falloon 2010), although this brings up particular issues in relation to learners with SLD/PMLD. While access to a tablet device is easier than to a smartphone or a computer using a mouse (and alternative access methods are becoming available), the idea of self-directed learning and mainly text-based communication may be beyond most of those in this group of learners. Another practice that has expanded more recently from its original home within specialist settings for learners with learning difficulties, as with touch-screens, is the use of graphic symbols for literacy (see also Chapter 28). Sheehy (2005) worked with a small group of learners with SLD using morphing software to change symbols (which the pupils could recognise) into words (which they could not). The use of graphic symbols as well as the expanded variety of information made easily available by the use of technology, for example pictures, photos and video, has made it easier for learners to access information as well as record achievement at a level they can relate to independently. A European Union project looking at internet access for those with cognitive and communication impairments (Poulson and Nicolle 2004) does not seem to have been implemented in any national or international way. However, there have been some local projects implemented by individuals. The SEVERI project (Starcic and Niskala 2010) set up a specialist e-learning interface for learners with SLD that allowed them to use the technology effectively in a way that they were able to access independently. The interface included learning materials, a diary and calendar, tasks and group discussion, all of which could be accessed by clear, simplified text, symbols, pictures, photos and speech. Cackett (2006) developed an integrated teaching environment for students at Somerset College that attempted to meet the needs of all those using the system: students and staff. Students were presented with learning modules that could be accessed via a mouse or switch and in a format accessible to non-readers, while staff were given the tools to assess progress and assemble data. In the corporate sector, Inclusive Technology (see useful websites at end of chapter) developed the MyZone programme to set up individual workspaces for learners in response to requests from teachers who wanted to limit the number of activities to which each learner had access.

Within Abbott's taxonomy referred to above, the expectation is that *'technology uses that enable learning'* will be emancipatory, innovative and ground-breaking. What is referred to here is not merely assisting learning or making it more efficient, important though that might be; rather the technology use in this case is helping to make learning possible where previously this may have been unachievable. The use of a VOCA to give a voice to a person unable to speak might fall into this category, as would many of the alternative interfaces, such as eye-gaze and other specialist switches designed for people with severe physical disabilities.

A taxonomy for SLD and PMLD contexts

However, neat as the above taxonomy might seem, the coherence tends to break down in the face of real learners in real situations with real needs. When considering the role of technology to support learners with SLD or PMLD, we suggest an alternative taxonomy is more appropriate:

- Technology for teaching.
- Technology for learning.
- Technology for communication.

Within this classification, 'technology for teaching' covers the use of computers, interactive whiteboards (IWBs) and handheld devices by teachers or others for didactic purposes. Also included under this heading would be the use of various technologies to record progress and indicate attainment. 'Technology for learning', on the other hand, would include the computers and software used by learners in classrooms, technology-enhanced sensory rooms and interactive devices to give feedback and provide motivation for learners. Finally, 'technology for communication' covers a wide range of AAC as well as low-technology communication aids such as pointing boards and technologies which enable access to these devices or their production by carers, parents and educators. The following text offers three vignettes of individual learners and their use of technologies for these three areas of use for technology, after some consideration of the issues involved in matching learner to technology.

Three learners and their use of technologies

The mainstream model of teaching ICT as a specific subject has, in some cases, migrated into special schools so that occasionally 'working on the computer' is considered as a separate skill or, perhaps less productively, as a reward for completion of 'work'. As learners with SLD and PMLD have a wide range of cognitive and physical abilities, teachers must personalise lessons for each learner. Depending on how the school organises its curriculum, there are likely to be personal targets for each learner in each lesson as well as subject content. Each school and every individual teacher will decide how to balance these two elements, but the important thing to note is that each learner will be learning in their own way and will need access to the materials in a way that is appropriate for them. The learning profile of each learner will also be idiosyncratic. Some may have outstanding abilities (relative to their peer group) in particular areas and this can be especially true of some learners with autism. Some of the learners with more complex needs will need personalised equipment to allow them to access the curriculum, to communicate, or for both purposes. They will often need to be supported by therapists and others with experience in issues such as positioning and available adaptive equipment. The provision of such equipment, personalised for the user, tends to be expensive and may need regularly replacing.

David is in a class of nine learners in the Post 16 unit of the school. There is a specific curriculum for this group, concentrating more on life skills and independence than traditional classroom subjects. As none of the learners in the unit remain together in class groups all week, the unit is laid out with computers in each teaching area and around other zones. Each teaching area has an IWB which is used in a variety of ways. As David is a reasonably independent computer user and needs no specialist access devices, he is able to use the computer for a range of activities. David has very limited literacy skills and finds handwriting very difficult, so he is encouraged to use pictures and symbols for recording. He is able to type single words into Communicate: Symwriter (a symbol word processing programme – www.widgit.com/products/symwriter/index.htm) and has used this, Clicker 6 (a literacy programme providing a range of materials to support early writers – www.cricksoft.com/uk/products/tools/clicker/home.aspx) and PowerPoint (part of the Microsoft Office suite for making slideshow presentations – http://office.microsoft.com/en-gb/powerpoint/) to record what he has done. He is able to send simple emails by attaching photographs and typing single words. He has carried out projects with other learners where they have worked together cooperatively and he has taken his own photographs. David has worked with the art teacher and his class making a stop animation film which was shown at a parents' evening. He is able to find items on the Internet and it is noticeable that his literacy skills improve when the activity is motivating enough – he is able to type all sorts of words into Google for searches and to remember web addresses. Outside school, David is able to use an X Box game controller independently and is about to acquire an adapted mobile phone with preset call buttons to support his independent travel. He also uses Skype video calling to talk to his cousins in Australia. It is hoped that David will be able to join a music and video workshop which runs at the local further education college with which the school has a link. This allows the learners access to equipment used by all Media Arts students such as video and radio editing suites and digital film creation – resources that could not be provided in school.

As can be seen, David has technology integrated into a range of activities both in school and at home. He is able to show his learning and provide evidence of a range of work and projects completed without being literate in the conventional sense. He is also able to carry out independent research. The staff have taken advantage of the motivation provided by using technology to develop his independence skills.

Lucy is in a small class of six learners, aged between 7 and 12, all of whom have PMLD. Although they are based in their classroom for the whole week, they have both formal and informal opportunities to mix with other learners in the school. There is a range of specialist equipment in the classroom, including computers, an interactive plasma screen which allows touch access on a large scale to anything that will appear on a computer monitor, switches, low tech communication aids such as BIGmacks (www.inclusive.co.uk/ablenet-bigmack-p2039) and switch operated toys. The school also has a sensory room which is timetabled for use by Lucy's class three times a week. It is also possible to use it at other times if it is free. Lucy's class follow an adapted version of the main school curriculum but with much greater emphasis on communication, independence and social skills. The class teacher keeps detailed records of the communication of all the learners which may or may not involve technology. Lucy's main form of communication is by looking at an object when it is held in front of her. She is able to show a preference for one object over another. She also uses a recordable single message communication aid during a variety of group and individual sessions. One of the items to bring up at her next review is a discussion of how valuable this is. As it is not possible to evaluate Lucy's language comprehension exactly, the staff are querying whether or not she knows what she is doing. It is known that she is able to respond to familiar language patterns as she appears to be able to anticipate actions or favoured choruses during songs, rhymes and games. As she has Rett's Syndrome which is associated with delayed motor responses, it also takes her a long time to carry out any motor tasks. Lucy also uses a switch attached to a mount on her wheelchair tray to access the computer, the plasma screen, items in the sensory room and toys. Again, she has difficulties with her motor planning, but it is noted that she appears to find most of these activities very rewarding, laughing and looking towards the response she has caused. She has participated in sensory story sessions using a variety of equipment and appears to particularly enjoy the SoundBeam music maker (www.soundbeam.co.uk/special-education-music-therapy/). These sessions generally take place in the sensory room as this is a distraction-free environment that can be set up with music, lights and video as required. Lucy enjoys music videos from YouTube and videos of herself played on the plasma screen. The staff are currently working on how to develop her choosing skills so that she can choose and then play her favourites. The school has recently had a demonstration of the SensoryEye software (http://sensoryguru.com/products/eyefx/) which allows access to a range of games and activities via eye gaze technology for learners with similar needs to Lucy. It is anticipated, if the money can be raised, that this will be an effective means of access for her.

At the moment, Lucy is making good use of a range of technology during a range of classroom activities, much of it led by her preferences. Close observation of her behaviour by the staff has led to a review taking place questioning the validity to Lucy of what she is doing. The importance of using technology to reinforce personalised learning means that the learner's needs are more important than either being seen to be using all the available devices or to be teaching the whole class in the same way.

Omar is in a small class of five learners, all of whom have a diagnosis of autism and SLD. The class is run according to the TEACCH (Treatment and Education of Autistic and related Communication Handicapped Children, see Bourgondien and Coonrod 2013) principles with individual workstations for each learner. As the class is part of the school's Early Years Department, the learners also have access to sensory and outdoor play several times a day. Although the classroom has a portable adjustable plasma screen computer, this is only brought into the room when it is to be used as several learners will do nothing else if they can see it. The class have an iPad which is proving to be very successful. Although Omar's concentration tends to be fleeting, he is able to touch the screen on both the plasma screen and the iPad to make something happen. As he smiles when he is doing this, it is presumed he enjoys it. He is beginning to show an aptitude for using the Let's Play with the Trains! app for the iPad. This turns lines and marks on the screen into tracks with trains running on them. It has been noticed that Omar responds better to a touch screen than to a traditional computer as he does not appear to be able to connect the pressing of a switch or key on the keyboard with what happens on the screen and can become frustrated. He has individual sessions on the ICT equipment as he cannot initiate the use of it. Omar does not use the computer at home as he becomes easily frustrated and finds it difficult to share with his siblings.

Whilst Omar only has limited access to technology, this is very motivating for him and it is noticeable that he will concentrate for longer on activities on the plasma screen or iPad than elsewhere. The class staff are gradually introducing him to a wider range of activities and encouraging him to concentrate for longer in the hope that he will eventually be able to generalise these skills to other areas.

Conclusions

Over the last 30 years, technology, along with increased specialist knowledge about how to teach, has made an increasing difference to the lives of learners with SLD/PMLD. Symbolic communication is now possible for those who would have been without it before. The advent of easily accessible, attention-grabbing pictures, video and music brings motivation and awareness to all learners, especially those who would have been in danger of withdrawing into self-stimulation. Access devices such as switches, eye gaze, adapted mice and touch screens allow those with physical disabilities to carry out tasks they are not able to do any other way. Contact across the world is now easily accomplished from the classroom and does not necessarily require literacy. None of this would have happened without a combination of government funding for computers in schools, the work of individual inventors creating one-off answers to particular problems which has then been taken up by commercial companies, and the imagination of teachers and other professionals who have found ways of answering the question: 'How can I develop this learner's language and learning?'

Questions for readers

- Where is the technology expertise in your school? – and how are you enabling those staff members to pass their expertise on to others?
- Are all the learners in your school using technology as well as they could in different areas of the curriculum?

- Do you have technology that is not being used to its full potential? If so, how could this be remedied?
- Who decides about new technology purchases, and what is considered before these decisions are made?
- What technology would you like to have in school in the future, and how might you acquire this?

Useful websites

Inclusive Technology (www.inclusive.co.uk): Company selling a wide range of specialist hardware and software for people with special needs and disabilities. They also have advice on how to use their products. MyZone is available through Inclusive Technology.

Widgit Software (www.widgit.com): Original developers of symbol software in the UK. Communicate: Symwriter 2 is available through Widgit Software plus a range of additional resources.

Crick Software (www.cricksoft.com): Make and sell Clicker software which has a range of uses for early literacy. Additional resources also available.

Liberator (www.liberator.co.uk): Company mainly specialising in communication aids who also sell a range of communication resources and switch operated toys.

Sensory Guru (www.sensoryguru.com): Make and sell a range of resources particularly eye gaze software for early learners.

Independent Life Technologies (www.independent-life-technologies.co.uk): Company making and selling a range of switch operated electronics. Will also adapt things to order.

Special Needs Toys (www.specialneedstoys.com) and **Rompa** (www.rompa.com). All make and install sensory rooms. Also sell a wide range of specialist switches and toys.

References

Abbott, C. (2007a) *e-Inclusion: Learning Difficulties and Digital Technologies*, Bristol: Futurelab.

Abbott, C. (2007b) 'Defining assistive technologies – a discussion', *Journal of Assistive Technologies*, 1, 6–9.

Abbott, C., Brown, D., Evett, L., Standen, P. and Wright, J. (2011) 'Learning difference and digital technologies: a literature review of research involving children and young people using assistive technologies 2007-2010'. Online. Available: www.kcl.ac.uk/sspp/departments/education/research/crestem/steg/recentproj/assistivetech.aspx (accessed 1 May 2013.)

Abbott, C., Brown, D., Evett, L. and Standen, P. (2014) 'Emerging issues and current trends in assistive technology use 2007-2010: practising, assisting and enabling learning for all', *Disability and Rehabilitation: Assistive Technology*, 9(6): 453–462.

Bober, M. J. (2004) 'The challenges of instructional accountability', *TechTrends*, 48(4), 48–51.

Bourgondien, M. and Coonrod, E. (2013) 'TEACCH: an intervention approach for children and adults with Autism Spectrum Disorders and their families, in S. Goldstein and J. A. Naglieri (eds) *Interventions for Autism Spectrum Disorders*, New York: Springer.

Brown, D. and Standen, P. (2011) 'Can participating in games based learning improve mathematical skills in students with intellectual disabilities?' In *IEEE 1st International Conference on Serious Games and Applications for Health (SeGAH)*, 1–9.

Cackett, P. (2006) 'An integrated teaching environment at Somerset College: providing a computer program that will present teaching modules in an efficient way', *The SLD Experience*, 46, 20–22.

DfE (Department for Education) (2012) *Training materials for teachers of learners with severe, profound and complex learning difficulties*. Online. Available: www.education.gov.uk/complexneeds (accessed 17 June 2013).

DfES (Department for Education and Skills) (2010) *Salt Review: Independent Review of Teacher Supply for Pupils with Severe, Profound and Multiple Learning Difficulties (SLD and PMLD)*. Online. Available: http://

webarchive.nationalarchives.gov.uk/20130401151715/https://www.education.gov.uk/publications/standard/publicationDetail/Page1/DCSF-00195-2010 (accessed 17 June 2013).

Galloway, J. (2009) *Harnessing Technology for Every Child Matters and Personalised Learning*, London: Routledge.

Herring, P (2009) 'Can computer assisted learning help autistic children communicate?' *The SLD Experience*, 53, 23–28.

Keay-Bright, W. (2008) 'ReacTickles Global: Can mobile technologies encourage playful social interaction?' *Journal of Assistive Technologies*, 2, 42–45.

Lee, D., McGee, A. and Ungar, S. (2001) Using multimedia to teach personal safety to children with severe learning difficulties, *British Journal of Special Education*, 28(2), 65–70.

Melhuish, K. and Falloon, G. (2010) Looking to the future: M-learning with the iPad, *Computers in New Zealand Schools*, 22(3), 1–16.

McGuiness, A. and Farrand, L. (2010) 'AAC and Autism. How are people really using voice output communication aids?' *Communication Matters*, 24(3), 35–37.

Millar, S. (2009) 'Meaningful technology for early level learners', *The SLD Experience*, 53, 15–22.

Mumtaz, S. (2000) 'Factors affecting teachers' use of information and communication technology: a review of the literature', *Journal of Information Technology for Teacher Education*, 9(3), 319–342.

Poulson, D. and Nicolle, C. (2004) 'Making the Internet accessible for people with cognitive and communication impairments', *Universal Access in the Information Society*, 3(1), 48–56.

Sheehy, K. (2005) 'Morphing images: a potential tool for teaching word recognition to children with severe learning difficulties', *British Journal of Educational Technology*, 36(2), 293–301.

Starcic, A. I. and Niskala, M. (2010) 'Vocational students with severe learning difficulties learning on the Internet', *British Journal of Educational Technology*, 41(6), 155–159.

Standen, P.J. and Brown, D.J. (2005) 'The use of virtual reality in the rehabilitation of people with intellectual disabilities', *Cyberpsychology and Behaviour*, 8(3), 272–282.

Standen, P.J., Brown, D.J. and Cromby, J.J. (2001) 'The effective employment of virtual environments in the training and rehabilitation of people with intellectual disabilities', *British Journal of Educational Technology*, 32(3), 289–299.

Ware, J. and Thorpe, P. (2007) 'How technology aids teaching of early cognitive skills to pupils with PMLD', *The SLD Experience Issue*, 47, 19–23.

34

PLAYING TO LEARN OR LEARNING TO PLAY?

Ideas on ensuring that the opportunity to play is continually accessible for learners with SLD/PMLD

Peter Imray and Robert Orr

In this chapter, the following questions will be addressed:

- Is play important?
- Why do children, young people and even adults with SLD/PMLD struggle to play co-operatively and freely with their peers?
- Do we learn to play, or is it an innate gift?

Is play important?

Play has many benefits in life, regardless of age. Play is fun, educational, creative, and stress relieving and encourages positive social interactions and communication.

(Blundon Nash and Schaefer 2011: 4)

Landreth (2002) has made the apposite observation that play is effectively a child's language, with the toys being the words, and Rudolph Steiner (1996) saw it as an open door to the unconscious, letting us in to the child's world. Drewes (2006) argues that play is a universal expression of children all over the world, transcending ethnicity, language and cultural issues. Huizinga (1949) saw play as being central to societal developments of the creative arts as well as the philosophies and social structures that make up the society. He was one of the first to note the significance of play across cultural, time and indeed species boundaries, since all animals play.

There is a growing interest in the apparent link between brain development and play from neuroscience research (Schore 2002; Lehrer 2012) as well as play's fundamental role in child development, typified by the observation that 'there seems to be a general consensus that play and learning are inextricably linked' (Stroh, Robinson and Proctor 2008: 11). Such is the recognition of the linkage that England's EYFS (Early Years Foundation Stage and effectively the national curriculum model for two to five year olds) has play as a central core, so that: 'each area of learning and development must be implemented through planned, purposeful play' (DfE 2012: 6).

Placing play as a central point in any curriculum for learners with SLD/PMLD, irrespective of the age of the individuals involved, also encourages the creativity and fun so necessary for effective teaching. It releases us all from the prison of 'age appropriateness' which rather strangely assumes that people no longer play once they have reached secondary school age, and certainly not once they are adults! Samuel and Maggs (1998) describe playing 'this little piggy' with a 31–year–old woman with PMLD. She, along with all the other clients, had previously been denied opportunities to play because the policy of age-appropriateness had 'become a tyranny' (p. 122). For some staff, 'introducing permission to be playful (had) been like turning on a switch' (p. 143).

Why do children, young people and even adults with SLD/PMLD struggle to play co-operatively and freely with their peers?

Do the difficulties with play, so obviously experienced by so many with SLD/PMLD, define the limitations of intellectual development in the same way as say, difficulties with generalisation and problem solving (Lacey 2009)? Defining things in terms of what cannot or does not happen is sometimes referred to as a 'deficit model' approach; the focus is on what is missing. In her seminal work, the late Lilli Nielsen, wondering what has to happen in order for exploratory play to emerge, concluded that the environment needs to change for children with complex needs to show to what extent they *can* play (Nielsen 1992). As noted elsewhere in this book (see Chapter 35), there has been remarkably little direct research conducted into how those with SLD (or PMLD) play, or perhaps more accurately, don't play. There are exceptions to this, though we might need to draw inferences from the numerous works on Intensive Interaction (Nind and Hewett 1994, 2001, 2006; Hewett and Nind 1998; Kellet 2000; Kellet and Nind 2003) as well as the writings of various authors on the more formalised elements of play evident in drama, storytelling and narrative (Grove and Park 1996 for example). What is evident is that the scenario witnessed by Stroh, Robinson and Proctor (2008) when three typical developing five–month–old children were introduced to a 'treasure basket' of ordinary household objects (see Goldschmeid and Jackson 1994) is unlikely to be repeated by a similar group of babies with severe or profound learning difficulties.

> None of the infants had seen the basket of objects before. The response of each of the five-month-old babies was dramatic, and although they each had their own style of response, their activity with the objects was remarkably similar. Each baby leaned forward eagerly, practically falling over with excitement, eager to touch and then pick up the objects.
>
> (Stroh, Robinson and Procter 2008: 12)

Nielsen's (1991) interventions with congenitally blind infants showed that where children are not visually alerted to the possibility of play or they cannot direct their reach and control their grasp, they will turn to their own bodies for playthings and may be locked into mouth and saliva play for example, as they can always access that on demand. To encourage outward reaching play and exploration outside of themselves, she would hang objects around children where their random movements would cause a contact in an enclosed 'Little Room', as well as lie them on a resonating platform so that all their movement sounds were accentuated.

While Lilli Nielsen's work has had a profound effect on encouraging free exploration and interaction with the world around the learner, it may be that for some with SLD/PMLD, even this is not enough. Imray (1996, 1997) – noted in Imray and Hinchcliffe (2014) – spent a year observing a small group of learners with PMLD and another year observing a small group of learners with SLD, both engaged with variations of treasure basket play. Unassisted by adults, the learners with PMLD took virtually no notice of any of the objects around them, continuing with their normal range of behaviours exhibited in every other setting where people were not involved. That is, they did not appear to exhibit any desire to play and certainly no play skills were evident. The learners with SLD did engage more directly with the objects, but fairly quickly fell into a routine, repeated more or less every week, revolving around the dominance and subservience of individual members of the group. These prolonged observations tie in with other reports redolent of learners with SLD, such as, they find the art of playing, especially co-operatively playing with their peers, extremely problematic (Simons 1977; Stagnitti, O'Connor and Sheppard 2012) and do not come to it naturally as typically developing children will.

There are likely to be a number of reasons for this which relate directly to the defining difficulties experienced by those with SLD/PMLD, namely that these learners:

- are less likely to learn spontaneously and may find the art of generalising one learned experience of play into another very difficult;
- are likely to miss the opportunities to generalise schemas and form concepts, even if they can amass the sequence of activities (Athey 2007);
- may have difficulties remembering what they played last time and with whom, and exactly what the rules were last time, and of course, the time before that;
- may have poor expressive and receptive communication skills, thus making for extreme challenges in joint play;
- may have difficulties in repairing communicative breakdowns so that misunderstandings and learners' natural squabbles will become insurmountable barriers to extended play experiences;
- may have poor concentration skills, may not be able to follow the 'rules' which they themselves may change from minute to minute, and may wander off to some other attraction within a very short time;
- may have difficulties with the abstract nature of creative play;
- may need many opportunities to learn one specific play scenario, such opportunities being denied by the constantly changing and developing scenarios evident in free play;
- may lack a sense of narrative which often drives play;
- may be delayed in their understanding of representation, which is critical to symbolic play.

We may add to the above the socially debilitating conditions of learners with SLD/PMLD with autism who:

- will probably have problems with flexibility of thought, perhaps engaging in rigid routines or rituals which prevent the development of play skills;
- may lack social reciprocity;
- may exhibit behaviours which may be circular, with repeating patterns;
- may naturally incline to preferring solitude and therefore lack the motivation to communicate socially;
- may lack social and emotional directedness;
- may have a high level of compulsions and rituals;
- may have only a limited ability to communicate in unstructured situations;
- may have a limited ability to communicate beyond simple requests;

- may use inappropriate language and have difficulties mapping language to the task;
- may have difficulties understanding non-verbal communications;
- will probably lack 'theory of mind' and an understanding of others thinking differently to themselves;
- will probably have difficulty with emotional involvement with people.

The above lists are of course limiting factors for learners with SLD/PMLD and may explain why they struggle to play. But may the fact that they struggle to play also contribute to the establishment and continued existence of these limiting conditions? If we can teach learners with SLD/PMLD to play, can we thereby help them to break into creativity, thinking, problem solving, formulating and maintaining relationships, purposeful self-engagement and the myriad other benefits of mastering the art of co-operative play? Daniel Stern (1985) and Colwyn Trevarthen (1979) suggest separately that an essential characteristic of the play companion for typically developing children is responsiveness – the best 'teacher' of play is one who responds to whatever in the child seems playful. For learners who are at the earliest stages of intellectual development, Intensive Interaction is the clearest presentation of how this is most effectively achieved, and from there it is a short step to playing games, which 'are not time out from real work; they are the most intensive developmental work you can do' (Nind and Hewett 2001: 66).

Do we learn to play, or is it an innate gift?

Typically developing children generally learn to play naturally, without conscious effort from 'teachers'. Parents, grandparents, aunts, uncles, older siblings and peers, and the more formal support coming from the likes of pre-school, nursery teachers and support staff may *facilitate* the learning of play but they do not consciously teach it. Bruce (1991) argued that planning and purposefulness were the antithesis of play, its key features being free flow and child-directedness with no particular outcome being sought.

> We can say that free-flow play seems to be concerned with the ability and opportunity to wallow in ideas, experiences, feelings and relationships. It is also about the way children come to use the competencies they have developed. It is the way children integrate all their learning.
>
> (Bruce 1991: 42)

This perspective appears again in Laevers' (1994) notion of 'involvement' and Csikszentmihalyi's (1990) state of 'flow' in self-directed activity or play, the sort of essential that Orr (2003) notes adults often dismissing as just 'messing about' especially with the oft heard phrase – they're *just* playing!

The ability to play freely and co-operatively comes more or less fully formed with the typically developing children by the time they enter the formal process of schooling at the age of 5 or 6, and such a scenario is supported by the fact that the English National Curriculum for pupils above the age of six years hardly mentions play, apart from its relationship with formal sports (Imray and Hinchcliffe 2014). There may be a need to refine and develop, especially with the introduction of more formalised rule-based play in games and sports, but the basic skills are probably pretty well established. The fact that this is not so with learners with SLD/PMLD is an indication that they do learn differently from typically developing children (Imray and Hinchcliffe 2012).

It is not that children with SLD and PMLD (or ASD for that matter) cannot play co-operatively, it is that they learn to do it differently and we must therefore teach them differently.

(Imray and Hinchcliffe 2014: 214).

Vygotsky's zone of proximal development (Vygotsky 1978) is key here, representing as it does, the space between the learner's known and safe area and the next step (into the unknown), which can be aided with another's help and support. It makes sense to assume that this help and support needs to revolve around structure, since structure is, by definition, the one consistent thing that is missing from free play, yet it is the one thing that those with SLD/PMLD (and of course with autism) often need the most. This is noted in the highly structured format advocated by Grove and Park in their seminal works on making literature accessible to all (Grove and Park 1996, 1999, 2000). This does not mean that the structure cannot be altered (Pulli 2012) but the structure is clear and unambiguous and acts as a guide to the journey. Play is of course very closely related to storytelling and narrative (Grove and Park 1996; Gussin-Paley 2004) as well as drama (Sherratt and Peter 2002) and McCaffrey notes a consistent theme in that 'play may need to be modelled for some children as it will not be a spontaneously occurring activity' (McCaffrey 2012: 26).

With typically developing children, formal and repeated structure is almost the last thing to come into play (though it will be evident in the 'rules' that children jointly establish), since firm rules and order are much more related to the formal playing of games and sports. Games such as chess and mahjong, Monopoly and Risk, cribbage and whist, football and cricket, which operate under a formal set of clearly defined rules, are played once the ability to play freely and co-operatively are well established. What we have here is a direct linear and developmental relationship between process (free) play and product (games) play. Process play does not have any end in mind, children are 'learning how to do it whilst doing it' (Peter 1997: 29) but the general and invisible rules of play become established over many, many hours of practice. Once these (invisible) rules are broadly understood, typically developing children are able to branch out into product play, which relates much more to the more formal rules and order that fits in with adult life. Here, play has a purpose (a product) in the game itself, with other more 'adult' considerations such as competition, co-operative and collaborative working, division of labour, team playing etc coming strongly to the fore. Here, process (freedom) precedes product (structure).

When working with learners with SLD/PMLD, this might need to be stood on its head, so that elements of structure are dropped in *before* the ability to engage in free play is established. In a similar vein, Imray and Hinchcliffe (2014) have noted that for those with SLD, the handling of money presents a particular problem because the basic skills involved in successfully counting are often not established. This is nobody's fault; it is directly related to the nature of severe learning difficulties and working memory. As McConkey and McEvoy (1986) have noted, in order to count successfully, one has to hold several pieces of information in one's head concurrently and relay them back on cue, entirely without error, every single time. Imray and Hinchcliffe (2014) therefore recommend starting at a much later point, with larger £1 and £2 coins and establishing coin recognition, coin handling and relative value in terms of purchase power. If (and only if) these basic rules can be established, can we then move to lower denominations such as 50p, 20p etc. In other words what we are doing here is recognising that those with SLD learn in a different way to typically developing children, and we should therefore be teaching them in a different way. Similar considerations apply in teaching thinking and problem solving, where for example, learners with SLD/PMLD often do not even recognise that there is a problem in the first place. In such situations, we need to make any and all thinking and problem-solving opportunities 'very explicit, or the children may not notice' (Lacey 2009: 22).

Stagnitti (2010) suggests that the act of play involves the 'doing' of play (the development of play skills), the 'being' of play (the expression of who they are) and the 'role' of player (engaging with others in meaningful interactions) and it is this doing which we would suggest is a necessary pre-condition before play can be extended out to co-operative play for learners with SLD/PMLD. With typically developing learners, these abilities tend to come together and develop alongside the communicative skills necessary to play co-operatively (McCune 1995; Lewis *et al.* 2000). For learners with SLD/PMLD, such communicative skills may never arrive, or at least take an awfully long time to evolve.

Introducing structure as an essential part of learning to play reduces the variables, and structure in play is most easily placed into games. The playing of games, and the teaching of the playing of games, may therefore provide the key to the teaching of play and learning about play.

What games might we play?

Readers might wish to refer to Imray and Hinchcliffe (2014) for a detailed list of games that might be open to a structured, supportive, modeled approach, but a shortened version would include:

- **One to one or small group games** with young learners such as Peek-A-Boo or Tickle Monster.
- **Activity games** that can quickly develop into free play for those learners who might be at that developmental level, such as Shark Attack or Beach Ball Catch.
- **Games in the ball pool**, especially when odd things are added, such as a ball that is too big, too heavy, or rattles. Time needs be allowed for becoming familiar with the properties of the playthings themselves before elaborate play becomes evident.
- **Sand and water play.** The Pen Green Family Centre in Corby, England, has two water play canal structures where children can shut off the flow and damn up the water. It is fascinating to see a little child up stream control the water for the players downstream and the heated debates that ensue. Bruce (1991) suggests that it is not until there is conflict in play that communication becomes necessary. If everybody is content to play along, then why talk? She once observed three children at a sand table with a train – one wanted to join the trucks together, one wanted to fill them with sand and one wanted to bury them (connecting schema, enclosure schema and enveloping schema). Adults who are 'facilitating' need to take considerable care that they do not miss the whole point of the vibrant communication and prevent the learners reaching a solution.
- **Small group or one-to-one games for any age** such as Hide And Seek; Pin The Tail On The Donkey; Pass The Parcel; Musical Chairs; Blind Man's Bluff; Musical Statues; Simon Says; Sleeping Lions; What's The Time Mr. Wolf?; Balloon And Spoon Relay Race; Barrel Relay Race; Three Armed Relay Race; Skittles; Flap The Kipper; Treasure Hunts, etc.
- **Board games** for older learners: Lotto/Bingo; Ludo; Kim's Game; Snakes and Ladders.
- **Card games** such as Snap or Pelmanism.

There are a number of published books on games, listed below, though only one of this list has been written specifically with those with learning difficulties in mind (Barratt *et al.* 2000). Even this will need some adaptation to be suitable for those with severe learning difficulties, but we would hope that such adaptations act as the catalyst for driving the play curriculum forward.

Conclusion

In many ways, play is not something that can be, or indeed, should be taught. Learning to play is a process that typically developing children need to approach in an entirely free and non-prescriptive manner; adults may facilitate and provide opportunities for play, they may ladder and scaffold, but generally, they will not 'teach'. Once the essential elements of this process play are established, children are generally introduced to more formalised games, which have rules, structure and purpose and might be described as product play. For very many learners with SLD/PMLD however, and especially for the increasing number of those with complex needs (Carpenter 2010; Carpenter *et al.* 2010) the demands placed on essential communication skills and flexibility of thought are often too great for process play to be effectively established. In these situations and with these learners and having established that free and open play presents too many difficulties, we may need to provide a basic structure, or in Vygotskian terms, a scaffold, upon which learners can safely climb *before* the greater freedom of process play is explored. Such a structure can be afforded by games, which can be as simple or complex as the situation demands, which are based around fun and as such, offer irresistible opportunities to learn. Games in this sense offer a halfway house to the freer process forms of play. For some, especially the more able, this halfway house may be only fleetingly and occasionally visited; for others, it may be a visit of many years. Play is for all learners, an essential rather than an option, and we need to recognise that it is as much the business of education, and as much a subject of education, as any other we might care to name.

Questions for readers

- Are learners of all ages and ability consistently given good opportunities to play and to develop the skills for play?
- Is the importance of play given due recognition in the whole curriculum?
- What do you personally bring in to your setting to develop learners' play?

Suggested books for games

Barratt, P., Border, J., Joy, H., Parkinson, A., Potter, M. and Thomas, G. (2000) *Developing Pupils' Social Communication Skills*, London: David Fulton.

Barron, P. (2008) *Classroom Gems: Practical ideas, games and activities for the orimary classroom*, Harlow: Pearson Education.

Barron, P. (2009) *Classroom Gems: Outdoor learning: games, ideas and activities for learning outside the primary classroom*, Harlow: Pearson Education.

Delmain, C. and Spring, J. (2003) *Speaking, Listening and Understanding: Games for young children*, Bicester: Speechmark

Leach, B.J. (2000) *10-Minute Games*, Witney, Oxfordshire: Scholastic.

Ludwig, A. and Swan, A. (2007) *101 Great Classroom Games*, New York: Mcgraw-Hill.

References

Athey, C. (2007) *Extending Thought in Young Children*, London: Sage.

Blundon Nash, J. and Schaefer, C.E. (2011) 'Play therapy: basic concepts and practices', in C.E. Schaefer (ed.) *Foundations of Play Therapy*, 2nd edition, Hoboken, NJ: Wiley.

Bruce, T. (1991) *Time to Play in Early Childhood*, London: Hodder Stoughton.

Carpenter, B. (2010) *Curriculum Reconciliation and Children with Complex Learning Difficulties and Disabilities*, London: Specialist Schools and Academies Trust.

Carpenter, B, Cockbill, B., Egerton, J. and English, J. (2010) 'Children with complex learning difficulties and disabilities: developing meaningful pathways to personalised learning', *The SLD Experience*, 58: 3–10.

Csikszentmihalyi, M. (1990) *Flow: the psychology of optimal experience*, New York: Harper and Row.

DfE (Department for Education) (2012) *Statutory Framework for the Early Years Foundation Stage: setting the standards for learning, development and care for children from birth to five*, London: Department for Education.

Drewes, A.A. (2006) 'Play-based interventions', *Journal of Early Childhood and Infant Psychology*, 2: 139–156.

Goldschmeid, E. and Jackson, S. (1994) *People Under Three: Young children in day care*, London: Routledge.

Grove, N. and Park, K. (1996) *Odyssey Now*, London: Jessica Kingsley.

Grove, N. and Park, K. (1999) *Romeo and Juliet. a multi-sensory approach*, London: Bag Books.

Grove, N. and Park, K. (2000) *Developing Social Cognition through Literature for People with Learning Disabilities: Macbeth in mind*, London: Jessica Kingsley.

Gussin-Paley, V. (2004) *A Child's Work: the importance of fantasy play*, Chicago: University of Chicago.

Hewett, D. and Nind, M. (eds) (1998) *Interaction in Action: Reflections on the use of Intensive Interaction*, London. David Fulton.

Huizinga, J. (1949) *Homo Ludens*, London: Routledge & Kegan Paul.

Imray, P. (1996) 'Heuristic Play: Report on secondary PMLD group', unpublished paper, London: Rosemary School.

Imray, P. (1997) 'Heuristic Play: Report on secondary SLD group', unpublished paper, London: Rosemary School.

Imray, P. and Hinchcliffe, V. (2012) 'Not fit for purpose: a call for separate and distinct pedagogies as part of a national framework for those with severe and profound learning difficulties', *Support for Learning*, 27(4): 150–157.

Imray, P. and Hinchcliffe, V. (2014) *Curricula for Teaching Children and Young People with Severe or Profound and Multiple Learning Difficulties: Practical strategies for education professionals*, London: Routledge.

Kellett, M. (2000) 'Sam's story: evaluating Intensive Interaction in terms of its effect on the social and communicative ability of a young child with severe learning difficulties', *Support for Learning*, 15(4): 65–71.

Kellett, M. and Nind, M. (2003) *Implementing Intensive Interaction in Schools: Guidance for practitioners, managers and coordinators*, London: David Fulton.

Lacey, P. (2009) 'Teaching thinking in SLD schools', *The SLD Experience*, 54: 19–24.

Laevers, F. (ed.) (1994) *Defining and assessing quality in early childhood education*. Studia Paedagogica, Leuven: Leuven University Press.

Landreth, G.L. (2002) *Play Therapy: the art of the relationship*, 2nd edition, New York: Brunner-Routledge.

Lehrer, J. (2012) *Imagine: How creativity works*, New York: Houghton Mifflin Harcourt.

Lewis, V., Boucher, J., Lupton, L. and Watson, S. (2000) 'Relationships between symbolic play, functional play, verbal and non-verbal ability in young children', *International Journal of Language and Communication Disorders*, 35(1): 117–127.

Lindon, J. (2001) *Understanding Children's Play*, Cheltenham: Nelson Thornes.

McCaffrey, B. (2012) 'What can teachers learn from the stories children tell? The nurturing, evaluation and interpretation of storytelling by children with language and learning difficulties', in N. Grove (ed.) *Using Storytelling to Support Children and Adults with Special Needs*, London: David Fulton.

McConkey, R. and McEvoy, J. (1986) 'Games for learning to count', *British Journal of Special Education*, 13(2): 59–62.

McCune, L. (1995) 'A normative study of representational play at the transition to language', *Developmental Psychology*, 31(2): 198–206.

Nielsen, L. (1991) 'Spatial relations in congenitally blind infants: a study', *Journal of Visual Impairment and Blindness*, 85(1): 11–16.

Nielsen, L. (1992) *Space and Self*, Copenhagen: Sikon Press.

Nind, M. and Hewett, D. (1994) *Access to Communication: Developing the basics of communication with people with severe learning difficulties through Intensive Interaction*, London: David Fulton.

Nind, M. and Hewett, D. (2001) *A Practical Guide to Intensive Interaction*, Kidderminster: British Institute of Learning Disabilities.

Nind, M. and Hewett, D. (2006) *Access to Communication*, 2nd edn, London: David Fulton.

Orr, R. (2003) *My Right to Play: a child with complex needs*, Maidenhead: Open University Press.

Peter, M. (1997) *Making Dance Special*, London: David Fulton.

Pulli, T. (2012) 'Describing and evaluating the storytelling experience: A conceptual framework', in N. Grove (ed.) *Using Storytelling to Support Children and Adults with Special Needs*, London: Routledge.

Samuel, J. and Maggs, J. (1998) 'Introducing Intensive Interaction for people with profound learning disabilities living in small staffed houses', in D. Hewett and M. Nind (eds) *Interaction in Action: reflection on the use of Intensive Interaction*, London: David Fulton.

Schore, A. (2002) 'Dysregulation of the right brain: a fundamental mechanism of traumatic attachment and the psychopathogenesis of Posttraumatic Stress Disorder', *Australian and New Zealand Journal of Psychiatry*, 36: 9–30.

Sherratt, D. and Peter, M. (2002) *Developing Play and Drama in Children with Autistic Spectrum Disorders*, London: David Fulton.

Simons, C. (1977) 'Learning to play together', *British Journal of Special Education*, 4(2): 17–19.

Stagnitti, K. (2010) 'Play', in M. Curtin, M. Molineux and J. Supyk-Mellson (eds) *Occupational Therapy and Physical Dysfunction Enabling Occupation*, 6th edn, London: Elsevier.

Stagnitti, K, O'Connor, C. and Sheppard, L. (2012) 'Impact of the Learn to Play program on play, social competence and language for children aged 5–8 years who attend a specialist school', *Australian Occupational Therapy Journal*, 59(4): 302–311.

Steiner, R. (1996) *The Education of the Child and Early Lectures on Education*, New York: Anthroposophic Press.

Stern, D. N. (1985) *The Interpersonal World of the Infant*, New York: Basic Books.

Stroh, K., Robinson, T. and Proctor, A. (2008) *Every Child Can Learn: Using learning tools and play to help children with developmental delay*, London: Sage.

Trevarthen, C. (1979) 'Communication and co-operation in early infancy: a description of primary intersubjectivity', in M. Bullowa (ed.) *Before Speech: The beginning of interpersonal communication*, Cambridge: Cambridge University Press.

Vygotsky, L. S. (1978) *Mind in Society: The development of higher psychological processes*, edited and translated by M. Cole, V. John-Steiner, S. Scribner, and E. Souberman, Cambridge, MA: Harvard University Press.

35

SUPPORTING PLAYFULNESS IN LEARNERS WITH SLD/PMLD

Going beyond the ordinary

Debby Watson and Margaret Corke

In this chapter, the following questions will be addressed:

- Why is playfulness important to learners with SLD/PMLD?
- What is meant by playfulness when thinking about learners with SLD/PMLD?
- What sort of environment do learners with SLD/PMLD need to feel playful?
- How can people encourage playfulness for this group of learners by naturally incorporating playfulness into their practice or daily routines?

Introduction

Many learners with SLD/PMLD will struggle to play in a recognisable way, but it is extremely rare to find a learner who does not express a 'playful disposition' in some form, be it a fleeting shiver of excitement, a blinking eye, an open mouth or a raised eyebrow. To those who know the learner well, signs of playfulness can be clearly recognised, but they can also be misinterpreted or may be missed altogether.

Playfulness has been described as not just a childish activity, but as: 'one aspect of the domain of activities which we find in all friendly or intimate activities' (Finlay *et al.* 2008: 532). Although this chapter is focusing on children and young people, it is important to recognise that adults with SLD/PMLD have a similar need for playfulness, as do we all. Playfulness can be seen in opportunities for meaningful and pleasurable interaction with people with SLD/PMLD, interactions which are not based on the usual agenda of care or instruction, even though they can arise during these activities if opportunities are taken. Playfulness has no timetable, it cannot be easily measured or rated, and yet its benefits are profoundly important. The urge to have playful interactions based on timing and rhythm appears to be an innate sense (Zeedyk 2008) and as a parent on a study being conducted by one of the authors (Watson 2014) stated:

> It's as fundamental to me as breathing. It's intrinsic to who we are and how we learn and how we develop... so this is why for me, it's about my daughter's posture... being proactive in that sense *and* being proactive about playfulness and engaging with my daughter and yes, things that she does are very, very small but in her world they are immense.

The importance of playfulness

There is a considerable amount of literature that provides evidence about the benefits of play (Moyles 2010). However, playfulness as a concept is rarely examined and playfulness in learners with SLD/PMLD is given hardly any direct attention in the literature (Corke 2012). Some of the literature around quality of life, wellbeing, mindfulness and happiness is relevant to the impact of playfulness in this group of learners (see Vos *et al.* 2010; Ivanic and Barrett 1997; Lancioni *et al.* 2002; Singh *et al.* 2004). Barnett asserts that it is important to focus on the 'internal predisposition to be playful' (Barnett 1990: 319) as this can inform us about both the learner's internal state and how he or she interacts with the external environment. Playfulness can be considered an outward expression of positive feelings, an indication that the learner is happy, relaxed and has a sense of wellbeing. These are important aspects for reflection and will affect practice. As the learners may not be able to say how they are feeling, their observable behaviour is perhaps the only means of knowing whether or not they are having 'a good life' (Kittay 2005).

Bundy (2008) states the disabled learner who is playful has more control, is more self-motivated and is capable of more interaction with others. It is in these respects that playfulness is particularly important for learners with SLD/PMLD as they often have very little control over the world that they find themselves in. Playfulness provides a 'way in' for the learner to engage with their surroundings without involving judgement or attainment as well as being, for the practitioner, a fantastic route to fostering attention and enthusiasm. Just the very act of having playful, phatic interaction (that is, sociable communication which is not based on instruction or ideas) has considerable benefit in terms of a learner's overall well-being (Hewett 2012a) and the value of cheerfully 'chatting' to and around learners with SLD/PMLD should not be underestimated. If that 'chatting' can turn into a lovely story that the learner can anticipate and be involved in, then all the better.

Playfulness, as Fogel maintains, results in 'spontaneous, creative, emergent achievements' (Fogel 1993: 58). Zeedyk (2008) also emphasises the importance of play, fun and joking to the growth of the social brain. Trevarthen simply asserts that 'fun does the brain good' (Trevarthen 2008: 29) and explains that infants or children functioning at an early developmental stage are attracted to extended engagement with the human voice and with gestures and seek 'playful duets', a subtle, musical form of communication. Trevarthen (2008) also describes how important it is for a child's early playful interactions to be interpreted correctly in order for attachment to occur (Bowlby 1958).

Recognising playfulness in learners with SLD/PMLD

Liebermann (1977) was one of the first people to examine playfulness, identifying five components: cognitive spontaneity; social spontaneity; physical spontaneity; manifest joy; and sense of humour. Liebermann's components have been examined by Barnett who added an overall playfulness factor, illustrating playfulness as part of the 'whole individual' (Barnett 1990: 333). Corke, one of the few to study playfulness in learners with SLD/PMLD, views playfulness as a place where 'emotional, cognitive and social dimensions can be explored and tested' (Corke 2012: 3), reiterating the encompassing nature of this elusive, loosely defined and yet vital concept.

For learners with SLD/PMLD, it is likely that we need to look more at this overall playfulness factor as individual components can be hard to spot or may not be appropriate. Physical spontaneity, for example, may be limited in learners who are quadriplegic. However, it is important to recognise that learners with SLD/PMLD possess a sense of humour as this is integral to developing playfulness. A respondent to the survey in Watson (2014) stated:

> Because playfulness is a state of mind, and although it is easier to develop if a child has appropriate physical skills, it does still exist in alert watchfulness, sense of humour/fun, interest etc. It is evident when children and young people with PMLD 'shine'. Sometimes it can't always be seen but it can be felt – a meeting of minds, a shared understanding.

This quote sums up nicely the elusive, yet recognisable quality of playfulness in learners if those around them are 'tuned in' to its possibilities. Recognising playfulness in learners is easier in those that have the ability to 'draw you in' by eye contact, reaching out, smiling and even giggling or chuckling. The example below illustrates how playfulness was recognised and built upon by a skilled practitioner:

> Peter, a lad with SLD and autism, finds the day challenging: he often chooses to sit with his back to everyone, he may scream when approached and often covers his ears to shut others out. Peter however is an expert at Intensive Interaction and his sense of fun is wonderful and engaging. He can draw you in with a look, he may lean his body towards another or tentatively approach and stand nearby glancing and waiting for a response; more likely he will throw an object for pleasure and to cause an effect. Peter sat with Sam at the table: she had won him over by playing a splash game with a water spray. Peter initiated a playful routine: he put his arm on the table and placed his head on it. Sam copied each time Peter assumed this position. There was a real sense that Peter was teasing and very soon shared smiles and laughter erupted. Peter sat upright and playfully took the lead; he made eye contact, vocalisations increased and mutual smiles and laughter ensued!

The adult response and openness to interaction, at the learner's level, was vital otherwise Peter's playfulness may have gone unnoticed. It is finding that trigger to playfulness that is all important here. Although the learner with SLD/PMLD may be intrinsically motivated to be playful, they may at times need someone or something to inspire them. What could trigger playfulness?: a tickling feather; a puff of wind or breath blown on the face; a 'walking round the garden' type game; a peek-a-boo game; bubbles; coming to get you games; seeing the funny side of a learner's movements and playfully drawing attention to this; funny or 'rude' sounds repeated within a play routine, gentle water splashes or water sprays and YOU being especially funny and using slapstick comedy in exaggerated form!

In many cases where playfulness is missed, it is because not enough time has been allowed for the learner to process what is happening. Reactions do not always happen straight away and the person interacting with the learner needs to be aware of this (Ware 2003). Similarly, a learner who has been deemed to have hearing or sight impairments may, in reality, be having difficulty processing what they see or hear or they may simply be in the wrong position to use what sight or hearing they have. It is therefore really important to take some time to observe a learner playing in order to work out what these delays mean and what playfulness looks like for the individual. Coupe O'Kane and Goldbart (1998) describe the 'Affective Communication Assessment' (ACA), which is useful in providing a framework for observation of learners with PMLD.

A learner may appear to be looking away from a playful activity that is happening, but on close observation, it becomes clear that this is more to do with poor positioning than a lack of interest in an activity. For example, if the playful activity is moved to the natural, maybe upward, direction of gaze of learners, they will be much more likely to engage with it. Interpreting a learner's behaviour requires sensitivity and an open-minded approach. It can sometimes be hard to recognise that, for example, a shocked, open mouthed expression can actually mean that a learner really enjoys having their feet tickled, or a tiny movement of the hand might be that learner's signal for 'more'. A 'play passport', a specific communication passport for encouraging playfulness, may be useful for those supporting a learner in, for example, a play scheme or short break service (see websites below).

Goodley and Runswick-Cole (2010) assert that most research on play and disabled children focuses on the mother–child relationship and they argue that not enough weight is given to wider, social factors. While agreeing that this is often the case, it is important to understand the early mother–child relationship, particularly regarding issues about interpretation and attachment. For learners with SLD/PMLD, early interactions with caregivers can be compromised by a range of factors; complex health issues, long periods of hospitalisation or sensory and physical impairment (Okimoto, Bundy and Hanzlick 2000). Understanding that the learner may be functioning at an early developmental stage is not to deny their right to be treated appropriately and respectfully, but we do them a disservice if we misjudge their developmental level and play with them at a level that they cannot make sense of.

'Intensive Interaction' (Hewett 2012b, and see Chapter 26) relies on an understanding of the processes involved in early interactions and can be an important tool or technique when encouraging playfulness as it is often in these close-up, learner-led interactions where playfulness occurs most rewardingly. Learners with SLD/PMLD have idiosyncratic and subtle ways of communicating and it is vital that people make huge efforts to recognise and respond to their playfulness appropriately. This can result in joyful moments that might be silly or quiet, but are well worth taking time to work towards.

We can think about different aspects of recognising playfulness as suggested in the cyclical model shown in Figure 35.1. The signs suggested above, which relate to step 4 in The Playfulness Cycle, may not, in practice, fit neatly into the categories but are divided in order for the observer to be fully aware of the range of responses that are possible. Co-regulation refers to the overt, observable regulation of behaviour, or 'reciprocity' – whereas attunement is emotional (covert) and sometimes difficult to assess. It is more likely to be a 'feeling' that playfulness is happening. Observation may be a prolonged period, where the observer is getting to know the learner and his or her responses and preparing for playfulness, or, if the observer already knows the learner well, may be a shorter period, useful to assess where the learner 'is' on that particular occasion.

So this process may at times be very rapid but it may also be a lengthy sequence of events, with some or all stages often repeated or with some stages such as the playful response taking a considerable time to appear. Attunement is likely to involve a sense of letting go for both partners and, essentially, trust. If two-way trust does not exist between the learner and the play partner then a 'true' connection is unlikely. Playfulness, undertaken with great sensitivity and empathy, can engender a sense of well-being between partners and this form of arousal may open the door to attunement, and enable the cyclical process of playful engagement to proceed.

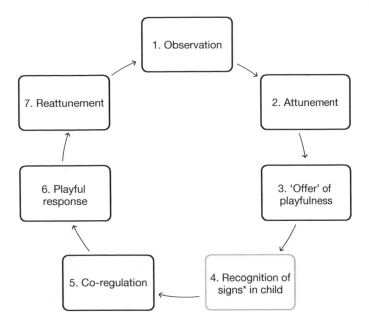

*The signs of playfulness will be very individual to each child but may include:

- physical – subtle changes in facial expression, stiffening, increased movement of body and eyes, finger flexing, relaxing, flapping, postural change
- emotional – twinkling eyes, open-wide eye gaze, smiling, laughing, raised eyebrows, open mouth, tongue out, increased expressive vocalisations, happy sounds
- social – moving nearer, reaching out, increased eye contact, leaning towards

Figure 35.1   The Playfulness Cycle

Making space for playfulness

If you capture and sustain a learner's attention and create a 'feel good' factor in the classroom, the learning environment becomes a much more satisfying place. This positivity encourages confidence and may increase social, physical and cognitive experimentation which, in turn, has a positive impact on a learner's psyche and learning outcomes. However, allowing playfulness to seep into all aspects of the curriculum may entail well thought out planning and requires the practitioner to possess certain attitudes, skills and competencies: being self-aware, reflective, empathic and thoughtful; actively listening and being responsive to the learner's signalling behaviours and to use these skills to reinforce, encourage and show appreciation. The playful practitioner has a sense of fun, a willingness to go with the learner's flow and confidence to 'dance in and out' of interaction to match the learner's mood and engagement levels.

It is important though, to understand the practical and theoretical principles underpinning playfulness as this knowledge supports and validates the inclusion of playfulness, giving the practitioners and carers 'permission' to be playful. There is a danger that playfulness can be side-tracked by daily routines, more formalised educational targets and structured events. Rather than being something that is seen as part of the curriculum, playfulness is more likely to occur, on and off, throughout the day when the opportunity arises. This 'random', spontaneous kind of playfulness is often wonderful and appealing but may be time-limited and infrequent and at worst, may not happen at all. Much will depend on the ability and willingness of individual practitioners and whether they have a playful disposition or not. Making space for playfulness, on the other hand, by actively and deliberately 'setting things up', is likely to raise the play profile and increase opportunities for playful learning throughout the day. By doing this we can exploit playfulness for all it's worth. When playfulness is not given priority it might remain cocooned, hidden away in rigid and often mundane curriculum delivery. If you make space for playfulness and are prepared to be spontaneous, there is a sense that you 'release the butterfly' and create a rich, fun-filled learning environment.

Promoting playfulness within the classroom requires thoughtful management. Offering an enabling environment, similar to the Early Years setting (DfE 2014), may be a good place to start. Having distinct areas for specific activities could help to reduce over-stimulation for a learner and make their environment easier to understand and feel comfortable in, especially for those learners with sensory impairments. A 'blank canvas' space can be helpful in gaining and maintaining a learner's attention. Here, there are limited environmental distractions, ensuring that the activities introduced become the focus of attention. In this way, sensory information can be processed by the learner in a more considered way. Very careful attention has to be paid to the learner's positioning in order for them to feel comfortable, both physically and emotionally. If learners are uncomfortable or unable to see, hear or feel what is going on, it is unlikely that they will feel playful, however stimulating or skilled the practitioners may be.

The planning stage is the time to think about playfulness and to consider what can be added to individual sessions. For example, if planning English 'writing' (mark making on paper or hands in sensory material), a 'Finger Dance' activity might awaken playfulness while drawing attention also to hands (Corke 2012: 81). During the mark making stage playful vocalisations made to mirror a learner's actions might extend the activity into a joint-action play routine enabling the whole experience to become more productive and fun.

> Claire, a support worker and James, a learner with autism, sat peacefully together. There was an observable sense of ease between them. James was flicking his fingers and turning away, turning towards and turning around. Claire's body language was open; she was available, gazing at his stereotypical behaviour admiringly then joining in, using Intensive Interaction, to celebrate his moves. Eye contact increased and James became more enlivened to a point where Claire decided to introduce a gentle tickling game: James fiddled and flicked, fiddled and flicked until Claire tentatively intervened with a little tickle. Claire used James' pace and timing to enhance the playful routine. They became fully engaged, sharing laughter and smiles until James signalled 'enough'.

At home, with parent/carers, siblings or peers, it might also be worth setting up a regular time and space for playful episodes – a kind of 'special time'. We can imagine this as time together using a dedicated bag or box of fun. Inside there might be, for example, noisy cause and effect toys, favourite twiddle materials, clowning props, strange and 'rude' sound makers, visual stimuli and material to hide under and to play with. Most important is having a playful partner because the human spirit and personality oozes with far more interactive playful possibilities than any bag of tricks. As a mum commented recently when discussing her 20-year-old son's playful relationship with a disabled 4-year-old sister: 'she thinks he's her age, just bigger: he breaks the adult rules to become childlike and this excites and intrigues her.' In the process there is no sense of dominance, rather openness to the emerging flow of play and interaction:

The interactive journey has to be taken 'with' the child and this means adopting a flexible, interactive style, taking on and using the behaviour and mannerisms similar to those naturally occurring in childhood.

(Corke 2012: 30).

Encouraging peer relationships with this group of learners can be a challenge but perhaps this is an area we might all explore a little more. Placing peers side by side on a play mat, for example, so that they can engage freely and explore the proximity of a friend without too much adult intervention, might engender a sense of togetherness and fun. Ensuring such a space is supervised, safe and secure would be paramount, but to prevent us from pre-empting danger and intervening too early we could think about the notion of 'positive risk taking' which Nind (2011) describes as 'letting go somewhat and sharing in exploring the unknown'. This play space may have unpredictable outcomes but it is likely to increase a learner's sense of identity and new friendships may ensue.

Encouraging playfulness

Opportunities for playful endeavour can be found in many activities and in particular in the creative arts such as drama, play and storytelling which are rich in language, emotional tones, role-play, exaggeration, slap-stick physical comedy and theatrical energy (Grove and Park 1996; Grove 2013); musical adventures that create opportunities for expression, interaction, exploration experimentation and playful pursuit (Corke 2002, 2012); dance and free-flow movement activities that engender spontaneity, body awareness and rhythmical associations (Tortora 2005); the 'splish-splosh' wonder of art, crafts and sensory play and the warmth of a hydrotherapy pool or during personal care where playfulness emerges quite naturally.

Approaches that incorporate a good deal of playfulness include Interactive Music; a multi-faceted approach used to develop a range of fundamental skills and competencies (Corke 2002). The facilitator is teacher, clown, magician, and performer using every interactive and multisensory means available to awaken the interest of each learner and encourage a communicative response. All aspects of delivery, in so far as it is possible, are personalised to meet each individual learner where they are developmentally, cognitively, physically and psychologically.

It is wise, however, to remember that while the creative arts seem quite naturally to lend themselves towards playful pursuit, playfulness can permeate and benefit all areas of the curriculum for learners with SLD/PMLD. Playfulness can be helpful in gaining and maintaining learners' attention, so as well as the possibility of using this special time to foster positive relationships, opportunities that focus upon developing specific skills or language and social communication ability could also be incorporated. The playful use of a balloon, for example, employed to increase early mathematical understanding, shows how a 'planned' playful approach can gain and maintain learners' attention so that learning can take place.

To teach counting Pauline, the teacher, holds a balloon, she makes a show of blowing it up saying 'and she huffed' (one exhale into balloon) 'and she puffed' (another exhale) and after several repeats the balloon is fully blown. All the learners watch with bated breath anticipating a range of outcomes; anything could happen! Pauline releases air slowly and teasingly, in bursts of three squeaks from the neck of the balloon, as she approaches each learner in turn. A mathematical pattern emerges (three squeaks and a pause) until Pauline counts 1, 2, 3 and the balloon is released to fly uncontrollably around the room. The learners' arousal and excitement are heightened; they laugh and squeal but immediately quieten when the process is repeated. There is much learning occurring: listening and attention are good, learners anticipate a range of outcomes (cognitive flexibility), learn about mathematical pattern and language. Burst-pause strategies, used later in the game, enable emerging counters to count and develop further skills and some are able to control the process by their actions and words. This balloon game has elements of heightened excitement and quiet anticipation so as a bonus the learners are also learning about self-regulation.

It is important to remember that 'an experimental frame of mind' emerges at the core of playfulness (Corke 2012: 25) as this is fundamental when considering ways of encouraging playfulness in practice. The practitioner's attitude and approach and their ability to transform the ordinary into something surprising, extraordinary and appealing are central.

Conclusion

Playfulness is not only possible, it is vital for learners with SLD/PMLD. However, as it can be such a fleeting and fragile phenomenon, unless playfulness is taken into consideration at all levels it can easily be missed or side-lined by 'the ordinary'. This would do a great disservice not only to the learners, but to those who interact with them. So, when planning curriculum delivery it is essential include playful elements; as a playful practitioner, try and develop an ease and spontaneity in your work, make sure learners have 'tuned in' support, acknowledge each learner's moods and pay attention to their positioning and environment. There is nothing so rewarding as seeing learners with SLD/PMLD 'shine' with playfulness and the benefits, although hard to measure, are truly extraordinary.

Questions for readers

- Is the learner you are working with comfortable, feeling safe and relaxed?
- Are you 'tuned in' to the learner, enjoying yourself and sensitive to the learner's playful cues?
- Is the environment one in which playfulness can thrive?
- What can you bring to the play space to awaken playfulness in the learner?

Useful websites

Frozen Light – multi-sensory theatre (www.frozenlighttheatre.com)
Imagining Autism – a research project exploring how drama-based activities may help learners with autism to communicate, socialise and play imaginatively (www.kent.ac.uk/ research/features/autism.html).
Information Exchange – covers multisensory resources and activities as well as use of 'iPads, tablets and apps (http://flolonghorn.com/).
Hirstwood Training – multisensory approach and resources (www.multi-sensory-room. co.uk/).

Oily Cart – theatre company, working with people with complex disabilities (www.oilycart. org.uk/).

Play Doctors – supports inclusion of all children by providing resources and training (www. theplaydoctors.co.uk).

Play Passport – a communication passport specifically for encouraging playfulness in learners with SLD/PMLD (www.debbywatson.co.uk).

Sounds of Intent – free downloadable framework for mapping and developing musical knowledge and skills of learners with PMLD (www.soundsofintent.org/).

Soundabout – charity that delivers training for people to use music and sound with children and adults with SLD/PMLD (www.soundabout.org.uk).

Tingly Productions – company providing multi-sensory experiences for learners with PMLD (http://tinglyproductions.org).

Us in a Bus – provides coaching, training and consultancy to develop communication with individuals with PMLD (www.usinabus.org.uk/).

References

Barnett, L. (1990) 'Playfulness: definition, design and measurement', *Play and Culture*, 3: 319–336.

Bowlby, J. (1958) 'The nature of the child's tie to its mother', *International Journal of Psychoanalysis*, 39: 1–23.

Bundy, A. (2008) 'Play and playfulness: what to look for', in L. Parham and L. Fazio (eds) *Play in Occupational Therapy for Children*, 2nd edn, St. Louis: Mosby.

Corke, M. (2002) *Approaches to Communication through Music*, London: David Fulton Publishers.

Corke, M. (2012) *Using Playful Practice to Communicate with Special Children*, Abingdon: Routledge/David Fulton.

Coupe O'Kane, J. and Goldbart, J. (1998) *Communication Before Speech: Development and assessment*, 2nd edn, London: David Fulton.

DfE (Department for Education) (2014) Statutory Framework for the Early Years Foundation Stage. Online. Available: www.gov.uk/government/publications/early-years-foundation-stage-framework --2 (accessed 4 February 2015).

Finlay, W.M.L., Antaki, C., Walton, C. and Stribling, P. (2008) 'The dilemma for staff in "playing a game" with a person with profound intellectual disabilities: empowerment, inclusion and competence in interactional practice', *Sociology of Health & Illness*, 30(4): 531–549.

Fogel, A. (1993) *Developing Through Relationships*, Chicago: The University of Chicago Press.

Goodley, D. and Runswick-Cole, K. (2010) 'Emancipating play: dis/abled children, development and deconstruction', *Disability and Society*, 25(4): 499–512.

Grove, N. (2013) *Using Stories to Support Children and Adults with Special Needs*, Abingdon: Routledge.

Grove, N. and Park, K. (1996) *Odyssey Now*, London: Jessica Kingsley.

Hewett, D. (2012a) 'Blind frogs: the nature of human communication and Intensive Interaction', in D. Hewett (ed.) *Intensive Interaction: Theoretical perspectives*, London: Sage.

Hewett, D. (2012b) (ed) *Intensive Interaction: Theoretical perspectives*, London: Sage.

Ivanic, M. and Barrett, G. (1997) 'A replication to increase happiness indices among some people with profound multiple disabilities', *Research in Developmental Disabilities*, 18(1): 79–89.

Kittay, E.F. (2005) 'At the margins of moral personhood', *Ethics*, 116(1): 100–131.

Lancioni, G., O'Reilly, M., Campodonico, F. and Mantini, M. (2002) 'Increasing indices of happiness and positive engagement in persons with profound multiple disabilities', *Journal of Developmental and Physical Disabilities*, 14(3): 231–237.

Lieberman, J.N. (1977) *Playfulness: Its relationship to imagination and creativity*, New York: Academic Press.

Moyles (2010) *The Excellence of Play*, 3rd edn, Maidenhead: Open University Press.

Nind, M. (2011) Keynote speaker 'The UK Intensive Interaction Conference 2011', notes in G. Firth (2011) *Intensive Interaction Newsletter*, Issue 36 Summer 2011, Leeds Partnership NHS.

Okimoto, A., Bundy, A., and Hanzlik, J. (2000) 'Playfulness in children with and without disability: measurement and intervention', *The American Journal of Occupational Therapy*, 54(1): 73–82.

Singh, N. Lancioni, G., Winton, A., Wahler, R., Singh, J., and Sage, M. (2004) 'Mindful caregiving increases happiness among individuals with profound multiple disabilities', *Research in Developmental Disabilities*, 25(2): 207–218.

Tortora, S. (2005) *The Dancing Dialogue: Using the communicative power of movement with young children*, Michigan: Paul H Brookes Pub Co.

Trevarthen, C. (2008) 'Intuition for human communication', in M. Zeedyk (ed.) *Promoting Social Interaction for Individuals with Communicative Impairments: making contact*, London: Jessica Kingsley.

Vos, P., De Cock, P., Petry, K., Van Den Noortgate, W. and Maes, B. (2010) 'What makes them feel like they do? Investigating the subjective well-being in people with severe and profound disabilities', *Research in Developmental Disabilities*, 31: 1623–1632.

Ware, J. (2003) *Creating a Responsive Environment for People with Profound and Multiple Learning Difficulties*, London: David Fulton.

Watson, D. (2014) *Go-getters and clever little cookies: a multi-method study of playfulness in children with profound and multiple learning disabilities (PMLD)*, PhD Thesis, University of Bristol.

Zeedyk, M. (Ed) (2008) *Promoting Social Interaction for Individuals with Communicative Impairments: making contact*, London: Jessica Kingsley.

36

CREATIVE TEACHING AND LEARNING FOR LEARNERS WITH SLD/PMLD

Melanie Peter

In this chapter, the following questions will be addressed:

- What are the characteristics needed to teach creatively with learners with SLD/PMLD?
- What strategies can the teacher use to facilitate creativity in learners with SLD/PMLD?
- Why is learning creatively so important for learners with SLD/PMLD?

Introduction

In order to achieve fulfilment in life, according to Maslow's (1954) humanistic theory, the flourishing of creativity is the pinnacle – no less for those with SLD/PMLD. Creativity has long been associated with achievement especially in the Arts, as implied by Gardner's (1983) influential theory of multiple intelligences, and as illustrated in the artistic talents of autistic savants such as Stephen Wiltshire's art and Derek Paravaccini's pianoforte. The introduction of the National Curriculum prompted curriculum development in special education to nurture progress in understanding and use of the arts – Craft's (2001) 'Big C' Creativity – for example, handbooks by Peter (1995, 1996, 1997) and Wills and Peter (1996). This was reflected in mainstream policy developments too (DfES 2007; QCA 2004).

The 'All our Futures' NACCCE Report (DfEE 1999) presented a view of creativity as universal potential within everyone. This metamorphosed to creativity regarded as divergent, flexible thinking as befits the adaptability needed by all within rapidly changing times – Craft's (2001) 'little c creativity'. Latterly, findings from neuroscience endorse emotion as being inextricably linked with cognition (Damasio 2003; Ramachandran 2003). Information comes into the brain via the five main senses, with multi-sensory activity favourably processed and 'feel good' sensations prioritised. Emotionally charged experiences are more likely to be etched in the memory, with emotional arousal in the mid-brain linked with cortical operations of thinking and problem-solving (Iverson 1996).

Chapter 12 of this book indicated the need for teachers' fundamental confidence in order to be able to teach creatively. They will need to feel emotionally secure to take risks to work in a more open-ended way, and to be in command of a repertoire of techniques (Peter 2013).

Teaching creatively

Teaching is essentially creative activity: it requires imagination, inspiration, preparation, engagement, improvisation and interactive relationships (Loveless 2009). Several studies have highlighted characteristics shared by creative teachers (Woods and Jeffrey 1996; QCA 2004; Jones and Wyse 2004; Cremin 2009). These all emphasise confidence and feeling at ease taking risks, underpinned by feeling secure emotionally and professionally. Teaching creatively requires rigorous understanding of development in order to be able to differentiate activity in both planned and spontaneous situations. In line with Vygotsky's (1978) social constructivist theory, this then enables the teacher to retain a covert structure within seemingly open-ended learner-led activity, and to recognise emerging signs of development and extend and shape responses accordingly towards achieving a next step in learning.

Not all activity that falls under the 'creativity' umbrella will be learner-led: practice tasks in which to explore and experiment with ideas and techniques will be crucial to enriching the range of options from which learners will eventually make informed decisions in their own original work. Creativity may also be a shared endeavour – a collaborative piece, in which case, social dynamics and groupings will be important, with thought given to principles of mixed ability teaching and adult support, balanced with opportunity for some learners to work together independently. This should not be taken as legitimation of staff hijacking the individual contribution and latent ability of learners with SLD/PMLD. An implication for teaching creatively will be freedom afforded by senior managers for staff to feel ownership and support for innovation and teachers exerting some autonomy in order to be flexible and responsive to individual needs and to adapt to different situations.

A key issue for facilitating creativity in learners with SLD/PMLD is the incubation of an idea and the time needed to process and co-ordinate a response, which implies a degree of forward planning but also willingness to be flexible in the moment. Theorists (Jones and Wyse 2004) identify 'flow' as a characteristic of creativity, with associated immersion as the muse takes hold and total absorption to the extent of apparent obliviousness to surrounding experience. Crucially, learners with SLD/PMLD will need this length of time to engage with techniques and processes, in order to be able to arrive at an original combination of ideas.

This may be challenging to accommodate within the busy, intensive special school day, already constrained with learners transported to and from school. However, it has to be recognised that to see some creative activities through fully will be time-consuming: a whole afternoon may be needed for art if learners are to be fully involved in organising and preparing the environment and clearing away afterwards, learning how to look after materials. Alternatively, for shorter time slots, continue one lesson over two sessions rather than rush, or else consider working with materials that are easier and quicker to organise – and allow learners to return to their work if unfinished with an area available in the classroom to facilitate this. All this may compromise balanced curriculum coverage of other areas, which will need to be redeemed at some point.

A further attribute which may require more personal work on oneself, is to dare oneself to innovate and brave the consequences if not immediately successful. However, teaching creatively can be collaborative, and planning with other teachers and with the class team will share the responsibility of this. Creative teachers will often have a strong sense of moral and political purpose (Woods and Jeffrey 1996; Cremin 2009). It is no coincidence that trainee teachers are so impressed by the dedication and creative practice witnessed on special school placements (Peter 2013).

The original National Curriculum inclusion principles (DfEE/QCA 1999) provided a framework to address the physical conditions to support learning: providing developmentally appropriate content presented multi-modally in an accessible way that appeals to the range of learning styles, and with consideration for overcoming individual barriers to learning and social dynamics. The inclusion statement is now much briefer in the Framework document for the 2014 National Curriculum in England (DfE 2013). It appears that the government wants to say as little as possible while confirming their determination for learners with SEN to achieve. It states that teachers should set high expectations for every learner and that lessons should be planned to ensure that there are no barriers to every learner achieving. Moreover, it asserts learners should be able to study the full National Curriculum, though an unspecified minority will need access to specialist equipment and different approaches.

An underestimated dimension is the teacher's 'X factor': the elusive quality that will entice the learner to engage in a shared experience. A crucial catalyst will be the teacher's ability to infuse an activity with sufficient emotional charge, taking account of learners' apparent preferences, interests and sensibilities, for example capturing the essence of their movement, rhythm or sound to express a shared feeling (Stern 1985; Prevezer 2000; Peter 2003). This may require making the activity appear pleasurable and larger than life, for learners with SLD/PMLD to associate the experience with excitement and arousal, for example through use of humour, melodrama and exaggerated expression (Potter and Whitaker 2001; Sherratt 1999, 2002; Peter 1994, 2003). Alternatively, some learners with SLD/PMLD may find this too confrontational, particularly those with autism (Williams 1996), and need a more oblique and less invasive approach. The level of dissonance has to be finely tuned: if the level of incongruity is too great or too little, interest levels and emotional engagement will quickly wane or become confused (Sherratt and Peter 2002; Peter 2003).

It will be apparent that meaningful learning in those with SLD/PMLD will not happen by accident. The pedagogical model in Figure 36.1 integrates the above generative conditions that

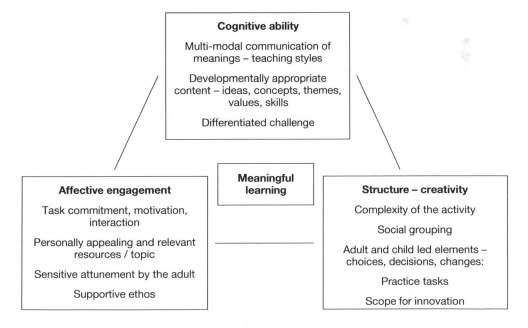

Figure 36.1 Pedagogical dimensions for meaningful learning

will be prerequisite, with creativity as a key dimension. The model develops an original multi-factional model proposed by Renzulli (1977) and Monks (1992) in relation to gifted and talented learners, that recognised pitching an activity at an appropriate developmental level will not be sufficient to unleash latent potential: essential too will be engaging the learners' commitment to the task and providing opportunity to explore, experiment and work with ideas and skills to make them their own. The three dimensions can provide a framework to support inclusive planning; strategies to facilitate the creative dimension are explored more fully in the next section.

Strategies for promoting learners' creativity

When working with learners with SLD/PMLD, clarification is needed to identify the teacher's role within NACCCE's (DfEE 1999: 29) influential view of creative activity as '*imaginative activity fashioned so as to produce outcomes that are both original and of value*':

> *Imaginative activity* – rather than something fantastical, imagination is perhaps better understood as 'creative use of memory' – embellishing a lived experience; learners with SLD/PMLD will often need support to prompt recall, for example using visual or tactile prompts of an experience – and the prerequisite direct experiences as inspiration, which may need to be very immediate rather than a delayed time-span.

> *Fashioned* – learners with SLD/PMLD need explicit instruction and time and opportunity to practise techniques prior to using them as independently as possible to shape and realise an idea, with the teacher sensitively providing just enough support 'one step behind'; it should be stated too, that exploration of materials themselves may mean that an idea emerges in process rather than starting out with a preconceived intention – or maybe remains an abstract exploration of the materials rather than a naturalistic representation that has to be 'about' something.

> *Purposeful* – this requires sustained engagement and resilience to setbacks towards achieving an outcome, which will mean positive support and encouragement from the teacher and explicit teaching to learners with SLD/PMLD of how to rework or research a step in a process; purpose may emerge after the event.

> *Original* – this can be interpreted at different levels: culturally and historically, or within the peer group and most significantly, in relation to an individual; it will depend on the teacher's knowledge of the learner's previous endeavour.

> *Judged of value* – this too will be socially and culturally situated, and be affected by an ethos that celebrates genuine effort and individual achievement, with regard for everyone's contribution as equally valid.

An appropriate ethos for meaningful learning, with creativity as a key dimension, has echoes with common principles shared with therapy (Peter 1999; Chesner 1995):

> *Patience* – belief that change is possible: time may be needed to adjust to a new experience (hence the importance of repetition) and for the creative process to flow; learners with SLD/PMLD may need explicit explanation of how the activity is relevant to them and will need positive praise or other reinforcer for effort, and encouragement to work through a challenge (akin to Piaget's concept of 'disequilibrium' as the learner wrestles to embrace this with their previous frame of reference).

Trust – an emotionally engaging experience entails investment and willingness to take a risk; the teacher will need to model a spirit of adventure and convey that they are reliably there to support the learners, and continue to be so through repeated experiences; using a personalised visual timetable may reassure that normality will be resumed.

Space – this may entail literally 'starting where the learner is', by identifying where in the environment the learner is most comfortable working, and perhaps creating a personalised space, which may be indoors or outdoors; creating a cosy nook for 'down time' may also support the flow for the learner and ease management of stress when faced with challenge during an activity to take positive time away.

Containment – providing clear structure and boundaries within which to create paradoxically will unleash rather than inhibit creativity, as learners with SLD/PMLD will feel more genuinely in control from making meaningful choices from options available and from knowing clear limits regarding activity or behaviour that would not be acceptable; this will provide emotional as well as physical security and reduce stress.

Doing and being – balancing demands and giving mental space to incubate and practise ideas and techniques will allow processing time – with learners with SLD/PMLD in particular, care needs to be taken not to over-prompt or to bombard the learner with different ways of explaining – or indeed, the temptation to fill the silence and question a learner when deeply immersed within an activity. Building in visual hooks (steps in a process) will allow a learner with short attention span to come and go and resume an activity.

Shared language – fundamental to teaching creatively is enabling learners with SLD/ PMLD to perceive the relevance of a novel activity to them: using multi-modal communication strategies to maximise engagement that will appeal to all preferred learning modes (visual props, objects of reference and signing to support meaning for the spoken and written word), and questioning to check understanding. Harnessing a personalised interest of a learner may help (for example, a special interest in cars), however, care should be taken that a theme does not become so overridingly significant that this inhibits rather than liberates free flow thinking and the possibility for extending with new challenge.

Timing – certain activity may be better at a particular time of the day or when the learner is most receptive: the teacher should be sensitive to mood and emotional states, and be prepared to be flexible and reschedule. Some learners with SLD/PMLD will be particularly resistant to change, and timing of this needs to be sensitively judged and learners prepared, for example by using a 'surprise' symbol (exclamation mark) on a visual timetable, and reassurance that this will be followed by a regular routine and order restored. Sensitively adjusting the pacing during an activity will enable an ebb and flow of tension and energy, and allow learners to refocus.

During creative activity the teacher will need to model appropriate behaviours (QCA 2004) and play a strategic role in facilitating them in learners with SLD/PMLD:

• *Questioning and challenging* – 'what if…?', 'I wonder what would happen if…?'… 'How high can you stretch?' 'How many different sounds can your drum make? Cremin (2009) highlights modelling curiosity and taking a speculative stance with large framing questions to generate interest, inquiry and thinking. Certainly learners with SLD/PMLD may struggle to generate a spontaneous sense of inquiry without these prompts. Constant bombardment however will be tuned out, and sensitive use of a range of questioning styles will be crucial to encourage initiative. Bloom (1956) indicated how questions can be differentiated, from following a request, factual recall and demonstrating comprehension, to higher order thinking that demands application of knowledge, analysis and synthesis of ideas and evaluation. Closed questions often receive bad press as limiting initiative, however these can be crucial for empowering reticent learners or those with restricted expressive powers: a carefully posed question that demands a yes/no answer or pointing gesture can enable a learner to make a creative decision ('Would you like this placed here?... No, ok, so what about here?').

- *Making connections and seeing relationships* – Cremin (2009) sees creative teachers encouraging links across limiting subject boundaries. However, for learners with SLD/PMLD, this runs deeper, as to a greater or lesser degree, their core difficulty lies with transferring and generalising learning across contexts, and seeing how aspects of experience connect. As previously, this will need to be made all the more explicit throughout the creative process, rather than assume learners are making links through imitating peer or adult role models.

- *Envisaging what might be* – flexibility of thought may be an inherent difficulty especially for those on the autistic spectrum, so how steps in a process contribute to a final outcome should be clarified at the outset. Care should be taken not to present this prescriptively, and to make explicit where there is scope for individual choices within a process.

- *Playing with ideas* – possibilities may need to be demonstrated, rather than rely on learners with SLD/PMLD finding the drive spontaneously from within: it is not that some learners (notably those with autism) cannot play, rather that they do not know how to (Sherratt and Peter 2002).

- *Representing ideas* – how one thing can stand for another will need to be explicitly talked through in order for learners with SLD/PMLD to understand how representation works and how objects and icons can be used symbolically ('If we put a blanket on this table, we can pretend it is a bed').

- *Evaluating the effects of ideas, actions, outcomes* – learners with SLD/PMLD need to be supported to focus on the impact of choices and decisions in their own and others' work. In the arts for example, this will mean explicitly focusing on use of the elements (such as pitch or rhythm in music, colour or pattern in art, body shape or use of space in dance, contrasts in light and dark or movement and stillness in drama).

There are teaching points to be gleaned from research into early years pedagogy, that thrives on child-led learning, in particular, the use of 'sustained shared thinking' and open-ended questioning in sensitive supporting adults (Siraj-Blatchford *et al.* 2002). The REPEY Report (Siraj-Blatchford *et al.* 2002: 720) explains that in sustained shared thinking, 'learning is achieved through a process of reflexive co-construction'. In other words, the adult and learner work together with both equally contributing, and thinking is deepened and extended. Pascal and Bertram (1997) signify the adult's sensitivity to a learner's feelings and emotional well-being – the degree of sincerity, empathy, responsiveness and affection. This relationship is fundamental for encouraging dialogic discourse based on adult mediation of learning, with positive questioning that leaves space for the learner's contribution (Siraj-Blatchford *et al.* 2002).

Sherratt and Peter (2002) describe a two-staged creative process of firstly, in a structured context, engaging the learner's curiosity in a stimulus, exploration through modelling and encouraging imitation and consolidation through supporting the learner to discover other possibilities. Secondly, in a free-flow learner-led context within a defined space with resources available, stepping back to allow the learner to make an experience 'their own', with the adult there to support as necessary and to evaluate it with the learner. This is summarised in Figure 36.2.

	Play Process	Child	Teacher
Structured	Curiosity	*What is it?*	Providing stimulus (play materials) Capturing interest and attention Infusing awareness of its significance
	Exploration	*What can it do?*	Encouraging and reinforcing initiative Mediating feelings of competence Demonstrating and modelling possibilities Supporting imitation by the child
	Consolidation	*What can I do with this?*	Reminding (prompting recall) of the experience Sensitively supporting the child practising the strategy or technique Reviewing the experience with the child
Free flow	Creativity	*What else can I do with this?*	Providing resources within a defined space Prompting recall of the previous experience Discussing intention Being available to support – especially for a new departure Evaluating the experience with the child

Figure 36.2 Supporting the creative process (based on Sherratt and Peter 2002)

Creative learning in learners with SLD/PMLD

Justification of any learning experience has to rest on whether it makes a difference. Assessing creativity is tricky, riddled with tensions between judging the process and/or a final outcome. Teachers need to familiarise themselves with development in those areas that are harder to pin down, such as the Arts. Intuitive assessment of artistic practice is not valid as teachers may be confidently wrong, also swayed by personal preference for a form of expression. As *The Arts in Schools Project* stressed:

> Effective teachers are assessing pupils' work all the time... The task is to make the processes of assessment explicit and coherent... to fulfil four essential roles in arts education:
> a)   facilitate individual achievement
> b)   facilitate curriculum continuity
> c)   improve co-ordination between disciplines
> d)   meet the needs of accountability
>
> (SCDC 1987: 60–61)

Figure 36.3 summarises a crude developmental framework to indicate progression in the Arts, which tracks increasing control over the elements in the respective art forms and growing awareness of audience in sharing and presenting work.

	Reactive	Active	Interactive	Proactive
Art	Scribbling Awareness and exploration of the art elements (pattern, texture, colour, line, tone, shape, form, space) in increasingly controlled mark-making	Pre-schematic Developing control and understanding of the art elements with an emerging sense of order in abstract and representational work	Schematic Refining subtlety and complexity of control over the art elements, with greater attention to detail and placement of images	Analytic Integrating the art elements to express ideas, thoughts and feelings in a range of media and artistic styles, with depth and form in original work
Music	Awareness and response to the music elements (pulse, rhythm, texture, dynamics, tempo, pitch, composition, silence) Creating patterns of sound	Developing control and understanding of the music elements Shaping patterns of sound as part of a group Recognising familiar pieces	Developing subtlety and complexity of control over the elements Refining patterns of sound within smaller groupings Reacting to familiar and unfamiliar pieces	Using the elements for original expression of ideas, thoughts and feelings in a range of styles Developing patterns of sound for others to play Recognising familiar and unfamiliar pieces
Dance	Developing awareness of movement possibilities (body shape, basic actions, dynamics, use of space, relationships)	Developing control over strength and co-ordination, poise and elevation Following a dance sequence	Refining quality in movement in relation to others/ accompaniment Devising simple solo/partner dance	Sensitivity in movement for expression and creating impression Using dance styles and traditions to create original sequence in groups
Drama	Attending – experiencing the drama Engaging in rituals, aware of teacher-in-role, Prescribed Drama Structures	Responding – imitating possibilities; Initiating with adult support; freeze-frame; structured play	Sustaining short then longer play sequences based on familiar social scripts Improvisation – 'living through'; responding to teacher in role; mantle of the expert; freeze-frame – fast forward, flashback	Creating complex, flexible imaginary play sequences Presenting – devising a play sequence to communicate meaning to others – rehearsal, tableau, hot-seating, physical theatre Ambiguous roles, conscience alley

Figure 36.3   Child development in the arts

It is also possible to assess progress in processes of arts-making. Possible indicators to evidence learners' 'little c creativity' (Craft 2001) across areas of learning could be (based on George 1992; DfEE 1999; Peter 2003):

- *Fluency of thought* – coming up with alternatives, solutions, expanding possibilities.
- *Flexibility of thought* – shifting thinking, considering several possibilities or perspectives.
- *Originality* – unusual or unique possibilities, combining or reinterpreting ideas in different ways
- *Elaboration* – applying to new situations, making unusual connections, analogies, seeing new relationships.
- *Embroidering* – developing, improving or changing an idea.

The Engagement Profile and Scale (DfE 2012) identifies indicators of learners' affective involvement and task commitment within an activity, and a way of gauging progress over time and tweaking activity to personalise a learning pathway. Evidence (verbal or non-verbal) may be noted and rated according to the extent to which a learner shows similar focus (none, emerging/fleeting, partly, mostly or fully sustained) within subsequent activity on a range of indicators:

- *Awareness* – response, consciousness, acknowledgement or recognition
- *Curiosity* – the need, thirst or desire to explore, know about, learn or make a connection with.
- *Investigation* – actively trying to find out more within or about an activity or experience.
- *Discovery* – a 'light bulb moment' where a new or repeated action or experience (planned or chance) causes realisation, surprise or excitement.
- *Anticipation* – shows expectancy or prediction as a result of previous knowledge, experience or skill.
- *Persistence* – 'sticking with it': continued effort (may be in short bursts), perseverance, determination, refusing to give up or let go.
- *Initiation* – a self-directed request, movement or indication, however small, which can be considered to express an intention, want or need

Conclusion

From the optimism and shared understanding on the importance of creativity in education that prevailed towards the end of the 2000s, with the change of government in the UK in 2010, core subjects (maths, English and computing) are prioritised at the expense of others. Cherishing creativity in the curriculum makes explicit the values of ownership and the co-construction of learning between teacher and student, and of fostering autonomy and individuality. It raises issues of an offered and received curriculum – whether learners progressed in what was intended, or whether they made other and no less worthwhile gains.

Whatever, creativity in its broader sense remains an essential characteristic both for teachers meeting diverse needs and for their own professional survival in times of rapid educational and social change, and for the learner as the key to social inclusion and fulfilment. The bottom line is that learners with SLD/PMLD will not do so effectively unless their route is personalised, unless they are engaged and have opportunity to apply and generalise their knowledge, skills and understanding. Creativity remains the order of the day; bring it on!

Questions for readers

- How would you describe the ethos and general policy of your school or organisation with regard to the status it gives creativity?
- How much creative teaching happens in the setting?
- What strategies do teachers use to promote creativity in the learners?
- What evidence is there of learning creatively?

References

Bloom, B. (1956) *Taxonomy of Educational Objectives*, London: Longman.

Chesner, A. (1995) *Dramatherapy for People with Learning Disabilities*, London: Jessica Kingsley.

Craft, A (2001) 'Little c creativity', in A. Craft, B. Jeffrey and M. Leibling (eds) *Creativity in Education*, London: Continuum.

Cremin, T. (2009) 'Creative teachers and creative teaching', in A. Wilson (ed.) *Creativity in Primary Education*, Exeter: Learning Matters.

Damasio, A.R. (2003) *Looking for Spinoza: Joy, sorrow and the feeling brain*, New York: Harcourt.

DfE (Department for Education) (2012) *Training Materials for Teachers of Learners with Children with Severe, Profound and Complex Learning Needs*. Online. Available: www.complexneeds.org.uk (accessed 14 July 2014).

DfE (Department for Education) (2013) *The National Curriculum in England: framework document*. Online. Available: www.gov.uk/government/uploads/system/uploads/attachment_data/file/210969/NC_framework_document_-_FINAL.pdf (accessed 14 July 2014).

DfEE (Department for Education and Employment) (1999) *All Our Futures: Creativity, culture and education*. Report by the National Advisory Committee on Creative and Cultural Education, Sudbury: DfEE.

DfEE/QCA (Department for Education and Employment/Qualifications and Curriculum Authority) (1999) *The National Curriculum. Handbook for Primary Teachers in England. Key stages 1 & 2*, London: DfEE.

DfES (Department for Education and Skills) (2003) *Excellence and Enjoyment*, London: HMSO.

DfES (Department for Education and Skills) (2007) *The Early Years Foundation Stage*, Nottingham: DfES.

Gardner, H. (1983) *Frames of Mind: The Theory of Multiple Intelligences*, New York: Basic Books.

George, D. (1992) *The Challenge of Able Children*, London: David Fulton.

Iverson, S.D. (1996) Communication in the mind. Paper to the International Congress of Psychology XXVI Montreal, *International Journal of Psychology*, 31: 254.

Jeffrey, B. and Craft, A. (2001) 'The Universalisation of Creativity', in A. Craft, B. Jeffrey and M. Leibling (eds) *Creativity in Education*, London: Continuum.

Jones, R. and Wyse, D. (eds) (2004) *Creativity in the Primary Curriculum*, London: David Fulton.

Loveless, A. (2009) 'Thinking about creativity: developing ideas, making things happen', in A. Wilson (ed.) *Creativity in Primary Education*, Exeter: Learning Matters.

Maslow (1954) *Motivation and Personality*, New York, NY: Harper.

Monks, F. J. (1992) 'Development of gifted children: the issue of identification and programming', in F.J. Monks and W. Peters (eds) *Talent for the Future*, Assen/Maastricht: Van Gorcum.

Pascal, C. and Bertram, T. (eds) (1997) *Effective Early Learning*, London: Hodder & Stoughton.

Peter, M. (1994) *Drama for All*, London: David Fulton.

Peter, M. (1995) *Making Drama Special*, London: David Fulton.

Peter, M. (1996) *Art for All, vols 1 & 2*, London: David Fulton.

Peter, M. (1997) *Making Dance Special*, London: David Fulton.

Peter, M. (1999) 'Good for them or what? the arts and pupils with SEN', *British Journal of Special Education*, 25(4): 168–172.

Peter, M. (2001) 'Art and Design', in B. Carpenter, R. Ashdown and K. Bovair (eds) *Enabling Access*, 2nd edition, London: David Fulton.

Peter, M. (2002) 'Play-Drama Intervention: an approach for creatively challenged children', *The SLD Experience*, 34: 6–10.

Peter, M. (2003) 'Drama, narrative and early learning', *British Journal of Special Education*, 30(1): 21–27.

Peter, M. (2009) 'Drama: Narrative Pedagogy and socially challenged children', *British Journal of Special Education*, 36(1): 9–17.

Peter, M. (2013) 'Training special educators: sustaining professional development in special school placements', *Support for Learning*, 28(3): 122–132.

Potter, C. and Whittaker, C. (2001) *Enabling Communication in Children with Autism,* London: Jessica Kingsley.

Prevezer, W. (2000) 'Musical Interaction and Children with Autism', in S. Powell (ed.) *Helping Children with Autism to Learn,* London: David Fulton.

QCA (Qualifications and Curriculum Authority) (2004) *Creativity: Find it, promote it!* London: QCA.

Ramachandran, V. (2003) 'The Emerging Mind: Lecture 5 – Neuroscience, the new Philosophy', Reith Lectures 2003, BBC Radio 4, 30 April.

Renzulli, J.S. (1977) *The Triad Enrichment Model: a guide for developing defensible programs for the gifted and talented*, Mansfield Center CA: Creative Learning Press.

SCDC (Schools Curriculum Development Committee) (1987) *A Special Collaboration (Arts in Schools Project)*, London: SCDC.

Sherratt, D. (1999) 'The Importance of Play', *Good Autism Practice*, September: 23–31.

Sherratt, D. (2002) 'Developing pretend play in children with autism: an intervention study', *Autism: the International Journal of Research and Practice*, 6(2): 169–181.

Sherratt, D. and Peter, M. (2002) *Developing Play and Drama in Children with Autistic Spectrum Disorder*, London: David Fulton.

Siraj-Blatchford, I.; Sylva, K.; Muttock, S.; Gilden, R.; Bell, D. (2002) *Researching Effective Pedagogy in the Early Years*, Research Report, Norwich: HMSO/DfES.

Stern, D. (1985) *The Interpersonal World of the Infant*, New York: Basic Books.

Vygotsky, L. (1978) *Mind in Society: The development of higher psychological processes*, Cambridge MA: Harvard University Press.

Williams, D (1996) *Autism: an inside-out approach*, London: Jessica Kingsley Publishers.

Wills, P. and Peter, M. (1996) *Music for All*, London: David Fulton.

Woods, F. and Jeffrey, B. (1996) *Teachable Moments: The art of teaching in primary schools*, Buckingham: Open University Press.

37

THE LEARNING ENVIRONMENT

Penny Lacey with Jodie Dunn, Yvonne McCall and Lisa Wilson

In this chapter, the following questions will be addressed:

- What do we mean by 'the learning environment'?
- How can we respond to particular disability-related needs in relation to the learning environment?
- What are the principles for designing physical learning environments for learners with SLD/PMLD?
- How can we make best use of the environment outside the classroom?

What do we mean by the learning environment?

In some circles, the term 'learning environment' refers exclusively to technology. That is *not* the definition we wish to employ in this chapter – see Chapter 33 in this book for a discussion of computers and other technology. The 'learning environment' in this chapter refers to the use of buildings, furniture, resources, both indoors and outdoors.

What is important for all learners is that the physical, social and emotional environment should be conducive to learning. As illustrated in Maslow's hierarchy, learners need to feel comfortable and safe, supported and encouraged before they can learn effectively (Maslow 1954). They also need to be motivated to learn and be stimulated by the world around them. Classrooms (indoor and outdoor) need to be exciting places to be. Wherever learners are, they need to be able to learn from their surroundings.

Specialist learning environments

Although generally there is little evidence for the need for a special pedagogy for learners with disabilities, Lewis and Norwich (2005) do suggest that there may be some aspects of teaching and learning that require some adaptation for particular groups of learners. In this section, we will explore some of the research and practice that can help us to optimise the physical learning environment for learners with SLD/PMLD, particularly focusing on aspects of visual impairment and autism. The section concludes with a brief consideration of multisensory environments often used with learners with PMLD.

Learning environments focused on visual impairment

Learners with visual impairment (see Chapter 15 in this book) require a range of adjustments to the physical environment to enable them to learn effectively. They may require access to an area where the lighting can be controlled, such as in a dark room and/or specialist equipment such as a magnifier, books in Moon (a raised reading system that is simpler than Braille) or objects to explore that are bright and provide contrast to a plain background. Trying to learn from a resource that is too small and does not stand out is unnecessarily difficult. There are also simple things that teachers need to consider, such as not standing with their backs to the light so their faces are in shadow or avoiding glare from shiny surfaces. Providing a running commentary of what is happening can be very important to some learners and all learners need to be warned of what is going to happen next, either with words, objects, music or touch cues.

There is a paucity of research on visual impairment in schools, colleges and centres for learners with SLD/PMLD and so there is a lack of evidence of what constitutes good practice for that specific group (Porter and Lacey 2008). However, one study that is specifically related to learners with SLD/PMLD, measured the results of adapting TEACCH (usually used for learners on the autistic spectrum) for use with learners with multiple disabilities and visual impairments (MDVI) (Taylor and Preece 2010). The researchers claim that using structured sound schedules led to improved communication, increased independence and gave a coherent framework to the activities of the day.

Learning environments focused on autism

It is relatively easy to find research that has been carried out in relation to the physical environment and learners with SLD who are on the autism spectrum. We know, for example, that an autism-friendly environment needs to take into account the individual's sensitivities to noise, light, temperature and strong colour (Giofrè 2010; Davidson 2010; Franklin *et al.* 2010). Davidson's (2010) study, in particular, recommends toning down 'toxic' stimuli such as fluorescent lights. He suggests that by listening to and observing the needs of people with autism, it is possible to design environments that reduce the elements that are potentially difficult for learners.

McAllister and Maguire's (2012a) study identifies 16 different aspects of designing a classroom for primary aged learners on the autistic spectrum. These range from considering classroom doorways and sightlines when entering the classroom, through to access to outside areas, toilet provision and a quiet area. Visual timetables and work stations also feature, as do computer provision and high level windows. McAllister and Maguire (2012a) suggest that there are three main challenges to designers:

1   Different levels of severity of individuals' sensitivities.
2   Different kinds of sensitivities of individuals.
3   The need to build in flexibility for learning to manage change.

It is undeniably difficult to get every element right for every learner with autism, but McAllister and Maguire (2012b) have produced an 'ASD Classroom Design Kit' to help designers and Henriksen and Kaup (2010) have produced a design matrix. Both offer useful practical advice.

Despite the need for some learners to have a very specifically bare and quiet environment, this is not necessary for all learners with SLD/PMLD and autism. The vignette below describes how a busy play environment was introduced in a special school.

The idea of having a role play area in our classroom (for eight KS2 children with SLD and autism and one child with Down syndrome) was met with some amusement and scepticism. We have always been told that children with autism are unable to use their imagination and find the concept of 'pretend' very difficult. However, as we have one child with Down syndrome, we wanted to meet her needs and so a very small area of the classroom was made into a kitchen area for role play.

Within a month we had to enhance the area by adding dressing up, then dolls and equipment and by the end of the year we also had a hairdresser's and a shop. This area was no longer for one child. Everyone in our class wanted to play there. It became so busy that we had to introduce 'Now and Next' boards and coloured bands to limit the number of children in the area at one time.

Recently we have adopted other Early Years principles and have created more themed or zoned areas in the classroom. Our classroom is very busy and the children have enjoyed learning to play. Much of the negative behaviour in the class has disappeared and children are in charge of their own learning. If we had continued down the road of what *we* thought was best, we would never have experienced the fantastic interactions and what we call 'Wow' moments that we have.

One of the aspects considered important to many learners on the autism spectrum is that of creating a structured learning environment. Van Bourgondien and Coonrod (2013) suggests that TEACCH is an effective intervention and educational strategy that provides structure to enable learners to function as meaningfully and independently as possible in their community. Mesibov, Shea and Schopler (2005) indicate there are four main components to TEACCH:

1   Physical structure (a clearly organised and planned environment).
2   Daily schedules (visual timetables telling learners what they are doing and when).
3   Work systems (tools to show what learners should do, when and for how long).
4   Visual structures (visual organisation and instruction related to activities).

Paying attention to these elements can make a difference to learners with autism. However, it is interesting to note that a meta-analysis of research studies on the evidence of best practice in educational provision for children on the autism spectrum by Parsons *et al.* (2011) concludes that there is insufficient evidence to promote any particular type of intervention, including those based on providing a structured environment.

Despite that warning about research evidence, there are plenty of examples from practitioners that structured environments based on visual cues can be very beneficial to learners with autism, as well as to other learners who display similar disabilities (Jordan 2013; Colley 2013).

Multi-sensory environments

One more specialist learning environment that would be useful to consider is the multi-sensory environment (MSE) found in so many schools, particularly special schools. These are often specially designed rooms containing very expensive and sometimes technically complicated equipment, such as computers, virtual environments and sound systems. There has been much criticism over the years of the grandiose claims for the efficacy of MSE with both practitioners and researchers questioning whether they are worth the enormous cost of the equipment (Mount and Cavet 1995; Orr 1993). There can be a tendency for staff to overstimulate individuals by using multiple pieces of equipment at a time rather than assessing and then designing specific stimulation for individuals as recommended by Pagliano (2012).

Research evidence for the efficacy of MSEs is very limited, especially in educational settings (Hogg *et al.* 2001). However, Lotan and Gold (2009) showed that adults with PMLD can benefit from relaxation in a Snoezelen environment, where the senses are stimulated using lights, sounds and scents, and Williams, Peterson and Brooks's (2007) study of 11 teenage learners suggests that the use of a personalised multisensory environment contributed to positive effects in their learning. For example, the learners increased hand–eye co-ordination, concentration duration and improved communication. In addition, van der Putten, Vlaskamp and Schuivens (2011) show how a multi-sensory environment helped teachers in functional assessments of the needs of learners with PMLD and enabled them to use this information in the classroom.

Some of the studies show an effect that does not require an expensive specialist environment. For example, Vlaskamp *et al.* (2003) studied increase in activity for adults with PMLD in 15 MSEs used by 177 individuals in the Netherlands and Belgium. They found that there was little evidence for increase in activity in the 20 individuals randomly selected for observation. However, the individuals did have strong responses towards the members of staff touching and talking to them, which occurred more in the MSE than in their ordinary living environment. Maybe they are worth the expense if they encourage more interaction between staff and individuals?

Heeding the advice of Pagliano (2012) will help teachers to get the best from their MSEs. For example, he suggests that design simplicity is very important. If the space is complicated and takes a long time to set up, staff will quickly lose interest and cease to use it. Instead, he extols the benefits of flexibility and the ability to control the environment so it can meet the needs of individual users. Pagliano (2012) introduces no less than 17 basic designs of MSEs, dividing up the kind of stimulation required (e.g. dark and white rooms, acoustically sharp or dull spaces, tactile space) so that individuals can have their needs met very specifically.

Principles for designing physical learning environments

Having considered the specifics of specialist environments suitable for learners with SLD/PMLD, it would be helpful to consider more general influences on environments found in settings where learners with SLD/PMLD are educated.

Early Years practice

We can learn a huge amount from the enabling environments encouraged in Early Years practice (DfE 2014). Despite their disabilities, young children with SLD/PMLD seem to be able to learn effectively in an Early Years environment. They may require more direction when learning from continuous provision, where resources are constantly available, or perhaps can only choose from a small number of activities but child-led learning is as vitally important as it is for typically developing learners.

In class 2 (for 8 Early Years children with PMLD) we aim to enable our environment to suit the children's needs and give them the optimum opportunity to explore and be independent. When developing the area as a team we consider the children's needs interests and abilities and from this we plan our environment in relation to the Early Years Foundation Stage Framework (EYFS) (DfE 2014) along with encouraging use of the children's senses and communication strengths.

The classroom is divided into themed areas, such as construction, music, and literacy, encouraging a variety of different learning opportunities both through independent and adult supported exploration.

When designing an area we follow a theme for half a term and promote this theme throughout our curriculum. The theme is extended into personalised stories, written for each child, which are a great success. The children love listening to the stories whilst in a themed area. For example, in the summer we had a seaside area and the children had lots of fun deciding what to pack in a bag to take to the beach.

Through enabling our environments and focusing on a theme that the children enjoy we promote learning throughout our curriculum and have fun!

As most learners with SLD/PMLD are still functioning at an academic level below the National Curriculum, the principles of Early Years practice could be considered relevant whatever the chronological age of the learners. It could certainly be argued that if older learners have yet to attain the Early Learning Goals (DfE 2013), they should continue to learn in ways that are known to be effective for typically developing young children, even if these approaches require specialised or 'high density' teaching (Lewis and Norwich 2005). This could be true for all learners whose attainment is measured within the P Scales (QCA 2009) (see Chapter 24 for an explanation of P-scales).

However, it could also be argued that older learners have needs that are different from their younger selves. Natural caution suggests that both can be considered, depending upon the needs of individuals. For example:

The classroom for a class of teenagers with SLD/PMLD is a lively place with Early Years influenced 'continuous provision' much in evidence. For example, there is a role play area, often taking the form of a shop or health clinic, where life skills can be practised. There is also a zone for 'Cognition' where various problem solving games and activities can be placed for independent work. There is a mix of pupil-led learning and adult-led teaching, as you would find in any Early Years classrooms.

James' pupil-led sessions are varied but cluster around his special interest in vehicles. He uses the computer to find images of various road vehicles and makes a Powerpoint presentation in

---

preparation for making a book. He also chooses to use a Scalextric track and races cars. Another young person takes photos of the races and together they download them onto the computer.

One of James' teacher-led sessions supports this interest by building on his understanding of mathematical concepts so he can work out the slowest and fastest vehicles. In another the teacher uses a map of Silverstone race track so James can connect that with a video of a Formula 1 race.

Active learning

Active learning has been promoted by many theorists over many years (for example, Dewey, Piaget, Vygotsky, Kolb and Bruner) and is the bedrock of Early Years pedagogy. Hedegaard and Fleer (2008) use Vygotskian theory to argue that child development occurs as the result of children's unique engagement with the materials they encounter in their social and cultural environment. The design of the physical environment is seen as vital to learning, especially at an early stage of development.

Learners who are engaged in playing, trying things out, talking and/or actively thinking are more likely to make sense of the world around them. Sylva *et al.*'s (2003) study found the highest quality Early Years provision where children were actively engaged in their learning through freely chosen play activities. Adults helped to develop children's understanding through joining in with the play and chatter and using open-ended question such as 'what else can we do?'

Other, more specific studies show how playing with objects in problem-solving situations leads to more effective learning than early introduction of symbolic representations (Gilmore, McCarthy and Spelke 2007). Problem solving is a process that is particularly difficult for learners with SLD/PMLD to grasp and plenty of practice with practical problem solving, in a supportive environment, is a fundamental requirement for learning for this group (Fidler *et al.* 2005). Lacey (1987) illustrates how a project such as 'Running the School Laundry' could enable young adults to get realistic work experience while learning the fundamentals of sorting, matching, counting, handling money as well learning to wash and dry clothes.

Early Years principles

Although it is not universally seen as a possibility, some special schools have taken the principles of the Early Years and adapted them for older learners who still need to learn through the kind of enabling environments found in Early Years classrooms. We have made a shortlist of what that might mean in practice in terms of classroom design. The list is adapted from High/Scope, an early years approach from the United States which is based on cognitive development (Hohmann and Weikhart 1995).

1   Classrooms should be attractive, fun places in which to learn.
2   There should be a range of different spaces in the classroom, where different activities can be encouraged.
3   Different activity areas should be arranged for ease of movement between them.
4   These areas should also be flexible so they can be changed with learners' interests.
5   Materials should be plentiful and support a wide range of activities.
6   The storage of materials should encourage learning (e.g. matching, sorting, categorising).

Classrooms can refer to traditional indoor spaces but also to outdoor spaces: anywhere where learning is taking place.

Environments outside the classroom

Although indoor classrooms are central to the education of learners with SLD/PMLD, learning outside the classroom is perhaps even more important. Learners with SLD/PMLD have particular difficulties with generalising their learning (Dockrell and McShane 1992) and need to have plenty of opportunities to practise skills and understanding in a range and variety of contexts. Some of these need to be real contexts: places where they will function in their daily lives and on into their adult lives.

A review of learning outside the classroom for all children from 0–18 entitled, 'Every Experience Matters' (Malone 2008) suggests that learning outside can positively change lives. Malone (2008: 5) suggests that learners:

- achieve higher results in the knowledge and skill acquisition;
- increase their physical health and motor skills;
- socialise and interact in new and different ways with their peers and adults;
- show improved attention, enhanced self–concept, self–esteem and mental health;
- change their environmental behaviours for the positive, along with changes in their values and attitudes and their resilience to be able to respond to changing conditions in their environment.

Considering how to achieve these outcomes for learners with SLD/PMLD is vitally important, especially as many learners lead restricted lives as a result of their physical and sensory disabilities and, sometimes, unconventional behaviour. If these restrictions are combined with the current anxiety around taking risks, for fear of retribution, educational establishments can find it very hard to run a full programme of learning outside the classroom. Schools, colleges and centres need to be very determined to make the best use of learning outside the classroom, especially in their commitment to training staff and creating an atmosphere of 'can do'.

Forest School (Knight 2011) offers a clear philosophy, practical ideas and training that can be applied to a range of educational situations. The Forest School movement has been an important part of Scandinavian education for many years and has been gaining momentum in the UK recently. Forest School provides outdoor education in a woodland environment where sessions are taught by trained Forest School leaders. Learners are encouraged to take risks, make choices and initiate their own learning while gaining an understanding and appreciation of the natural world (Slade, Lowery and Bland 2013).

Although the Forest School movement is mainly aimed at primary–aged children, there is no reason why older learners should not be able to benefit from the experiences (Knight 2011). Searching for insects, identifying trees, building shelters, following a map and developing tool skills are all useful learning activities for older learners.

Research evidence on Forest Schools is still small, especially in relation to learners with special educational needs, but evaluations by O'Brien and Murray (2007), Roe and Aspinall (2011), Ridgers, Knowles and Sayers (2012) and Slade, Lowery and Bland (2013) suggests that Forest School outdoor experiences give rise to gains in confidence, social skills, written and oral skills, motivation and concentration, physical skills and stamina, knowledge and understanding, especially with learners with special educational needs. Slade, Lowery and Bland's (2013) research shows the importance of both teacher–led and learner–led activities. For example, participants suggest building on the outside experiences, back in the classroom, to embed the learning. They also felt it was important to stand back to let learners explore their environment.

If you go down to the woods today...

Eight children are in the Forest School at the far end of the school field. There is a circle of logs for them to sit on, under a canopy of branches, while they have a collection of leaves, twigs and other natural objects to explore. They have a magnifying glass to investigate the environment. There are various teddy bears hidden in the trees, bushes and undergrowth.

During the lesson, they search the leaf litter and undergrowth to find woodland treasure like unusual leaves, sticks and mini beasts, extending their investigation with the use of magnifying glasses. They lift small logs to see what shelter they provide for the insects beneath. They hunt for the teddy bears and help to construct a den for themselves and the bears. Staff work with individuals or pairs of children, providing them with opportunities, through play, to develop children's vocabulary, take risks, make choices and initiate learning. Children develop practical skills in a context where they can really achieve, and grow in confidence. Children use iPads to capture images of interest to use in the future, to recall and sequence events and support their working memory. Everyone enjoys their outdoor classroom; it offers a dynamic, challenging, stimulating and informal environment to help facilitate children's interest and enjoyment in learning through play with and in the real world. The lesson ends with a game, singing songs and drinking hot chocolate before tramping back to school.

Learning outside the classroom can mean anything from Early Years play, outdoor adventure, sports and leisure skills to work experience and life skills. Planning a meal, going to the supermarket to buy the ingredients and cooking and eating it in the kitchen is a regular activity in many schools and colleges. It is vital practice for life after formal education.

Other activities outside the classroom might include creating a large-scale junk model in the garden, growing vegetables for soup, running the school or college laundry, providing a shopping service for housebound people, simple orienteering in the countryside, keep fit in the local gym, attending a brass band concert, travelling on a train to a museum, taking landscape photos for a calendar, taking a dog for a walk, going bowling and volunteering in the local hospital. There is almost no limit to what can be done and they are all activities that could become lifetime enjoyments.

Conclusions

It is impossible in a chapter such as this to cover all aspects of developing the learning environment for learners with SLD/PMLD. A common theme has been evident throughout the aspects chosen to explore: good Early Years practice. It has been argued that the principles behind good Early Years practice can be applied to learners with SLD/PMLD of any age. Active learning through exploration in carefully designed environments leads young typically developing children to begin to understand the way the world works and so it can with older learners with SLD/PMLD who are functioning at a similar intellectual level. There must be a proviso though as older youngsters with SLD/PMLD are not the same as typically developing young children. They will have had several years of experience, even if their general knowledge and understanding may be more limited than their typically developing peers.

Nevertheless, employing the principles of learning that have been found successful with typically developing children at an early developmental stage must be a good place to start. Intensive Interaction has been shown to be successful (Kellett 2004; Barber 2008; Nind 2009; Drysdale 2011) although there is little research evidence to support adopting other Early Years practice with learners with SLD/PMLD. There is clearly a need to adapt the learning environment in the light of sensory or physical impairments or other additional needs associated with SLD/PMLD (such as VI or autism) but providing learners with SLD/PMLD exciting and challenging environments, to provoke thinking and developing lifelong skills, is paramount.

Questions for readers

- Is my learning environment based on sound principles and evidence of efficacy?
- How far can/does it take into account learners' needs?
- Does my learning environment excite my learners and motivate them to learn?

Resources

Professional journals such as *GAP: Good Autism Practice*, *PMLD Link* and *SLD Experience* often publish exemplar articles relating to the learning environment.

The Autism Education Trust (www.autosmeducationtrust.org.uk) has a useful tool that can help schools to audit and improve their learning environments.

'Christina's Adventures' is a website with photos and explanations of Christina's classroom for learners with autism (http://christinasadventures.com/2011/10/my-classroom.html).

References

Barber, M. (2008) 'Using Intensive Interaction to add to the palette of interactive possibilities in teacher–pupil communication', *European Journal of Special Needs Education*, 23(4): 393–402.

Colley, A. (2013) *Personalised Learning for Young People with Profound and Multiple Learning Difficulties*, London: Jessica Kingsley.

Davidson, J. (2010) '"It cuts both ways": a relational approach to access and accommodation for autism', *Social Science & Medicine*, 70(2): 305–312.

DfE (Department for Education) (2013) *Early Years Outcomes: A non-statutory guide for practitioners and inspectors to help inform understanding of child development through the early years*, London: DfE.

DfE (Department for Education) (2014) *Statutory Framework for the Early Years Foundation Stage*, London: Department for Education.

Dockrell, J. and McShane, J. (1992) *Children's Difficulties in Learning: A cognitive approach*, Oxford: Blackwell.

Drysdale, H. (2011) *Effects of Intensive Interaction on the Social and Communication Behaviour of Three Students with Profound/Multiple Disabilities*. Online. Available: http://researcharchive.vuw.ac.nz/handle/10063/1730 (accessed 11 August 2014).

Fidler, D.J., Philofsky, A., Hepburn, S.L. and Rogers, S.J. (2005) 'Nonverbal requesting and problem-solving by toddlers with Down syndrome', *American Journal on Mental Retardation*, 110(4): 312–322.

Franklin, A., Sowden, P., Notman, L., Gonzalez-Dixon, M., West, D., Alexander, I., and White, A. (2010) 'Reduced chromatic discrimination in children with autism spectrum disorders', *Developmental Science*, 13(1): 188–200.

Gilmore, C.K., McCarthy, S.E. and Spelke, E.S. (2007) 'Symbolic arithmetic knowledge without instruction', *Nature*, 447 (7144): 589–591.

Giofrè, F. (2010) 'Rethinking the home space and autism spectrum disorder (ASD) in Italy: architectural design guidelines towards discomfort reduction', Conference paper. Online. Available: http://research.arc.uniroma1.it/xmlui/handle/123456789/310 (accessed 13 August 2013).

Hedegaard, M. and Fleer, M. (2008) *Studying Children: A cultural-historical approach*, Maidenhead: Open University Press.

Henriksen, K. and Kaup, M.L. (2010) 'Supportive learning environments for children with Autism Spectrum Disorders', *Undergraduate Research Journal for the Human Sciences*, 9(1). Online: http://kon.org/urc/v9/henriksen.html (accessed 10 August 2014).

Hogg J., Cavet, J., Lambe, L. and Smeddle, M. (2001) 'The use of "Snoezelen" as multisensory stimulation with people with intellectual disabilities: a review of research', *Research in Developmental Disabilities*, 22: 353–372.

Hohmann, M. and Weikhart, D. (1995) *Educating Young Children,* Yspsilanti: High/Scope Press.

Jordan, R. (2013) *Autism and Severe Learning Difficulties*, London: Human Horizon.

Kellett, M. (2004) 'Intensive interaction in the inclusive classroom: using interactive pedagogy to connect with students who are hardest to reach', *Westminster Studies in Education*, 27(2): 175–188.

Knight, S (2011) *Forest School for All*, London: Sage.

Lacey, P (1987) 'Project work with children with severe learning difficulties', in B. Smith (Ed.) *Interactive Approaches to the Education of Children with Severe Learning Difficulties*, Birmingham: Westhill College.

Lewis, A. and Norwich, B. (eds) (2005) *Special Teaching for Special Children?* Maidenhead: Open University Press.

Lotan, M. and Gold, C. (2009) 'Meta-analysis of the effectiveness of individual intervention in the controlled multisensory environment (Snoezelen®) for individuals with intellectual disability', *Journal of Intellectual and Developmental Disability*, 34(3): 207–215.

Malone, K. (2008) *Every Experience Matters: an evidence based research report on the role of learning outside the classroom for children's whole development from birth to eighteen years*, Report commissioned by Farming and Countryside Education for UK Department Children, School and Families, Wollongong, Australia.

Maslow, A. (1954) *Motivation and Personality*, New York: Harper.

McAllister, K. and Maguire, B. (2012a) 'Design considerations for the autism spectrum disorder-friendly Key Stage 1 classroom', *Support for Learning*, 27(3) 103–112.

McAllister, K. and Maguire, B. (2012b) 'A design model: the Autism Spectrum Disorder Classroom Design Kit', *British Journal of Special Education*, 39(4): 201–208.

Mesibov, G., Shea, V. and Schopler, E. (2005) *The TEACCH Approach to Autism Spectrum Disorders*, New York: Kluwer.

Mount, H. and Cavet, J. (1995) 'Multisensory environments: an exploration of their potential for young people with profound and multiple learning difficulties', *British Journal of Special Education*, 22(2): 52–55.

Nind, M. (2009) 'Promoting the emotional well-being of people with profound and multiple intellectual disabilities: a holistic approach through intensive interaction', in J. Pawlyn and S. Carnaby (eds) *Profound Intellectual and Multiple Disabilities: nursing complex needs*, Oxford: Wiley-Blackwell.

O'Brien, L. and Murray, R. (2007) 'Forest School and its impacts on young children: case studies in Britain', *Urban Forestry & Urban Greening*, 6 (4): 249–265.

Orr, R. (1993) Life beyond the room? *Eye Contact*, 6: 25–26.

Pagliano, P. (2012) *The Multisensory Handbook: A guide for children and adults with sensory learning difficulties*, London: Routledge.

Parsons, S., Guldberg, K., MacLeod, A., Jones, G., Prunty, A., and Balfe, T. (2011) 'International review of the evidence on best practice in educational provision for children on the autism spectrum', *European Journal of Special Needs Education*, 26(1): 47–63.

Porter, J. and Lacey, P. (2008) 'Safeguarding the needs of children with a visual impairment in non-VI Special schools', *British Journal of Visual Impairment*, 26(1): 50–62.

QCA (Qualifications and Curriculum Authority) (2009) *The P Scales: Level Descriptors P1-P8*, London: QCA.

Ridgers, N. D., Knowles, Z. R. and Sayers, J. (2012) 'Encouraging play in the natural environment: a child-focused case study of Forest School', *Children's Geographies*, 10(1): 49–65.

Roe, J. and Aspinall, P. (2011) 'The restorative outcomes of forest school and conventional school in young people with good and poor behaviour', *Urban Forestry & Urban Greening*, 10(3): 205–212.

Slade, M., Lowery, C. and Bland, K. (2013) 'Evaluating the impact of Forest Schools: a collaboration between a university and a primary school', *Support for Learning*, 28(2): 66–72.

Sylva, K., Melhuish, E., Sammons, P., Siraj-Blatchford, I., Taggart, B. and Elliot, K. (2003) *Effective Provision of Pre-school Education (EPPE) Project: Findings from the Pre-school Period*. Online. Available: www.ioe.ac.uk/RB_summary_findings_from_pre-school(1).pdf (accessed 10 August 2014).

Taylor, K. and Preece, D. (2010) 'Using aspects of the TEACCH structured teaching approach with students with multiple disabilities and visual impairment Reflections on practice', *British Journal of Visual Impairment*, 28(3): 244–259.

Van Bourgondien, M. E. and Coonrod, E. (2013) 'TEACCH: An intervention approach for children and adults with autism spectrum disorders and their families', in S. Goldstein and J.A. Naglieri (eds) *Interventions for Autism Spectrum Disorders*, New York: Springer.

van der Putten, A., Vlaskamp, C. and Schuivens, E. (2011) 'The use of a multisensory environment for assessment of sensory abilities and preferences in children with profound intellectual and multiple disabilities: a pilot study', *Journal of Applied Research in Intellectual Disabilities*, 24(3): 280–284.

Vlaskamp, C., De Geeter, K.I., Huijsmans, L.M. and Smit, I.H. (2003) 'Passive activities: The effectiveness of multisensory environments on the level of activity of individuals with profound multiple disabilities', *Journal of Applied Research in Intellectual Disabilities*, 16(2): 135–143.

Williams, C., Petersson, E. and Brooks, T. (2007) 'The Picturing Sound multisensory environment: an overview as entity of phenomenon', *Digital Creativity*, 18(2): 106–114.

PART VI

Towards a new understanding of education for learners with SLD/PMLD

38

ENGAGING WITH RESEARCH

Jill Porter

In this chapter, the following questions will be addressed:

- How does research support teachers' professionalism?
- How do we make judgements about the strength of research?
- What are good designs for different research projects?
- How do we forge better links between researchers and schools?

Introduction

The place of research in education has long been the subject of debate. Politically, this is driven by attention to the allocation of scarce financial resources. In 2013 at the request of the Department for Education, Ben Goldacre published a paper on 'Building evidence into education' (Goldacre 2013) that has been highly instrumental in driving changes in the funding and use of research toward developing an evidence informed approach to education. There have been mixed responses among educationalists, who are concerned that there could be a narrowing of the type of research that is carried out with an over-emphasis on quantitative research and a decontextualised view of the findings. The rhetoric can easily be simply 'what works' rather than 'what works for whom and in what context', an issue that is particularly important where learners have quite varied profiles of attainment.

In 2005 Penny Lacey and I wrote *Researching Learning Difficulties* and reviewed the previous 10 years research in the field (Porter and Lacey 2005). We found that over that period educational research, particularly research concerned with teaching and learning, was diminishing. For a whole variety of reasons, some of which I will explore below, it is still relatively difficult to find robust research that concerns the education of learners with SLD/PMLD. Doing an online literature search, either by topic or by research participants, suggests that while the field of autism attracts researchers' (and funders') interest there is remarkably little with *children* with SLD/PMLD. Of course, much of the research that is carried out with children with autism may well be relevant. Emerson and Baines (2010) estimate that some 30 per cent of children with learning disabilities also have autism, with previous estimates ranging from 12–72 per cent, so it is up to the teacher to test out the relevance of this research. Dockrell, Peacey and Lunt (2002) and Hegarty (2001) writing more broadly in relation to special educational needs have also commented on the fragility of the evidence base for strengthening practice and Hassiotis and Sturmey (2010) estimate that only 5 per cent of the papers in the field of adult learning disability concern interventions. This appears to reflect a divide between those who 'do' and those who carry out research. It is timely to consider how we bridge the gap, how best to support research that can inform classroom and school practices.

With the questions expressed at the beginning of the chapter in mind, I set out in this chapter to enable the reader to become a better user of research, motivated to look at how the research was carried out to make a judgement about its strength. I also hope this chapter will encourage teachers to carry out their own research and to disseminate it within and across schools. The starting point is to consider the place of research in teachers' professional practice.

Professionalism and research

A recent review of teachers' views on engaging with research commissioned by the British Educational Research Association and RSA concludes on some of the benefits that teachers report. This includes the way in which research can focus 'thinking beyond the accountability culture of a performative system' (Leat, Lofthouse and Reid 2013: 8) to consider issues that are fundamental to decisions about what to teach and how to teach, and to be given permission to be innovative. It supports teachers in the move away from normal routines, to a more risk-taking approach that enables them to take challenges and 'to step out of their comfort zone' and examine the effectiveness of new practices (Leat, Lofthouse and Reid 2013: 8). Furlong and Salisbury (2005), in an evaluation of the Best Practice Award scheme, illustrate the powerful gains of teachers engaging in research into their practice:

> I read a great deal indeed! The research has made me read things I would not have read before. Some sources were hugely influential – they have changed the way I look and think about pupils … I just feel it makes you more PROFESSIONAL because you've had to go and examine something instead of just thinking of lesson plans and little Freddie in the front row who is being naughty.
>
> (Furlong and Salisbury 2005: 56)

This statement is from a teacher undertaking a project on inclusive provision. Her head teacher also comments:

> It's amazing isn't it, you can have someone who has been at the school for over 20 years who is a very good teacher actually … one of my best! She has actually increased her skills base and feels more confident about her teaching. That says quite a lot doesn't it about the scheme … she feels even at this stage in her career a much better teacher.
>
> (Furlong and Salisbury 2005: 59)

Leat, Lofthouse and Reid (2013) argue that engaging in research can also be reinvigorating, affecting the identity of the teacher. Research is integral to the professional development of the teacher. As Goldacre (2013) argues, it supports their independent decision-making, enabling them to make evidence-based judgements.

Looking at the evidence base

One of the outcomes of the Goldacre report (2013) has been to direct attention towards the strength of the evidence base, making research users more aware of the quality of the research. Take the following example from the Better Communication Centre:

> The Talking Mats [a low tech communication framework involving sets of symbols] approach has an indicative evidence level, with limited evidence available. It is included here because of the strength of its face validity and significant use in practice. It is therefore seen a useful approach to consider, especially when services determine where and when it is most effective for the children they work with.
>
> (Law *et al.* 2012: 139)

This statement illustrates the ways in which approaches are graded by their effectiveness – 'indicative' being used to signal that the methods used to evaluate an intervention are not sufficiently strong to conclude that they are effective. They require further testing.

The hierarchy of evidence

Randomised control trials are often portrayed as the gold standard (Beail 2010). This involves randomly assigning children to two groups, carrying out a pre-test of both groups, intervening with one group and then re-testing both groups. This design allows conclusions to be drawn that changes in the intervention group did not happen by chance, but are as a result of the treatment they received. These designs are used relatively infrequently in the field of learning difficulties – the challenges of finding sufficient participants, the hugely varied profiles of individuals with SLD/PMLD, of developing outcome measures that are generic to the group, and the challenges of gaining informed consent have all been cited as problematic. Instead educationalists are more likely to use methods that don't require random allocation but compare parallel control and intervention groups in a quasi-experimental design. Although the evidence base is weaker, if the groups are matched on a dimension that's pertinent to the intervention then the evidence is relatively strong. The Education Endowment Foundation provides a useful DIY guide for practitioners to use to design robust evaluation research (Coe *et al.* 2013).

For practitioners investigating a particular topic area, reviews of existing evidence are particularly helpful. The EPPI Centre provides detailed reviews although there is little that relates directly to special educational needs, and less still in relation to learning disabilities. However, drawing on work with adults with learning difficulties it is possible to find reviews including meta-analyses, where the authors combine data from across studies to make a further analysis. A recent example of this is a paper by Ogg-Groenendaal, Hermans and Claessens (2014) who draw evidence from 20 studies that intervene by providing exercise for children and adults with intellectual disabilities with challenging behaviour. This meta-analysis concludes on the positive effect of such interventions. Table 38.1 provides a summary of the strengths and limitations of these and other methods.

Small-scale evaluations

Goldacre (2013) emphasises how practitioners should also be producers of research – adding to the body of knowledge of what we know by systematically collecting evidence in much the

Table 38.1 Engaging with Different Research Designs

Research Design	Example Research Questions	Description	Strengths	Limitations	Example/ Further Reading
Meta-analyses	What works best for who	Systematically reviews and evaluates the strength of existing evidence by only including studies that meet criteria for good research design.	Some reviews take the data from a collection of studies and re-analyse it, benefiting from the larger sample size.	Insufficient attention usually paid to contextual issues– including the sustainability of an intervention Often excludes the majority of studies for failure to meet criteria.	Ogg–Groenendaal *et al.* (2014) Mayton *et al.* (2013)
Randomised Control Trials	What works (best)	Allocates participants randomly to an intervention or a control group taking pre and post test measures from both groups.	Provides large scale data on the effect of an intervention compared to alternative practice/ provision (or no provision).	Changes in average outcomes can mask differences between individuals.	Durand *et al.* (2012) Hassiotis and Sturmey (2010)
Quasi Experimental Designs	What works (best)	As above but there is no random allocation of participants.	Uses groups that are already formed.	Conclusions are dependent on having identified relevant matching criteria.	Gersten *et al.* (2000) Coe *et al.* (2013)
Single case (N=1)	What works for X	Baseline measures followed by intervention with a single participant.	Usually studies include a good level detail about the intervention and the context in which it took place.	Needs good evidence of a stable base-line so that changes are not a reflection of normal fluctuations.	Smith *et al.* (2014) Kellet (2004)
Survey	What practices are being used and with whom \n\n What are the issues or priorities	Collects data to describe, compare or determine relationships often through questionnaire.	With careful testing of questions to ensure that the meaning is interpreted as intended and there are appropriate response options, provides.	Conclusions are dependent on getting good return rates from a representative sample of the population under study.	Emerson *et al.* (2005) Malley *et al.* (2010)

Table 38.1 (continued)

Research Design	Example Research Questions	Description	Strengths	Limitations	Example/ Further Reading
Ethnography	What are the everyday life experiences of a particular group ?	Naturalistic study of the meanings of events, actions, behaviours in the contexts in which they take place.	Detailed analysis and description of the social structure and culture of a group	Two particular threats – insider knowledge producing "blind spots" and the production of stand-alone snap shots rather than a holistic picture especially where limited time is spent on observation	Nind *et al.* (2010) Davis *et al.* (2008)
Action Research	How can I ?	Usually focused on changing professional practice in cycles of plan act, observe, reflect.	Addresses practical problems and supports professional development and organizational change	Limited by what is feasible and permissible in a particular work setting.	Rayner (2011) Lacey (undated)

same way as General Practice doctors contribute to clinical trials. This need not be carried out on a large scale. Indeed if every teacher contributed a single case study using a robust design we could build a picture of whether a particular practice is effective, for whom and in what context.

One such example is provided by Smith, Hand and Dowrick (2014), using a technique known as video feedforward to provide quite dramatic changes in the use of PECS (see Chapter 27) by four participants (one with Down syndrome and three with autism). The use of video in classrooms is quite common practice but this technique involves editing video to provide a self-model of the child performing a task without help. Although some individuals learn to use PECS quite rapidly, others can be quite dependent on prompts, either to initiate the selection of the picture, to present it in communication or then to select the desired item. Watching the video of themselves completing the task (apparently) unaided led to rapid learning in the participants. It is worth looking at the methodology used in this study.

1   Clear target behaviours were specified for each of the individuals.
2   Three baseline measures were taken for each participant, that is his/her performance on the target behaviours when no prompts were provided. A criterion was set of 80–100 per cent correct performance on at least two days.
3   A video was made of each participant performance when prompted through the task and this was then edited to provide a model of his independent performance. This was followed by a further baseline just in case the filming on its own had led to new learning.

4   The videos were shown to the participants – this varied between once or twice a week to once a day. Independent performance of the task was logged together with occasions when prompts were needed.

5   When each participant met the criterion the video was no longer used with them but performance continued to be logged using different communication partners and novel items with a follow-up at six weeks.

The study has the characteristics necessary for robust research. Clear measures, several baseline measures so that any variability in performance was recorded, the use of a checklist to ensure fidelity to the intervention procedure, a check that observations of performance are accurate (inter-observer agreement), post-intervention checks on performance that include a longer-term follow-up (maintenance of the learning) and checks that the learning was used with novel items and new communication partners (generalisation). Interestingly, the study also inspired another member of staff to use the method to facilitate dressing. Alongside having hard evidence we also need an explanation of why this should be effective. One explanation lies with the strength of visual learning for many groups of learners. A video of themselves is likely to be highly engaging and provides them with a clear view of the target behaviour. The expression 'learning from the future' has been used and there can be no doubt that being presented with a recording of successful performance can be an empowering experience.

Classroom-based research has traditionally taken a different form – with variations around a more cyclical approach to research where the outcomes of teacher action are reflected on to inform the planning and evaluation of the next action. The emphasis lies as much, or sometimes more with (changing) teacher action as on the pupils' responses and learning. There are a confusing array of models: some are grouped together under an umbrella description of Action Research; others are referred to as Practitioner Inquiry; and we can add Appreciative Inquiry and Design-based research. All include some variation in principles and procedures. Hopkins (2008) provides a useful starting point for understanding some of the variants in design. Researcher reflexivity is central: a conscious self-awareness of values and biases in drawing conclusions. Working with others can be a great support in developing criticality to the interpretation of the findings. Rayner (2011) describes using action research to develop a curriculum in his school to meet the needs of the pupils with severe and profound learning difficulties, and 'at the same time as developing professional practice via progressive problem solving' (Rayner 2011: 25). Lacey and Smith (2010) describe working with librarians in an action research project to enable them to meet the needs of people with SLD/PMLD. Bailey (2012) describes her collaborative practitioner inquiry to develop the effectiveness of teaching assistants in her school for learners with SLD/PMLD. Lacey (undated) provides a guide to getting started on action research.

The place of qualitative research

There is an important place for qualitative research where the focus is on understanding subjective experiences, the interpretations people make about the world around them. It can be useful both in further understanding why something works (or not) and for generating practice that can then be tested out more extensively. Unless we understand why something works we are not well placed to understand the elements of an intervention that are critical and to make adaptations that reflect their criticality. Guskey (2000, 2002) draws attention to the different levels of evaluation:

- Participant reaction.
- Participant learning.
- Organisational support and change.
- Participant use of knowledge and skills.
- Pupil learning outcome.

Qualitative research plays an important part in providing insights into this 'bigger picture'.

Often (but not always) qualitative research relies on the use of language to understand people's experiences usually through interviews. Much has been written elsewhere about interviewing young people with learning difficulties, and the importance of providing the appropriate means and context for communicating views that are not constrained by the researchers' expectations (see Nind 2008; Porter 2014).

Ethnographic studies use observation as a key method of investigating real-world experiences often to analyse patterns of social interaction. A good example of this is an ethnographic study by Nind, Flewitt and Payler (2010) who describes the experiences of young children both at home and in different educational settings. The study uses video and live observations over periods of a week in the spring and summer, field notes, documentary analysis, parent diaries and interviews. Together these provide a picture using 'active listening' which is illustrated below in the short excerpts taken from the study:

> Opportunity Group: Together on the floor with Helen both adults are holding the book they have selected and giving verbal input in support of each other and the activity. Questioning is accompanied by pointing but few pauses: 'What are those Helen? What are those? What are they? What are those?' Little response from Helen leads to the adults filling the gaps – 'are they ducks? Let's give you a hand today'. The adults are warm in their comments and they seize on interest shown when Helen lifts a flap: 'Shall we look under the cushion? What's that? What is it sweetheart?' Helen glances but gives no further answer. The adults sign cat and answer for her 'cat…cat… good girl'.
>
> (Nind, Flewitt and Payler 2010: 661)

> At home: Helen and her father are looking at books together on the settee. Helen's dad leads, pointing, 'what number's that?' Helen replies 'one', her dad repeats 'one… two… what's that?' Helen responds, 'three' and dad confirms 'that's it'. Helen's competence is assumed and she responds accordingly in a competent way. She leans in, looks carefully and is fully involved. The questions and pointing continue with Helen wringing her hands and curling up her upper body apparently in pleasure and concentration.
>
> (Nind, Flewitt and Payler 2010: 662)

The data from this and other similar studies draw attention to the different experiences of participation and interaction that learners receive in different settings, their experience of being initiator and responder and the different expectations that operate in different contexts. They provide an insight into the differing cultures of provision and of home and the affordances these provide to learners' developing sense of agency. Differing communication modes were presented in the two settings and the study illustrates how the learners negotiated these. Ethnographic studies pay a particular role where participants are not able to narrate their experiences. They avoid some of the challenges of relying on the views and interpretations of others but can raise some ethical dilemmas where practices are observed that might at best be viewed as questionable. This possibility needs to be addressed at the outset.

Participatory research

Increasingly there is a concern for research to be developed and carried out *with* rather than *on* participants. There are many ways and degrees to which this can take place but at the heart lies a concern that if what is important in research is subjective experiences and perspectives, then it should reflect and incorporate what is meaningful from the outset. Put another way, if the aim of the research is, for example, to understand the meaning of friendships or relationships then the questions to be asked and answered need to incorporate what is important from the perspective of the young people themselves. O'Brien, McConkey and García-Iriarte (2014) report on a national study with co-researchers with intellectual disabilities:

> At each stage of the study, the presence of the co-researchers kept us rooted in their realities. Their lived experiences became our lived experience. As university researchers we gained a much deeper appreciation and insight into their daily lives as they exchanged anecdotes of past and present experiences in which their hurt, isolation and helplessness was evident as well as the joys, achievements and improvements that they had witnessed. These insights were especially valuable when the university staff undertook the initial data analysis of the focus group audio-recordings as it helped them to appreciate better the deeper meanings underlying participants' contributions that may have been incompletely expressed verbally.
>
> (O'Brien, McConkey and García-Iriarte 2014: 73)

The strength of this research lies with the enhanced integrity of participatory research. Arguably participants have a Right to be involved. As the authors go on to state:

> the move internationally towards greater public and user involvement in determining the research that is funded through public monies suggests that strong arguments need to be marshalled for excluding persons whose lives are likely to be affected by the research rather than having to argue for their inclusion.
>
> (O'Brien, McConkey and García-Iriarte 2014: 73)

The article also provides important insights into how to support involvement that is useful not just for those researching with adults but also with children.

Disseminating research

Goldacre (2013) draws attention to the need: for better dissemination of research; for good quality accessible information and resources for schools to support the dissemination of research; and for teachers to have better understanding of the strengths and limitations of different types of research. This is best achieved by involving teachers in research. He portrays a 'dating system' where teachers in turn inform the type and nature of research that is carried out and the practice questions that they want answered.

Collins (2012) highlights the lack of communication about research both within and across schools, often a result of lacking time, resources, skills or a belief that research has something to offer the classroom teacher. Campbell and Levin (2012) suggest that there needs to be a focus on building networks between consumer, producers and commissioners of research, and that this needs to be coupled with a building of capacity in schools through organizational changes that support teachers in accessing, understanding and evaluating, sharing and using research findings to inform their teaching. One suggestion they make is that schools nominate a member of staff to take the lead on this. They also suggest: that senior management staff model and facilitate research use and demonstrate that they recognize its value; that it becomes embedded into routine events such as staff meetings; and that stronger links are forged throughout the education system so that knowledge is transferred across the system as a whole. In turn researchers need to look beyond dissemination to consider actual support for the use of research.

In parallel to the call on schools for greater engagement with research, is a change in emphasis for university researchers to identify the impact of their research. This is changing the currency of research from 'Who has read and cited the research?' to address 'How has it actually changed practice, policy or provision?' All researchers, whether they are based in research centres, schools or universities, are universally encouraged as part of their research planning to develop a strong 'knowledge mobilization' plan. Most research funders now require a substantial plan for drawing out the implications and engaging relevant stakeholders in the findings of the research. The use of the internet and open access publications make disseminating research more egalitarian, providing of course that it is written in the appropriate manner. Within the field of learning difficulties there are good examples of easy access reports to imitate with a turning point occurring in the publication of the document 'Nothing About Us Without Us' by the Department of Health (2001), demonstrating a commitment to enabling everyone to read important information. Mobilizing knowledge suggests a two-way flow of information, one that requires a strong commitment from each side (Levin 2014). Durbin and Nelson (2014) provide a useful review of some of the strategies used by schools to improve their use of evidence including the role of teacher-led research and enquiry.

Conclusions

This chapter has set out to support the teacher in becoming a more discerning reader of research. It is hoped that they will be inspired to carry out their own small-scale studies following a robust and systematic design. This is more likely to happen where schools have a strategy in place to share and use research findings. Research should not be seen as an individual activity but one that is best carried out as a collaborative venture. We must all do our part to forge those links if we are to improve the strength of the evidence base to guide good practice in schools.

Questions for readers

- How can I contribute to the development of a stronger evidence base for good practice in SLD/PMLD?
- What resources and systems does the school have to engage with research? How could these be strengthened?
- Who should I approach to support these changes?

Resources

SLD Experience: The only journal to target the education of pupils with SLD. It contains a 'Recent Research' column by Dawn Male that keeps readers in touch with the latest research. This journal is published by the British Institute of Learning Disabilities who also publish *The British Journal of Learning Disabilities* and *Journal of Applied Research in Intellectual Disabilities*. Members also receive a monthly *Current Awareness Service* that provides details of new resources, publications, projects, events etc. (www.bild.org.uk/)

PMLD Link: a journal for sharing good practice in supporting adults and children with PMLD for staff and carers (www.pmldlink.org.uk)

Educational Endowment Foundation who together with the Sutton Trust form part of the government's What Works Network. Details of the effectiveness of different strategies for disadvantaged children can be found at http://educationendowmentfoundation.org.uk/ toolkit

What Works at the Communication Trust: This website provides evidence of the effectiveness of different methods of supporting children with speech and language difficulties including those with complex needs. www.thecommunicationtrust.org.uk/projects/what-works/

EPPI Centre: Set up in 1993 to support the development of evidence-based policy and practice it hosts a library of systematic reviews as well as a data base of educational research. (http:// eppi.ioe.ac.uk)

Accessible Research: The Norah Fry Research Centre provides good examples of how to make information accessible, including research studies www.bristol.ac.uk/norahfry/easy-information/

References

Bailey, S. (2012) 'Developing pedagogy with teaching assistants', *Teacher Leadership*, 3(1). Online. Available: www.teacherleadership.org.uk/volume-3-issue-1-july-2012.html (accessed 9 July 2014).

Beail, N. (2010) 'The challenge of the randomised control trial to psychotherapy research with people who have learning disabilities', *Advances in Mental Health and Learning Disabilities*, 41: 37–41.

Campbell, C. and Levin, B. (2012) *Developing Knowledge Mobilisation to Challenge Educational Disadvantage and Inform Effective Practices in England*, Discussion Paper, University of Toronto, November 2012.

Coe, R., Kime, S., Nevill, C. and Colman, R. (2013) *The DIY Evaluation Guide*, Education Endowment Foundation. Online. Available: http://educationendowmentfoundation.org.uk/evaluation/diy-evaluation-guide/ (accessed 9 July 2014).

Collins K. (2012) 'Foreword', in C. Campbell and B. Levin *Developing Knowledge Mobilisation to Challenge Educational Disadvantage and Inform Effective Practices in England*, Discussion Paper, University of Toronto, November 2012.

Davis, J., Watson, N. and Cunningham-Burley, S. (2008) 'Disabled children, ethnography and unspoken understandings: the collaborative construction of diverse identities', in P.M. Christensen and A. James (eds) *Research with Children: Perspectives and practices*, New York, USA: Routledge.

Department of Health (2001) *Nothing about Us Without Us: the report from the Service Users Advisory Group*. Online. Available: http://web.archive.org/web/20030315162917/http://www.doh.gov.uk/ learningdisabilities/access/nothingabout/nothing2.htm (accessed 9 July 2014).

Dockrell, J., Peacey, N. and Lunt, I. (2002) *Literature Review: meeting the needs of children with special educational needs*, London: Institute of Education, University of London. Online. Available: http:// eprints.ioe.ac.uk/749/1/Dockrell2002Literature.pdf (accessed 9 July 2014).

Durand, M., Hieneman, M., Clarke, S., Wang, M. and Rinaldi, M. (2013) 'Positive family intervention for severe challenging behavior – I: a multisite randomized clinical trial', *Journal of Positive Behavior Interventions*, 15(3): 133–143.

Durbin, B. and Nelson, J. (2014) *Why Effective use of Evidence in the Classroom Needs System-wide Change* (NFER Thinks: What the Evidence Tells Us), Slough: NFER.

Emerson, E. and Baines S. (2010) *The Estimated Prevalence of Autism among Adults with Learning Disabilities in England*. Online. Available: www.improvinghealthandlives.org.uk/publications/936/The_ Estimated_Prevalence_of_Autism_among_Adults_with_Learning_Disabilities_in_England (accessed 9 July 2014).

Emerson, E.B., Davies, I., Spencer, K. and Malam, S. (2005) *Adults with Learning Difficulties in England 2003/4*, London: National Statistics/NHS Social Care and Information Centre. Online. Available:

www.lancaster.ac.uk/staff/emersone/FASSWeb/Emerson_05_ALDE_Main.pdf (accessed 10 August 2014).

Furlong, J. and Salisbury, J. (2005) 'Best practice research scholarships: an evaluation', *Research Papers in Education*, 20(1): 45–83.

Gersten, R., Baker, S. and Lloyd, J.W. (2000) 'Designing high quality research in special education: group experimental design', *The Journal of Special Education*, 34(1): 2–18.

Goldacre B. (2013) *Building Evidence into Education*. Online. Available: www.gov.uk/government/uploads/system/uploads/attachment_data/file/193913/Building_evidence_into_education.pdf (accessed 9 July 2014).

Guskey, T.R. (2000) *Evaluating Professional Development*, Thousand Oaks, CA: Corwin Press.

Guskey, T.R. (2002) 'Professional development and teacher change', *Teachers and Teaching: Theory and Practice*, 8(3/4): 381–392.

Hassiotis, A. and Sturmey, P. (2010) 'Randomised controlled trials in intellectual disabilities and challenging behaviours – current practice and future challenges', *European Psychiatric Review*, 3(2): 39–42.

Hegarty, S. (2001) 'Discussant response, Chapter 3', in Standards and effectiveness in special educational needs: questioning conceptual othodoxy, Policy Paper 2, Series 4, Tamworth: NASEN. Online. Available: www.nasen.org.uk/policy-option-papers/ (accessed 9 July 2014).

Hopkins, D. (2008) *A Teachers Guide to Classroom Research*, Maidenhead: Open University Press.

Kellett, M. (2004) 'Intensive Interaction in the inclusive classroom: using interactive pedagogy to connect with students who are hardest to reach', *Westminster Studies in Education*, 27(2): 175.

Lacey, P (undated) Action research: when the practitioner becomes the researcher: an essay by Dr Penny Lacey. Online. Available: www.teamaroundthechild.com/allnews/researchsurveys/1035-action-research-when-the-practitioner-becomes-the-researcher-an-essay-by-dr-penny-lacey.html (accessed 9 July 2014).

Lacey, P. and Smith, P. (2010) 'Inclusive libraries', *Journal of Assistive Technologies*, 4(2): 44–48.

Law, J., Lee W., Roulstone, S., Wren Y., Zeng B. and Lindsay, G. (2012) '"What Works": interventions for children and young people with speech, language and communication needs: technical Annex', DfE Research Report 247-BCRP10. Online. Available: www.gov.uk/government/uploads/system/uploads/attachment_data/file/219624/DFE-RR247-BCRP10a.pdf (accessed 9 July 2014).

Leat, D., Lofthouse, R. and Reid, A. (2013) 'Teachers' views: perspectives on research engagement', *Research and teacher education: the BERA-RSA inquiry*. Online. Available: www.bera.ac.uk/wp-content/uploads/2013/12/BERA-Paper-7-Teachers-Views-Perspectives-on-research-engagement.pdf (accessed 9 July 2014).

Levin B. (2014) 'To know is not enough: research knowledge and its use', *Review of Education*, 1(1): 2–31.

Malley, J., Caiels, J., Fox, D., McCarthy,M., Smith, N., Beadle-Brown, J. Netten A. and Towers, A. (2010) *A report on the developmental studies for the National Adult Social Care User Experience Survey*, PSSRU Discussion Paper 2721, University of Kent/London School of Economics, University of Manchester: Personal Social Services Research Unit. Online. Available: www.pssru.ac.uk/pdf/dp2721.pdf (accessed 10 August 2014).

Mayton, M.R., Menendez, A.L., Wheeler J.J., Carter S. and Chitiyo, M. (2013) 'An analysis of Social Stories research using an evidence-based practice model', *Journal of Research in Special Educational Needs*, 13(3): 208–217.

Nind, M. (2008) *Conducting Qualitative Research with People with Learning, Communication and Other Disabilities: methodological challenges*, Economic and Social Research Council's/National Centre for Research Methods Review Paper. Online. Available: http://eprints.ncrm.ac.uk/491 (accessed 10 August 2014).

Nind, M., Flewitt, R. and Payler, J. (2010) 'The social experience of early childhood for children with learning disabilities: inclusion, competence and agency', *British Journal of Sociology of Education*, 31(6): 653–670.

O'Brien, P., McConkey, R. and Garcıa-Iriarte, E. (2014) 'Co-researching with people who have intellectual disabilities: insights from a national survey', *Journal of Applied Research in Intellectual Disabilities*, 27: 65–75.

Ogg-Groenendaal, M., Hermans, H. and Claessens, B. (2014) 'A systematic review on the effect of exercise interventions on challenging behavior for people with intellectual disabilities', *Research in Developmental Disabilities*, 35: 1507–1517.

Porter, J. (2014) 'Research and pupil voice', in L. Florian (ed) *Handbook of Special Education*, 2nd Edition, London: Sage.

Porter J. and Lacey P. (2005) *Researching Learning Difficulties: A guide for practitioners*, London: Sage.

Rayner, M. (2011) 'The curriculum for children with severe and profound learning difficulties at Stephen Hawking School', *Support for Learning*, 26(1): 25–42.

Smith, J., Hand, L. and Dowrick, P.W. (2014) 'Video feedforward for rapid learning of a picture-based communication system', *Journal of Autism and Developmental Disorders*, 44: 926–936.

39

THE WAY AHEAD

Penny Lacey, Rob Ashdown, Phyllis Jones,
Hazel Lawson and Michele Pipe

Identifying themes in the book

The coverage in this book is extremely wide and one of the book's strengths is that so much information is gathered together in a single volume with clear references to different sources of further information. Each chapter has ended with some questions for readers to ponder and we hope that these will stimulate consideration of issues pertinent to their context, e.g. their own professional development needs, the development needs of their local community or place of work and the services that are required by the learners and their families with whom they work. This chapter is intended to tie together the whole book and offer a vision about what the future may hold. The authors of the chapters and their collaborators come from a variety of different backgrounds and have equally varied enthusiasms and aspirations for learners with SLD/PMLD. Therefore, it would not be sensible to try and summarise everything that they have written and it would be repetitious to provide a brief overview of each chapter and its key messages. Instead, we have contented ourselves with recording some key themes that keep recurring throughout the book; some appear in just a few chapters and some in most. These themes, we believe, must be fully explored and all issues addressed if there is to be a genuine impact on the quality of education for learners with SLD/PMLD and on their quality of life and that of their families.

Theme 1: Human rights

Learners with SLD/PMLD are, like every other learner, unique individuals. We categorise them as having SLD or PMLD because it can be a helpful way of recognising their common needs and organising effective approaches to teaching them. However, we should not just be focussing on their difficulties and problems; we need also to be clear about their rights and must work systematically to identify and remove any barriers that might prevent them achieving their rightful place in society as other children and young people do. We may not yet be able to fully understand their learning difficulties or compensate fully for their disabilities, but several chapters have given us a historical background to this field of special education and reminded us that much progress has been possible due to increasing respect for diversity and valuing individuals for who they are. They also help to address an important question: What meaning can 'citizenship' have for this group of learners?

We need to continue to fight for their equal rights that all too often in the past have been significantly neglected. Successive UK and regional governments have tried to reform the special educational needs system. We have read that there is a spasm of legislation that is seeking to provide new rights and protections to learners from birth through to 25 years in terms of education and training. This legislation offers families personal budgets to give them more control over their support arrangements and aims to improve cooperation between all the services so that they work together to provide the support that is needed by children, young people and their families. The objective is transparency in all that is said and done and local authorities and health authorities have been told that they must fully involve children, young people and parents in reviewing and developing provision for education, health and social care. Yet, these reforms, as with past reform attempts, are taking place in the context of wider reforms: changes to funding systems and formulae; changes in the school curriculum and assessments; new approaches to providing teacher education; different ways of managing schools, with increasing numbers of academies and free schools that are not maintained by local authorities; and sweeping changes in the funding and organisation of health services. It is essential to their success that the people in responsible positions fully understand the human rights issues, that sufficient resources are made available by strategic planners, and that people at all levels are given the training and support to implement these innovations.

Theme 2: Working with families

Several chapters present evidence that many parents find the whole system for supporting children, young people with SEN and families far too complex and unnecessarily bureaucratic and adversarial. They want and deserve better information and explanations by people who have understanding of their child's learning difficulties and disabilities. We have also seen that professionals may not understand the circumstances, beliefs and culture of people from varying ethnic minority groups. Parents from culturally-diverse backgrounds find it harder to form effective partnerships with schools if their communication skills and confidence levels are not good, especially when the delivery of information by the services is not sensitive to their particular needs. We now know that parents with disabled children have higher levels of stress and a poorer quality of life than parents with non-disabled children. In this book, several authors have made plain why and how the needs and interests of the families can be addressed in schools in many ways and it is crucial that partnership is of a high quality, sincere and proactive.

The problem for teachers is that they cannot go it alone, although they can do a lot to improve their own practice. They do not have the skills and knowledge of, say, a social worker or a housing officer, hence the need for close working between schools and other agencies. However, it has been pointed out that there is a widespread need to develop formal integrated systems of public services. Schools have to be fully a part of these systems: informal good practice is not enough. Staff from schools and other agencies require proper training, support and regulation if they are going to significantly improve the quality of life of these families. Without these preparations, children and young people and their families will continue to be placed at social and material disadvantage.

Theme 3: Learner participation

Several chapters have explored in their different ways concepts of 'participation' and 'voice' for learners designated as having SLD/PMLD. Although some special schools have long pursued developments in 'advocacy' and 'self-advocacy', schools overall have been tardy in developing these practices: for instance, it may be argued that learner involvement in assessment for learning is now so much to the fore only because of new expectations of Ofsted inspectors. However, chapters in this book offer answers for some pertinent questions: e.g. What does meaningful participation look like? How can learners' 'voices' be sought and listened to? We have seen how improvements in our knowledge about ways of communicating with all learners, and especially those with the most profound impairments in communication ability, can help to give every learner a voice if we remain sensitive and responsive ourselves. For instance, several chapters assert the value of Intensive Interaction as an entirely positive approach, which accords well with ideas of justice and fairness. They recognise the human right of the learners to have their communicative attempts acknowledged and acted upon, as well as the importance of teaching better ways of communicating wherever possible.

Theme 4: Professional development for the school workforce

Most, if not all, chapters have made observations and/or recommendations that have implications for the professional development of teachers and support staff in both mainstream and special education settings, i.e. preschools, nurseries, play groups, schools and academies, and colleges. There have long been concerns about the supply of appropriately trained teachers for working with learners with SLD/PMLD. Within the book there are concerns expressed or reported about the quality of teacher education and anticipated changes in teacher training, but there are also concrete suggestions for school leaders and others to consider about what they can do to enhance induction of new staff and continuing professional development of existing staff. It has been interesting to read what teachers themselves consider to be critical aspects of their role and work and there is a chronic need for greater understanding of the needs and beliefs of existing teachers if diminishing resources are going to be appropriately targeted. Can listening to teachers' voices make a difference? It is fervently to be hoped that school leaders and others keep in touch with the aspirations and needs of teachers and support staff, and increasingly that includes therapists and nurses and others employed by schools.

Theme 5: Making the most of learning opportunities

Learners spend perhaps one fifth of their waking hours at school, about six to six and one-half hours per day for just 190 days per year. Indeed, in terms of teaching time for the school curriculum, as defined by legislation which excludes play breaks, assemblies, lunch times, etc., the number of hours is probably more like 850 or 900 hours per year, or getting on for 15,000 hours over their entire school career. These estimates of the limited time available simply serve to underline the need for careful planning to ensure best possible use of the available time in school. It also reinforces the importance of learners' families becoming involved in their education so that it can be extended into the waking hours at home in appropriate ways.

A strong case has been made by some authors in this book for recognising that daily routines and other activities in school, such as the activities surrounding arrival and departure or care routines or play activities or snack times and lunchtimes or physiotherapy, offer many real opportunities for teaching and learning, for developing communication and social interaction, for developing thinking and understanding and for developing independence to the greatest degree practicable. These activities need to be seen as an integral part of the whole school curriculum rather than an addendum to it. They are far too important and time–consuming to be treated as though they are somehow 'beneath' the teacher and are not truly educational.

The quality of planning is important in maximising opportunities for learning. This entails careful consideration of potential and desirable learning outcomes which are often hard to put into behavioural targets. Just as important is the quality of assessment during and after activities that identifies whether learners are indeed making progress. How well assessment is carried out has obvious implications for the quality of planning for the next steps in their development. Several chapters have provided overviews of the various forms of assessment that have informed practice and have offered descriptions of holistic and learner-centred assessment processes that can enable staff to respond more effectively to the evident achievements and needs of each unique learner.

Theme 6: Appropriate learning environments

What are the effects of the different learning environments on learners with SLD/PMLD? Developments in special schools have informed developments in mainstream schools and other education settings for learners with SEN: for instance, approaches in specialist settings emphasising visual information systems and clarity of thought about room organisation have been useful in mainstream schools too. Good and appropriate practice for learners in mainstream settings has also transferred, with modifications, to special schools: for instance the Early Years Foundation Stage framework highlighted the influence of the learning environment, both inside and outside the classroom, and encouraged early years practitioners to review their learning environments with obvious implications for the delivery of the curriculum, teaching styles and children's learning in all settings. Similarly, we have seen how developments in the teaching of literacy and mathematics to learners with or without learning difficulties in mainstream schools have been shown to have applicability to a proportion of learners with SLD in special schools. In many respects, such developments reflect the importance of inclusion agenda which have created to a certain extent opportunities to share good practice. However, there remains a need for greater partnership between mainstream and special schools with a focus on the applicability and effectiveness of different learning environments as well as pedagogies. Also, much has been said in this book about the key features of different learning environments in special schools and colleges because, after all, these are where most learners with SLD/PMLD can be found.

Theme 7: The development of the school curriculum

As might be expected, a prodigious amount of the book is concerned with the development of appropriate curricula for schools catering for learners with SLD/PMLD. Chapters have presented accounts of the development, over time, of the curricula that have been and are now offered to them. There is coverage in the book not just of curriculum models but also of teaching goals and approaches that provide opportunities for learning key knowledge and skills and developing positive attitudes through a range of activities: literacy, mathematics, the creative arts, physical development activities, sex and relationships education, and religious education. Chapters emphasise key curriculum drivers: helping learners to become effective and willing communicators, enhancing language learning, promoting their independence and self-reliance, fostering creativity and curiosity. Above all, authors stress the importance of making opportunities for learning meaningful and fun. Teachers tend to stick with approaches that distinguish between play and work; a particular challenge is to ensure that play features much more within the curriculum because some learners, if not all, have to be taught the art of play and because playfulness is important for all.

Theme 8: Personalisation

Inclusive education, in mainstream or specialist settings, is only possible when there is personalisation of teaching and intended learning outcomes so that each individual's needs are met. Personalisation has been insisted on by successive UK governments and ministers and is enshrined in the SEND Code of Practice 0–25 years and in policies on inclusion and promoting high standards of teaching and learning. Various chapters have emphasised the importance of person-centred, or learner-centred, approaches that permit flexibility in curricula so that teaching and learning can be made relevant to each learner. Again, they emphasise that every learner with SLD or PMLD is unique: a 'one size fits all' approach is wholly inappropriate. The implications are that all teachers and support staff need to develop a full understanding of the range of teaching approaches that may suit the differing needs of the individual learners. They also need to be able to identify what their individual needs are. These chapters gives us much useful guidance about the knowledge, skills and attitudes that are required to teach an increasingly wide range of learners.

Theme 9: Multidisciplinary working

It is not just teachers who teach. In special schools for learners with SLD/PMLD teachers tend to be a minority group on the staffing establishment and there are many support staff who can have different education and care roles depending on the school organisation. Overall, there may be almost as many staff as learners in special schools and in mainstream schools there have been significant increases in the number of support staff over the past few decades. Moreover, all schools have outside support from NHS staff (nurses, therapists, paediatricians, dieticians and others) and from local authority visiting specialists (psychologists, teachers of pupils with physical or sensory impairments, social workers and others). Health and therapy support is mainly provided by the NHS, although increasingly schools employ their own therapists or paramedical staff or social workers. So chapters have stressed the importance of multidisciplinary teamwork to enable schools to meet learners' individual needs in school and at home. This calls for careful, integrated planning and for all key professionals to work together in a sensitive and coordinated way to ensure needs are met. This approach cannot rely on informal ways of relating to one another: it requires established well-regulated systems and procedures for the different professionals negotiated by service managers and school leaders in consultation with their teams.

Theme 10: Mental health and well-being

Recognising and interpreting behaviour that reflects mental health issues is a difficult matter as regards learners with SLD/PMLD. Teachers and other professionals may often interpret bizarre or disturbing behaviour as symptoms of a diagnosed condition such as autism spectrum disorder or as a reflection of profound learning difficulties or other disabilities. We have been shown that one danger of labels is that they can often overshadow or obscure significant needs in learners. Professionals working in, or with, special and mainstream schools need to acquire additional skills, knowledge and understanding of mental health issues in order to be able to recognise needs and provide appropriate support. School environments can ensure that the mental health needs of all learners are met. There has been coverage too of learners' emotional responses to loss, adverse life experiences and bereavement and how the whole school community can care for each other, including the adults, in the face of death and loss. Dealing successfully with habitual challenging behaviours is another major issue to be faced and the key to success lies in adopting a positive approach, avoiding or most carefully considering the use of punishments and other negative consequences. Challenging behaviour is after all a means of communicating unmet needs or anxieties or fears. The adult has to understand the needs of the learner, the probable triggers for the behaviour and positive methods for teaching a better way of communicating.

Theme 11: The teacher as investigator or researcher

A clear and omnipresent message has been that there is a need for more research to throw more light on issues and to identify different or better solutions. Yet, we have read that it is still relatively difficult to find new and robust research reports concerning the education and care of learners with SLD/PMLD. We have also read that there is something of a revolution in the government's demand for education to be based around evidence of what works, although it might be thought that this is driven in part by considerations surrounding the allocation of scarce resources. The interest in evidence-based practice, it has been argued, will result in improved outcomes for learners but it could also support the professional independence of teachers and others working in or with schools in making evidence-informed decisions about what works best. So these professionals need to become better consumers and users of research, who are motivated to keep abreast of new research as it is published and who know enough to make a judgement about its quality and its relevance. The other challenge to them is to carry out their own research and to disseminate it to their colleagues, both positive and negative outcomes.

One of the most aggravating problems in education, and this particular field of special education is no exception, is the lack of communication both within and across schools, often a result of lacking time, resources, skills or motivation to read or design and report investigations. This is a key issue for strategic planners, including school leaders. School leaders in particular should model and facilitate research into the use of pedagogies; they should make plain that they recognise the value of systematic problem-solving and investigation and ensure that research is routinely discussed and promoted both in staff meetings and training events and also in their support for enthusiastic individuals. We have been urged to recognise that being a good teacher or educator is not about uncritically copying approaches reported in the research literature; nor is it about ignoring the evidence from research, and just relying on hunches and personal preferences or beliefs. We do best by the learners with SLD/PMLD, if we develop the right combination of knowledge and skills, borrowing eclectically but critically, to do the best job we can.

A vision for the future

One of us (Penny Lacey) did some research for the UK charity Mencap to inform its vision for an effective education for children and young people with learning disabilities for the next 10–20 years (Lacey 2011). Analysis of the responses from schools and others to an online questionnaire revealed considerable variation in the educational provision for learners with SLD/PMLD: special schools with and without links with mainstream schools; special schools with and without residential provision; special schools next door to or even inside mainstream schools; units or special classes in mainstream schools; special and mainstream schools sharing pupils; and mainstream schools with and without links to special schools. Some of the provision was in new, well-designed premises but some was in old and inadequate accommodation. Most of the schools had learners with a range of needs, not only those with SLD/PMLD, and almost half of the schools reported a change in their population over the previous five years both in terms of increased numbers overall and the numbers of learners with multiple disabilities. There were also differences in staffing arrangements, particularly in terms of support from external specialists such as local authority visiting professionals and health and therapy support provided by the NHS.

As regards their vision for the future, all the respondents indicated a commitment to inclusion but only if all learners' individual needs can be met. Generally, the stated aspiration was that learners with SLD/PMLD should be educated in their own neighbourhood but not if that endangered their entitlement to having their educational and other needs met. The favoured option appeared to be that special schools or classes should be built right next to or inside a mainstream school.

The Mencap website sets out the charity's policy of supporting inclusive education (www. mencap.org.uk/campaigns/what-we-campaign-about/children-and-young-people/mencaps-education-policy). This policy recognises that for some learners, because of the nature of their individual needs, there may be a requirement for specialised support, but asserts that this can and should be delivered in local community education settings. This is a considered and not unreasonable policy. Mencap acknowledges that this desire for inclusive education can only be realised when all mainstream schools provide a good quality of education and care for all learners that has the confidence of both the learners and their parents. Yet as we have seen, UK education is undergoing massive change and even well-intentioned changes can cause both uncertainty and anxiety. The UK political, economic and education systems mean that special schools and other specialist settings will remain an important part of the continuum of provision for the foreseeable future.

So it is right that we should reaffirm here that we should all be campaigning for some basic entitlements for all learners with SLD/PMLD. Wherever they are placed, they should be guaranteed four things:

- appropriately trained teachers, support staff, therapists and other professionals who work together with the learners and their families;
- a curriculum and teaching approaches that are tailored to learners' specific individual needs;
- participation in meaningful and engaging learning experiences;
- inclusion in their learning community, whether that be a specialist or a mainstream setting.

We hope that this book helps readers to campaign for and achieve these guarantees in their own local communities.

References

Lacey, P. (2011) 'Educational provision for pupils with severe and profound and multiple learning difficulties'. Unpublished report to Mencap, University of Birmingham School of Education.

GLOSSARY

CAMHS Child and Adolescent Mental Health Services are specialist NHS services which offer assessment and treatment when children and young people have emotional, behavioural or mental health difficulties. Referral is often by the learner's family Doctor or a consultant.

Colleges Many further education (FE) colleges offer courses to learners with SLD and MLD and some for learners with PMLD. FE colleges may work collaboratively with special schools with provision for learners aged 16 to 19 years and may offer provision to 25 years.

DfE The Department for Education is the central government department with duties and responsibilities relating to the provision of education in schools in England. There have been several name changes for the department over the years, most recently. Department for Education (1992–1995), Department for Education and Employment (DfEE) (1995–2001), Department for Education and Skills (DfES) (2001–2007) and the Department for Children, Schools and Families (DCSF) (2007–2010). The Department for Education in Northern Ireland, the Learning Directorate for the Scottish Government, and the Department for Education and Skills for the Welsh Government perform similar functions within their education systems.

DoH The Department of Health is responsible for government policy on health and adult social care matters in England. It oversees the English National Health Service (NHS).

EFA The Education Funding Agency is responsible for distributing funding for state education in England for 3–19 year olds.

Ethnicity In this book 'ethnicity' refers to a group of people that share distinctive features, such as origin of descent, language, culture, physical appearance, religious affiliation, customs and values. Terminology referring to minority ethnic groups is often inconsistently used. The UK Office for National Statistics uses the term Black and Minority Ethnic to describe persons from ethnic minority groups resident in the United Kingdom.

Key stages Used to refer to identifiable phases in each learner's education in the UK. They are: Key Stage 1, 5–7 years; Key Stage 2, 7–11 years; Key Stage 3, 11– 4 years; Key Stage 4, 14–16 years. The equivalent year groups are Years 1 and 2; Years 3–6; Years 7–9; Years 10 and 11 respectively. Also recognised as important stages of education are the Early Years and Foundation Stage for children aged under 5 years, and the Post-16 stage, 17–19 years, sometimes called Key Stage 5 or 6th Form.

Key worker Key workers are people who work with learners, such as health visitors, teachers, social workers and school nurses. A key worker can work with parents and professionals to ensure a learner has one clear and effective plan of support.

LA Local authorities are locally-elected bodies that have a number of duties laid down by Parliament, including the provision of schools and ensuring an appropriate education for all. Thirty years ago, the LA managed all state schools in its area and controlled what they did. Successive legislation has reduced the role of the LA and strengthened that of schools and the DfE. Schools are now largely self-governing, although LAs receive and delegate their funding to them. The majority of primary and special schools are still 'maintained' schools in this sense. However, many other schools have become so-called 'academies' or 'free schools' and LAs have no control over their funding. Each LA also has responsibility for a range of children's social care services. There are 152 LAs in England.

Level descriptions In previous versions of the National Curriculum attainment in subject areas was assessed against eight level descriptions. Level descriptions indicated the types and range of performance a learner was expected to demonstrate for each level. Level descriptions have been dropped in the revised National Curriculum for 2014.

LSC The Learning and Skills Council was a non-departmental public body in England. It was replaced in 2010 by the Skills Funding Agency (SFA), which funds adult FE and skills training in England, and the Young People's Learning Agency.

National Curriculum All maintained schools in England must teach a range of subjects according to National Curriculum programmes of study. The National Curriculum was first established in 1989. From 2014 there was a revised National Curriculum for England. Wales, Scotland and Northern Ireland curriculum requirements are being reviewed.

NHS The National Health Service is provides a comprehensive range of health services, most of which are free in the UK. A range of NHS professionals work directly with children and young people and their families and in schools: paediatricians, school nurses, occupational therapists (OTs), physiotherapists (PTs), speech and language therapists (SaLTs), dieticians, orthotists, clinical psychologists, to name but a few.

NCTL The National College for Teaching and Leadership is responsible for administering the training of new and existing teachers in England, and offers school leaders and children's services leaders opportunities for professional development. It was established on 1 April 2013, when the Training Agency (TA) which replaced the Training and Development Agency (TDA) for schools merged with the National College for School Leadership (NCSL).

Ofsted The Office for Standards in Education is a non-ministerial government department which has responsibility for the inspection of all schools in England.

'P' levels In 1998, the Department for Education and Employment and Qualifications and Curriculum Authority produced eight level descriptions for each attainment target in English and Mathematics leading up to Level 1 of the National Curriculum. In 2001, P-levels were developed for all National Curriculum subjects and PSHE and RE. Since National Curriculum level descriptions have been abandoned, there is some doubt about how P levels will be used with the 2014 National Curriculum.

QCA The Qualifications and Curriculum Authority was formed in 1997 as an advisory body on all aspects of the curriculum and its assessment in schools, as well as examinations. Predecessor agencies were SCAA (School Curriculum and Assessment Authority) and prior to that the NCC (National Curriculum Council). QCA was revamped as the QCDA (Qualifications and Curriculum Development Agency), itself abolished in 2011. The Standards and Testing Agency took on QCDA's functions.

SEND Special Educational Needs and Disabilities. The term Special Educational Needs (SEN) is used when referring to pupils who, for a variety of intellectual, physical, social, sensory, psychological or emotional reasons, experience learning difficulties which are significantly greater than those experienced by the majority of pupils of the same age. Not all learners with disabilities actually have special educational needs because their needs are well met in school without extraordinary adjustments or arrangements.

Special Educational Needs and Disability Code of Practice: 0 to 25 years This replaces the former SEN Code of Practice (2001). It applies in England only and gives guidance to local authorities and governing bodies of schools on the discharge of their functions in related to pupils with SEND. It also provides legal and operational guidance for school leaders, other professionals and parents.

Statements of special educational needs A statement is a legal document detailing a pupils' formal assessment and identification of learning difficulties and the special educational help which she or he must receive. In England since September 2014 these are being progressively replaced by Education Health and Care Plans. An EHC plan details the education, health and social care support that is to be provided to a child or young person, from birth to 25 year old, who has SEN or a disability.

INDEX

Page numbers in **bold** indicate tables and in *italics* indicate figures.